THE INTERDICT IN THE THIRTEENTH CENTURY

The Interdict in the Thirteenth Century:

A Question of Collective Guilt

PETER D. CLARKE

OXFORD
UNIVERSITY PRESS

OXFORD
UNIVERSITY PRESS

Great Clarendon Street, Oxford OX2 6DP

Oxford University Press is a department of the University of Oxford.
It furthers the University's objective of excellence in research, scholarship,
and education by publishing worldwide in

Oxford New York

Auckland Cape Town Dar es Salaam Hong Kong Karachi
Kuala Lumpur Madrid Melbourne Mexico City Nairobi
New Delhi Shanghai Taipei Toronto

With offices in

Argentina Austria Brazil Chile Czech Republic France Greece
Guatemala Hungary Italy Japan Poland Portugal Singapore
South Korea Switzerland Thailand Turkey Ukraine Vietnam

Oxford is a registered trade mark of Oxford University Press
in the UK and in certain other countries

Published in the United States
by Oxford University Press Inc., New York

British Library Cataloguing in Publication Data

Data available

Library of Congress Cataloging-in-Publication Data

Clarke, Peter D.
The interdict in the thirteenth century: a question of collective guilt/Peter D. Clarke.
p. cm.
Includes bibliographical references.
ISBN-13: 978-0-19-920860-9
1. Interdict (Canon law) 2. Excommunication (Canon law) 3. Guilt (Canon law)
4. Punishment (Canon law) 5. Canon law—History. I. Title.
KBR3607.C53 2007
262.9'2—dc22   2007023160

Typeset by Laserwords Private Limited, Chennai, India
Printed in Great Britain
on acid-free paper by
Biddles Ltd, King's Lynn, Norfolk

ISBN 978-0-19-920860-9

3 5 7 9 10 8 6 4 2

Preface

The interdict is a subject of great contemporary relevance. This was a sanction of the medieval church normally imposed on an entire community because of the conduct of its secular leaders. The interdict, therefore, raises issues of collective guilt and punishment, the responsibility of the governed for the actions of their governors, the justice and efficacy of imposing sanctions on a people for the deeds of its leaders, the question of individual or collective consent to the wrongs of others, and even the idea of individual or collective duty to prevent others from committing such wrongs in the first place. These issues are still of importance today, as much as they were in the thirteenth century, not only for historians but also for lawyers, theologians, social and political scientists, and moral philosophers. This book addresses these issues as they were understood by medieval thinkers and churchmen, but hopefully this wider academic audience will find something in this book which resonates with their own work. Nevertheless this is fundamentally a historical study which explores a largely neglected aspect of papal, ecclesiastical, legal, and political history of the Middle Ages. It started life as a Manchester University PhD thesis completed in 1995 with a grant from the British Academy and under the enthusiastic and expert guidance of Professor Jeff Denton. I only realized while extensively rewriting the thesis as a book the truth of his many perceptive observations as my supervisor. I am grateful to him and to my PhD examiner Professor Anne Duggan of King's College London, who recognized that I had made a 'good start' but needed to do further research on manuscripts and in archives. The latter was carried out largely between 1995 and 1998 in Rome, where I received the generous support of a Leverhulme Trust Study Abroad Studentship. I benefited there from the advice of Dr Martin Bertram of the German Historical Institute, Rome, who knows more about thirteenth-century canon law manuscripts than anyone else. I am grateful to him and to his institute for providing a welcoming academic home for a British scholar at Rome. I also made frequent visits to the Stephan Kuttner Institute of Medieval Canon Law at Munich University, and I am grateful to its director, Professor Dr Peter Landau, for allowing me free access to its extensive microfilm collection and for encouraging me to write this book. Its preparation has incurred many debts to many other people, especially since this book has been so long in the making, and I hope to have acknowledged below all others who helped to bring it to fruition: the staff of the Vatican Library (in particular the late Fr. Leonard Boyle and Dr Christine Grafinger), and of the British Library (London), Bayerisches Staatsbibliothek (Munich), Bodleian Library (Oxford), Cambridge University Library, John Rylands University Library of Manchester, Bibliothèque royale (Brussels), Bibliothèque Nationale and Bibliothèque de l'Arsenal (Paris), Nationalbibliothek (Vienna), the libraries of Gonville and Caius College and Trinity College (Cambridge) and Merton College (Oxford), Eton College Library, Durham Cathedral Library, Archivio di Stato di Firenze (Florence), Archivio Comunale di San Gimignano, National Archives (London), Archives départementales de l'Hérault (Montpellier), Cumbria County Record Office (Carlisle), British School at Rome (in particular Valerie Scott and Maria Pia Malvezzi), and the Keeper of the Archivio Vescovile (Volterra); as well as the following colleagues and friends: Professor Dr Ludwig Schmugge; Professor Henry Mayr-Harting; Professor Richard Sharpe; Dr Patrick Zutshi; Dr Jörg Müller; Brenda Bolton; Professor David d'Avray; Dr Christoph Egger; Dr Rosemary Morris (PhD internal examiner); Professor Jack Watt (for kindly reading a first draft of chapter 1); Dr Joe Canning; Professor Ken Pennington; Professor John Baldwin; Dr Martin Brett; Professor Manlio Bellomo; Dr Frances Andrews; Alexander Murray; James Willoughby; Dr Magnus Ryan; Dr Bill North; Dr Victoria Morse; Dr Kirsi Salonen; Dr Cordelia Warr; Dr Donal Cooper; Dr Michèle Mulcahey; Dr Mary Sommar; Giulio Marcelli (a great friend and flatmate in Rome); Bruno Boute of Leuven, the Courty family of Paris, the Egger family of Vienna, the prior of St Albert and abbot of St Boniface in Munich for their kind hospitality in those cities; and Lia, Angelo, and other friends at the Vatican Library coffee bar. I am also grateful to Rupert Cousens and his colleagues at Oxford University Press for publishing my book, and its anonymous readers for their incisive and helpful comments. Finally I thank my fiancée, Barbara Bombi, for her support and brightening my life while I wrote the book, and my parents, Douglas and Edith, for their love and encouragement throughout; this book is dedicated to them.

Peter D. Clarke
September 2006

Contents

Abbreviations

N.B. Any abbreviations not listed below are to be found in the Bibliography.

A.	anno, annum
AMN	Analecta Medievalia Namurcensia
ASV	Archivio Segreto Vaticano
BAV	Biblioteca Apostolica Vaticana
BL	British Library
BJRL	*Bulletin of the John Rylands Library*
BMCL	*Bulletin of Medieval Canon Law*
BN	Bibliothèque Nationale
CCSL	Corpus Christianorum Series Latina
Coll. I	*Collectio prima* (collection of the canons of Lugd. Conc. I); followed by the number of the canon.
Coll. III	*Collectio tertia* (definitive collection of Innocent IV's *Novelle*); followed by the number of the chapter.
dist.	distinctio (in works other than Gratian's *Decretum*)
JL	P. Jaffé, *Regesta pontificum Romanorum ab condita ecclesia ad annum post Christum natum MCXCVIII*, revised by S. Löwenfeld et al., 2 vols. (Leipzig 1885–88).
Lat. Conc. II	Second Lateran Council (1139)
Lat. Conc. III	Third Lateran Council (1179)
Lat. Conc. IV	Fourth Lateran Council (1215)
Lugd. Conc. I	First Council of Lyon (1245)
Lugd. Conc. II	Second Council of Lyon (1274)
PL	*Patrologiae cursus completus ... series Latina*, ed. J.-P. Migne, 221 vols. (Paris 1844–64).
Po.	A. Potthast, *Regesta pontificum Romanorum inde ab anno post Christum natum MCXCVIII ad annum MCCCIV*, vol. 1 (Berlin 1874).
q.	questio
reg.	regula
v.	verbum, verba
ZRGKA	*Zeitschrift der Savigny-Stiftung für Rechtsgeschichte, Kanonistische Abteilung*

Methods of citing legal texts:

Gratian's *Decretum*: In Part I texts are cited by distinctio and canon, e.g. D.1 c.1 (the first canon in the first distinctio). In Part II they are cited by causa, questio, and canon, e.g. C.1 q.1 c.1 (the first canon in the first questio of the first causa), except at C.33 q.3 which forms the treatise *De penitentia* and where texts are cited by distinctio and canon, e.g. De pen. D.1 c.1. In Part III (*De consecratione*) texts are cited by distinctio and canon e.g. De con. D.1 c.1.

Decretal collections: In *Compilationes prima-quinta* (1–5 Comp.), *Liber extra* (X), *Liber sextus* (VI), *Clementine* (Clem.), *Extravagantes communes* (Extrav. comm.), and the collections of Alanus (Alan.) and Gilbertus (Gilb.) texts are cited by book, title, and chapter, e.g. X 1.1.1 (the first chapter of the first title in the first book of the *Liber extra*).

Roman law: In the Code of Justinian (Cod.) texts are cited by book, title, and lex, e.g. Cod. 1.1.1. In the Institutes of Justinian (Inst.) and the Digest (Dig.) texts are cited by book, title, and fragment e.g. Dig. 1.1.1. In the *Novellae* of Justinian (Nov.) texts are cited by *collatio*, title, and fragment e.g. Nov. 1.1.1.

Introduction

By the thirteenth century the interdict and excommunication were the chief spiritual sanctions of the Western Church. By this time the two were sharply differentiated in ecclesiastical doctrine. An interdict might affect an entire community for the faults of one or more of its members, but St Augustine had taught that excommunication might be imposed only on individuals for their own sins, a view that Innocent IV confirmed as law.[1] Hence an interdict did not signify collective excommunication (outlawed by 1246). Nevertheless it needs to be pointed out that by the thirteenth century canon law distinguished between two forms of excommunication, known as 'major' and 'minor', and that the interdict corresponded closely to 'minor excommunication' in terms of its effects. Both kinds of excommunication involved exclusion from church services, the Eucharist and other sacraments, as did the interdict with certain exceptions, but 'major excommunication' also involved total social exclusion with all the consequences that implied.[2] Interdicts did not cut anyone off from the Church as the body of the faithful, but, like minor excommunication, it suspended the spiritual benefits of membership.

Distinct as the interdict was from excommunication by the thirteenth century, it has received little separate and specific attention from historians. Admittedly some interdicts are well known to historians, such as the interdict imposed by Innocent III on King John's England in 1208, and this and other such cases have been the subject of several detailed studies.[3] But it is some time since a general overview of interdicts has been attempted. The only historical monograph on interdicts in English appeared in 1909 and focused on Innocent III's pontificate.[4] By contrast excommunication has received far more recent general treatment, though the abundant literature concerning it refers very little to interdicts.[5] This book attempts to remedy this neglect but cannot claim to be comprehensive. Several obstacles face a general history of interdicts in the Middle Ages. Firstly,

---

[1] C.24 q.3 c.1; VI 5.11.5.   [2] Vodola, *Excommunication*, 36, 41–2.

[3] See e.g. Cheney, 'Interdict'; 'Reaction'; 'A recent view'.

[4] Krehbiel. An excellent but older German monograph is Kober, 'Das Interdict'. See also the useful but brief treatment in Vodola, 'Interdict'; Maisonneuve, 'L'interdit'; and Hinschius, *System*, v.19–31.

[5] See e.g. Vodola, *Excommunication*; Logan; Helmholz, 'Excommunication'; id. *Spirit*, ch. 14; Murray, *Excommunication*; etc.

interdicts occurred with increasing frequency by the later Middle Ages; therefore
sources regarding them multiply in this period. Indeed two fourteenth-century
interdicts are so well documented that a monograph has been devoted to each of
them.[6] Hence the evidence is simply too abundant to allow anything other than
a superficial account of the development of the interdict across the whole Middle
Ages, especially after 1300. Secondly, it is necessary to understand the changing
political, ecclesiastical, and social context in which the interdict developed, but I
cannot claim any particular expertise in early medieval history. An unpublished
doctoral thesis over a century ago sought to trace the interdict's origins and
evolution down to the twelfth century, and the time is ripe for a specialist in this
period to reassess such issues.[7]

These might seem negative reasons for restricting this study of the interdict
to the thirteenth century, but there are also positive reasons for doing so. First
of all it is in this period that the medieval papacy most fully developed its
claims to intervene in the affairs of secular rulers,[8] and the interdict was a vital
tool of such interventionism. Indeed a community was subjected to an interdict
usually because its secular ruler had violated ecclesiastical rights. For example,
Innocent III imposed an interdict on France in 1199 because its king refused to
abandon his mistress and return to his wife despite papal refusal of a divorce;
in other words the interdict was meant to punish the king's disregard for the
Church's marriage law and its jurisdiction over matrimonial disputes. Innocent's
exploitation of the interdict as a political weapon was much imitated by his
successors, and this development needs to be understood in the context of a
revolution in papal ideology largely initiated by Innocent himself, since this gave
rise to growing assertions of papal authority over lay rulers. The papacy, indeed,
increasingly used the interdict to bolster such claims in the thirteenth century.

Another good reason for concentrating on this period is that the papal registers
survive in a virtually continuous series from 1198.[9] They record outgoing
papal letters and give vital evidence of papal relations with lay rulers. Hence
they shed much light on the operation of the interdict, since they include letters
threatening or pronouncing interdicts on recalcitrant rulers. Some letters indicate
why interdicts were imposed and how they were observed in practice. Others
provide accounts of princely and popular reactions to interdicts, usually derived
from petitions of clergy seeking papal support in enforcing such interdicts.
Thus they illustrate how popes responded to princely and popular opposition to

[6] On the interdict against Lewis of Bavaria and of his supporters (1324): Kaufhold. On the
Florentine interdict (1376): Trexler.

[7] Summarized in Howland, 'Origin'. Documents on early interdicts were edited by Richter, *De
origine*.

[8] See e.g. Watt, *Papal Monarchy*.

[9] A critical edition of the registers of Pope Innocent III is in progress superseding older editions
in *PL* (see Bibliography s.v. Innocent III). Calendars of registers of other thirteenth-century popes
have also been published (see Bibliography s.v. Reg. Alexander IV–Urban IV).

interdicts. Papal letters also show that popes intervened not only over their own interdicts but also those of other ecclesiastical authorities. Sometimes this was a response to appeals against such sentences, since by the thirteenth century the pope was seen as the church's supreme judicial authority, or 'universal ordinary'. Papal letters might not only quash such interdicts as invalid but even grant immunity from the interdict or at least from some of its effects. Finally these letters show how the papacy developed and applied standard procedures with regard to the interdict.

Indeed the main reason for focusing on this period is that popes established a common law of interdicts between the late twelfth and the early fourteenth centuries. This effectively regulated the operation of interdicts until the end of the Middle Ages and beyond, since it formed part of the *Corpus iuris canonici* that remained binding on all Catholics till 1917.[10] The thirteenth-century papal registers hence illustrate this law in action as it was being formed and the issues that influenced its formation. It is, therefore, a fundamental assumption of this book that ecclesiastical law and practice cannot be studied in isolation from one another. As Brundage has recently observed, most records created by the medieval church were legal in nature (and papal letters especially), so we cannot make full and proper sense of them without a knowledge of the law that informed them.[11] Conversely medieval canon law ought not to be treated simply as part of intellectual history or the history of ideas; it affected people's lives across the Western Church in various ways. Indeed it is necessary to observe how the law was applied in practice and understand how interpretation of it by commentators influenced how it was applied. Furthermore a symbiotic relationship existed between legal theory and practice in the thirteenth-century Western Church, since most papal legislation of the period was essentially case law. For centuries popes issued decretal letters in reply either to requests for judgement on specific cases or for clarification of a point of law. But from the mid-twelfth century, as papal jurisdiction expanded, these decretals proliferated dramatically in response to external demand and came to form a growing body of new law. They are also historical sources since many clearly refer to actual cases, and indeed some letters cited below from the papal registers as evidence of practice also entered canonical collections. Finally it must be recalled that growing numbers of clergy studied canon law at universities from the late twelfth century, and that they included many future popes and prelates who laid interdicts as well as lower clergy charged

---

[10] The formation of this *Corpus* is discussed below. Literature on medieval canon law is too extensive to cite fully; much of it is listed in the detailed bibliographies of the *Bulletin of Medieval Canon Law*, 1– (1955–). Excellent introductions are Brundage, *Canon Law*, and Helmholz, *Spirit*. Standard guides to medieval commentaries on the *Corpus* are Kuttner, *Repertorium*, and Schulte, *Quellen*, ii. *Dictionnaire de Droit Canonique* is also useful. A multivolume *History of Medieval Canon Law*, ed. K. Pennington and W. Hartmann, has also begun to appear; an online version of the last volume, a Bio-bibliographical Index of Medieval Canonists, is currently available at http://faculty.cua.edu/pennington

[11] Brundage, *Canon Law*, 1.

with enforcing these sentences. Canon law and the commentaries on it written by their university teachers thus undeniably influenced their application of the interdict. Indeed we cannot fully appreciate how interdicts worked at this time without knowing how they were meant to work according to canon law and its commentators.

Although this argument holds true for almost all the Church's activities in the thirteenth century, not only interdicts, a negative attitude to canon law has not entirely disappeared among medievalists over forty years after Charles Duggan berated it: 'A curiously myopic view *still* survives, even among medievalists, that canonical studies are merely of peripheral or highly specialist interest.'[12] Duggan indeed concluded that it was far 'from being a true opinion'. A basic aim of my book is to demonstrate how canon law is central to our understanding of the Church and its relations with society in the thirteenth century, and in particular the interdict. In the first chapter the ideas of twelfth- and thirteenth-century writers on canon law, theology, and Roman law will be examined to understand how churchmen could justify a sanction like the interdict that seemed to punish the innocent along with the guilty, in that it usually fell on an entire community for its ruler's fault. Evidence will be given of the influence of these ideas on those using interdicts in the thirteenth century, especially Innocent III.[13] Lay forms of collective punishment were admittedly also potential influences, notably penalties laid on a whole family or tribe for the crimes of one of its members. But these secular sanctions were largely developed in the early Middle Ages and thus need to be studied in relation to the interdict's origins, which I am not proposing here. And arguably the ideas of our twelfth- and thirteenth-century thinkers constituted a more immediate and demonstrable influence on those using interdicts in this period. In subsequent chapters explaining the interdict's operation canonical theory is presented along with examples of actual practice. Hence canon law forms the essential backbone of the book.

In order to make this book accessible to those who are not specialists in canon law, it is necessary here to sketch its development during the central Middle Ages. This development will be traced from the appearance of Gratian's *Decretum* in about 1140. This canon law collection does not refer to the interdict, but it includes texts that aroused debate on the related issues of punishment of the innocent and collective punishment. Generally it marked a fundamental turning point in the history of canon law and the Church. Earlier collections had been compiled and they were an important source of texts for Gratian's own collection, but none of them had superseded the rest as the definitive summation of the Church's legal tradition. Gratian's compilation was increasingly accepted as such across the West by the late twelfth century. First within twenty years of its appearance it became the standard textbook for the study of canon law

---

[12] Lawrence (ed.), *English Church*, 108. The italics are mine.
[13] See also my 'Peter the Chanter' and 'Popular Resistance'.

in Bologna, where Gratian himself had probably taught the subject. By the mid-twelfth century Bologna was already acquiring an international reputation for Roman law studies, and the *Decretum* also stimulated the growth of a canon law school there. The earliest extant commentary on the *Decretum* was written at Bologna in *c*.1148 by Paucapalea, possibly a pupil of Gratian. The most important of these early Bolognese commentaries were completed in the 1150s by Rolandus (once erroneously identified with the future Pope Alexander III), in *c*.1164 by Rufinus, and in *c*.1171 by Johannes Faventinus.[14] Those who lectured and wrote on the *Decretum* soon became known as decretists, and decretist schools sprang up outside Italy in France, the Anglo-Norman realm, and the Rhineland. A French school was established at Paris by the 1160s when Stephen of Tournai wrote his commentary on the *Decretum*; another early decretist work of this school was the anonymous *Summa Parisiensis* (*c*.1170). The Anglo-Norman school was centred on Oxford by the 1180s, and teachings of two Oxford early decretists, Simon of Southwell and John of Tynemouth, are reported in a commentary to the *Decretum* in Cambridge, Gonville and Caius College MS 283/676.

A major reason for the *Decretum*'s success was that it was perfectly designed for the classroom, and it is probable that Gratian originally compiled the book for his own teaching. What made his book attractive as a teaching tool was its 'dialectical' arrangement. The dialectical method was a common literary technique among early twelfth-century scholars and involved assembling the authorities for (*pro*) and against (*contra*) a particular proposition. It had been popularized by the theologian Abelard's *Sic et Non*, which collected contradictory passages in the Bible, and similarly Gratian gathered conflicting legal authorities and sought to resolve the contradictions between them through interpretation. Accordingly Gratian entitled his collection a 'concordia discordantium canonum' (*Decretum* was a later appellation), and the canons there are interspersed with his interpretative comments or *dicta*. His canons comprised extracts from the Bible and Church Fathers, notably St Augustine, decrees of church councils, and papal decretals. Recent research has demonstrated that the *Decretum* appeared in at least two recensions, the first completed before 1139, perhaps as early as the 1120s, and the second after 1139 and no later than 1158.[15] The second recension incorporated much extra material, including extracts from Roman law, and was twice as long as the first. It has been argued that Gratian was not responsible for this recension because it broke up the structure and argument of the original, but it was this later version which was generally adopted. Commentators on this recension continued Gratian's work of harmonizing its

---

[14] Twelfth-century decretist literature is described by Kuttner, *Repertorium*, 1–58, 123–271. For editions of Paucapalea, Rolandus, Rufinus, Stephen of Tournai, and *Summa Parisiensis*, see the Bibliography.

[15] See Winroth. On the 'dialectical' method see Meyer.

dissonant texts by interpretation. This process culminated in twelfth-century Bologna with Huguccio's *Summa* (*c*.1188), the summation of four decades of decretist doctrine.[16] By Huguccio's day Bologna was the main centre for the study of canon law in western Europe, attracting students and teachers from north of the Alps. But their interests had begun to shift away from the old law of the Church, as codified in the *Decretum*, towards new canon law that appeared after the *Decretum*.

Ironically the *Decretum* partly stimulated the growth of this new law. Gratian had exposed gaps in existing canon law and emphasized the papacy's role as supreme judicial authority in the Church, the 'universal ordinary'. Indeed from the mid-twelfth century the *Decretum* was effectively supplemented by the papacy's rulings on cases referred to it as 'universal ordinary'. But one must be wary of seeing this case law as self-conscious legislation from the outset. Though the papacy sought to extend papal and ecclesiastical jurisdiction from the mid-twelfth century, judicial business at the curia largely expanded in response to external demand. Appeals to Rome from most parts of the West proliferated from the mid-twelfth century, and papal decretals were essentially a by-product of this process. But it was not the papacy that initially made decretals into a body of law. Decretals were first assembled in private collections by their recipients; they were indeed addressed to specific individuals. But, as interest in the latest papal rulings grew, they began to circulate and canonists copied them from various sources into their own collections. Many early collections were compiled in England, and indeed English prelates were especially assiduous in soliciting decretals partly as a response to the growing claims of royal jurisdiction from the mid-twelfth century. This English interest in canon law also became evident in the schools as we will see, but first let us return to early decretal collections.[17]

These were initially haphazard affairs, but by the 1170s systematic collections where decretals were organized under subject headings appeared. The most important of these late-twelfth century collections was the *Breviarium extravagantium* compiled by Bernard of Pavia (*c*.1188–92).[18] It became the model for most subsequent decretal collections. It was split into five books, each concerning a broad area of decretal law: judicial powers (book 1); procedure (book 2); clerical duties and privileges (book 3); marriage (book 4); crime and punishment (book 5). Each book was further subdivided into sections or 'titles' (*tituli*) that concerned specific aspects of its main theme. Most decretals on interdicts appear in the title 'De sententia excommunicationis' in book 5 not only in Bernard's decretal collection but also most that followed it; Gilbertus was apparently the only canonist to include a separate title 'De sententia interdicti' in his collection.[19]

---

[16] See Müller, *Huguccio*.   [17] See e.g. Duggan, *Decretal Collections*.

[18] The 'extravagantes' of the title referred to decretals 'wandering outside' the *Decretum*.

[19] Heckel, 'Gilbertus und Alanus', 217.

Bernard's collection was the first of five generally used in courts and schools of canon law before 1234, the *quinque compilationes antique*; hence his *Breviarium extravagantium* became more widely known as *Compilatio prima*. The first decretal collection officially approved by the papacy for use 'tam in iudiciis quam in scholis' was *Compilatio tertia*. It contained decretals from the first twelve years of Innocent III's pontificate and was compiled by a papal chaplain Petrus Beneventanus in 1210.[20] There is no evidence that Innocent commissioned it but he did authenticate its content. This was largely a response to growing forged decretals, and such papal approval was significant. Apparently Innocent did not endorse *Compilatio quarta*, where Johannes Teutonicus assembled his decretals not found in *Compilatio tertia* and canons of the Fourth Lateran Council convened by him in 1215, and indeed canonists were slow to accept this collection. Between these two Innocentian collections *Compilatio secunda* had appeared. The work of a Welshman Johannes Galensis, it was said to be *secunda* even though *Compilatio tertia* had appeared before it, for it contained chronologically earlier material including twelfth-century decretals not collected in *Compilatio prima*. Galensis largely derived these from the collections of Gilbertus Anglicus (1202) and Alanus Anglicus (1205), two other canonists from the British Isles active at Bologna. Finally Honorius III issued a collection of his own decretals as *Compilatio quinta* in 1226, and unlike *Compilatio tertia* there is no question whether the pope ordered the making of this collection, because its bull of promulgation addressed to its compiler, Tancred of Bologna, makes this explicit.[21]

These decretal collections, like the *Decretum* before them, became the subject of canonistic commentary. Most of this activity was centred at Bologna, and canonists from the British Isles were again deeply involved in this. Both Richardus Anglicus (*c*.1197) and Alanus Anglicus (*c*.1201–10) wrote commentaries on *Compilatio prima*, and Johannes Galensis likewise on *Compilatio tertia* (*c*.1212). Iberian canonists were also active at Bologna; both Vincentius Hispanus and Laurentius Hispanus composed commentaries on *Compilatio tertia* before 1215, as did the German canonist Johannes Teutonicus (*c*.1217). The international character of the Bolognese 'decretalist' school (decretalists being commentators on decretals) indicates not only its reputation but the extent of canon law's influence. Furthermore the Bolognese decretalist commentaries circulated across Europe, and in the early thirteenth century the Paris school of Petrus Brito also produced commentaries on *Compilatio prima*.[22] Some canonists even wrote on

[20] See Pennington, 'Making'.
[21] The first four *compilationes* were printed in A. Agustin, *Antiquae collectiones decretali-um* ... (Illerda 1576). Friedberg's 'edition' of all five *compilationes* (see Bibliography) is unsatisfactory as it omits the text of decretals included in the *Liber extra* (see below) though its compiler often amended the texts he derived from the *compilationes*. For manuscripts of the *compilationes* and their commentaries: Kuttner, *Repertorium*, 322–85.
[22] See e.g. my 'Collection'.

their own collections, notably Bernard of Pavia in his *Summa* on *Compilatio prima* (1192–8), Alanus in a commentary on his decretal collection (*c*.1206), and Johannes Teutonicus in that on *Compilatio quarta* (*c*.1215).[23] The literary activity of canonists thus concentrated on new decretal law by the early thirteenth century, but they did not neglect the *Decretum* entirely. In *c*.1210–15 Alanus and another unknown Bolognese writer (identified by some as Laurentius Hispanus) wrote commentaries on it, known respectively as the *Apparatus* 'Ius naturale' and *Glossa Palatina*. Several anonymous decretist commentaries also survive from the French school of this period, notably the *Apparatus* 'Ecce vicit leo' (1202–10) and *Summa* 'Animal est substantia' (1206–10).[24]

Commentaries generally took the form of marginal notes surrounding the legal text and relating to key words or passages in it. It was a common scholarly technique to 'gloss' authoritative texts in this way, and interlinear and marginal glosses had also been written on scriptural and Roman law texts since at least the early twelfth century; Roman law indeed supplied many of the concepts and terms of canonistic thought, as we will see, and influenced canonistic writing strongly by the early thirteenth century. 'Glosses' not only elucidated the meaning of a particular text but also noted analogies and contradictions between it and related texts. In legal glosses these cross references were given in a highly abbreviated form and were called *allegationes*.[25] Early glosses often comprised mere strings of them, notably on the *Decretum* where they continued its work of identifying conflicting legal authorities. But increasingly teachers of law added their own comments in the gloss, and these originated largely as notes for their lectures in the schools, for the lectures were based on close reading of the legal texts. Where they cited an opinion of another teacher, they usually acknowledged him in the gloss with an abbreviated form of his name, a *siglum*.[26] They also identified their own opinions by *sigla*, e.g. 'io.' for Johannes Teutonicus. But not all glosses were authored and circulated by the teachers themselves. Some are reported versions of their lectures such as that on *Compilatio prima* (*c*.1205) by a pupil of Parisian canonist Petrus Brito or the decretist gloss in a Cambridge manuscript noted above.[27]

Besides glosses other genres of canonistic literature existed, notably the *summa*, a treatise summarizing the rulings in a collection rather than analysing them closely. It was normally transmitted separately from the legal text, e.g. Huguccio's *Summa*. Terse summaries of individual rulings were given in *casus*, *notabilia*, or *brocarda*, e.g. *notabilia* of Paulus Hungarus (*c*.1220) on *Compilatio secunda* and *tertia*. Finally canonists discussed specific legal problems or hypothetical cases

---

[23] Alanus's commentary in Vercelli Cathedral MS 89 is described by Kuttner, 'Alanus'.

[24] See Kuttner, *Repertorium*, 59–92, 206–7.

[25] These abbreviations are listed and extended by Mollat, *Introduction*. Methods for citing canon law are clearly explained by Brundage, *Canon Law*, 190–202.

[26] Numerous *sigla* are listed and identified by Mollat, *Introduction*.

[27] Reported Brito gloss: n. 22. Cambridge manuscript: Kuttner, 'Anglo-Norman Canonists', 317–19.

in *questiones* which often reported disputations in the schools. A *questio* usually noted the legal authorities for and against and then gave a 'solutio' reconciling these authorities and hence applied Gratian's dialectical method; the second part of his *Decretum* indeed comprised a series of *questiones*.[28]

The profusion of this literature was doubtless bewildering to students who had to master it; hence for many texts a standard gloss or *glossa ordinaria* that synthesized opinions of various commentators was established. The *Glossa ordinaria* to the Bible begun by Anselm of Laon and his circle had paved the way in the twelfth century. In *c*.1215 Johannes Teutonicus completed his *glossa* on the *Decretum* that was accepted as *ordinaria*, but it was revised by Bartholomew of Brescia thirty years later, and this later version accompanied virtually all copies of the *Decretum* from the mid-thirteenth century into the age of early printing. Certain glosses were also regarded as *ordinaria* on the *quinque compilationes*, notably those completed by Tancred of Bologna around 1220 on the first three *compilationes*. Indeed his gloss appears in most manuscripts of those collections. The only gloss on *Compilatio quarta* was by its compiler Johannes Teutonicus and hence became *ordinaria* by default. Nevertheless the Fourth Lateran Council canons in that collection also circulated independently and were glossed by Vincentius Hispanus and Damasus (*c*.1215). Finally Zoën Tencarius and Jacobus de Albenga wrote glosses (*c*.1230) on *Compilatio quinta*, and Jacobus's was the most widely diffused of these and hence effectively *ordinaria*.[29]

The decretal collections to which these glosses were attached were short-lived, however, as the *quinque compilationes* were superseded in 1234 by the *Liber extra*, so called because it was 'extra' to the *Decretum*. It was also known as the *Decretales* of Gregory IX, rather misleadingly for it largely comprised decretals of his predecessors derived from the *quinque compilationes* (which became *antique* after the *Liber extra* appeared). Nevertheless Gregory IX had commissioned it from his chaplain, Catalan canonist Raymond de Peñafort, whom he allowed a free hand in editing this material, and the *Liber extra* included some 200 decretals of his own, some of which he drafted specifically for it.[30] This marked a major step towards more self-conscious papal lawmaking, and Gregory, following the lead of his immediate predecessors in *Compilatio tertia* and *quinta*, further enhanced the pope's role in making definitive, exclusive, and authoritative collections of decretal law.

The *Liber extra*'s rapid reception is illustrated by the writing of commentaries on it within a few years of its promulgation on 5 September 1234. This did not mean that glosses on the *quinque compilationes* ceased to be important as these

---

[28] On *summe* etc. see e.g. Kuttner, *Repertorium*, 123–256, 386–433, esp. 411–13 on Paulus Hungarus.

[29] On these various ordinary glosses and their manuscripts, see Kuttner, *Repertorium*, 93–122, 322–85.

[30] See e.g. Kuttner, 'Raymond', and Michaud-Quantin, 'Remarques'.

collections lost legal force, for as most of the decretals collected there passed into the *Liber extra*, so these older glosses travelled with these rulings into literature on the new collection. Indeed one of the first commentaries on the *Liber extra* was by Vincentius Hispanus (*c*.1236), who copied there many of his earlier glosses on *Compilatio prima* and *tertia* and the Fourth Lateran Council canons, often revising and updating them. Other early literature on the *Liber extra* comprised the *Summa* of Johannes Hispanus de Petesella (*c*.1236), who taught at Bologna and Padua, and the *Lectura* and *Summa* of Cardinal Goffredus de Trano (d. 1245).[31] Bolognese canonist Bernard of Parma also drafted a marginal gloss on the *Liber extra* by 1239 and repeatedly revised it until his death in 1266. It was treated as *ordinaria* by the mid-thirteenth century and is found in almost all manuscripts of the *Liber extra*. It cited many commentators on the *compilationes antique*, thus maintaining the influence of the older decretalist glosses. Alongside the *glossa ordinaria*, the most influential commentaries on the *Liber extra* were those of Innocent IV and Hostiensis. Innocent completed his, the *Apparatus*, around 1251, and though it draws on earlier literature that he studied as a law student at Bologna, it also displays great originality of thought, particularly on the question of collective guilt.[32] Meanwhile Henricus de Segusio, known as 'Hostiensis' since he was cardinal bishop of Ostia, wrote a *Summa* (*c*.1252) and an extensive commentary by the time he died in 1271, and these treatments of the *Liber extra* are subtle but less innovative than Innocent's. Other mid-thirteenth-century commentators on the *Liber extra* were southern French canonist Pierre Sampsona and his pupil Bernard de Montmirat (d. 1296), the latter being dubbed 'Abbas antiquus' as abbot of Montmajour, but they 'collaborated so closely that it is easy to confuse their works'.[33]

Meanwhile papal legislation continued to grow and was appended to copies of the *Liber extra*. It comprised Innocent IV's *Novelle* and Gregory X's *Novissime*. The *Novelle* circulated in at least three different collections, the first consisting of decrees of the First Council of Lyon (1245).[34] The second largely comprised parts of Innocent IV's decretal 'Romana Ecclesia' (1246); this specifically addressed a dispute between the Archbishop of Reims and his suffragans but was clearly also conceived as general legislation, since it was reissued as such a month after its original appearance. Finally Innocent IV confirmed his decrees, this decretal, and eight further rulings in his third and definitive collection (1253). His laws were glossed by Bernardus Compostellanus junior (before 1253) and 'Abbas Antiquus'

---

[31] On these commentaries see Schulte, *Quellen*, i.193; ii.81–3, 88–91. On Vincentius see Ochoa Sanz.

[32] On his *Apparatus* see Schulte, *Quellen*, ii.92–3, and Bertram, 'Angeblicke Originale'. On Bernard's *Glossa* see Kuttner, 'Glossa'.

[33] Hostiensis: Pennington, 'Henricus'; 'Earlier recension'. Sampsona and 'Abbas': Pontal, 'Quelques remarques'; Vodola, *Excommunication*, 233–6 (quotation from p. 233); Bertram, 'Pierre de Sampson'.

[34] See Kuttner, 'Decretalistica' and 'Konstitutionen'; Kessler, 'Untersuchungen'.

(1260) among others. Though Bernardus's gloss was apparently seen as *ordinaria*, Innocent's gloss on his own laws, included in his *Apparatus*, was unremarkably more influential. His 41 *Novelle* were supplemented by Gregory's 31 *Novissime* issued at the Second Council of Lyon (1274).[35] The gloss on the *Novissime* by Johannes Garsias Hispanus (1282) was immediately accepted as *ordinaria*; thus it was the most widely diffused. Other glosses included that of French canonist William Durand the Elder (1289), noted as author of an important procedural manual titled the *Speculum iudiciale*.

Subsequently the *Novelle*, *Novissime*, and other papal legislation issued since 1234 were incorporated in a new canon law collection promulgated on 3 March 1298 by Boniface VIII.[36] This was called the *Liber sextus* as it supplemented the five books of Gregory IX's collection. Boniface had commissioned three canonists to compile it in 1296, one of whom was Bérenger Frédol, bishop of Béziers. Bérenger subsequently wrote a treatise on excommunication and interdicts; thus it has been supposed that he redacted the texts on these sentences in the *Liber sextus*. However, it is clear that the pope himself contributed significantly to the *Liber sextus*, as Bérenger's treatise itself indicates, as over half the texts in this collection are ascribed to Boniface and many of them appear there for the first time. Some were admittedly adapted from the rulings of his predecessors, whilst others resolved canonistic disputes about points of law, often affirming opinions of Hostiensis.[37] Nevertheless it was a highly original compilation which represented the culmination of self-conscious papal lawmaking, and canonists immediately recognized it as authoritative. Johannes Andreae glossed it (*c*.1302) and his gloss was *ordinaria* in his university of Bologna whereas the gloss of French cardinal Johannes Monachus (*c*.1305) was *ordinaria* at Paris. Guido de Baysio (d. 1313), nicknamed 'Archdiaconus' since he was archdeacon of Bologna University, also wrote a commentary on the *Liber sextus* (and another on the *Decretum* known as his *Rosarium*). Manuscripts of the *Liber sextus* were often accompanied by two or all three commentaries, particularly in England. After 1317 they also normally included another canonical collection, the *Clementine*, so called as it contained constitutions of Clement V, many of them allegedly based on rulings of his Council of Vienne (1311–12).[38] Although it was redacted by his death in 1314, it was not promulgated till 1317 (by his successor John XXII). The gloss on the *Clementine* by Johannes Andreae was generally recognized as *ordinaria*, and he also wrote bulky commentaries, both called *Novella*, on the *Liber extra* and *Liber sextus* before his death in 1348. By then decretal legislation and its codification

[35] See Kuttner, 'Conciliar'; Johanek, 'Studien'; Bertram, 'Wissenschaftlichen' and 'Commentaire'.
[36] See Gagner; Le Bras, 'Boniface VIII'; Schmidt, 'Bonifaz VIII' and 'Frühe Anwendungen'; and my 'Two Constitutions'.
[37] On Bérenger see Schmidt, 'Bonifaz VIII', 230–2.
[38] See Menache, 288–305, and Müller, *Vienne*. On this early fourteenth-century literature see Schulte, *Quellen*, ii.186–90, 191–3, 205–29. On Johannes Andreae see Kuttner, 'Andreae'.

had largely ceased;[39] the last major collection was John XXII's *Extravagantes* compiled and glossed by French canonist Jesselin de Cassagnes (*c*.1325). This along with the *Extravagantes communes*, a fifteenth-century collection of papal legislation issued since 1298, completed the *Corpus iuris canonici*. This body of law also comprising the *Decretum*, *Liber extra*, *Liber sextus*, and *Clementine* was first published at Paris in 1500 and frequently reprinted thereafter. A definitive edition commissioned by Gregory XIII was published at Rome in 1582; this 'Editio Romana' remained the standard version of the *Corpus* until the appearance of Emil Friedberg's edition in 1881, though the latter is far from being the much needed critical edition.

Clearly medieval canon law and canonistic literature represent a large, complex body of material. Nevertheless various canonistic treatises on the interdict have enabled me to penetrate this vast legal labyrinth, although most are late. The two most significant are an anonymous treatise dated 1270 and generally attributed to Hermann of Minden, a German Dominican,[40] and a treatise of the Bolognese canonist Johannes Calderinus, the pupil and adopted son of Johannes Andreae, completed shortly before 1359.[41] The first is the earliest known treatise on the interdict and draws heavily on Innocent IV's *Apparatus*; the second is the most thorough and original monograph on interdicts by a medieval canonist. Beyond these treatises, I have investigated almost all the canonical collections and commentaries cited above, largely in manuscripts; hence this book can claim to be reasonably comprehensive on canonical theory in the 'classical' period of canon law (1140–1317). It cannot make a similar claim for canonical practice, though I have thoroughly searched editions and calendars of the papal registers of 1198–1303 for evidence of this. Chapter 5 contains case studies of three interdicts based on these and other records, but the scope remains for many similar studies, and this book aims to provide a framework in which these can be understood. More generally it seeks to illuminate the relationship between the spiritual and temporal powers in the thirteenth century. Though my subject may suggest an emphasis on episodes of conflict between these powers, it also provides examples of cooperation, for secular powers might aid the enforcement of interdicts and conversely church authorities might use interdicts to defend secular interests.

---

[39] By the early fourteenth century papal legislation largely took the form of constitutions, i.e. general abstract rulings, rather than decretals responding to individual cases. Indeed by then cases referred to the papal curia were largely heard by the judges of the *Rota*, rather than the pope himself; consequently the *Rota* increasingly made the case-law of the Western Church.

[40] Hermann of Minden (attrib.), 'De interdictis'. Hermann was identified as the author by Denifle and Ehrle, *Archiv*, ii.232. He was Dominican prior of the German province in 1286–90. Manuscripts of this treatise are listed by Kaeppeli, *Scriptores*, ii.227–8 (no. 1878).

[41] Calderinus, 'De interdicto'. Another Bolognese canonist, Johannes de Legnano, observed in his own treatise on the interdict dated 1359 (Legnano, 'De interdicto', fol. 335ra) that Calderinus had published a treatise on the interdict at Bologna University 'very recently'. Calderinus took his doctorate in canon law at Bologna in 1326 and taught there from 1330 to 1359 (Schulte, *Quellen*, ii.247–53).

Furthermore this study of a collective sanction seeks to raise important questions about medieval notions of community, especially the relationship between the head of a community and its members. Therefore this book explores three fundamental dualities of medieval life: spiritual and temporal; individual and society; and legal theory and practice.

1

The Justification of the Interdict in Medieval Thought

1.1 PUNISHMENT OF THE INNOCENT

An interdict was usually imposed on a community or place since its ruler had sinned against the Church. Consequently, it punished the innocent along with the guilty. This raised a moral and legal problem that twelfth- and thirteenth-century canonists and theologians attempted to resolve in their writings. They were familiar with a number of authorities that argued against the punishment of the innocent. In Ezechiel 18:20, for instance, God had taught that each soul should suffer for its own sin; therefore a son should not bear the burden of his father's wickedness. The same general principle was expressed in Roman law maxims: 'penalties ought to bind their authors'; 'nobody ought to be deprived of his right without guilt'; 'the deeds of some may not prejudice others'; and 'one person's wrong ought not to result in a church's loss'.[1] Nevertheless, the interdict was one of several penalties approved by canon law and papal authority that departed from this principle of restricting punishment to the guilty. In 1199, for instance, Pope Innocent III responded to the growth of heresy at Viterbo in the papal patrimony by ordering the disinheritance of the orthodox sons of heretics. This order circulated widely, was included in the official body of canon law from 1210 onwards, and remained in force until the inquisition fell into decline in the eighteenth century.[2] Contemporary canonists and theologians, therefore, had to apply all their ingenuity to the problem of justifying the Church's use of such exceptional sanctions.

Gratian had approached the problem in one of his *cause* in the *Decretum*, that is, hypothetical cases designed to stimulate student debate in the classroom. This way of teaching law was a central purpose of his text and indeed revolutionary; from the mid-twelfth century teachers of Roman and canon law generally adopted

---

[1] Cod. 9.47.22: 'peccata suos debent tenere auctores' (cited in X 3.11.2). The other principles cited above were treated by the canonist Ricardus Anglicus at the end of the twelfth century; his treatment has been edited and discussed in Piergiovanni, ii.1–19. See Piergiovanni in general on this subject.

[2] See my 'Punishment of the Guiltless', esp. 271–8, and Pennington, 'Pro peccatis patrum puniri'.

this method. It involved posing questions, and at C.1 q.4 Gratian asked whether it was legitimate for sons to be punished for their fathers' sins. He answered in his classic dialectical fashion by assembling authorities for and against, notably Exodus 20:5 where God had threatened to visit the sins of the fathers on the sons down to the third and fourth generations. He resolved the contradiction between this text and others opposing such apparently indiscriminate severity by quoting St Augustine. The latter had commented on this text that it showed divine mercy not severity, for God postponed judgement in expectation of repentance until the fathers' sins were repeated in the third and fourth generations. In other words descendants were punished for imitating their forebears' sins, which they thereby made their own. Gratian then cited many examples in the Old Testament of divine punishment falling on whole communities but concluded with the same interpretation: 'by these examples none are proven to be held responsible for the sins of others except imitators of their wickedness.'[3] Most twelfth-century theologians from Peter Lombard onwards adopted this line, observing that the God of Exodus 20:5 had threatened to extend punishment to the third and fourth generations 'of those who hated him' in imitation of their forebears.[4] Stephen Langton, a master of theology at Paris till 1206, observed that since a man usually lived long enough to see the fourth generation of his descendants, they would see his sinful example and imitate it, which they might not have done had they not seen him.[5] Conversely Innocent III, a one-time theology student at Paris, used this imitation argument to limit a son's responsibility for certain paternal sins. For example in 1200 he ruled that illegitimate sons might be excluded from clerical office only where they imitated their fathers' incontinence.[6]

Although this interpretation of Exodus 20:5 restricted the punishment of third parties to imitators, it conceded that a community could be lead astray by the example of its head or members. Indeed a text of the third-century theologian Origen included in the *Decretum* observed that a people could be polluted by one sinner just as a flock could be infected by one diseased sheep.[7] Likewise in Leviticus 4:3 God had taught that a sinful priest caused his people to stray. Innocent III quoted this text in a letter of 1198 and two of his sermons to warn

---

[3] C.1 q.4 *dictum post* c.11, §12. On Gratian and the dialectical method see Meyer, 144–77.

[4] Landgraf, 'Vererbung'.

[5] Langton on Exodus 20:5, Oxford, Trinity College MS 65, fo. 125ra; Durham Cathedral MS A.I.7, fol. 42ra: 'Ego sum visitans ... Sed quare dicitur "In terciam et quartam generacionem", cum in qualibet generacione puniatur imitator paterni flagicii? Solutio. Ideo dicit quia tamdiu solent patres vivere. Prima, enim, generacio a xv annis et supra et sic usque ad lxx annos sunt quatuor generaciones, et quod semper est vite hominis labor et dolor. Et ideo hoc dixit quia filii videntes patres eos pocius imitantur quam si non viderent. Quod enim videmus pocius imitamur quam quod non videmus.' Another version in Durham Cathedral MS A.III.12, fol. 192ra: 'In terciam et quartam generationem ... usque ad has generationes solent antiquitus homines vivere et posteritatem suam videre, sicut constabit si anni computentur. Homo, enim, in xvᵃ etate potest generare, quae etas, si per v multiplicetur, erunt fere lxxx anni ... ' For a fuller treatment of such views on Exodus 20:5 see my 'Peter the Chanter', 4–6.

[6] X 1.6.20. Cf. X 1.9.10 §6. See my 'Punishment of the Guiltless', 279–80. [7] D.45 c.17.

clergy not to set a bad example to their flock. He observed in his sermons on this text that if priests committed sins, laity would simply follow their example and excuse themselves with the words of John 5:19: 'A son can only do what he sees his father doing.'[8] The Paris master Peter the Chanter (d. 1197) and Stephen Langton had glossed Leviticus 4:3 in similar terms; hence Innocent III, possibly a pupil of the Chanter, was again following Parisian moral theology.[9] These theologians had also argued that sons might suffer divine punishment to prevent them imitating their fathers' sins. According to the Chanter and Langton God's destruction of the Sodomites' children was merciful since, if he had spared them, they might have followed their parents' example and suffered a fate worse than death: to lose sight of God.[10] But Langton had denied that human justice was likewise justified in killing a son for his father's sin. Indeed an anonymous French canonist pointed out (*c.*1206–10) that God alone might inflict such physical punishment on innocent sons, since only he could foresee that they would become imitators of their parents' vice.[11]

When most canonists debated punishment of the innocent, they did not pursue this notion of sin corrupting others. They were mainly concerned to

---

[8] X 3.34.7. *PL* 217.650–1, 654, 678 (sermons). See my 'Peter the Chanter', 8–9.

[9] Langton on Leviticus 4:3, Durham Cathedral MS A.I.7, fol. 56vb: 'Delinquere faciens populum. per exemplum suum, quia componitur orbis reg. ad exemplum, unde sacerdos per quodlibet peccatum alios corrumpit. Vel intellige hoc, quando peccatum adeo est apertum quod omnes corrumpebat ... unde dicit Osea. "Erit populus sicut sacerdos", et dominus sicut servus.' The Chanter on Leviticus 4:3, Paris, Bibliothèque de l'Arsenal MS 44, p.135a; London, BL, Royal MS 2.C.viii, fol. 69va: 'peccaverit. in omittendo vel faciendo ... negligens aut peccans aut non iudicans populum peccare facit ... eum ad peccandum provocans ... quia sacerdos sicut populus et econtrario'.

[10] The Chanter on Genesis 19:25, Eton College MS 14; Paris, Bibliothèque de l'Arsenal MS 44, p.29b: 'Et habitatores urbium et cuncta terre virencia ... Infantes cum parentibus in Sodomis cremati sunt ... et provisum est illis ne diu viventes parentum exemplum sequerentur et sic sevius punirentur. Parentes quoque tam pro eis quam pro se rei sunt. Mors enim filiorum est parentum, ideo futuri sunt accusatores eorum ... Quomodo cum parvulis Sodomorum actum est misericorditer? Sed pena ibi accipitur pro dampno. Nullum maius dampnum est homini quam non videre deum'. Langton makes the same points in his gloss on Genesis 19:25 v. *parvuli pro peccatis parentum,* Oxford, Trinity College MS 65, fol. 48rb, adding that God's angers condemns these children 'temporaliter', presumably sparing them the eternal damnation which they would have endured, had they lived to follow their parents' bad example.

[11] Langton on Deuteronomy 24:16, Oxford, Trinity College MS 65, fol. 270ra; Durham Cathedral MS A.I.7, fol. 91rb: 'Non occidentur patres pro filiis. Nota dominus dixit Moysi qualiter ipse deberet punire. Dominus autem aliter punit et ita aliud est de hiis quos dominus punit et aliud de hiis quos punit Moysis.' Id. on 4 Kings 14:6, Oxford, Bodleian Library, Rawlinson MS C.427, fol. 47ra; Cambridge, Peterhouse MS 112: 'sicut precepit dominus Moysi in Deuteron. xxiiii c. Non morientur patres pro filiis etc. Sed contra in Iosue c. vii. [Joshua 7:24–6] Achor lapidatus est cum filiis. Ecce pro peccato patris puniti sunt filii. Item in Exodo xx c.: "Ego sum deus tuus fortis, zelotes, visitans iniquitates patrum in filios." Solutio. Sententia divina puniuntur filii pro patribus temporaliter sed non eternaliter, sed sententia humana non puniuntur, ut supradictum est.' *Summa* 'Animal est substantia' on C.24 q.3, Bamberg Staatsbibliothek MS Can. 42, fol. 119ra: 'consumpti ... Sed que est ratio quod Dominus ita corporaliter punivit eos pro peccato parentum? Potest dici quod Deus bene sciebat eos futuros paterne luxurie imitators ... visitans. Idest puniens etiam corporaliter. Sed hoc nulli licet nisi Domino'.

distinguish which penalties might be imposed on the innocent and which not. The *Decretum* included a letter in which St Augustine had castigated an episcopal colleague for anathematizing a whole household for the sin of its head. Gratian had thus distinguished that children might suffer a physical penalty for their parents' sins but not a spiritual one. Therefore most canonists taught that a community might not be excommunicated, but Gratian's distinction did not explain why a community might still suffer the spiritual penalty of the interdict.[12] Canonists could resolve this contradiction through theological doctrine on the original sin. All mankind suffered death for Adam's original sin. St Augustine had taught that those who were baptized and remained in a state of grace at death were at least safe in eternity. From this teaching Peter Abelard (d. 1142) and later twelfth-century theologians concluded that God punished children for their forebears' sins by a 'pena temporalis', that is, suffering confined to this earthly life, but never an eternal one, that is damnation.[13] Hence canonists from Rufinus (*c*.1164) onwards argued that one might not be excommunicated for another's sin because this involved an eternal penalty (it consigned those dying unrepentant to eternal damnation). Conversely, one anonymous canonist recognized (*c*.1185–7) that an entire city might be interdicted for another's sin since this was a 'pena temporalis'.[14] The same distinction was drawn by the English canonist Alanus (*c*.1201–10).[15] And the interdict was only one of several penalties that late twelfth-century canonists classified as a *pena temporalis* in order to justify their extension to the innocent. Others were fines, loss of status, and physical penalties, although some canonists still doubted whether human justice might punish the innocent physically.[16] Innocent III had even used this idea in 1199 when he sought to justify disinheritance of the orthodox sons of heretics: 'in many instances, even according to divine judgement, sons may suffer a *pena temporalis* on account of their fathers, and, according to canonical sanctions, retribution may be inflicted not only on the authors of crimes but also on the offspring of the condemned.'[17]

Such arguments thus excused the application of some penalties to the innocent in terms of their lesser severity, in that they entailed suffering only in this life, but

---

[12] C.24 q.3 c.1 (St Augustine). Cf. Gratian's *dictum* before this canon and VI 5.11.5.

[13] Landgraf, 'Vererbung', esp. 221.

[14] Rufinus, *Summa* on C.1 q.4 (Ed. p. 230). Anonymous gloss on C.24 q.3 *dictum ante* c.1 v. *Quod autem* (inserted in Huguccio's *Summa* on the *Decretum*), BAV, Vat. lat. MS 2280, fol. 253rb: 'Pena duplex est, eterna et temporalis. Ad eternam non imputatur alicuius peccatum alii. Ad temporalem id imputatur. Sed temporalis alia est corporalis, alia est spiritualis. Corporalis pro peccato alterius alteri infertur ... Spiritualis etiam quandoque infertur alteri pro altero ut apparet in filiis sacerdotum adulterorum fornicatorum qui ab ordine repelluntur. Item pro peccato alterius quandoque civitas tota interdicitur'.

[15] Alanus on 1 Comp. 2.17.6 v. *in terram*, München, Bayerische Staatsbibliothek Clm 3879, fol. 28va: 'Ecce pro peccato unius alii punientur, quod non est absurdum de pena temporali. Perpetua nullus pro peccato alterius punietur, ut i. q.iiii. Iam itaque [C.1 q.4 c.8].'

[16] See Piergiovanni, ii.21–58.

[17] X 5.7.10 ('Vergentis'). See the literature on this decretal quoted in n. 2.

not for eternity, as under anathema. Indeed the *Glossa Palatina* on the *Decretum* (*c*.1210–15) observed that for another's sin one might not be anathematized but one might well suffer a *lesser* spiritual penalty, one that forbade all sacraments except infant baptism and penance of the dying, in other words an interdict.[18] St Thomas Aquinas similarly justified interdicts despite Innocent IV's ban on collective excommunication when he noted (*c*.1252) that, though the innocent were denied the Eucharist under an interdict, excommunication was a greater penalty since it cut them off from the Church.[19] The interdict's severity was, as we will see, gradually reduced by papal rulings during the thirteenth century, which made it more bearable for the innocent and more defensible for canonists. Nonetheless, even if canonists accepted that it was licit for the innocent to suffer an interdict, it was licit only in certain circumstances and for certain reasons. It was indeed a commonplace maxim of thirteenth-century canonists that one might be punished without guilt but not without cause.[20]

The canonist Damasus (*c*.1210–15) held that one was punished 'temporaliter' on certain occasions where the seriousness of the crime required it or a deterrent was needed.[21] Indeed the punishment of the innocent was usually reserved in Roman and canon law for the most serious crimes. In Roman law treason was the ultimate crime and its punishment involved not only the traitor's execution but the confiscation of his assets, thereby depriving his sons of their inheritance. In 1199 Innocent III extended this penalty to heretics, since he argued that heresy was treason against Christ and so more heinous than that against any temporal authority. His provision that the catholic sons of heretics suffer disinheritance even exceeded Roman law on heresy, which had at least permitted orthodox heirs to succeed to a heretic's estate.[22] Despite its severity canonists generally called for strict enforcement of this ruling except for Tancred, who argued for its moderation. But even he accepted (*c*.1220) that a serious crime justified the suffering of the innocent under interdicts, remarking that when it was the doing of a lord or father, his household might be deprived of Communion as a result.[23]

---

[18] *Glossa Palatina* on C.24 q.3 d.a.c.1 v. *Quod autem pro peccato*, BAV, Pal. lat. MS 658, fol. 71vb: 'Nota in hac questione iii. quod unus pro alio non debet anathatazari, ut infra e. Si habes [C.24 q.3 c.1], sed alia minori pena spirituali bene preter baptisma parvulorum et penitentia morientium, xvii. q.iiii. Miror, extra. de spon. Non est vobis [C.17 q.4 c.8; 1 Comp. 4.1.13]'. These were indeed the classic exceptions to the ban on the sacraments in interdicted lands (see pp. 145–7, 148–52 below).

[19] Thomas Aquinas, *Scriptum*, IV dist. 18, ii, 3, q.3.

[20] E.g. Raymond of Peñafort, *Summa*, 375: 'Licite quis punitur sine culpa sed non sine causa.' In 1298 Boniface VIII would make this a rule of law at VI 5.12.23.

[21] Damasus, 'Brocarda', fol. 26rb (reg. 22): 'Nullus punitur eternaliter pro peccato alterius, ut c. Nullius [C.1 q.4 c.1], sed quandoque temporaliter quis punitur vel propter enormitatem delicti, ut in §Verum [C.6. q.1 *dictum ante* c.1], vel propter terrorem, ut in c. Cum multe [C.15 q.8 c.3].' The latter canon 'Cum multe' sought to enforce clerical celibacy by threatening to reduce the sons of clergy to serfs of their fathers' churches.

[22] On 'Vergentis' and its canonistic reception see the literature cited in n. 2.

[23] Tancred on 2 Comp. 3.5.2 v. *administrationis*, BAV, Vat. lat. MS 1377, fol. 121ra: 'hii sunt casus in quibus quis privatur iure suo sine culpa sua non tamen sine causa … propter scelus enorme

Following Damasus canonists also recognized that one might be deterred from committing or persisting in serious crimes by the penal consequences for one's nearest and dearest. In other words the punishment of the innocent was understood to have a psychological effect on the guilty. For instance, the canonist Johannes Teutonicus (*c.*1217) observed that Innocent III's ruling on heresy still permitted heretics to recover their assets *ex indulgentia* if they returned to the Catholic faith. The pope's intention was thus not wholly vindictive but coercive: to drive heretics back into unity with the Church by threatening their heirs where threats to themselves alone were ineffectual.[24] Likewise an early thirteenth-century French canonist had remarked that a son rightly suffers a *pena temporalis* for his father, for a father sometimes suffers more through his son's punishment than his own. The canonist Guido de Baysio (d. 1313) subsequently elaborated on this point that if parents were not deterred from wrongs by the penalties inflicted on themselves, at least they might be deterred by those inflicted on their children, since parents feared more for their children than for themselves.[25]

The notion that a wrongdoer was most vulnerable through those closest to him had already been recognized in late twelfth-century Paris theology circles. Thus Peter the Chanter had observed that when God had threatened to visit the sins of the fathers on their offspring down to the third and fourth generations, the sinful father was most severely punished by seeing his offspring suffer on his account, since men were used to living long enough to see the fourth generation of their descendants.[26] It is implied here that the father might be induced to repent

patris vel domini spoliatur familia communione, xxiiii. q. iii. Si habes, supra. de sponsalibus. Non est vobis lib. i. [C.24 q.3 c.1; 1 Comp. 4.1.13] ... t.'

[24] Johannes Teutonicus on 3 Comp. 5.4.1 v. *filiorum* (http://faculty.cua.edu/Pennington/edit 501.htm). See my 'Punishment of the Guiltless', 277.

[25] *Apparatus* 'Ecce vicit leo' on C.15 q.8 c.3 v. *in progeniem*, Paris, BN, MS lat. nouv. acq. 1576, fol. 210va: 'bene potest puniri <filius> pro patre pena temporali quia magis quandoque punitur pater in filio quam in se ipso, ut ff. quod metus causa. Isti quidem §ult. [Dig. 4.2.8 §3], sed numquam pena eterna punitur unus pro alio.' Guido de Baysio, *Rosarium*, ibid.: 'Ut si non terrerentur parentes pro penis sibi illatis, saltem terreantur pro his que filiis infliguntur, nam plus timent parentes de filiis quam de seipsis, ff. quod me. causa. Isti quidem.' Cf. Azo (d. 1220), *Summa* on Cod. 2.19 (Ed. p.39a): 'pro affectu magis terrentur parentes in liberis quam in seipsis'.

[26] Peter the Chanter on Exodus 20:5, Eton College MS 14; Paris, Bibliothèque de l'Arsenal MS 44, p. 86a.: 'Iniquitates patrum in filios usque in terciam et quartam generationem. Non solum de patre, cum peccat, ultionem sumo, sed etiam in filium, nepotem et pronepotem vindictam temporalem extendo, ut in illis etiam puniatur pater et auctor cladis videns eos sic cruciari. Usque ad quartam generationem et non ultra dicit se punitura peccata patrum, quia usque ad has generationes solent vivere homines et posteritatem suam videre.' Id. on Deuteronomy 5:9, Eton College MS 16; Paris, Bibliothèque de l'Arsenal MS 44, p. 306a: 'Reddens iniquitatem patrum super filios ... idest. temporaliter puniens filios et nepotes propter peccata patrum, ut sic pater gravius puniatur in morbo et flagello filii, eum videns furiosum vel leprosum, ut de Achab legimus et Iehu vindictam sumptam.' Id. on Ezechiel 18:2, Paris, BN, MS lat. 16793, fol. 30va: 'Quid est vertitis parabolam in proverbium ... Temporaliter autem sepe punit deus filios pro peccatis parentum, quia in hoc ipso punitur pater, ut in leprosia filii'.

when he realized the suffering that his sins had brought on his family. Indeed a pupil of the Chanter, Stephen Langton, saw this as the motive for the divine punishment that had fallen on Israel in 2 Kings 24. Its cause was King David's murder of Uriah and adultery with Beersheeba, and David had expressed remorse at his people's plight in 2 Kings 24:17: 'I am the sinner. It is my wrong. What have these sheep done? O Lord, I beg you, spare your people from your wrath.' Langton noted Gregory the Great's remark on this biblical passage that the wrath of God that struck the people physically also prostrated the king with grief, and Langton added that contrition was punishment in itself, for the king suffered no other penalty than the contrition that he felt on seeing his people die. And contrition, according to twelfth-century doctrine on penance, was prerequisite for reconciliation of sinners to the Church.[27]

It is also significant that Innocent III had studied theology at Paris, perhaps under the Chanter himself, and he quoted this verse from Kings in a letter of 1199 in order to justify the papal interdict on the kingdom of Lèon. The king of Lèon's refusal to break off his illicit betrothal had caused the sentence. Innocent's use of this verse makes it clear that the king's responsibility for his subjects' suffering was meant to induce him to repent like King David. And, even before becoming pope, Innocent had written in his theological treatise *De miseria conditionis humanae* that a lord's guilt entailed his serf's punishment, and quoted approvingly Horace's epigram that whatever wrongs kings commit, their subjects shall pay for.[28] It is small wonder that as pope he readily imposed interdicts on communities for their rulers' faults and ruled in the first year of his pontificate that orthodox sons of heretics be disinherited.

By the late twelfth century various arguments had evolved that could justify the suffering of the innocent under certain penalties. Theology was the main source from which canonists and popes, notably Innocent III, adapted these for their own ends. It is doubtful whether they would have exploited such arguments if the church authorities had not regularized usage of such sanctions, especially under Innocent III. Following the reform movement of the late eleventh century, the papacy had become increasingly assertive of its authority over laity and clergy, and no more strongly than under Innocent III. It exploited sanctions

[27] Stephen Langton on 2 Kings 24:1, Oxford, Bodleian Library, Rawlinson MS C.427, fol. 30ra; Cambridge, Peterhouse MS 112, fol. 136va: 'Et addidit furor. Nota glosam Gregorii [i.e. Gregory the Great, *Moralia in Iob*, XXV, xvi, ed. CCSL 143B, 1260–2] ... "Ira enim que corporaliter populum pertulit ipsum quoque dolore prostravit." Ex his verbis glose videtur quod contritio sit pena quia David non fuit punitus alia pena quam contritione quam habebat videns populum mori'. On contrition see Anciaux, 463–73.

[28] Innocent III, Reg. 2, p. 132; Innocent also interpreted the 'sheep' of 2 Kings 24:17 as 'innocents' in a sermon (*PL* 217.644). Id. *De miseria*, 21. The quotation is from Horace, *Epistulae*, i. 2, 14. It was also cited by the anonymous *Apparatus* 'Servus appellatur' (*c*.1215) on 3 Comp. 1.3.4 v. *excessibus*, Bamberg Staatsbibliothek MS Can. 19, fol. 120ra: 'Quicquid delirant reges, plectantur Achivi, extra. de spon. Non est vobis et supra. de officio iud. del. Sane quia. l.i. [1 Comp. 4.1.13, 1.21.16].' Incidentally the text being glossed here (3 Comp. 1.3.4) was a decretal of Innocent III concerning an interdict on Le Mans.

touching the innocent in order to bolster that authority, in particular to defend
the Church against violations of its liberties, as in the case of the interdict,
and to combat heresy, as in the case of Innocent's disinheritance provision.
Such collective penalties were not only a result of growing papal claims but
also a reaction to secular forms of social organization emerging in the twelfth
century. These created claims to collective loyalty that often conflicted with those
asserted by the Church. City communes had often been founded in defiance of
episcopal temporal jurisdiction, and some of those in northern Italy sometimes
banded together to oppose the papacy during its clashes with the empire. And
Innocent III often retaliated against such Italian communes with interdicts, trade
embargoes, exposure of their citizens and goods to seizure, and loss of their
see.[29] Moreover the rise of the communes promoted the growth of legal thought
in northern Italy on the nature of an organized community, or *universitas* as
jurists called it, from the late twelfth century onwards.[30] And it was in this
intellectual context that jurists began to confront the issue of corporate liability,
as a modern-day lawyer would term it, or collective guilt and punishment.

1.2 COLLECTIVE GUILT AND PUNISHMENT

The revival of Roman law in the twelfth century, largely stimulated by the
recovery of the complete text of Justinian's Digest in around 1070, supplied the
emerging science of canon law with many of its concepts, procedures, and terms.
In particular, it enabled canonists to formulate their ideas about corporations
and was the source of the notion *universitas* itself. On the problem of corporate
liability, however, it gave them unclear guidance in two conflicting texts of the
ancient Roman jurist Ulpian. At Dig. 4.2.9 §1 he had admitted the possibility of
a people or collegiate body as well as an individual being guilty of intimidation
but had not elaborated. Yet at Dig. 4.3.15 he had stated that, in legal circles in
his time, it was doubted that a citizen body (*municipes*) might be charged with
fraud. He had even suggested that it was incapable of doing anything fraudulent.
Nevertheless he had conceded that legal action might be brought against it if it
had benefited as a result of fraud committed by those administering its affairs,
and he had compared this with a lord being sued for his proctor's fraud. In other
words an organized community might be held responsible for the wrongs of its
rulers or agents; canonists would elaborate significantly on this view after 1200.

Despite Ulpian's vague and equivocal position, medieval Roman lawyers were
in no doubt that a community was capable of wrongdoing. In his *glossa ordinaria* on the Digest Accursius (d. 1263) interpreted Ulpian's question—'Quid

[29] Tillmann, 45 ff.; my 'Punishment of the Guiltless', 278.
[30] See Michaud-Quantin, *Universitas*, for an excellent discussion of medieval notions of
community.

enim municipes facere possunt?'—to mean that they could not commit fraud 'easily'.[31] His reading had been a juristic commonplace since *c*.1200. Another Roman law commentator, Azo (d. *c*.1220), stated the same view in response to Ulpian's question: a citizen body can do nothing easily because of men's natural facility to disagree.[32] Both Azo and Accursius recognized that it was hard for a community to reach a consensus on collective action, but Accursius added that a corporation might be held legally responsible for deeds of the majority of its members, as if they were done by the whole body, and for deeds of its rulers, since it seemed to have given a mandate for them.[33] Likewise, another early thirteenth-century Roman lawyer, Pilius, concluded that Ulpian's question expressed the relative difficulty but not absolute impossibility of corporate wrong-doing.[34] Mid-thirteenth-century canonists, notably Pope Innocent IV, would adopt these views in their own treatment of this issue, as we will later see.

Canonists did not confront the question of corporate liability until after 1200, perhaps because only then did Romanist corporation theory fully open their minds to the complexities of the problem, and even then they first considered it with regard to internal discipline, namely wrongs attributed to ecclesiastical bodies rather than lay communities. One of the first canonists to discuss corporate liability at any length was Johannes Teutonicus. In his *glossa ordinaria* on the *Decretum* (*c*.1215) he conceded that a church might be accused of admitting bretheren simoniacally, i.e. for payment, as Innocent III had ruled in his decretal 'Dilectus filius' (1201). But he contrasted this example with Ulpian's doubts about a community's capacity to commit fraud and St Augustine's teaching against collective excommunication. He went on to point out the procedural difficulty in bringing criminal charges against a corporation. He noted that a community defended itself in court through a proctor or legal representative, but the Romano-canonical procedure of the church courts did not allow the use of proctors in criminal cases; hence a community might not be summoned on criminal charges. He admitted, however, that another kind of legal action, an *inquisitio*, might be brought against a community.[35]

---

[31] Accursius, *Glossa* to Dig. 4.3.15 v. *facere possunt*.   [32] Azo, *Summa* on Cod. 2.20, p. 42b.

[33] Accursius, *Glossa* to Dig. 4.2.9 §1 v. *collegium*.

[34] Pilius, *Summa super Tres Libros* (Books X–XII of the *Codex*, in continuation of the *Summa* on Books I–IX by Placentinus (d. 1192), Pilius's teacher) at Cod. 11.29, London, BL, Arundel MS 492, fol. 170va: 'Item si metum vel vim aliquam fecerit, sicut quilibet conveniretur, ut ff. quod metus causa l. Metum §Animadvertendum [Dig. 4.2.9 §1]. Quamvis dicatur alibi quod universitas consentire non poterit, vel dolo facere, illud enim non inpossibilitatem sed facti notat difficultatem, ut in pandectarum volumine t. de dolo l. Sed ex dolo §Sed an in municipes. [Dig. 4.3.15 §1] notavimus'. Azo and Accursius echoed this point, observing that Ulpian's question denoted the rarity but not impossibility of collective fraud (see their glosses cited in nn. 32–3). See Ullmann, 'Delictal Responsibility', 79–81 and 83 ff., on further civilian discussion of this question.

[35] Johannes Teutonicus on C.12 q.2 c.58 v. *accusandi*, BAV, Vat. lat. MS 1367, fol. 142vb; 'Editio Romana', i. 3139–40: 'Ergo videtur quod alius posset accusare ecclesiam, ut scilicet accusatur quod simoniace elegit aliquem, ut extra.ii. de symonia. Veniens, vel quod metum intulit alieni, ut ff. quod me. c. Metum §ii [2 Comp. 5.2.1; Dig. 4.2.9 §1]. Sed contra, universitas non potest

His views were supported by and perhaps derived from the *Glossa Palatina* on the *Decretum* (*c*.1210–15), which also stated the procedural impossibility of charging a church or community with a crime, even intimidation, as Ulpian had conceded. An *inquisitio*, it recognized, might be brought against a community, such as a church for holding a simoniacal election, but in this instance only its senior members were to be punished.[36] Johannes would reach a similar but more elaborate conclusion in his gloss (*c*.1217) on Innocent III's decretal 'Dilectus filius'. This had ordered an *inquisitio* into monasteries accused of admitting brethren in return for payment, and, where it was proven, the imposition of penances on the prelates and officials of the offending monastery. Johannes wondered why only such individuals were to be punished and not the whole community if all of the monks had done wrong and were understood to know as much as their superiors. His answer was that the prelates and officials alone were punished since everything was done at their counsel and instigation. Hence he concluded that a community might not be charged or punished but its senior members were to be punished.[37] In other words those in charge of a community were to suffer the legal consequences of any wrong attributed to it. This inverted the idea behind the interdict, that a community suffered for wrongs of its rulers. Johannes and the author of the *Glossa Palatina* admittedly conceded that an action might be brought against a church where its bishop or agent was accused of a crime committed with its counsel, but neither drew out the implications of this point in terms of collective responsibility.

dolum committere, ut ff. de dolo. Si ex dolo, nec dicitur aliquid possidere, ff. de acq. pos. l.i. §ult., nec civitas potest excommunicari, ut xxiiii. q.iii. Si habes [Dig. 4.3.15, 41.2.1 §22; C.24 q.3 c.1]. Preterea universitas per actorem vel procuratorem suum se defendere sed in crimine non interveniat procurator, ergo universitas non potest de crimine conveniri, quod verum est. Dicas ergo hic poni verbum "accusandi" pro verbo "agendi", vel intellige cum episcopus accusatur de crimine quod commisit de consilio universitatis, ut xvi. q.vi. Placuit [C.16 q.6 c.2]. Item in modum inquisitionis potest agi contra universitatem prout legitur, extra.ii.de sy. Veniens. [Vel dic quod non proceditur contra universitatem sed potius contra singulos. Io.]' The text in square brackets is in the 'Editio Romana' but not in the manuscript and was probably added by Bartholomew of Brescia (*c*.1245), perhaps quoting another Johannes.

[36] *Glossa Palatina* on C.12 q.2 c.58 v. *accusandi*, BAV, Pal. lat. MS 658, fol. 51va; BAV, Reg. lat. MS 977, fol. 145va: 'Quilibet potest de universitate accusare, ar. C. si reus vel accus. mor. l.i [Cod. 9.6.1], nam ibi plures de eodem crimine fuerint accusati. Sed numquid ecclesia vel universitas potest accusari, cum et quandoque violentiam inferat, ff. quod metus causa. Metum §Animadvertendum [Dig. 4.2.9 §1]. Non, propter iuris impossibilitatem et quia in crimine non posset se defendere per actorem. Utitur ergo verbi "accusandi" improprie pro verbo "agendi". Vel hoc intellige cum episcopus vel actor ecclesie accusatur de aliquo crimine quod commisit consilio universitatis, puta rapina vel aliquo alio, ar. xvi. q.vi. Placuit [C.16 q.6 c.2]. Vel hoc intellige cum per inquisitionem proceditur contra universitatem, extra. de symo. Veniens [2 Comp. 5.2.1].' Id. on C.25 q.2 c.25, v. *Ita nos*, BAV, Pal. lat. MS 658, fol. 73r: 'Sed nunquid potest universitas de isto crimine accusari? Videtur quod non, cum lex dicat quod universitas non potest aliquid dolo facere, ff. de dolo. Si ex dolo §i [Dig. 4.3.15 §1]. Dicimus tamen quod potest et accusabitur nomine universitatis procurator vel amministrator, ff. de con. Et de municipibus, C. de episcopali. audi. Decrevimus, et punientur maiores, ar. extra.ii. de symo. Veniens [Dig. 35.1.97; Cod. 1.4.13; 2 Comp. 5.2.1].'

[37] Johannes on 3 Comp. 5.2.2 v. *officialibus* (edited at http://faculty.cua.edu/pennington/edit 501.htm).

In contrast to their strict theoretical opposition to collective punishment, other canonists adopted a more pragmatic line. Alanus Anglicus agreed (*c*.1201–10) that no formal charges could be brought against a community although an *inquisitio* might be conducted into its wrongdoings, but he added that if this established guilt, it might be punished as often happened in practice; he gave no examples of this, but the interdict is an obvious one.[38] Tancred found a middle way between Johannes and Alanus. He copied the commentary of Johannes on 'Dilectus filius' into his own *glossa* (*c*.1220) on that decretal and appended Alanus's view that a community might be canonically punished following an *inquisitio* into its excesses. But Tancred qualified the latter in line with Johannes's conclusions, arguing that its senior members were to be punished more severely.[39] Tancred's synthesis not only harmonized conflicting views but better described contemporary practice, since when a community suffered an interdict, those who had occasioned it normally fell under the harsher sanction of excommunication.

Although Johannes's position was based on a rather literal reading of Roman law, his pragmatic opponents could find support in recent writings of Roman lawyers. When Bartholomew of Brescia revised Johannes's *Decretum* commentary in 1245, he added to its discussion of corporate liability that a community might be accused for it could commit fraud, albeit not easily; he clearly followed the Roman lawyers' views on Ulpian that had appeared since Johannes's commentary. Like Alanus, he referred to actual practice too, observing that a chapter or civic council was often accused and 'excommunicated'.[40]

Another canonist, Zoën Tencarius, had been even more dependent on Romanist doctrine. He had treated corporate liability (*c*.1230) in response to one of Frederick II's ecclesiastical edicts in *Compilatio quinta*. The edict threatened the imperial 'ban' on any community or person under his rule

---

[38] Alanus on 1 Comp. 1.10.4 v. *accusandi*, München, Bayerische Staatsbibliothek Clm 3879, fol. 9rb: 'Ar. quod universitas non potest accusari, et ar. vii. q.i. Sicut vir, extra. ne clerici vel mona. c. penult., ff. quod metus causa 1. Metum §Animadvertendum [C.7 q.1 c.11; 1 Comp. 3.37.7; Dig. 4.2.9 §1]. Ar. contra ff. de acquir. pos. l.i §ult., ff. de dolo. Sed ex dolo §i [Dig. 41.2.1; 4.3.15]. Solutio: Cum iuris sollempnitate non potest accusari universitas, sed ea omissa de delictis eius potest inquiri et, si et culpa inventa fuerit, puniri, ut extra. ne cleri. uel mo. c. penult., et ita sepe de facto. Vel hic exponatur "accusare", idest "agere". Similis expositio C. de edendo. Qui accusari [Cod. 2.1.4].'

[39] Tancred on 3 Comp. 5.2.2 v. *officialibus*, BAV, Vat. lat. MS 1377, fol. 262rb: '[following gloss in n. 37] Ego dico quod licet universitas non possit accusari, potest tamen inquisitio de excessibus universitatis vel collegii fieri et canonice puniri, sed maiores gravius sunt puniendi, ut supra. e. t. Veniens l.ii., et xliiii di. Commessationes, ff. de condic. Et de municipibus, et xxv. q.ii. Ita nos silanorum [2 Comp. 5.2.1; D.44 c.1; Dig. 35.1.97; C.25 q.2 c.25] t.'

[40] Bartholomeus Brixensis on C.12 q.2 c.58 v. *accusandi*, BAV, Vat. lat. MS 1367, fol. 42rb; 'Editio Romana', i.1340: '[following the gloss at n. 35] Ego credo <quod> universitas ubi non sunt infantes et similes persone accusari potest quia dolum committere potest. Nec obstat lex illa, ff. de dolo. Si ex dolo, quia quod ibi dicitur "non potest committere", suple "de facili". Et vides quod sepe capitulum accusatur et excommunicatur et consilium civitatis [Et delictum quod maiores de universitate committunt ad omnes refertur, ff. de re. iu. l. Aliud [Dig. 50.17.160]] b.' The closing passage in square brackets appears in the 'Editio Romana' not the manuscript.

remaining excommunicate for over a year. Firstly Zoën asked why a community was punished when, according to Roman law, it was not considered capable of sin. He cited Ulpian's doubts about collective fraud, a Digest text that argued against the possibility of collective consent, and a well-known maxim in the Codex, which urged that punishment be restricted to actual wrongdoers. However, he noted that some jurists, including the Roman lawyer Pilius, had responded to these objections that a community was understood to act and thereby sin through its ruler; hence it was rightly held responsible for the deeds of its ruler. He attributed this opinion to his own teachers at Bologna, which reinforces our impression gained from Tancred and others that Johannes's contrary opinion was not widely accepted. Zoën then developed what he considered an even stronger argument, tacitly borrowed from Azo and Pilius, that a community was capable of sin because of its capacity for collective decision-making, such as in making laws and appointments. He acknowledged the difficulty of a community reaching agreement because of men's natural facility for dissent, but concluded that, since they rarely 'consented', i.e. came to a *consensus*, a community was rarely said to sin, but it sinned sometimes and when it did, it was to be lawfully punished.[41] Earlier canonists had already categorized the interdict as a legitimate punishment for a community, and a subsequent canonist, Pope Innocent IV, would explicitly link the interdict with collective consent to wrongdoing.

Innocent (d. 1254) made a decisive contribution to juristic debate on collective guilt and punishment, firstly by banning excommunication of organized communities in his decretal 'Romana Ecclesia: Ceterum' (1245). His intention stated in his law was to avoid imperiling innocent souls, and he added in a gloss on his own law that it was absurd for one-day-old infants and absent members

41 Zoën on 5 Comp. 5.18.3 v. *communitas*, Tours, Bibliothèque municipale MS 565, fol. 41rb: 'Sed quomodo est quod communitas punitur cum non intelligatur peccare posse? Quid enim municipes dolo facere possunt, ut ff. de dolo. Sed ex dolo §Si autem municipes? Nam quomodo peccare qui non potest consentire? Et universitas non potest, ut ff. de libertis univer. l. una [Dig. 38.3.un.], ergo nec peccare, quare ergo punitur cum non debeat protendi pena quam reperiatur delictum, ut supra de hiis que fiunt a ma. par. c. Quesitum, et accedit, supra de regula. et trans. ad relig. e. Que §Porro lib. e. et C. de penis. Sancimus [2 Comp. 3.9.2; 2 Comp. 3.18.(?); Cod. 9.47.22]. Respondent quidam et dicunt ut Pi<leus> quod communitas intelligitur tunc demum peccare quando peccat is qui universitati preest, de cuius facto communitas facit, ar. ff. de condict. et demon. Municipibus, et sic intelligunt legem, ff. quod metus causa. Metum §Animadvertendum [Dig. 35.1.97; 4.2.9 §1]. Sed tu dicas quod, licet communitas teneatur bene de facto eius qui communitati preest, ar. dicte 1. Municipibus, quod et nostri senciunt preceptores, tu tamen aliter et melius respondeas et dicas communitatem illam peccare posse nam et bene potest peccare, ut vides in lege condenda, C. de legibus et constit. Humanum, sic in electione, ut ff. de off. questoris l.i. et supra. de elec. Quia propter l.iiii. [Cod. 1.14.8; 1.131; 4 Comp. 1.3.9]. Quod ergo dicitur eos non posse consentire intelligendum est de facili, ar. ff. de orig. iu. l.ii. §Demum cum populus, et ita intelligitur lex illa de libertis universitatum et quod dicitur ff. de dolo. Sed ex dolo [Dig. 1.2.2 §22; 38.3.un.; 4.3.15]. Raritatem notat in possibilitate, naturalis est enim hominum ad dissenciendum facilitas, ut ff. de arbitris. Item sumus §Principaliter [Dig. 4.8.17 §6], unde, cum raro consenciant, ipsa communitas raro peccare dicitur. Peccat tamen interdum, quo casu communitas que peccat legittime est punienda. Zo.' See n. 34 on Pilius's views cited here.

to fall under the excommunication of their community.[42] His law thus limited excommunication to the guilty members of a community. He merely turned a traditional canonistic view into law, but his grounds for doing so, as revealed in his commentary on his own and his predecessors' decretal law, appear to negate the idea of collective guilt. Indeed in one much misinterpreted gloss he argued that a community could not be excommunicated for it was impossible for it to do wrong, and this was because 'community' was the name of a right not of a person.[43] That is to say, only an individual person was capable of wrongdoing. He did not conceive of a community as a mere group of individuals who might collaborate in a wrong but as something above and beyond its members: the right to association. In his view any social group did not automatically constitute a community in the juristic sense; this was a right conferred on it by a prince or another competent authority, and without this no group might exercise corporate rights, such as appointing officials and representatives, and making majority resolutions binding on the whole community.[44]

This precise juristic notion of a community also informed a gloss on 'Romana Ecclesia: Ceterum', in which he argued that a chapter as a mere conceptual term and not a physical thing can do nothing except through its members.[45] That is to say, they alone might be guilty of a canonical crime and suffer the canonical punishment for it, i.e. excommunication. Novel as his arguments were, they articulated a similar position to that of Johannes Teutonicus. Like the latter he also accepted that under Roman law only individual wrongdoers might face criminal charges and criminal punishment but a civil action might be brought against a community. Nevertheless Innocent admitted that the latter might result in civil sanctions for the community, such as a fine imposed on account of its rulers' wrongdoing.[46] He elaborated on this point that if the rulers

---

[42] Coll. III 40 (=VI 5.11.5; Po. 12062). Innocent IV, *Apparatus* (Venice 1578) on Coll. III 40 [=VI 5.11.5] v. *in universitatem*. All citations in this chapter from his *Apparatus* refer to this 1578 edition.

[43] Innocent IV, *Apparatus* on X 5.39.53 v. *consiliarios*. See n. 50 on misinterpretation of this gloss.

[44] See Eschmann, 'Studies', 8. Innocent IV, *Apparatus* on X 5.31.14: 'Societas ... non constituit collegium ... vel corpus ... societas non est collegium per se, nisi aliter constituatur per principem vel senatusconsultum, vel alio modo.' Id. on X 1.31.13: 'Intellige de illa universitate que constituta est per superiorem sic quod sit universitas, nam, si tot essent homines simul collecti quot sunt Rome et non haberent tacitum vel expressum consensum a superiore, non possent sibi constituere iudicem nec haberent alia iura et privilegium universitatis.' In reality such *iura universitatis*, for example, those granted in royal municipal charters in England, often simply gave formal recognition to existing corporations and confirmed collective rights established by custom. Nevertheless once a superior had made the 'creation' of a *universitas* his prerogative, he could also claim the right to dissolve one, a legitimate collective punishment in itself, as Innocent IV observed on X 5.39.53 v. *consiliarios*: 'privabitur privilegio universitatis, ut ulterius non sit universitas. Et sic patietur capitis diminutionem.' On Innocent's corporate thought see also Melloni.

[45] Innocent IV, *Apparatus* on Coll. III 40 (=VI 5.11.5) v. *culpabiles*.

[46] Id. on X 5.3.30 v. *abbatibus* and on X 5.39.53 v. *consiliarios*. He went on to point out in the latter gloss that under certain Roman laws (Cod. 9.16; Dig. 48.6), a criminal action might be

of a community or others committed a wrong with the mandate of the whole community, or the majority of it, even if they acted against the will of the rest, or even if they had acted without a mandate but the community subsequently ratified that the wrong had been done in its name, the community might suffer the spiritual penalty of an interdict or temporal one of a fine.[47] That is to say, an organized community might bear legal responsibility for crimes committed by its rulers or agents with its prior or subsequent consent, and the interdict was an appropriate penalty, like civil sanctions, for this kind of fault. In drawing a distinction between collective responsibility and individual guilt and the penalties appropriate to these different kinds of fault, excommunication being reserved to the latter kind, Innocent struck a more satisfying compromise than Zoën or Tancred between the conservative Johannes Teutonicus and his pragmatic opponents.

Innocent's views on this issue were widely accepted. The canonist Hostiensis (d. 1266) found them so compelling that he simply copied them into his own glosses. Hostiensis merely reinforced Innocent's view that excommunication might not apply to a community by adding that such a sentence bound the soul, and only an individual possessed a soul. Likewise the theologian St Thomas Aquinas argued (*c*.1252–6) with regard to 'Romana Ecclesia: Ceterum' that one ought to be excommunicated only for mortal sin, which consisted in action, and action was proper to individuals; hence they might be excommunicated but not a community, although it might be interdicted.[48] Later commentators on 'Romana Ecclesia: Ceterum', notably the fourteenth-century canonists Johannes Monachus, Johannes Andreae, and Guido de Baysio, found little of originality to add or oppose to Innocent IV's ideas. Monachus (*c*.1303), for instance, remarked that a community was not a person in any real sense but only figuratively, a *persona representata*, and because excommunication might only bind a real person, it was inadmissible against communities; this simply reformulated Innocent's notion of community as 'the name of a right', like *persona representata* a juristic abstraction.[49]

By the time of Innocent IV canonists had, therefore, reached a consensus that, as a matter of general principle, a community might in certain circumstances

brought against a *universitas* but in such instances capital punishment was usually commuted to a civil penalty, i.e. a fine.

[47] Innocent IV, *Apparatus* on X 5.39.53 v. *consiliarios*: 'Fatemur tamen quod, si rectores alicuius universitatis vel alii aliquod maleficium faciunt de mandato universitatis totius, vel tante partis, quod invitis aliis maleficium fecerint, vel etiam sine mandato fecerint, sed postea universitas quod suo nomine erat factum, ratum habet: quod universitas punietur speciali [*recte* spirituali] pena suspensionis et interdicti, 17 q.4 Uxor et c. Miror [C.17 q.4 c.33 & 8], supra. de spon. Non est [X 4.1.11] et etiam temporali puta pecuniaria, ff. quod met. cau. Metum §Animadvertendum, ff. de vi. et vi. arma. Si vi [Dig. 4.2.9 §1; 43.16.4], 23 q.2 Dominus [C.23 q.2 c.2].'

[48] Thomas Aquinas, *Scriptum*, IV dist. 18, ii, 3, q.2.

[49] Johannes Monachus, *Glosa* on VI 5.11.5 v. *universitatem* (fol. 402va). On the other canonists named here, see my 'Theory and Practice', 52–9.

be held to account for a certain kind of fault and suffer certain appropriate penalties. This was in part an acknowledgement of the realities of legal practice, notably interdicts. It also reflected a growth of canonistic concern, stimulated by Roman law doctrine, with the nature of an organized community, in particular the relationship between its head and members. By the mid-thirteenth century canonists did not think in terms of collective guilt, since guilt for a crime under canon and Roman law was specific to individuals; only they were capable of sin. Neither did they think of a community as a mere group of individuals who might unite in wrongdoing. In their view an organized community might only technically act through its head or agents, but it might be held responsible to some extent for their wrongs committed in its name. Hence they thought in terms of collective responsibility rather than collective guilt. Innocent IV had provided the most original statement of this view. He was the first canonist to use it as an apologia for the interdict, and he introduced a new idea to canonistic thought in community as the 'name of a right', a notion influenced by the contemporary reception of Aristotle, especially his idea of universals.[50] Nevertheless Innocent's view that one might suffer for wrongs done by others with one's consent or in one's name had a long tradition in both theological and canonistic thought going as far back as the early twelfth century. One of the first commentators on the *Decretum*, Paucapalea (*c*.1148), had qualified St Augustine's teaching, that members of a household might not be excommunicated for the sin of its head, with the words, 'unless they clearly supported the excommunicate', i.e. the sinner.[51] The rest of this chapter will trace the growth of this doctrinal tradition regarding consent, agency, and sin from the early twelfth century, for it laid the crucial intellectual foundations on which Innocent IV would build his significant justification of collective responsibility and collective punishments, notably the interdict.

---

[50] Aristotle had taught that universals, general terms like *universitas* itself, were abstractions of the mind, *essentiae*, but only individual entities, the *substantia* that embodied these *essentiae*, had physical existence in the world: 'the concepts being less real than the physical substances in their motions and activities' (Knowles, *Evolution*, 109). The Aristotelian view was generally accepted by the schools of philosophy in the thirteenth-century Latin West and known as 'moderate' realism. Hence Innocent, in speaking of a *universitas* as a *nomen iuris*, was a man of his time and not ahead of it as some have argued. Indeed Gierke (*Genossenschaftsrecht*, 3. 279) and others claimed that he had thereby invented the idea of a corporation as a fictitious 'legal person', actually a construct of nineteenth-century jurisprudence. Rather, as Ullmann ('Delictal Responsibility', 81) rightly stated: 'all Innocent IV was interested in proving was the legal inadmissibility of excommunicating a corporate body.' For other refutations of Innocent's paternity of the fiction theory, see Eschmann, 'Studies', 33–4, and Rodriguez, 'Innocent IV'.

[51] Paucapalea, *Summa* on C.24 q.3 *dictum ante* c.1 v. *quod autem pro peccato alicuius tota familia non sit excommunicanda* (Ed. p. 105). Cf. Sicard of Cremona (*c*.1179) on C.24 q.3, BAV, Pal. lat. MS 653, fol. 98ra: 'familiam non esse excommunicandam pro peccato unius nisi faveat eum et in delicto foveat vel nisi gravissime moveatur ecclesia, ut Si habes.' Gratian based his *dictum* on C.24 q.3 c.1 ('Si habes'), a letter in which Augustine had stated that he would not anathematize a household for the sin of its head unless he was very seriously moved.

1.3 CONSENT TO ANOTHER'S SIN

Twelfth-century canonistic doctrine on this issue was based on St Paul's teaching in Romans 1:32, that not only wrongdoers ought to suffer punishment but also those who consented to their wrongdoings. This view was echoed in some *Decretum* texts which ruled that a similar penalty binds both those doing wrong and those consenting to it.[52] Consequently twelfth-century commentators on the *Decretum* had not limited guilt to individual wrongdoers, as Innocent IV and other thirteenth-century jurists influenced by Roman law did. It was a commonplace among those earlier canonists at least since Rufinus (*c*.1164) that he who consented to another's sin was guilty of it, for through consent he made it his own.[53] The source of this canonistic view was theology, for as early as *c*.1150 the theologian Rolandus had stated that the sins of others become our own where we approve of them or imitate them.[54]

Theology also shaped canonistic definitions of consent to sin. Peter Lombard (d. 1160) and subsequent Bible commentators often copied a gloss of St Ambrose (d. 397) on Romans 1:32. It had distinguished two kinds of consent to sin: keeping silent when one could oppose sin (i.e. *tacit* consent); supporting sin with praise (i.e. *active* consent).[55] This distinction was widely adopted by twelfth-century canonists. Rufinus likewise identified two kinds of consent of sin: *negligence*, when one ought to oppose a sin but failed to do so; *cooperation*, when one defends or in any way aids a sin. The canonist Johannes Faventinus (*c*.1170) added a third: *licence*, i.e. granting permission to sin either before or after the fact.[56] This was the same kind of consent that Innocent IV described some eighty years later as grounds for an interdict: authorizing a ruler's or agent's wrong by a prior mandate or subsequent approval.

---

[52] C.2 q.1 c.10; C.17 q.4 c.5.

[53] Rufinus, *Summa* on D.83 d.a.c.1 v. *Providendum* (Ed. p. 173). The same point was made by Stephen of Tournai, *Summa* on D.83 d.a.c.1 (Ed. p. 105); Johannes Faventinus on D.83 d.a.c.1 v. *Providendum*, BAV, Borgh. lat. MS 71, fol. 56ra; *Summa Parisiensis* on C.1 q.4 (Ed. p. 94); and *Summa Reginensis* on D.83 *dictum ante* c.1 v. *providendum*, BAV, Reg. lat. MS 1061, fol. 15va. See Kuttner, *Schuldlehre*, 43–7, on which this section of this chapter develops.

[54] Rolandus, *Sentenzen*, 253. The views expressed here were copied almost verbatim in the *Summa Parisiensis* (*c*.1170) on C. 1 q.4 (Ed. p. 94).

[55] Peter Lombard on Romans 1:32 (*PL* 191.1336): '[Ambros.] Consentire est tacere cum possis arguere, vel errorem adulando fovere.' Reiterated in the *Glossa ordinaria* on Romans 1:32 v. *qui consentiunt*.

[56] Rufinus, *Summa* on D.83 *dictum ante* c.1 v. *providendum* (Ed. p. 173); cf. Stephen of Tournai, *Summa* on D.83 *dictum ante* c.1 v. *admittas* (Ed. p. 105). Johannes Faventinus on D.86 c.1 v. *rector*, BAV, Borgh. lat. MS 71, fol. 56v: 'tribus enim modis prelatus consentire dicitur: per negligentiam; per licenciam; per <co>operationem ... Si per licenciam assentit, <is> quam principalis auctor reus constituitur, sive sit licencia iam in facto sive in faciendo, sicut presumi potest ex illo c. quod est in xii. q.ii. De rebus [C.12 q.2 c.22].'

If canonists derived much of their thinking on consent to sin from theology, their debate on the issue would be given further impetus by the rulings of two popes trained as theologians: Alexander III and Innocent III. Alexander has been identified with the theologian Rolandus, whose views on consent to sin we have noted. Indeed, Peter the Chanter (d. 1197) claimed that this pope tolerated the contemporary practice of executing the sons of forgers and traitors when they had consented to their fathers' sins.[57] Meanwhile it will be demonstrated below that Innocent III was influenced by the Chanter's views on consent to sin. Indeed all of Innocent's important rulings on this matter are from the first year of his pontificate, which shows that his views were already formed when he became pope. The rulings of both popes on this issue, in the decretals 'Sicut dignum', 'Mulieres', and 'Quante presumptionis', threatened penalties for consent to attacks on the clergy.[58] Hence these rulings and canonistic responses to them are relevant to interdicts, since an interdict was usually imposed on a community because its ruler had attacked the persons, property, or rights of the clergy.

In the first of these decretals, 'Sicut dignum' (1173; JL 12180), Alexander III judged those variously associated with the murder of Thomas Becket, Archbishop of Canterbury, in 1170. The international notoriety of Becket's martyrdom encouraged the rapid reception of this decretal in canonical collections. Significantly it adopted the canonistic distinctions between kinds of consent to sin when it categorized those who shared in the guilt of Becket's killers. First those who had confessed to seizing Becket with the aim of killing, harming, or holding him captive had thereby facilitated his death and were to perform a penance similar to that enjoined on the actual killers. The first canonist to gloss this decretal, Ricardus Anglicus (c.1197), recognized that these men had consented to the murder by cooperation, the *active* form of consent to sin identified by Rufinus. In support of the pope's decision he cited a ruling from the *Decretum* that a like penalty binds those committing a sin and those consenting to it.[59]

---

[57] Identity: Noonan, 'Who was Rolandus?', esp. 34–6. Peter the Chanter on 4 Kings 14:6, Oxford, Bodleian Library, Bodley MS 371, fol. 62va: '<Non> morientur pro patribus. Modo tamen filii falsariorum et reorum crimine lese maiestatis plectuntur morte pro peccato patris. Papa tamen Alexander [III] hoc noluit pati nisi peccato patris consenserint. Pena pecuniaria etiam non consentientes sepe puniuntur pro peccato patris.' In another version of this gloss (Eton College MS 16; Paris, Bibliothèque de l'Arsenal MS 44, p. 407b) he made a similar point, that the pope had disinherited a forger's sons of everything except their mother's goods, since she had not consented to her husband's sin: 'Non morientur patres pro filiis etc. Pecunia tamen sepe puniuntur usque in terciam et quartam generationem, uti a domino papa filiis cuiusdam suspensi et rem<???>sis non est restituta patris hereditas, sed matris hereditatem que non consenserat marito habuerunt filii. Etiam sepe pro facinore filii exulant.'

[58] X 5.12.6, 5.39.6 and 47. The decretal 'Quante presumptionis' was excerpted by canonists from the letter copied into Innocent III, Reg. 1, no. 24.

[59] Ricardus Anglicus on 1 Comp. 5. 10.7 (=X 5.12.6) v. *pari pena*, BAV, Pal. lat. MS 696, fol. 102vb: 'Consenserunt enim cooperando, ut infra xvii. q.iiii. Omnis [C.17 q.4 c.5].'

Another early commentator on this decretal defined active consent differently, in terms of the sinful intention which those seizing Becket shared with his murderers. A pupil of the northern French canonist Petrus Brito, he observed (*c.*1205) that one who intended to kill but did not do so was still a killer by virtue of his will and hence deserved a penalty similar to, if not as severe as, that inflicted on the actual killer.[60] In support of this view he cited a canon from the *Decretum*, which ruled that where a mob attack on someone ended with their death, he who had dealt the fatal blow was judged the killer, but others present who intended to kill the victim had to perform a similar penance to the killer. Hence collective punishment was justified where there was a collective intention to commit a sin.

This reflected a fundamental development in the twelfth-century doctrine of sin. Peter Abelard (d. 1142) had taught that what made a sin was not the nature of the deed itself but the intention which lay behind it. According to Abelard God might determine guilt from intentions in our minds, but human judges, including ecclesiastical ones, might only infer it from the actual effects of those intentions.[61] Likewise the canonist Huguccio (*c.*1188) agreed that only God might judge our inner will but he argued that human justice might punish will that had been translated into outward actions, even if its fulfillment had not been achieved. He even observed that under some canons intention and premeditation were still punished even if they had not been put into effect, although less harshly than if they had been.[62]

Indeed by the early thirteenth century popes and canonists agreed that acts expressing either consent to sin or intention to sin were both as bad as the sin itself and entailed a similar punishment.[63] Nevertheless canonists did not consider

---

[60] Anon. on 1 Comp. 5. 10.7 v. *pari pena*, Brussels, Bibliothèque royale MS 1407–9, fol. 80vb: 'Verum est in genere non in asperitate quia, quando quis vult occidere et non occidit, homicida est voluntate, vi. q.i. Verum, et ff. quod le. eos. de sicariis l.v. [C.6 q. 1 d.a.c.22; Dig. 43.3.5]. Et hec est ratio quare omnes tenentur quando dubium <est> quis interfecit, ar. ff. ad 1. aquil. l. Item mela §Si plures [Dig. 9.2.11 §4] ... ne crimina remaneant inpunita ... Idem est si multi sint in domo et adsit de domo eiectus et effusus ... Omnes illi qui in domo sunt tenentur, scilicet de eiecto et effuso, ibi. §ult. et xxxiii. q.ult. Si quattuor homines [C.23 q.8 c.34].' Similar views are found in another French canonistic work, the decretist *Summa* 'Animal est substantia' on C.23 q.8 c.34 v. *affluerunt*, Bamberg Staatsbibliothek Can. MS 42, fol. 117rb. On the first commentary see my 'Collection', 133–8.

[61] Kuttner, *Schuldlehre*, 25.

[62] Huguccio on C.6 q.l c.22 v. *voluntatem*, BAV, Arch. S. Pietro MS C.114, fol. 161vb; Vat. lat. MS 2280, fol. 147r: 'Ecce hic punitur voluntas et cogitatio sine effectu, tamen minus quam si effectus sequeretur, ar. de pen. di.i. Si cui, et di.xviiii. Nulli Anastasius, di.xxii. Omnes [De pen. D.1 c.30; D. 19 c.5; D.22 c.l]. In maleficiis enim voluntas spectatur non exitus, ut ff. ad 1. cor. de sic. Divus. Ar. contra, de pen. di.i. §Contra eodem 1. Cogitationis [Dig. 48.8.14; De pen. D.1 *dictum ante* c.14]. De interiori quidem voluntate deus iudicat non homo, di.xxxii. Erubescant, et xxxii. q.v. Christiana [D.32 c.11; C.32 q.5 c.32]. Sed hic intelligitur de illa cogitatione et voluntate que non stetit in suis finibus sed processit ad actum exteriorum licet non sit consecuta effectum.'

[63] E.g. Innocent III's decretal 'Tua nos duxit discretio consulendos' (1207; 3 Comp. 5.2.6; Po. 3235), which judged clerks accused of simony guilty on the grounds of intention; they had granted property to a church on the condition that its clergy elected them to prebends. Cf. Johannes Galensis on 3 Comp. 5.2.6 v. *culpabiles*, München, Bayerische Staatsbibliothek Clm 3879, fol. 249vb: 'Non

that a community might consent to sin through actions that supported the actual sinners or shared their intentions, though this might happen in practice. But, after valuables were stolen from Regensburg Cathedral and the city was consequently 'excommunicated', or more likely interdicted, in 1146, Gerhoch of Reichensberg argued that it could be held accountable if it had supported these crimes and harboured their authors from justice, but he doubted that all citizens had thus despised justice. Hence he condemned the sentence on the grounds that only the wrongdoers should suffer not the whole populace, and that the innocent should be separated from the guilty. It may be that as a theologian he was articulating ideas of the schools.[64]

Popes and canonists not only condemned active support for sin but also failure to resist it, or tacit consent. In 'Sicut dignum' Alexander III ruled that those who had aided Becket's killers against their opponents were not free from guilt for the murder, for 'he who could free a man from death, and did not, killed him', and so they were to be punished though less harshly than the actual killers. Tancred (c.1220) inferred that this applied to the archbishop's subjects, who should have resisted his killers by force in the first place. A pupil of the French canonist Petrus Brito had compared (c.1205) those who failed to intervene with Saul, who was called a killer of St Stephen since he had held the cloaks of those who stoned the martyr.[65]

The source of Alexander's maxim in this ruling is unidentified, but Alanus and other early commentators noted that it echoed the argument of several *Decretum* texts, that he who failed to reproach the wicked, when he can ('cum potest'), supported their wickedness.[66] Jesus had also commanded his followers in Matthew 18:15 to correct brethren who sinned against them. By the twelfth

dicit quod sint simoniaci ad parem penam tamen tenentur propter intentionem et opus subsecutum, ar. de bi. c.i. lib. e. [3 Comp. 1.14.1] la<urentius>. Nisi velis dicere quod sola intentio facit hominem simoniacum, ut i. q.i. Qui studet, et c. Reperiuntur, et q.iii. Non solum [C.1 q.l c.11, 7; C. 1 q.3 c.11], sicut sola spes facit hominem usurarium, ut xiiii. q.iii. c.i [C.14 q.3 c. 1].'

[64] *Codex Chronologico-Diplomaticus*, i.215–16 (no. 229).

[65] Tancred on 1 Comp. 5. 10.7 v. *debebant*, BAV, Vat. lat. MS 1377, fol. 87va: 'Idest "parabant" ala<nus>. Vel sicut littera per se plane significat, quia subditi archiepiscopi debebant illos sua violentia impedire ab incepto. t.' Anon. on 1 Comp. 5.10.7 v. *obviare*, Brussels, Bibliothèque Royale MS 1407–9, fol. 80vb: 'lxxxiii. d. Error, et ii. q.vii. Negligere [D.83 c.3; C.2 q.7 c.55]. Unde Paulus fuit dictus homicida beati Stephani quia levavit vestimenta lapidantium eum.' On Paul's part in Stephen's martyrdom, Acts 7:58, 8:1: 'et <Stephanum> eicientes extra civitatem lapidabant. Et testes deposuerunt vestimenta sua secus pedes adulescentis, qui vocabatur Saulus ... Saulus autem erat *consentiens* neci eius.' The italics are mine.

[66] Alanus on 1 Comp. 5.10.7 v. *qui*, München, Bayerische Staatsbibliothek Clm 3879, fol. 85va: 'Supra di.lxxxiii Error, supra di.lxxxvi Facientis, supra xxiii <q.iii> Qui potest, infra lombar. tu. l.penult, supra xxiii q.v Reos, supra di.l Si quis viduam, supra xxiii q.ult c.ult [D.83 c.3; D.86 c.3; C.23 q.3 c.8; *Lombarda Casinensis* 1.3.39 (Henry II, 2); C.23 q.5 c.7; D.50 c.8; C.23 q.8 c.34].' The Lombarda law text cited is edited in *Liber Papiensis*, 584, and listed in *Lombarda Casinensis*, 608. Other pertinent texts besides these are C.23 q.3 c.11 (see n. 91) and D.86 c.21, which ruled that anyone who could save a man dying from hunger and did not, killed him. Johannes Faventinus had hence judged (c.1170) on D.86 c.21 v. *occidisti* (BAV, Borgh. lat. MS 71, fol. 57rb) that one who does not give a dying man food 'reus est mortis'.

century the power of ecclesiastical discipline had been reserved to prelates; thus some theologians and canonists, notably Gratian and Peter Comestor, insisted that only prelates were obligated under Christ's commandment and similar rulings in the *Decretum*.[67] For canonists of this persuasion, the key phrase in these rulings on correcting sin was 'cum potest', which they clearly associated with the idea of 'potestas' or power over others. For example the pupil of the French canonist Petrus Brito observed (*c*.1205) that a lord who had sons and did not correct them was at fault, for he had not done what he could do. Hence only those with such power might bear guilt and punishment for consenting to a sin by failing to oppose it. Therefore Vincentius Hispanus conceded in relation to Alexander's maxim that one who knew of another's sin but was powerless to stop it was free of blame.[68]

But this restriction was not accepted by all canonists and theologians. Rufinus (*c*.1164) considered that subjects ('minores') as well as prelates could consent to sin in this way, but he distinguished that prelates who did so were as guilty as the actual sinners, while subjects were far less so, unless the crime was truly reprehensible and one they might easily have prevented, notably murder. His contemporary Stephen of Tournai went even further, accepting that not only was a prelate to resist a subject's error, but a subject ought to resist a prelate's error. Stephen recognized that a subject lacked the power to coerce verbally and physically which a prelate had, but he might accuse a prelate of error if it was worthy of accusation and the subject had evidence.[69] Finally Huguccio noted that correction of sin appeared to be restricted to prelates by virtue of their office, but in his view it was a duty to which everyone was bound.[70]

---

[67] Alanus, *Apparatus* 'Ius naturale' on C.23 q.3 c.8 v. *esset*, BAV, Ross. lat. MS 595, fol. 187va (second layer of glosses): 'Et spectat ad prelatum, ar. prox. q.iii. Tam sacerdotes [C.24 q.3 c.14].' Johannes Teutonicus, *Glossa ordinaria* on D.83 c.3 v. *possis*, BAV, Vat. lat. MS 1367, fol. 56ra; 'Editio Romana' i.533: 'Ex officio, hoc enim intelligunt quidam de prelato, arg. xxiii. q.iiii. Ita plane [C.23 q.4 c.6], sed H<uguccio> de quolibet, xxiiii. q.iii. Tam sacerdotes.' On Peter Comestor see n. 72.

[68] Anon. on 1 Comp. 5.31.2 v. *occident*, Brussels, Bibliothèque royale MS 1407–9, fol. 87va: 'quia dominus erat in culpa qui habet filios et non corrigit eos, tunc ei imputatur quia non fecit quod facere potuit, xlvii. d. Necesse et xxxvii. d. Legatum et ii. q. vii. Accusatio [D.47 *dictum post* c.8; D.37 c.5; C.2 q.7 c. 15]'. D.47 *dictum post* c.8 and D.37 c.5 referred to the example of Elias in 1 Kings 2, who failed to correct his errant sons and hence suffered divine punishment together with them. Vincentius Hispanus on 1 Comp. 5.10.7 v. *potuit hominem*, Leipzig Universitätsbibliothek MS 983, fol. 52vb: 'Alias culpa caret qui scit sed prohibere nequid, ff. de re. iu. di. Culpa, supra de heretic. c.ii. [Dig. 50.17.60; 1 Comp. 5.6.2].'

[69] Rufinus on D.83 *dictum ante* c.l v. *providendum* (Ed. p. 173); Stephen of Tournai on D.83 c.3 v. *cui non resistitur* (Ed. pp. 105–6). Johannes Faventinus copied this view of Rufinus in his *Summa* at D.83 *dictum ante* c.l v. *providendum* and that of Stephen at D.86 c.l v. *rector* (BAV, Borgh. lat. MS 71, fols. 56ra, 56vb).

[70] Huguccio on D.83 c.3 v. *nichil est aliud quam fovere*, BAV, Arch. S. Pietro MS C.114, fol. 99va: 'Idest qui negligit arguere perversos, cum possit, videtur eorum malo consentire.' Id. on v. *cum possis*: 'In quantum ex officio suscepto, et secundum hoc restringitur tantum circa prelatos. Ego autem credo quod ad hanc correctionem teneantur omnes, ar. ii. q.vii. Quapropter, et v. q.v. Non vos, et xxiiii. q.iii. Tam sacerdotes [C.2 q.7 c.47; C.5 q.5 c.1; C.24 q.3 c.14].' Cf. Anonymous

Some later canonists also recognized a universal duty to resist other's sins. For example, after a decretal of Pope Innocent III declared those supporting the forgery of papal letters excommunicate, one anonymous canonist commented (*c.*1215) that this applied to anyone who knew of this crime and could prevent it but did not do so. This commentator admitted that doubts existed about who could perform this duty, and that a superior might do so by virtue of his authority; he cited a *Decretum* text that stressed the duty of any head of a community to correct its sinful members. However, he added that someone lacking this authority could report this crime to one 'who could help and not hinder', presumably a superior, just as Stephen of Tournai had held that a subject could resist a prelate's error by accusation. Our commentator hence concluded in line with Huguccio that this was the duty of any Catholic.[71] This assumption also underlies Tancred's view, such that Becket's subjects should have resisted his killers and papal judgement fell on them for their failure to do so. This doctrinal development had clear implications for subjects who failed to resist their ruler's sin, as they thereby appeared to consent to it and merit punishment, such as an interdict. And the canonists were not alone in developing this doctrine; the Paris theologian Peter the Chanter (d. 1192) also contributed to it, and this is important for it is supposed that he taught the future Pope Innocent III, and his views arguably influenced Innocent's own on this matter.

Peter the Chanter commented on Christ's exhortation to fraternal correction in Matthew 18:15 that he who sees someone sinning and keeps silent sins himself. He then noted that some (*quidam*), notably the theologian Peter Comestor, stated that this command was aimed only at prelates. But he was also aware that others, including the canonists Rufinus and Johannes Faventinus, argued the opposite, that it was enjoined on all, as St Augustine had taught: on superiors with regard to subjects; and subjects with regard to superiors.[72] The Chanter agreed with

---

Anglo-Norman decretist (*c.*1200) on D.83 c.3 v. *negligere*, Cambridge, Gonville and Caius College MS 283/676, fol. 50rb: 'Hoc non tantum de prelato sed etiam de quolibet fideli laico intelligendum est, ut infra ii. q.i. Si peccaverit in te, infra xxiiii. q.iii Tam sacerdotes, infra d. lxxxvi. Facientis, infra ii. q.vii. Negligere, infra xxiiii. q.iii. Qui errorem [C.2 q.1 c.19; c.24 q.3 c.14; D.86 c.3; C.2 q.7 c.55; C.24 q.3 c.32].' See Kuttner and Rathbone, 'Anglo-Norman Canonists', 317–19, on this *Decretum* commentary.

[71] *Apparatus* 'Servus appellatur' on 3 Comp. 5. 11.4 v. *innodatos*, Bamberg Staatsbibliothek MS Can. 19, fol. 211vb: 'Est ergo canon late sententie et colligantur fautores, sed qualiter intelligit "fautores" ... credo fautorem hic accipere qui scit et potest prohibere et non prohibet, nam talem, dicit lex, pena falsi teneri, ut ff. ad 1. cor. de fal. 1. Lege Cornelia et di. lxxxiii. Error [Dig. 48.10.5; D.83 c.3], sed super hoc qualiter debeat prohibere dubitari potest. Sed potest dici quod si esset eius superior, auctoritate sua, ut xxiii. q.iiii. Si forte duo ista nomina [C.23 q.4 c.35]. Alias potest denuntiare ei qui possit prodesse et non obesse, ad quam denuntiationem dico omnem catholicum teneri, ut xxii. q.v. Hoc videtur [C.22 q.5 c.8]'.

[72] Peter the Chanter on Matthew 18:15, Paris, BN, MS lat. 15585, fol. 124vb; Oxford, Merton College MS 212: 'Attendite ... Ita enim peccat qui peccantem videns tacet ... Sed si peccaverit etc .... Hoc capitulum ad solos prelatos dicunt quidam pertinere eo quod in antiquibus codicibus invenitur: "Respiciens dominus discipulos dixit ad Petrum, Si peccaverit, etc." Alii econtra asserunt,

the latter opinion and so reached the same conclusion as Huguccio. This was not the only occasion when Peter's views coincided with Huguccio's, but there is no evidence that either of these contemporary masters was directly familiar with the other's teachings. Significantly Innocent III, at the very beginning of his pontificate, would implement the same principle concerning non-resistance to others' sins in the decretal 'Quante presumptionis' (1198; Po. 24). It is possible that Huguccio had inspired his ruling, as Kuttner and others have perceived his influence on Innocent, but Pennington has argued that there is no evidence that the pope was taught by Huguccio or that he studied canon law for more than a few years, if at all, during his stay at Bologna in the late 1180s.[73] The evidence for the Chanter's influence on Innocent is certainly much stronger in the case of this particular decretal.

Innocent's decretal was admittedly based on canon law, in particular a canon of the Second Lateran Council (1139) which imposed excommunication on those who physically attacked a clerk.[74] His decretal extended this sentence to any who failed to defend the clerk when they could do so, thereby supporting the attacker, for 'catholic authority condemns those doing the deed and those consenting to it to be bound by a similar penalty'. This argument and the Lateran canon both occurred in the *Decretum*, but Innocent's ruling was founded more on the Chanter's work than Gratian's. Indeed the Chanter had collected many contemporary and biblical examples of non-resistance as a 'remote' kind of consent to another's sin. He concluded that any Christian failing to defend another Christian from injury, when able to do so, was guilty of a crime and deserved to be accused before God, for 'those doing a deed and those consenting to it are to be punished by a similar penalty'. In direct anticipation of Innocent's ruling he also stated that those who saw a clerk being attacked and said nothing, as if it pleased them, ought to incur the same penalty of excommunication as the attacker, for silence meant consent when one could intervene very easily, and it was as if one had ordered the clerk to be attacked. Even more significantly he recognized that a 'multitude' was capable of non-resistance, arguing that none of its members might excuse themselves like Pilate because the rest allowed a sin to occur, since every single person could and ought to resist and speak against sin.[75]

---

ut Io. Fa[ventinus] et Rufinus, eo quod vitio scandali omnibus sit inhibita. Et ad hoc pertineat hoc capitulum, sicut etiam testatur Augustinus, dicens, "Hoc precipi omnibus et paribus in pares, et maioribus in minores et minoribus in maiores". Item Theodorus in penitentiali: "Quicumque fratrem peccare viderit nec increpat non modica pena dignus est." Huic opinioni consentimus'. A marginal note in the Oxford manuscript indicated that Peter Comestor was one of those limiting the command of Matthew 18:15 to prelates: 'Ita m<agister> P<etrus> Mandu<cator>.' See my 'Theological Views', 17–18.

73 Pennington, 'Legal Education'; 'Further Thoughts'. However, see n. 75.
74 See Helmholz, ' "Si quis suadente" (C.17 q.4 c.29)', on this canon.
75 Peter the Chanter, *Summa*, II, AMN 7, pp. 271–5, esp. 275; ibid. III 2a, AMN 16, p. 397. Id. *Verbum abbreviatum* (long version), BAV, Reg. lat. MS 106, fol. 92v (short version in *PL* 205. 217): 'Quod peccatum unius redundat in universos ... Totum unusquisque qui potest debet resistere

The Chanter would elaborate elsewhere on this idea of collective non-resistance, but before we consider this and its clear implications for the interdict, we must first examine how canonists reacted to Innocent III's ruling, for this indicates that canonists were still divided on this question of non-resistance.

Alanus Anglicus was the first to include 'Quante presumptionis' in a decretal collection and gloss it (*c*.1206). Alanus recognized the Christian obligation to defend one's neighbour, as noted in the *Decretum*, but he regarded Innocent's interpretation of this as 'new law' contradicting the old law 'Si quatuor' that had deemed innocent those present but not collaborating in a physical attack.[76] Under the pope's 'new law' there was no longer any such person as an 'innocent' bystander. Perhaps the compiler of *Compilatio tertia*, Petrus Beneventanus, also thought the pope's law controversial, for he did not include it in his collection. Johannes Teutonicus, nevertheless, included it in *Compilatio quarta* and made an important distinction in his commentary on it. He observed that whatever one ought to do in defence of lay persons, anyone was obliged to defend a clerk by the *ius publicum*, that is, Roman law.[77] He added that anyone who did not defend another when he could, if only by clamour and weeping, intended sin and murder. Nevertheless he admitted that some canonists only applied this principle to judges or those holding power. One such canonist was a French decretist who had distinguished (*c*.1206–10) that anyone who could constrain a delinquent 'de iure' and failed to do so approved his wrong and was accountable before God and man in civil proceedings, for example, a bishop obliged to coerce his subjects, but anyone, such as a subject, who could only constrain another 'de facto' was only answerable to God.[78] Innocent's ruling was clearly controversial, and it remained

---

et contradicere vel impedire. Ille vero qui se excusat et excipit a peccato multitudinis vel delicto et per multitudinem vel etiam per prelatum se credit, similis est Pilato, qui immundam habens conscientiam manus suas lavit.' cf. ibid. fol. 94ra: '[same heading] ... Qui excusant se ab occasione peccati prestita nisi manu peccaverint, se reos non putantes ... similes sunt Saulo consentienti in necem prothomartyris Stephani, et eum in manibus omnium lapidantium servando eorum vestes lapidanti [Acts 7:58–8:1; cf. Anon. gloss in n. 68].' Huguccio also discussed this general obligation to defend another in the context of a vassal's duties: see Pennington, 'Feudal Oath', 63–4.

[76] Alanus on Alan. 5.22.1, v. *possunt*, Vercelli Cathedral MS 89, fol. 127va: 'Comodum qualiter unus alium debeat defendere diximus, xxiii.q.iii.in prin. et c. Non inferenda [C.23 q.3 c.7], ubi ergo tenetur defendere proximum in illo casu. Si non defendat clericum, per interpretationem Innocencii incidit in canonem ut hic dicitur, et est ius novum, sed xxiii.q. ult. c. ult. [C.23 q.8 c.34 ('Si quatuor')] contra ar.'

[77] Johannes Teutonicus on 4 Comp. 5.15.3 v. *interpretans*, BAV, Vat. lat. MS 1377, fol. 316rb: 'dicunt tamen quidam solos iudices vel qui habent potestatem aliquam ad istud teneri, ut xxiii. q.iiii. Forte [C.23 q.4 c.11]. Sed quicquid sit de defensione laicorum, quilibet tenetur ad defensionem clerici, nam hoc ad ius publicum spectat, ut supra di. i. Ius publicum [D.1 c.11].' The rest of this gloss is too long to quote but many canonists copied it into their commentaries on this decretal, notably Goffredus Tranensis (Vienna, Nationalbibliothek MS 2197, fol. 157va) and Vincentius Hispanus (see n. 79).

[78] *Summa* 'Animal est substantia' on D.83 c.2–3, Bamberg Staatsbibliothek Can. MS 42, fol. 47ra: 'Istud non est generaliter verum sed tantum de his quos de iure prohibere potest, ut si videro servum delinquentem et non corripio, approbo errorem, et obligor et quo ad Deum et quo ad

so even after its inclusion in the *Liber Extra* (1234). In his commentary on that collection Vincentius Hispanus held (*c.*1236) that this ruling should only apply to those with the power and authority of defending others, such as podestàs, officials, and judges, or lords in regard to their serfs, though he agreed that all were obliged to resist wrong.[79]

The Chanter's doctrine that inspired Innocent's ruling was thought radical not only by canonists but even by his pupil and fellow Paris theologian, Stephen Langton. Commenting on Peter Lombard's gloss to Romans 1:32, which interpreted silence as consent to sin, Langton had noted that Christ's command to correct one's brother in Matthew 18:15 would thereby appear to apply to all, such that if one saw a king sin or someone entering a brothel and kept silent, one consented and hence sinned. But he concluded that in practice the power to resist others' sins was restricted to prelates by virtue of their office.[80] And many early-thirteenth-century canonists, including Alanus and even Johannes Teutonicus, accepted this general rule in accordance with Gratian, though Johannes and others recognized exceptions to it, notably Innocent III's ruling, in the case of serious sins.[81]

Nevertheless canonists admitted that silence might be taken as consent to sin, even if they debated whether it spelled penal consequences for all. The *locus*

---

homines civiliter, ff. de noxalibus actionibus. In delictis et l. In omnibus [Dig. 9.4.4, 3], sed illorum errorem quos non nisi de facto corripere possum nunc corripendo non teneor nisi quantum ad Deum, nec tunc etiam nisi credidero me posse prodesse, ergo prelatus tenetur civiliter et quo ad Deum subditos cohercere, xliii c.i. et c. Ephesiis [D.43 c.1, 4]'.

[79] Vincentius on X 5.39.47 v. *interpretans*, Paris, BN, MS lat. 3967, fol. 207va: '[added to gloss in n. 77] ego Vinc. distinguo <quod> scelus <quod> est commissum vel committendum omnes tenentur obviare, xxiiii. q.iii. Tam sacerdotes, xiii. di. Nervi [C.23 q.4 c.14; D.13 c.2], non tamen omnes non inpedientes eos qui volunt percutere clericos credo incidere in canonem sed illos qui consentiunt habentes in loco auctoritatem et potestatem defendendi, ut potestates et officiales et iudices locorum, vel domini super servos, vel patres super filios, vel viri super uxores, vel paterfamilias super familiam'.

[80] Stephen Langton on Peter Lombard's gloss (see n. 55) on Romans 1:32, Paris, BN, MS lat. 14443, fol. 259vb; Cambridge University Library MS Ii. 4. 23, fol. 166ra: 'Consentire est tacere cum possis arguere. Ex hoc videtur quod illud preceptum, "Si peccaverit in te frater tuus, corripe eum inter te et ipsum solum" [Matthew 18:15], ad omnes pertineat, et ita si video regem peccare et taceo, consentio et ita pecco, et si video aliquem intrantem lupanar et taceo, pecco. Ista maiori indigent inquisitione, sed quantum ad expediens dicimus quod hic dicitur de posse officii esse intelligendum. Unde sensus est, consentire est tacere cum possis de officio arguere. Et hoc ad solos pertinet prelatos. Tamen in glosa media dicitur cum possis corrigere et planum est.' No authentic tradition of Langton on Matthew has survived.

[81] E.g. *Glossa Palatina* on C.2 q.7 c.55 v. *perturbare*, BAV, Pal. lat. MS 658, fol. 34rb: 'Idest, prohibere et removere a malo. Et dicit h[uguccio] quod est preceptum ad omnes et quod quilibet tenetur prohibere iniuriam ad proximum xxiii. q.ii<i>. Non inferendam [C.23 q.3 c.7]. Ego hic similia intelligo tantum de prelatis, ar. xxiii. q.ult. Preterea, lxxxiii. <di.> §i, xxv q.<i> generali [C.23 q.8 c.12; D.83 *dictum ante* c.l; C.25 q.l c.11]. Vel intellige de atrocibus, ut tunc quilibet teneatur ar. extra de sententia excom. Quante, xxiii. q.iii. c.ult., de pen. di.i Periculose [Po. 24; C.23 q.3 c.11; De pen. D.1 c.23]. Vel dic quod quilibet tenetur prohibere proximum a committendo xxii. q.v. Hoc videtur [C.22 q.5 c.8].' Repeated with minor variants by Johannes Teutonicus at C.2 q.7 c.55 v. *perturbare* (BAV, Vat. lat. MS 1367, fol. 97rb; 'Editio Romana', i.939). See also n. 67.

classicus in the *Decretum* was a text which ruled that, if a lord knew that his serf had taken holy orders, which freed him from servile status, but the lord said nothing then he lost his rights over the serf. Stephen of Tournai, Huguccio, and subsequent canonists thus interpreted silence plus knowledge of the deed as consent to it.[82] And they applied this principle to consent to sin. Stephen had compared the lord to a prelate who ought to correct and prevent the evils of his subjects and sinned if he did not speak against these; but this implied that only those with the power to correct sin consented to it by their silence.[83] Certain canonists qualified the principle of silence as consent even further and noted a Roman law maxim which doubted whether silence always meant consent; it could be ambiguous, somewhere between consent and contradiction, as Damasus (*c.*1210–15) observed.[84] Johannes Teutonicus (*c.*1215) added that silence might not be taken as consent when express consent was required, notably in marriage.[85] Nevertheless the principle was applied in some instances that silence meant consent to sin and was thus punishable. A text in *Compilatio Prima* stated that a husband who knew of his wife's adultery but continued to sleep with her was judged an accomplice to her sin and thus guilty along with her. As Ricardus Anglicus commented (*c.*1197), he was presumed to consent and sinned

---

[82] D.54 c.20. See Stephen's *Summa* on this text at v. *preter voluntatem* (Ed. p. 82). Cf. Huguccio, ibid., v. *sciente et non contradicente*, BAV, Arch. S.Pietro MS C.114, fol. 72ra; Vat. lat. MS 2280, fol. 56vb: 'Videtur enim consentire. Hic enim scientia et taciturnitas pro consensu habentur, et hoc propter favorem libertatis et religionis sepe contingit ut hic et xx. q.ii. c.i. et ii. et di. xxvii Diaconus, et di. xxviii Diaconi [C.20 q.2 c.1,2; D.27 c.1; D.28 c.11].' In 1298 Boniface VIII would make the principle 'Qui tacet consentire videtur' a rule of law in his *Liber Sextus* at VI 5.12.43.

[83] Cf. Alanus on 1 Comp. 2.16.6 v. *tacendo*, München, Bayerische Staatsbibliothek Clm 3879, fol. 27vb: 'Ar. qui tacet consentit, liiii. di. Si servus [D.54 c.20]. Dic quod ubi per proibicionem meam possum prohibere quod fit, tunc taciturnitas mihi nocet quia videor consentire. Si vero per proibicionem meam non possum proibere quod fit, tunc taciturnitas mea mihi non nocet, ut ff. de re. iu. Sepe. in medio le. [Dig. 42.1.63].'

[84] Ricardus on 1 Comp. 2.16.6 v. *tacendo*, BAV, Pal. lat. MS 696, fol. 34vb: 'Verum est quod qui tacet non loquitur. Tamen verum est non negare.' Alanus on 1 Comp 4.11.3 v. *nec*, München, Bayerische Staatsbibliothek Clm 3879, fol. 7lva: 'Nota qui tacet nec consentit nec negat quod est verum, ff. de reg. iuris. Qui tacet. [Dig. 50.17.142]'. Damasus, 'Brocarda', fol. 27rb (reg. 48): 'Solutio. tacere medium est inter contradictionem expressam et consensum expressum ... ut ff. de reg. iur. Qui tacet.'

[85] Johannes on D.27 c.l v. *tacuerit*, BAV, Vat. lat. MS 1367, fol.19vb; 'Editio Romana', i.173: 'taciturnitas semper habetur pro consensu nisi ... in casibus ubi requiritur expressus consensio, ut in servitute imponenda ... in procuratore constituendo ... in solvendo matrimonio ... Vel distingue an tale sit factum quod possit fieri me prohibente. In eo casu non obest taciturnitas ut rem meam potest vendere quis me invito et ideo ibi non nocet taciturnitas, ut ff. de contrahen. emp. Rem alienam [Dig. 18.1.28]. Si autem tale factum est quod non potest fieri me prohibente ibi taciturnitas habetur pro consensu, ut extra. i. de hiis que fiunt a pre. c. Continebat [1 Comp. 3.9.2]. Sic distinguit lex ff. de re. iudi. Sepe, sic xi. q.iii. Quando [Dig. 42.1.63; C. 11 q.3 c.23].' Cf. Huguccio on D.86 c.24 v. *interim tacemus*, BAV, Arch. S. Pietro MS C.114, fol. 102rb; Vat. lat. MS 2280, fol. 79rb: 'non semper qui tacet consentit nec semper idem est tacere quam voce consentire, ar. de con. di. iiii. Cum pro parvulis [De con. D.4 c.77]'. The *Glossa Palatina* repeated these remarks at D.86 c.24 v. *tacemus*, BAV, Pal. lat. MS 658, fol. 2lra.

mortally by not calling her to repentance. Likewise the Chanter had condemned the wicked silence of those, especially prelates, who did not reproach one close to them when they saw his wickedness.[86]

If the Chanter's view was provocative, that any individual might suffer for not correcting another's sin, this principle appeared even more radical when he and other Paris theologians applied it to whole communities. They did so largely on the basis of St Augustine's view blaming the Jews for Christ's crucifixion. Augustine commented on Psalm 81:4 that the Jewish people bore some guilt for this crime as they had not constrained their leaders from having Christ executed, when their leaders would have feared them owing to their 'multitude'.[87] Notably he concluded that they could have freed their leaders from this deed and themselves from consent to it, because whoever fails to resist, when he can, consents. Peter Lombard adopted this interpretation in his own gloss to Psalm 81:4, adding that it was aimed at 'minores'.[88] Clearly 'minores' possessed the power to resist sin and derived it not from office, as their 'maiores' did, but from their sheer force of numbers. The Chanter recognized this power of the mob when he assimilated Augustine's gloss.[89] But he also developed this view on Jewish responsibility for the Crucifixion into a general ethical principle, that any people had a duty to resist its sinful rulers. In his commentary on 2 Kings 24 he asked why divine judgement had fallen on the people of Israel as well as King David after the latter had murdered Uriah and committed adultery with Bethsheba. He noted Pope Gregory the Great's explanation that a ruler's sin reflected the sinfulness of his people, and hence they suffered punishment when he sinned. The Chanter went on to argue that God had punished Israel for both David's sin and its own, which consisted in its failure to resist David and its consent to his acts of murder and adultery. In one manuscript a marginal note, probably of the Chanter, concluded that we ought to fear for ourselves when we do not resist our prelates' sins. In a longer version of his commentary he observed that a prince's sin falls on his subjects since a multitude of them ought to restrain him from evil, when it was able to do so. He then quoted Augustine on Psalm

[86] Ricardus on 1 Comp. 5.13.3 v. *reus*, BAV, Pal. lat. MS 696, fol. 104vb: 'Presumitur enim consentire, vel dico quod mortaliter peccat si eam ad penitentiam non denuntiet, ut ii. q.i. Si petra [C.2 q.l c.19]'. The Chanter's view is expressed in his *Verbum abbreviatum* (*PL* 205.19).

[87] C.23 q.3 c.11 (derived from Augustine's gloss on Psalm 81:4). See Watt, 'Parisian Theologians'.

[88] *PL* 191.778. Augustine's gloss was also repeated with this remark, 'Hoc modo minoribus dicitur', in the *Glossa ordinaria* to Psalm 81:4.

[89] Peter the Chanter on Psalm 81:4, London, BL, Royal MS 10.C.V, fol. 99va: 'Et liberate egenum de manu peccatoris. Pilati, scilicet, et maiorum Iudeorum potestate. "Per hoc ostenditur", ut ait Augustinus [a marginal note quotes his gloss in n. 87] plebem Iudeorum non esse immunem a morte Christi, cum pre multitudine timerentur, facultatem haberent resistendi. Ut enim ait Augustinus: "Qui non resistit, cum potest, consentit." ... Sed numquid plebs potuerit liberare adductum \innocentem/ patibulo a principe, cum summa rerum gerendarum non sit penes populum? Numquid nisi liberavit pro posse suo peccabit? Ita maiores et minores dominum crucifexerunt.'

81:4 in order to demonstrate that this ability came from force of numbers.[90]
Consequently, the Chanter held that a people had both the power and a duty to
resist the sins of their ruler, and if they neglected this collective responsibility,
they thus deserved collective punishment. Hence he concluded in his *Summa*
that if King David had feared that the people would resist his wrongs, he would
not have had Uriah murdered, and therefore the people had incurred guilt and
punishment for Uriah's death.[91]

The Chanter was not thereby advocating popular rebellion against sinful kings,
however. Baldwin has argued that, when Peter considered whether the people
had the right to liberate those condemned in princely miscarriages of justice,
'Peter concluded that the people do not have the right of insurrection in such
cases'. Similarly Baldwin found that Stephen Langton agreed with this position,
for while he felt that the Jewish people had been obliged to liberate Christ
from the cross, resistance to authority in the face of an injustice was to consist
of prayers and petitions. Hence Baldwin concludes: 'Since recourse to violent
rebellion against an unjust government was denied to the people, the Parisian
theologians must be seen in the last analysis as supporting Paul's principle,
which made political obedience a divine command.'[92] Admittedly Langton in
his own gloss on 2 Kings 24 noted the interpretation that when a king did
wrong, his people ought to resist him in so far as they could, otherwise they
sinned, and that therefore divine vengeance fell on King David's people since
they did not resist him. But Langton considered this view 'disputabilem' though
he tactfully attributed it to St Jerome rather than contradict his master, the
Chanter, directly.[93] Even the Chanter had adopted Gregory the Great's views on
civil obedience to sinful kings in his own gloss on 2 Kings 24, as did the authors

---

[90] Id. on 2 Kings 24:1, Oxford, Bodleian Library, Bodley MS 371, fol. 31r; Eton College MS
16: 'Et addidit furor domini etc. Iam enim ultio facta fuerat in David et domo eius pro interfectione
Urie sed nondum in populo qui vel non resistit David vel consentit adulterio et homicidio
David ... dixit rex ... Punitus est ergo populus pro superbia David numerantis populum ... et pro
peccato proprio quia non resistit David interficienti Uriam vel quia ei consensit.' In Bodley
MS 371 a marginal note added: 'ergo timere debemus nobis pro peccatis prelatorum cum eis
non resistimus.' Another expanded version of this gloss in Paris, Bibliothèque de l'Arsenal MS
44, p. 380b: 'Addidit furor domini. Iam enim ultio facta fuerat in David et in domo eius
sed non in populo qui non resistit David vel ei consensit. Ecce peccatum principis redundat
in subditos et quod multitudo, cum posset, debet principem cohibere a malo. Unde super
Psalmum lxxxi versum "Eripite" etc. Augustinus: "Per hoc ostendit ... [continues as n. 87] ... se a
consensu".'

[91] Id., *Summa*, III 2a, AMN 16, p. 193.

[92] Baldwin, i.167–9. See also Buc, 350–67, 379–98, which discusses many of the texts and
questions raised here in a wider scholastic context.

[93] Stephen Langton on 2 Kings 23:59–24:1, Cambridge, Peterhouse, MS 112, fol. 136rb:
'Urias et Echeus: <Nota> glossam disputabilem Ieronimi que sic dicit... "Iam enim ultio
domini facta fuerat in David et in domo eius sed non in populo, vel quia non resistit
Dauid vel <ei> consensit". Simul glosam secundum illud Psalmi, "Eripite pauperem et
egenum" etc., quando ergo rex delinquit, populus debet ei resistere in quantum potest, vel
si non facit peccat'. Cf. *Ps*. Jerome, *Quaestiones Hebraice in libros Regum et Paralipomenon*
(*PL* 23.1363).

of the *glossa ordinaria* to the Bible and Langton.[94] Gregory had held that a sinful king might be judged only by God but his subjects were to take care that his deeds did not displease them, lest they came to scorn or disrespect him, and, if he could amend what displeased them, this ought to be suggested humbly. Langton added that subjects should still respect a ruler who displeased them if he was constrained by the law. As Gregory himself had concluded, subjects faced with sinful rulers had to follow a subtle path of rectitude and humility. In other words, a fine line divided resistance from disobedience, and in practice it was hardly easy for subjects to toe this line and thereby avoid punishment for their ruler's sinful conduct.[95]

Hence Paris theologians taught that subjects had a duty to call on a sinful ruler to correct his faults but not rebel against him. This teaching arguably influenced Pope Innocent III, who had of course studied theology at Paris. Early in his pontificate his decretal 'Etsi necesse' (25 May 1199) cited God's punishment of David's subjects in 2 Kings 24 in order to justify a papal interdict imposed on the kingdom of Lèon for its king's uncanonical marriage. Indeed in the same decretal it is stated that when the people of Lèon saw that they were subjected to the interdict together with their prince, they believed that they bore a degree of guilt for his sin, because they consented to it by keeping silent. But Innocent's decretal was replying to the petition of some Iberian prelates and this observation occurs in a summary of their petition, so it may represent their view rather than his own. Nevertheless it agrees significantly with the teachings of Innocent's masters at Paris, and before becoming pope he had noted that subjects suffered for their rulers' sins. Even more strikingly in one of the first letters as pope, in February 1198, Innocent called for all the German princes to press for the release of the Archbishop of Salerno; otherwise, all of Germany would fall under an interdict. The archbishop had been captured by their emperor Henry VI, and since the latter's death he had been in the custody of Henry's brother Philip of Swabia, a prime candidate to succeed Henry. In other words, if subjects did not resist

---

[94] Gregory the Great, *Moralia in Iob*, XXV, xvi, *CCSL* 143B, 1260–2. Summarized in the Chanter's gloss on 2 Kings 24:16, Oxford, Bodleian Library, Bodley MS 371, fol. 31rb; Paris, Bibliothèque de l'Arsenal MS 44, p. 380b: 'Percutienti populum. Gregorius ... Sed quia rectores habent iudicem suum, non temere iudicent subditi vitam regentium. Per semetipsum effudit dominus es nummulariorum et cathedras <vendentium> evertit, significans quia per magistros iudicat vitam plebium, per semetipsum facta magistrorum ... Dum ergo salva fide res agitur, virtutis est meritum quicquid prioris est tolerare, debet tamen humiliter suggeri si forte valeat quod displicet emendare. Sepe autem prelati in subditos et viceversa committunt, quia prelati subditos minus sapientes arbitrantur, et subiecti rectorum facta iudicant, et si regnum tenere contingeret, se melius agere putant ... prelatis curandum est ne eorum corda <estimatione> singularis sapientie locus superior extollat, ita subditis providendum est ne sibi facta rectorum displiceant, ita quod illos contempnant vel non venerentur, sed semper humilitas conservetur.'

[95] Langton on 2 Kings 24:1 (summarizing Gregory's gloss), Oxford, Bodleian Library, Rawlinson MS C.427, fol. 29vb; Cambridge, Peterhouse MS 112, fol. 136va: 'Si autem magistrorum vita iure reprehenditur, oportet ut subditi eos etiam cum displicent venerentur'. The *Glossa ordinaria* adds to its summary of Gregory on 2 Kings 24:1: 'Subtilis enim via tenenda est rectitudinis et humilitatis, ut sic magistrorum facta displiceant, ut subditorum mens a magisterii reverentia non recedat.'

a sin committed by their ruler (and perpetuated by their potential ruler), they deserved a collective punishment. It is also notable that this sin was a violation of clerical immunity and that Innocent's letter included a general condemnation of the failure to defend clerks from attack, the ruling incorporated in decretal collections as 'Quante presumptionis' and discussed above.[96]

Stephen Langton likewise applied the doctrine of the Paris theology schools to the interdict when he wrote to the English people on the eve of Innocent's interdict on England.[97] As is well known, this interdict was occasioned by King John's refusal to accept Langton as papal nominee to the see of Canterbury; hence Langton wrote to his flock from exile in France. He begged them not to consent in any way to persecution of the English Church 'since a like penalty binds those consenting to a deed and those performing it'. He defined consent as giving counsel, defence, or protection to wrongdoers, and as we will see, canonists and Innocent III had also identified these forms of consent to sin. He added that anyone who rejoiced in or turned a blind eye to wrongs also consented to them when he could reasonably have prevented them in part or even altogether. Hence non-resistance implied consent to sin, and Langton did not restrict this to prelates as some canonists and even he himself did in their scholastic writings. His question 'Is there one of you who cannot help somehow?' implied that resistance was a universal duty, and in particular he reminded knights that they were invested by the Church in order to defend her. Even those unable to oppose a prince directly might offer him sound warnings, oppose wicked counsel, and restrain their retainers, subjects, and friends from consent to evil, Langton argued. In effect he instructed the English to follow Gregory the Great's teachings on 2 Kings 24. They were to remain obedient to their king, he warned, but if they consented to John's disobedience toward God and the Church, they were to repent and urge others to do the same in the knowledge that, if they sought justice for the Church, it would be just as meritorious for them to lack divine offices under the imminent interdict as to participate in them at the proper time.

Canonists also took up this theological notion that a people had the power and duty to resist its prince's sins. Gratian had included in his *Decretum* Augustine's gloss on Psalm 81:4 blaming the Jews for not preventing the Crucifixion.[98] But only in the late twelfth century, following the Chanter's response to this text, did canonists begin to realize its sociopolitical implications. Huguccio was apparently the first, and he stated the Chanter's view that the text was directed at 'minores', who sinned since they could have restrained their leaders from Christ's murder but failed to do so and hence consented to it. Huguccio thus inferred

[96] Innocent III, Reg. 1, no. 24; 2, no. 72. On his remark before becoming pope see n. 28.

[97] *Acta*, 6. The phrase 'interdictum … expectate' in this letter dates it between Innocent III's first threat of this interdict on 27 August 1207 and its proclamation on 23 March 1208. Innocent's decretal 'Nuper a nobis' (X 5.39.29) specifies the same forms consent to sin as this letter.

[98] See n. 87.

that subjects might resist their secular or ecclesiastical superior if they saw him act against God. This was consistent with his teaching that any Christian should correct another's sin when he could and sinned if he did not, and notably it coincided again with the Chanter's view. Indeed Huguccio likewise argued that a multitude's power over its leaders lay in its superior numbers.[99]

Subsequent decretists followed this interpretation of Augustine's gloss. Alanus (*c*.1210–15) likewise understood it to mean that a people might resist a sinful prince, but he noted that Augustine had also commented on Psalm 1:6 that a king was only to be punished by God.[100] As Paris theologians taught, obedience placed limits on popular resistance to a king's sin. The contemporary author of the *Glossa Palatina* made the same comments; it is unclear who is borrowing from whom, but his other remarks on Augustine's gloss are less circumspect. Firstly he observed that the Jews had failed to prevent the Crucifixion by keeping silent, that is to say, they had tacitly consented to it. He added that one had the power to resist injury to another when one had jurisdiction. But he did not reserve this power to prelates and others in authority as some canonists and theologians did. Rather he argued that the people had this power since it had jurisdiction and retained this even though it had transferred sovereignty to the prince.[101] In a period when it was widely accepted that power came from God, the idea that it came from the people was radical, even when French and English kings were crowned with the formal acclamation of their subjects. This notion reflects the growing influence of Roman law on canonists, because it was based

---

[99] Huguccio on C.23 q.3 c.11, BAV, Vat. lat. MS 2280, fol. 245r; Admont Stiftsbibliothek, MS 7, fol. 319va: 'Ostendit propheta. In illo versu scilicet David ... "Eripite pauperem et egenum" etc. ubi loquitur David minoribus iudeis qui poterunt principes arcere ab interfectione Christi et eis non consentire, quia qui non fecerunt, peccaverunt ... cum pro multitudine. Quia multo plures erant minores quam principes, et est argumentum quod neminem sociam habentem multitudinem excusat allegatio inpotentie, ar. xxxi. q.ii. Lotarius [C.31 q.2 c.4] ... a facto ... est argumentum subditos posse resistere suo prelato seculari vel ecclesiastico, si videant eum contra deum agentem, ar. xi. q.iii. Qui resistit [C.11 q.3 c.97]'.

[100] Alanus, *Apparatus* 'Ius naturale' on C.23 q.3 c.11 v. *principibus*, Paris, BN, MS lat. 15393, fol. 182va: 'Argumentum posse quem(?) resistere principi malefacienti, sed Augustinus dicit super illum verbum Psalmi "Tibi soli peccavi" [Psalm 1:6] quod rex a Deo tantum est puniendus.' Peter Lombard (*PL* 191.486) and the compilers of the *glossa ordinaria* on the Bible (ii.516a) also knew this gloss on Psalm 1:6 but attributed it to Cassiodorus; Cassiodorus's commentary on Psalm 1:6 (*CCSL* 97.457) is similar but lacks this exact phrase.

[101] *Glossa Palatina* on C.23 q.3 c.11, Cambridge, Trinity College MS O.10.2, fol. 13rb: 'permiserunt. Tacendo, xxxiii. q.v. Qui uxorem [C.33 q.5 c.10] ... timerentur. Per hoc videtur probari quod supracantavimus, scilicet quod proximus a proximo non tenetur repellere iniuriam corporalem nisi iurisdictionem habeat, sed dic quod populus propter<ea> bene hoc facere potest, cum populus iurisdictionem habeat, licet imperatore imperium transtulerit, ut inst. de iure naturali §quis [Inst. 1.2.6], et principi et sibi retinuit ... obviare. Quod possit quilibet resistere imperatori suo si ipse in tempore(?) delinquit, sed ar. contra habes in Psalmum "Misere mei, Deus, tibi soli peccavi" [Psalm 1:6]; dicit ibi in glosa Augustini quia rex tantum a Deo puniendus est.' Goffredus de Trano (d. 1245) stated the issue of tacit consent more forcibly, as Guido de Baysio noted in his *Rosarium* on C.23 q.3 c.11 v. *obviare*: 'intelligit Gof. consentire tacendo, lxxxiii. di. Error et c. Consentire [D.83 c.3, 5].'

on a particular interpretation of the *Lex regia* in Roman law developed by the Roman lawyer Azo (d. 1220) among others.[102]

Radical as this notion was, Johannes Teutonicus nevertheless adopted it in his *glossa ordinaria* on the *Decretum*.[103] He noted that Augustine's gloss on Psalm 81:4 contradicted the view that nobody was bound to protect another from harm unless he had jurisdiction and that a people had no jurisdiction. According to Johannes the *Lex regia* stated that the people had such a right and had transferred it to the emperor. He thus concluded that if a people or city had no jurisdiction, one could not explain why it was punished for its judge's fault, and he cited a *Decretum* text which held a people or city responsible for punishing improper acts of its members and making restitution of any losses resulting from such acts.

The *Glossa Palatina* similarly concluded on Augustine's gloss that, because a people had jurisdiction, it had the power and duty to resist its king when he wished to fight an unjust war or do anything wrong. In support another passage from Augustine in the *Decretum* was cited such that if an earthly power commanded anything contrary to divine law, a subject ought to disobey and serve the higher power of God before the emperor, since although the emperor might threaten the disobedient with prison, God might threaten hell![104] Strikingly similar ideas are stated in the *Forma interdicti*, which prescribed the terms of the papal interdict on England (1208–14).[105] It required parish priests to preach to their parishioners that they ought to obey God before man and not fear those who had the power to kill them physically. Priests were then to say prayers for the peace of the Church and for the king that Christ might guide him onto the path of salvation and grant him the spirit of counsel that he might see God's will and carry it out.[106] Such sermons and prayers were clearly propaganda meant to win the people over to the Church's side but not to promote insurrection against the king. The *Forma interdicti* encouraged the same non-violent resistance to his sin as Stephen Langton's letter to the English people on the eve of the interdict.

[102] Laurentius Hispanus, possibly author of the *Glossa Palatina*, is credited by McManus, 50–74, with a decisive role in this 'Romanisation of canon law'. On the *Lex regia* see *Cambridge History of Renaissance Philosophy*, ed. Q. R. D. Skinner, E. Kessler, and J. Kraye (Cambridge, 1988), 391–4.

[103] *Glossa ordinaria* on C.23 q.3 c.11 (Venice, 1496), fol. 214va; Cambridge University Library, MS Dd.VII.20: 'Ostendit propheta ... Hic est evidens ar. contra illos qui dicunt quod socius non tenetur iuvare socium, nisi habeat aliquam iurisdictionem [*manuscript adds*: in eum qui infert iniuriam. Sed] isti dicunt quod populus non [*Ed.* bene] habet iurisdictionem, licet dicat lex [Inst. 1.2.6] quod transtulit ius suum in imperatorem. Nam si civitas vel populus non haberet iurisdictionem, quare punitur propter defectum iudicis, ut supra. e. q.ii. c. Dominus [C.23 q.2 c.2]? Io.'

[104] As n. 101: 'Cum potest Cum iurisdictionem habet, et ita intelligo extra. de homic. Sicut §i [1 Comp. 5.10.7]. Item probatur ex hoc c. quod populus debet resistere regi, cum contra ius voluerit arma movere, vel aliquid mali facere, ar. xi. q.iii. Qui resistit [C.11 q.3 c.97].' In his *Rosarium* on the *Decretum* at C.23 q.3 c.11 Guido de Baysio (d. 1313) copied Huguccio's gloss v. *cum pro multitudine* (see n. 99) and the above gloss, which he specifically attributed to Laurentius.

[105] See p. 132 below on this source.   [106] *Thesaurus*, i.812–13.

Therefore it seems that interdicts were intended not only to punish a people's failure to resist its ruler's sin but also to coerce it into such resistance. Indeed as early as 1111 Abbot Geoffrey of Vendôme had described how an interdict had had exactly this effect. This interdict had fallen on the county of Vendôme because of the count's persecution of the Church, and, according to Geoffrey, it had prompted all the people to proclaim against him, being aware of and greatly displeased by his wickedness, so that clamour and the fear of men caused him to desist. This account recalls, probably not coincidentally, Gregory the Great's gloss on 2 Kings 24 and Augustine's on Psalm 81:4. Likewise the *Gesta Innocentii III* alleged that the papal interdicts imposed on France and England in 1199 and 1208, respectively, provoked popular clamours which prompted the rulers of these kingdoms to seek terms with Innocent III. No source outside this curial chronicle supports this version of events, but it at least shows what effect the curia expected an interdict to have.[107] As a sanction meant to turn subjects against their ruler the interdict was an extreme and desperate measure. Raymund de Peñafort (*c.*1233) indeed noted that a household, city, or province suffered an interdict when its lord committed a grave sin and could not be compelled to make amends otherwise.[108] An interdict might be lifted once he who had occasioned it submitted to ecclesiastical authority, and it was meant to induce those who suffered it along with him to persuade him to do so.

However, not only those who aided or failed to resist sin were said to consent to it and share blame for it, but also those inciting another to sin. Gratian's *Decretum* included a text suggesting that those who counselled and exhorted another to commit murder were also murderers. The text comprised excerpts from Augustine reiterating his view that the Jews were responsible for Christ's death, as it argued that they had killed him, albeit not with their hands, but with their tongues crying 'Crucify, crucify him'.[109] Rufinus and subsequent decretists agreed that the Jews bore more guilt for Christ's death than Pilate and the Roman soldiers who had actually executed Christ, for Christ had said to Pilate: 'He has greater sin who delivered me to you.'[110] These canonists therefore concluded on the basis of this and another *Decretum* text (C.24 q.3 c.32) that those defending a sin were more guilty than those committing it and

---

[107] *PL* 157.84 (Geoffrey); see my 'Popular Resistance', esp. 78–81.

[108] Raymund de Peñafort, *Summa*, 372.

[109] De pen. D.1 c.23. *Glossa Palatina* (BAV, Pal. lat. MS 658, fol. 85vb) summarizes it thus: 'Casus. Qui consilium dat ad occidendum homicida est. Unde Iudei probantur fuisse homicide Christi, quia illum etsi non manibus tamen lingua occiderunt et magis peccaverunt quam Pilatus vel milites qui eum crucifixerunt.' Cf. id. on v. *acutus*: 'Dum clamarent "crucifige, crucifige". Et hii etiam fecerunt mortem ut gladius accutus.' Both glosses were copied by Johannes Teutonicus in his *Glossa ordinaria* at De pen. D.1 c.23 (BAV, Vat. lat. MS 1367, fol. 254vb).

[110] Rufinus, *Summa* on D.83 *dictum ante* c.1 v. *providendum* (Ed. p. 173), quoting John 19:11. Much the same was said by Stephen of Tournai on D.83 *dictum ante* c.1 v. *admittat* (Ed. p. 105) and Johannes Faventinus on D.83 *dictum ante* c.1 v. *providendum*, BAV, Borgh. lat. MS 71, fol. 56r.

so they deserved harsher punishment. The *Decretum* even recorded a case where punishment was inflicted not on the actual sinner, a bishop acquitted on grounds of senility, but on those who counselled his sin.[111] These were exceptions to the rule that a 'like penalty' bound those committing a sin and those consenting to it.

Canonists clearly considered that consent to sin varied in its gravity and so the punishment should vary accordingly. Failure to correct another's sin was deemed less worse than the actual sin and so merited a lesser punishment, although early decretists further distinguished that a prelate who consented in this way might be punished more severely than a subject. Those who actively consented by cooperating with the sinner had sinned as much as him and so were to be punished likewise. Canonists considered counselling and defending sin the most sinful form of consent for various reasons. An anonymous decretist (*c*.1185–7) explained that it granted others the authority to sin.[112] Johannes Galensis of Wales (*c*.1210) also observed that Innocent III's decretal 'Nuper a nobis' (Po. 700; 1199) extended excommunication to those who had counselled a canonical crime for the actual wrongdoer would not have committed it otherwise.[113] Alexander III had likewise ruled in the decretal 'Sicut dignum' that those who had provoked Henry II by their suggestions to order Becket's murder should be punished as severely as Becket's killers, and Tancred justified (*c*.1220) this on the grounds that Henry might not have done so otherwise.[114] Such papal rulings did not follow canonistic doctrine strictly, for they had threatened the same penalty on those counselling and those committing a sin. However, Innocent III's decretal 'Vergentis' toed the more draconian canonistic line; according to Tancred it punished defenders of heretics more than the actual heretics because they sinned

---

[111] D.86 c.24. Huguccio, ibid. v. *duobus mensibus*, BAV, Arch. S. Pietro MS C.114, fol. 102rb; Vat. lat. MS 2280, fol. 79r: 'Ecce casus ubi magis puniuntur consiliarii, quam auctor, ar. di. xcvi. Duo, et xi. q. iii. Qui consentit [D.96 c.10; C.11 q.3 c.100]. Sed quare magis hic puniuntur consentientes, quam auctor? Resp. parcitum est ei, quia senex et simplex erat sed in istis non inveniebatur, quare cum eis dispensaretur. Postea presumebatur quia isti plus pecassent, quia ille senex et simplex erat, unde quicquid fecit eius consiliariis inputari debebat'.

[112] Added to Huguccio's *Summa* at C.24 q.3 c.32 v. *Qui aliorum*, BAV, Vat. lat. MS 2280, fol. 254rb: 'Hic habetur quod consentiens plus peccat quam faciens ... Plus peccat qui defendit quia et ipse peccat et auctoritatem peccandi aliis prestat.' Cf. *Glossa Palatina*, ibid. v. *defendit*, BAV, Pal. lat. MS 658, fol. 72rb: 'Consensus ... <quartus> per auctoritatem prestando, patrocinium, et favorem et auctoritate facienti, xxiiii. q.iii. Qui aliorum ... In quarto magis peccat consentiens quam faciens. Quandoque tamen minus est facere quam auctoritatem prestare, ff. de act. ep. Iul. §Sed cum in facto [Dig. 19.1.13 §7].'

[113] Johannes Galensis on 3 Comp. 5.21.3 v. *ei consilium*, München, Bayerische Staatsbibliothek Clm 3879, fol. 261vb: 'Qui alias non erat facturus, ff. de hiis que no. infa. l.i [Dig. 3.2.1], idest favorem ei qui alias non erat facturus'. Cf. C.11 q.3 c.103.

[114] Tancred on 1 Comp. 5.10.7 v. *provocasset*, BAV, Vat. lat. MS 1377, fol. 87ra: 'forte alias non facturum.' Cf. Zoën on 5 Comp. 1.1.1 v. *consiliarios*, Tours, Bibliothèque Municipale MS 565, fol. 1rb: 'Abstinendum est ergo a consilio fraudulento etiam si alias sic facturus esset is cui datur consilium, non enim oportet laudando augeri maliciam aliis, ut ff. de servo cor. l.i §Sed utrum [Dig. 11.3.1 §4]. Et hoc est quod vulgo consuevit dici: Lauda malum et facies eum currere.'

more.[115] Indeed this is comparable to the tendency of medieval chroniclers to blame the faults of rulers on wicked counsellors. Counsel and consent were thus closely related in medieval thought on collective guilt as on other matters.

By the early thirteenth century theologians and canonists had developed fairly sophisticated notions of collective guilt on the basis of consent to another's sin, which in turn formed the doctrinal foundation for Innocent IV's justification of the interdict. Although they condemned the consent of a *multitudo* or *populus*, tacit or otherwise, it was only after 1200 that they discussed this issue in the context of corporation theory, that is to say, in relation to an organized community or *universitas*. The only canonist who came close to doing so before 1200 was Rufinus, who had argued that if a prelate alienated his church's dues with his brethren's consent, the church might suffer loss as a result, but if he acted on his own authority without their consent, then only he would be punished and the church would not suffer.[116] This example is oblique and specific but raises a key distinction: only the head of an organized community was responsible for his conduct if the rest of the community did not approve it; but they too were held accountable if he acted with their approval. This reflected the decretist doctrine that consent to another's sin made it one's own. After 1200, as corporation theory evolved, canonists applied this doctrine more explicitly to organized communities. One of the first was a pupil of the French canonist Petrus Brito, who said (*c*.1205) of a ruling of Alexander III on simony that a whole monastery was at fault when all of its brethren consented to admission of novices in return for money. Likewise Johannes Teutonicus conceded (*c*.1217) that an abbot's fraud ought to harm his church if the whole church body had given him its consent.[117] Tacit consent was also attributed to a *universitas*. Alexander III's decretal 'Continebatur' had provided that if an abbess alienated tithes of her church and its convent knew but did not object, then her grant was valid, for, as Alanus noted (*c*.1201–10), their silence was taken as consent. And such a body might suffer for its silence.[118] Johannes Teutonicus observed on Innocent III's decretal 'Cum secundum aspostolum' that where a bishop ordained a clerk but failed to assign him a benefice, the bishop's church was penalized for this

---

[115] Tancred on 3 Comp. 5.4.1 v. *defensare*, BAV, Vat. lat. MS 1377, fol. 264va: 'Plus peccant defensores hereticorum quam ipsi heretici et ideo gravius puniendi sunt, ut <xxiv> q.iii. Qui aliorum [C.24 q.3 c.32] t.'

[116] Rufinus, *Summa* on C.16 q.6 v. *quod autem ea que ecclesia debentur* (Ed. pp. 366–7).

[117] Anon. on 1 Comp. 5.2.10 v. *edere*, Brussels, Bibliothèque Royale MS 1407–9, fol. 74va: 'extra. Innoc. [*recte* Alex.] iii. Veniens [2 Comp. 5.2.1] ... ad illam decretalem dicitur quod totum illud monasterium fuit in culpa quia omnes monachi consenserunt receptioni pecunie'. Johannes Teutonicus on 3 Comp. 2.4.un. v. *ipsius dolum* (Ed. p. 194).

[118] Alanus on 1 Comp. 3.9.2, München, Bayerische Staatsbibliothek Clm 3879, fol. 42va: 'contradicente. Nota in alienatione rerum ecclesie taciturnitas pro consensu habetur. Contra ar. xii. q.ii. Sine ex., x. q.ii. §Hoc ius por. in fi. [C.12 q.2 c.52; C.10 q.2 c.2]. concessit. Hoc ideo dicit quoniam, si multum tempus elapsum esset et conventus semper tacuisset, videtur consensisse, ar. infra. de privil. Si de terra [1 Comp. 5.28.9]'. Johannes Teutonicus on 3 Comp. 3.5.1 v. *vel successores eorum* (edited at http://faculty.cua.edu/pennington/edit301.htm).

negligence by having to maintain the clerk, for it did not oppose the bishop over this appointment and no bishop carried out ordinations without his church's counsel. Johannes thus concluded that those who had not resisted a wrongdoer were punished.

A prelate was not to make decisions touching the rights of his church without consulting its clergy, as Johannes indicated. Though Johannes and the pupil of Petrus Brito spoke of a whole church body consenting to a prelate's deeds, this did not mean unanimous consent necessarily. Canonists accepted that collective decisions might be made by a majority (*maior et sanior pars*). For example, a majority vote was enough to elect a prelate, since, as Vincentius Hispanus (*c*.1210–15) noted from Roman law, 'what the majority does, all are understood to do'. As early as the 1190s Bernard of Pavia had equated majority support with the general consent of a church body, and he concluded that a dissenting minority was thereby overruled and bound by the majority decision.[119] This also applied to collective wrongs, for Vincentius observed that if the majority of a church body committed a wrong, it might result in loss for the church as a whole.[120]

Therefore Innocent IV was strongly supported by canonistic tradition when he argued that a *universitas* might be interdicted if its leaders or agents had done wrong with the approval of all or most of its members. The kind of *universitas* that most concerned canonists was an ecclesiastical one, notably the bishop and chapter, which, as the examples above show, practised this consensual form of government. Bolognese canonists who developed corporation theory were also influenced by the example of civic communes in northern Italy. Yet, when canonists noted interdicts in papal letters, they described these as falling mostly on a territory for the sin of its lord or prince and only occasionally on a city or church.[121] Alanus (*c*.1210–15) remarked that it could be imposed on subjects for their superior's contumacy. More tellingly Jacobus de Albenga (*c*.1230) observed

[119] Vincentius Hispanus on 1 Comp. 5.2.21 v. *perturbata*, Leipzig Universitätsbibliothek MS 983, fol. 49va: 'Videtur ergo quod canonice electus fuit, supra. de hiis que fiunt a maiore parte capituli c.i [1 Comp. 3.10.1], et quod maior pars facit omnes facere intelliguntur, ff. ad inimici. Quod maior [Dig. 50.1.19]. Et in istis sufficit quod maior pars consentiat, supra de etate. Licet [1 Comp. 1.8.4]'. Bernard was applying this principle to a chapter or collegiate church specifically. Bernardus Papiensis, *Summa*, III.10 §1 (Ed. p. 75). On this principle see Landau, 'Bedeutung', 42.
[120] Vincentius Hispanus on 1 Comp. 1.35.4 v. *suo iure*, Leipzig Universitätsbibliothek MS 983, fol. 11rb: '<Si> vero maior pars ecclesie delinquid in faciendo, etiam in dampnum ecclesie redundat, ut xxv. q.ii. Ita, ff. quibus mo. usufru. a. l. Si usus [C.25 q.2 c.25; Dig. 7.4.21].'
[121] Ricardus Anglicus on 1 Comp. 4.1.13 v. *tota*, BAV, Pal. lat. MS 696, fol. 77ra: 'Sic ergo pro delicto unius tota provincia interdicitur, ut supra de off. iu. de. Sane quia [1 Comp. 1.21.16] b<ernardus(?)>.' Anon. on 1 Comp. 2.17.6 v. *celebrari*, Brussels, Bibliothèque Royale MS 1407–9, fol. 23va: 'Patet quod terra alicuius pro eius delicto potest interdici, xvii. q.iiii. Miror [C.17 q.4 c.8]'. Vincentius Hispanus on 1 Comp. 4.1.13 v. *provincia*, Leipzig Universitätsbibliothek MS 983, fol. 39va: 'pro delicto principis tota terra subponitur interdicto'. Regarding an interdict on a city, *Glossa Palatina* on C.17 q.4 c.8 v. *domus tue*, BAV, Pal. lat. MS 658, fol. 61ra: 'Ar. quod delictum unius et civitas debeat interdici, extra. de spon. Non est vobis [1 Comp. 4.1.13]'. Regarding an interdict on a church, Alanus on 1 Comp. 3.33.17 v. *terras*, München, Bayerische Staatsbibliothek

that an interdict on a place might be caused by the delict of the person holding lordship there.[122] Feudal ties might justify why people in that place suffered an interdict for their lord's fault. Land was the basis of relations between a lord and his subjects. His vassals held land from him in return for counsel and aid, military and financial, which might involve them in supporting his sins. Indeed Innocent III's decretal 'Nuper a nobis' (1199) had extended excommunication to any knowingly associating with an excommunicate in a crime by offering him aid, counsel, or support; this had clear implications for feudal retainers.[123] Canonists had, moreover, defined counsel, cooperation, and defence as forms of consent to another's sin that merited punishment, and on the eve of the English interdict Stephen Langton likewise condemned those who consented to persecution of the English Church by giving counsel, defence, or protection to wrongdoers. Thomas Aquinas also justified a *pena temporalis*, which punished one for another's sin, such as an interdict, in terms of medieval social relations, arguing that one man belonged 'temporaliter' to another—sons to fathers, serfs to lords—and hence shared their punishment.

However, though a feudal ruler required the counsel and aid and thus consent of his principal vassals, he did not govern with the active consent of the majority of his subjects. Only in the late thirteenth century did English kings require communities to consent to grants of taxation through representatives in Parliament. And even this was formal not free consent. Hence before the late thirteenth century subjects might only consent to deeds of their ruler in the tacit sense of failing to resist his wrongs. It was certainly in this sense that Paris theologians and Bolognese canonists understood a people to consent to its ruler's sin and thereby deserve punishment, and we have seen that Innocent III and Stephen Langton applied this way of thinking to interdicts. But scholars and popes were not advocating popular revolt against abuses of temporal power. After King John submitted to Innocent III, ending the conflict that occasioned the papal interdict on England, the pope supported John against his rebellious subjects and condemned Magna Carta as damaging to royal rights. Rather scholastic doctrine on consent to another's sin and the use of interdicts that

---

Clm 3879, fol. 58va: 'ar. propter peccatum sacerdotis, patroni, vel domini terre ecclesia interdicto supponi'.

[122] Alanus, *Apparatus* 'Ius naturale' on C.24 q.3 d.a.c.1 v. *pro peccato*, BAV, Ross. lat. MS 595, fol. 207rb (second layer of glosses): 'Minori <excommunicatione> que est separatio a sacramentis excommunicari possunt subditi pro superioris delicto si contumax fuerit, ut infra. de of. iud. del. Sane quia nos, supra xvii. q.iiii. Miror [1 Comp. 1.21.16; C.17 q.4 c.8]'. (Alanus here defines the interdict as collective minor excommunication). Jacobus de Albenga on 5 Comp. 2.16.1 v. *interdicti*, London, BL, Royal MS 11.C.vii, fol. 257ra: 'Quod quandoque fit propter delictum persone que dominium habet in loco, ut supra de officio iud. del. Sane l.i., et de iure patro. Ex insinuatione, et de spon. Non est vobis lib. i. [1 Comp. 1.21.16; 3.33.7; 4.1.13]'.

[123] 3 Comp. 5.21.3 (=X 5.39.29). Cf. Alanus (*c*.1201–10), who had said that one who gave a thief aid and counsel might be judged his accomplice and guilty too, at 1 Comp. 5.26.6 v. *partitur*, München, Bayerische Staatsbibliothek Clm 3879, fol. 91rb: 'Sive consilium sive auxilium in participando.'

it justified were meant to reinforce a sense of popular collective duty to the Church authorities above, but not necessarily in derogation of, that owed to lay rulers. An interdict was meant both to punish subjects for not resisting their ruler's sins against the Church and to coerce them into persuading him to make amends for these sins. Hence the interdict can be seen as the Church's reaction to lay forms of social organization emerging in the twelfth century, notably kingdoms and communes, that made claims to collective loyalty sometimes in conflict with those asserted by the Church.

1.4 SIN IN ANOTHER'S NAME

So far we have considered collective guilt in terms of a group's consent to a wrong of its head. Canonists also considered the problem from another perspective, in terms of the formal relationship binding a community and its head. We have already seen how feudal relations justified an interdict falling on a land for its lord's wrong. Organized communities might also be answerable for wrongs of their representatives. From the early thirteenth century canonists increasingly perceived the head of an ecclesiastical body as its proctor, i.e. its legal representative empowered by its mandate to act on its behalf and bind it by his actions.[124]According to Post jurists had argued since the late twelfth century that proctors were to receive a general mandate granting them full power or *plena potestas*; this bound a client to consent to the decision of the court in a suit brought by his proctor.[125] This mandate was issued by the mid-thirteenth century to ambassadors despatched to negotiations and by 1300 to representatives summoned to Church councils, general chapters of religious orders, and popular assemblies in England, France, and Aragon. Canonistic discussion of proctorial power was based on Roman law, whose revival in the twelfth century had introduced procedures involving proctors to ecclesiastical courts. Civil charges might be brought against a *universitas* via its proctor, and a *univeritas* or even an individual client might be held accountable for their proctor's conduct. Johannes Galensis (*c*.1210) noted the juristic commonplace that one was often said to do what one did through another. Similarly Laurentius Hispanus (*c*.1210) observed that whatever an advocate said on behalf of his client, the client was deemed to have said.[126] Hence canonists recognized that a proctor's statements in court might prejudice his client, especially if the client did not refute them. Alanus (*c*.1206) had argued that a client was not prejudiced

---

124 See Tierney, 117–27.   125 Post, 91–162.
126 Johannes Galensis on 3 Comp. 3.26.5 v. *inutiles*, München, Bayerische Staatsbibliothek Clm 3879, fol. 229vb: 'Id enim sepe quis dicitur facere quod per alium facit, ut infra de sen. ex. Ut fame, C. ubi et apud quem. l.iii, ff. de ami. tu. ita. Tamen §Quod si quis [3 Comp. 1.21.8; Cod. 2.46.3; Dig. 26.7.5].' Laurentius Hispanus on 3 Comp. 3.37.5 v. *advocatus ipsius* (Ed. pp. 534–5).

by his proctor's statements unless he had ratified them or given the proctor a mandate to make them. However, Alanus conceded that what a clerk said in court might prejudice his church, even if this were not true of a proctor, at least not without the above qualifications.[127] Johannes Galensis agreed that a proctor's statements might not prejudice the client unless he ratified them, but he added that they might still prejudice the client when he did not refute them, for it would be as if he approved them; in other words his silence might be taken as consent.[128]

The fullest discussion of this problem among the early decretalists is found in the writings of Johannes Teutonicus. His view, repeated in many glosses on both *Compilationes tertia* and *quarta*, was that whatever a proctor said or did wrong in his client's name might prejudice the client, unless he exceeded the terms of his mandate, i.e. the general one empowering him to act in his client's name. But Johannes required no specific mandate or ratification approving such wrongs, as Alanus had. Johannes conceded that a client ignorant of his proctor's wrongs might not be held responsible for them, presumably because he could not refute what he did not know. Knowledge of a fact was seen as crucial in tacit consent to it, as we noted above. This also applied to a proctor exceeding the terms of his mandate, for Johannes argued that this would prejudice the client if he knew of it but not otherwise. Johannes also observed that a proctor's fraudulent conduct, contumacy, or negligence might count against his client, since the client might be accused of appointing a bad and incompetent proctor.[129]

Such views on proctors could apply to a *universitas*, for it could appoint a proctor or, strictly speaking, a syndic, notably to swear an oath in court in its name.[130] They were especially pertinent to an ecclesiastical body, whose head

---

[127] Alanus on Alan. 1.5.5 (=3 Comp. 1.4.1) v. *non negavit*, Vercelli Cathedral Chapter MS 89, fol. 55vb: 'Que confessio presumptionem inducebat, domino tamen non preiudicabat, ut ff. de inter. ac. Si defensor, et ff. de confessis. Certum §Sed an, et ff. ad l. Aquil. Proin. §Si procurator [Dig. 11.1.9 §4; 42.2.6 §4; 9.2.25 §1], nisi dominus confessionem ratam habuerit hic, ff. de int. ac. Qui servum [Dig. 11.1.20], vel sic confiteri mandaverit, ar. supra de procura. c.i. lib. i., et supra. de procu. Cum pro causa lib. ii. [1 Comp. 1.29.1; 4 Comp. 1.16.1].' Id. on Alan. 1.16.4 (=3 Comp. 3.29.un) v. *confessus*, fol. 67ra: 'Sic ergo confessio illius presbyteri ecclesie preiudicavit, quod est verum sine mala fide sic confessus, ar. infra. de his que fiunt ab episcopis. Cum olim, et infra. de censi. Olim [4 Comp. 1.12.1; 3 Comp. 3.37.5]. Secus de procuratoris confessione, ut dictum est supra. de postu. prela. Ad hec in glo. [Alan. 1.5.5].'

[128] Johannes Galensis on 3 Comp. 1.4.1 v. *negavit*, München, Bayerische Staatsbibliothek Clm 3879, fol. 154vb: 'Hec confessio sibi non preiudicabat ... ff. de inter. ac. Si defensor, ff. de confessis. Certum §Sed an, ff. ad l. Aquil. Provid. §i. [Dig. 11.1.9 §4; 42.2.6 §4; 9.2.25 §1], nisi ipse confessionem ratam haberet, ar. de procurat. c.i. lib. i., de procurat. Ex insinuatione l.i [1 Comp. 1.29.1; 2 Comp. 1.18.3].' Id. on 3 Comp. 3.29.un. v. *confessus*, fol. 231va: 'Hec confessio ... ubi non revocata quasi approbata preiudicat, ff. de procurat. l.ii [Dig. 3.3.2]. Alias autem nisi approbaretur domino non nocet, ff. de confessis Certum §Sed cui [Dig. 42.2.6].'

[129] Johannes Teutonicus on 3 Comp. 1.4.1 v. *idem magister* (Ed. p. 32); 1.18.11 v. *protinus* (Ed. p. 127); 2.3.1 v. *propter contumaciam* (Ed. pp. 182–3). Id. on 4 Comp. 1.12.1 v. *recusare*, BAV, Vat. lat. MS 1377, fol. 288va: 'imputet ergo sibi quod malum procuratorem elegit'.

[130] Tancred on 3 Comp. 1.24.1 v. *procuratorem*, BAV, Vat. lat. MS 1377, fol. 184va: 'Hic videtur quod universitas possit constituere procuratorem, ut infra de iuramento calumpnie c.uno

was increasingly regarded as its proctor and was elected by its members. And the latter were obliged to elect a suitable candidate; otherwise, according to many decretals of Innocent III, their voting rights might be transferred to a superior. A gloss on the *Decretum*, possibly by Alanus (*c*.1210–15), had even said that subjects might suffer because of a bad prelate, since he would lead them astray by his bad example and, if they had elected him, they would be punished unless he was removed.[131] Subsequently Innocent IV affirmed that if a church's proctor was negligent, it might be punished not for his wrong but rather its own fault in failing to elect a trustworthy and competent proctor.[132] Twelfth- and thirteenth-century theologians also argued that a sinful people deserved a sinful ruler, notably Israel suffering divine punishment for King David's sin in 2 Kings 24.[133] Though medieval kings were said to be elected with the acclamation of their people in England and France, not until the late Middle Ages did jurists impute the sins of kings to their subjects for 'electing' one who was unworthy of office.[134]

A potential obstacle to such arguments was Gratian's maxim that the wrong of one person, namely a prelate, ought not to result in loss for his church. Rufinus had distinguished that a church might suffer as a result of alienations made by its prelate with its clergy's advice but not on his own authority alone.[135] Other canonists drew another broader distinction. Johannes Faventinus discerned that a prelate's negligence could result in loss for his church, for example, as Rolandus (*c*.1150) had also observed, a bishop's failure to convert heretics subject to his see, but the wrongdoer alone was to suffer for actual crimes like adultery or murder.[136] The *Summa Parisiensis* expressed this distinction in terms of wrongs of commission, such as adultery, which were not to result in a church's loss,

---

[3 Comp. 1.26.un.], sed ibi sindicus dicitur ... t.' Laurentius Hispanus on 3 Comp. 1.24.1 v. *negligenter* (Ed. p. 327).

[131] Innocent III's decretals on chapters electing unworthy prelates and thereby forfeiting voting rights: 3 Comp. 1.3.7, 1.4.1, 1.6.8, 15; 4 Comp. 1.3.8–11. Alanus(?) on C.1 q.4 d.p.c.11 v. *inmeregeretur*, BAV, Ross. lat. MS 595, fol. 96ra: 'in vita subditorum deprivatur propter malum prelatum, racione mali exempli, ut supra e. q. Homini [C.1 q.4 c.9], quia si subditi malum eligant, puniuntur, alias removebitur, supra lxiii. Miramur [D.63 c.5].'

[132] Innocent IV, *Apparatus* on X 2.6.1 v. *sciens*: 'in predictis non punitur ecclesia pro delicto procuratoris, sed pro sua culpa, in qua fuit quod non elegit et in fide et in facultatibus bonum procuratorem.'

[133] E.g. Thomas Aquinas, *Summa theologiae*, II^a II^{ae}, 108, art. 4, ad 1.

[134] Eschmann, 'Notion of Society', 6 n. 21, noted the opinion of Spanish jurist Franciscus de Vitoria (d. 1546): 'It is permitted to punish the whole "commonweal" (*res publica*) for the sin of the king ... The commonweal is indeed bound to entrust power to no one else but he who exercises and uses it justly.'

[135] C.16 q.6 c.3. On this principle see Landau, 'Bedeutung', 42–3. On Rufinus see n. 116.

[136] Johannes Faventinus on C.16 q.6 c.3 v. *delictum persone*, BAV, Borgh. lat. MS 71, fol. 122va: 'Non est hic intelligendum de omni delicto. Sunt enim quedam prelatorum que in dampnum ecclesie convertendum, ut eius negligentia qui hereticos ad suam cathedram pertinentes convertere noluit ... delicti ergo nomine hic intellige crimen, ut adulterium, homicidium et similia'. Rolandus, *Summa* on C.16 q.6 (Ed. p. 55).

and those of omission, i.e. negligence, which might.[137] This formula became a commonplace in subsequent canonistic discourse. But it was soon qualified, since some canonists accepted that a church might sometimes suffer for its prelate's wrongs of commission. For example Peter of Blois (*c*.1180) combined this distinction with that of Rufinus, arguing that a prelate's wrong might result in loss for his church if it was committed with the consent of his church or the majority thereof; albeit this applied to wrongs against the church's goods, like alienations, not personal crimes like heresy. But not all canonists agreed that a church suffered for its prelate's wrongs if it authorized them, even alienations.[138] Nevertheless one influential canonist reached a synthesis similar to Peter's; Tancred argued that one person's wrong did not result in a church's loss if it was not 'contemplated' by the church, for example theft, but it did if it arose from the dictate of a prelate's office or his church, whether it was a wrong of commission or omission. Damasus (*c*.1210–15) likewise concluded that a prelate's wrong of commision resulted in his church's loss when he acted on its behalf and in its defence.[139] In other words a church might be held responsible for any wrong that its prelate committed in his official capacity, acting in its name with its authority, but not as a private person acting of his own volition. This may explain why canonists did not hold clients responsible for proctors who exceeded the terms of their mandates without their knowledge, as these proctors were acting not as their agents but of their own free will. Agents needed authorization from those in whose name they claimed to act, even if only a general mandate, and the canonists also discussed this issue.

Huguccio had identified 'licence' as one of the forms of consent to another's sin, observing that whoever granted licence to a sinner approved his sin and so ought to suffer the same penalty as him.[140] Early-thirteenth-century canonists

---

137 *Summa Parisiensis* on C.16 q.6 (Ed. p. 186).
138 Peter of Blois, *Speculum* (Ed. p. 29). Cf. The French *Summa* 'De iure canonico tractaturus' (*c*.1185) on C.16 q.6 c.1 v. *detrimentum cause*, Laon, Bibliothèque communale MS 371bis, fol. 141ra: 'nec tamen inde ecclesie preiudicabitur nisi auctoritate collegii hoc factum fuerit, dico.' Added in a marginal note: 'Quidam tamen dicunt et forte verius quod si etiam auctoritate ecclesie rem propriam ecclesie invadat episcopus, non preiudicat ecclesie'. Vincentius Hispanus on 1 Comp. 1.35.4 v. *ignorante*, Leipzig Universitätsbibliothek MS 983, fol. 11rb: 'Hic valet argumentum contrario sensu: delictum enim persone in dampnum ecclesie redundare non debet, xvi. q.vi. Si episcopum [C.16 q.6 c.3]. Resp. dicunt quidam quod illud intelligitur quando prelatus solus perpetrat ad instar tutoris, nam eius temeritas pupillo nocere non debet etiam si culpa precesisset, C. unde vi. Meminerit [Cod. 8.4.6]. Secus si cum collegio dampnum dedit, viii. q.iii. Placuit, xxv. q.ii. Ita nos [C.16 q.3 c.8; C.25 q.2 c.25]. Vel melius distingue inter delictum in omittendo et in faciendo.'
139 Tancred on 2 Comp. 2.14.2 v. *successoribus*, BAV, Vat. lat. MS 1377, fol. 114rb: 'Unde sic solvo: delictum personale quod non contemplatione ecclesie committitur, ut furtum, adulterium et similia, non redundat in dampnum ecclesie. Illud vero quod intuitu prelationis vel ecclesie committitur, sive in faciendo sive in negligendo consistat, redundat in dampnum ecclesie. t.' Damasus, 'Brocarda', fol. 26vb.
140 Huguccio on D.86 c.1 v. *negligentes*, BAV, Arch. S. Pietro MS C.114, fol. 100va; Vat. lat. MS 2280, fol. 78ra: 'Tribus modis dicitur quis consentire scilicet ... Per licentiam, cum approbationem

preferred to speak of granting 'authority' to a sinner and considered it more serious than the actual sin, arguing that it should be punished more harshly.[141] Vincentius Hispanus (*c*.1210–15) thus remarked that when consent consisted of authority in the form of commands, such as those from a father to a son or a lord to his retainer, it was more incriminating than other forms of consent to sin.[142] One *Decretum* text had even suggested to the author of the *Summa Reginensis* and other decretists that anyone who ordered a death, except for a judge imposing a capital sentence, was guilty of murder along with the killer.[143] There was much canonistic debate on this point and it had been stimulated by Alexander III's decretal 'Mulieres'. It had ruled that any authorizing or ordering an attack on a clerk required papal absolution, for 'he truly commits the wrong by whose authority or mandate it is proven to be committed', an idea based on the Roman *lex Aquilia* on murder.[144] Ricardus Anglicus (*c*.1197) inferred that the person ordering the attack incurred the same penalty that the canon 'Si quis suadente' (C.17 q.4 c.29) imposed on a clerk's attacker, i.e. papal excommunication, even though Huguccio had doubted this.[145] Ricardus went on to argue that he incurred this penalty even if he repented his order before the attack. Repentance spared him from excommunication, Alanus added (*c*.1201–10), only if he revoked his

concedit et tunc equaliter peccat consentiens et faciens, ut xi q.i<ii> Qui consentit in fine [C.11 q.3 c.100]'. Id. on C.11 q.3 c.100 v. *qui consentit*, BAV, Arch. S. Pietro MS C.114, fol. 198rb; Vat. lat. MS 2280, fol. 180rb: 'In hoc capitulo facit Ysidorus mentionem de duobus consensibus ad malum. Primo de illo qui fit per cooperationem, ubi gravius peccat consentiens quam faciens. Postea de illo qui qui fit per licenciam, ubi equaliter peccat consentiens et faciens.'

[141] *Glossa Palatina* on C.11 q.3 c.100 v. *qui consentit*, BAV, Pal. lat. MS 658, fol. 48vb: 'Per cooperationem et auctoritatem.' Johannes Teutonicus, *Glossa ordinaria* on C.2 q.1 c.10 v. *et consentientem*, BAV, Vat. lat. MS 1367, fol. 84vb; 'Editio Romana', i.533: 'dicitur consentire cum defendit peccantem vel quando sua auctoritate delinquitur, xi. q.iii. Qui consentit, xxiiii. q.iii. Qui aliorum [C.11 q.3 c.100; C.24 q.3 c.32], et talis magis punitur quam faciens ut ibi dicitur ... Io.' Id. on C.11 q.3 c.100 v. *consentit* (BAV, Vat. lat. MS 1367, fol. 135ra) copies the *Glossa Palatina*.

[142] Vincentius Hispanus on 1 Comp. 5.2.7 v. *reatum*, Leipzig Universitätsbibliothek MS 983, fol. 48rb: 'agentes et consentientes par pena constringit ... Est consensus auctoritatis que in preceptis consistit, ut de patre ad filium, de domino ad famulum, hic magis obligat, ut xxiiii. q.iii. Qui aliorum. Est consensus negligentie huius pena minor, i. q.i. Quicquid [C.1 q.1 c.101]. Est consensus licencie huius par pena, ii. q.i. Notum [C.2 q.1 c.10].'

[143] *Summa Reginensis* on D.50 c.8 v. *aut facto*, BAV, Reg. lat. MS 1061 fol. 9ra: 'nam et qui mandavit et consilium prestitit homicidii reus est'.

[144] 1 Comp. 5.34.7 (=X 5.39.6). Cf. Dig. 43.16.1 §12.

[145] Ricardus on 1 Comp. 5.34.7 v. *auctoritate vel mandato*, BAV, Pal. lat. MS 696, fol. 114vb: 'Quidam solvendo concedunt de plano quod mandator incidit in canonem quibus consentio. Dicit tamen magister Hucg<uccio> quod non incidit sed in detestationem criminis mittitur ad curiam et illi consentirem si Celestinus [Pope Celestine III] non contradiceret.' Cf. Huguccio on C.17 q.4 c.29 v. *iniecerit violentas manus in clericum*, BAV, Arch. S.Pietro MS C.114, fol. 248r: 'Quid si quis non percutit clericum sed facit eum percuti, idest, iussu eius percutitur, numquid in hunc canonem inciditur? Et dicunt quidam quod sic, ar xxii q.v c.i [C.22 q.5 c.1] et decretalis Alex. "Mulieres", ubi hec questio determinatur et respondent quod ille intelligitur facere cuius precepto et autoritate fit. Mihi tamen videtur quod talis ipso iure non sit excommunicatus. Debent enim verba istius capituli sicut dictum est cum affectu accipi. Graviter tamen peccat nec in illa decretale "Mulieres" dicitur quod sit excommunicatus sed quod ad curiam Romanam sit mittendus quod forte in detestatione criminis et terrore malefactorum dictum est et in pene exasperatione.'

order before the attack;[146] anyone then proceeding with the attack clearly acted of his own volition. Thus canonists were careful not to let those in whose name wrong was done evade responsibility for it.

A common view of early thirteenth-century canonists, based upon Roman law, was that ratification, i.e. subsequent approval, was equivalent to a mandate in regard to crimes. Although Alanus was one of the first canonists to state this view, he did not apply it to the decretal 'Mulieres', arguing that the text did not expressly refer to one ratifying an attack on a clerk, and he cited a Roman law maxim that penalties were to be limited rather than extended.[147] Johannes Galensis (*c*.1210) was less cautious. Though no glosses of his on 'Mulieres' are known, he held that ratification was comparable to a mandate in regard to crimes, especially when they had been carried out in the name of him who ratified them; thus he who ratified a murder committed in his name might be judged a murderer. Another contemporary canonist likewise pointed out that one might *only* ratify deeds done in one's name or with one's contemplation.[148] Damasus (*c*.1210–15) reviewed the canonistic debate on this point. He questioned the view that one who ratified but did not order an attack on a clerk incurred excommunication. He noted in favour of this view that ratification was comparable to a mandate in regard to crimes and that the one ratifying was involved in a crime and with a criminous person, which under Innocent III's decretal 'Nuper' merited papal excommunication. He also noted opposing arguments, such that it was remarkable that anyone might be punished for approving another's deed, for approval consisted only of 'will' and not action, and that one could only ratify what was done in one's name. Despite the latter argument of Johannes Galensis

---

[146] Ricardus on 1 Comp. 5.34.7 v. *mittendi*, BAV, Pal. lat. MS 696, fol. 114vb: 'Sed pone quod peniteat dominus mandasse antequam clericus percutitur? Ex eo sequitur quod incidat in canonem anathematis et iuste.' Alanus on 1 Comp. 5.34.7 v. *auctoritate*, München, Bayerische Staatsbibliothek Clm 3879, fol. 95va: 'Pone quod mandavit sed ante manuum iniectionem penituit. Resp. nichilominus incidit in canonem nisi mandatum revocaverit'.

[147] Alanus (*c*.1206) on Alan. 5.2.4 (=3 Comp. 5.2.5) v. *postea consenseris*, Vercelli Cathedral Chapter MS 89, fol. 115rb: 'Si enim post consenserit crimine symonie, ut videtur, errat, quia in maleficiis ratihabitatio mandato comparatur, ut ff. de vi et vi l.i §Quotiens in fi. et ff. de re. iu. Hoc iure §Dictis [Dig. 43.16.1 §13; 50.17.152 §2]' id. (*c*.1201–10) on 1 Comp. 5.34.7 v. *auctoritate*, München, Bayerische Staatsbibliothek Clm 3879, fol. 95va: 'Item pone quod non mandet sed ratum habet. Resp. non incidit cum hoc in iure non exprimatur et pene emoliende sunt non extendende, ar. de pen. di.i. Pene [de pen. D.1 c.18], ar. contra ff. de vi et vi l.i. §Quotiens.'

[148] Johannes Galensis on 3 Comp. 5.2.5 v. *consenseris*, München, Bayerische Staatsbibliothek Clm 3879, fol. 249va: 'Quia in maleficiis ratihabitatio mandato comparatur, ff. de vi. et vi. ar. l.i §Quot. [Dig. 43.1.16 §13], maxime in hiis que nomine eius gesta sunt qui ratum habet, ff. de neg. g. Si pupilli §Item queritur [Dig. 3.5.5 §11]'. Id. on 3 Comp. 5.14.3 v. *auctoritate*, fol. 256ra: 'incidit in homicidium et forte ... si ratum habuit homicidium nomine suo commissum, ar. supra de simo. Sicut lib. e. [3 Comp. 5.2.5], ff. de vi et vi ar. l.i §Quotiens.' Cf. *Apparatus* 'Servus appellatur' on 3 Comp. 2.6.5 v. *ratam*, Bamberg Staatsbibliothek Can. MS 19, fol. 153rb: 'Nota quia illud solum possum habere ratum quod meo nomine gestum, ut ff. de neg. g. <Si> pupilli §Sed si ego, ff. de calump. l.ii, ff. de preca. Si servus [Dig. 3.5.5 §8; 3.6.2; 43.26.13] ... alias non, sed negotium non meum, si mei contemplatione geratur, possum ratum habere, ut ff. de neg. g. Si pupil. §Item quare [Dig. 3.5.5 §11]'.

and Alanus's view, Damasus concluded that one who ratified an attack on a clerk might incur excommunication, a view also expressed in the contemporary *Glossa Palatina*.[149] Tancred went further still, stating his belief that anyone who could forbid an attack on a clerk and held jurisdiction or power of coercion over the attacker effectively ratified the attack by not forbidding it and was therefore excommunicate in accordance with 'Quante presumptionis', Innocent III's decretal which imposed this penalty on those who could resist an attack on a clerk but failed to do so.[150] We thus return to the notion that tacit consent to another's wrong deserved punishment.

On the basis of this canonistic debate Innocent IV argued forty years later that a *universitas* might be interdicted if it ratified a wrong committed in its name. But he was not the first canonist to state that a *universitas* might suffer as a result of ratifying its leader's faults. Even Alanus had admitted that a chapter might not reclaim property of its church if its bishop had alienated this with their consent, but only if he had acted alone and his alienation was not confirmed as valid by their ratification. Zoën likewise commented on Honorius III's decretal 'Dilecti filii', which held an abbey liable for debts its abbots contracted with its consent, that the abbey was thereby understood to have *ratified* the abbots' actions by universal or majority consent, and what a whole body or the majority of it did was referred to all its members.[151]

---

[149] Damasus, *Questiones,* BAV, Borgh. lat. MS 261, fol. 44va: 'Item pone quod aliquis non mandet quod clericus percutiatur, sed ratam habeat percussionem, numquid incidit in excommunicationem? Et videtur quod sic, quia in criminibus ratihabitatio mandato comparatur, ut infra. de simo. Sicut. lib. iii. et de restit. spo. Cum ad sedem lib. iii. [3 Comp. 5.2.5; 2.6.5], ff. de vi. et vi. ar. l.i §Quotiens. Item queritur dubita\<n\>s hic nonne iste qui ratum habet participat crimine et criminoso, ergo incidit in eamdem excommunicationem in quam incidit ille qui iniecit, ut infra extra. de sententia excom. Nuper lib. iii [3 Comp. 5.21.3]. Sed contra mirabile est quod dicis. Approbatio facti alicuius penes voluntatem tantum consistit, nec progreditur ad aliquem actum, unde, licet puniatur adeo, non est tamen punienda per ecclesiam, ut de pe. di.i §Cogitationis [De pen. D.1 c14]. Item non potest quis negotium gestum ratum habere, nisi nomine ipsius sit gestum, ita quod inde oriatur obligatio, ff. de neg. g. Si pupilli §Sed si ego, et de precario. Si servus. Solutio. dicit Ala. non incidere et Io. Galensis, si nomine eius non fuit factum. Verius tamen videtur quod incidat.' Cf. *Glossa Palatina* on C.17 q.4 c.5 v. *et consentientes,* BAV, Pal. lat. MS 658, fol. 60vb: 'Quid si quis percussit clericum et alius percussit postea, numquid incidit in canonem? Videtur quod sic, quia in delictis ratihabitatio retrotrahitur, unde si me eiecisti de possessione et alius postea prestitit auctoritatem, ille tenetur interdicto, ff.de vi et vi ar. l.i. §Quotiens. Credo tamen contrarium in hoc casu, ar. ff. de his que no. infa. Quid ergo §i, ff. manda. Si vero §Si post creditam [Dig. 3.2.13; 17.1.12 §14]'.

[150] Tancred on 1 Comp. 5.34.7 v. *committi,* BAV, Vat. lat. MS 1377, fol. 96va: 'ego credo quod, si potest prohibere et est talis qui percutit in quo iurisdictionem vel cohertionem habet, is qui ratum habet, si non prohibet, est excommunicatus, ut dicit illud capitulum et extra. Alani. e.t. Quante presumptionis [Alan. 5.22.1]. t.'

[151] Alanus on 1 Comp. 3.9.3 v. *ratam,* München, Bayerische Staatsbibliothek Clm 3879, fol. 42va: 'Nota rei ecclesiastice alienationem, que de iure valuit, ratihabitatione posse confirmari, ut xvi. q.i. c.ult., infra de iure patro. Cum pastorali [C.16 q.1 c.58; 1 Comp. 3.33.13].' Zoën on 5 Comp. 3.8.3 v. *aut maioris,* Tours, Bibliothèque municipale MS 565, fol. 26va: 'Unde ratum intelligitur fieri de consensu totius conventus nam refertur ad universos ut ff. de re. iu. Aliud refertur [Dig. 50.17.160], et quod maior pars facit omnes facere intelliguntur ut ff. ad inimic. Quod maior [Dig. 50.1.19]. Nam et in alienationibus idem seruatur ut x q.ii. Hoc ius [C.10 q.2 c.2] Zo.'

1.5 CONCLUSION

By the mid-thirteenth century ecclesiastical authorities and canonists could, therefore, draw on a wide range of arguments, developed in scholastic circles over the preceding century, in order to justify interdicts. Canonistic doctrine reserved excommunication to individual wrongdoers, for it bound the soul, a principle confirmed as papal law in 1245, but doctrine also accepted that others associated with wrongdoers might suffer a *pena temporalis*, such as interdicts, the effect of which was limited to this earthly life. The knowledge that serious wrongs had penal consequences for others was meant to deter one from committing them in the first place, or, failing that, make the undeterred feel guilty and make amends. Such punishment was designed to impose psychological pressure both before and after the fact not only on the wrongdoer but also on third parties. It was meant to restrain them from supporting the wrongdoer, by actively aiding and collaborating with him, tacitly failing to resist him physically or verbally, or even inciting and authorizing him to do wrong. From the late twelfth century the canonists argued that all these ways of consenting to another's sin merited punishment together with the sin itself. Some, notably Gratian, admittedly asserted that only those who had the power to correct sin, such as prelates, might suffer for not resisting others' sin, but by the late twelfth century Peter the Chanter and many Bolognese canonists, including Huguccio, believed that all Christians had a duty to resist another's sin, even subjects with regard to a sinful ruler, and they deserved punishment for neglecting this duty. Augustine had also argued that the power to resist another's sin came from numbers as well as office and hence blamed the Jews for not restraining their leaders from killing Christ. The Chanter developed this into a general condemnation of any people who did not resist its ruler's sin, and canonists adopted this line of thought. Hence an interdict was designed both to punish the failure of subjects to restrain their ruler from sin and to turn them against him, compelling him to make amends.

Theology arguably gave the initial impetus for such doctrinal developments, and theology continued to exert a strong influence on all aspects of canonistic thought till at least 1200. It is also significant that the two popes who were most innovative in introducing interdicts and other penalties touching third parties into regular canonical usage, Alexander III and Innocent III, were both trained in twelfth-century theology schools. The Chanter's influence on Innocent is particularly noticeable in this regard. Already, in Innocent's pontificate, however, Roman law was supplanting theology as the prime intellectual influence on canonistic thought, and it stimulated new thinking on the nature of communities. Jurists began to define certain ecclesiastical and secular bodies endowed by a ruler with collective rights as corporations or *universitates*. And Roman law denied that a corporation could be charged with a crime; it could only be held responsible in a civil action for crimes of its ruler or agent. This led Johannes Teutonicus to doubt whether punishment of a community was licit. Other canonists, notably Alanus and Tancred, were sufficiently pragmatic to admit that it was already valid in reality. Zoën and Innocent IV finally accommodated these civilian principles within the canonistic justification of collective punishment, and Innocent in particular argued that only individuals could do wrong and therefore only they were to suffer the penalty for a canonical crime, namely excommunication. He made a law to this effect that thus harmonized Roman judicial procedure and traditional canonistic thought. The interdict remained the appropriate punishment, like civil penalties in Roman law, for a community, in Innocent's view. While he subtly reformulated canonistic thought on collective punishment, rebutting the idea of collective guilt, but accepting a notion of collective responsibility, he followed deep-rooted canonistic tradition when he held that this responsibility arose from consent to another's sin. His notion of collective responsibility was also based on civilian ideas of representation, which had penetrated canonical procedure and canonistic thought by 1200, whereby a community was held accountable for whatever a plenipotentiary did in its name.

It might appear ironic to modern eyes that the same ideas of consent, counsel, and representation that gave rise to a theory of popular government, now generally admired, also provided Innocent IV with a justification of the general interdict, a penalty now seen as unjust and abolished under the modern Code of Canon Law. Yet medieval thinkers would have seen little contradiction between communities bearing both collective rights *and* responsibilities with regard to their leaders. It must be added that the growth of canonistic thought on this issue was not simply a response to intellectual currents but also to ecclesiastical practice. The increasingly sophisticated views of canonists on collective responsibility were more a reaction to than a vehicle for changes in legal practice, notably Alexander III and Innocent III's radical innovations in penal law mentioned above. Nevertheless, canonistic doctrine helped to reinforce and defend current trends in ecclesiastical practice and supplied the ecclesiastical authorities with an apologia for the interdict, much needed in the face of the popular and princely hostility that the sanction often provoked. Above all the use of the interdict and the doctrine which justified it helped to reinforce the idea of Christian society as one corporate unity, one unity in which subjects bore a share of responsibility for their ruler's crimes against the Church, over and above but not totally in disregard of individual rights and responsibilities.

2

Kinds of Interdict

It might be assumed that there was only one sort of interdict in the thirteenth century, that imposed on a whole territory, such as the sentence that Innocent III laid on King John's England. But from the beginning of the thirteenth century popes and canonists increasingly distinguished between an interdict on places and an interdict on persons and defined how one worked differently from the other. They further distinguished between general and particular (or specific) forms of such interdicts. For example a personal interdict might be applied specifically to an individual. This may come as a surprise given that we tend to assume that an interdict normally affected a community, while excommunication was the canonical penalty for individual sinners. A general local interdict imposed on a territory or city is, admittedly, the kind of interdict most often encountered in papal letters and other thirteenth-century sources, and it certainly produced the better known and more dramatic cases of interdict. Nevertheless it was clearly not the only kind of interdict, and one must understand how the various kinds of interdict differed or were meant to differ in their usage and operation.

2.1 THE GENERAL LOCAL INTERDICT

An interdict was sometimes already defined as a *generale interdictum terre* in letters of the first year of Innocent III's pontificate, and it was clearly an established formula of the papal chancery by 1198. It was normally found in grants to bishops and regular clergy of freedom to celebrate the offices 'cum generale interdictum terre fuerit',[1] but recipients of these grants did not always know what this clause meant. Early in 1199 the Pope had to clarify it at the request of the Portuguese episcopacy; he intended it to describe the interdict of a kingdom, province, or even a castle or town. His definition became a canonistic commonplace after its inclusion in *Compilatio tertia* and then in the *Liber extra*.[2] However, it was a rather prosaic definition and it failed to resolve the ambiguities in the phrase *generale interdictum terre*. After Innocent III

---

[1] Innocent III, Reg. 1, nos. 287, 549 etc.
[2] Ibid. no. 551; 3 Comp. 5.23.1; X 5.40.17.

pronounced an interdict on 'terra regis Francorum' later in 1199, for example, the bishop of Auxerre argued that his diocese was immune from the sentence for the king had no land there. Innocent had overlooked the then key political distinction between the royal demesne and the kingdom of France. In a decretal of 1200 he explained that the legate who had published his sentence on 'totam terram regis Francorum' had correctly interpreted it as relating to that land 'que regi tunc temporis adherebat', in other words all the land then under royal jurisdiction. In some subsequent sentences of general local interdict Innocent was, therefore, careful to specify that they were pronounced on the territory or city where the guilty parties exercised lordship or temporal jurisdiction.[3] His more rigorous definition also rapidly entered canon law and was adopted by canonists,[4] for example Jacobus de Albenga, who stated that an interdict was sometimes imposed on a place because of the delict of the person who had lordship in that place.[5]

The pope thus defined the general local interdict in response to the demands of practice. Canonists subsequently introduced subtle refinements to this papal definition in order to cover various hypothetical situations. Vincentius Hispanus commented (*c*.1210–15) that the interdict on 'totam terram regis Francorum' included land the king held as his wife's dowry, for a husband was the lord of a dowry.[6] This interpretation was apparently followed in practice since Gregory IX made a special exception to it in 1232, allowing a noblewoman to hear divine offices in her dowry lands whenever her husband's lands were laid under an interdict.[7] By 1342 Johannes Andreae could add many further distinctions. For instance an interdict on a lord's land was not to include land he acquired after the sentence had been laid, but it was to remain in force on land that he sold or lost subsequently until it was removed by the judge who laid it. A pupil of

[3] Innocent III, Reg. 8, no. 84 (domain); 10, nos. 111, 125 (manors); 12, no. 80.

[4] Alan. 1.5.5; 3 Comp. 1.4.1; X 1.5.1. Alanus's collection was compiled *c*.1206, only a few years after this decretal was issued.

[5] See p. 49 n. 122. Cf. Tancred on 3 Comp. 1.4.1 v. *propriam*, BAV, Vat. lat. MS 1377, fol. 154va: 'Et licet rex in illa diocesi terram propriam non haberet, tamen tota est iurisdictioni subiecta et ideo de regno dicitur esse ... et ideo totum regnum intelligo iuste fuisse suppositum interdicto'. Goffredus de Trano (d. 1245) on X 1.5.1 v. *rex propriam*, Vienna, Nationalbibliothek MS 2197, fol. 7rb: 'Quamvis enim in diocese illa rex non teneret aliquam terram sed totam teneret barones, nichilominus tamen tota erit regis Francie iurisdictione subiecta et ideo intelligendum erat totam interdicto suppositam ut infra. de of. del. Sane, infra. de spon. Non est nobis [X 1.29.11, 4.1.11]. Gof.'

[6] Vincentius Hispanus on 3 Comp. 1.5.1 v. *totam*, BAV, Vat. lat. MS 1378, fol. 5vb (repeated by him on X 1.5.1 v. *totam terram*, BAV Vat. lat. MS 6769, fol. 17rb): 'ista terra est interdicta, quia licet non esset sua quoad mensam, erat tamen sua quoad coronam, vel hec terra erat dotalis, unde subicitur interdicto quia maritus est dominus dotis, inst. de rerum di. §Per traditionem, ff. de auro et ar. le. Quinto et C. de rei ven. Dote ancillam [Inst. 2.1 §40; Dig. 34.2.10; Cod. 3.32.9]'. Cf. also *Apparatus* 'Servus appellatur' on 3 Comp. 1.4.1 v. *rex*, Bamberg Staatsbibliothek MS Can. 19, fol. 121va: 'Idest quam per se ipsum teneat immediate, nam sua est licet sui re dotarii'. Vincentius added in the above gloss that an interdict on the land that one held also included that which had been pledged to one as a creditor.

[7] Reg. Gregory IX, no. 989.

Andreae Johannes Calderinus likewise added that an interdict on a king's or duke's land applied to land held from them in fief, even if outside their kingdom or duchy.[8]

Behind these canonistic nuances lay the assumption that all land bound to a lord by feudal ties was subject to the interdict that he provoked. Those who held fiefs from that lord shared in his punishment presumably because they shared in his crime by reason of their feudal obligations. Retainers held lands from their lord in return for aid (military and financial) and counsel and this might involve them in supporting him in a canonical wrong. Hence Johannes Teutonicus (*c*.1215) interpreted Innocent III's interdict on 'terra regis Francorum' as applying to all lands that offered the king aid, and he cited a ruling of Innocent's that extended excommunication to those who gave aid to an excommunicate. Likewise over a century later Johannes Calderinus held that an interdict was imposed on a king's land for assisting him 'ratione feudi vel alias' in the delict that had occasioned the sentence.[9]

This canonistic teaching was also applied in practice. Innocent IV expressed it both as a jurist in his *Apparatus* and as pope in his sentences of interdict.[10] In 1246 he ordered various French clergy to enforce an interdict on lands *supporting* the recently deposed emperor, Frederick II, and his allies. Of course it was not the actual lands that were at fault for supporting him but the people living there. Nevertheless land was the basis for raising finance and mounted troops to aid enemies of ecclesiastical authority. Likewise in 1248 Innocent declared an interdict on all castles and places in Salzburg province where people had bound themselves by an oath to aid Frederick against the Church. It is unclear whether a feudal oath was meant, but it is evident that the pope felt that those pledging support to a wrongdoer deserved punishment along with him. The Franciscan Monaldus hence wrote in his canon law manual (1270s) that when a prince's land was interdicted, the men of that land were affected only as long as they remained under his lordship. Monaldus inferred that if they moved elsewhere because of the interdict and in opposition to the prince so that nothing of theirs remained under his lordship to provide him with aid, they no longer belonged to his interdicted land. But another mendicant manualist John of Freiburg doubted (*c*.1280) that such drastic action could release subjects from a local interdict unless it was relaxed specifically in relation to them. Nevertheless this teaching

---

[8] Johannes Andreae, *Novella* on VI 5.11.5 v. *domini*; Johannes Calderinus (*attrib.*), *De censura*, BAV, Pal. lat. MS 797, fol. 12vb: 'Et est sciendum quod interdicta terra regis vel ducis etc. et talis propter delictum, terra assistens regi vel duci etc. in delicto ratione feudi vel alias, licet in regno vel in ducatu non sit sita, tamen est interdicta.' The view that an interdicted land remained so after its lordship was transferred to another by sale had first been stated in the earliest treatise on the interdict (Hermann of Minden, §84) and also noted by John of Freiburg, *Summa*, III, xxxiii, q.226.

[9] Johannes Teutonicus on 3 Comp. 1.4.1 v. *rex terram propriam* (Ed. p. 33). See n. 8 for Calderinus.

[10] Innocent IV, *Apparatus* on X 1.5.1 v. *regi*; Reg. Innocent IV, nos. 2344, 3572.

confirms that an interdict on a lord's land was meant to punish those bound to aid him by virtue of holding that land.[11]

Occasionally a lord's land was interdicted not because of a wrongdoing of his own but of his subjects. As Innocent III pointed out in 1213 to a commune lamenting an interdict imposed on its land for the excesses of its lords, biblical examples taught that 'superiors are sometimes punished for an offence of subjects and subjects for the guilt of superiors'.[12] Indeed by the early thirteenth century various canon law rulings held a superior penally responsible for a wrong that a subordinate committed with his consent. Even if he had not expressly authorized the wrong, his failure to restrain the subordinate from committing it or correct him after the fact might be considered tacit consent. The only canonical excuse for such negligence was ignorance of a subject's wrongdoing. Indeed the few cases in the thirteenth-century papal registers of a lord's land being interdicted for a subject's fault are where the lord appealed on this ground. For example early in 1213 Duke Henry of Brabant informed Innocent III that judges delegate had imposed excommunication on him and an interdict on his land after one of his servants had physically injured a clerk 'although he [the duke] was absent and unaware of this fact'; thus he petitioned the pope to relax these sentences. Some lords even secured papal grants of immunity from interdicts laid on their land for wrongs of their subjects committed without their support. For example in 1298 Boniface VIII forbade the imposition of interdicts on the lands of Duke Robert of Burgundy for the crimes of his bailiffs or officials unless the duke or his deputy refused full justice for these crimes when warned or requested. Presumably such refusal was to be taken as tacit approval of an agent's crimes.[13]

Where subjects committed crimes without the consent of their lord, express or tacit, he could deny responsibility since they acted as private individuals of their own volition. Canonistic doctrine supported this view from the early thirteenth century, for it taught that a client was not answerable for what his proctor did without his authority or knowledge, and likewise that a church was not to suffer for crimes which its prelate committed without its consent and as a private person. Consequently in 1265 when a provost and chapter in the Clermont diocese complained to the pope that papal legates and judges delegate laid interdicts on their parish for the wrongs of private persons who held neither temporal lordship nor public office there, they were on solid legal ground, and the pope recognized this in 1265 by granting their parish immunity from such interdicts. But this and similar papal grants show that the canonistic distinction between 'public' and 'private' wrongs was not always observed in practice.[14]

---

[11] Monaldus, *Summa*, fol. 95vb; John of Freiburg, *Summa*, III, xxxiii q.271.

[12] Innocent III, Reg. 16, no. 20. See pp. 32–5, 36–7 with regard to what follows.

[13] Innocent III, Reg. 16, no. 56; cf. Reg. Honorius IV, no. 172. Reg. Boniface VIII, no. 2722.

[14] Reg. Clement IV, no. 144; cf. Reg. Alexander IV, no. 1721. See pp. 52–3 for canonistic discussion of this point.

A general local interdict was not always laid on the jurisdiction of a temporal ruler and thereby justified in terms of social relations. It was sometimes laid on places associated with the wrong that provoked it. The wrong in most instances was seizure of property or persons under ecclesiastical protection. Sometimes an interdict was laid on the stolen property itself to compel restitution to its rightful owners. Innocent III in 1209 warned King John of England to restore lands belonging to his brother's widow; otherwise, he would impose an interdict on them. Innocent was indeed mindful of the Church's duty to protect widows and orphans, as his biographer noted.[15] More often an interdict was laid on places where captured persons and goods were held. Pilgrims and crusaders enjoyed ecclesiastical protection; thus when a party returning from 'the service of Christ' overseas was seized at Cremona, Innocent ordered the local bishop and bishops of dioceses where the pilgrims were held to warn their captors to release them and their goods in fifteen days. Otherwise the bishops were to interdict the places where they were held and excommunicate their captors.[16]These interdicts punished inhabitants of these places presumably for harbouring the captors and in order to turn them against these violators of ecclesiastical immunity. The interdict was chiefly used in this way to defend property and personnel of the Church itself against lay hostility. Anyone attacking a clerk already incurred excommunication under the canon 'Si quis suadente' (1139), and interdicts were increasingly used during the thirteenth century to reinforce this ruling. For example in 1248 Innocent IV confirmed a statute of the Archbishop of Mainz, such that all places in the latter's province where goods stolen from clergy were brought, clerks were held captive, or the wrongdoers involved were given refuge should remain interdicted until amends were made.[17] General as well as local ecclesiastical legislation laid interdicts on places tainted by anti-clerical crimes. In 1298 Boniface VIII decreed that a city incurred an interdict and loss of its see if it gave counsel, aid, or support to those attacking or seizing a cardinal or failed to punish his attackers in a month. Some fifteen years later a constitution of Clement V likewise declared an interdict on any place where a bishop was attacked, seized, or held. These rulings applied canonistic notions of collective guilt in condemning the connivance of local communities at canonical crimes committed in their midst.[18]

An interdict on the scene of a violent crime against a clerk also recognized that the place was profaned by this sacrilegious act and thereby rendered unfit for religion. In one case such places even seemed cursed. Clement IV allegedly laid an interdict on some places in Tuscany after their inhabitants

---

[15] Innocent III, Reg. 11, nos. 223–4; *Gesta* c.150 (*PL* 214.ccxxviii). On his use of interdict to protect widows and orphans, see Innocent III, Reg. 13, no. 74; 14, no. 8.
[16] Innocent III, Reg. 12, no. 77.   [17] C.17 q.4 c.29; Reg. Innocent IV, no. 3626.
[18] VI 5.9.5; Clem. 5.8.1.

had collaborated in seizing and killing a bishop, and, as they came under Clement's temporal jurisdiction in the papal state, he also withdrew their right of *municipium* and *universitas* in perpetuity, i.e. freedom of civic and corporate self-government. Some twenty years later in 1285 the places were said to be deserted and uninhabitable. Allegedly no priest or clerk dared to officiate or even stay there, and anyone still living there was to be refused the sacraments unless they abjured the right to live there. The consequences of this interdict were unusually harsh and barely accord with the Church's teachings on penance and redemption, but they suggest that even at this late time general local interdicts still owed something to the maledictions that Benedictines had uttered against the persons, families, and lands of their enemies in tenth- and eleventh-century France.[19] Indeed local interdicts were still associated with curses in sermon *exempla* of the Dominican preacher Stephen of Bourbon in the mid-thirteenth century.

Perhaps in reaction to such superstitions, popes and canonists were concerned that local interdicts should not appear irrational. Tancred admitted (*c*.1210–15) that it was more 'honest' to interdict persons than churches since churches did no wrong but persons did.[20] Indeed about this time, early in 1213, Innocent III maintained that royal chapels in France might not be interdicted for the wrongs of their chaplains, since this would do injury to the king, but rather the offending chaplain might be interdicted not the place 'so that the penalty bound its author'. The latter was a Roman law maxim in favour of limiting punishment to the guilty, and here it also reflected the juristic idea noted above that a superior was not accountable for wrongs done by subjects without his approval.[21] By the mid-thirteenth century the absurdity of the idea of punishing a place struck many canonists, but they carefully distinguished that it was the people of that place and not, in any real sense, the place itself that was the object of an interdict. Bernard of Parma indeed observed that a place could not be suspended or interdicted literally since it was a *res inanimata*. This might signify not only an inanimate object but also matter lacking a soul (*anima*) and thus unable to receive spiritual punishment. Innocent IV added that a place could not receive or confer the sacraments. Hostiensis synthesized these views, arguing that a place was incapable of sacraments and offices and could not do wrong or be considered disobedient, in other words give a canonical cause for an interdict,

<hr>

[19] Reg. Honorius IV, no. 172; Little, esp. 12, 36, 60, 62–6, 84–5, 123–6, 129–49, 161, 163–4, 168–70, 182–5, 213–15, 255, 258, 260–1, 263–5, 267. On Stephen of Bourbon see Winkler, 'The Excommunicated Castle', esp. 245, 252–3.

[20] Tancred on 2 Comp. 3.9.2 v. *ecclesiam*, BAV, Vat. lat. MS 1377, fol. 122va: 'non nego tamen honestius esse personas interdicere, non enim ecclesie delinquunt sed persone, ut in aut. de manda. prin. §oport. coll' iii, et supra. de penis. Licet. libro i, xvi. q. vi. Illud [Nov. 17.1; 1 Comp. 5.32.3; C.16 q.6 c.7] la.' The *siglum* indicates that Tancred was citing an opinion of the canonist Laurentius Hispanus (d. 1248).

[21] Innocent III, Reg. 15, no. 227. The maxim cited is from Cod. 9.47.22; Celestine III also cited it in his decretal 'Quesivit', glossed by Tancred in n. 20 above.

for it lacked the powers of intellect, reason, and the senses.[22] It was the *communis opinio* of these canonists that a place fell under an interdict because of the men living there; hence it was they and not the place itself who were denied the sacraments. An early fourteenth-century treatise on the interdict attributed to Johannes Andreae therefore explained that when a city, town, castle, or church was put under an interdict, this did not mean that its walls and buildings were interdicted but that priests might not celebrate the offices in those places.[23]

Nevertheless because a local interdict was imposed on a place and not directly on the persons living there, it was meant to operate in a way different from a personal interdict. Tancred taught (*c.*1220) that when a city was laid under an interdict, clerks might go outside it and celebrate the offices in another uninterdicted place, for it was the city that was interdicted and not the clerks. This teaching was generally accepted among canonists by the mid-thirteenth century;[24] hence it is probable that Tancred had simply been describing current practice. Innocent III and his successors even ordered clerks to leave interdicted cities on occasion, though it was never explicitly stated that the fugitive clergy might thereby escape the effects of a local interdict.[25]

By the mid-thirteenth century canonists also debated whether laity were free from a local interdict outside the area affected. This was a more contentious point, for there was a danger that those whom the interdict was meant to punish would elude its hardships. Innocent IV hence distinguished that laity were free to hear the offices and receive sacraments outside an interdicted place provided that they had not done wrong or otherwise given cause for the interdict, but not if they had. Conversely, he added, if an interdict was laid on people and not a place, they were excluded from the offices or sacraments wherever they went. Although Innocent was expressing a juristic opinion and not issuing a papal ruling, he was pope and thus his view commanded respect and was widely accepted by contemporary canonists. The first known treatise on interdicts (dated 1270) copied it *verbatim* and explained how it might work in practice:[26] those who had

---

[22] Bernard of Parma on X 5.31.18 v. *inanes*; Innocent IV, *Apparatus* on X 5.31.18 v. *interdicti violationem*; Hostiensis, *Lectura* on X 5.31.18 v. *post interdicti violationem* (vol. 2, fol. 77rb).

[23] Johannes Andreae (attrib.), *De modo*, BAV, Pal. lat. MS 797, fol. 8va (Ed. fol. 7v): 'Et quando dico ecclesiam interdici, non intelligo lapides interdici sed presbiteros ne in ea celebrant. Similiter cum interdicitur civitas, villa vel castrum, non intelligo muros vel edificia sed ne in dictis locis celebrentur divina.'

[24] Tancred on 3 Comp. 1.3.4 (= X 1.4.5) v. *interdicto*, BAV, Vat. lat. MS 1377, fol. 152vb: 'In hoc clerici non sunt interdicti sed locus, unde si egrederentur civitatem, celebrare possunt divina in alio loco non interdicto, quia locus est interdictus et non persone.' Repeated almost *verbatim* by Vincentius Hispanus (*c.*1236) on X 1.4.5 v. *non servabant*, BAV, Vat. lat. MS 6769, fol. 15vb, and Goffredus de Trano on X 1.4.5 v. *etiam interdicto*, Vienna, Nationalbibliothek MS 2197, fol. 6va. Cf. also Innocent IV, *Apparatus* on X 1.4.5 v. *in civitate*.

[25] Innocent III, Reg. 6, no. 182; 7, no. 41; 11, no. 143, etc. See pp. 189, 207 for further examples.

[26] Innocent IV, *Apparatus* on X 5.33.24 v. *regularium*; X 5.33.25 v. *qui causam*. Hermann of Minden, 'De interdictis', §§76–8 (fol. 346va). Cf. Also Hostiensis, *Lectura* on X 5.33.25 v. *qui causam* (vol. 2, fol. 86vb).

not caused an interdict on their locality might accompany their parish priest to an
uninterdicted place and there he could celebrate the offices for them in a church
with its priest's permission. But not all canonists accepted that innocent laity
enjoyed this freedom outside of interdicted places. Bernard of Parma believed
that they should not be admitted to any offices or sacraments, since anyone who
was under interdict in one church was under interdict in all of them. That is he
made no distinction between personal and local interdicts in terms of their effect
on the innocent, and his reasoning was that interdicts might thereby induce the
guilty to come to terms more quickly and be feared more. John of Freiburg
stated a similar hardline view that when a place was interdicted, those under the
jurisdiction of the guilty party were also understood to be interdicted personally
and thus excluded from offices and sacraments in uninterdicted churches.[27] Who
could this leave out, except perhaps the clergy? There is insufficient evidence to
show whether this or the more liberal view generally obtained in practice. In
1200, admittedly, the dauphin and count of Ponthieu had visited Normandy,
part of the 'terra regis Anglorum', to have their betrothals blessed since this was
forbidden in the interdicted 'terra regis Francorum'. This suggests that Innocent
IV was describing customary practice, but it might be an untypical case and
these dignitaries might have received a special freedom. Conversely the proctors
of the dean and chapter of Laon accused the citizens of Laon of violating a papal
interdict laid on their city in 1296, in that they heard offices in churches outside
the city in the Laon diocese. Nevertheless the sentence was provoked by a rising
of the commune against the dean and chapter, and so if the latter perceived all
the people of Laon as guilty, there were no innocents free to hear offices outside
the city in accordance with Innocent IV's teaching.[28]

No papal legislation on the matter appeared until Boniface VIII published
his constitution 'Si sententia' in 1298. This allowed innocent citizens of a city
interdicted because of its lord or ruler to hear divine offices outside it provided
that they were not interdicted personally. Boniface then pointed up the contrast
with a personal interdict, ruling that no member of an interdicted people might
hear the offices or receive the sacraments anywhere. In other words he made
Innocent IV's teaching into law. In common with other rulings of his it was
written specifically for his law code the *Liber sextus* to settle a canonistic debate
definitively. But his rulings in the *Liber sextus* not only responded to academic
controversies but also to practical problems of his day.[29] By the late thirteenth
century it was hard to define in practice where an interdict on a city ended and
where the 'outside' began. Rapid population growth across the West, notably
in Italian towns close to papal lands, meant that cities were no longer defined

[27] Bernard of Parma on X 5.33.25 v. *causam*; John of Freiburg, *Summa*, III, xxxiii q.259.
[28] Interdict on France: Howden, iv.115; Krehbiel, 119. Interdict on Laon: Reg. Boniface VIII,
no. 1533; Denton, 'Laon', esp. 79–82.
[29] VI 5.11.16. On the *Liber sextus* in general: Le Bras, 'Boniface VIII'; Schmidt, 'Papst Bonifaz
VIII'; Clarke, 'Two Constitutions'.

simply by a circuit of walls; they were increasingly girdled by sprawling suburbs with their own churches. Nicholas IV, Boniface's predecessor, had reacted to this situation by laying interdicts on a city *and* its suburbs. Suburbs came under the jurisdiction of a city's governors, and a general local interdict was meant to apply throughout the jurisdiction of the temporal ruler who provoked it. Boniface hence ruled in his constitution 'Si civitas' that an interdict on a city, castle, or vill automatically included its suburbs and adjacent buildings. His concern was that the sentence would be scorned if offices might be licitly celebrated in such neighbouring places.[30] But how was 'neighbouring' to be defined? The canonist Johannes Andreae (d. 1348) observed that it included the buildings adjacent to the city, but then potentially buildings adjacent to those, and so on indefinitely until an interdict embraced the whole world. This absurd scenario was hardly what Boniface intended, and Johannes concluded that in practice it was left to a judge to interpret what was neighbouring and what was not.[31]

While the innocent might escape the effects of a local interdict outside the area affected, at least after 1298, conversely those coming to that area from outside were to be excluded from its churches along with its inhabitants according to Innocent IV.[32] It seems that this had been a given since the late twelfth century, when the papacy began issuing grants permitting the military orders and other religious arriving in interdicted places to open churches and celebrate offices there once a year, as it would have been a meaningless freedom unless outsiders were normally excluded.[33] A Christian burial was likewise prohibited to any who happened to die in an interdicted place according to Innocent IV. Again he apparently described customary practice, for the papacy had made exceptions to this unwritten rule in favour of the military orders during the late twelfth century and all clergy under Innocent III. Such freedoms were of course open to abuse, and since the late twelfth century popes had warned those who enjoyed them not to admit those who did not, particularly laity, to divine offices and Christian burial in interdicted places.[34] By the mid-thirteenth century canonists also doubted that such freedoms might be so extended, even though the papal documents granting them only required the exclusion of excommunicated and interdicted persons. The issue was not settled definitively till 1298, when Boniface VIII's constitution 'Licet' forbade those free to celebrate offices in private during

---

[30] Reg. Nicholas IV, nos. 616, 717; cf. Reg. Urban IV, no. C107, which granted Troyes Cathedral and churches in the city's suburbs immunity from interdicts laid by legates, judges delegate, or subdelegate. VI 5.11.17 ('Si civitas').

[31] Johannes Andreae, *Novella* on X 1.5.1 v. *adherebat*; id. *Glossa* on VI 5.11.17 v. *continentibus*. Cf. Johannes Calderinus, 'De interdicto', Pt 1 §§25–6 (fol. 326rb).

[32] Innocent IV: as n. 22. Cf. Hostiensis, *Lectura* on X 5.33.25 v. *interdictis* (vol. 2, fol. 86ra).

[33] 1 Comp. 5.28.3 §3 (= X 5.33.3 §3). 4 Comp. 5.12.7 (= X 5.33.24). Innocent III, Reg. 6, no. 10; 7, nos. 95, 139; 10, no. 121; etc.

[34] Innocent IV: as n. 22. 1 Comp. 5.28.3 §§3–4 (= X 5.33.3 §§3–4). 4 Comp. 5.12.7 (= X 5.33.24). 4 Comp. 5.14.3 (= X 5.38.11).

general local interdicts from admitting those coming from elsewhere, except those privileged in this regard.[35]

By the late twelfth century general local interdicts were directed against places associated with a wrongdoer or the wrong itself. This association was often defined in feudal terms. A general local interdict might cover all lands under the lordship of the guilty party and so punish his retainers, as he acted with their advice and aid. It might also affect places linked with crimes against property and persons under ecclesiastical protection, for either the complicity of the inhabitants was assumed or they harboured the wrongdoers with their thefts or victims. Thus this interdict was normally provoked by wrongs of a temporal power against those associated with the spiritual power. The 'rules' governing its operation were largely a matter of customary practice and juristic opinion until they were defined in law at the end of the thirteenth century. It was thus gradually differentiated from personal interdicts. The latter were meant to follow one wherever one went like a shadow, but a general local interdict was to affect everyone settled or passing within its physical limits except those granted immunity or innocent inhabitants passing outside those limits. It was as if the place were polluted by sin and so declared unfit for religious worship until cleansed of that sin, an idea which will be encountered more forcibly in the next section.

2.2 THE PARTICULAR LOCAL INTERDICT

When Innocent III had defined a *generale interdictum terre* in a decretal of 1199 as an interdict on a kingdom, province, town, or castle, he was trying to differentiate it from an *interdictum particulare*. He issued this decretal to advise Portuguese bishops who had asked how one determined whether an interdict was 'general' or 'particular'. This reveals that the distinction was current by the late twelfth century even if it was not generally understood. Laurentius Hispanus glossing this decretal (*c.*1210) defined an *interdictum particulare* as one laid on specific churches or chapels. His definition was copied by Tancred in his ordinary gloss on *Compilatio tertia* and generally accepted by subsequent canonists.[36] Nevertheless

---

[35] Innocent IV, *Apparatus* on X 5.33.24 v. *qui causam*; Pierre Sampsona (1267), *Distinctio* on X 5.38.11, BAV, Pal. lat. MS 656, fols. 155vb–6ra; Bernard de Montmirat on X 5.33.25, BAV, Vat. lat. MS 2542, fol. 80rb (Ed. fol. 144vb); Johannes Andreae (attrib.), *De modo*, BAV, Pal. lat. MS 797, fol. 9r (Ed. fol. 8v); see also pp. 166, 192–5, 203 below on abuse of clerical immunities. VI 5.7.11 ('Licet').

[36] Tancred on 3 Comp. 5.23.1 (= X 5.40.17) v. *nomine*, BAV, Vat. lat. MS 1377, fol. 278rb: 'nullum sit interdictum particulare, immo si eorum oratoria interdicerentur vel ecclesie, supra. de privil. Sane. lib. i. [1 Comp. 5.28.8]. La<urentius>. Verumtamen quotienscumque aliqua terra magna vel parva totaliter supponitur interdicto, generale interdictum dicitur ut hic in fine. T<ancredus>.' Vincentius Hispanus (*c.*1210–15) on 3 Comp. 5.23.1 v. *intelligi*, Bamberg Staatsbibliothek MS Can. 20, fol. 179va, also copied Laurentius's gloss, and again (*c.*1236) on X

thirteenth-century papal letters rarely refer to an interdict as *particulare*, though they record interdicts on churches from at least the late twelfth century.[37] In contrast to a general interdict the papacy used this interdict more to exert authority over disobedient clergy than to coerce secular rulers. Indeed Pope Celestine III and his successors often interdicted cathedral or collegiate churches when chapters resisted papal provisions to canonries there. In one case from late 1203 an interdict was laid on Clermont Cathedral and unusually other churches belonging to its chapter, because the bishop and canons had refused to admit a papal candidate.[38] Occasionally a papal interdict was placed on a monastic church in order to discipline its community. In one extreme case monks were associated with a brutal attack on a P. de Sancto Albino, who had tried to reform their degraded house near Vercelli. In 1212 Innocent III used canonistic notions of collective guilt to justify an interdict on the monks' church: none of them were free from guilt or negligence, since some had aided the attack and others had neglected to stop it.[39] Lesser prelates also resorted to interdicts on churches of regular clergy who opposed their authority, especially their powers of visitation and procuration, although such cases were often only recorded in the papal registers when the monks appealed on grounds of exemption.[40] However, an interdict on a church was not always provoked by its clergy. When possession of a church was disputed, it might be interdicted to compel rival claimants, lay or clerical, to come to terms.[41]

Examples of interdicts on churches are relatively rare in the thirteenth-century papal registers, however, perhaps because of their extremely localized nature, and even canonists and canon law said little about the phenomenon. Innocent IV distinguished in his *Apparatus* that parishioners of interdicted churches might hear offices and bury their dead at uninterdicted churches, if the clergy had provoked the sentence (which in practice was generally the case), but not if the parishioners themselves or their lord had caused it. In other words he taught that a particular local interdict should work in a way similar to a general local one: innocent laity might escape its effects outside its bounds. The only striking difference was that clergy were not meant to enjoy the same immunities as

5.40.17 v. *intelligi*, Paris, BN, MS lat. 3967, fol. 210ra, where he appended Tancred's addition, misattributing it to Laurentius. Cf. Hermann de Minden, 'De interdictis' §10–11 (fol. 345rb).

[37] 1 Comp. 5.28.8: Alexander III confirmed papal immunity of Hospitallers' churches from interdict. 2 Comp. 3.9.2 (= X 3.11.2); see p. 102 below.

[38] Innocent III, Reg. 6, no. 195. Other papal interdicts laid on churches for resisting provisions: ibid. 1, nos. 55 (ordered by Celestine III), 418, 477; 2, no. 186 (?laid under Celestine III); 5, no. 145; 6, nos. 37 (?laid under Lucius III), 207; 7, no. 71; 9, no. 57 (?laid under Celestine III); Reg. Nicholas IV, no. 657.

[39] Innocent III, Reg. 15, no. 105.

[40] E.g. Innocent III, Reg. 1, no. 60; 15, no. 144; Reg. Gregory IX, no. 1738.

[41] E.g. Innocent III, Reg. 1, no. 221; 8, no. 47; 9, no. 49. Another example of laity provoking interdicts on churches is when Venetians looted the Haggia Sophia in Constantinople after the Fourth Crusade, and the Latin Patriarch laid an interdict on all churches 'in parte sacrilegorum ipsorum' (Innocent III, Reg. 9, no. 1077).

they did under general local interdicts. Innocent held that the freedom of clergy (granted in 1215) to receive burial without rites in interdicted places did not apply to interdicted churches.[42] Presumably the freedom of certain clergy to celebrate offices behind closed doors during a general local interdict might not be enjoyed if the recipients' church was specifically interdicted. Indeed Petrus Bonetus, a minor early fourteenth-century canonist, taught that members of the military orders who arrived at an interdicted church might celebrate there in accordance with their privileges if it lay under a general interdict but not if it had been specifically interdicted.[43] Given that an interdict on a church was usually caused by clergy, canonists such as Bonetus were no doubt concerned that clerical immunities should not protect the guilty from its effects. Whether the papacy took this view is not, however, certain on the available evidence.

The only papal law on particular local interdicts during the thirteenth century was Boniface VIII's constitution 'Si civitas' (1298), which ruled that when a church was interdicted, offices were not to be celebrated in its chapels nor the dead buried in any cemetery adjoining it, just as an interdict on a city was to include its suburbs: lest the sentence be scorned as a result. Boniface did not except the clergy from the ban on burial; hence he appears to confirm Innocent IV's teaching on this point.[44] Otherwise, the few canonistic opinions noted above were the only guide to practice.

Canon law and its commentators had much more to say on a phenomenon that closely resembled a particular local interdict: the suspension of worship in a 'violated' church. The canon 'Si motum' in Gratian's *Decretum* said that a church was violated by murder or adultery, while the canon 'Ecclesiis' that immediately followed it in the *Decretum* stated more generally that a church was 'polluted' by bloodshed or semen, though it did not specify these as products of the above sins.[45] Laurentius Hispanus (*c*.1210) argued regarding 'Ecclesiis' that a church polluted by blood and coition ought to be considered 'quasi interdictam'; this teaching was later copied by Tancred in his *glossa ordinaria* to *Compilatio secunda*. Another contemporary canonist, Vincentius Hispanus, likewise taught (*c*.1210–15) that if a church was violated, those holding the freedom to celebrate in an interdicted church once a year, such as the military orders, might not enjoy it 'in tali interdicto'.[46] It would seem that these canonists were simply describing

---

[42] Innocent IV on X 5.31.18 v. *interdicti violationem* and X 5.33.24 v. *regularium*; his teachings here were noted by Johannes Andreae (attrib.), *De modo*, BAV, Pal. lat. MS 797, fol. 7rb–va (Ed. fol. 5r).

[43] Petrus Bonetus on X 5.33.3 v. *admittantur*, BAV, Borgh. lat. MS 228, fol. 193vb: 'si autem ecclesia esset specialiter interdicta, non possunt in ea celebrare, ut infra c. Tuarum §Eos [X 5.33.11]'.

[44] VI 5.11.17.

[45] De con. D.1 c.19–20. These canons contradicted each other on whether 'violated' churches were to be reconsecrated before worship might be resumed in them, on which see pp. 246–7 below.

[46] Tancred on 2 Comp. 3.9.2 v. *observare*, BAV, Vat. lat. MS 1377, fol. 122va: 'Supple. Nec tanquam interdictam ecclesiam habere nisi etc. et tunc non ratione interdicti cum nullum sit, ut

what ecclesiastical authorities, especially the papacy, saw as good practice. In 1198 the Archbishop of Lund had complained to Innocent III that when a bishop in his province had forbidden celebration of offices in a Hospitaller church since it was violated by an attack on its priest, the Hospitallers had disobeyed.[47] The pope reacted by ordering the suspension of those illicitly celebrating in that church. But later thirteenth-century canonists would have perceived the Lund case as anomalous. The French canonists William Durand and Petrus Bonetus argued that a 'violated' church had been interdicted by the law itself and not by a man, such as a bishop. Innocent IV had argued that a 'violated' church was not interdicted at all, but rather its 'organs of worship' were suspended.[48] Both arguments were used to justify the view that clergy officiating in 'violated' churches did not incur the canonical penalties for disregarding interdicts. This view later became law in the *Liber sextus* (1298).[49]

In the course of the thirteenth century canonists also tried to reconcile the two definitions of 'violation' in the *Decretum*. Many appear to have accepted the narrow sense in 'Si motum' on the question of bloodshed and held that injury might result in 'violation' only if it was intentional, such as murder, and not accidental. That is to say these canonists understood that 'violation' only arose when a sin was involved, since according to the canonistic doctrine of guilt it was not the act but the intention behind it that made it a sin. Moreover they agreed that a church was only 'violated' if the sin was actually committed inside it, not outside, and a danger existed that scandal might arise if it became public knowledge, but not if it was known only under the seal of the confessional.[50] These qualifications still left room for doubt. The canonist Bernard de Montmirat stated (*c*.1259–66) that if someone killed in self-defence inside a church, it was not strictly speaking 'violated', but he thought it safer to assume that it was.[51] In regard to 'violation' by semen canonists found it even

---

infra, sed ratione delicti debet eam quasi interdictam reputare, puta si sanguine sit perfusa aut coitu polluta, ut supra. de con. di. i. Ecclesiis. La<urentius>.' Vincentius Hispanus on 3 Comp. 5.16.1, BAV, Vat. lat. MS 1378, fol. 101ra: 'Sed nonne poterant ibi celebrare ex privilegio semel in anno, supra. e. Cum et plantare lib. i [1 Comp. 5.28.3]? Non admitto privilegium eorum in tali interdicto quia locus excipiendus<est>.'

[47] Innocent III, Reg. 1, no. 450. Included in canon law as 3 Comp 5.16.1 (= X 5.33.11).

[48] William Durand, *Speculum*, I, §*De legato*, fol. 26r. Petrus Bonetus on X 3.40.10 v. *semine*, BAV Borgh. lat. MS 228, fol. 122va: 'ubi ecclesia polluta est sanguine est, interdicta est a iure, sed celebrans in ecclesia interdicta a iure non est irregularis. Secus si a iure [*recte* homine], infra. de privil. Tuarum [X 5.33.11].' Innocent IV, *Apparatus* on X 5.31.18 v. *interdicti violationem*. Even Laurentius's gloss copied by Tancred (n. 46) seemed to doubt that a 'violated' church was technically interdicted.

[49] VI 5.11.18.

[50] Hostiensis, *Lectura* on X 3.40.10 v. *aut sanguinis effusione* (vol. 2, fol. 160va); Bernard de Montmirat on X 3.40.10 v. *sanguinis*, BAV, Vat. lat. MS 2542, fol. 67vb (Ed. fol. 120rb); Petrus Bonetus on X 3.40.10 v. *semine*, BAV, Borgh. lat. MS 228, fol. 122va.

[51] Bernard de Montmirat's addition to Pierre Sampsona's *Lectura* on X 3.40.4 v. *proposuisti*, Vienna, Nationalbibliothek MS 2083, fol. 39ra; MS 2113, fol. 64va: 'Quidam voluerunt dicere quod si aliquis se defendendo aliquem in ecclesia interfecerit, ecclesia non est reconcilianda. Sed

harder to determine whether a sin was involved. For them adultery was clearly a sin and therefore it might 'violate' a church, as stated in 'Si motum', but some canonists also debated whether sex between a married couple in church was a sin even if it was licit elsewhere. The canonist Pierre Sampsona noted that *doctores antiqui* agreed that a church was not 'violated' in the latter instance but that the Spanish canonist Johannes de Deo had disputed this view. Hostiensis and Sampson's pupil, Bernard de Montmirat, agreed that a man sinned by having sex with his wife in church, though Hostiensis added that the wife did not sin as she was simply doing her marital duty! But the question was still open to canonistic debate in the early fourteenth century, when Petrus Bonetus claimed that a church was not 'violated' by sex between a married couple. These canonists at least agreed that a church was polluted by human and not animal semen, presumably since only human copulation involved sin, and only when the sin was known publicly and not confided to a priest under the seal of the confessional.[52] That they found it necessary to debate such hypothetical questions indicates their attitude to contemporary sexual morality.

The *Decretum* had specified other acts which made a church unfit for worship: its total devastation by fire; its consecration by a simonist or excommunicate; if it was built for the sake of profit; if it was dedicated without the local bishop's permission or relics in its altar.[53] A pupil of the French canonist Petrus Brito added (*c.*1205) that if patrons of a church disagreed over the appointment of a priest there, the bishop might suspend celebration of offices in it until they came to terms, and this instance was also noted by later canonists. Since the late twelfth century disputes over the patronage of churches had likewise occasioned interdicts on such churches.[54] Moreover cemeteries might become unfit for

---

puto tutius esse quod debeat reconciliari. B.' 'Reconciliation' made the church fit again for worship, on which see pp. 246–7. The siglum 'B.' identifying this as Bernard's gloss is absent in MS 2113, which implies that it is an original gloss of Sampsona. The writings of Bernard and his teacher Pierre de Sampson are often confused: Pontal, 'Quelques remarques', esp. 134–8, 141–2; Vodola, *Excommunication*, 233–6.

[52] Pierre Sampsona on X 3.40.10 v. *cuiuscumque*, Vienna, Nationalbibliothek MS 2083, fol. 39ra; MS 2113, fol. 64vb. Bernard de Montmirat on X 3.40.10 v. *si ecclesia*, BAV Vat. lat. MS 2542, fol. 67vb (Ed. fol. 120ra); Hostiensis, *Lectura* on X 3.40.10 v. *semine* (vol. 2, fol. 160va); Petrus Bonetus on X 3.40.10 v. *consecranda*, BAV, Borgh. lat. MS 228, fol. 122rb. In 1172–3 Alexander III declared in the decretal 'Significasti' (1 Comp. 5.13.6; X 5.16. 5) that a church was 'violated' after it became public knowledge that a woman had repeatedly committed adultery inside that church with a priest.

[53] C.1 q.4 c.11; C.16 q.5 c.10; De con. D.1 c.5, 10, 26. Noted by later canonists: Johannes Teutonicus on 3 Comp. 3.31.3 v. *dedicationes* (edited at http://faculty.cua.edu/Pennington/edit323 .htm); Tancred on 3 Comp. 3.31.3 v. *reconciliari*, BAV, Vat. lat. MS 1377, fol. 245rb; Pierre Sampsona on X 3.40.4 v. *proposuisti*, Vienna, Nationalbibliothek MS 2083, fol. 39ra; Hostiensis, *Lectura* on X 3.40.4 v. *reconciliari* (vol. 2, fol. 159va); Johannes Calderinus, 'De interdicto', Pt 1 §14 (fol. 325vb).

[54] Anon. on 1 Comp. 3.33.1 v. *perlatum est*, Brussels, Bibliothèque royale MS 1407–9, fol. 52ra: 'Si quilibet heredum patronorum suum voluerit instituere in ecclesia et concordare noluerint, episcopus precipiat ne divina celebrentur in illa ecclesia donec concordent.' Cf. William

Christian use if excommunicates were buried there, according to a decretal of Innocent III (1213) included in *Compilatio quarta* and the *Liber extra*. Boniface VIII later added in the *Liber sextus* (1298) that the 'violation' of a church by bloodshed or semen also applied to its adjoining cemetery; hence burial was forbidden there, but conversely 'violation' of the churchyard alone was not to affect the church. This ruling echoed his constitution on the observance of particular local interdicts.[55] It can be seen at work a year later at Ardembuch parish in Tournai diocese, where it was said that the clergy refused to officiate, since one of their number had allegedly been dragged from the parish church and murdered, another had been beaten up there until blood flowed, and a third had been wounded in the churchyard. In common with the Lund case a century earlier and many interdicts laid on the scene of a canonical crime, this suspension of offices was occasioned by violence against clergy and intended to encourage deeper respect for them and their churches.[56]

Another phenomenon similar in effect to a particular local interdict was also a means of clerical self-defence: the so-called *cessatio a divinis*, where the clergy of a specific church agreed not to celebrate offices. It was already in use by 1215, when it was regulated by the Fourth Lateran Council.[57] It was the practice in the churches of Lyon, Vienne, and Clermont, Johannes Garsias Hispanus observed (1282), and Arras and elsewhere, according to William Durand (*c*.1289). Indeed the cases recorded in thirteenth-century papal registers mainly come from France.[58] It was a measure that chapters of some cathedral or collegiate churches claimed to exercise by custom or privilege against attackers of their property, persons, or liberties. For example regular clergy and other clerks in Würzburg and its suburbs initiated a *cessatio* by May 1249 following a mob attack by local citizens on clergy celebrating mass in its cathedral.[59] Hence it was a protest designed to air a grievance, a kind of clerical strike. But since the early thirteenth century canonists had been careful to distinguish that it was not an interdict. An interdict was a judicial sentence, and, as Johannes Teutonicus (*c*.1217) and subsequent canonists explained, nobody might impose this on themselves as if they were their own judge; it was a commonplace maxim of

---

Durand, *Speculum*, I, §*De legato*, fol. 26rb, and Johannes Calderinus, 'De interdicto', Pt 1 §12–13. Interdicts on churches caused by disputed patronage are noted above on p. 69.

[55] Innocent III, Reg. 16, no. 26 (= 4 Comp. 3.14.1; X 3.40.7). VI 3.21.un.; cf. VI 5.11.17.

[56] Reg. Boniface VIII, no. 2834.   [57] Lat. Conc. IV, c.7; 4 Comp. 1.13.1; X 1.31.13 §1.

[58] Johannes Garsias Hispanus on Lugd. Conc. II c.17 (VI 1.16.2) v. *ecclesiis*, BAV, Pal. lat. MS 629, fol. 280ra: 'Ut in Lugdunense, Viennense, et Claromontense ecclesiis'. William Durand, ibid. v. *ex consuetudine* (Ed. fol. 58r). French cases: Reg. Honorius III, no. 5342 (Langres); Reg. Gregory IX, no. 2309 (Laon); Reg. Honorius IV, nos. 42 (Lyon), 767 (Châlons-sur-Marne); Reg. Nicholas IV, nos. 420 (Reims), 2115 (Cambrai), 4299 (Reims); Reg. Boniface VIII, nos. 355 (Reims), 2912 (Châlons-sur-Marne).

[59] Reg. Innocent IV, no. 4569.

Roman law that nobody might be judge in their own case.⁶⁰ Innocent IV and Hostiensis thus agreed that clergy might officiate with impunity in any church where its canons observed a *cessatio*, and Johannes Garsias Hispanus added that priests might celebrate offices there in a low voice, 'which might not be done had the church been interdicted'.⁶¹

Nevertheless a *cessatio* was sometimes extended beyond the church in which it started to others nearby. In 1286, at the request of the cathedral chapter of Cambrai, Honorius IV required that whenever the chapter held a *cessatio*, it was to be observed by clergy in other churches of the city as long as it lasted.⁶² Apparently this practice was not uncommon by the early fourteenth century. A constitution of Clement V then observed that chapters and clergy of collegiate and conventual churches occasionally claimed by custom or otherwise the freedom to hold a general *cessatio* of cities, lands, and other places. In other words it resembled a general local interdict; the constitution indeed obliged regular clergy to observe a general *cessatio* in the same way as general local interdicts regardless of their freedoms. In his gloss on this constitution Johannes Andreae therefore applied the distinction between general and particular interdicts to *cessationes*, noting that *speciales cessationes* were observed only in churches where they began.⁶³

In conclusion a particular local interdict, in the proper sense of the term, was used mainly as a tool of internal discipline, unlike the general local interdict, though it was to be observed in much the same way as one, namely the innocent might take part in offices outside its ambit. Two other phenomena had the same effect of suspending services in specific churches, namely 'violation' and *cessatio a divinis*, but by contrast they were usually occasioned by much the same cause as a general local interdict, i.e. lay hostility against the clergy, and hence likewise concerned external discipline. By the mid-thirteenth century canonists also distinguished that neither phenomenon was strictly speaking an interdict, since neither carried the same penal consequences as an interdict for clergy who

---

⁶⁰ Johannes Teutonicus on 4 Comp. 1.13.1 (= X 1.31.13) v. *manifesta*, BAV, Vat. lat. MS 1377, fol. 289ra: 'Item non videtur quod capitulum possit suspendere ecclesiam quia iam se ipsos supponerent interdicto, quod esse non potest quod aliquis se ipsum suspendat, nec possint esse iudices in proprio facto, ut extra. iii. de conces. preben. non va. Post electionem [3 Comp. 3.8.4]'. Cf. Damasus (*c*.1215) on Lat. Conc. IV c.7 (= X 1.31.13) v. *maxime in contemptum episcopi* (*Constitutiones*, 422). Cf. also Vincentius Hispanus (*c*.1236) who copied Johannes's gloss on X 1.31.13 v. *manifesta*, BAV, Vat. lat. MS 6769, fol. 52ra; and Goffredus de Trano on X 1.31.13 v. *cessaverint*, Vienna, Nationalbibliothek MS 2197, fol. 25vb.

⁶¹ Innocent IV, *Apparatus* on X 1.31.13 v. *manifesta*; Hostiensis, *Lectura* on X 1.31.13 v. *manifesta* (vol. 1, fol. 165ra); cf. also Bernard of Parma on X 1.31.13 v. *cessaverint a divinis*. Johannes Garsias Hispanus on Lugd. Conc. II c.17 (VI 1.16.2) v. *cessare*, BAV, Pal. lat. MS 629, fol. 280ra: 'presbiteri medio tempore infra ecclesiam etiam cum canonicis submissa voce officiant et celebrant, quod non fieret si esset ecclesia interdicta, ut patet infra. de cleri. ex. min. Postulasti [X 5.27.7]'.

⁶² Reg. Honorius IV, no. 444; cf. n. 59 above.

⁶³ Clem. 5.10.1. Johannes Andreae, *Glossa* on Clem. 5.10.1 v. *generalibus*.

officiated in spite of them. The only exception was a general *cessatio*, which by 1317 was virtually equivalent to a general local interdict.

2.3 PERSONAL INTERDICTS

Thirteenth-century canon law and its commentators differentiated a personal interdict from a local interdict to such a degree in terms of form and observance that they seem almost separate institutions and had probably originated as such before they came to share a common name. According to the canonists Alanus Anglicus (*c*.1210–15) and Zoën, a personal interdict was the same in effect as minor excommunication, in that it denied access to the sacraments and church services but did not imply the loss of legal rights and social exclusion as major excommunication did.[64] Paulus Hungarus indeed remarked (*c*.1215) that interdicted persons might bring lawsuits or appoint proctors to do so on their behalf. And according to the canonist Petrus Bonetus, writing a century later, one might associate with an interdicted person but not with an excommunicate, presumably meaning one bound by major excommunication.[65]

Canonists drew a distinction between major and minor excommunication by the late twelfth century. When *Decretum* texts imposed excommunication for contact with excommunicates, notably Gregory VII's canon 'Quoniam multos' (1078), they interpreted it to mean the lesser form of the sanction. By the end of the century papal decretals confirmed this teaching, and Innocent III's decretal 'Nuper a nobis' (1199) ruled that association with an excommunicate incurred major excommunication only where this contact involved collaboration in a crime.[66] Hence it seems likely that the general personal interdict originated as the extension of minor excommunication to an entire community in

---

[64] Alanus, *Apparatus* 'Ius naturale' on C.24 q.3 *dictum ante* c.1 v. *pro peccato*, BAV, Ross. lat. MS 595, fol. 207rb (second layer of glosses): 'Minori<excommunicatione>que est seperatio a sacramentis excommunicari possunt subditi pro superioris delicto si contumax fuerit, ut infra. de of. iud. del. Sane quia nos, supra. xvii. q. iiii. Miror [1 Comp. 1.21.16; C.17 q.4 c.8]. Excipiuntur penitentias <morientium> et baptismas parvulorum, que nulli pro peccato alterius sunt deneganda, infra. de spon. et matrim. Non est vobis \ex. lib. i./, infra. e. q. Si habes. [1 Comp. 4.1.13; C.24 q.3 c.1] A.' Zoën on 5 Comp. 1.18.1, Tours, Bibliothèque municipale MS 565, fol. 7vb: '<u>interdicto</u>. Idest minori excommunicatione que aliquem separat ab ecclesie sacramentis. <u>excommunicatione</u>. Maiori que seperat aliquem a communione fidelium, sicut de his duabus habes, supra. de excep. c.i. vel iii. q. iiii. Engeltrudam [5 Comp. 2.16.1; C.3 q.4 c.12]'.

[65] Paulus Hungarus, *Notabilium* on 3 Comp. 5.23.7, BAV, Borgh. lat. MS 261, fol. 89rc: 'Item nota ex hac decretali quod interdictus potest agere vel procuratorem constituere in agendo.' Petrus Bonetus on X 2.28.37, BAV, Borgh. lat. MS 228, fol. 112vb: 'cum interdicto participari potest, non autem cum excommunicato, ff. de pen. l. Moris, ff. de servis. expor. l. Cui pacto, supra. Quod metus causa. Sacris [Dig. 48.19.9, 18.7.5; X 1.40.5]'.

[66] Vodola, *Excommunication*, 41–2; C.11 q.3 c.103 ('Quoniam multos'); X 5.39.29.

non-criminous contact with wrongdoers. Alanus Anglicus indeed distinguished that no one might be bound by major excommunication for another's sin but minor excommunication might punish subjects for their superior's delict; and the two decretals that he cited in support of this view make it clear that he had an interdict of a community in mind. Furthermore when a community was interdicted, its guilty members and their collaborators, with whom the rest of the community was inevitably in contact, were normally excommunicated. For example before May 1235 the Bishop of Savona had excommunicated the podestà and councillors of Noli and others of that commune who had personally participated in destroying a castle of the bishop, and he had interdicted the rest of the people of Noli.[67] Given the similarity between general personal interdicts and minor excommunication, it is not surprising that communities were sometimes said to be under excommunication when an interdict was meant. The terms were used almost interchangeably in two papal letters referring to Cremona in 1201, and as we have seen, the canonist Alanus still equated minor excommunication with an interdict some ten years later.[68] Nevertheless from the early thirteenth century canonists increasingly distinguished between excommunication as a sanction reserved for individuals and the interdict as applicable to communities. Popes still occasionally imposed full excommunication on groups, such as Honorius III's sentence of 1222 on the masters and scholars of Paris, but Innocent IV outlawed the practice in 1245. And by the mid-fourteenth century the canonist Johannes Calderinus observed that minor excommunication was rarely if ever imposed and the interdict had taken its place.[69]

A general local interdict also affected those associated with wrongdoers, often also in conjunction with the excommunication of the guilty. Canonists did not state in which circumstances a general personal interdict was more appropriate, but in practice the latter was mainly used against communes and other urban communities, whereas a general local interdict might apply to a whole territory under the jurisdiction of a lord or feudal monarch. Personal interdicts were also meant to work in a way distinct from local ones. Although canonists distinguished between excommunication and interdict, they maintained that those under a personal interdict were to be excluded from church services in the same manner as excommunicates. Indeed since at least the late twelfth century, papal grants of the freedom to celebrate behind closed doors during a general local interdict specifically forbade the admission of excommunicated *and* interdicted persons. By the mid-thirteenth century Innocent IV held that interdicted persons were to

    [67] Reg. Gregory IX, no. 2579.
    [68] Krehbiel, 133. The opinions of Alanus discussed above are those in n. 64 above.
    [69] Reg. Honorius III, no. 4012. Innocent IV: VI 5.11.5 (see pp. 25–6). Johannes Calderinus (attrib.), *De censura*, BAV, Pal. lat. MS 797, fol. 11rb: 'Sed quia minor excommunicatio numquam vel rare ab homine infligitur, videtur per abusum de medio recessisse et interdictum quodammodo in locum eius mutato nomine successisse.'

be excluded from church services anywhere, and Boniface VIII later confirmed this teaching as law in the *Liber sextus*.[70] In fact the papacy seems to have considered this the correct practice since at least the early thirteenth century. In 1221 Honorius III had forbidden prelates of the Esztergom and Vesprém dioceses in Hungary to admit excommunicated and interdicted persons of a certain parish to divine offices, as some prelates had done presumably; otherwise they would face due punishment.[71]

By the 1270s Monaldus could give priests detailed guidance in his canon law manual on how to deal with interdicted persons. A priest in a church that he was not bound to serve was not to celebrate divine offices there if he suspected that interdicted persons were among his congregation. But if the priest could identify the interdicted, he might warn them to leave and then celebrate the offices for the non-interdicted. By contrast, a priest who was obliged to serve a church had to celebrate the offices there even if he knew some persons present to be interdicted and they refused to leave, but he was to shun them at communion like excommunicates. This was true, Monaldus asserted, even if the interdict had not been publicized but simply made known to him by trustworthy persons. If the interdict was publicized and a priest knowingly received the interdicted at divine offices, Monaldus concluded that the rest of the congregation was not obliged to leave and did not sin by hearing those offices, but the priest alone sinned, unless they approved of his conduct. Priests no doubt faced these hypothetical situations outlined by Monaldus in practice, but it cannot always have been easy for them to discriminate between the guilty and the innocent. Another manualist John of Freiburg conceded this point when he warned priests not to assume someone to be an excommunicate or interdicted because they did not enter church during services but listened to them from outside.[72] Though these guidelines were never expressed in law, they doubtless represented the ecclesiastical authorities' notions of good practice. In northern Italy as early as 1207 the patriarch of Grado had warned clerks of the church of Santa Maria Formosa on pain of excommunication not to participate in the offices with their interdicted provost, the Archdeacon of Castello. Likewise some forty years later, when supporters in Basel of the deposed Frederick II incurred excommunication and

---

[70] See pp. 134–40 below on such papal grants; cf. X 5.40.17. The view expressed by Innocent and other canonists (see pp. 65–6 and n. 26 above) was confirmed by VI 5.11.16. Likewise Goffredus de Trano on X 5.38.11 v. *quod audiri*, Vienna, Nationalbibliothek MS 2197, fol. 153rb: 'Si ergo non licet interdictis audire divina etiam extra ecclesiam constitutis, multominus hoc licet excommunicatis. Indigni enim sunt divina audire a quibus sunt exclusi, ut extra. de excep. A nobis, infra. t. prox. c. penult. [X 2.25.2, 5.3959].' Cf. Pierre Sampsona (1267), *Distinctio* on X 5.38.11, BAV, Pal. lat. MS 656, fol. 155vb–6ra.

[71] Reg. Honorius III, no. 3273; cf. ibid. no. 4366, which warned the papal legate not to allow any of the excommunicated or interdicted Cremonese to have communion (*communicare*) with him.

[72] Monaldus, *Summa*, fol. 97r; John of Freiburg, *Summa*, III, xxxiii q.263–6, esp. q.266.

interdict for destroying their bishop's palace, Innocent IV required the Bishop of neighbouring Strasbourg to enforce these sentences and order friars, Hospitallers, and other religious specifically not to celebrate the offices if these persons were present.[73]

A papal law on personal interdicts did not appear, however, till as late as 1298, when Boniface VIII's constitution 'Si sententia' ruled that if a people were laid under an interdict, its individual members were understood to be interdicted. This countered the juristic notion of a *universitas* as an abstract entity above and beyond its members, which Innocent IV had conceived in order to deny the capacity of a *universitas* to suffer excommunication. In Boniface's law a community was nothing other than the persons who composed it. But his main point was more practical than conceptual: members of an interdicted community even outside of it were to be excluded from the sacraments and divine offices anywhere.[74] No distinction was drawn between guilty and innocent, unlike under a general local interdict. According to Johannes Andreae's commentary on this ruling (*c.*1342), 'multi religiosi' contended that the interdict of a community should bind those present at the wrong that occasioned it and who seemed to support it by keeping silent, but not those who were absent or opposed it. In other words only those who bore collective responsibility for another's sin ought to suffer a collective penalty for it. Andreae, however, denied that those who did not were to be excepted.[75] Other innocents not excepted were those who became members of a community after the wrongdoing. Canonists resolved this problem by referring to the juristic notion of a *universitas* as a sempiternal community, one which remained conceptually the same even if its actual members changed. Innocent IV held that a community existing at the time of the wrong was the same one as in the future, but he did not see this as a reason for excommunicating a community, since he felt that it would be very wicked if future members who had no part in the wrong were thereby affected.[76] Conversely Johannes Andreae remarked (*c.*1302) that an interdict might still bind a community if it had not been relaxed after a hundred years, since the community remained the same; there are indeed cases of interdicts lasting for such long periods.[77] Johannes Calderinus, a pupil of Andreae, likewise observed that an interdict on a people affected anyone becoming a member of that people even if the sentence had preceded him, for a community was not changed by new members. As Johannes Andreae had concluded, it was harsh

---

[73] Innocent III, Reg. 10, no. 178; Reg. Innocent IV, no. 3109.

[74] VI 5.11.16. See pp. 65–6.   [75] Johannes Andreae, *Novella* on VI 5.11.16.

[76] Innocent IV, *Apparatus* on X 5.39.53 v. *consiliarios*. On the sempiternal community see Rodriguez, 'Innocent IV', 295, and Kantorowicz, 291–313.

[77] Johannes Andreae, *Glossa* on VI 5.11.16 v. *non competano*. Cf. Baldus de Ubaldis (d. 1417) on Dig. 5.1.76 n. 4 as quoted in Kantorowicz, 295 n. 50. An interdict could last for 12 years (Portugal), 30 years (Italian towns), 60 years (Sicily), and sometimes more than a century (Le Bras, *Institutions*, 248 n. 26). See also p. 174 on an interdict lasting some 40 years noted by Andreae.

that innocent persons were bound by an interdict, but a harsh sentence imposed by a judge or the law was to be observed, and the innocent remained so in the eyes of God.[78]

The only exception that 'Si sententia' admitted was that the clergy were not to be considered interdicted when the people were interdicted, and vice versa, unless the sentence stated otherwise. This distinction had been foreshadowed by Innocent III's decretal 'Ex parte' (1203), which had referred to separate interdicts laid on the people and clergy of a place. The sentence on the clergy was evidently superfluous unless, as Hostiensis later observed, that on the people was not understood to include the clergy. However, it is unclear whether this applied in practice before 'Si sententia' confirmed this canonistic deduction as law.[79] Hostiensis had also noted that when a church was interdicted and not its clergy, they might celebrate offices elsewhere; hence when the clergy were interdicted and not their church, other clergy coming to it from elsewhere might celebrate in it.[80] Johannes Andreae (*c.*1302) repeated this comment, but neither canonist stated whether laity might attend offices celebrated by outsiders. Certainly an interdict on the people of a place did not technically forbid those not belonging to that people, laity or clergy, from hearing offices or receiving sacraments there. Johannes Calderinus conceded that such persons were not bound by this sentence and the law did not prevent clergy from celebrating offices in a loud voice in a place where only its people were interdicted. Nevertheless he advised clerks against public celebration during such an interdict, lest the interdicted could hear the celebrants' voices and see the Eucharist openly, and so ecclesiastical discipline would be disrespected.[81] But it is unclear whether interdicts of peoples ever indirectly affected outsiders in practice.

Certainly canonists held that outsiders who joined an interdicted people were thereby interdicted, but did the corollary follow, that those who ceased to belong to an interdicted people thereby ceased to be interdicted? Calderinus held that incarceration or banishment might exclude a person from an interdicted people but he still remained interdicted. Entry to a monastic community was a more effective escape route. By the mid-thirteenth century the papacy was granting the prelates of various religious orders the power to absolve interdicted persons who wished to join their houses. Calderinus later observed that profession of monastic vows totally severed a person's ties with an interdicted people, so that he might

[78] Johannes Calderinus, 'De interdicto', Pt 1 §34 (fol. 327ra); Johannes Andreae, *Novella* on VI 5.11.16.

[79] VI 5.11.16 ('Si sententia'). 3 Comp. 5.16.3; X 5.33.13 ('Ex parte'). Hostiensis, *Lectura* on X 5.33.13 v. *populum* (vol. 2, fols. 80vb–81ra).

[80] Hostiensis, *Lectura* on X 5.33.13 v. *et in clerum* (vol. 2, fol. 80vb). Johannes Andreae, *Glossa* on VI 5.11.16 v. *in clerum*.

[81] Johannes Calderinus, 'De interdicto', Pt 1 §32 (fol. 327ra).

be ordained.[82] Apparently, therefore, the sentence no longer had any effect on him, for an interdict normally prevented ordination.

A person might be interdicted not only by virtue of belonging to an interdicted people, however. As early as 1179 a canon of the Third Lateran Council had referred to persons interdicted *nominatim*, which Alanus Anglicus (*c.*1201–10) and Innocent IV interpreted to mean those specified in a sentence by name. Thus an interdict might be laid on individuals. The canon required that those interdicted *nominatim* be shunned along with excommunicates; hence a person interdicted individually was to be treated more harshly than someone belonging to an interdicted people.[83] Indeed Innocent IV distinguished that regular clergy who had the freedom to open churches in interdicted places annually in order to collect alms might admit interdicted persons to the offices, but not those interdicted *nominatim*. Likewise Johannes Andreae inferred (1326) that since Clement V's constitution 'Eos qui' prohibited the burial in cemeteries of those interdicted *nominatim*, it did not apply to those interdicted 'non nominatim' provided that they were not buried in an interdicted place.[84]

In effect the canonists appear to have been drawing a distinction between the innocent and the guilty. Innocent IV had added that those who provoked an interdict on themselves were also excluded from the services of alms-collecting regular clergy, even if they were interdicted as members of a community and not *nominatim*. In fact, whereas most members of an interdicted community were suffering for the wrongs of others, it seems that persons were interdicted *nominatim* for their own wrongs just as excommunicates were. In the few cases recorded in thirteenth-century papal registers of interdicts imposed on individuals, the sanction was mostly used to punish faults of clerks. For instance in 1207 the patriarch of Grado had interdicted the Archdeacon of Castello and the church of Santa Maria Formosa where he was provost because of his disobedience: he had failed to read out a mandate of the patriarch addressed to clerks of that church. Indeed, in 1213 Innocent III had warned the Bishop, dean, and cantor of Paris that no French royal chapel was to be interdicted for its chaplain's wrongdoing, but rather the chaplain himself ought to be interdicted.[85] Although an interdict on an individual was less harsh than major excommunication and

[82] Johannes Calderinus, 'De interdicto', Pt 1 §§35–7 (fol. 327rb). Papal grants: Reg. Innocent IV, no. 2474 (minister general of Trinitarians); Reg. Alexander IV, nos. 312 (Carmelite priors), 900 (Cistercian priors), 3255 (Carthusian priors); Reg. Clement IV, no. 1720 (Dominican priors).

[83] Lat. Conc. III c.9 (= 1 Comp. 5.28.3; X 5.33.3). Alanus Anglicus on 1 Comp. 5.28.3 v. *nominatim*, München, Bayerische Staatsbibliothek Clm 3879, fol. 92ra: 'Nominatim interdictus est qui nomine suo vel aliis circumstantiis denotatur ut infra. instit. de exhereda. lib. §masculos [*recte* Emancipatos; Inst. 2.13 §3].' Innocent IV, *Apparatus* on X 5.33.3 v. *excommunicatis*; cf. ibid. on X 3.5.31 v. *nominatim*.

[84] Innocent IV, *Apparatus* on X 5.33.24 v. *excommunicatis*. Johannes Andreae, *Glossa* on Clem. 3.7.1 v. *nominatim*.

[85] Innocent IV: as n. 84. Innocent III, Reg. 10, no. 78; 15, no. 227. Cf. also Reg. Honorius III, no. 5513.

barely distinguishable in effect from minor excommunication, it represented a double punishment for clerks in that it forbade them from participating in the celebration of offices and administration of the sacraments as well as in hearing and receiving these.

A sanction which had a similar effect was the interdict on entry to church (*ab ingressu ecclesie*). An undated decretal of Alexander III (1159–81) had threatened this against a monastic community, but it was more often used against individuals. A canon of the Fourth Lateran Council (1215) imposed it for a month on prelates who did not follow the procedure laid down by that canon for excommunicating someone, and it was also incurred for other clerical offences under some subsequent papal laws. Alexander IV (1254–61) reserved it as a mitigated penalty for prelates, who were only to incur the harsher penalties of suspension from office and excommunication if they persisted in their disobedience; the latter applied to lower clergy in the first instance. Hence a canon of the Second Council of Lyon (1274) placed an interdict *ab ingressu ecclesie* on prelates taking procurations in cash instead of in kind but punished lower clergy doing likewise by suspension from office and benefice. Popes also applied this preferential treatment in practice. In 1286 Honorius IV moderated a judges delegate's sentence of excommunication on some clerks of Canterbury diocese in a debt case to an interdict *ab ingressu ecclesie* for their archbishop, but he provided that the latter's punishment might be increased in accordance with Alexander IV's ruling.[86] This kind of interdict might also affect laity, albeit cases in the thirteenth-century papal registers are rare. For example after the Bishop of Oporto fled to the curia alleging persecution by the king of Portugal, Innocent III warned the king in 1211 to make amends to the bishop; otherwise he would be interdicted from entry to church and all the sacraments. Certainly lay dignitaries perceived it as a serious enough danger by the mid-thirteenth century to request Innocent IV and Alexander IV for immunity from it. By the 1290s it was inflicted on both laity and clergy by church courts in England as a penalty for failure to respond to summons.[87]

An interdict *ab ingressu ecclesie* prohibited entry to church not only for the purpose of celebrating or hearing offices. According to Innocent IV it even forbade access to church for the sake of private prayer, and any who died under this interdict were also denied burial in a church or cemetery. Hostiensis adopted these views, and Monaldus similarly distinguished that persons under a general interdict might pray in private in church, even in an interdicted one, but not excommunicates or those under an interdict *ab ingressu ecclesie*. That is to say

[86] On monastic community: X 2.24.9. Automatic penalty: Lat. Conc. IV c.47 (= X 5.39.48); cf. VI 5.7.8, 5.11.1 (see p. 104). Lugd. Conc. II c.24 (= VI 3.20.2). Alexander IV: VI 1.14.2. Reg. Honorius IV, no. 605.

[87] King of Portugal: Innocent III, Reg. 13, no. 75. Immunity: Reg. Innocent IV, nos. 491 (Count of Toulouse), 7363 (King of Bohemia); Reg. Alexander IV, no. 1285 (Queen of Navarre). Church courts: e.g. *Select Cases*, 425–7, 507–8.

the innocent were again to be treated less harshly than the guilty. By 1298 Boniface VIII had confirmed as a rule of canon law Innocent IV's teaching on burial. Nevertheless Johannes Andreae commented on this ruling that the ban on celebrating offices only applied within church, so that those under this ban might celebrate outdoors, in a tent, or private house.[88]

To sum up, since the late twelfth century canon law had distinguished between general and specific forms of the personal interdict as in the case of the local interdict. A general personal interdict was normally imposed on a community for the wrong of its head or some of its members. Its evolution can be associated with the development of minor excommunication as a sanction against those in non-criminous contact with excommunicates, and with the emergence of organized communities, against which a general personal interdict was chiefly aimed. Indeed juristic notions about organized communities largely shaped canonistic doctrine on its application. In particular they led canonists to draw no distinction between treatment of guilty and innocent under a general personal interdict, in contrast to their teaching on a general local one, though they admitted that wrongdoers interdicted by name were to be treated more severely. Canonistic doctrine also seems to have been describing customary practice in relation to general personal interdicts, though, in common with teaching on general local ones, it was not confirmed in canon law till the end of the thirteenth century. Canon law on specific personal interdicts was laid down earlier, and in practice these were directed largely against the clergy, in common with specific local interdicts. Personal and local interdicts were, nevertheless, meant to operate in different ways, but sometimes their effects might be combined.

2.4 MIXED SENTENCES

Interdicts were occasionally laid on a people *and* its place of habitation. Pope Martin IV used this double punishment in 1282–3 against Perugia, Spoleto, and other places in Italy associated with supporters of the Aragonese occupation of Sicily.[89] He regarded Sicily as a papal fief and Charles of Anjou as rightful vassal king of the island; hence this use of the interdict was motivated by extreme political circumstances, and indeed it was exceptional. Canonists only alluded to such a double interdict as a hypothetical possibility and none classified it as a distinct kind of interdict, as it was very much an expedient of judicial practice.

Canonists gave a little more attention to another sentence that brought together aspects of the personal and local interdict in a different way: the so-called ambulatory interdict. This sentence was imposed on an individual but it

---

[88] Innocent IV, *Apparatus* on X 5.39.48 v. *ingressum*. Hostiensis, *Lectura* on X 5.39.48 v. *ingressum ecclesie* (vol. 2, fol. 117rb). Monaldus, *Summa*, fol. 96rb. Boniface: VI 5.11.20. Johannes Andreae, *Glossa* on VI 5.11.20 v. *in ea*.

[89] Reg. Martin IV, nos. 280–1, 283, 310, 460, 467, 469.

affected any place where he or she happened to stop. It followed them like a shadow, such that 'they were never outside interdicted territory'. As Innocent IV noted, a judge might impose an interdict that came into effect against churches at certain times, such as whenever the local lord was present. A treatise on interdicts attributed to Johannes Andreae added that such a sentence was to be observed in a place as long as that person remained there. It might even remain in force for three days after that person departed according to Johannes Calderinus.[90] Presumably the aim was to turn people against a carrier of the sentence wherever he went. For example in 1203 Innocent III had declared that the murderers of Bishop Conrad of Würzburg and their heirs were to be deprived in perpetuity of all fiefs and benefices belonging to the church of Würzburg, and any diocese where they tried to obtain other ecclesiastical fiefs or benefices was subject to interdict until they ceased trying or the inhabitants of the diocese opposed them. This was perhaps not an ambulatory interdict in the strict sense, but it demonstrates that in practice as well as in theological and canonistic theory interdicts were designed to induce the innocent to resist the sins of the guilty.[91]

Innocent III and successive popes frequently imposed ambulatory interdicts on excommunicates, especially the persistently obdurate, thereby reinforcing their pariah status. For example in 1199 Innocent III declared that all places where Markward of Anweiler and his supporters arrived fell under interdict. Markward and his supporters were already excommunicated for scorning the pope's authority as overlord of Sicily and ward of Frederick II, heir to the kingdom, and Innocent III had even proclaimed a crusade against them. Thirty years later Gregory IX likewise laid the excommunicate Frederick II under an ambulatory interdict.[92] Sometimes ambulatory interdicts formed part of a whole battery of sanctions including excommunication. In a few cases it was combined with an interdict on places under a guilty party's jurisdiction, i.e. a general local interdict. In one extreme case in 1256 Alexander IV threatened an ambulatory interdict and excommunication on the duke of Silesia if he failed to free the Bishop of Wratislava and other clerks in his custody, besides an interdict on his land and places where these hostages were held. In other cases ecclesiastical authorities applied such penalties sequentially rather than together. For example a general local interdict was sometimes an aggravation of an ambulatory interdict.

---

[90] Krehbiel, 78 (quotation). Innocent IV, *Apparatus* on X 5.33.24 v. *interdicto*. Johannes Andreae (attrib.), *De modo*, BAV, Pal. lat. MS 797, fol. 8ra (Ed. fol. 6v). Johannes Calderinus (attrib.), *De censura*, BAV, Pal. lat. MS 797, fol. 15ra: 'interdicitur divinorum celebratio in locis ad que venerint et per triduum post eius recessum'. Reg. Clement IV, no. 144, also referred to ambulatory interdicts that were to last in places for three days after those under these sentences had passed through.

[91] Innocent III, Reg. 6, no. 113. On the theory see pp. 39–45.

[92] Markward: Innocent III, Reg. 2, no. 212. Frederick II: Reg. Gregory IX, no. 332. Cf. Innocent III, Reg. 1, no. 121; 6, no. 17; 7, no. 46; 9, no. 154; 11, no. 26; 13, no. 75; Reg. Gregory IX, nos. 757, 1639, 2158, 3615, 4453, 4777; Reg. Innocent IV, nos. 5279, 5469; Reg. Honorius IV, no. 768.

In 1199 when King Philip II of France refused to leave his mistress and return to his wife, at first the papal legate in France threatened ambulatory interdicts on Philip, his mistress, and members of their households, before proclaiming a papal interdict on the whole kingdom of France two months later. By the late thirteenth century an ambulatory interdict might form a stage in a scale of penalties which increased in severity with the delinquent's obduracy. The concordat between the king and church of Portugal approved by Nicholas IV in 1289 stipulated, for example, that if the king, his successors, or officials failed to amend any violation of the concordat in two months, the king's chapel was to be interdicted, and after four months he incurred an ambulatory interdict, then after a further two months excommunication, and if he still remained obdurate after that, his kingdom was to fall under a general interdict and his vassals were absolved of fealty to him.[93] The various forms of the interdict could thus be applied progressively as circumstances required.

In conclusion the ecclesiastical interdict embraced a range of sanctions that excluded from the sacraments, divine offices, and church burial. As Vodola stated, the interdict brought together 'a number of earlier disciplinary practices of the Church'.[94] The derivation of general personal interdicts from minor excommunication as a penalty for those innocently associating with excommunicates has been noted, for example. The different forms of the sanction might be used for different purposes; for instance the particular interdict, local or personal, helped reinforce internal discipline, whereas the general interdict was aimed more at external coercion, notably of secular rulers and other lay violators of ecclesiastical liberty. Therefore it was a highly adaptable and flexible sanction, which could even give rise to such peculiar variants as interdict *ab ingressu ecclesie* and so-called ambulatory interdicts.

Thirteenth-century canonistic doctrine on the operation of these various kinds of interdict reflected the papacy's approach in practice, though the teachings and the customary observances that they described were often not approved in canon law till 1298. Indeed many points remained obscure and disputed until they were clarified by papal rulings, notably the definition of a *generale interdictum terre* or access of laity to churches outside their interdicted land. In attempting to fill the gaps left by the law canonists were guided not only by papal practice but also their own ideas of collective guilt, notably in their teachings on general interdicts. In their *opinio communis* those associated with the guilty by feudal ties, by membership of the same community as the guilty, or even by sheltering the guilty and their crimes were held responsible and thus punishable under a general interdict. Nevertheless canonists often distinguished that those who committed a wrong should be treated more harshly than those simply associated with a

---

[93] Silesia: Reg. Alexander IV, no. 1557. France: Innocent III, Reg. 2, no. 188; cf. id. Reg. 7, no. 171. Portugal: Reg. Nicholas IV, no. 717; cf. Reg. Honorius IV, no. 96.
[94] Vodola, 'Interdict', 494.

wrongdoer. Individual delinquents were thus often excommunicated in practice, and interdicts were meant to punish the guilty more severely, for example if they were named in a personal interdict or caused a general local interdict. Canon law and canonistic doctrine on the interdict, therefore, tried to balance the competing concerns of maintaining ecclesiastical discipline and mitigating it for the innocent.

3

Laying of Interdicts

From the mid-twelfth century canonists and theologians increasingly distinguished between the internal and external *fora* of ecclesiastical discipline.[1] By the thirteenth century penance was enjoined in the *forum internum* for private sins disclosed in the confessional, whereas excommunication, interdict, and other canonical penalties were imposed in the *forum externum* for public crimes tried in open court. This bifurcation resulted partly from the evolution of the Church's administrative structures during the twelfth century and the concomitant separation of canon law from theology. From the mid-twelfth century canonists increasingly left sacramental matters, notably penance, to theologians and devoted themselves to juridical issues, notably canonical crime and punishment.[2] Canon law and its commentators increasingly defined who had power to excommunicate and how it was to be exercised, and interdicts largely followed these procedural rules during the thirteenth century. The reservation of excommunication and interdict to the *forum externum* would have a profound influence on these rules.

3.1 THE POWER TO INTERDICT

From the mid-twelfth century the question of internal and external *fora* was connected with another duality, orders and jurisdiction. It was agreed that those in priest's orders and above might enjoin penance and absolve sins in the *forum internum*, but canonists taught by the thirteenth century that only those holding ecclesiastical jurisdiction by virtue of an office (e.g. bishops) or commission (e.g. judges delegate) might impose and remove sanctions in the *forum externum*. Orders were not even a prerequisite for the exercise of such jurisdiction.[3] In canonistic doctrine this distinction was based on Gratian's interpretation of the power of binding and loosing. This was the 'power of the keys' that Christ had conferred on St Peter (Matthew 16:18–19),[4] and Gratian understood it in two senses. He accepted the traditional explanation that it represented the sacerdotal power to administer penance in the *forum internum*, and Christ had

---

[1] Russo, 436–59; Vodola, *Excommunication*, 35–6; Benson, 45–55.
[2] Cf. Huizing, 298.   [3] Vodola, *Excommunication*, 36.
[4] D.20 *dictum ante* c.1. Cf. C.24 q.1 *dictum post* c.1. See Tierney, 30–6, and Benson, 47–50.

also granted this power to absolve sin to all the apostles on another occasion. But Gratian also interpreted the power of the keys as the judicial authority to decide legal disputes, and he discussed this with reference to the pope alone. He held that 'knowledge' and 'power' were required to exercise this jurisdiction, and these were granted to St Peter through the keys. One 'key' was knowledge needed to judge between parties in court; the other was power to eject members from the Church, i.e. excommunication. This implied that all ecclesiastical jurisdiction, including the power to interdict, inhered in the pope as St Peter's successor; hence the decretist Rufinus argued before the Third Lateran Council (1179) that the judicial authority of bishops was ultimately derived from the papacy.[5]

Such an extreme claim on behalf of papal power would not be fully elaborated until the fourteenth century, and indeed Gratian's novel interpretation did not have an immediately wide impact. The theologian Rolandus still asserted in *c*.1150: 'omnibus sacerdotibus indifferenter he claves conferantur ex verbis Domini dicentis Petro'.[6] But the idea that the 'keys' in a judicial sense, and power to excommunicate and interdict, was reserved to prelates was accepted among canonists by the thirteenth century.[7] The canonist Bérenger Frédol argued (*c*.1298) that priests held 'potestas ligandi et solvendi' only in the limited sense of absolving sin but bishops received a fuller power (*amplior potestas*) that included excommunication.[8] He did not maintain that this was derived from the pope but that bishops as vicars of Christ and successors of the apostles held the 'keys' that Christ had conferred on the apostles and their successors. Indeed most thirteenth-century canonists, notably Hostiensis, did not accept that judicial authority was simply delegated to prelates by the pope but rather it was a right they exercised autonomously. This limitation of papal power was later challenged by the friars in the early fourteenth century, who claimed that the pope had supreme jurisdiction over the Church and distributed all jurisdiction to lesser prelates.[9] Hence when the canonist Johannes Calderinus considered who could interdict in the mid-fourteenth century when the Avignon papacy was at its zenith, this absolutist view of papal monarchy underlay his definition: it was the pope who principally imposed interdicts, and others received this power of coercion from him, since he alone had universal jurisdiction. In support of his view Johannes cited an influential text of Augustine from the *Decretum* which

---

[5] Benson, 85; cf. Pennington, 59 ff.   [6] Roland, *Sentenzen*, 267. See also Russo, 446.

[7] Anon. (*c*.1206) on 1 Comp. 3.33.16 v. *archidiaconi*, Brussels, Bibliothèque royale MS 1407–9, fol. 54rb: 'ar. quod archidiaconus potest excommunicare, supra. de officio archid. Pleni ius [*sic*; 1 Comp. 1.15.5(?)]. De hoc planum est enim quod nemo excommunicare potest nisi qui claves habet.'

[8] *Bérenger Frédol*, 49–50.

[9] Johannes Calderinus (attrib.), *De censura*, BAV, Pal. lat. MS 797, fol. 12rb: 'Videndum est de his qui interdicere possunt, et principaliter dominus papa interdicit, de excess. prelata. Tanta [X 5.31.18], a quo ceteri potestatem percipiunt cohercendi cum solus habeat universalem ordinariam iurisdictionem, xxiiii. q. i. Quodcumque [C.24 q.1 c.6].'

suggested that when St Peter received the keys, he 'signified' the Church; this had significant implications for the pope's position.[10]

Although thirteenth-century canonists conceived papal power in more limited constitutional terms, they recognized that the pope as 'universal ordinary' exercised jurisdiction throughout the Church and issued laws for the whole Church. This power was demonstrated through interdicts among other means. The pope alone pronounced interdicts on entire kingdoms or provinces. Only he or ecumenical councils convened by his authority attached interdicts to laws that ran throughout the Church so that any violator of these laws incurred this penalty. And the pope might even intervene in the jurisdiction of local ordinaries (e.g. bishops) by granting those nominally subject to it immunity from interdicts laid without papal consent and other more limited freedoms from interdict, as well as quashing invalid interdicts referred to the curia on appeal.[11] The interdict thus gave practical expression to the pope's wide interventionist powers, but he could not exercise them effectively without the cooperation of lesser prelates. When the pope declared an interdict, he relied on prelates and other clergy in the area or community which it concerned to publicize it and see that it was observed. In this respect it was a test of his authority over local churches. The English interdict is a case in point. In a letter of 27 August 1207 Innocent III instructed the Bishops of London, Ely, and Worcester to publish an interdict on England and have it 'inviolably' observed if they failed to persuade King John to yield to papal demands.[12] The monks of Canterbury had made two disputed elections to their vacant archiepiscopal see then accepted a candidate proposed by the pope, Stephen Langton. John's refusal to accept Langton was the cause of the interdict. The bishops charged with laying it delayed for some months, however, before they had the interdict promulgated on 23 March 1208.

Fear of the king's immediate power perhaps initially overtook their duty to a distant pope. The chronicler Roger of Wendover claimed that John reacted furiously to the bishops' 'tearful' entreaties to yield to the pope, allegedly uttering blasphemous oaths against the pope and cardinals and threatening to expel all clergy from England, confiscate their property, and send all Roman and papal clerks back to the curia with their eyes torn out and noses slit if the interdict were laid.[13] Wendover is a notoriously unreliable source, and we will consider later the king's actual countermeasures to this interdict, but the bishops were wary enough to flee into exile shortly after proclaiming the interdict. Possible intimidation and fear of reprisals were not the only factors that made the bishops' position difficult. Their loyalties were split between king and pope. As prelates they owed

[10] C.24 q.1 c.6. See Tierney, 34–6.
[11] On the thirteenth-century 'constitutional' view see Pennington, 62–74, and Watt, 75–92. Interdicts imposed by papal legislation are discussed below at pp. 126–8.
[12] *SLI*, no. 30. See Cheney, 'Interdict', for an unsurpassed account of the English interdict.
[13] Wendover, *Flores*, ii. 45–6; Gervase, ii. 101, 107. On King John's reaction see below at pp. 170–1, 176, 180–1.

obedience to the pope and had frequently been entrusted with executing papal mandates, but they had also served the king before becoming bishops. And all three, especially the Bishop of Worcester, probably owed their bishoprics to royal patronage.[14] Indeed the key issue in John's dispute with Innocent was that the pope consecrated Langton as archbishop without royal consent, contrary to English custom, and had rejected the king's preferred candidate. Moreover as magnates the bishops also held the temporalities of their sees from the king and were his subjects. A papal interdict hence severely tested the loyalties of local prelates who were expected to enforce it against their secular ruler.

Indeed they might fail to do so for the reasons already discussed. In May 1203 Innocent III had threatened King John with an ambulatory interdict if he did not recall the Archbishop of Dublin from exile and restore his temporalities within a month. The execution of the sentence was delegated to Hubert Walter, Archbishop of Canterbury and John's chancellor, and the Bishop of Ely who later had to declare the interdict on England. A year and a half later Innocent reproved them for neglecting their mandate and it was renewed with a two-month deadline. It is dubious whether the interdict was ever imposed, and the rationale for it ceased in 1205 when Hubert Walter brought the king to an agreement with the exiled archbishop.[15] On occasion, clearly, it was more expedient for local prelates to deal with their lay ruler by less confrontational means than a papal interdict.

The pope could also use agents to impose his interdicts who were less prone to such divided loyalties: papal legates. Normally cardinals or others attached to the curia, they were usually sent to places with which they had no personal ties. In 1198 the legate in France was Italian cardinal Peter of Capua, and the pope then instructed him to persuade the French king to leave his mistress and return to his wife; otherwise Peter was to lay an interdict on the king's 'land'. After the king had ignored frequent warnings, Peter finally summoned a general council of all prelates of the kingdom to meet at Dijon on 6 December 1199 where he ignored a royal appeal and promulgated the interdict, issuing orders to prelates in the king's land (not all of whom attended the council) to have it observed.[16] Peter had been acting on a specific papal mandate, and similarly in 1227 Gregory IX instructed the papal legate in England not to pronounce excommunication or interdict against its king or his brother the count of Poitou, as the previous pope Honorius III had required, without a specific papal mandate.[17] Legates sometimes received a general papal mandate to coerce any opponent of their mission by interdict or other canonical penalties, but it was more common for the mandate to specify which offenders they might use such measures against.[18] On other occasions

[14] See *SLI*, nos. 6, 9.
[15] Innocent III, Reg. 6, no. 64; 7, no. 171; Cheney, *England*, 304 n.; Krehbiel, 92.
[16] Innocent III, Reg. 1, no. 347; Krehbiel, 111–15.   [17] Reg. Gregory IX, no. 94.
[18] E.g. Reg. Urban IV, no. 594; the legate sent by Urban to negotiate peace between Henry III and his barons in England was authorized to coerce the rebels by ecclesiastical censure. Cf. Reg. Honorius III, no. 244; Reg. Clement IV, no. 116; Reg. Nicholas IV, nos. 225–6.

popes employed other curial agents, notably papal scribes, vicars, chaplains, and non-legatine cardinals, to proclaim an interdict to enforce papal judgements.[19] Nicholas IV often granted more freedom to inquisitors, allowing them to deploy excommunication and interdict against those obstructing their work regardless of papal immunities; one mandate specified these opponents as uncooperative civic officials, another as those who harboured or otherwise assisted heretics.[20]

In most of the instances above clergy on the ground had to act as executors of a sentence pronounced by the pope in a case already considered by him. As universal ordinary the pope claimed authority to judge all cases referred to him from across the Church, and his was a court of first instance, to which a case might be appealed even from the lowest church court.[21] Appeals to Rome rose so dramatically and inexorably from the mid-twelfth century, however, that the pope was increasingly unable to hear them all in person. A common solution was to refer cases back to the provinces from which they came and commission local prelates as papal judges delegate to hear them on the pope's behalf. In an undated decretal Alexander III made it a point of principle that a papal judges delegate was superior to all parties in the case referred to him, even bishops or others outside his jurisdiction; hence he might coerce them by an interdict if they defied his authority; with regard to a bishop, by an interdict on entry to church or even on his land. In another undated decretal Alexander added that a judges delegate might punish the defiance not only of those involved in the case but also of their chief supporters 'since, according to scripture, those doing wrong and those consenting to it should suffer a like penalty', a principle that also justified collective sanctions like the interdict. Both rulings entered canonical collections, notably the *Liber extra*, and thus were recognized by thirteenth-century canonists.[22]

These rulings also applied to subdelegates. Alexander III provided that judges delegate might subdelegate their commission if they could not discharge it because of illness or another serious reason and the case could be settled without them. Innocent III recognized in 1207 that judges delegate subdelegated their power of coercion with their jurisdiction. Consequently subdelegates might impose interdicts to enforce their judgements.[23] These rulings also passed into canon law, and they can be seen at work in a letter of Alexander IV from early 1260. It recorded that judges delegate had been appointed to settle a dispute in Ireland between the Bishop and chapter of Lismore and their metropolitan, the Archbishop of

---

[19] E.g. Reg. Honorius III, no. 2161 (scribes); Reg. Gregory IX, no. 1968 (chaplain); Reg. Innocent IV, no. 4681 (vicar); Reg. Nicholas IV, no. 4497 (cardinal); Reg. Boniface VIII, no. 1089 (nuncio).

[20] Reg. Nicholas IV, nos. 320, 430 (officials), 892 (harbourers), 2777. See pp. 46–7 on how canonistic doctrine called for the punishment of those defending heretics together with the heretics themselves.

[21] On the growth of papal appellate jurisdiction see, for example, Cheney, *Becket*, 47–75.

[22] 1 Comp. 1.21.16 (= X 1.29.11); 1 Comp. 1.21.2 (= X 1.29.1).

[23] 1 Comp. 1.21.4 (= X 1.29.3); 3 Comp. 1.18.8 (= X 1.29.29).

Cashel, and his chapter over possession of some monasteries, churches, and chapels. They had then subdelegated the case to the Bishop and Archdeacon of Kilmacduagh and Archdeacon of Mayo, who had decided in favour of the archbishop and his chapter and, at their request, imposed excommunication and interdict on the Bishop of Lismore and some of his chapter.[24]

A judges delegate's or subdelegate's power to coerce and hence to interdict was restricted to the case over which he was granted jurisdiction. From the early thirteenth century canonists also agreed that a legate might not exceed the limits of his mandate, especially when it came to laying interdicts.[25] This view was based on Innocent III's decretal 'Novit ille' (1200). It had responded to the French king's complaint that the interdict on his kingdom was invalid since the pope's legate had proclaimed it outside the boundaries of the kingdom.[26] Although the legate had first published the sentence at Dijon, he then travelled outside the kingdom and announced it again at a council at Vienne. Nevertheless his legation, Innocent explained, included not only the kingdom of France but also the provinces of Vienne, Lyon, and Besançon (whence prelates had come to attend the second legatine council). Though this was an expedient reaction to events, it contributed significantly to the general canonistic view that an ecclesiastical judge might only pronounce interdicts on those subject to his jurisdiction, and by the early thirteenth century one might legitimately appeal against an interdict laid 'a non suo iudice'. Indeed in 1193 Clement III's decretal 'A nobis' had ruled that a general sentence of excommunication only bound those subject to the one imposing it.[27]

Consequently an archbishop might not impose interdicts *ex officio* outside his province. But there was some debate among canonists whether an archbishop was the judge ordinary of his suffragan's subjects and might use interdicts against them. From the early thirteenth century canonists generally agreed that this was not true except in specific cases admitted by canon law: the suffragan was negligent or gave his consent; a case was referred to the archbishop on appeal; a

---

[24] Reg. Alexander IV, no. 3063.

[25] Alanus (*c*.1206) on Alan. 1.5.5 (= 3 Comp. 1.4.1) v. *metas*, Vercelli Cathedral Chapter MS 89, fol. 55vb: 'Si ergo metas legationis transisset legatus, ipsius iurisdictio expirasset et in homines legationis, ar. ff. de offi. prefec. et leg. l. ult. ff. de off. presidis. Preses. [Dig. 1.12.3, 1.18.3] sed contra ff. de officio procon. et l. l. ult. [Dig. 1.16.16]. Solutio. Secus de delegato pape quam delegato proconsulis, vel dic quod iurisdictionem contentiosam amittit statim ex quo provinciam exiverit, ut hic ammititur, voluntariam non, ut supra. de sent. ex. Ad eminentiam. lib. ii [2 Comp. 5.18.9].' Vincentius Hispanus on 3 Comp. 1.19.5, v. *fines*, BAV, Vat. lat. MS 1378, fol. 27rb: 'Ultra metam non teneret sententia, ff. de of. prefec. et leg. l. ult. ff. de of. pre. l. iii. [Dig. 1.12.3, 1.18.3] sicut nec antequam ingrediatur, ut ff. de of. proconsulis l. ii. et iii. in fi. [Dig. 1.16.2, 3] sicut nec etiam ultra iurisdictionis mensuram ff. de iurisdictione o. iud. l. ult. [Dig. 2.1.20]. Ordinarii autem sententia ex iurisdictione lata tenet, ar. contra xi. q. i. Si quisquam. De con. di. i. Hic ergo [C.11 q.1 c.16, De con. D.1 c.14]. Vin.' Cf. likewise Johannes Teutonicus on 3. Comp. 1.19.5 v. *terminos sue* (Ed. pp. 132–3), which gloss Tancred copied, BAV, Vat. lat. MS 1377, fol. 180vb.

[26] 3 Comp. 1.19.5 (= X 1.30.7); see glosses in previous note.

[27] 2 Comp. 5.18.10 (= X 5.39.21).

dispute arose between the suffragan and a subject of his; a case concerned a delict or property of the suffragan's subject in the archbishop's diocese; the archbishop was conducting a visitation; the suffragan's see was vacant.[28] Controversy on this issue was not confined to the schools but also broke out in practice. In 1245 suffragans of Reims province complained to Innocent IV that their archbishop judged cases from their jurisdiction not appealed to him and arbitrarily laid excommunication and interdicts on their subjects. The archbishop was cited before the pope to account for himself and responded that he laid these sentences when clergy of his province resisted his visitation. Innocent lifted these sentences and ruled that the archbishop might excommunicate only those subject to his jurisdiction. His ruling appeared in the decretal 'Romana Ecclesia' (1246), which was conceived and circulated as an addition to canon law and presumably also applied to interdicts.[29] An archbishop might, nevertheless, excommunicate or interdict his suffragans, if not their subjects, as Vincentius Hispanus had observed (*c*.1236); after all an archbishop was, according to Goffredus de Trano, the judge ordinary of his suffragans.[30] Likewise by the early thirteenth century, it was a canonistic commonplace that a bishop might lay an interdict *ex officio* only on persons and places subject to his jurisdiction, i.e. within his diocese. Hence in 1290, after nobles forced the Bishop of Trent out of his diocese, he had to secure papal permission to exercise his jurisdiction from just outside it and proclaim excommunication and interdicts on his persecutors.[31]

[28] Anon. (*c*.1206) on 1 Comp. 1.22.un v. *sive metropoleos*, Brussels, Bibliothèque royale MS 1407–9, fol. 12vb: 'Metropolitanus de causis subditorum sui suffraganei potest cognoscere si causa defertur ad ipsum per appellationem ut hic, si negligens fuerit \episcopus/, ix. q. iii. Cum simus [C.9 q.3 c.3], si vacaverit episcopatus, ix. q. iii. Conquestus [C.9 q.3 c.8], quando clericus agit contra episcopum suum secundum quosdam; alii dicunt quod arbitri sunt obligandi in hoc, xi. q. i. Pervenit [C.11 q.1 c.39].' Vincentius Hispanus on 3 Comp. 1.20.5 v. *exceptis*, BAV, Vat. lat. MS 1378, fol. 27vb: 'Potest archiepiscopus iudicare de subditis sui suffraganei in casibus specialibus et in casu d. xii. De hiis [D.12 c.13]. Item ubi deliquit in diocesi eius, vi. q. iii. Placuit [C.6 q.3 c.4], vel si habet predium, supra. de foro compe. Sane. lib. i. [1 Comp. 2.2.4], vel tenet feudum ab eo, supra. de iud. Ceterum. lib. i. [1 Comp. 2.1.7]. Item si criminalis causa est inter episcopum et suum subditum, vi. q.ii. c.i [C.6 q.2 c.1] … Item ubi lis est inter episcopum et subditum suum in civili, xi. q.i. Si clericus [C.11 q.1 c.46]'. Tancred on 2 Comp. 5.13.4 v. *aliquid*, BAV, Vat. lat. MS 1377, fol. 141vb: 'Ar. quod archiepiscopus non est iudex ordinarius totius provincie … La<urentius> notavit in illa decretali "Pastoralis" [Po. 2350], quod est iudex ordinarius totius sed non cuiuslibet, vel est iudex omnium sed habet iurisdictionem impeditam an est pro eo. infra. de prescrip. Cum ex officii. lib. iii. [3 Comp. 2.17.6]. Mihi autem videtur quod non est iudex in diocesibus suorum suffraganeorum, nisi in casibus supradictis ut expresse dicit illa decretalis "Pastoralis". t.' Id. on 3 Comp. 3.5.9 v. *excommunicationis*, BAV, Vat. lat. MS 1377, fol. 223rb: 'Ideo valet hec sententia excommunicationis ab archiepiscopo in subditos suffraganeorum suorum lata quia delegatus domini pape fuit in hac parte, vel quia consensus episcopi loci accessit ut supra patet, alias esset contra, supra. ix. q. ii. Nullus primas, et supra. de of. iudicis ordina. Pastoralis. lib. e. [C.9 q.2 c.3, 3 Comp. 1.20.5] t.'

[29] Reg. Innocent IV, nos. 1625, 1652–8; Po. 12062.

[30] Vincentius Hispanus on X 5.39.52 v. *promulgata*, BAV, Vat. lat. MS 2546, fol. 243va: 'Potest ergo metropolitanus suspendere suffraganeum suum, ut hic, et excommunicare, xviii(?). di. De hiis. v. q.iii. Si egrotans [D.12 c.13, C.5 q.3 c.1], sed subditum eius non. supra. de offi. ord. Pastoralis [X 1.31.11].' Goffredus de Trano, *Summa*, p. 109 (*De officio ordinarii*, §6).

[31] Reg. Nicholas IV, no. 2616.

A bishop had power to discipline his subjects once his metropolitan confirmed his election according to a decretal of Celestine III (1191–8); therefore
a bishop-elect might excommunicate and interdict in his diocese even before
his consecration.[32] The power to excommunicate indeed pertained to jurisdiction (conferred by confirmation) and not orders (received at consecration), as
Laurentius Hispanus and later canonists observed.[33] And this distinction was
applied in practice; Innocent IV affirmed that an Archbishop-elect of Cologne
had sufficient ordinary jurisdiction to correct wrongdoers in his diocese, even by
interdicting their lands.[34]

A bishop's judicial power was, however, subject to a constitutional limitation.
In several decretals incorporated in canon law Alexander III had exhorted prelates
not to administer their churches without their chapter's advice, and his decretal
'Pervenit' specifically required them not to lay interdicts 'sine iudicio capituli'.[35]
Hence by the early thirteenth century canonists generally agreed that an interdict
laid by a bishop without his chapter's consent was invalid. Exceptions to this
rule were allowed only by privilege or special custom according to Tancred.[36]
Clearly the chapter was meant to restrain its prelate from arbitrary and excessive
sentences, and Hermann de Minden argued in his treatise on the interdict (1270)
that the chapter's consent was especially necessary when the bishop intended to
impose a perpetual or long-lasting interdict.[37]

It was a far more complex issue whether the chapter had the power to
interdict without its bishop. As canonistic doctrine had reserved this power
to those exercising ecclesiastical jurisdiction, the key point was whether this
included chapters. Canonists increasingly perceived that a bishop derived his
jurisdiction from his chapter through its electing him and thus this authority
devolved to the chapter in a vacancy. Rufinus had argued that a chapter might
exercise its bishop's judicial powers *sede vacante*. In 1184 Lucius III's decretal 'Ad
abolendam' reinforced this view when it assigned the episcopal role of judging

---

[32] 2 Comp. 1.3.7 (= X 1.6.15). See Benson, 108–15, esp. 111–12.

[33] Tancred on 2 Comp. 1.3.7 v. *excommunicationi*, BAV, Vat. lat. MS 1377, fol. 103ra:
'Confirmatus ergo excommunicare potest non solum electus in episcopum sed electus in abbatem,
ut infra. de simonia. Sicut nobis. lib. iii. [3 Comp. 5.2.5]. Unde patet quod excommunicare
iurisdictionis est non ordinis, unde et visitator ecclesie excommunicare potest, cum liberam habeat
administrationem, ut supra. vii. q.i. Quamvis triste [C.7 q.1 c.14] ... La<urentius>.' Also quoted
by Vincentius Hispanus on X 1.6.15 v. *confirmatione*, BAV, Vat. lat. MS 6769, fol. 19vb, and
Goffredus de Trano on X 1.6.15 v. *statuendi habeas*, Vienna, Nationalbibliothek MS 2197, fol. 8vb.

[34] Reg. Innocent IV, no. 354.

[35] 1 Comp. 3.9.4–5 (= X 3.10.4–5); 1 Comp. 5.27.1 (= X 5.31.1).

[36] Tancred on 3 Comp. 1.3.4 v. *interdicto*, BAV, Vat. lat. MS 1377, fol. 152vb: 'Ad hoc
dicendum quod nec episcopus nec aliquis inferiorum prelatorum potest hoc facere sine consensu
capituli sui, nisi hoc optineat ex privilegio vel consuetudine speciali iam prescripta, ar. ad hec xv.
q. vii. Episcopus nullius causam et supra. de excessibus prelatorum. Ad hec. lib. i. [C.15 q.7 c.6, 1
Comp. 5.27.1] t.'

[37] Hermann de Minden, 'De interdictis', §17 (fol. 345va). Cf. Johannes Calderinus, 'De
interdicto', Pt 1 §55 (fol. 328rb).

heretics to chapters in vacancies.[38] From the early thirteenth century canonists hence understood that the bishop's jurisdictional power might revert to his chapter, and one French canonist (*c.*1206) even inferred that the chapter might excommunicate in a vacancy (and presumably also interdict).[39] But in practice various arrangements existed for the administration of vacant dioceses, and often it fell to the bishop's official, his deputy in judicial affairs, to exercise episcopal jurisdiction *sede vacante* not the chapter.

Outside of vacancies canon law appeared to deny that chapters might exercise jurisdiction. Celestine III's decretal 'Quesivit' (*c.*1191–5) ruled that canons might not impose interdicts without the consent of their bishop and the rest of their cathedral chapter. It was the converse of Alexander III's ban on episcopal interdicts laid without the chapter's consent, and like that ban it was subject to exceptions.[40] A decretal of Innocent III suggested in 1206 that a dean and chapter might interdict, but Goffredus de Trano's commentary on this decretal doubted whether a chapter might interdict or excommunicate 'iure ordinario' unless it held this power by custom or privilege.[41] In 1208 another decretal of Innocent III had recognized that a dean might interdict even without his chapter's consent, but canonists likewise qualified this ruling. Johannes Teutonicus noted that it went against canon law, notably 'Quesivit', but he admitted that a dean might interdict by special custom, and Vincentius Hispanus argued that he might do so by a special privilege of his church. Such views were widely held among canonists by the mid-thirteenth century and they reflected contemporary practice.[42] As early as 1232 a bishop had allowed his chapter to use excommunication and interdict against wrongdoers in his diocese, and subsequently popes granted certain deans and chapters the power to interdict. Such papal grants usually justified this as a means of self-defence against those violating their property,

[38] Rufinus, *Summa* on D.23 c.1 (Ed. p. 52); 1 Comp. 5.6.11 (= X 5.7.9). See Benson, 85, 106, and Tierney, 127–30.

[39] Anon. on 1 Comp. 5.6.11 v. *sede vacante*, Brussels, Bibliothèque royale MS 1407–9, fol. 79ra: 'Quia sede vacante clerici bene possunt excommunicare, cum potestas episcopi devoluta sit ad capitulum, lxv. d. Si forte [D.65 c.9].' Cf. Jacobus de Albenga on 5 Comp. 1.18.1 v. *pro bono pacis*, London, BL, Royal MS 11.C.vii, fol. 251ra: 'Igitur videtur quod de iure communi vacante ecclesia, prelati transferatur potestas ad capitulum ... sicut vacante sede capitulum potest absolvere excommunicatos, ut supra. de hereticis. Ad abolendam. lib. i. [1 Comp. 5.6.11] et alia facere'.

[40] 2 Comp. 3.9.2 (= X 3.11.2).

[41] 3 Comp. 1.3.4 (= X 1.4.5). Goffredus de Trano on X 1.4.5 v. *vel a vobis*, Vienna, Nationalbibliothek MS 2197, fol. 6va: 'Capitulum, autem, non credo quod ordinario iure possit excommunicare vel interdicere, nisi hoc ei competat ex privilegio vel consuetudine'.

[42] 3 Comp. 2.19.13 (= X 2.28.55). Johannes Teutonicus on 3 Comp. 2.19.13 v. *promulgavit* (Ed. p. 358); copied by Tancred, ibid. v. *interdictum*, BAV, Vat. lat. MS 1377, fol. 218ra. Vincentius Hispanus, ibid. v. *cessaretur*, BAV, Vat. lat. MS 1378, fol. 55va: 'credo quod hoc <excommunicare> potest decanus ex speciali privilegio ecclesie illius.' Cf. Goffredus de Trano on X 2.28.55 v. *interdictum*, Vienna, Nationalbibliothek MS 2197, fol. 75ra: 'Erat enim de consuetudine illius ecclesie ut decanus posset eam subicere interdicto, quod tamen erat contra ius scriptum'. Cf. also Innocent IV, *Apparatus*, ibid. v. *post modicum tempus*; Bernard de Montmirat, ibid. v. *appellavit*, BAV, Vat. lat. MS 2542, fol. 52rb (Ed. fol. 90rb); Hostiensis, *Lectura*, ibid. v. *decanus episcopum monuisset* (vol. 1, fol. 191vb). Reg. Gregory IX, no. 891.

persons, and liberties. A decretal of Innocent IV to the dean of Orléans conceded that he might protect himself against the temporal power by the spiritual sword; hence the dean's use of excommunication and interdict against a *ballivus* who had seized his property was lawful. Innocent reissued this decretal as an addition to canon law in 1251 and it entered the *Liber sextus*, but canonists did not see it as a revocation of 'Quesivit'.[43] Johannes Andreae maintained the traditional view that the dean held this *potestas fulminandi* by custom or privilege. Indeed late-thirteenth-century popes had continued to grant this power of self-defence to certain deans and chapters as a special freedom.[44]

Such a freedom was symptomatic of the growing autonomy of chapters during the thirteenth century, and they increasingly claimed the power to exercise jurisdiction independently of their bishop. This inevitably caused friction with prelates, especially when a dean and chapter laid an interdict. For example shortly before 1208 the Bishop of Auxerre had jailed and excommunicated a priest for an alleged misdemeanour, but the dean of Auxerre claimed jurisdiction over the priest, requiring the latter's transfer to his custody. When the bishop refused, the dean convened the chapter and, despite its opposition, interdicted the cathedral so that services were to cease there whenever the bishop was present. But this sentence was overruled since the bishop appealed to his metropolitan, the Archbishop of Sens. The dean still tried to enforce the interdict by disrupting services held in the bishop's presence and even excommunicating the bishop's chaplain for chanting the offices; hence the bishop excommunicated the dean. The dean retaliated by reissuing his interdict, this time with the chapter's support, and ordering its observance. Ultimately the case was referred to Innocent III, who quashed the sentences issued by both sides. Innocent did not dispute the dean's right to lay this interdict, in effect against his superior, but after his judgement entered canon law, mid-thirteenth-century canonists expressed concern about the sentence, especially its effect on the bishop's flock.[45] They agreed that the bishop had appealed against the interdict so that his subjects might receive the sacraments, hear the offices, and be instructed in the faith, since he was accountable for their spiritual welfare.[46] In addition Hostiensis thought it monstrous that a subordinate might presume to castigate and even punish a superior contrary to clerical obedience, and Innocent IV had agreed that the dean was not the bishop's judge in this case, but added that he might protest against

[43] Coll. III. 41 (= VI 5.11.6). Johannes Andreae, *Glossa* on VI 5.11.6 v. *decano*.

[44] Reg. Martin IV, no. 381; Reg. Nicholas IV, nos. 2740, 4092.

[45] Innocent III, Reg. 10, no. 189; see n. 42 above.

[46] Bernard de Montmirat on X 2.28.55 v. *se et suum*, BAV, Vat. lat. MS 2542, fol. 52ra (Ed. fol. 90ra): 'Vide formam appellationis: appellat episcopus pro se et suis subditis ... quia subditi tenentur ab episcopo recipere sacramenta ... et divina officia audire in ecclesiis, per que populus reddatur bene instructus in fide. Et si minus bene instructus esset, episcopus tenetur reddere rationem ... unde ne ecclesia interdicatur in qua populus instruitur, potest episcopus pro se et suis subditis appellare'. Cf. Innocent IV, *Apparatus*, ibid. v. *civitatis*, and Hostiensis, *Lectura*, ibid. v. *decanus episcopum monuisset* (vol. 1, fol. 191vb).

a legitimate grievance. This concern to balance the rights of both bishop and chapter was reflected in another papal judgement on a similar case in 1290.[47] The dean and chapter of Lyon enjoyed a papal grant to use the spiritual sword against anyone doing them injury (like Innocent IV's concession to the dean of Orléans), but they turned this weapon against their archbishop as their alleged persecutor. He sought papal arbitration, and Nicholas IV confirmed both the grant to the dean and chapter *and* their archbishop's position as head of his church, so that they might not use the spiritual sword against him and any excommunication, suspension, or interdict they declared on him were void. Probably it was to curb such abuses that thirteenth-century canon law and canonists did not admit that every dean and chapter had an inherent power to interdict.

A related power that some chapters also held by custom or privilege was that of imposing a *cessatio a divinis*. It is often difficult to distinguish in practice whether a chapter was observing an interdict or *cessatio* on its church, as in the Auxerre case, before these sanctions were more sharply differentiated in the mid-thirteenth century. The effects of a *cessatio* and interdict were similar, and likewise chapters were meant to use a *cessatio* in self-defence but turned it against superiors. As in the cases above the consequent breakdown in relations often meant papal arbitration was required. In 1287 Honorius IV tried to settle a dispute between the bishop and chapter of Châlons-sur-Marne which had resulted in a particularly dramatic *cessatio*. The bishop claimed that when his archbishop came to consecrate him, the canons barricaded the doors of the cathedral and its bell-tower and removed the service books, so that the bells could not be rung to call the people or mass celebrated. According to the chapter the bishop had the cathedral doors forced open and people and clergy assembled to hear him hold mass in defiance of the *cessatio*. The dispute and *cessatio* were still continuing twelve years later when Boniface VIII tried to resolve the matter.[48] The papacy had seen this use of the *cessatio* as an abuse and tried to curb it through legislation since 1215, not apparently altogether successfully (see pp. 109–11 below).

The papacy also sought to regulate the power to interdict among other clergy subordinate to bishops. Canon law had long recognized archdeacons as their bishop's deputies, who as *oculi episcopi* in the parishes might exercise correction on his behalf. Huguccio and other canonists thus understood that archdeacons held a *cura animarum* in a jurisdictional sense delegated by their bishops, though some canonists argued that it was attached to their office.[49] The former view

47 Reg. Nicholas IV, no. 2649.
48 Reg. Honorius IV, no. 767; Reg. Boniface VIII, no. 2912.
49 Tancred on 1 Comp. 1.15.4 v. *consuetudinis*, BAV, Vat. lat. MS 1377, fol. 11r: 'Hug<uccio> dixit quod archidiaconus non habet curam animarum nisi sibi demandetur ab episcopo, xvi. q. vii. Nullus [C.16 q.7 c.11], et respondet ad omnia capitula que videntur dicere quod habeat curam animarum quod intelliguntur ex delegatione et ita solvit contraria, s. e. t. Archidiaconis cum suis concordantiis [1 Comp. 1.15.5]. Bazianus vero contrarium dixit, scilicet quod habet curam

was underscored by Alexander III's decretal 'Archidiaconis', which ruled that archdeacons might not proclaim sentences without the consent and authority of bishops. Alanus Anglicus took this to mean that they might not excommunicate in their own right (*de iure*), but he and other canonists recognized that they might and did do so as a matter of custom (*de consuetudine*), and even other decretals of Alexander III supported this view.[50] It was officially endorsed when Gregory IX's decretal 'Dudum' (1228) conceded that an archdeacon imposed interdicts *de consuetudine* on parish churches under his supervision and this pertained to his *cura animarum*. The assumption of 'Archidiaconis' that an archdeacon derived his jurisdiction from his bishop was also challenged by another canonistic argument.[51] Tancred asserted that this ruling did not apply to archdeacons who were elected by the ecclesiastical body over which they presided, since the latter were judges ordinary and might excommunicate *de iure communi*. This view was widely adopted by subsequent canonists, including Goffredus, who argued that a prelate elected by a collegiate body held jurisdiction, and since jurisdiction was nothing without the power to coerce, any prelate holding it might excommunicate. But Innocent IV questioned this assumption and distinguished that although some archdeacons received jurisdiction from the body electing them, only bishops might grant them power to excommunicate.[52]

animarum eo ipso quod episcopus <qui> instituit eum dat ei generalem administrationem. Pro eo facit infra. de preben. Referente et s. e. t. Ut archidiaconus [1 Comp. 3.5.9, 1.15.2] cum suis concordantiis ... [fol. 11rb] ... Vinc<entius>. Ego puto opinionem Hug' prevalere, ar. infra. de exces. pre. Ad hec lib. e. infra. de instit. Cum venissent lib. iii. [1 Comp. 5.27.2, 3 Comp. 3.7.3] ... t.' The first part of the gloss is copied, as Tancred acknowledges, from Vincentius Hispanus, ibid. v. *cuilibet* (Leipzig Universitätsbibliothek MS 983, fol. 6va). This canonistic debate was later synthesized by Johannes Hispanus de Petesella, *Summa* on X 1.23, BAV, Vat. lat. MS 2353, fol. 150va; the latter agreed not with Tancred but with Laurentius Hispanus and Johannes Teutonicus that archdeacons held customary not delegated jurisdiction. On archdeacons as episcopal deputies see D.93 c.6 and D.88 c.7.

[50] 1 Comp. 1.15.5 (= X 1.23.5). Alanus Anglicus on 1 Comp. 1.15.2 v. *corrigat*, Munich, Bayerisches Staatsbibliothek Clm 3879, fol. 10rb: 'Ergo habet cohertionem archidiaconus, ar. infra. de iure pa. Cum seculum. infra. de ap. Reprehen. supra. de elec. et e. p. Cum in cunctis [1 Comp. 3.33.16, 2.20.42, 1.4.16], quod est verum, scilicet modicam, sine qua nulla est iurisdictio, ut ff. de officio eius cui man. est iuris l. ult. [Dig. 1.21.5]. Sed numquid potest excommunicare? Non credo de iure suo, ar. infra. e. c. ult. xvi. q. ii. Visis. in fi. xxiiii. q. iii. Corripiantur [1 Comp. 1.15.5, C.16 q.2 c.1, C.24 q.3 c.17]. De consuetudine, tamen, excommunicant archidiaconi secundum quam intellige omnia illa que dicunt quod potest excommunicare, ut extra. de iure pa. Cum seculum. de ap. Reprehen. et si qua sunt similia' (copied by Tancred; BAV, Vat. lat. MS 1377, fol. 10vb).
[51] X 1.6.54 §4.
[52] Tancred on 1 Comp. 1.15.5 v. *sententiam*, BAV, Vat. lat. MS 1377, fol. 11ra: 'Hoc ubi archidiaconi non eliguntur ab universitate cui presunt, sicut alicubi eliguntur, xciii. d. Legimus [D.93 c.24]. Quo casu cum iudex sit ordinarius, credo quod anathematizare possit de iure communi, ut infra. de of. iu. or. Cum ab ecclesiarum [1 Comp. 1.23.3], et quod hic dicitur'; Zoën cited this view on 5 Comp. 1.13.1 v. *starent* noting that 'in qua opinione sunt moderni doctores ut plene notatur xxv. di. Perlectis [D. 25 c.1] in quadam glosa Io<hannis> que incipit "hic videtur"' (Tours, Bibliothèque municipale MS 565, fol. 5va). Goffredus de Trano on X 1.23.5 v. *promulgare*, Vienna, Nationalbibliothek MS 2197, fol. 20vb: 'archidiaconus eligatur ab universitate, ut xciii. di.

This canonistic controversy reflected the archdeacon's increasingly ambiguous position in practice. By the late thirteenth century many archdeacons established their own courts and tried to make these independent of their bishops, but the latter equally tried to resist such encroachments on their jurisdiction.[53] A case referred to Boniface VIII in 1301 indicates how archdeacons might assert their claim to impose sentences not as episcopal judges delegate but *ex officio*. The case involved a property dispute between the Franciscan convent of Burgos and Benedictine abbey of San Domenico de Silos. The monks had evicted the friars from a house allegedly belonging to their abbey. But the friars claimed that it was theirs, complaining to the local bishop that the monks had seized books and other things of theirs from it. He ordered restitution of these goods on pain of excommunication and interdict. But the friars had also made this complaint to the Archdeacon of Polenzuela, in whose archdeaconry both the friary and abbey lay; hence he claimed jurisdiction over the case *de consuetudine*. When the monks allegedly ignored his summons, he excommunicated the abbot, prior, and other monks and interdicted the abbey. The bishop only intervened at his request when the monks disregarded his sentences, which suggests that the bishop respected his claim over the case.[54]

The power of a *plebanus* to impose sentences was also increasingly recognized from the late twelfth century. *Plebani*, known in England as rural deans and elsewhere as archpriests, came to handle more and more judicial matters in this period, at least in England.[55] Indeed a decretal of Alexander III included in canon law ordered that if a *plebanus* imposed excommunication or interdict *rationabiliter* on a parishioner of his, his bishop was to observe them as sentences declared by prelates on wrongdoers that were binding.[56] Alanus Anglicus was apparently the only canonist to deny that a *plebanus* thereby had power to excommunicate and interdict *ex officio* under canon law; rather Alanus held that, like an archdeacon, a *plebanus* might only impose such sentences by a special indulgence or approved custom. Most canonists immediately recognized this decretal as an important statement of general principle, affirming the right to interdict and excommunicate as a judicial prerogative of prelates. Laurentius defined a prelate as the head of a church elected by its clergy, and under this decretal, he argued, any prelate was a judge ordinary, even if subject to a bishop, and had jurisdiction to hear cases and excommunicate, and this included a *plebanus*.[57] Tancred adopted his views and canonists generally accepted them by

---

Legimus [D. 93 c.24], et qui ab universitate eligitur habet iurisdictionem, ut in aut. de defensa. civi. §Nos igitur coll. iii. [Nov. 15 pref.]. Si habet iurisdictionem, ergo potest excommunicare, ut infra. de of. del. Ex litteris [X 1.29.29]'. Innocent IV, *Apparatus* on X 1.23.5 v. *sententiam excommunicationis*.

[53] See e.g. Brundage, 'Cambridge Faculty', 36–41.   [54] Reg. Boniface VIII, no. 4112.
[55] Cheney, *Becket*, 146–7.   [56] 1 Comp. 1.23.3 (= X 1.31.3).
[57] Alanus on 1 Comp. 1.23.3 v. *tulerit*, Munich, Bayerisches Staatsbibliothek Clm 3879, fol. 14vb: 'Quod licuit ei ex speciali indulgentia vel consuetudine approbata. Alias de iure

the mid-thirteenth century.[58] They were no doubt responding to contemporary practice, at least in England where 'much [judicial] business fell to [*plebani*] which in a more highly developed bureaucracy went to full-time officials'.[59] Officials were episcopal deputies who came to administer a bishop's court on his behalf; even archdeacons' courts were run by their own officials in time. Though officials gained competence over cases formerly passed to *plebani*, canon law did not grant them the latters' power to interdict *ex officio*. A constitution of Boniface VIII, based on an earlier ruling of Alexander IV, forbade officials to impose penalties, including interdicts, unless the power to do so was specifically delegated to them.[60]

Outside the hierarchy of secular clergy the heads of monastic houses certainly had powers of ecclesiastical discipline, but early-thirteenth-century canonists debated whether they included excommunication, and thus interdict. Tancred summarized this debate: Alanus and others reserved *de iure* power to excommunicate to bishops and claimed that it might only extend to abbots by privilege or custom; this was consistent with Alanus's similarly conservative views on archdeacons and *plebani*. But Tancred agreed with Johannes Teutonicus that abbots and priors fitted Laurentius's definition of a prelate (they were elected by the clergy over whom they presided) and thus held jurisdiction and might excommunicate.[61] Tancred, Johannes, and some later canonists also agreed that

communi plebanus non habet potestatem excommunicandi, quia nec archidiaconus, supra. de officio archid. c. ult [1 Comp. 1.15.5].' Cf. Vincentius Hispanus on 1 Comp. 1.15.3 v. *voluit*, Leipzig Universitätsbibliothek MS 983, fol. 6va: 'Eo quod episcopus iurisdictionem committit archidiacono intelligitur committere etiam archipresbitero.' Tancred on 1 Comp. 1.23.3 v. *firma*, BAV, Vat. lat. MS 1377, fol. 14va: 'Hoc tenendum quilibet prelatus collegiate ecclesie, licet subsit episcopo, est iudex ordinarius et habet iurisdictionem de causis cognoscendi et excommunicandi, in aut. de defensoribus civitatum §ii. et hic et xv. q.iiii. c.i, ar. infra. de iudic. c. ii, ar. C. de iur. dic. o. iu. l. ult. [Nov. 15.2, C.15 q.4 c.1, 1 Comp. 2.1.2, Cod. 3.13.7]. Illum autem dico prelatum qui ab universitate vel collegio eligitur, ar. s. de elect. c.i etc. [1 Comp. 1.4.1] la<urentius>.'

[58] See n. 57 on Tancred. Vincentius Hispanus on X 1.31.3, BAV, Vat. lat. MS 6769, fol. 50va: 'Possunt ergo isti excommunicare, xvi. q. i. Alia est causa [C.16 q.1 c.6], ergo iudices ordinarii sunt, infra. de iudic. c.i ar. xxiiii. di. Quando [X 2.1.1, D.24 c.5], et habent curam animarum, supra. de elect. Cum in cunctis [X 1.6.7].' Goffredus de Trano on X 1.23.5 v. *promulgare* (as n. 52): 'Sed cum plebanus habeat iurisdictionem, qui minor est archidiacono, excommunicare possit, ut infra. de off. ord. Cum ab ecclesiarum [X 1.31.3].' Cf. id. *Summa* on X 1.23 (Ed. p. 87); Innocent IV, *Apparatus* on X 1.31.3 v. *prelates*. Bernard de Montmirat on X 1.31.3, BAV, Vat. lat. MS 2542, fol. 25rb; Borgh. lat. MS 231, fol. 37va (Ed. fol. 43rb). Petrus Bonetus on X 1.31.3, BAV, Borgh. lat. MS 228, fol. 57vb: 'Casus. Archipresbyter et plebanus excommunicat vel etiam interdicit qui etiam collegio preest.'

[59] Cheney, *Becket*, 147.

[60] VI 1.13.2. Johannes Andreae, *Glossa*, ibid., noted a precedent in Alexander IV's decretal 'Dudum (dilectis filiis)'. Cf. Reg. Nicholas IV, no. 7351.

[61] Tancred on 2 Comp. 3.18.6 v. *sententias*, BAV, Vat. lat. MS 1377, fol. 126rb; Borgh. lat. MS 264, fol. 89rb; Vat. lat. MS 2509, fol. 120va: 'Excommunicationis. Potest enim abbas cohercere eum, alias iurisdictio nulla esset, ut ff. de officio eius cui mandata est iurisdictio l. ult. [Dig. 1.21.5]. Quod autem possit excommunicare quibusdam placet. Alii contra, inter quos magister Ala<nus>, vero enim iure hoc ad episcopum spectat, ar. xxiiii. q. iii. Corripiantur, xvi. q. ii. Visis in fi., ar. contra ii. q. i. Nemo [C.24 q.3 c.17, C.16 q.2 c.1, C.2 q.1 c.11]. Illi ergo dicunt quod hoc esset ex

abbots received this power to excommunicate on the confirmation of their election, in the same way as bishops. Vincentius even classified abbots as judges ordinary like bishops.[62] But no canonist pretended that regular prelates might operate courts *ex officio* and impose canonical penalties in judgements on cases. A decretal of Innocent III (1211) decried abbots in Perugia diocese for venturing into matrimonial cases beyond their competence and excommunicating and interdicting their bishop's subjects. Canonists generally restricted abbots' and priors' use of such penalties to the correction of monks subject to their authority for deviations from monastic obedience. Innocent III approved this in his decretal 'Cum in ecclesiis', and in another decretal of 1198 he reserved this power of correction to abbots and priors unless their negligence necessitated the local ordinary's intervention.[63] The thirteenth-century papal registers do not record such use of interdicts probably since there was no appeal from monastic correction, but sometimes they include papal grants to abbots of extraordinary powers to interdict. They were usually meant as a defensive measure in common with similar grants to deans and chapters. In 1286 Honorius IV confirmed a grant of Celestine III in 1192 which allowed the abbots of Cluny to impose excommunication and interdict on any from the province of Lyon who did them and their abbey wrong, if the bishops and prelates of these wrongdoers failed to correct them when requested three times.[64]

If the power to interdict was normally circumscribed for abbots and priors, it was denied altogether to abbesses and prioresses. A decretal of Celestine III (1191–8) stated that owing to her sex an abbess might not absolve nuns from excommunication. Alanus, who appended this ruling to his decretal collection,

---

privilegio vel ex consuetudine A<lanus>. Michi videtur quod omnes prelati qui per electionem collegio creantur hoc possunt, ar. hic et supra. de appell. Reprehensibilis lib. i, supra. de officio iudicis or. Cum ab ecclesiarum lib. i, supra. de iure patro. Cum seculum, infra. de institutionibus. Cum venissent lib. iii, xxiiii. q.iii. De illicita, infra. de symonia. Sicut nobis lib. iii [1 Comp. 2.20.42, 1.23.3, 3.33.16, 3 Comp. 3.7.3, C.24 q.3 c.6, 3 Comp. 5.2.5] t.'

[62] See n. 33. Vincentius Hispanus on 3 Comp. 1.20.1, BAV, Vat. lat. MS 1378, fol. 27va: 'exequi. Ar. quod abbates et priores possunt excommunicare suos subiectos ... compellas. Hoc est hic notabile quod correctio monachorum, ut abbas est negligens, defertur ad episcopum. Primo loco defertur abbati, ar. supra. <de ap.> Reprehensibilis lib. i [1 Comp. 2.20.42] ... sentio abbates esse iudices ordinarios non solum episcopum, supra. de of. prela. Cum ab ecclesiarum lib. i. et supra. de iud. c.ii. lib. i [1 Comp. 1.23.3, 2.1.2] dummodo sit creatus ab aliqua universitate, ad illud c. De persona [D.65 c.4].' Cf. Johannes on 3 Comp. 1.20.1 v. *si prelati* (Ed. p. 134; copied by Tancred, ibid., BAV, Vat. lat. MS 1377, fol. 181ra); and on 4 Comp. 1.14.2 v. *excommunicationis*, BAV, Vat. lat. MS 1377, fol. 289va: 'Nota quod prior potest excommunicare monachum, sic et electus in abbatem, supra. de symo. Sicut. lib. iii [3 Comp. 5.2.5].'

[63] 4 Comp. 1.14.2 (= X 1.33.10), 2.10.2. Johannes Teutonicus on 4 Comp. 2.10.2 v. *supponebant*, BAV, Vat. lat. MS 1377, fol. 295va: 'Quod solus episcopus potest, supra. de his. que fi. a ma. parte ca. Quesivit [2 Comp. 3.9.2].' See Johannes and Vincentius in n. 62. Goffredus de Trano on X 1.33.10 v. *excommunicationis*, Vienna, Nationalbibliothek MS 2197, fol. 26vb: 'Possunt igitur abbates et priores excommunicare ut hic et infra. de symo. Sicut [X 5.33.3]. Correctio enim monachorum ad ipsos pertinet, ut supra. e. t. Quanto [X 5.33.26]'.

[64] Reg. Honorius IV, no. 410. Cf. Reg. Nicholas IV, no. 7362.

thus doubted whether she might excommunicate deviant nuns in the first place.[65] However, Vincentius thought that an abbess held jurisdiction as she was elected by her convent and thus, according to canonistic doctrine, a prelate. He even conceded that she might impose an interdict *ab ingressu ecclesie*.[66] Honorius III's decretal 'Dilecta' (1222) also recognized that an abbess had power to discipline disobedient subjects, but it ruled that she might not excommunicate them. This settled the issue definitively. It rapidly passed into canon law and its earliest commentator Jacobus de Albenga explained its doctrinal rationale: women might not exercise the power of the keys, for Christ had conferred the keys on men, namely the apostles, but not women, notably the blessed Virgin; hence abbesses had no power to loose and bind, in the jurisdictional or penitential sense, and therefore might not excommunicate or absolve.[67] Celestine III's ruling on absolution alluded to this argument, and it is still invoked against female ordination in the modern Catholic Church. It was adopted by all subsequent commentators on 'Dilecta', including Pierre Sampsona, who observed that women might not impose an interdict or suspension, as these were reserved to prelates as heirs to the keys of St Peter. Canonists, including Innocent IV, generally agreed that abbesses might not interdict, albeit Vincentius had conceded that they might 'interdict' their chaplains from celebrating divine offices.[68]

[65] Decretal edited by von Heckel, 'Gilbertus und Alanus', 317–18; cf. 3 Comp. 5.21.6 (= X 5.39.33). Alanus on Alan. 5.22.5, Vercelli Cathedral Chapter MS 89, fol. 128ra: 'solvere. Sed numquid abbatissa potest sororem incorrigibilem excommunicare ... disciplinam. Que abbatisse reservanda est.'

[66] Vincentius on 1 Comp. 1.4.17 v. *abbatissa*, Leipzig Universitätsbibliothek MS 983, fol. 2vb: 'Que iurisdictionem habet ratione officii, et hoc quia creatur ab uni<versi>tate et habet iurisdictionem a lege, in aut. de defensoribus civita. l. xiiii [Nov. 15.6?], si in plebibus et infra. de of. Cum ab ecclesiarum lib. e., si cum et quandoque femina habet ex consuetudine, infra. de arbitris. Cum dilecti lib. iii. [3 Comp. 1.25.3] et potest hic interdicere ingressum ecclesie et egressum, xviii. q. ii. Diffinimus [C.18 q.2 c.21].'

[67] 5 Comp. 1.18.3 (= X 1.33.12). Jacobus de Albenga, ibid. v. *compellas*, London, BL, Royal MS 11.C.vii, fol. 251rb: 'Quidam dicunt quod non potest excommunicare quia nec etiam absolvere potest, ut ex. iii. de senten. ex. De monialibus [3 Comp. 5.21.6], et est hoc propter fragilitatem sexus ... tu dicas hanc esse rationem quare mulier excommunicare non possit, quia non sexui femineo sed virili tradite fuerunt claves regni celorum, quia licet beata virgo dignior <et> excellentior fuerit apostolis universis, non tamen ipse sed apostolis tradidit deus claves regni celorum. Unde cum mulier claves non habeat, sed vir tantum, non potest mulier claudere vel aperire, unde nec excommunicare nec absolvere potest, extra. iiii. de pe. et re. c. Nova quedam [4 Comp.5.14.1] Iac.'

[68] Pierre Sampsona on X 1.33.12 v. *suspendat*, Vienna, Nationalbibliothek MS 2083, fol. 15rb; MS 2113, fol. 25ra: 'Abbatissa enim suspendere, interdicere, vel excommunicare non potest, nam ista tria ex collatione clavium facta beato Petro, et ipsum prelatis ecclesie, supra. e. Solite [X 1.33.6]'; this view was also adopted by his pupil Bernard de Montmirat, ibid. (Ed. fol. 46r). Cf. Pierre de Sampson (1267), *Distinctiones*, ibid., BAV, Pal. lat. MS 696, fol. 127v; Goffredus de Trano, ibid. v. *mandata*, Vienna, Nationalbibliothek MS 2197, fol. 26vb; Innocent IV, *Apparatus*, ibid. v. *suspendat*. Vincentius, ibid. v. *suspendat*, BAV, Vat. lat. MS 6769, fol. 53va: 'Concedo tamen quod abbatissa ex causa prohibere vel interdicere large capellanis ne celebrent vel accipiant portiones illa die, et ipsi sunt ab ea interdicti large, idest prohibiti, nec tamen sunt re vera prohibiti, suspensi, privati, vel interdicti.'

In order to determine whether prelates below bishops might excommunicate or interdict, canonists defined jurisdictional power as a prerequisite. Female prelates fell foul of this criterion at least by 1230, but even more significantly it posed a challenge for priests. Canonists noted that some ancient authorities in the *Decretum* affirmed the power of priests to excommunicate.[69] But by the late twelfth century many canonists argued that priests had no jurisdiction in the *foro externo*, except if delegated to them, and hence no *ex officio* power to excommunicate and indeed interdict as this pertained to the external forum.[70] According to Alanus priests might only exercise discipline in the internal or penitential forum. Hostiensis later suggested that the penitential forum retained the sanction of minor excommunication (significantly comparable in effect to a specific personal interdict), for he claimed that priests might still impose it to correct sinners; but 'this never became common teaching and was not the English custom'.[71]

No papal ruling specifically deprived priests of the *ex officio* power to interdict or excommunicate, but Celestine III's decretal 'Quesivit' forbade individual canons to interdict their cathedral without the consent of the bishop and the rest of their chapter. This ruling responded to the Bishop of Clermont's claim that some of his chapter had done so without this consent. Laurentius observed that canons in Spain and Italy were also accustomed to interdict churches.[72] Nevertheless Innocent IV's commentary on 'Quesivit' held that no valid custom might allow an individual canon to lay interdicts, even on parishioners of his prebend or their lands, for he held no jurisdiction and they were not his subjects but his bishop's. Subsequent canonists generally agreed, and it was also accepted

---

[69] Anon. on 1 Comp. 1.23.3, Brussels, Bibliothèque royale MS 1407–09, fol. 13ra: 'in clericos. Ar. quod sacerdos excommunicare potest clericos in sua parrochia constitutos. Similiter etiam monachos excommunicare potest in sua parrochia constitutos, lxxxi. d. Ad reatum, xvi. q. i. Alia [D.81 c.33, C.16 q.1 c.6] ... observare. Ecce quod presbyter auctoritate sua excommunicare potest, ii. q. i. Nemo [C.2 q.1 c.11].' Alanus on 1 Comp. 1.16.5 v. *cuncta*, Munich, Bayerisches Staatsbibliothek Clm 3879, fol. 11ra: 'Presbyter, autem, simplex de iurisdictione contentiosa nihil habet. Ubicumque invenitur habere, dicatur quod hoc ex speciali delegatione vel secundum iura antiquissima, ut ibi. ii. q. i. Nemo. xcv. Ecce [C.2 q.1 c.11, D.95 c.6]. De voluntaria iurisdictione habet penitentias iniungere.'

[70] Ricardus Anglicus on 1 Comp. 1.16.5 v. *opus exerceant*, BAV, Pal. lat. MS 696, fol. 12vb: 'Ar. quod archipresbyter vel presbyter iurisdictionem non habeat ... nam cum contentiosa iurisdictio consistat in iurgiis iurgium, ad episcopum et archidiaconum pertineant, ut d. xxv. Perlectis [D.25 c.1]. Patet quod sola voluntaria iurisdictio ad sacerdotes, non contentiosa, ii. q.i. Nemo, xi. q.i. Experientie [C.2 q.1 c.11 C.11 q.1 c.15], quia primum c. de presbyteris delegans intelligitur, secundum sub nomine presbyterorum intelligit episcopos. Non est contra infra. de officio. i. or. Cum ab ecclesiarum [1 Comp. 1.23.3], quoniam a specialis fuit indulgentia.' Cf. Alanus in n. 69 above.

[71] Hostiensis, *Summa* on X 5.39 §5; Logan, 14 n. 6.

[72] 2 Comp. 3.9.2 (= X 3.11.2). Tancred, ibid. v. *ecclesiam*, BAV, Vat. lat. MS 1377, fol. 122va: 'Et intellige hoc ubi canonicus non habet ius episcopale in ipsa ecclesia. Alias si haberet et eidem negaretur debitus census uel aliqua offensa excommunicatione digna perpetraretur, bene supponeret ecclesiam interdicto, ut fit in Hyspania et etiam in Italia ... La<urentius>.'

that canons might only interdict as a chapter.[73] Indeed the power to interdict was normally granted to them as a corporate body, notably during a vacancy.

From the late twelfth century popes and canonists tried to reserve the power to interdict to ecclesiastical judges, chiefly popes and bishops. But the formation of the Church's judicial machinery stimulated growing legal business that quickly exceeded the capacity of popes and bishops to deal with it all in person. They increasingly had to pass on some business to deputies, popes to their legates and judges delegate, and bishops to their archdeacons and *plebani*. The latter indeed acquired jurisdiction over parishes by custom if not by right. It was a canonistic commonplace that jurisdiction was nothing without coercion; hence the power to interdict was necessarily delegated with it.[74] Despite the withdrawal of this power from priests, individual canons, and female prelates, popes and canonists were quick to accept its extension to lesser prelates. But the severity of the interdict and the need to curb its arbitrary and excessive use meant that the papacy had to regulate the laying of interdicts in ways other than reserving the power to impose them to a specific but ever-growing body of clergy.

3.2 THE CANONICAL PROCEDURE

From the late twelfth century popes laid down procedural rules for excommunication, and these were largely applied to interdicts. First, according to Alexander III's canon 'Reprehensibilis' (1179) prelates needed to issue a warning before excommunicating their subjects. This ruling was meant to end the 'reprehensible custom' of bishops and archdeacons imposing excommunication without warning in cases where appeals were anticipated. This effectively denied the right of appeal since canonical procedure only permitted an appeal from excommunication before the sentence was laid and not afterwards.[75] Canonists recognized that 'Reprehensibilis' confirmed a principle stated in a ninth-century *Decretum* text: ecclesiastical punishment ought to be preceded by a warning.[76] As early as *c*.1173–4 Alexander III had applied this principle to interdicts. During one of Henry II of England's many quarrels with his sons, he had their

---

[73] Innocent IV, *Apparatus* on X 3.11.2 v. *non debes*. Quoted approvingly by Hostiensis, *Lectura*, ibid. v. *ecclesiam tuam* (vol. 2, fol. 49ra). Cf. Bernard de Montmirat, ibid., BAV, Vat. lat. MS 2542, fol. 57va; Borgh. lat. MS 231, fol. 86vb (Ed. fol. 100vb).

[74] This view was based on Dig. 1.21.5. Cited by Hostiensis, *Summa* on X 5.39 §5 (fol. 291rb), among others.

[75] Lat. Conc. III c.6 (= 1 Comp. 2.20.42; X 2.28.26). See pp. 249–54 below on the appeals procedure.

[76] C.12 q.2 c.21. Thus Ricardus Anglicus (*c*.1197) on 1 Comp. 4.1.13 v. *moneatis*, BAV, Pal. lat. MS 696, fol. 77ra: 'Nam amonitio debet precedere vindictam, ut infra. xii. q. ii. Indigne et supra. de appell. Cum sit contra [C.12 q.2 c.21, 1 Comp. 2.20.5] b<ernadus(?)>.' Ricardus is apparently citing a gloss of Bernard of Pavia, who compiled 1 Comp. (*c*.1191) and wrote a *Summa* on it. Cf. Alanus (n. 88).

wives abducted, and Alexander required him to release them within forty days of receiving his written warning to do so; otherwise an interdict would be placed on the province where the captives were held.[77] This case illustrates that even when wrongdoing was evident and hence an appeal was not at issue, a warning gave the guilty party a chance to correct their fault and so avoid the sentence. Indeed the aim of an interdict was not punitive but coercive; it was meant to persuade the guilty party to come to terms with the ecclesiastical authorities. Sometimes a threat of an interdict was enough to achieve this. In 1200, during the struggle between Otto of Brunswick and Philip of Swabia for the imperial throne, Otto complained to his chief supporter, Innocent III, that Hermann, landgrave of Thuringia, had defected to Philip, breaking his oath of allegiance to Otto; hence the pope ordered the Archbishop of Mainz to warn Hermann to keep his oath or be compelled to do so by a papal interdict and excommunication.[78] There is no proof that this threat was ever carried out but a letter of 1203 from Otto to the pope suggests that it had prompted Hermann's return to his service.[79] Interdicts were also threatened on other occasions but not laid apparently. In effect it was a last resort to be used only when warnings failed to move the guilty party. Indeed when Innocent III reprimanded Philip II of France in 1202 for his continued failure to leave his mistress and return to his wife, the pope observed that his kingdom was interdicted because of this only after frequent warnings.[80]

Despite 'Reprehensibilis', Alanus and a pupil of French canonist Petrus Brito still held in the 1200s that excommunication was still valid without a warning, even if the judge laying it thereby sinned.[81] However, Innocent III had written to Hungarian prelates in 1199 that if they imposed excommunication or interdict against retainers or councillors of their king without canonical warning, their sentences were not binding. His Fourth Lateran canon 'Sacro' (1215) reaffirmed this principle, forbidding anyone to impose excommunication without proper warning. It further required that warning be given before suitable persons who could attest to its existence if necessary. Anyone violating this canon was to incur an interdict *ab ingressu ecclesiae* for a month and, if appropriate, a fine, even if the excommunication that they had imposed was justified. And this was also understood to apply to interdicts, at least by 1298 if not before.[82] It provided safeguards

---

[77] 1 Comp. 4.1.13 (= X 4.1.11).   [78] Innocent III, *RNI*, no. 27; cf. ibid. nos. 120–1.

[79] Innocent III, *RNI*, no. 106; Krehbiel, 94.

[80] Innocent III, Reg. 5, no. 49; *Gesta* c.51 (*PL* 214.xcvi). Cf. Krehbiel, 127; Innocent III, Reg. 5, no. 66 (see n. 91); 7, no. 83.

[81] Anon. on 1 Comp. 2.20.42 v. *commonitione*, Brussels, Bibliothèque royale MS 1407–9, fol. 29vb: 'Que semper est necessaria, xii. q. ii. Indigne, ii. q. i. Si peccaverit [C.12 q.2 c.21, C.2 q.1 c.19]. Si tamen non premittatur, tenet excommunicatio, xi. q. iii. Si episcopus [C.11 q.3 c.40], sed peccat sic excommunicans, contra c. Veniens [1 Comp. 5.25.un.].' Alanus on Alan. 5.21.6 v. *non tenere*, Vercelli Cathedral Chapter MS 89, fol. 127ra: 'Sententia excommunicationis sine ammonitione vel iuris ordine omisso tenet, ut xi. q. i. c. i, ii et iii [C.11 q.1 c.1–3].'

[82] Hungary: Innocent III, Reg. 1, no. 511; cf. ibid. 10, no. 120. 'Sacro': Lat. Conc. IV c.47 (= 4 Comp. 5.15.5; X 5.39.48). See p. 106 on its application to interdicts.

for both ecclesiastical judges and their subjects. The latter might appeal against excommunication on the ground that it was laid without warning, but equally judges might challenge such appeals if they could produce witnesses to testify to their warning. The canonist Pierre Sampsona maintained that at least two such witnesses were needed, but Innocent IV had argued that one was sufficient besides the judge himself.[83] Nevertheless Innocent seemed more cautious in practice. In 1251 the Pope made careful provision so that the duke of Swabia could not deny being warned before he incurred papal sentences. The Archbishop of Vienne and Bishop of Grenoble were to warn him in person to make amends in two months for persecuting the church of Turin; otherwise they were to excommunicate him and interdict his lands.[84] If they failed to meet him, they were to issue this warning often at public gatherings in places where it might easily come to his attention.

But not all ecclesiastical authorities were this scrupulous in observing 'Sacro'. Within some ten years of its appearance, popes were responding to appeals to quash sentences laid without warning.[85] In 1237 Gregory IX had even had to instruct French archbishops and bishops to proceed with maturity and seriousness when pronouncing interdicts, since their king had claimed that some of them were laying interdicts on his land prematurely, presumably without warning.[86] The papacy clearly saw warnings as vital to curb such arbitrary sentences and ensure that excommunication and interdicts were only imposed in extreme necessity. Innocent IV even affirmed in a canon of the First Council of Lyon (1245) that if a judge excommunicated without warning those communicating with excommunicates, his sentence was invalid.[87] Canonists took an even stricter line. In the 1200s Alanus had taught that judges should issue a warning *three times* or at least once peremptorily before resorting to a sentence. Subsequent commentators on the Fourth Lateran ruling, including Johannes Teutonicus, generally agreed. In particular Pierre Sampsona and his pupil Bernard de Montmirat insisted that the three warnings be spaced at least a day apart.[88]

---

[83] Pierre Sampsona on X 5.39.48 v. *personis idoneis*, Vienna, Nationalbibliothek MS 2113, fol. 73ra: 'Sed quot personas sufficere? Dicit Innoc. quod una sufficit cum per unam possit probari monitio, supra. de testibus. In omni negotio [X 2.20.4]. Sed illa loquitur de monitione que fit in denunciatione, unde oportet esse duas personas adminus et sufficiunt, quia ubi numerus testium non adicitur, et c. iv. q. iv. §Item in criminali, versu "Nisi numerus" [C.4 q.4 *dictum post* c.2].' Innocent IV, *Apparatus*, ibid. v. *personis*. Bernard of Montmirat, ibid. v. *personis*, BAV, Borgh. lat. MS 231, fol. 135vb; MS 260, fol. 107va (Ed. fol. 150ra), also noted this difference of opinion between Innocent and his 'magister' Sampsona.

[84] Reg. Innocent IV, no. 5343.

[85] Reg. Honorius III, no. 5894; Reg. Gregory IX, no. 2289. Regular clergy were even granted immunity from excommunication and interdict laid without warning: Reg. Honorius III, nos. 1753, 2640.

[86] Reg. Gregory IX, no. 3901.   [87] Lugd. Conc. I c.12 (= Coll. III 38; VI 5.11.3).

[88] Alanus on 1 Comp. 2.20.5 v. *inrequisitum*, Munich, Bayerisches Staatsbibliothek Clm 3879, fol. 31rb: 'Sed nonne semper ammonitio debet precedere vindictam, ut xii. q.ii. Indigne [C.12 q.2 c.21] ... Melius puto aliquem dupliciter requiri, vel ad emendationem quod fieri debet cum triplici ammonitione ut xvi. q. ult. Omnes decime [C.16 q.7 c.5], vel ad iudicium, et hoc trinis edictis vel uno peremptorio, ut xxiv. q. iii. De illicita [C.24 q.3 c.6].' Johannes Teutonicus on 4 Comp. 5.15.5

Gregory X confirmed this idea as law in a canon of the Second Council of Lyon (1274), requiring judges to observe appropriate intervals of a few days between the three warnings or at least between the peremptory warning and the sentence. This was clearly meant to allow the guilty party time to reconsider their position. This canon required that a warning name the party at whom it was directed, lest there be any grounds for doubt. This canon was specifically designed to bolster the Lyon I canon on excommunication, but Boniface VIII ruled in 1298 that it also had to be observed strictly in regard to interdicts; otherwise they were considered invalid.[89] This ruling apparently had an immediate impact, so one Spanish case suggests. This was the dispute between the Franciscans of Burgos and monks of San Domenico de Silos referred to Boniface in 1301.[90] The Archdeacon of Polenzuela had summoned the monks *three times* to no avail before excommunicating them and interdicting their abbey. In fact repeated warnings before interdicts seem to have been observed for at least a century, as Innocent III demonstrated as early as 1202.[91]

Often a warning was attached to a summons before a church court. This gave the guilty party a formal opportunity to come to terms with the church authorities and so avoid an interdict. For example Innocent IV issued a summons at Lyon, calling on reprobate excommunicate Ponzard de Duno to obey ecclesiastical mandates and make amends by 29 June 1251; otherwise he would take further action against Duno. When Ponzard not only failed to represent himself before the pope but even seized Sienese merchants travelling on papal business, Innocent carried out his threat, interdicting all Ponzard's lands in Besançon and Lyon provinces and placing an ambulatory interdict on Ponzard. Boniface VIII likewise used threats of excommunication and interdict in 1296 to compel the citizenry of Verdun to represent themselves before him; this gave them the chance either to contest their bishop's charges against them or make amends for their alleged wrongs.[92]

If warning and summons went unheeded, an ecclesiastical judge might publish an interdict so that, as Johannes Teutonicus and later canonists said, 'ignorance would excuse nobody from observing it'.[93] Innocent III's decretal 'Ad hec' (1200) stated that it was unnecessary to notify all interested parties of an interdict by

---

v. *competenti*, BAV, Vat. lat. MS 1377, fol. 316va: 'Idest trina, ut xxiv q. iii. De illicita.' Pierre Sampsona on X 5.39.48 v. *ammonitione premissa*, Vienna, Nationalbibliothek MS 2113, fol. 73ra: 'Sed numquid dicitur quis ter monitus ... sine interpolatione iuris, videtur sic quia tales monitiones pro una sumuntur, xxxi. q. ii. Lotarius [C.31 q.2 c.4], quod Vin. non credit nam oportet adminus quod quelibet admonitio contineat unum diem, ut ff. de publico iud. Accusatore [Dig. 48.1.13].' Cf. Bernard de Montmirat, ibid. v. *competenti*, BAV, Borgh. lat. MS 231, fol. 135vb; MS 260, fol. 107va (Ed. fol. 150ra). Sampsona attributes this view to Vincentius but it has not been found in any of the latter's glosses on this canon.

[89] Lugd. Conc. II c.29 (= VI 5.11.9); VI 5.11.13.   [90] As n. 54 above.
[91] See n. 80. Cf. Reg. Innocent III 5, no. 66.
[92] Reg. Innocent IV, no. 5469; Reg. Boniface VIII, no. 1253. Cf. Reg. Nicholas IV, no. 2168.
[93] Johannes Teutonicus on 3 Comp. 1.4.1 v. *aut publice* (Ed. p. 33); Tancred had a similar view on 3 Comp. 1.4.1 v. *publice* and *observari*, BAV, Vat. lat. MS 1377, fol. 154va. Reg. Honorius IV, no. 807, required sentences against James of Aragon to be published by written proclamation nailed

special mandate or letter; anyone had to observe it who knew of it, Johannes Teutonicus observed, even by rumour alone.[94] The interdict on France, which this decretal concerned, was made known in both ways; a legate proclaimed it at a general council of French clergy, who could spread the news in their dioceses, and then he announced it to all prelates of the kingdom by letter. Usually executors of papal interdicts had to have them published in churches on Sundays and feast days, when parishioners would hear them.[95] Canon law required no solemnities for publication, but when an interdict was accompanied by the excommunication of those provoking it, proclamation with bell, book, and candle was often required.

Some papal interdicts had to be publicized not only in the area affected but also in neighbouring places. This is understandable given that a general interdict was meant to affect outsiders arriving in interdicted places and members of an interdicted people wherever they went. Thus after a legate had declared excommunication on the king of Navarre and an interdict on his land, Innocent III ordered these sentences to be published across Spain in 1198. But normally publication was limited to neighbouring dioceses.[96] In 1233 Gregory IX required that the excommunication of certain citizens of Bergamo and interdict on its churches be published on Sundays and feast days with bells and candles in all cities and places of Lombardy, Romagna, and the Marche.

Though Innocent III did not insist on written notice of interdicts, Innocent IV issued a canon at the First Council of Lyon requiring ecclesiastical judges to publish excommunication in writing, stating clearly the reason for the sentence. In addition the excommunicate might request a copy of the sentence, which the excommunicator had to provide within a month in the form of a public instrument or testimonial letter bearing his genuine seal, i.e. a formal document properly witnessed and authenticated. If the judge failed to comply with this request, he was to suffer automatic suspension and interdict *ab ingressu ecclesie* for a month. And if he participated in divine offices while under these penalties, he also incurred 'irregularity', which prevented him from receiving and exercising holy orders and was removable only by a papal dispensation. Presumably given that the other penalties were imposed by papal law, absolution from them was likewise reserved to the papacy. Innocent IV further ruled that the judge's superior might relax his invalid excommunication without the usual formalities, order him to compensate the party whom he excommunicated, and otherwise punish him to teach him the gravity of threatening excommunication *sine maturitate*

on the doors of the church where the Pope declared them so that 'none might feign ignorance'. Cf. Reg. Clement IV, no. 695; Reg. Nicholas IV, no. 2178.

[94] 3 Comp. 1.4.1 (= X 1.5.1). Johannes Teutonicus, ibid. v. *per speciale mandatum* (Ed. pp. 32–3); copied by Tancred, ibid. v. *mandatum* (BAV, Vat. lat. MS 1377, fol. 154va). Cf. Herman de Minden, 'De interdicto', §70 (fol. 346rb).

[95] France: *Gesta* c.51 (*PL* 214.xcvii). Proclamation in churches: Innocent III, Reg. 6, no. 190; 12, no. 77; etc.

[96] Innocent III, Reg. 1, no. 192; Reg. Gregory IX, no. 1668.

debita.[97] These penalties were comparable with those imposed under Innocent III's canon of 1215 for excommunication laid without warning, and they were likewise intended as deterrents against arbitrary sentences. Innocent IV added that they were also applicable to judges disregarding this constitution when laying sentences of interdict or suspension. And in common with Innocent III's canon it was not always observed. Over forty years after its appearance violations of it were so common that between 1289 and 1291 Nicholas IV gave several archbishops and bishops power to absolve and dispense prelates and clerks of their dioceses who incurred suspension and irregularity by issuing sentences 'sine scriptis contra tenorem constitutionis Innocentii pape IV'.[98]

Aside from these procedural formalities of warnings and publication, the basic prerequisite for a canonical sentence of excommunication or interdict, at least by 1215, was a 'manifest and reasonable cause'. In fact Innocent III had been warning prelates not to lay interdicts 'sine manifesta et rationabili causa' since becoming pope. In 1198 he granted St Vaast Abbey at Arras immunity from these arbitrary sentences after its monks complained that prelates involved in disputes with them laid interdicts on their churches, and he also ordered removal of these sentences.[99] Over the following fifteen years he made numerous grants of immunity from excommunication and interdict laid 'sine manifesta et rationabili causa', often in response to such appeals, occasionally to secular dignitaries and their lands, but usually to religious houses often as part of their exemption privileges.[100] That such an immunity had to be granted suggests that it was not yet a common right under canon law, but the principle was widely recognized for appeals against such sentences were even made by laity not granted this immunity. In 1211 the commune of Laon petitioned Innocent that their bishop-elect and clergy laid excommunications and interdicts on them, their lands, and households 'sine rationabili causa ac pretermisso iuris ordine'. He granted them immunity from such sentences for 'ecclesiastical censure ought not to oppress the innocent but correct the guilty', and in 1212 when they alleged that the same clergy violated this grant, he ordered the lifting of sentences 'temere promulgatas' on them.[101] Three years later at the Fourth Lateran Council he confirmed as law in his canon 'Sacro' that if a judge excommunicated his subject without manifest and reasonable cause, the aggrieved subject might appeal to a higher court which might order his absolution.[102] As he added, such a great

[97] Lugd. Conc. I c.19 (= Coll. III 36; VI 5.11.1).

[98] Reg. Nicholas IV, nos. 1241 (Mainz), 2379 (Lyon), 3115 (Oviedo), 3389 (Patti), 5062 (Salzburg).

[99] Innocent III, Reg. 1, no. 160; cf. ibid., no. 286.

[100] Innocent III, Reg. 1, no. 511 (see n. 82); 2, nos. 43, 70; 6, nos. 42, 115, 206; 7, nos. 30, 62; 8, no. 32; 10, nos. 33, 59, 68, 93, 120; 12, nos. 21, 52, 166; 13, nos. 51, 81; 14, nos. 45, 54, 63; 15, nos. 16, 100.

[101] Innocent III, Reg. 14, no. 63 ; 15, no. 124; 16, no. 57. Cf. id. Reg. 7, no. 151; 10, nos. 68, 85, 125.

[102] See n. 82 above.

penalty was not to be imposed for a trivial reason. And this ruling apparently also applied to interdicts, for in 1220 Honorius III forbade German prelates to lay interdicts on lands of their emperor, Frederick II, 'pro levi causa', ordering them to lift such sentences.[103]

By the thirteenth century it was a canonistic commonplace that anyone might be punished without guilt but not without cause, and popes were certainly concerned that a canonical penalty that largely affected the guiltless, the interdict, should appear justified.[104] However, as this German example indicates, Innocent III's canon did not secure immediate compliance, and following its appearance his successors continued to grant magnates and monasteries freedom from excommunication and interdict laid without manifest and reasonable cause.[105] In 1230 when Marseilles came under papal protection and gained this immunity, Gregory IX required its citizens to pay an annual tribute of a hundred gold coins for the privilege. Similarly in 1243–4 Innocent IV gave the Archbishop of Mainz and Bishops of Beauvais and Amiens immunity for five years from sentences laid by judges delegate without a specific mandate, for they stated that judges delegate often excommunicated, suspended, or interdicted them 'pro levi causa minus quam rationabiliter'.[106] Continuing requests for such immunities indicate that arbitrary sentences remained common and that 'Sacro' was not seen to give adequate protection against them, at least until the mid-thirteenth century when papal grants of such immunities cease.

Rules of procedure similar to those governing excommunication and interdict were also laid down by the thirteenth-century papacy regarding the *cessatio a divinis*. Another Fourth Lateran canon 'Irrefragibili' provided that if a chapter held a *cessatio* without manifest and reasonable cause, especially in contempt of its bishop, he might celebrate in the cathedral despite the *cessatio* and at his request his archbishop might intervene to correct the chapter. Clearly this ruling was designed to curb wilful abuse of a *cessatio* by chapters against ecclesiastical superiors, and it perhaps responded to complaints of prelates at the Fourth Lateran Council.[107] But, as Vincentius observed, if a chapter had a reasonable cause to hold a *cessatio*, their bishop had to observe it.[108]

Nevertheless misuse of the *cessatio* was still a cause for papal concern when Gregory X regulated its use further in the canon 'Si canonici' (1274). It required that before canons proceed to a *cessatio*, they should state its cause in a formal

---

[103] Reg. Honorius III, no. 2637.

[104] E.g. Raymond de Peñafort, *Summa*, III, 6 (p. 375b): 'Licite quis punitur sine culpa sed non sine causa'. See p. 18 above.

[105] Reg. Honorius III, nos. 324, 646, 1753, 2640, 5826, 5854; Reg. Gregory IX, nos. 432, 1972, 2795, 4278; Innocent IV, nos. 245, 437, 468, 812, 2351, 5040, 7887. In two of these instances (Reg. Honorius III, nos. 1753, 2640), the immunity also extended to sentences imposed without due canonical warning.

[106] Reg. Gregory IX, no. 432; Reg. Innocent IV, nos. 245, 437, 812.

[107] Lat. Conc. IV c.7 (= 4 Comp. 1.13.1; X 1.31.13).

[108] Vincentius on Lat. Conc. IV c.7 v. *absque manifesta et rationabili causa* (*Constitutiones*, 297).

document authenticated by their seals and send this to the party against whom the *cessatio* was directed.[109] In other words the provisions of Innocent IV's Lyon I canon concerning excommunication and interdict were extended to the *cessatio*.[110] If a chapter failed to comply or their cause was not canonical, they had to repay income received from their church during the *cessatio*. Conversely if a superior judged their cause canonical, he was to coerce the other party to compensate them and their church for loss of divine service. The canonist William Durand later argued (*c*.1289) that this compensation should even cover alms and offerings that the church and other religious foundations were deprived of during the *cessatio*, adding that he had introduced this practice into Italy and had it observed at Modena, Pisa, Forlì, and elsewhere while he was rector of the papal patrimony.[111] Clearly Gregory X's main concern was the negative effects of such ecclesiastical disputes for pastoral care, and a written warning of a *cessatio*, as of an interdict, was meant to give the parties a chance to settle their differences and thus avoid a suspension of religious services altogether. The *cessatio*, like the interdict and excommunication, was only to be used as a last resort and when justified.

This legislation on the *cessatio* was not wholly effective in containing tensions between bishops and their increasingly autonomous chapters, however. A case in point is the dispute between the Bishop-elect of Châlons-sur-Marne and his chapter that led to a *cessatio*. Both sides claimed to have observed the terms of 'Si canonici'.[112] They contradicted each other and only agreed on the dispute's cause: the jailing of a baker by the bishop's provost. The chapter alleged that they warned their bishop to free the baker and make amends to them, and that when he refused, they held a *cessatio*. But according to the bishop, when the dispute arose, he sent a representative to negotiate a settlement with them, offering to release the baker and make amends to them, but they rejected his offer and, despite his appeal to Rome, they began the *cessatio*. He asked Honorius IV to force them to resume their offices and make amends to him, punishing them for the *cessatio*, 'according to Gregory X's constitution'. In 1287 Honorius tried to arbitrate but Boniface VIII was still seeking to resolve the dispute in 1299.

Boniface himself recognized the need to tighten up current papal legislation on the *cessatio* in his constitution 'Constitutioni felicis recordationis' (4 April 1296).[113] It required that before the chapter or convent of a collegiate church held a *cessatio*, they should summon their absent members to determine by majority consent whether their cause was canonical. If this was agreed, the party occasioning the *cessatio* was to be notified of this cause, and in fifteen days, or such time as distance required, proctors were to represent both sides

---

[109] Lugd. Conc. II c.17 (= VI 1.16.2).   [110] Lugd. Conc. I c.19 (= Coll. III 36; VI 5.11.1).
[111] William Durand on Lugd. Conc. II c.17 v. *occasione* (fol. 60v).
[112] See p. 96 above and n. 48. Both sides claimed temporal jurisdiction over the baker.
[113] ASV, A. A. Arm. C. 139. It is discussed more fully and edited in my 'Two Constitutions'.

before the pope with all documents regarding the dispute and seek papal justice. Boniface also extended the penalties in Gregory X's canon to those approving or ratifying an uncanonical *cessatio* as well as those observing one. Such strict regulations were meant to discourage use of the *cessatio*, promote peaceful settlement of ecclesiastical disputes, and strengthen the central power of the papacy to intervene in local church affairs. In particular it can be seen as part of Boniface VIII's concerted effort at this time to increase papal control over the French Church. In April 1296 his bull 'Clericis laicos' was also circulated in France, forbidding royal taxation of ecclesiastical wealth without papal consent, and 'Constitutioni' likewise responded to events in France. It was apparently occasioned by a dispute between the Archbishop of Reims and his chapter. The canons had stopped services in the cathedral and other churches of the city, and both sides appealed to the pope. On 28 April 1296 Boniface appointed judges delegate to settle the dispute, but oddly he did not refer them to his recent constitution.[114] Nevertheless their mandate shares many of its basic concerns: gathering of evidence from both sides; settlement of the dispute by papal arbitration; and minimizing the disruption of religious worship.

It is not certain how widely this constitution circulated for it only survives as a unique original document, an office copy already noted in the papal archives in 1366, though it is sealed and all formalities for issuing had been completed.[115] Nevertheless a revised version of this constitution, 'Quamvis super', was issued in the *Liber sextus* (1298).[116] It significantly reworded the original text but did not alter its basic aims, rather it reinforced them. Admittedly the prerequisite of a majority decision for a *cessatio* was dropped, but the party whose offence or injury gave rise to the *cessatio* had a chance to make amends for this. 'Quamvis super' also made more practical arrangements for settlement at the curia. If a *cessatio* was unavoidable, representations were to be made in a month, not fifteen days, or as soon as possible, and the pope might settle the case even if only one of the parties were present. Finally the deterrents were increased: the pope might impose arbitrary penalties on the guilty party as well as to those laid down in canon law; and a *cessatio* might be disregarded if a chapter held it without fulfilling the preconditions or making the representations required under 'Quamvis super'.

These procedural rules were meant to ensure that no *cessatio* or interdict might be held without manifest and reasonable cause, but what did this mean? Innocent III's decretal 'Ex parte' (1205) had defined contumacy and offence as the two basic causes of a sentence of excommunication or interdict.[117] He distinguished that a sentence was imposed on someone for contumacy alone where they

---

[114] Varin, *Archives*, 1. 1099–101.

[115] On its diplomatic features see *Schedario*, iii. 613 (no. 4539). The reference to it in the inventory of 1366 of the papal archive was printed by Muratori, *Antiquitates*, vi.189, xv.

[116] VI 1.16.8 (printed with the earlier version in my 'Two Constitutions', 125–6).

[117] 3 Comp. 5.23.7 (= X 5.40.23). See Logan, 47.

disobeyed a summons to appear before an ecclesiastical judge, but it was also laid for an offence where they disobeyed the judge's orders to make amends for their wrong. It was contempt for ecclesiastical authority not the wrong itself which was manifest and reasonable cause. Therefore the purpose of an interdict was not vindictive, to punish wrong, but coercive, to persuade wrongdoers to come to terms with the ecclesiastical authorities. It might be laid only after they had ignored warnings to do so and lifted once they sought reconciliation.

Nevertheless canonists had long recognized that a superior's wrong ultimately caused an interdict on the land or people under his jurisdiction. There were almost as many kinds of such wrong as there were interdicts. As Johannes Calderinus observed, no precise rule could be given about what constituted the causes of an interdict, since they were so diverse, and it was ultimately left to the judge concerned to decide what they were.[118] The thirteenth-century papal registers indicate a number of such causes, and these are broadly classified in the following list with their frequency:

i)	Supporting/defending a deed/person condemned by the Church[119]	106
ii)	Misappropriation of ecclesiastical property/revenues[120]	95
iii)	Political opposition to papal temporal interests[121]	54

---

[118] Johannes Calderinus (attrib.), *De censura*, BAV, Pal. lat. MS 797, fol. 12ra: 'Propter quas causas feratur interdictum perstringemus, et non est facile, nec potest dari certa regula, sed secundum diversitatem casuum et modum agendi poterit poni et non poni, et relinquendum est hoc arbitrio iudicis cuius officium latius est, ff. de iurisd. omni. l.i [Dig. 2.1.1], nam regulariter pro quacumque causa potest excommunicare, potest interdicere suo rectu, idest generaliter vel specialiter.'

[119] Innocent III, Reg. 1, no. 382; 5, nos. 135, 154; 6, nos. 37, 113, 190; 7, no. 14; 8, no. 84; 10, nos. 113, 160, 190; 11, nos. 26, 173; 12, nos. 63, 107; 14, nos. 8, 40, 64, 74, 79, 126; 15, nos. 15, 105, 159; 16, nos. 28, 48, 56; id. *RNI*, nos. 27, 120; id. Suppl. no. 63; *Gesta* c.22, 133 (*PL* 214.xxxiii, clxxx); Reg. Honorius III, nos. 832, 1240, 1136, 1686, 3524, 4517, 4549–51, 4555, 4583, 5720; Reg. Gregory IX, nos. 481, 834, 1197, 1668, 2603, 2615, 4498; Reg. Innocent IV, nos. 201, 2344, 2779, 3109, 3210, 3572, 3625, 3817, 4096–7, 4103, 4333, 4459, 5083, 5279, 5343, 7486; Reg. Alexander IV, nos. 24, 679–80, 2368; Reg. Urban IV, no. 649; Reg. Clement IV, nos. 86–7, 124–5, 143, 413–14, 693–5, 699; Reg. Gregory X, nos. 162–5; Reg. Martin IV, nos. 266, 277–8, 281, 283, 300, 309–10, 471, 482, 489; Reg. Honorius IV, nos. 172, 807; Reg. Nicholas IV, nos. 320, 892, 6028, 6590, 6840.

[120] Innocent III, Reg. 1, nos. 3, 121, 268; 2, nos. 56, 272; 5, no. 68; 7, no. 147; 8, nos. 119, 154; 9, nos. 49, 243; 10, nos. 69, 112, 125, 172; 11, nos. 87, 175; 13, nos. 136, 190; 14, nos. 8, 52, 128, 133; 15, nos. 40, 193; 16, no. 98; id. Suppl. nos. 55, 60, 73, 179; Reg. Honorius III, nos. 1097, 1451, 1925, 2155, 3993, 4364, 4430, 4500, 4594, 4636, 4674, 5513, 5808, 6187–8; Reg. Gregory IX, nos. 470 (theft of body of St Francis), 481, 734, 757, 1327–9, 1968, 1997, 2376, 2603, 2753, 3615, 3630, 3861, 3862, 4453; Reg. Innocent IV, nos. 3626, 3928, 4338; Reg. Alexander IV, nos. 751, 2232, 2845; Reg. Nicholas III, no. 553; Reg. Martin IV, nos. 317, 574; Reg. Honorius IV, nos. 65 (icon), 172, 412, 432, 680; Reg. Nicholas IV, nos. 420, 512, 552, 616, 678, 717, 2115, 2140, 2366, 2616, 2740, 3533, 3888, 4092, 4497, 4573, 5200, 7494; Reg. Boniface VIII, nos. 1110, 1574, 3340, 3727, 4112.

[121] Innocent III, Reg. 1, no. 552; 14, no. 74; Reg. Honorius III, nos. 1451, 1589, 3524; Reg. Innocent IV, nos. 2344, 3109, 3210, 3572, 3817, 4097, 4103, 4333, 4459, 5083, 5279, 5343; Reg. Alexander IV, nos. 24, 2368; Reg. Clement IV, nos. 86–7, 124–5, 143, 413–14, 694–5, 699; Reg. Gregory X, nos. 162–5; Reg. Martin IV, nos. 266, 277, 281, 283, 462–6, 471, 482,

iv)	Destroying/attacking churches/ecclesiastical property[122]	41
v)	Attacking/killing ecclesiastical persons[123]	35
vi)	Defiance/non-payment of ecclesiastical dues[124]	31
vii)	Disobedience to ecclesiastical judgements/mandates[125]	30
viii)	Violating ecclesiastical liberties (miscellaneous or unspecified)[126]	27
ix)	Disobedience to ecclesiastical authority (miscellaneous)[127]	26
x)	Mistreating laity under the protection/in the service of the Church[128]	25

489, 573–5, 577–8; Reg. Honorius IV, no. 807; Reg. Nicholas IV, nos. 6590, 6840, 7040; Reg. Boniface VIII, no. 1123.

[122] Innocent III, Reg. 2, nos. 27, 272; 6, no. 148; 7, no. 46; 9, no. 243; 14, no. 128; id. Suppl. no. 73; *Gesta* c.16 (*PL* 214.xxix); Reg. Honorius III, nos. 951, 1097, 2295, 2553, 3669, 3993, 4674, 5808, 6188; Reg. Gregory IX, nos. 734, 757, 1697, 1997, 2603, 2753, 3615, 3861–2, 3988; Reg. Innocent IV, nos. 399, 3109, 3626, 5011; Reg. Gregory X, no. 948; Reg. Honorius IV, nos. 486–7; Reg. Nicholas IV, no. 552, 678, 2140, 2616, 4497, 6028; Reg. Boniface VIII, no. 1110.

[123] Innocent III, Reg. 1, no. 299; 2, no. 27; 5, no. 133; 6, nos. 17, 113, 148; 7, no. 46; 8, no. 124; 11, no. 26; 15, nos. 15, 119; 16, no. 144; Reg. Honorius III, nos. 1097, 1271, 4191; Reg. Gregory IX, nos. 734, 757, 1197, 2615, 3615, 3859, 3861, 4453; Reg. Innocent IV, nos. 353–4, 3626, 4569; Reg. Alexander IV, no. 751; Reg. Urban IV, no. 649; Reg. Gregory X, no. 166; Reg. Martin IV, no. 317; Reg. Honorius IV, no. 172; Reg. Nicholas IV, no. 2140; Reg. Boniface VIII, nos. 1253, 2142, 2834.

[124] Innocent III, Reg. 2, nos. 138, 233; 7, no. 41; Reg. Honorius III, nos. 1635, 2415, 5513, 5690; Reg. Gregory IX, nos. 1328, 2520; Reg. Innocent IV, nos. 497, 3871, 6115; Reg. Alexander IV, nos. 750, 1219, 2661; Reg. Urban IV, no. 1130; Reg. Martin IV, no. 502; Reg. Honorius IV, nos. 95 (crusader tithe), 123, 608, 704 (tithe for Aragon), 874; Reg. Nicholas IV, nos. 452, 1007 (for Aragon), 3863–6, 5906 (for Aragon against Moors), 6316 (for French king); Reg. Boniface VIII, no. 3051 (as previous).

[125] Innocent III, Reg. 1, no. 114; 7, no. 27; 10, nos. 57, 178; 12, no. 107 (surrender heretics); 14, no. 36; Reg. Honorius III, nos. 589, 4364, 4594, 5180; Reg. Gregory IX, nos. 481, 1315 (ban on usury), 1519 (summons), 2603 (surrender heretics), 2753; Reg. Innocent IV, nos. 1290, 5469 (summons), 5474; Reg. Alexander IV, no. 3032 (summons); Reg. Martin IV, nos. 464–6, 482 (papal embargo), 503, 573–4, 577–8; Reg. Nicholas IV, no. 6840 (expel excommunicate); Reg. Boniface VIII, no. 4112 (summons).

[126] Innocent III, Reg. 2, no. 232; 5, no. 35; 7, no. 41; 10, no. 222; 14, no. 8; Reg. Honorius III, nos. 1136, 1160, 1271, 2161, 2910, 4143, 4776, 6188, 6194; Reg. Gregory IX, nos. 834, 1327 (forcing clerks to do military service, etc.), 1499, 1997, 2753 (as 1327), 4015, 6029; Reg. Innocent IV, nos. 354, 7486; Reg. Alexander IV, nos. 751, 2851; Reg. Honorius IV, no. 432; Reg. Nicholas IV, no. 3533.

[127] Innocent III, Reg. 1, no. 68 (visitation); 2, no. 30; 6, no. 189; 10, no. 57; 15, no. 144 (visitation); Reg. Honorius III, nos. 3233, 3745 (visitation); Reg. Gregory IX, nos. 781, 1275, 1299, 1738 (all except 781 regarding visitation); Reg. Innocent IV, no. 1652 (visitation); Reg. Urban IV, no. C229; Reg. Clement IV, no. 116; Reg. Martin IV, nos. 277, 573–4, 577–8; Reg. Honorius IV, no. 807; Reg. Nicholas IV, nos. 225–6, 320, 892, 1127 (visitation); Reg. Boniface VIII, nos. 1253, 2142, 3340.

[128] Innocent III, Reg. 7, no. 153; 12, no. 77 (pilgrims); 13, no. 74 (widow); 14, no. 8 (orphans); 15, no. 15 (allying with Saracens against fellow Christians in Spain); Reg. Honorius III, nos. 558, 1271, 2725 (papal ward); Reg. Gregory IX, nos. 757, 2579, 3861–2, 4498; Reg. Innocent IV, nos. 4459, 5343; Reg. Alexander IV, no. 1557; Reg. Urban IV, no. 1130; Reg. Gregory X, no. 948; Reg. Honorius IV, no. 172, 432, 807; Reg. Nicholas IV, nos. 552, 582, 2140, 6028.

[129] Innocent III, Reg. 1, no. 24; 8, no. 87; 10, no. 112; 14, no. 8; 16, no. 144; *Gesta* c.22 (*PL* 214.xxxii–xxxiii); Reg. Honorius III, nos. 980, 1271, 3837; Reg. Gregory IX, nos. 734, 757 (both for ransom), 1202, 1639 (extortion), 3859, 3861; Reg. Innocent IV, nos. 3626 (for ransom), 5343; Reg. Alexander IV, nos. 751, 1557; Reg. Gregory X, no. 166; Reg. Nicholas IV, nos. 552, 4573 (collusion), 6028; Reg. Boniface VIII, no. 1253.

[130] Innocent III, Reg. 1, nos. 55, 418, 477; 2, no. 186; 5, no. 145; 6, nos. 37, 195; 7, no. 71; 9, no. 57; Reg. Honorius III, nos. 1130, 5690; Reg. Gregory IX, nos. 2679, 3859; Reg. Innocent IV, nos. 1611 (abuse of provisions), 2403, 3871; Reg. Alexander IV, no. 2733; Reg. Nicholas IV, nos. 211, 236, 3772, 5858, 5964, 6105; Reg. Boniface VIII, no. 4102.

[131] Innocent III, Reg. 1, no. 242; 11, no. 223; 12, nos. 80, 107, 120; 13, nos. 67, 190; id. *RNI*, no. 27; Reg. Honorius III, nos. 1451, 3837; Reg. Gregory IX, nos. 1328, 1968, 2603, 2753, 3630; Reg. Nicholas III, no. 553 (crusader tithe); Reg. Martin IV, no. 574; Reg. Honorius IV, nos. 412, 680; Reg. Nicholas IV, nos. 420, 616, 678.

[132] Innocent III, Reg. 1, nos. 164, 221; 8, no. 47; 15, no. 228; Reg. Honorius III, nos. 622, 658, 1323; Reg. Gregory IX, nos. 1769, 2294 (non-residence); Reg. Innocent IV, nos. 530 (chapter's status), 1632, 7211, 7462, 7629; Reg. Alexander IV, no. 3063; Reg. Martin IV, no. 352; Reg. Honorius IV, no. 767 (temporal jurisdiction); Reg. Nicholas IV, no. 211 (providee and presentee); Reg. Boniface VIII, nos. 4112, 4299 (chapter's rights).

[133] Innocent III, Reg. 6, no. 182; 7, no. 41; 10, no. 222; 11, nos. 87, 175; 13, nos. 43, 67; 14, no. 133; Reg. Honorius III, nos. 1561, 2151, 3962; Reg. Gregory IX, nos. 1327–8, 1997, 2753; Reg. Alexander IV, no. 1702; Reg. Martin IV, no. 349; Reg. Boniface VIII, no. 2140.

[134] Innocent III, Reg. 6, no. 189 (papal appointee); 7, no. 153; id. *RNI*, nos. 27, 120; *Gesta* c.25 (*PL* 214.xlviii); Reg. Honorius III, nos. 1686, 4296, 4517, 4940, 4949–51, 4955; Reg. Innocent IV, no. 4459; Reg. Urban IV, no. 598; Reg. Clement IV, nos. 44, 120; Reg. Martin IV, no. 300; Reg. Honorius IV, no. 807 (backing usurper).

[135] Innocent III, Reg. 6, no. 13; 8, no. 31; Reg. Honorius III, nos. 1235, 4430, 6187–8; Reg. Gregory IX, nos. 1765, 1882, 2178, 2820 (church), 3745, 4758 (ecclesiastical fiefs); Reg. Innocent IV, nos. 201 (commune seizing bishop's temporal jurisdiction), 6115; Reg. Alexander IV, nos. 750 (*novalia*), 2368; Reg. Boniface VIII, nos. 1253 (commune seizing bishop's temporal jurisdiction), 2034.

[136] Innocent III, Reg. 1, nos. 92, 249,355, 552; 6, no. 162; 8, nos. 1 (impeding crusade), 114 (unjust war); id. Suppl. no. 233; *Gesta* c.84 (*PL* 214.cxxxvii; attending tournaments); Reg. Honorius III, nos. 558, 1057, 4302, 4583; Reg. Innocent IV, no. 2616 (general unrest), 5016 (thieves, robbers, and their harbourers); Reg. Nicholas III, no. 225; Reg. Nicholas IV, no. 7040; Reg. Boniface VIII, no. 3445.

[137] Reg. Honorius III, nos. 939, 3760; Reg. Gregory IX, nos. 675, 998, 2391, 3461; Reg. Innocent IV, nos. 6537, 7529; Reg. Alexander IV, no. 28; Reg. Martin IV, no. 492; Reg. Honorius IV, no. 605; Reg. Nicholas IV, nos. 2264, 3653; Reg. Boniface VIII, nos. 1084, 4656.

[138] Innocent III, Reg. 1, no. 3; 7, no. 147; 14, no. 126; 15, no. 105; Reg. Honorius III, nos. 1589, 1834, 5265; Reg. Gregory IX, nos. 1327, 1668 (heretics), 2603 (heretics),

3918; Reg. Innocent IV, no. 1290 (failing to coerce excommunicates); Reg. Boniface VIII, no. 2722.

[139] Reg. Honorius III, nos. 1511, 3962, 4961, 5768; Reg. Gregory IX, nos. 1080, 1327, 2753, 3083; Reg. Innocent IV, no. 7190; Reg. Martin IV, nos. 148, 349; Reg. Honorius IV, nos. 479–80.

[140] Innocent III, Reg. 1, nos. 130, 142, 552; 2, nos. 40, 187; Reg. Honorius III, no. 4302; Reg. Alexander IV, nos. 2379, 2938; Reg. Martin IV, no. 503 (concordat); Reg. Honorius IV, nos. 96, 432; Reg. Nicholas IV, no. 717 (concordat); Reg. Boniface VIII, no. 3445.

[141] Innocent III, 2, no. 30; Reg. Honorius III, nos. 3745, 5513, 5690; Reg. Gregory IX, nos. 2294, 3343; Reg. Innocent IV, nos. 497, 3871; Reg. Urban IV, no. 1130; Reg. Nicholas IV, nos. 3888, 4497, 6130, 6545.

[142] Reg. Honorius III, nos. 832, 1097, 4822 (intimidating witnesses); Reg. Gregory IX, nos. 1327, 2753, 2213; Reg. Innocent IV, no. 201; Reg. Alexander IV, no. 751; Reg. Honorius IV, no. 96 (impeding appeals to Rome); Reg. Nicholas IV, no. 430; Reg. Boniface VIII, nos. 1253, 2142.

[143] Innocent III, Reg. 1, no. 298; 2, no. 75; 7, no. 83; 8, no. 85 (heretic); 10, no. 111 (aspostate); Reg. Honorius III, nos. 5265, 5720; Reg. Gregory IX, no. 1498 (Muslims and Jews); Reg. Innocent IV, no. 4096 (Frederick II's allies); Reg. Nicholas IV, no. 6840 (excommunicate); Reg. Boniface VIII, no. 864.

[144] Innocent III, Reg. 10, no. 222; 11, no. 175; Reg. Honorius III, nos. 3669, 4818; Reg. Gregory IX, nos. 734, 1277, 2376; Reg. Alexander IV, no. 2845; Reg. Clement IV, no. 1914; Reg. Nicholas III, no. 134.

[145] Innocent III, Reg. 1, no. 298; 2, no. 42; id. *RNI*, nos. 27, 120; *Gesta* c.25 (*PL* 214.xlviii); Reg. Honorius III, nos. 1130, 4517; Reg. Gregory IX, nos. 1668, 3630; Reg. Martin IV, no. 277.

[146] Innocent III, Reg. 15, no. 186 (exacting procurations); Reg. Gregory IX, nos. 1371, 1566 (harassing monastery), 1824 (frustrating visitation), 2192; Reg. Innocent IV, no. 1611; Reg. Alexander IV, nos. 2448, 2661 (abuse of papal letters); Reg. Honorius IV, no. 608 (exacting procurations).

[147] Innocent III, Reg. 1, nos. 92, 347; 2, no. 188; 5, no. 51; 7, no. 93; 10, no. 143; Reg. Innocent IV, no. 3366; Reg. Urban IV, no. C376.

[148] Innocent III, Reg. 1, no. 364; 6, no. 73; 7, no. 171; 14, no. 8; *Gesta* c.131 (*PL* 214.clxxv–clxxvi); Reg. Gregory IX, nos. 757 (citizenry adopting anti-bishop), 1327, 2753.

[149] Innocent III, Reg. 15, no. 228; Reg. Honorius III, no. 658 (no episcopal investiture); Reg. Gregory IX, no. 3859; Reg. Innocent IV, no. 7462; Reg. Alexander IV, no. 680 (bishopric); Reg. Boniface VIII, no. 4102.

[150] Innocent III, Suppl. no. 233; *Gesta* c.84 (*PL* 214.cxxxvii); Reg. Gregory IX, no. 1957; Reg. Innocent IV, no. 2054; Reg. Nicholas III, no. 225.

xxxiii)	Heresy/apostasy/schism[151]	4
xxxiv)	Imposing secular jurisdiction on ecclesiastical persons[152]	4
xxxv)	Not compensating injured party[153]	3
xxxvi)	Others[154]	7

This classification is necessarily arbitrary; hence this list is less scientifically precise than it appears. Some interdicts had more than one cause and are therefore represented several times in the above figures. Some causes are naturally related, notably ii, iv, and v, since ecclesiastical property was seized in most instances by laymen, and this often involved violence against clergy and the property itself. A chain of causation may also be at work, for example where refusal of restitution (xiii) concerned seizure of church property or lay property under ecclesiastical protection (ii, x); such a chain arose from canonical procedure: wrongdoers were warned to make restitution or be coerced to do so by interdict. Similarly disobedience to ecclesiastical mandates (vii) and refusal to compensate injured parties (xxxv) were usually responses to warnings and therefore procedural reasons for interdicts, albeit the underlying causes in these cases, the actual wrongs, are not always clear. Indeed the papal registers rarely give the full facts about particular cases. Often only a threat of interdict is recorded and it is uncertain whether a sentence was actually imposed. Sometimes the cause of an interdict was unspecified and was even disputed by the parties concerned, which was why the case was referred to the pope. Hence this list cannot be comprehensive even for the papal registers.

Despite its limitations the list clearly shows that interdicts were used mostly as a weapon of self-defence in reaction to attacks, usually by laymen, on ecclesiastical property, persons, and liberties (ii, iv, v, vi, viii, xi, xv, xxi, xxvi, xxxiv). The interdict was used far less as a tool of internal discipline, in disputes only involving clergy (xii, xiv, xxiii, xxxi). As a judicial sanction it was sometimes used against both clergy and laity to enforce decisions on cases where the church courts had exclusive competence, notably debts, oaths, and marriage (vii, xvii, xix, xxii, xxiv, xxvii, xxix, xxxv). Above all the list illustrates the explicit application of canonistic ideas of collective guilt, as the single most frequently cited cause of an interdict in the papal registers was consent to the wrongs of others, usually express (i) but sometimes tacit (xx).

Some interdicts were laid for what seemed arbitrary or frivolous causes (xxvii, xxxvi); these usually arose from jealous disputes among clergy. In two cases the

---

[151] Innocent III, Reg. 14, no. 8 (keeping sorceress); 16, no. 48 (heresy); Reg. Honorius III, nos. 1240 (schism), 2030 (apostasy).

[152] Innocent III, Reg. 7, no. 41; Reg. Gregory IX, nos. 1327, 2753; Reg. Alexander IV, no. 751.

[153] Innocent III, Reg. 13, no. 74; Reg. Honorius III, no. 3837; Reg. Nicholas IV, nos. 2140.

[154] Innocent III, Reg. 6, no. 182 (building latrines by cathedral cemetery); Reg. Honorius III, no. 4674 (bringing prostitutes to clerks' homes); Reg. Gregory IX, nos. 1296, 1327 (seizing clerical concubines); Reg. Nicholas IV, nos. 1281, 5836; Reg. Boniface VIII, no. 3675 (refusing to free a prisoner-of-war).

cause was hostility of secular clergy to mendicant popularity. In 1233 a widow protested to Gregory IX that interdict and excommunication were declared against her since local secular canons resented her decision to found a Dominican priory on her land. In 1289 Franciscans of Orense diocese likewise complained to former Franciscan Nicholas IV that their bishop threatened interdict and excommunication on any laity who attended their preaching, made confession to them, gave them alms, had contact with them, or brought to their churches the bodies of those who had arranged to be buried there.[155]

Interdicts arising from disputes between clergy and laity could have peculiar causes too. The citizens of Cagli were interdicted and their officials excommunicated in 1291 as a result of a planning dispute: they opposed the papally approved extension of the city's cathedral. Conversely buildings authorized by the commune of Bergamo had occasioned Innocent III's threat of an interdict in 1203. When local clergy refused to pay taxes to the commune, its podestà had toilets built by the cathedral's cemetery! Bergamo was to be interdicted unless taxes collected from clergy were refunded and the toilets removed. Another lurid means was apparently used to humiliate clergy into giving money to the lay power in Portugal; it was one of many anti-clerical abuses which provoked interdicts there. The Bishop of Oporto complained to Gregory IX that a royal statute ordered the arrest of any woman found with a clerk. It was maybe meant to enforce clerical celibacy originally, but the bishop claimed that royal officials and vassals used it to extort hush money from embarrassed clergy. Under Honorius III the Bishop of Lisbon had even declared excommunication and interdict on royal officials who abused the statute by planting prostitutes (*mulierculas*) in clergy's houses.[156]

However, the purpose of an interdict that strikes us as most controversial was as a political weapon. The interdicts that Innocent III declared on France in 1199 and England in 1208 are famous examples. It is even arguable that Innocent regularized papal use of interdicts as a means of intervening in temporal affairs. Initially interdicts were used in conflicts with lay powers largely to enforce an issue of canon law, as in the case of France in 1199, or punish violations of ecclesiastical liberty, as in the case of England in 1208.[157] But during the thirteenth century the papacy came to exploit interdicts more and more to bolster its own temporal power. This went hand in glove with the papacy's increasing concentration on its territorial interests in Italy, arguably at the expense of its wider pastoral and reform agenda. The precedent for

---

[155] Reg. Gregory IX, no. 1296; Reg. Nicholas IV, no. 1281.

[156] Cagli: Reg. Nicholas IV, no. 5856. Bergamo: Innocent III, Reg. 6, no. 182. Portugal: Reg. Honorius III, no. 4674; Reg. Gregory IX, no. 1327; cf. ibid. no. 2753.

[157] The French interdict was to enforce the canon law of marriage by compelling Philip II to leave his mistress and return to his wife (Innocent III, Reg. 1, no. 347; Krehbiel, 110–25); the English interdict punished King John's interference in the appointment of the Archbishop of Canterbury (Innocent III, Reg. 10, no. 113; Cheney, 'Interdict').

interdicting those who threatened the papal state was already set by the end of the twelfth century. Under Celestine III an interdict was laid on Pisa and his successor Innocent III lifted it in 1198 on the condition that Pisa joined the Pope's Guelf allies in the Tuscan League; otherwise the sentence would be reimposed.[158] Guelfs were traditionally opponents of the pro-imperial Ghibellines in northern Italian communes, and this usage of interdicts intensified with the growing papal struggle against the empire. Innocent III employed interdicts against supporters of emperor-elect Otto IV after he invaded the papal state in 1211.[159] This trend grew under Gregory IX and his successsors, especially Innocent IV, in their conflict with the emperor Frederick II and his heirs. They saw the union of the Sicilian kingdom and German empire in Frederick as a threat to their overlordship in Sicily and to the papal state. The military manoeuvres of Frederick and his heirs in Italy and uncertain loyalties of the communes there heightened such fears. Frederick's pretensions to universal monarchy and his leadership of a crusade and crown-wearing in Jerusalem while under papal excommunication were also seen as challenging papal claims. Hence countless interdicts were laid in the mid-thirteenth century on lands and cities of Frederick's dynasty and its allies in the empire, northern Italy, the kingdoms of Sicily and Jerusalem (these comprise most of the interdicts in the list at iii).[160] In 1257 an interdict was even threatened on England since its king had failed to send his son Edmund with troops to conquer Sicily from Frederick's heirs in the Pope's name. This use of the interdict for temporal ends was justified by papal rhetoric. Innocent IV threatened excommunication and interdict on the duke of Swabia since he had backed the deposed Frederick II in 'rebellion against God' when he should have been zealous for 'catholic liberty' and 'risen in common faith with Mother Church and stood before her as a wall against all enemy attacks'.[161] Even when the imperial threat ceased with Charles of Anjou defeating Frederick's last heir in 1268, the papacy soon renewed its sanctions and rhetoric in defence of its temporal claims. Charles's displacement as its vassal king of Sicily by the Aragonese in 1282 resulted in interdicts against these new invaders and their Sicilian allies.[162]

---

[158] Innocent III, Reg. 1, no. 552; Krehbiel, 102–3.

[159] Innocent III, Reg. 14, nos. 74, 79; 16, no. 56.

[160] Reg. Gregory IX, nos. 308–9 (crown-wearing provokes papal interdict on Jerusalem); Reg. Innocent IV, nos. 2344, 2779, 3109, 3210, 3572, 3625, 3817, 4096–7, 4103, 4333, 4459, 5083, 5279, 5343; Reg. Alexander IV, nos. 24, 2368; Reg. Clement IV, nos. 86–7, 124–5, 143, 413–14, 694–5, 699; Reg. Gregory X, nos. 162–5; Reg. Martin IV, no. 266. On the background see Abulafia, 165–70, 194–200, 341–66, and Morris, 559–67. The classic account of the conflict after 1250 is Runciman.

[161] England: Reg. Alexander IV, no. 2379. Swabia: Reg. Innocent IV, no. 5343. Innocent had deposed Frederick as emperor in 1245.

[162] Reg. Martin IV, nos. 310, 453, 471, 482, 489–90, 571, 577; Reg. Honorius IV, nos. 479–80, 807.

Outside Italy the thirteenth-century papacy sometimes also used interdicts for temporal ends, but ironically largely in defence of the rights of secular rulers (x, xvi). This was especially true of Honorius III, who was more moderate than his successors in his claims for papal power in the temporal sphere but still used interdicts to defend papal vassal kings and thereby reinforced papal suzerainty over their realms. He was especially protective of Henry III, heir to King John of England; John had surrendered England and Ireland to Innocent III as papal fiefs in 1213 and assigned his infant son to papal wardship at his death in 1216. Consequently in 1220 Honorius authorized use of excommunication and interdict to restrain John's widow and her accomplices from treachery against Henry, and in 1223 he ordered the English episcopate to publish the excommunication of Llewellyn, *soi-disant* prince of North Wales, and his supporters and place the strictest interdicts on their lands for rebelling against John and Henry.[163] In 1223 he similarly ordered the use of excommunication and interdict to compel the count of Zwerin to free the king of Denmark, who held his realm as a papal fief. Thus Honorius like any dutiful lord used the weapons at his disposal to protect his vassals, even from their subjects, and to encourage lay powers to accept papal protection. His successors Urban IV and Clement IV continued his policy in the 1260s, approving use of excommunication and interdict by papal legates to compel rebel English barons and their allies to cease defying Henry III.[164]

Thus the interdict could be used to preserve the status quo, and in fact it seems to have originated as a means of maintaining social order. One of the first known uses of interdict was at the council of Limoges in 994. The chronicler of the event, Adémar of Charbannes, wrote some thirty years later that Bishop Alduin of Limoges had had all monasteries and churches cease divine service 'in order to punish the rapine of the *milites* and the devastation of the poor'.[165] Adémar called this a new practice ('novam observantiam') and recorded that it was adopted again at another council of Limoges in 1031, when a 'public excommunication' was proclaimed on all the land of Limoges owing to peace-breakers. This measure was necessitated by the decline of royal power and judicial institutions in late tenth-century France which left society, and especially the clergy, vulnerable to the arbitrary rule and ruthless exploitation of local lords, the rampaging *milites* deplored by Alduin. Political and social circumstances had changed by the thirteenth century, but the papacy sometimes still used the interdict to enforce truces among secular powers (see list above, xviii). In particular it was threatened on the lands of those who broke the general peace that was normally

---

[163] Reg. Honorius III, nos. 2725, 4517; Sayers, 162 ff. Cf. *Acts*, no. 220: Welsh princes complained to Innocent III that the Archbishop of Canterbury interdicted their lands whenever English invaded them.

[164] Denmark: Reg. Honorius III, nos. 4549–51, 4555. England: Reg. Urban IV, no. 755; Reg. Clement IV, nos. 44, 116, 120.

[165] Little, 213–14; Mansi xix.541–2 (council of 1031). See also Howland, 'Origins', 444.

declared along with a crusade, even if they only attended tournaments.[166] The late eleventh-century papacy initiated the crusades in response to the anarchic conditions that also gave rise to the interdict, and they were meant to direct *milites* from fighting fellow Christians towards defending Christendom from its external enemies. Given their common origin and purpose in keeping social order, it is not surprising that the interdict was still used in support of crusading by thirteenth-century popes, especially to compel fulfilment of crusader vows (list, xxxii) and surrender of tithes for crusades or other holy wars.[167]

Apparently unlimited as the causes of an interdict were, not all uses of it were approved by the papacy. Celestine III's decretal 'Quesivit' (*c*.1191–5), for example, condemned canons who interdicted their cathedral because of debts owed to it or the wrong of a clerk or parishioner. In such instances, the canonist Laurentius observed, it was more appropriate to interdict the persons involved since they had done wrong and not the church. Indeed 'Quesivit' concluded with the civilian maxim that sins ought to bind their authors. This also echoed Gratian's *dictum* that a church ought not to suffer because of one person's wrong.[168] But an interdict was often imposed on a community for the wrongs of its head, and Tancred hence distinguished that a church might suffer for its prelate's wrong done in his official capacity but not as a private individual. And 'Quesivit' had apparently condemned interdicts laid for the faults of private persons. Certainly in 1257 Alexander IV forbade judges acting on papal authority to interdict the churches or parish of Clermont-Ferrand on account of lawsuits concerning private persons, for this prejudiced all parishioners, and he observed in words echoing those of 'Quesivit': 'a penalty ought not to bind those whom innocence frees from guilt'. In 1265 Clement IV also used this argument when he gave a parish in Clermont diocese immunity from interdicts laid by judges delegate without a specific papal mandate for the delict or contumacy of private persons.[169] Presumably such interdicts were widely seen as improper, for the protest of the parish's provost and chapter at such sentences had prompted the grant.

But the closest canon law came to banning interdicts laid for faults of private individuals was in debt cases. Boniface VIII's constitution 'Provide' (1302) forbade ecclesiastical judges to interdict a place because rulers, officials, or *individuals* there defaulted on debts, except by specific papal permission.[170] As the preamble observed, interdicts were very often laid 'not without reason but

---

[166] Innocent III, Reg. 8, no. 1; id. Suppl. no. 233; *Gesta* c.84 (*PL* 214.cxxxvii); Lat. Conc. IV c.71 (see *Constitutiones*, 115–17); Reg. Nicholas III, no. 225.

[167] Tithes: Reg. Nicholas III, no. 553; Reg. Honorius IV, no. 95; Reg. Nicholas IV, no. 5906.

[168] 2 Comp. 3.9.2 (= X 3.11.2). On Laurentius see p. 64 n. 22. The maxim is from Cod. 9.47.22 (see p. 14 n. 1 above). Gratian's teaching and Tancred's distinction are discussed at pp. 52–3.

[169] Reg. Alexander IV, no. 1721; Reg. Clement IV, no. 144. See also p. 62 above.

[170] Reg. Boniface VIII, no. 5019; *Extrav. comm.* 5.10.2.

without the guilt of many' and some judges were too inclined to use them in lawsuits said to proceed 'more from the root of greed than charity', with negative spiritual results for the faithful. The canonist Johannes Monachus observed that cases involving merchants' contracts gave rise to this ruling. Indeed it was specifically occasioned by such a case from Ascoli in the Marche. The town's commune protested to Boniface that the Bishop of Osimo had interdicted Ascoli at the request of secular judges, proceeding against them to recover debts owed by an Ascoli merchant to a Florentine merchant. In a letter dated four days earlier than 'Provide' and anticipating its rulings Boniface ordered the bishop to relax the interdict and not to proceed further against the commune in debt cases without a specific papal mandate.[171] A century earlier Celestine III had simply been concerned about interdicts laid for debts owed to churches, but since then a system of international banking and commerce had developed, largely run by Italians. Popes, princes, and merchants came to rely increasingly on loans from Italian bankers, and use of ecclesiastical sanctions against defaulters became all too common. It has been assumed that the diocese with the highest incidence of excommunication in later medieval Europe was Florence, for so many of its citizens were involved in papal finances.[172] As 'Provide' makes clear, Boniface VIII deplored overuse of interdicts for such worldly ends at the expense of pastoral care. But, apart from 'Provide' and the rule that interdicts might only be laid with manifest and reasonable cause, thirteenth-century popes did not seek to regulate what ends interdicts might be used for.

Nevertheless the papacy granted certain dignitaries and communities freedom from excommunication and interdict, not simply when imposed without manifest and reasonable cause but in many cases *tout court*, although it was often specified that this immunity might be disregarded on papal or legatine authority. From an early stage it formed a significant element in 'exemption', the freedom from episcopal jurisdiction that the papacy allowed a growing number of religious houses to claim from the late eleventh century.[173] By Alexander III's pontificate such claims had to be recognized by papal documents specifying that the monastery was directly subject to the holy see 'nullo mediante', and thus subject only to its interdicts. But grants of exemption were rare outside Cistercian, Cluniac, and other reformed houses in the late twelfth century. In 1215 only one Augustinian and six Benedictine houses in England were 'exempt'. By contrast in 1184 Lucius III had affirmed that houses and brethren of the Cistercian order held immunity from interdicts as part of their exemption.[174] This immunity had been extended to new religious orders enjoying a special relationship with the papacy, notably the Hospitallers, Templars, and Premonstratensians by

---

171 Johannes Monachus on *Extrav. comm.* 5.10.2 v. *radice.* Ascoli: Reg. Boniface VIII, no. 4656.
172 Brucker, 'Ecclesiastical Courts', esp. 255.
173 Robinson, 223 ff., esp. 234–5; Knowles, 'Exemption'; Cheney, *Visitation*, 36–46.
174 England: Knowles, 'Exemption'; Denton, *Free Chapels*, 16. Cistercians: *PL* 201.1301–2 (discussed in Schreiber, 'Studien').

the late twelfth century, and the Dominicans and Franciscans in the early thirteenth.[175]

But the danger inherent in such grants was that delinquent clergy might abuse them to evade ecclesiastical justice, and canonists aware of this argued for limitation of this immunity. A pupil of the French canonist Petrus Brito observed (*c.*1206) that the freedom of Hospitallers and their churches from episcopal excommunication and interdict applied unless they fell into heresy or committed a manifest act of plunder.[176] Tancred was similarly concerned that immunities should not supply an excuse for sin, and while he argued that bishops might not include exempt churches within a general local interdict, he conceded that local ordinaries might punish exempt religious who committed wrongs in their jurisdiction.[177] Tancred and other early thirteenth-century canonists limited this exception to notorious wrongs (as opposed to hidden ones) and wrongs in a non-exempt matter, notably homicide (as opposed to those in an exempt matter, such as misconduct in ecclesiastical office).[178] But Innocent IV later ruled at the First Council of Lyon that while the exempt might be summoned before their local ordinary for any wrong, contract, or lawsuit of

---

[175] The immunity of the military orders was old enough to be regulated in Lat. Conc. III (1179) c.9 (= 1 Comp. 5.28.3; X 5.33.3). Cf. Innocent III, Reg. 13, no. 11 (Spanish military order of St James); Reg. Honorius III, nos. 203–4 (Franciscans, Dominicans), 2554 (Premonstratensians); Reg. Alexander IV, no. 2988 (Templars); Reg. Clement IV, no. 1758 (Hospitallers).

[176] Anon. on 1 Comp. 5.28.8 v. *presumatis*, Brussels, Bibliothèque royale MS 1407–9, fol. 86vb: 'Supra. de parochiis. Licet [1 Comp. 3.25.4]. Et verum nisi ceciderint in heresim, supra de hereticis [1 Comp. 5.6]. Item si <???> manifestam fecerint depredationem, ut vi. q. iii. Placuit [C.6 q.3 c.4], vel nisi ceciderint in canonem, tunc possunt eos denunciare, sicut iudex delegatus posset denunciare excommunicatum qui magis numquam potest ligari denunciationem, ut extra Inno. iii. Pastoralis §Qui [Po. 2350], quia non datum privilegium ad tutionem iniquitatis sicut nec appellatio, infra. de appellationibus. Ad nostram [1 Comp. 2.20.3].'

[177] Tancred on 1 Comp. 5.28.3 v. *enervant*, BAV, Vat. lat. MS 1377, fol. 93rb: 'Pone quod privilegiatus in parrochia alicuius episcopi deliquid, non potest episcopus loci eum excommunicare? ... Solutio. Quia episcopus non potest eorum ecclesias interdicere, quando totam terram interdicto subponit. Preterea pro levibus et minimis causis ab episcopo non possunt excommunicari ... Et hec ratio quare puniuntur, nam papa nichil aliud eis concessit nisi quod eos suos filios fecit, et hoc facto aliis episcopis iurisdictionem quo ad hoc non abstulit, nam alias nichil aliud esset nisi materiam peccandi dare.' Immunity was rarely so qualified in papal grants, e.g. Innocent III, Reg. 8, no. 167.

[178] Tancred on 3 Comp. 5.16.1 v. *interdicas*, BAV, Vat. lat. MS 1377, fol. 271rb: 'Hic patet quod iudex ordinarius potest punire exemptos, ut supra. de heretic. Ad abolendam l. i. in fi. [1 Comp. 5.6.11] ubi dicitur quod nullum privilegium prodest talibus ... Ad hoc dicunt quidam quod pro occultis delictis tales non possunt puniri ab episcopis sed pro notoriis, ar. huius decretalis. Melius dices quod si privilegiatus deliquit circa rem non exemptam, ut in contractu vel maleficio occidendo videlicet hominem vel adulterando cum aliqua, tale delictum potest punire episcopus loci, quia etsi persona sit exempta, tamen res in qua delinquitur non est exempta. Si vero deliquit circa rem exemptam, puta male gerendo se in officio suo vel alienando res ecclesie sue, tunc a solo papa punitur.' Cf. id. on 2 Comp. 1.6.2 v. *excessus*, 2.5.1 v. *irritam*, 5.14.2 v. *per te* (BAV, Vat. lat. MS 1377, fols. 103vb, 110rb, 142ra). Cf. also *Apparatus* 'Servus appellatur' on 3 Comp. 5.16.4 v. (?)*decernimus* (Bamberg Staatsbibliothek MS Can. 19, fol. 215ra); Zoën on 5 Comp. 5.12.1 v. *privilegio* (Tours, Bibliothèque municipale MS 565, fol. 39rb); Johannes Hispanus de Petesella, *Summa*, §*De privilegiis* (BAV, Vat. lat. MS 2343, fol. 221rb).

theirs done outside their monastery or an exempt place, they might not be interdicted or excommunicated as a result, unless they were moved to priories subject to the ordinary. In the decretal 'Veniens' he also explained that those recognized in papal privileges as 'speciales et proprios ecclesie Romane filios' were not technically exempt but immune from excommunication and interdict laid by anyone other than the pope or his legates, and this especially applied to churches built by religious in uninhabited places or those under Muslim rule.[179]

The papacy had long defended grants of this immunity and the jurisdiction that it reserved over their recipients, despite canonistic misgivings. Many prelates resented this freedom from coercion and especially exemption as eroding their judicial powers, and some asserted jurisdiction by interdict and excommunication over those claiming such rights. An early test case was a dispute between the Bishop of Paris and Abbot of Ste-Geneviève in 1201. The bishop held that traditionally the priest of a certain parish received its cure of souls from him and excluded from the offices anyone interdicted or excommunicated by him. When the abbot chose a priest for this parish but refused to present him to the bishop, the latter forbade its parishioners on pain of excommunication to hear offices or receive sacraments in the abbey church, unless the celebrant had received his cure from him. The parishioners initially obeyed, but then the abbey enlisted a former abbot and eminent canonist, Stephen of Tournai, to preach to them that no archbishop, bishop, or archdeacon might lay excommunication or interdict on them. The abbot claimed that the abbey and its locality were exempt and subject only to papal and legatine sentences; therefore, Stephen argued, the bishop's sentence was invalid being 'a non suo iudice lata'. It was a cogent canonistic argument: Innocent III quashed the sentence as violating the abbey's immunity, confirming that no interdict might be observed on the parish church.[180] Honorius III also used this argument when he condemned the Bishop of Transylvania for using excommunication and interdict in lands which 'had no bishop or prelate other than the Roman pontiff'; he instructed the Bishop of Esztergom in 1223 to declare the sentences null as issued 'a non suo iudice' unless the first bishop revoked them.[181] Gregory IX likewise had to intervene in 1233 when English prelates tried to compel three abbeys to submit to visitation by interdict and excommunication despite their immunity from such sentences.[182] Often religious houses, especially Cistercian and Cluniac ones, complained that local ordinaries tried to circumvent such immunity by laying sentences on their patrons and servants. Since the late twelfth century the papacy had responded by

[179] Coll. III 32 (= VI 5.7.1), 41 (= VI 5.12.1). Bernard de Montemirat noted (early 1260s) on Coll. III 41 ('Veniens') that this distinction applied to the order of St James in Spain (BAV, Vat. lat. MS 2542, fol. 88va). Cf. Innocent III, Reg. 13, no. 11.

[180] Innocent III, Suppl. no. 53.   [181] Reg. Honorius III, nos. 4608, 4618.

[182] Reg. Gregory IX, nos. 1275, 1299, 1738.

extending this immunity to these associates.[183] Honorius III even made such a concession regarding the Cluniac order, and though his ruling entered canon law, his successors were still asked to confirm it and make similar grants to Cistercian houses down to the late thirteenth century.[184]

Some laity might thus share the freedom of religious from excommunication and interdict, but popes also gave this immunity to certain lay dignitaries in their own right, notably kings and magnates, as well as ecclesiastical dignitaries like bishops; it was often even extended to their chapels and lands.[185] These grants apparently had a long tradition by the thirteenth century; in 1213 Innocent III confirmed the freedom of the king and queen of Aragon from excommunication and 'interdiction' allegedly first granted by Urban II (1088–99).[186] These were personal grants that did not necessarily extend beyond their recipients' lifetime to their heirs, though they might be renewed, and some were limited to even shorter periods, especially under Innocent IV. In 1251 he granted Simon de Montfort, earl of Leicester and the English crown's vicegerent in Gascony, personal freedom for two years from excommunication and interdict laid by anyone in Gascony without a special papal mandate.[187] On succeeding him as pope Alexander IV revoked all Innocent's grants of freedom from excommunication and interdict to laity and clergy and their lands, perhaps since he had issued so many, and perhaps to counter forgeries and raise funds from issuing new grants of this much sought-after freedom.[188] Another limitation was that some grants only gave immunity from sentences laid by papally commissioned judges without a special papal mandate, and not local ordinaries, or vice versa.[189]

However limited, such grants often rewarded lay dignitaries for service to the Church. Immunity from interdict regularly formed part of the ecclesiastical protection extended to crusaders' lands. Indeed in 1235, after the king of

---

[183] E.g. Innocent III, Reg. 10, no. 205; Innocent III, Suppl. nos. 4, 19, 42, 79, 86, 92, 124. Cf. Alanus on Alan. 3.23.1 (= 2 Comp. 3.26.2) v. *in aliis locis tantum pro se et familia sua*, Vercelli Cathedral MS 89, fol. 104ra: 'Quo nomine servos et mercenarios intelligo comprehendi. Et est ar. quod servientes privilegiatorum non possunt a diocesano excommunicari, ar. supra. de statu. mona. Quanto nos [2 Comp. 3.22.4].'

[184] 5 Comp. 5.12.1 (= X 5.33.26). Papal grants: Reg. Honorius III, nos. 4177, 5564, 5859; Reg. Gregory IX, nos. 1727, 1741; Reg. Innocent IV, no. 477; Reg. Nicholas III, no. 455; Reg. Honorius IV, no. 411; Reg. Nicholas IV, nos. 4902, 7365.

[185] E.g. Innocent III, Reg. 5, no. 43 (king of Armenia); 9, no. 245 (duke of Dijon's chapel); 16, no. 87 (king and queen of Aragon); Reg. Honorius III, nos. 1690 (king of Scotland), 2128 (Latin empress of Byzantium and her chapels); Reg. Gregory IX, nos. 1121 (bishop), 1399 (Portuguese infanta and his kingdom of Majorca), 1677–8 (king and queen of France's chapels), 1746 (ex-bailiff of Latin empire of Byzantium and his land), 2642 (earl of Pembroke, his brothers, and their lands in Ireland and Wales), 2756 (king of Hungary, his wife, children, and lands), 2805 (crusader king of Navarre and his land), 3898 (queen of France's lands), 4603 (chapel of heir to Byzantium empire); etc.

[186] Innocent III, Reg. 16, no. 87.　　　　[187] Reg. Innocent IV, no. 5019.

[188] Reg. Alexander IV, no. 1006.

[189] E.g. without a specific papal mandate: Innocent III, Reg. 16, no. 87; Reg. Gregory IX, nos. 1399, 1677–8, 2756, 2805, 3898, 4469, 4603; etc.

Navarre took the cross, Gregory IX prohibited anyone to excommunicate him or interdict his lands without a special papal mandate until his death or return from crusade was certain.[190] Innocent III had even rewarded a prodigal's return to ecclesiastical obedience in 1214, when he agreed to King John's request that nobody might excommunicate him or interdict his chapel without a special papal mandate; ironically Innocent did not lift the interdict on England provoked by John till ten weeks after this grant.[191] Conversely princes might forfeit such immunities if they turned against ecclesiastical authority. Innocent IV in 1249 ordered the Bishop of Ratisbon to annul freedoms given to the duke of Bavaria by Gregory IX, including freedom from interdicts and excommunication laid without manifest and reasonable cause, unless the duke submitted by 15 August.[192] When the deadline passed and the duke still supported the deposed Frederick II against the pope, Innocent authorized the bishop to declare the duke and his supporters excommunicate and his land interdicted, despite his former freedoms, until he returned to the service of the Church by joining the crusade against Frederick.

On at least one occasion immunity was granted to protect victims of arbitrary and excessive sentences, although in a sense this is simply a variation on the grants of immunity from interdicts laid without manifest and reasonable cause.[193] In late 1210 Innocent III required the Archbishop of Sens and Bishops of Troyes, Langres, Châlons-sur-Marne, and Auxerre not to lay ill-considered sentences of excommunication and interdict on subjects and lands of Countess Blanche of Champagne as she alleged they were doing. This warning did not have a lasting effect, as the pope had to intervene again in 1214. He granted Blanche and her son protection against prelates, officials, and chapters of Reims province, notably the Bishop of Châlons who allegedly tried to enforce claims over her temporal jurisdiction by excommunication and interdict. He also reminded the Archbishop of Reims and Bishops of Soissons and Châlons-sur-Marne of his warning of 1210 such that if they disobeyed, his executors would use the same ecclesiastical sanctions against them. Ultimately he had to grant Blanche and her son immunity from interdict and excommunication.

Such grants invalidated sentences imposed specifically on their recipients and sometimes also their churches, lands, and subjects, but it was uncertain whether these grants also freed them from observing general interdicts on the area or community to which they belonged. This was a point of contention between Innocent III and some exempt Cistercian houses under the English interdict, and this issue was not settled in canon law definitively until a constitution of Clement V ruled that the exempt should observe general sentences. Indeed a

---

[190] Reg. Gregory IX, no. 2805.
[191] *SLI*, p. 175 (15 April 1214). The interdict was not relaxed until 2 July 1214 (Cheney, 'Interdict', 295).
[192] Reg. Innocent IV, no. 4333. Freedom granted in Reg. Gregory IX, no. 2795.
[193] Po. 4135a, 4943, 4946, 5269; Krehbiel, 143–4.

grant of Gregory X to Philip III of France in 1273 was unusual in that it
forbade extension of general sentences of excommunication and interdict to the
king's person unless he was expressly named in them.[194] Certainly by the early
thirteenth century canonists had agreed that immunities did not guard against a
certain kind of general sentence, one laid by canon law itself.[195]

3.3 INTERDICTS *A IURE*

This chapter has so far only treated interdicts laid by ecclesiastical judges,
termed by canonists interdicts *ab homine* or *ferende sententie*. But the thirteenth-
century papacy also attached penalty clauses to some of its legal rulings, whereby
any violating them automatically incurred excommunication or interdict. This
sentence was in effect laid by the law itself, not a judge, and was hence known as
excommunication (or interdict) *a iure*, *a canone*, or *late sententie*.[196] The sentence
had indeed already been laid before the wrong that occasioned it, as opposed
to a sentence to be laid (*ferenda*) by a judge after the fact. By the late twelfth
century canonists hence recognized that no warning was necessary before an
interdict *late sententie*, unlike an interdict *ferende sententie*, since the warning
was contained in the law that imposed it.[197] Some laws blurred this distinction
in that they deferred the sentence for a fixed period after their violation; in
this time the violator might make amends, so the sentence came into effect
only after he failed to do so in common with an interdict *ferende sententie*, but
such laws were exceptional. Canonists classified this kind of sentence as *lata sub
conditione*.[198]

Provision for automatic excommunication was found in canon law long before
canonists began to analyse it.[199] They observed that the *Decretum* included laws
that laid this sentence for several crimes, chiefly heresy, resisting papal decisions,
simony, priests living in concubinage, lay investiture, and violence against clergy.
Canon law had only introduced automatic penalties in the last three instances
under the eleventh-century reform papacy, and after the *Decretum*'s appearance

---

[194] Clen. 5.10.1; see p. 203 below. Reg. Gregory X, no. 149. Cf. grant to Philip's father Louis
IX in Reg. Clement IV, nos. 412, 419.

[195] Paulus Hungarus, *Notabilium* on 3 Comp. 5.16.1, BAV, Borgh. lat. MS 261, fol. 88rc–va:
'Item nota subtiliter quod interdicto lato ab homine possunt privilegiati in suo privilegio, secus
autem in interdicto lato a iure.' See also n. 176 ('nisi ceciderint in canonem').

[196] Huizing, 279–80.

[197] Richardus Anglicus on 1 Comp. 5.34.14 v. *excommunicatos*, BAV, Pal. lat. MS 696, fol.
115ra: 'Sed qualiter potest canon aliquis esse date sine peremptoria ... Responsio. Est ammonitio
hominis, de qua habetur in capitulo "Si peccaverit" [C.2 q.1 c.19], et ammonitio legis, ut hic
Innocentius [*recte* Alexander] enim cotidie ammonet.' Alanus on 1 Comp. 2.20.42 v. *nisi*, Munich,
Bayerisches Staatsbibliothek Clm 3879, fol. 36ra: 'In hoc ergo casu non est necessaria precedens
ammonitio, quod verum est ubicumque sententia fertur a iure, sed ubi a iudice ferenda debebit
precedere.'

[198] Huizing, 310–15.   [199] Ibid. 281–309.

such instances multiplied rapidly as a means to advance reform and punish abuses condemned by the reformers. The earliest instances of interdict *a iure* were apparently the suspension of worship in polluted or violated churches, but thirteenth-century canonists disputed whether these were strictly interdicts. The interdict was only defined by the late twelfth century as a distinct sanction, and automatic sentences were first specified as interdicts in the early thirteenth century and these only affected individual offenders like excommunication, notably interdicts *ab ingressu ecclesie* which ecclesiastical judges incurred for various breaches of canonical procedure.[200] Penalty clauses in papal legislation only imposed general interdicts after the mid-thirteenth century, perhaps as a result of Innocent IV's ban on collective excommunication in 1245. Thereafter instances of automatic general interdict proliferated so much, notably under Boniface VIII, that compilations of them became a minor canonistic genre by the mid-fourteenth century.

Popularizing knowledge of such sentences was meant to provide scant excuse for incurring them. One of the earliest and most widely circulated treatises about them is a case in point. It was compiled by French canonist Bérenger Frédol when Bishop of Béziers and following his collaboration on the *Liber sextus* (1298). Indeed it was the situation he found in Béziers on completing this papal commission that probably gave rise to his treatise. In his absence the consuls of Béziers had taxed its clergy contrary to 'Clericis laicos' (1296), Boniface VIII's well-known bull forbidding lay taxation of clerical wealth without papal consent. Under the terms of the bull the consuls incurred excommunication and the city was interdicted.[201] Bérenger thus wrote the treatise, as his preface explains, to teach his flock how to avoid automatic sentences in future. He listed twelve instances of interdict *a iure*, citing 'Clericis laicos' and other recent papal rulings also included in the *Liber sextus*. By the mid-fourteenth century continuators of his treatise had added nine more instances from subsequent canonical collections, notably the *Clementine* and *Extravagantes* of John XXII.[202]

The twenty rulings other than 'Clericis laicos' included provision for automatic interdicts against:

a) a city where a papal election was held and its rulers and officials did not observe the rules regarding the conclave;[203]

b) a city, castle, or place where its *universitas* levied tolls (*pedagia*) on churches or clergy;[204]

---

[200] E.g. Lat. Conc. IV c.47 (= 4 Comp. 5.15.5; X 5.39.48); cf. Coll. III 35 (= VI 5.11.1), VI 5.7.8.

[201] Treatise: *Bérenger Frédol*, 42–53. *Clericis laicos*: VI 3.23.3; Reg. Boniface VIII, no. 1567. Béziers: Ibid., no. 2140; see also pp. 225–33 below.

[202] *Bérenger Frédol*, 25 (preface), 59–121 (continuations).

[203] Lugd. Conc. II c.2 (= VI 1.6.3), i.e. issued by Gregory X in 1274.

[204] VI 3.20.4 (first issued by Boniface VIII in 1298).

c) a *universitas* which did not expel usurers arriving in its territory;[205]
d) a *universitas* which allowed seizure of pledges (*repressalie*) against ecclesiastical persons and their property;[206]
e) churches and cemeteries where clergy had induced someone to choose burial and failed to hand over the bodies within ten days of their burial;[207]
f) the land of anyone who attacked, seized, or exiled a bishop, or ordered, advised, supported, defended, or collaborated in such deed, any city doing the same, and any place for as long as the bishop was held there.[208]

The sentences laid *a iure* on those levying tolls on churches or clergy were to be publicized by diocesans according to a constitution of Clement V. In practice it had probably long been the duty of local ecclesiastical authorities to identify and publicize violations of canon law that carried an automatic sentence.[209]

Automatic sentences were not only laid by canon law that applied throughout the Latin West, but also by the local ecclesiastical law that supplemented it in specific provinces. A mid-fourteenth-century series of *casus* of excommunication and interdict *a canone* from the Carlisle diocese in northern England hence included instances from the conciliar and legatine legislation of the English Church as well as the common law of the Universal Church. A notable example comes from the Danish Church. In 1257 Alexander IV confirmed the constitution 'Cum ecclesia Daciana' issued by a council of the Archbishop of Lund and his suffragans. This had decreed that if the Danish king or any of his nobles should order, consent to, or connive at the capture or mutilation of any of the bishops within his realm, it would fall under an interdict so that priests and chaplains were forbidden on pain of excommunication from celebrating divine offices in the presence of nobles or any of their retainers or otherwise in public or private.[210] Violence by the secular power against the spiritual was clearly a particular problem in Denmark, and this law significantly bolstered Alexander III's decretal 'Mulieres' that already laid automatic excommunication on those ordering attacks on clergy.

During the thirteenth century canon law and canonistic doctrine came to specify with increasing precision how and by whom an interdict might be imposed, even for which offences it was mandatory. Ecclesiastical judges alone might use

---

[205] Lugd. Conc. II c.26 (= VI 5.5.1). Individuals violating this canon incurred suspension, if prelates, or otherwise excommunication. If they or the interdicted *universitas* remained obdurate for a month, their lands fell under an interdict for as long as the usurers lived there.

[206] Lugd. Conc. II c.28 (= VI 5.8.un.). Individuals violating this incurred excommunication.

[207] VI 3.12.1 (first issued by Boniface VIII in 1298).   [208] Clem. 5.8.1.

[209] Clem. 3.13.3.

[210] These *casus* were appended to a copy of Cardinal Ottobuono's constitutions for the English Church (1268) and inserted in a composite volume of the registers of the fourteenth-century bishops of Carlisle (Carlisle, Cumbria County Record Office, DRC/1/2, pp. 393–5; see my 'Fragment', 133). Denmark: Reg. Alexander IV, no. 2268. 'Mulieres': 1 Comp. 5.34.7 (= X 5.39.6); see pp. 54–5 above.

it and only if clearly justified and as a last resort, where warnings, summons, and all other means had failed to secure compliance with their commands. It was not a vindictive penalty intended to avenge a wrongdoing but a coercive one designed to bring a wrongdoer to repentance and reconciliation. It was primarily used to defend ecclesiastical persons, property, and liberties from the violence of the secular power, to which they were highly vulnerable. In practice, however, interdicts were sometimes subject to arbitrary and excessive use. Even the papacy used the sanction as a political weapon to intervene in secular affairs, not always in defence of ecclesiastical liberty but increasingly to protect its temporal interests in Italy. Regulation was, therefore, insufficient to constrain use of interdicts, and many, especially religious houses and secular rulers, sought protection from them in papal grants of immunity. Regulation would probably never have arisen in the first place had there not been a tendency to overuse and abuse interdicts. The interdict and excommunication were the only means of coercion that the spiritual power had under its direct control, which accounts for both this tendency and papal concern to regulate their usage, lest they came to lose their efficacy and diminish respect for ecclesiastical authority. Whether the interdict was effective at all is another issue, and it can only be judged when it is understood what the interdict was meant to accomplish according to canon law and its commentators. Hence the next chapter will examine what the terms of the interdict were and the evidence for their observance in the thirteenth century.

4

The Terms of an Interdict

By Innocent III's time an interdict was generally understood to involve suspension of divine offices, withdrawal of the sacraments, and prohibition of ecclesiastical burial in regard to the persons or places on which it was laid. But it was not usually meant as a ban on all religious ministrations. By the late twelfth century papal interdicts normally permitted infant baptism and penance of the dying. And though evidence of interdicts is sparse before this period, it seems that these exceptions were customary as early as the ninth century at least in the French Church, whence the earliest recorded interdicts come.[1] Indeed canonists agreed by the early thirteenth century that these sacraments should always be allowed during interdicts, since, as Richardus Anglicus argued, they were necessary for salvation.[2] Nevertheless Alanus held that they might be refused in extreme circumstances, when absolute severity was required; he observed (c.1201–10) that Innocent III was then applying this against the Piacenzans, presumably owing to their persistent disobedience in the face of his interdict and other sanctions.[3]

Beyond the usual exception of these sacraments, however, papal mandates for interdicts rarely specified the terms of the sentence. Neither were such terms generally defined in canon law or canonistic doctrine at the beginning of the thirteenth century. Consequently those required to execute such mandates on behalf of Innocent III often had to write to him for clarification of the terms of his interdicts. His extant responses to prelates ordered to enforce his interdicts in France (1200), England (1208), Ferrara (1209), and Naples (1211)

---

[1] Alexander III's decretal 'Non est vobis' (c.1173) was the legal *locus classicus* for these exceptions: 1 Comp. 4.1.13 (= X 4.1.11). An interdict on Laon diocese was condemned and lifted for denying these exceptions in 869: see p. 146 and Howland, 'Origins', 439–40. These exceptions were allowed when the council of Limoges imposed a 'public excommunication' on its diocese in 1031 (Mansi, xix.541).

[2] Ricardus on 1 Comp. 4.1.9 v. *preter baptisma*, BAV, Pal. lat. MS 696, fol. 76va: 'Ista enim semper debent excipi, nam sacramenta sunt necessitatis, que etiam ab heretico essent sumenda, ut xxiiii. q. i. Si quem forte, et de con. di. iiii. Sanctum est [C.24 q.1 c.40; De con. D.4 c.36]; secus de aliis, ut xxiiii q. i. c. Cepit [C.24 q.1 c.42].'

[3] Alanus on 1 Comp. 4.1.9 v. *baptisma*, Munich, Bayerisches Staatsbibliothek Clm 3879, fol. 63vb: 'Omnia enim alia sacramenta uni interdicuntur pro peccato alterius quando res postulat, ut hic et infra. e. Non est vobis, supra. de iure patro. Ex insinuatione [1 Comp. 4.1.13, 3.33.17]. Ista vero nulli pro <peccato> alterius interdicuntur, ut xxiiii. q. iii. Si habes [C.24 q.3 c.1], nisi ex maximo rigore, quem observat papa modo circa Placentinos.' Innocent III interdicted Piacenza in 1198; see Krehbiel, 101–2.

shows how widespread the uncertainty was.[4] The English interdict illustrates the problem well.[5] A letter of Innocent III dated 27 August 1207 instructed the Bishops of London, Ely, and Worcester 'to publish a general sentence of interdict throughout England' and, according to the usual concise formula, 'permitting no ecclesiastical office except the baptism of infants and the confession of the dying'.[6] The bishops had presumably found this mandate insufficient, for the pope had to write to them again three months later, explaining that his sentence, not yet imposed, was to be observed by all clergy, secular and regular, including the military orders, and that it also applied to Wales, a point he admitted to omitting in his original mandate. But this still left many points unclear, and he had to reply to queries from the bishops in a third letter seven weeks after they published his interdict on 23 March 1208.[7] They asked how infants might be baptised with chrism if the interdict prohibited consecration of chrism; he suggested alternative arrangements. He also ruled that the last Communion, the *viaticum*, was not allowed along with confession of the dying during the interdict.[8] Finally he added that he would not have minded if from the start religious orders had been permitted to celebrate the offices behind closed doors with excommunicates and those under interdict excluded, as their privileges conceded. This seemed to contradict his earlier letter requiring regular and secular clergy to observe the interdict regardless of any privilege or liberty, and when he wrote to the three bishops again on 22 August 1208, he had to refute allegations of inconsistency.[9] This matter was then left to their discretion, and Innocent did not expressly mitigate the interdict for regular clergy till 12 January 1209, when he permitted all conventual churches observing the interdict to celebrate mass once a week behind closed doors, though Peter of Blois, Archdeacon of London, observed that many clergy in his diocese found this concession still left many issues unclear.[10] In 1212 the English interdict was mitigated further by the concession of the *viaticum*, reversing Innocent's earlier ruling; hosts might be consecrated for the dying at the masses permitted since 1209.[11]

If the papal line on observance of the interdict was ambiguous and vacillating, local attempts to supplement papal instructions contradicted each other even more blatantly. Indeed the two fullest definitions of the interdict's terms did not

[4] X 5.38.11 (France); X 5.39.43 (Ferrara); Innocent III, Reg. 14, no. 74 (Naples).

[5] See Cheney, 'Interdict', 298–300, and id. *England*, 300–6; cf. Parker, 'Terms'.

[6] *SLI*, no. 30 (Innocent III, Reg. 10, no. 113).

[7] His second letter of 15 November 1207 is *SLI*, no. 31 (Innocent III, Reg. 10, no. 161); his third of 14 June 1208 is *SLI*, no. 36 (Innocent III, Reg. 11, no. 92).

[8] He had, however, permitted the *viaticum* under the French interdict (1200); see pp. 149–50 below.

[9] Innocent III, Reg. 11, no. 141.

[10] *SLI*, no. 37 (Innocent III, Reg. 11, no. 211); *Peter of Blois*, 118–19 (Letter 24). This concession was noted in various contemporary monastic chronicles: *Annales*, iv.54, 397; Coventry, *Memoriale*, ii.201.

[11] Coggleshall, *Chronicon*, 165; Coventry, *Memoriale*, ii.205. Coggleshall suggests that this mitigation was granted by the Bishops of Ely and London; see Cheney, 'Interdict', 299 n. 4.

apparently come from the pope. One is admittedly titled the 'Forma interdicti ab Innocentio III in Angliam consituta', but it probably emanated from one or all of the sentence's bishop-executors, as Cheney argues, or another English ecclesiastical authority.[12] The other is an interpolated version of the pope's third letter to the bishop-executors (from 14 June 1208); it may represent the application of the interdict in Canterbury diocese.[13] Both documents show that local ecclesiastical authorities were prepared to tolerate religious practices that Innocent's sentence did not technically ban, notably preaching, but they also 'point to divergent practices in different parts of the country'.[14] Another source, the Dunstable annals, noted observance of the interdict, probably in Lincoln diocese, in similar but not wholly identical terms to the 'Canterbury' document.[15] In particular, the issue of closing churches to laity was variously interpreted. The 'Forma interdicti' held that no layman might enter church even for private prayer, except a powerful one who was not excommunicated, devoutly sought admittance, and could not be refused without dire repercussions; even then he might be admitted only to hear a sermon. But the 'Canterbury' document required that churches remain closed except on important feast days, when they might be opened to parishioners and others for prayer; whereas the Dunstable annals record that priests granted access to the altars to anyone wishing to make offerings. These sources also differed on provision for infant baptism and on whether priests might distribute holy water and *panis benedictus*. In addition a letter of Peter of Blois described, at the Bishop of Salisbury's request, arrangements in London diocese for Candlemas and Ash Wednesday during the interdict. These had to be devised by the dean and chapter in the Bishop of London's absence; he was one of the interdict's executors who had fled into exile soon after promulgating it, and Peter had to write at the chapter's behest in 1209 seeking his advice on other observances.[16]

Hence at the beginning of the thirteenth century the terms of an interdict were, apart from the usual exception of infant baptism and penance of the dying, largely *ad hoc* and a matter of local custom. Admittedly Innocent III issued advice on request in specific cases, but it was not immediately clear whether these rulings were intended to apply generally. For example Peter of Blois' letter to the Bishop of London had to ask whether the interdict might be mitigated in his diocese in accordance with Innocent's letter to the Bishop of Paris that

[12] Martène and Durand, i.812–13; these eighteenth-century editors used the text in a manuscript then at Mont St Michel, now Avranches, Bibliothèque municipale MS 149, fol. 109rb–va (identified by Cheney, 'Collections', 466). On its possible authors: Cheney, 'Interdict', 298; Parker, 'Terms', 259–60.

[13] Gervase, II, pp. xcii–xciii. It is found in a collection of documents about the disputed Canterbury election that occasioned the interdict, probably compiled by a monk of the cathedral priory contemporary with its chronicler Gervase (Ibid., p. xvi).

[14] Cheney, 'Interdict', 298; cf. Parker, 'Terms'.   [15] *Annales*, iii.30 (A. 1208).

[16] *Peter of Blois*, 110 (Letter 20, to Bishop of Salisbury), 118–21 (Letter 24, to Bishop of London).

had relaxed the terms of the papal interdict on France. Nevertheless from the mid- to late twelfth century canonists increasingly collected such rulings in papal decretals as a new source of canon law. In 1210 Innocent approved a collection of his decretals for use in courts and schools, and this included some of his rulings on the terms of interdicts.[17] It marked the start of a common law of interdicts, and as decretal law evolved during the thirteenth century, regulation of interdicts grew with it. This process of gradual legal clarification and codification regarding interdicts was largely completed by Boniface VIII's *Liber sextus* (1298).

Canonistic literature also proliferated alongside this growing body of decretal law in the thirteenth century, supplementing and complementing it. A close symbiotic relationship developed between the two, not found as markedly in any other period of canon law. Notably the *Liber sextus* confirmed many traditional canonistic teachings on the interdict, although these in turn may have been describing customary practices. The purpose of this chapter is, therefore, to trace the evolution of the interdict's terms from the customary practices of the early thirteenth century to the fully articulated and systematic definition that existed in law and legal doctrine a century later. The lines of development are not always clear, however, and the evidence of practice that emerges from the thirteenth-century papal registers and other sources is patchy. Hence it is not possible to do more than assemble a few illuminating scraps of detail at certain points. The evidence is organized under three main headings, each concerning a broad area of religious observance: *divine offices* and other non-sacramental liturgical practices; the *sacraments*, namely baptism, confirmation, Eucharist, marriage, holy orders, penance, and extreme unction; and *ecclesiastical burial*.

4.1 DIVINE OFFICES

By the late twelfth century local interdicts forbade celebration of divine offices in the churches affected; it was likewise understood that those under personal interdict were denied participation in the offices.[18] Offices are church services and so include mass, wedding, and funeral services. Innocent IV even suggested that an interdict affected all liturgical rites that only the ordained might perform, and ecclesiastical authorities and canonists certainly recognized by the early thirteenth century that it might have broad implications.[19] Before we consider these in detail, it must be pointed out that positive evidence of the offices ceasing during interdicts is generally hard to find; the violation of an interdict

---

[17] E.g. 3 Comp. 5.21.16 (= X 5.39.43).

[18] Alexander III's decretal 'Ex rescripto' contains one of the earliest express statements of the ban on offices under interdicts (1 Comp. 2.17.6; = X 2.24.9).

[19] Innocent IV, *Apparatus* on X 5.31.18 v. *violavit*; cf. Calderinus, 'De interdicto', Pt 1 §§2 and 60–1.

was usually thought more worthy of comment than its observance. The English interdict is a case in point. Cheney found only a few contemporary references to closed and silent churches that the faithful surely faced everywhere. The chronicler Geoffrey of Coldingham mourned the bareness and desolation of the altars in his own Durham diocese; the 'Forma interdicti' had indeed required altars to be stripped.[20] He went on to lament the silence that had descended on churches as a result of cessation of sung services and bell-ringing. In nearby York diocese the Cistercian Matthew of Rievaulx evoked the same scenario in dark moralizing terms, for he saw the interdict as divine retribution for sins against the English Church, in particular appointment of unworthy candidates to ecclesiastical offices: 'And this apostacy is the principal and definite reason why the voice of the turtle-dove, Mother Church, is not heard in our land. Mainly on this account has the Lord of Hosts stopped the mouths of those celebrating him, and abandoned us in derision and hissing, so that people and priest lack rites and masses.' A less colourful allusion to the absence of offices was the comment of the Tewkesbury annalist that, after the interdict was relaxed, services were resumed on 5 July 1214, which implies that they had been suspended.[21]

Scanty as the evidence is, it would seem that the interdict disrupted the normal round of services in English churches. But the general ban on church services was not meant to be total. When Innocent III said that the privileges of English clergy did not free them from observing the sentence, its bishop-executors apparently interpreted his instructions more strictly than he intended, since he later expressed regret that monks had not been allowed to enjoy their freedom to celebrate the offices in private, and, as already mentioned, he extended this freedom to all conventual churches in early 1209. In fact papal grants of this freedom to monastic orders and specific houses, churches, other religious institutions, and prelates were already commonplace by the late twelfth century, so much so that *Compilatio tertia* included a decretal interpreting their terms from the first year of Innocent's pontificate.[22] By then the papal chancery had strictly formulated such terms: recipients of such grants might celebrate divine offices in their churches during a general local interdict in a low voice, behind closed doors, with the excommunicated and those under interdict excluded, and no bells being rung.[23] Such conditions were obvious precautions against violation of the interdict. Bells normally summoned the laity to worship, and sung masses might be heard even outside closed churches, while locked doors were necessary

[20] *Historiae Dunelmensis*, 25; Martène and Durand, i.813.
[21] Wilmart, 'Mélanges', 83; *Annales*, i.61.
[22] 3 Comp. 5.23.1 (= X 5.40.17); Innocent III, Reg. 1, no. 551.
[23] So many of these grants are recorded in the thirteenth-century papal registers that it would be tedious to list them all, but an illustrative selection is found in Innocent III, Reg. 1, nos. 287, 549; 2, nos. 7, 31, 71, 92, 102; 5, no. 9; 6, nos. 88, 115, 118, 206; 7, nos. 30, 95, 149, 185; 9, nos. 67, 242; 10, nos. 33, 59, 192, 205; 11, nos. 61, 92, 111, 141, 145, 193, 214, 217; 12, nos. 9, 10, 21, 166, 169; 13, nos. 11, 31, 81; 14, nos. 24, 62, 106; 15, nos. 16, 79, 126, 143, 234; 16, no. 146.

to prevent laity not only entering church but also seeing the services within, in which they were largely passive spectators even at normal times.[24] Indeed when some regular canons of Le Mans claimed that custom allowed them to celebrate in a loud voice with bells ringing during a general interdict, Innocent III quashed this custom as damaging to ecclesiastical discipline in a decretal of 1206, conceding the canons the freedom to celebrate under the normal circumspect conditions.[25] Sometimes a further reasonable qualification was placed on such grants: they might not be enjoyed by those who had caused the interdict or who were interdicted by name.[26] In a few instances the freedom to celebrate services in private was limited to a certain interdict as in the English case, or interdicts caused by a certain lay power, notably the local lord.[27] Initially this freedom mainly featured in grants of exemption or papal protection to monastic, notably Cistercian, houses, but at the Fourth Lateran Council Innocent III extended it to all bishops under the normal conditions, including disqualification of those who caused the interdict even through fraud.[28] And grants of this freedom to regular clergy grew until 1298, when Boniface VIII ruled that masses and other divine offices might be held daily in all churches and monasteries in private during general local interdicts. He even required clergy to attend such services on pain of the loss of their daily allowances in churches where they were distributed.[29] He was determined to maintain such observances, for, as the preamble to his ruling explained, infinite spiritual dangers might arise from the privations of the interdict. Nevertheless he was also concerned not to undermine ecclesiastical discipline; in another ruling he added that those who gave any cause for an interdict might not enjoy this freedom to celebrate or hear offices during it, and clergy free to hold services behind closed doors might not admit others from outside their church unless they shared this freedom.[30]

And such freedoms were not always restricted to the clergy. In 1205 Innocent III had confirmed that monks of exempt Cluniac houses might admit their servants to their services held behind closed doors during interdicts. This arrangement was also permitted in some other religious houses, and certain bishops might likewise celebrate the offices in the presence of their household. Occasionally the papacy allowed other favoured members of the laity to attend

[24] The need for such conditions was understood by Vincentius Hispanus on X 5.38.11 v. *voce*, Paris, BN, MS lat. 3967, fol. 202va: 'Patet quod non licet excommunicato extra ecclesiam stare prope cum celebrantur divina, cum et omnes prohibeantur audire exterius in interdicto, ut hic colligitur, et plenius in integra ubi dicebatur voce ita dimissa quod exterius non possint audiri.' On the ban on bell-ringing: Guido de Baysio, *Lectura* on VI 5.11.24 v. *non pulsatis* (fol. 126ra).
[25] 3 Comp. 1.3.4 (= X 1.4.5); Innocent III, Reg. 8, no. 212.
[26] E.g. Innocent III, Reg. 1, no. 287; Reg. Honorius III, nos. 1992, 3113, 3910, 6129, 6131; Reg. Gregory IX, nos. 1194, 2469, 4706; Reg. Innocent IV, nos. 23, 5176; etc.
[27] E.g. Innocent III, Reg. 14, no. 24; 15, nos. 126, 143; etc.
[28] Lat. Conc. IV c.58 (= 4 Comp. 5.12.8; X 5.33.25).
[29] VI 5.11.24. On the origin of this ruling see my 'Two Constitutions', 120–1, 126.
[30] VI 5.7.11.

such 'private' services. In 1212 Innocent III conceded that if the Archbishop of Bourges interdicted a certain church subject to the abbey of Dol, chaplains presented to the church by the abbey might still hold services there behind closed doors and admit their servants, the poor, and sick.[31] The devotion of laity doing pious works was similarly rewarded. According to his biographer Innocent III let prelates hold private services during the French interdict (1200) for crusaders who had asked him for this freedom.[32] The laity who composed the third orders of the Humiliati, Franciscans, and Dominicans also obtained freedoms to take part in offices behind closed doors like regular members of these movements.[33] Unordained members of religious institutions, such as nuns and sometimes brethren of leper hospitals, might also be allowed to have the offices celebrated for them.[34]

However, these extensions of clerical freedoms were unusual and a subject of controversy among canonists. Johannes Teutonicus even doubted whether a cathedral chapter might join their bishop in celebrating offices behind closed doors, and he was concerned that broad interpretation of such freedoms might result in interdicts being violated.[35] His concern was widely shared. After friars had admitted scholars to their churches in interdicted Avignon, mid-thirteenth-century canonist Pierre Sampsona saw this as an abuse of their freedom to hold services behind closed doors. In his view only those given this freedom might enjoy it; otherwise ecclesiastical discipline would be scorned.[36] Nevertheless

---

[31] Cluniacs: Innocent III, Reg. 7, no. 185. Dol: id. Reg. 15, no. 126; cf. Reg. Gregory IX, no. 4706.

[32] *Gesta* c.84 (*PL* 214.cxxxv–cxxxvi).

[33] Humiliati: Reg. Innocent IV, no. 2193. Most of these grants were localized: Reg. Honorius III, no. 5740; Reg. Alexander IV, nos. 714; 1310; Reg. Urban IV, nos. 749, 1906; Reg. Honorius IV, no. 886. Likewise by 1285 Franciscans could admit their servants, proctors, and craftsmen to such offices (Reg. Honorius IV, no. 203).

[34] For nuns: Reg. Honorius III, no. 6131; Reg. Gregory IX, no. 1194; Reg. Innocent IV, no. 5176; Reg. Urban IV, no. 749; Reg. Nicholas IV, nos. 243, 869, 7502. For members of hospitals: Reg. Clement IV, no. 1626; Reg. Nicholas IV, nos. 2098, 3738, 4566.

[35] Johannes Teutonicus on 4 Comp. 5.12.8 v. *quandoque*, BAV, Vat. lat. MS 1377, fol. 314vb: 'Numquid canonici tunc poterunt interesse? Non, ne per hoc vilescat rigor, ut supra. c. prox. [4 Comp. 5.12.7].' Vincentius Hispanus and Damasus agreed, on Lat. Conc. IV c.58 v. *celebrare divina*, that not all canons might join the bishop but only those he invited (*Constitutiones*, 371, 453). Vincentius modified his view on X 5.33.25 v. *possint*, BAV, Vat. lat. MS 6769, fol. 135rb: 'Item queritur an canonici sui tunc [fol. 135va] possunt cum eo ibi interesse. Dixit Io. quod non ... Dixit <Bernadus> Compos <tellanus> quod possunt quasi de familia, et satis credo quia pars corporis eius sunt, supra viii. q.i. Verum [C.8 q.1 c.22].'

[36] Bernard de Montemirat on X 5.33.25, BAV, Vat. lat. MS 2542, fol. 80rb (Ed. fol. 144vb): 'Nunquid canonici cum episcopo possunt interesse? Sic audivi magistrum meum [Sampsona] determinantem in questione facti satis isti simili: ecce quod Avinione civitas fuit supposita interdicto, habent minores et predicatores privilegium quod possunt tempore interdicti celebrare divina, interdictis et excommunicatis exclusis, veniebant scholares ad eorum ecclesias et admittebantur ab eis. Dicebat magister meus quod hoc fieri non deberet quia stricte erat interpretandum privilegium, ne vilesceret rigor discipline ... et ideo tantum ipsi predicatores celebrare debebant et alii admittendi non erant.' Copies of this gloss in BAV, Borgh. lat. MSS 231 (fol. 129vb) and 260 (fol. 103rb), have 'P. de San.' instead of 'magistrum meum', and 'magister P.' instead of 'magister meus'.

Innocent IV taught that bishops and other individuals who secured this freedom might admit their servants, at least clerical ones, to participate in their services, but a convent might not do so, unless this freedom was extended to its servants expressly; and as pope he made express grants of this kind. His teaching was confirmed as law by Boniface VIII in the *Liber sextus*. But this extension of clerical freedom to laity was somewhat curtailed when a constitution of Clement V prohibited Franciscans on pain of excommunication to admit members of their third order to hear offices during interdicts, despite previous grants to the contrary.[37]

Nevertheless there were more significant exceptions to the exclusion of laity from services. Since the early thirteenth century popes had increasingly granted some lay dignitaries the freedom to hear divine offices in interdicted places. In a handful of instances access was merely conceded to the offices of clergy who were free to hold them.[38] But usually such grants allowed their recipients to have offices celebrated by their chaplain. Often it was specified who might accompany them at these services, in the case of male addressees normally their wife and children, and sometimes members of their household or retinue.[39] In 1244 Innocent IV simply permitted Count Henry of Vienne to admit ten knights, and another nobleman to be accompanied by two or three 'honest persons'.[40] Of course he taught that persons free to take part in offices during general interdicts might admit their servants; presumably he meant royal and noble as well as episcopal recipients of this freedom. Johannes Andreae understood as much in *c*.1302 after this teaching became law, but Innocent's successors continued to specify companions in grants to lay dignitaries until then.[41] Otherwise the conditions of such grants were the same as those to religious houses: offices were to be held behind shut doors, etc.; and, according to some grants, only if the recipient and their companions had not caused the interdict and were not interdicted by name.[42] Sometimes the terms were even more specific. In 1232 Gregory IX gave one noblewoman freedom to hear services in her dowry lands if her husband's land was interdicted.[43] In 1217 another noblewoman had gained a similar grant from Honorius III alleging that her husband's land was interdicted by no fault of hers. Other grants were also explicitly designed to spare innocent

[37] Innocent IV, *Apparatus* on X 5.33.25 v. *et interdictis*; cf. Reg. Innocent IV, no. 7557. Boniface VIII: VI 5.7.11. Clement V: Clem. 5.10.3.

[38] Reg. Gregory IX, no. 852; Reg. Innocent IV, nos. 4005, 6452, 6458; cf. grant in n. 32.

[39] Reg. Honorius III, nos. 1241, 4504 (prince with army), 5854; Reg. Gregory IX, nos. 3919, 4277; etc.

[40] Reg. Innocent IV, nos. 407, 598; cf. ibid. nos. 405, 5956, 6435.

[41] E.g. Reg. Alexander IV, nos. 177, 429, 1849; Reg. Urban IV, no. 2665; Reg. Gregory X, no. 148, etc. Johannes Andreae, *Glossa* on VI 5.7.11 v. *persone*.

[42] E.g. Reg. Gregory IV, no. 3919; Reg. Innocent IV, nos. 5956, 6435; Reg. Alexander IV, no. 177, etc.

[43] Reg. Gregory IX, no. 989; Reg. Honorius III, no. 314; cf. Reg. Urban IV, no. 2665, grant to a widow in lands interdicted because of the Hohenstaufen.

parties. After the papacy interdicted Sicily to punish the expulsion of its papally approved Angevin rulers, Boniface VIII granted members of the dynasty and its supporters seeking to reconquer the island in 1302 the freedom to have offices celebrated there. These and other grants were also meant to reward lay service to the Church, notably crusading. Innocent III's grant to crusaders in interdicted France has been noted; in 1238 Gregory IX likewise gave the *crucesignatus* Richard of Cornwall freedom to hear offices in interdicted places on his land with his wife and son.[44]

Such grants often allowed lay dignitaries to hear offices only in their chapels, but some also allowed them to do so in any interdicted place where they happened to arrive.[45] Indeed royal and noble households were often mobile, and Nicholas IV even made this concession to Queen Elizabeth of the Romans together with a grant for her chaplain to celebrate offices at a portable altar if necessary.[46] No such concessions to monastic houses are known, but religious were not usually meant to leave the cloister. But interdicts could be mobile. When the king of Portugal came under an ambulatory interdict in 1238, Gregory IX permitted friars and other exempt religious to celebrate offices behind closed doors in any town of the kingdom where he was present.[47] It is unclear whether this was an exceptional grant, but some clergy secured the freedom to celebrate in any interdicted places where they arrived. As missionaries and preachers friars often travelled outside their convents, hence Franciscans obtained this freedom from Innocent IV in 1246.[48] By the mid-thirteenth century these grants were usually made to clergy on papal missions, notably legates and those preaching crusades. The Archbishop of Tyre enjoyed such a grant whilst preaching the cross in France in 1263, and in 1265 he was further authorized to admit crusaders and those intending to take the cross to services behind closed doors in interdicted places.[49]

Such a concession was intended to reward and encourage acts of lay devotion, especially necessary when interdicts removed the usual stimuli to piety. This freedom to admit laity to churches in interdicted places was indeed most often granted to those seeking lay charity. By the late twelfth century the papacy permitted Hospitallers and Templars to open a church once a year on reaching an interdicted place. This applied especially to brethren sent to collect alms,

---

[44] Reg. Boniface VIII, nos. 4620, 4691. Reg. Gregory IX, no. 4277; cf. ibid. nos. 1627, 2565; see above, n. 32.

[45] E.g. Reg. Honorius III, nos. 1483, 3314; Reg. Gregory IX, nos. 1627, 2125–6; Reg. Innocent IV, no. 3184; Reg. Alexander IV, nos. 826–7; Reg. Urban IV, no. 2184 (bishop), etc.

[46] Reg. Nicholas IV, nos. 3490 (altar), 3491. See n. 59 on concession of portable altars to bishops.

[47] Reg. Gregory IX, no. 4247; cf. Reg. Urban IV, no. 749, discussed on p. 140 below.

[48] Reg. Innocent IV, no. 1959. On other mendicant freedoms during interdicts see n. 33.

[49] Reg. Urban IV, no. 385; Reg. Clement IV, nos. 1571–2. Cf. ibid. no. 321; Reg. Gregory X, nos. 522, 524; Reg. Nicholas III, no. 292; Reg. Martin IV, no. 472 *et seq.*; Reg. Honorius IV, no. 796; Reg. Boniface VIII, nos. 793 (nuncio), 798, 1615, 3369, etc.

and similar freedoms were conferred in the thirteenth century on those raising funds for their hospitals, and even on one occasion those soliciting contributions to a church's fabric fund.[50] In the latter grant from 1253 it was specified that churches might be opened in interdicted places and services held there so that the faithful might become more devout and hear sermons exhorting them to offer alms. These grants normally excluded excommunicates and those interdicted *nominatim*, but otherwise the laity might attend such 'open' services.[51] The charitable work of lay confraternities might win similar papal recognition. In 1255 members of a Milanese confraternity who contributed to paupers' funeral expenses secured freedom to hear offices in their church behind closed doors during a general interdict. But such direct grants to lay bodies were very rare.[52]

Perhaps less uncommon were grants allowing regular clergy to admit laity to their services during general interdicts on certain feast days. In 1257 Alexander IV permitted a nunnery in Genoa diocese to ring its bells and call people to hear offices in its church on any feast of the Blessed Virgin during a general interdict. In that year Dominicans of the shrine church of St Peter Martyr in Milan won a similar freedom, to be enjoyed on the saint's feast day and its vigil.[53] Indeed Johannes Andreae implied that by 1298 many friars and other exempt clergy had won grants to celebrate offices freely during interdicts on their special feast days, even for up to a week afterwards.[54] In 1298, however, these and similar freedoms of clergy and laity to participate in the offices during interdicts were largely revoked by Boniface VIII's constitution 'Alma mater'.[55] It replaced them with two general rights. One has already been noted, that allowing clergy to celebrate offices. The other regarded lay access to these services: on the principal holy days of Christmas, Easter, Pentecost, and Assumption churches might be opened with bells ringing and those under interdict admitted to hear offices celebrated solemnly in loud voices.[56] The usual conditions applied: excommunicates were to be excluded and those occasioning the interdict might not approach the altar. Boniface hence intended to mitigate the severity of the interdict for the innocent while maintaining its force against the guilty. His motives for so doing will be examined in the context of popular reactions to interdicts later, but contemporary

[50] Grant to military orders regulated in Lat. Conc. III c.9 (= 1 Comp. 5.28.3; X 5.33.3). Hospitals: Reg. Honorius III, nos. 2993, 5829; Reg. Alexander IV, nos. 1553, 2037, 2373; Reg. Nicholas IV, no. 842.

[51] Cf. Innocent IV, *Apparatus* on X 5.33.24 v. *excommunicatis*. His grant was made to assist the church of St Just, Lyon, to reward its clergy's hospitality during the pope's exile in Lyon (Reg. Innocent IV, no. 6361).

[52] Reg. Alexander IV, no. 774; cf. Reg. Gregory IX, no. 2565; Reg. Boniface VIII, no. 104.

[53] Reg. Alexander IV, nos. 1664, 2195.

[54] Johannes Andreae, *Glossa* on VI 5.11.24 v. *concessis*.

[55] VI 5.11.24. As understood by Johannes Andreae in n. 54 and his *Novelle* on VI 5.11.24 v. *celebrent*; cf. Guido de Baysio, *Lectura* on VI 5.11.24 v. *non obstantibus* (fol. 126rb).

[56] Guido de Baysio stated on VI 5.11.24 v. *celebrentur* (fol. 126r) that offices might be celebrated from the vespers of the vigil until the vespers of the feast inclusive.

canonists saw his ruling as a deserved amendment of the injustice of punishing some for others' sins.[57]

It was promulgated in the *Liber sextus*, as well as circulating separately,[58] and in the spirit of that compilation it established a common code of practice for observing general interdicts. It superseded the freedom of the military orders to open churches in interdicted places and most similar grants to groups and persons. Albeit other rulings in the *Liber sextus* still recognized grants permitting some individuals to hear offices with their households in general interdicts, and one even let prelates celebrate them at portable altars in interdicted places if churches were inaccessible.[59] Nevertheless while Boniface extended certain freedoms during general interdicts to most clergy and laity, he also restricted those freedoms. Papal grants of such freedoms had proliferated over the previous century, and this was not the first papal attempt to regulate their growth. In 1263 Urban IV had noted that since his predecessor Alexander IV had interdicted many places in Italy for supporting the papacy's political opponents, many clergy and laity had sought papal grants to celebrate these offices in such places.[60] Therefore Urban had revoked these grants, forbidding use of them on pain of excommunication, so that the interdict might be observed more strictly. His aim was to increase pressure on the interdicted communities to submit, but his ruling did not have the desired effect and it concerned him that clergy in such communities were denied the offices through others' wickedness. He thus backtracked, permitting clergy of collegiate churches and religious houses to celebrate only before their *conversi* and visiting clerks; unordained religious such as nuns and Humiliati might also have offices celebrated for them. Like Boniface 35 years later Urban replaced private freedoms with common rights, though only in parts of Italy. More significantly he sought to strike a balance between coercing the guilty and sparing the innocent, a basic problem in imposing an interdict as a collective punishment, and one that the thirteenth-century papacy tried to resolve in its ever closer definition of the terms of the interdict through general legislation and specific grants, and nowhere more explicitly than in 'Alma mater'.

By Innocent III's time canonists had agreed that the ban on offices applied especially to mass services and that these might be held during interdicts only by those enjoying this freedom.[61] But they also observed that some

---

[57] Johannes Andreae, *Glossa* on VI 5.11.24 v. *appropinquent*; cf. Johannes Monachus, *Glossa*, ibid. (fol. 418vb).

[58] Po. 24523 (1 June 1298); Schmidt, 'Frühe Anwendungen', 123.

[59] VI 5.7.11 (households); VI 5.7.12 (portable altars), in effect an extension of the grant in n. 28.

[60] Reg. Urban IV, no. 749; cf. ibid. no. 2665.

[61] Tancred on 1 Comp. 4.1.13 v. *celebretis*, BAV, Vat. lat. MS 1377, fol. 64vb: 'Tali posito interdicto, quero an, hostio clauso, populo non admisso, licet in ecclesiis divina celebrare? ... missam vero etiam secreto dicere non audent nisi sit eis concessum per privilegium, ut extra. iii. de ver. si. Cum in partibus [3 Comp. 5.23.1].' Likewise: Richardus Anglicus, ibid., BAV, Pal. lat. MS 696, fol. 77ra; Alanus, ibid., Munich, Bayerisches Staatsbibliothek Clm 3879, fol. 64ra; Vincentius

other offices were excepted, notably canonical hours. Alanus taught that during an interdict any clerk was free to recite the hours as a private devotion even if interdicted himself.[62] This reflected contemporary practice. When Peter of Capua published the interdict on France in 1199, he allowed clergy to say hours outside church provided that no laity might hear; this practice was also tolerated under the English interdict, at least in Canterbury diocese.[63] Moreover a decretal of Innocent III even allowed clergy to read the hours *together* in twos and threes in conventual churches.[64] The same conditions applied as to grants to celebrate offices during general local interdicts; namely the hours were not to be sung but said behind closed doors with the excommunicated and interdicted excluded and in a voice so low that nobody outside might hear. The decretal appeared in Alanus's collection with the Bishop of Paris as its addressee, and it seems to be a response to his queries concerning observance of the French interdict in 1200.[65] But it was not immediately understood to have general force. Peter of Blois, Archdeacon of London, knew of it but asked his bishop in 1209 whether it applied in his diocese during the English interdict. And in 1213, after King John admitted Stephen Langton as Archbishop of Canterbury, Langton allowed the hours to be sung during the interdict in a low voice in conventual churches and even in parish churches by priests before their congregations, regardless of Innocent III's more restrictive concession.[66] Tellingly the latter was not included in *Compilatio tertia* (1210). It appeared in *Compilatio quarta* (1215), but canonists were slow to accept that collection; Tancred recognized Innocent's ruling but cited it from Alanus's collection. Certainly canonists accepted its general force after its inclusion in the *Liber extra*.[67] They agreed that hours might be said in churches by secular priests singly or conventual clerks in pairs but others might not attend unless privileged to do so. Innocent IV unusually claimed that in monastic churches the whole convent might say the

Hispanus on 1 Comp. 4.1.13 v. *divina*, Leipzig Universitätsbibliothek MS 983, fol. 39va; id. on 3 Comp. 1.4.1 v. *suspenderant*, BAV, Vat. lat. MS 1378, fol. 5vb; etc.

[62] Alanus on 1 Comp. 5.23.2 v. *presumpserit*, Munich, Bayerisches Staatsbibliothek Clm 3879, fol. 90va: 'in modum enim privati suffragii dicere horas suas, quod etiam potest laicus, ut xxviii. di. Presbiterum, xi. q. iii. Si quis episcopus in concilio [D.28 c.16; C.11 q.3 c.7].' Cf. id. on Alan. 5.20.1 v. *legere*, Vercelli Cathedral Chapter MS 89, fol. 124va: 'Non tamquam officiando <in> ecclesia. Sic etiam clericus interdictus potest horas dicere, ar. xi. q. iii. Si quis episcopus in concilio.'

[63] France: Martène and Durand, iv.147. England: Gervase, II, pp. xcii–xciii (except when laity present).

[64] Alan. 5.20.1 (= 4 Comp. 5.14.3; X 5.38.11).

[65] See von Heckel, 'Gilbertus und Alanus', 301–2; cf. Innocent III, Suppl. nos. 35–6.

[66] *Peter of Blois*, 120 (Letter 24); Wendover, *Flores*, ii.83–4.

[67] Tancred on 1 Comp. 4.1.13 v. *celebretis*, BAV, Vat. lat. MS 1377, fol. 65ra: 'Tali posito interdicto, quero an, hostio clauso, populo non admisso, licet in ecclesiis divina celebrare? Respondeo non licet tamquam ecclesias officiando ... sed tanquam privata suffragia singulariter possunt bini binique, ut videantur potius legere quam cantare, ut extra. Alani. de penitentia et re. Quod [Alan. 5.20.1].' In his *Lectura* on X 5.38.11 v. *et in conventualibus* (vol. 2, fol. 101rb) Hostiensis distinguished that during a general interdict a secular clerk might recite the hours with a colleague in his room but alone in church.

offices together for burials of its deceased members *and* the canonical hours.[68] Indeed in 1289 Nicholas IV gave a female convent in Mainz diocese freedom to recite the hours together, but such a concession was exceptional.

Such private observances of clergy aside, the ban on offices generally affected rites involving laity that only ordained clerks could perform. Notably priests could not admit women to church during the French and English interdicts for ritual purification after childbirth, known in England as churching.[69] Parish clergy usually received new mothers at the church door, aspersed them with holy water, and led them into mass with prayers and psalms of thanksgiving for God's gift of a child.[70] Innocent IV taught that such rites were offices and the function of those in clerical orders and thus banned by an interdict. But alternative arrangements that the sentence did not technically ban had been tolerated during the French and English interdicts.[71] In interdicted France priests were to advise women that at times when they would have been churched they might pray with their neighbours outside church, but they might not enter church, even to act as godmothers at infant baptisms permitted during the interdict, until a priest inducted them after it was lifted. In interdicted England mothers could also observe churchings outside church, according to a Canterbury source, and the Dunstable annalist said that they were done in church porches with gospel reading, implying clerical involvement, but this perhaps only applied in his own Lincoln diocese. Later practice is unclear, but according to Johannes Calderinus it was customary by the mid-fourteenth century for mothers to confess their sins and enter church offering thanks, provided that they were not interdicted by name and did not cause the interdict, which indicates an even more relaxed arrangement.[72]

Evidence for other minor observances reserved to the clergy is scant and rather inconsistent, especially on the blessing of objects. Peter of Blois recorded in 1209 that under the English interdict the dean and chapter of London had banned the blessing of candles at Candlemas but permitted the blessing of ashes on Ash Wednesday.[73] Local ecclesiastical authorities clearly had to make their own arrangements in the absence of general papal rulings on such points, but this led to regional variations in practice. For example under the English interdict clergy were not to bless bread or water according to the 'Forma interdicti', but a Canterbury document stated that they might bless and distribute bread and water in churchyards on Sundays, and the Dunstable annals said that this was indeed done (at least in Lincoln diocese).[74] But when Peter of Capua had promulgated the interdict on France, he forbade the use of holy water, even in

[68] Innocent IV, *Apparatus* on X 5.38.11 v. *horas*; Reg. Nicholas IV, no. 7502.
[69] Martène and Durand, i.813 (England); iv.147 (France).
[70] Johannes Calderinus, 'De interdicto', Pt 1 §89 (fol. 330va); Hamilton, *Religion*, 113.
[71] Innocent IV, *Apparatus* on X 5.31.18 v. *violavit*.
[72] England: Gervase, II, p. xciii; *Annales*, iii.30. See n. 70 for Calderinus.
[73] *Peter of Blois*, 108 (Letter 20).
[74] Martène and Durand, i.813; Gervase, II, p. xciii; *Annales*, iii.30.

stoups outside churches, though he allowed the blessing of pilgrims' staffs outside church.[75] The inconsistencies of practice were reflected in the distinctions of thirteenth-century canonists on this issue. Innocent IV argued that an interdict did not forbid blessing of tables, as this was not reserved to the ordained, but the opposite was true of blessing water, since only the ordained might do this; Hostiensis and William Durand agreed.[76] Clearly this distinction was widely understood by 1291 when Nicholas IV permitted two archbishops to bless abbesses, nuns, chalices, altar cloths, and chrism during an interdict on Aragon. By the mid-fourteenth century Johannes Calderinus understood that this ban on blessings reserved to the ordained comprised the blessing of chalices, vestments, palms on Palm Sunday, and candles at Candlemas as well as consecration of churches and altars. But he felt that clergy might publicly and solemnly bless water to asperse people on the four feasts when churches were opened during interdicts.[77]

Though it was not fully clear which offices the interdict banned, ecclesiastical authorities generally encouraged secular clergy to continue with those pastoral duties it was not thought to forbid, notably preaching. The legate who published the interdict on France instructed priests to preach the word of God in church porches on Sundays in place of mass.[78] This was intended to keep alive a sense of community religion in the absence of the usual stimuli to devotion. Likewise priests in interdicted England were expected to maintain regular pastoral contact with their flock by calling them to hear a sermon in the churchyard on Sundays and feast days. But in England preaching also had another purpose. The 'Forma interdicti' sanctioned it as church propaganda, to teach the laity to put their loyalty to God before that owed to man, in other words to take the Church's side in its dispute with King John; after preaching clergy might also lead prayers for the peace of the Church and Christ's guidance of the king towards the will of God.[79] The aim of an interdict was to turn the innocent against the guilty, and preaching was to facilitate this. Innocent III likewise allowed preaching to bolster the coercive aim of an interdict on Ferrara in 1209. Its bishop had asked whether he might call excommunicates and those under interdict to church weekly or monthly to preach God's word to them and induce them to repent.[80] Innocent's positive reply passed into canon law immediately; hence preaching

---

[75] Martène and Durand, iv.147.

[76] Innocent IV: as n. 71. Hostiensis, *Lectura* on X 5.31.18 v. *violavit* (vol. 2, fol. 77ra); the views of all three canonists, Durand included, are reported by John of Freiburg, *Summa*, III, xxxiii, q.255. Aragon: Reg. Nicholas IV, nos. 3979–80.

[77] Johannes Calderinus, 'De interdicto', Pt 1 §§91–2 (fol. 330va); he also taught that bishops might not bless crowds when visiting interdicted places (§93). A German early-fourteenth-century treatise on interdicts agreed that they banned blessings of water, of palms on Palm Sunday, candles at Candlemas, and ashes on Ash Wednesday (Ludeco Cappel, *Summarius*, fol. 1v).

[78] Martène and Durand, iv.147.   [79] Martène and Durand, i.812–13.

[80] Innocent III, Reg. 11, no. 267 (= 3 Comp. 5.21.16; X 5.39.43).

became generally permitted during interdicts. In fact the military orders and other religious doing missionary work and collecting alms had long held grants to preach annually at churches in interdicted places.

Bible readings were naturally associated with sermons, but initially they were not automatically tolerated along with preaching. The legate who permitted preaching in interdicted France forbade clergy to read the New Testament aloud to laity. During the English interdict the 'Forma interdicti' likewise approved only private readings by clergy behind closed doors, but the Dunstable annals alleged that Gospel readings took place at churchings and weddings in church porches, at least in Lincoln diocese.[81] The latter practice probably became the norm, since Innocent IV taught that Innocent III's toleration of preaching also extended to public Bible readings by clergy, and this was generally accepted by later thirteenth-century canonists.[82]

Partly through such pastoral activity church authorities encouraged the usual expressions of lay piety that interdicts did not technically forbid. During the English interdict priests were to exhort parishioners to observe prayers and vigils to make up for the loss of masses.[83] The sources for this interdict disagree on whether laity might be admitted to church for prayer, but Hostiensis subsequently taught that those under interdict might enter church to pray alone as long as they had not caused the sentence and were not interdicted by name, and his opinion was widely adopted by subsequent canonists.[84] Lay observance of the church calendar had also been encouraged during the English interdict; priests were to announce feast days and fasts and might set up a cross outside church on Easter Sunday for the customary adoration of parishioners, a practice that Johannes Calderinus considered widely tolerated during interdicts by the mid-fourteenth century since no office was involved.[85] Furthermore pilgrimage could still provide an outlet for popular religious feeling. Priests in interdicted France were allowed to bless pilgrims' staffs outside churches. And a Canterbury source recorded that religious might admit pilgrims to their churches through a side door for the sake of prayer in interdicted England; Cheney noted many examples of pilgrims flocking to shrines and witnessing miracles there.[86] Indeed the papacy sometimes rewarded the devotion of pilgrims and crusaders with the freedom

[81] France: as n. 78. England: Martène and Durand, i.812; *Annales*, iii.30.

[82] Innocent IV, *Apparatus* on X 5.31.18 v. *violavit*. Cf. Hermann de Minden, 'De interdictis', §53 (fol. 346ra); John of Freiburg, *Summa*, III, xxxiii q.257; Petrus Bonetus, *Lectura* on X 5.31.18 v. *violavit*, BAV, Borgh. lat. MS 228, fol. 193ra.

[83] Martène and Durand, i.812 ('Forma interdicti').

[84] Hostiensis, *Summa* on X 5.27 §1 (fol. 257vb). Cf. Monaldus, *Summa*, fol. 96rb; John of Freiburg, *Summa*, III, xxxiii q.260; Johannes Calderinus (attrib.), *De censura*, BAV, Pal. lat. MS 797, fol. 13va.

[85] Calderinus, 'De interdicto', Pt 1 §90. But, according to an early-fourteenth-century German treatise, the office might be performed at the cross on Good Friday secretly and silently during interdicts before the laity might approach it and make offerings (Ludeco Cappel, *Summarius*, fol. 3r). England: Martène and Durand, i.813; Gervase, II, p. xciii.

[86] Martène and Durand, i.147; Gervase, II, p. xcii; Cheney, 'Interdict', 316.

to hear offices during interdicts, such as that granted by Gregory IX to those visiting St Vincent's shrine at Valencia.[87] The activity of lay confraternities was likewise encouraged, and by the mid-fourteenth century Calderinus taught that such bodies might sing litanies, rogations, and lauds to God and the Blessed Virgin in church and publicly in interdicted places, which implies that popular religious processions, which these associations held, were also tolerated.

The interdict's ban on offices was prone to many exceptions and uncertainties in the early thirteenth century. Clergy and laity increasingly requested papal grants of freedom to celebrate or hear offices in general local interdicts; such grants continued to proliferate until largely replaced by two general rights in 1298, which allowed most clergy and laity some degree of participation in the offices. The terms of the ban were left largely to local church authorities to determine, until they were likewise clarified and codified by Innocent IV's teaching that interdicts forbade all functions reserved to holy orders. This definition became a canonistic commonplace, and canonists applied it systematically when they came to write treatises describing the terms of an interdict from the late thirteenth century, notably Calderinus. In fact observances not reserved to clergy had long been tolerated during interdicts before this definition so that some sense of community religion was sustained. But these could hardly compensate for the cessation of church services and most significant loss under interdicts: the sacraments.

4.2 SACRAMENTS

4.2.1 Baptism

By the late twelfth century interdicts normally forbade administration and reception of all the sacraments except infant baptism and penance of the dying. Infant baptism had long been allowed under interdicts, for the church considered it essential to salvation, as noted above. Indeed when the Archbishop of Naples asked Innocent III whether children of its excommunicated and interdicted citizens might be baptized, he replied in 1211 that baptism might not be refused for their parent's sins, since it was a sacrament of necessity.[88] Monaldus taught in the 1270s that it could not be delayed by interdicts without imperiling a child's salvation. According to doctrine if a child died unbaptized, its soul went into limbo, whereas the soul of a baptized child went straight to Heaven; hence the church allowed even a lay person to baptize a newborn infant if it was in danger of death. This was because baptism was said to cleanse a child's soul from original sin and confer membership of the Church. Probably because of

---

[87] Reg. Gregory IX, no. 4706. Calderinus, 'De interdicto', Pt 1 §82 (fol. 330ra).
[88] Innocent III, Reg. 14, no. 74; cf. n. 2.

the latter, the *Glossa Palatina* suggested that those born in a community or place under interdict were not bound by that sentence till after baptism; this further explained why baptism was excepted.[89] Hence ecclesiastical authorities usually made arrangements for infant baptism during interdicts by the late twelfth century. When Peter of Capua ordered the closure of all churches in interdicted France, he granted access only to laity bringing infants for baptism. During the English interdict arrangements varied from one place to another. A Canterbury source recorded that baptisms might be performed in church behind closed doors in the usual manner but with no laity present except godparents; which compares with the French practice. The Dunstable annalist, writing in Lincoln diocese, also noted that priests baptized in churches. By contrast the 'Forma interdicti' provided for infant baptism at home; a portable font could be brought to parishioners' houses for baptizing their children.[90]

It was exceptional and controversial to forbid infant baptism during interdicts. As early as 869, when Bishop Hincmar of Laon had attempted to do so, the clergy of his diocese had protested to his uncle and metropolitan, Hincmar of Reims, who lifted the ban and castigated his nephew. Even as late as 1286, when the exception of infant baptism from an interdict was traditional doctrine, the citizens of Liège complained to Honorius IV that their bishop had specifically included infant baptism in his sentence on the city. In response a papal mandate required that if this was true, the bishop was to relax his interdict; otherwise this would be done by papal executors, since the pope felt that the loss of this sacrament would result in spiritual dangers and offend God.[91]

Although infant baptism was usually allowed during interdicts, it was unclear whether anointing of the baptized with chrism was allowed along with it before 1298. The latter was performed by parish priests, and fresh chrism had to be consecrated for this purpose by local bishops and distributed to their clergy every Maundy Thursday. The old chrism was then burned, for a text in the vulgate recension of the *Decretum* had prohibited its usage in baptism.[92] However, an interdict forbade consecration of chrism, since Innocent IV taught that it banned all functions reserved to holy orders, and this was already understood in England

---

[89] Monaldus, *Summa*, fol. 96ra; on baptism see Hamilton, *Religion*, 112, and Moorman, 83. *Glossa Palatina* on C.24 q.3 c.1 v. *in mortis periculo*, BAV, Pal. lat. MS 658, fol. 71vb: 'Sed pone quod posset anathematizari familia sic pro peccato alicuius, vel civitas tota. Numquid erunt excommunicati qui nascuntur? Sic, quam primo sunt baptizati, ante non. Pro hoc facit quia eadem familia est, vii. q. i. Denique, ff. de iud. Proponebatur [C.7 q.1 c.9; Dig. 5.1.76]. Quidam tamen dicunt quod qui nascuntur non sunt excommunicati.' Cf. C.1 q.4 c.10.

[90] 90 France: Martène and Durand, iv.147. England: Gervase, II, pp. xcii–xciii; *Annales*, iii.30; Martène and Durand, i.813. It was not uncommon even outside interdicts for newborn infants to be baptized in an emergency at home by lay persons, usually the midwife or mother, lest the child die and its soul enter limbo (Hamilton, *Religion*, 112–13; Moorman, 84); this may be the practice tolerated by the 'Forma interdicti'.

[91] Howland, 'Origins', 439–40 (Laon); Reg. Honorius IV, no. 698.

[92] *De con.* D.4 c.122; see Winroth, esp. chs. 2–4, on such additions to Gratian's original recension. Johannes Andreae, *Glossa* on VI 5.11.19 v. *dubium non existit*, explains this practice.

by 1208. Shortly after the executors of Innocent III's interdict had imposed it there, they asked him how the baptized might be anointed if new chrism might not be prepared during the interdict. He conceded that old chrism might be used and, if necessary to prevent a shortage, mixed with oil by bishops or even priests; hence the 'Forma interdicti' told English clergy to conduct baptisms with chrism and all due solemnity.[93] But Innocent's ruling did not pass into canon law, and it is not known what provision was normally made for chrism during subsequent interdicts, but as it was not essential to baptism, clergy might have omitted it. Nevertheless Hostiensis argued that since baptism was permitted during interdicts and it normally involved chrism, the latter should also be tolerated. Subsequently in 1290 Nicholas IV allowed the Bishop of Barcelona to consecrate chrism secretly and anoint the baptized in his diocese during an interdict on Aragon, but such grants were apparently exceptional.[94] Finally Boniface VIII ruled on this matter in his constitution 'Quoniam', which followed Hostiensis by stating that chrism might be consecrated for use in baptism during interdicts.[95] 'Quoniam' did not simply ratify canonistic doctrine but also marked a significant departure by allowing adult baptism during interdicts. In the 1270s Monaldus had accepted that baptism might be excepted from interdicts only for infants, for adults did not risk damnation through lack of the sacrament and might be saved by faith. Adult baptism was normally required only by converts, for children of Catholic parents were usually baptized on the day of their birth or shortly thereafter.

4.2.2 Confirmation

The baptized received this in order to complete their initiation into the faith. According to doctrine those lacking it might not attain full membership of the Church nor receive the gifts of the Holy Spirit. It was normally performed by the local bishop and involved marking the sign of the cross with chrism on the foreheads of candidates.[96] Owing to its close association with baptism it was permitted along with the latter during interdicts by the early thirteenth century.

[93] Papal concession: *SLI*, no. 36 (= Innocent III, Reg. 11, no. 92); cf. Gervase, II, pp. xcii–xciii. Martène and Durand, i.813 ('Forma').

[94] Hostiensis, *Lectura* on X 5.39.57 v. *non negatur* (vol. 2, fol. 123ra). Reg. Nicholas IV, no. 2943.

[95] VI 5.11.19; Johannes Andreae recognized in his *Glossa* on VI 5.11.19 v. *quoniam* that this confirmed Hostiensis's teaching. Monaldus, *Summa*, fol. 96ra; cf. John of Freiburg, *Summa*, III, xxxiii, q.237.

[96] Laurentius Hispanus on 3 Comp. 5.21.16 v. *confirmatione* (Ed. p. 614): 'Sine qua non est plene christianus aliquis, ut de con. di. v. Omnes, si illam contemptu omittat, ut e. di. De hiis in fine [De cons. D. 5 c.1, 3].' This gloss was copied by most contemporary canonists, including Johannes Galensis (Munich, Bayerisches Staatsbibliothek Clm 3879, fol. 264ra), Johannes Teutonicus (edited at http://faculty.cua.edu/pennington/edit517.htm), Vincentius Hispanus (Bamberg Staatsbibliothek MS Can. 20, fol. 179ra), and Tancred (BAV, Vat. lat. MS 1377, fol. 277vb); cf. Hostiensis, *Lectura* on X 5.39.43 v. *ad confirmationem* (vol. 2, fol. 119rb); Guido de Baysio,

In 1209 the Bishop of Ferrara asked Innocent III whether he might confirm with chrism children baptized in his interdicted city, and Innocent's affirmative response quickly passed into canonical collections and thereby acquired general force.[97] This ruling did not, however, address the issue of the supply of chrism during an interdict, and, as we have seen above, this was not settled until 1298. Hence in 1290 Nicholas IV had to grant the Bishop of Barcelona power to consecrate chrism to confirm those baptized in his diocese during an interdict on Aragon.[98] The constitution 'Quoniam' not only resolved this question but also extended confirmation to adults as well as children, in line with its ruling on baptism, though as early as *c*.1236 Vincentius Hispanus had assumed that adolescents might be confirmed.[99] Nevertheless if Hamilton's claim is correct that most medieval laity were never confirmed, these concessions can only have mattered to the devout.

4.2.3 Eucharist

However, few can have been unmoved by the loss of the Eucharist. Its consecration was the high point of the mass, and laity came to mass largely to witness this event even if they did not take Communion. In fact only those absolved of their mortal sins might receive the sacrament. In 1215 the Fourth Lateran Council required all laity to seek absolution and take Communion at least once a year at Easter.[100] This was a very basic minimum, and it indicates how irregular participation in the Eucharist then was. Indeed previously many laity only took Communion at their final absolution on the point of death, as heavy penances prescribed by the Church before the twelfth century discouraged most from seeking absolution in their lifetime. By the late twelfth century absolution of the dying was a traditional exception to the interdict, but it was unclear whether the final Communion might be granted along with it during interdicts. When Peter of Capua proclaimed the French interdict, he allowed priests to celebrate

---

Lectura on VI 5.11.19 v. *confirmationem* (fol. 124vb). On the scriptural basis for the sacrament: Acts 2:1–4, 8:14–17.

[97] See n. 80.

[98] Reg. Nicholas IV, no. 2943; cf. nos. 3879–80. Apparently an interdicted bishop might not consecrate chrism or administer confirmation. Bernardus Compostellanus junior implied as much in his *glossa* on Innocent IV's *Novelle* at Coll. I 21 (= VI 5.11.4) v. *periculosum* (BAV, Vat. lat. MS 1365, fol. 589vb): 'in multis enim consistit officium episcoporum que necessitatem inducunt, ex quorum dilatione pericula imminerent in crismatis confectione, sine quo baptismus non fit, confirmatione pontificali, ordinum collatione ... et que per alios prelatos inferiores fieri non possunt.'

[99] VI 5.11.19; Vincentius on X 5.39.43 v. *confirmationem*, Paris, BN, MS lat. 3967, fol. 207rb: '[copies gloss of Laurentius as in n. 96 then] ... Numquid tempore interdicti possunt adolescentes confirmari? Sic, ar. illius c. de con. di. v. De hiis [De con. D.5 c.3], ubi dicitur quod baptismus et confirmatio sunt connexa, et est iudicandum in eis. Vinc.' See Hamilton, *Religion*, 113.

[100] Lat. Conc. IV c.21 (= 4 Comp. 5.14.2; X 5.38.12). See n. 139 on pre-twelfth-century penance.

mass alone weekly late on Friday mornings in order to consecrate the Eucharist for the sick. Nevertheless the Bishop of Paris still sought reassurance from the pope that the *viaticum*, the final Communion, might be administered. In 1200 Innocent III replied that as absolution was not refused to the dying, neither might the *viaticum*, provided that they were truly penitent.[101] This ruling was included in Alanus's decretal collection (*c*.1206), but it was not immediately applied to Innocent's interdict on England. In 1208, shortly after three English bishops had proclaimed it, they asked Innocent III whether the *viaticum* might still accompany absolution of the dying, but the pope's reply was ambiguous. Hence the 'Forma interdicti', which probably emanated from these bishop-executors, discouraged clergy from administering the Eucharist to the penitent.[102] But in 1209 the Archdeacon of London Peter of Blois urged his bishop, who was one of these executors, to exploit Innocent's ruling on the French interdict permitting the *viaticum*. Finally in 1212 this bishop and the Bishop of Ely, another of the executors, allowed priests to grant the *viaticum* to the truly penitent *in extremis*; they were to obtain hosts from conventual churches where the pope had allowed mass once a week in private since 1209.[103] Hence the arrangements were broadly similar to those tolerated during the French interdict, as Peter of Blois would have wished. But they were permitted by local ecclesiastical authorities; the pope did not authorize the extension of his earlier ruling on the *viaticum* to England.

Significantly it was not included in *Compilatio tertia*, nor was it recognized by contemporary canonists, except in an oblique gloss of Vincentius Hispanus, observing that when divine offices alone were interdicted, mass might still be celebrated and the Eucharist offered to the dying along with absolution.[104] Admittedly Innocent's ruling was included in *Compilatio quarta* but canonists were slow to accept this collection. Nevertheless a similar ruling entered other contemporary decretal collections, where it was described as a canon of Alexander III issued at the Council of Tours (1163). It proclaimed an interdict on the lands of lords (*castrenses*) who attacked ecclesiastical property, but it excepted Communion 'timore mortis' and allowed priests to celebrate mass alone once a week behind closed doors in a nearby town in order to consecrate the host. But Somerville doubts the historical authenticity of this text, observing that it was

---

[101] Martène and Durand, iv.147 (France). Innocent III's ruling was addressed to the Bishop of Paris in Alan. 5.20.1 (= 4 Comp. 5.14.3; X 5.38.11); it echoes D.50 c.63 in its insistence that no dying person might be denied the *viaticum*. It was so called since it sustained the dying on the way (via) to Heaven.

[102] *SLI*, no. 36, pp. 108–9 (= Reg. Innocent III 11, no. 92); cf. Gervase, II, p. xcii. Martène and Durand, i.813 ('Forma').

[103] *Peter of Blois*, 120 (Letter 24). See Gervase, II, p. xcvii, on the papal concession of 1209 (solicited by Stephen Langton).

[104] Vincentius on 1 Comp. 4.1.10 v. *celebrari*, Leipzig Universitätsbibliothek MS 983, fol. 39rb: 'Celebretur ergo missa, licet terra sit interdicta, ut per eucharistiam subveniatur morientibus, et secundum hoc expone penitentias [*in another hand*:] idest, fructus penitentie, scilicet perceptione eucharistie.' It is unclear whether the addition was Vincentius's or generally transmitted with this gloss, since no other copy of his commentary is known to survive.

transmitted only in collections much later than 1163, notably that of Alanus.[105] Indeed Alanus commented on this canon in his collection that it only had local force, presumably in Tours province, and that its provision for the *viaticum* was novel. His collection was nevertheless the likely source for its inclusion in *Compilatio secunda*, a collection generally accepted in the schools and glossed by several canonists, notably Laurentius Hispanus, who remarked on the exception of the *viaticum* in this canon.[106] It was not included in the *Liber extra*, but it was superseded there by 'Permittimus', a chapter that Gregory IX drew up specifically for this collection commissioned by him. 'Permittimus' basically confirmed the arrangements for the *viaticum* under the French interdict and in words similar to those of the Tours canon, allowing clergy to celebrate mass once a week during interdicts in order to consecrate the host for the dying.[107] In common with grants to celebrate offices during interdicts, it required the celebrant to take the precautions of saying mass in a low voice, behind closed doors, with no bells ringing, and interdicted and excommunicated persons excluded. In addition the *Liber extra* included Innocent III's ruling on the French interdict, reinforcing the principle of offering the *viaticum*. Hence it was generally recognized as a regular exception to interdicts after 1234 along with infant baptism and penance of the dying.[108] Indeed when the Bishop of Dax interdicted his city in 1243, he authorized a priest from his cathedral to administer the *viaticum* as well as baptize children and hear confessions of the sick. Moreover when the citizens of Liège complained to Honorius IV in 1286 that their bishop had specifically prohibited these three sacraments during his interdict on the city, the pope ordered the sentence's removal.

Otherwise interdicts generally excluded clergy and laity from participation in the Eucharist. It was celebrated secretly and reserved for the dying in closed churches. There were few exceptions to this general rule even amongst privileged clergy. Early thirteenth-century canonists agreed that the freedom to celebrate offices behind closed doors excluded the mass, and clerks might not even recite it in secret during interdicts except where this was specifically conceded.[109] Admittedly Vincentius claimed that Templars and Hospitallers who were free to open churches once a year in interdicted places might have mass celebrated there,

---

[105] Alan. 3.24.3 (= 2 Comp. 3.27.1). This so-called canon ten of the council of Tours (Mansi, xxii.1179) is discussed by Somerville, 45–8, 50–1, esp. 45, where he calls it 'a maverick canon'.

[106] Alanus on Alan. 3.24.3, Vercelli Cathedral Chapter MS 89, fols. 104vb–5ra: 'sacramento. Hoc locale est et fere quidquid dicit in hoc capitulum … [fol. 105ra] semel in hebdomada. Hoc est novum.' Tancred quoted Laurentius on 2 Comp. 3.27.1 v. *communione*, BAV, Vat. lat. MS 1377, fol. 131ra: 'Hic additur hoc tertium illis duobus permissis [*infant baptism and penance of the dying*] que habes, supra. de spon. Non est vobis. lib. i. [1 Comp. 4.1.13] La.'

[107] X 5.39.57. On the need to consecrate fresh hosts every week, see Hostiensis, *Lectura* on X 5.39.57 v. *ministris* and v. *semel* (vol. 2, fol. 123ra).

[108] Reg. Innocent IV, no. 201; Reg. Honorius IV, no. 698. See pp. 218–25 below on the Dax interdict.

[109] See n. 61.

but only Tancred adopted this view among subsequent canonists.[110] Nevertheless by the mid-thirteenth century the papacy had granted the freedom to hold mass in private and even receive the sacraments during interdicts to some clergy, mainly friars. In 1267 Clement IV affirmed that Dominicans might hear mass daily in their convents during interdicts behind closed doors, with no ringing of bells, and all those outside their order excluded; he also conceded that they might take Communion during interdicts, and Nicholas IV confirmed similar freedoms to the Franciscans in 1288.[111]

Laity might also receive such rare freedoms, notably as a reward for religious devotion. In 1225 Honorius III ordered all prelates in Italy to administer sacraments to laity of the mendicant third orders during interdicts.[112] Johannes Teutonicus had even suggested (*c.*1213–18) that pilgrims might receive the Eucharist during interdicts. His view was adopted by several canonists, and a treatise on interdicts added in 1301 that crusaders and those on long-distance pilgrimages enjoyed such a freedom, but there is little evidence to support this assertion and it was not a canonistic *opinio communis*.[113] The only comparable concessions were made by Gregory IX in 1235 to the knights of Jesus at Parma, probably a crusader confraternity, and by Boniface VIII in 1299 when he allowed the despatch of priests to interdicted Sicily to administer the sacraments to those fighting a papal 'crusade' against the Aragonese occupation.[114] But these were exceptional grants, and the latter was largely meant to avoid the injustice of punishing the pope's allies along with his enemies. Communion was generally denied to healthy laity during interdicts. Even after Boniface VIII's constitution 'Alma mater' allowed lay participation in the offices during interdicts on the four main annual feast days, the canonist Guido de Baysio observed that this did not extend to the Eucharist. Likewise Guido's pupil Johannes Andreae concluded that when Boniface conceded absolution from sin for the healthy and infirm, the Eucharist was not conceded along with it but reserved to the penitent *in articulo mortis*.[115]

[110] Vincentius on 1 Comp. 5.28.7 v. *in anno*, Leipzig, Universitätsbibliothek MS 983, fol. 57rb: 'qui primus de templariis venerit habebit ecclesie relaxationem, vel potius concedo quod non erit relaxatio sed in ecclesia interdicta potest missa celebrari ... et istud licitum est.' Copied by Tancred on 1 Comp 5.28.7 v. *semel*, BAV, Vat. lat. MS 1377, fol. 93rb.
[111] Reg. Clement IV, nos. 509, 578; Reg. Nicholas IV, no. 205; cf. ibid. nos. 71–2, 683 (Franciscan nuns), 4566 (leper hospital); Reg. Honorius IV, nos. 203–4.
[112] Reg. Honorius III, no. 5740; cf. Reg. Urban IV, nos. 2144, 2155, 2159.
[113] Johannes on 3 Comp. 5.21.16 v. *confirmationem* (http://faculty.cua.edu/pennington/edit517.htm); copied by Tancred, ibid. (BAV, Vat. lat. MS 1377, fol. 277vb), and Goffredus de Trano on X 5.39.43 v. *ad confirmationem* (Vienna, Nationalbibliothek MS 2197, fol. 157va). Likewise Petrus Bonetus on X 5.38.11, BAV, Borgh. lat. MS 228, fol. 167va: 'Sed pone quidam vult confiteri tempore interdicti et vult recipere eucharistiam, numquid potest? Dic quod non nisi vadat ad aliquam peregrinationem, ut hic in dec. Quod in te.' Cf. Johannes Andreae (attrib.), *De modo*, BAV, Pal. lat. MS 797, fol. 6rb (Ed. fol. 3r): 'cum eisdem personis sanis non est tempore interdicti huiusmodi eukaristia danda nisi crucem receperunt vel peregrinari debent ad partes longinquas.'
[114] Reg. Gregory IX, no. 2565; Reg. Boniface VIII, no. 3073; cf. n. 44.
[115] Guido de Baysio, *Lectura* on VI 5.11.24 v. *divinorum* (fol. 126rb); Johannes Andreae, *Glossa*, ibid. v. *admittantur*. Cf. id. *Novella*, ibid. v. *divinorum*. Cf. also n. 113.

Although an interdict excluded the majority from receiving the host, it did not technically prohibit people from seeing and revering the host, especially when it was brought to the dying, at least according to Johannes Calderinus in the fourteenth century. Admittedly thirteenth-century sources indicate that ecclesiastical authorities had objected to the host being displayed publicly during interdicts.[116] Nevertheless use of *panis benedictus* was tolerated during some early thirteenth-century interdicts in order to compensate for loss of the Eucharist. This was traditionally bread set aside for mass but not consecrated. When Peter of Capua published the French interdict, he permitted reception of *panis benedicti* outside church on Easter morning. In interdicted England the practice varied.[117] A Canterbury source allowed distribution of *panis benedictus* in churchyards on Sundays, and the Dunstable annals noted that this was done in Lincoln diocese, but the 'Forma interdicti' forbade its use. Canon law, however, never defined observance on this point. Innocent IV taught that bread might be administered as a *viaticum* during interdicts if a consecrated host were unavailable. But apparently no canonist commented on its distribution to the healthy until the fourteenth century. In 1301 a treatise attributed to Johannes Andreae opposed 'customary' use of *panis benedictus* instead of the host during interdicts; Andreae's pupil Johannes Calderinus agreed, observing that this bread was distributed on Sundays in certain areas, notably France.[118] In fact the custom of giving *panis benedictus* had been dying out generally since the thirteenth century except in parts of France, perhaps since church authorities preferred laity to receive the Eucharist in accordance with the Fourth Lateran ruling.[119]

4.2.4 Marriage

The Eucharist might be celebrated only by priests and thus came under Innocent IV's definition of an interdict as a ban on offices performed by the ordained; this was not true of the sacrament of marriage. According to doctrine this sacrament was performed by the couple alone through the free exchange of consent; canon law did not require this to be done in church before a priest. Hence according to Innocent IV's definition an interdict did not technically impede marriage, and indeed Innocent argued that marriage might be contracted by those under an interdict, for it was even canonical between infidels.[120] There were clearly also moral and practical reasons to allow marriages during

---

[116] Calderinus, 'De interdicto', Pt 2 §§3–4 (fol. 331va). On earlier objections see p. 190 below.

[117] France: Martène and Durand, iv.147. England: see n. 74. See also Hamilton, *Religion*, 116.

[118] Innocent IV, *Apparatus* on X 5.38.11 v. *viaticum*; Johannes Andreae (attrib.), *De modo* (Ed. fol. 3v) and Johannes Calderinus (attrib.), *De censura*, BAV, Pal. lat. MS 797, fols. 6va and 13va.

[119] Hamilton, *Religion*, 116; see n. 100 for this ruling.

[120] Innocent IV, *Apparatus* on X 4.1.11 v. *officia*. Hostiensis, *Lectura* on X 4.1.11 v. *morientium* (vol. 2, fol. 4vb); the latter's view was repeated by Petrus Bonetus, ibid., BAV, Borgh. lat. MS 228, fol. 134va.

interdicts given clerical denunciation of sex outside marriage as sinful and its issue as illegitimate. Nevertheless Hostiensis considered that even if interdicts did not forbid marriage, they forbade its solemnization. After all this had to be performed by a priest, for it comprised a blessing that he pronounced on the couple knelt before him at the church porch after their exchange of vows and a nuptial mass that he celebrated after leading the newly weds into church. These teachings probably reflected customary practice. During the English interdict the Dunstable annals record in 1208 that marriages took place in church porches, at least in Lincoln diocese, albeit according to another source betrothals and marriages could not be contracted.[121] It is thought that weddings were held in churchyards under the French interdict, though the legate who imposed it did not expressly permit marriages.[122] Certainly it appears that marriages were not solemnized in interdicted France, since some couples had to travel outside this territory for nuptial blessings. The chronicler Roger of Howden recorded that in 1200 the dauphin Louis and Blanche of Castile were wedded by the Archbishop of Bordeaux in Normandy then outside the kingdom 'for the kingdom of France was then under an interdict'; likewise the count of Ponthieu had his marriage to the French king's sister blessed at Rouen.[123] In interdicted England the Dunstable annals simply noted that the Gospels were read at weddings, a function not reserved to the ordained. Hence it seems that interdicts suspended solemnization in practice. By the fourteenth century, however, Johannes Calderinus noted a possible exception to this. He argued that marriages might be solemnized at Assumption (15 August) since Boniface VIII permitted laity to attend church services on this and three other feasts during general local interdicts; solemnizations were not permitted on the other feasts even outside an interdict.[124] Nevertheless Calderinus also argued that a priest might not solemnize a marriage if one or both partners were under a personal interdict, though he conceded that it might be done in non-interdicted places if the bride alone were interdicted, not *nominatim* but simply by belonging to an interdicted community.

4.2.5 Ordination

While marriage was not a sacrament in the Church's gift and so not in its power to withhold, ordination might be received only from ecclesiastical superiors, normally the diocesan; hence it was more readily included under the interdict's ban on the sacraments. Vincentius Hispanus indeed doubted (*c*.1236) whether

---

[121] *Annales*, iii.30 (A. 1208); Martène and Durand, i.813 ('Forma').

[122] Krehbiel, 119, cites the view that in interdicted France 'marriages were solemnized at graves instead of altars', but he found no proof of this, not even in the legatine 'Forma' (Martène and Durand, iv.147).

[123] Howden, iv.115; Krehbiel, 119.

[124] Calderinus, 'De interdicto', Pt 2 §§9–10, 18 (fols. 331vb, 332rb).

bishops might ordain in interdicted lands and noted that Cistercians might do so, which implied that others might not.[125] Innocent IV distinguished that in interdicted lands laymen might not take holy orders but ordained clergy might be promoted to higher orders provided that they were not personally interdicted. In practice sentences of interdict did not ban ordination explicitly, but equally papal grants sometimes allowed it during interdicts, suggesting that it was normally refused at such times. Nicholas IV granted licences to confer and receive ordination in interdicted lands, for example, allowing the monks of San Salvatore, Messina, to be ordained by bishops authorized by him to confer orders on friars in interdicted Sicily.[126] Other evidence of a ban on ordination during an interdict is hard to find. One late example concerns a prior who asked Boniface VIII in 1301 to dispense some of his monks from irregularity; since they had been ordained during an interdict on their abbey in Burgos diocese.[127] Clergy who violated interdicts incurred irregularity; hence the prior evidently understood that interdicts prohibited ordination. Canonistic theory was clearer on this issue than practice. Johannes Calderinus argued that orders might not be conferred on interdicted persons or in interdicted places. But he admitted two exceptions to this rule.[128] Members of an interdicted people might be ordained after monastic profession, since they thereby ceased to belong to that people. And clergy might be promoted to higher orders not in interdicted places, as Innocent IV had argued, but in places where the people were interdicted, since the clergy there were not interdicted according to Boniface VIII's constitution 'Si sententia'.

In addition to ordination most aspiring clergy sought ecclesiastical offices and benefices, and interdicts might also affect appointment to these. By 1199 Innocent III had accepted that interdicted persons might not elect to ecclesiastical offices or obtain benefices, and he was ready to quash appointments that violated this principle.[129] His decretal 'Cum dilectus' (1209), which recorded one such intervention, quickly entered canon law and established the rule that no interdicted person might be elected or elect to offices.[130] Canonists subsequently agreed that such elections were invalid. Johannes Galensis and Tancred also accepted Innocent's view that interdicted persons could not obtain benefices,

---

[125] Vincentius on X 5.33.25 v. *possint*, BAV, Vat. lat. MS 6769, fol. 135rb: 'Sed numquid <episcopus> potest ordinare illum qui ei concelebret? Hoc tempore Cisterciensi possunt ordines ordines conferre.'

[126] Innocent IV, *Apparatus* on X 4.1.11 v. *officia*; Reg. Nicholas IV, nos. 3847 (Messina), 3979–80 (faculty for the Archbishops of Tarragona and Barcelona to ordain).

[127] Reg. Boniface VIII, no. 4112.

[128] Calderinus, 'De interdicto', Pt 1 §§36–7, Pt 2 §11 (fols. 327rb, 331vb).

[129] Innocent III, Reg. 2, nos. 30, 232. The first of these letters also entered canon law at 3 Comp. 1.6.1 (= X 1.6.16).

[130] 3 Comp. 1.3.7 (= X 1.4.8). E.g. Paulus Hungarus, *Notabilium* on 3 Comp. 1.3.7, BAV, Borgh. lat. MS 261, fol. 80vb: 'Cum &c .... Item suspensus nec eligere nec eligi potest.' Cf. id. on 3 Comp. 1.6.1, fol. 81ra: 'Cum inter &c .... Item electio facta a suspensis vel interdictis non valet.'

but other canonists were apparently silent on this issue.¹³¹ However, several canonists debated whether a bishop under ecclesiastical censure might collate to benefices or prebends in his cathedral. Tancred concluded in the negative, and his view was adopted by Goffredus de Trano and more significantly Bernard of Parma.¹³² The thirteenth-century papal registers shed no light on actual practice in these matters. Papal interventions in elections involving interdicted persons have been noted above, but they were not always negative. The papacy was not unaware that vacancies could disrupt the administration and pastoral direction of dioceses and religious houses, and hence Innocent IV authorized some elections contrary to 'Cum dilectus'. One French abbey had lacked an abbot for so long that he feared that 'serious spiritual privations' would arise; therefore in 1252 he suspended all sentences on its monks and permitted them to elect a new abbot in response to their 'prayers'.¹³³

Canon law did not, however, forbid elections to church offices or collation of benefices in interdicted places, where these did not involve interdicted persons. True, Tancred observed that it was wrong to hold an election in an interdicted church, and he cited Innocent III's decretal 'Cum inter' (1199) that had quashed such an election, but, as Johannes Calderinus pointed out over a century later, the electors in this case also lay under ecclesiastical censure.¹³⁴ Indeed Calderinus maintained that elections might be held in interdicted places, for an election was akin to marriage and marriage was allowed in such places; he was, of course, drawing on Innocent III's metaphor of episcopal election as a spiritual marriage between a bishop and his church. But except for Tancred thirteenth-century canonists were silent on this issue, although it might be inferred that Innocent IV's approval of promotion to higher orders in interdicted

¹³¹ Johannes Galensis on 3 Comp. 1.6.1 v. *a suspensis*, Munich, Bayerisches Staatsbibliothek Clm 3879, fol. 158vb: 'Quod excommunicatorum electio non teneat liquet ix. q. i. Nos in hominem, infra. de hereticis. Vergentis [C.9 q.1 c.6; 3 Comp. 5.4.1] ... similiter nec beneficii susceptio, supra. de etate. Cum littere lib. ii [2 Comp. 1.8.5]. Idem hic in suspenso, scilicet quod nequit eligere.' Tancred on 2 Comp. 1.8.5 v. *suspensi*, BAV, Vat. lat. MS 1377, fol. 104vb: 'Suspensi eligere non possunt, ut ix. q. i. Nos in homine, infra. de elec. c.i. nec potest eligi suspensus, ar. supra. de ap. Constitutus lib. i. infra. de elec. Per inquisitionem lib. iii [3 Comp. 2.19.4, 1.6.11], et beneficia ecclesiastica sunt ei interim deneganda, ut infra. de appell. Pastoralis in fi. lib. iii [3 Comp. 2.19.11].'
¹³² Tancred on 3 Comp. 1.3.7 v. *suspensis*, BAV, Vat. lat. MS 1377, fol. 153vb: 'Suspensus non potest eligere nec eligi ut hic ... nec investire, ut infra. de concessione preben. non vaca. Quoniam diversitate [3 Comp. 3.8.2]. Sed nonne iudicare et prebendas dare iurisdictionis est utique ... et excommunicare ... Quidam dicunt quod episcopus suspensus potest excommunicare et prebendas dare ... alii dicunt et credo verius quod episcopus suspensus non potest excommunicare nec prebendas dare ... beneficium dare et habere posse competit ratione ordinis.' Cf. Johannes Teutonicus, who took the contrary view on 3 Comp. 1.3.7 v. *suspensis* (Ed. p. 29); this gloss was adapted by Tancred. Goffredus de Trano, *Lectura* on X 1.4.8 v. *a suspensis*, Vienna, Nationalbibliothek MS 2197, fol. 6vb, and Bernard of Parma, ibid., base themselves on Tancred's gloss.
¹³³ Reg. Innocent IV, no. 5865; cf. ibid. nos. 8160, 8172.
¹³⁴ Tancred on 3 Comp. 1.24.1 v. *eligerent*, BAV, Vat. lat. MS 1377, fol. 184va: 'Et male si interdictum erat monasterium, ut supra. de electione c.i. supra. de consuetudine c. ult. lib. e. [3 Comp. 1.6.1, 1.3.7] t.' Calderinus (attrib.), *De censura*, BAV, Pal. lat. MS 797, fol. 13r (Ed. p. 275).

lands extended to elections to higher offices. Nevertheless Calderinus apparently described customary practice. For example bishops were elected with papal approval to vacant sees at Chichester, Exeter, Lichfield, and Lincoln during the English interdict.[135] But they were not consecrated, and while it is true that their archbishop Stephen Langton was exiled in France, it appears that metropolitans could not consecrate suffragans in interdicted places. Indeed the election quashed in Innocent III's decretal 'Cum inter' was judged invalid partly since it was confirmed and the elect was consecrated in an interdicted church. After all consecration was a liturgical ceremony and hence clearly came under the terms of the interdict. Consequently in 1220 Honorius III had to grant the Archbishop of Cagliari a faculty to consecrate his suffragans despite an interdict on his province.[136] This suggests that the thirteenth-century papacy tolerated elections, if not consecrations, in interdicted places, but occasionally it inhibited elections in local papal interdicts. In 1255 a letter of Alexander IV noted that his predecessor Innocent IV had reserved appointments to churches in the kingdom of Sicily when he laid it under interdict. Indeed the previous year Innocent had provided a bishop to Tricarico there, quashing the election of another candidate to the see by its cathedral chapter.[137] Such inhibitions apparently often accompanied papal interdicts on places in Italy and might be removed along with these sentences. In 1264 Urban IV gave his legate in Umbria a faculty to relax all papal interdicts and inhibitions on elections within his legation, and Clement IV granted a similar power to his legate in the kingdom of Sicily in 1266.[138] Otherwise an election was not technically prohibited during local interdicts, since, as Calderinus observed, it was not a sacrament.

4.2.6 Penance

Marriage and ordination were necessary for Christians wishing to follow certain paths in life, but they were not essential to salvation. According to doctrine the sacrament of penance was, however, necessary to maintain the soul in a state of grace. Before the twelfth century penance had to be performed in order to obtain absolution from sin but the penances prescribed were generally so onerous that many only sought absolution at their deathbed, when they feared that their salvation might otherwise be imperilled.[139] Thus it was customary not to refuse absolution to the dying even during interdicts. But in the twelfth century the doctrine of penance was transformed; notably absolution might be granted before penance was performed and the scale of penances was reduced encouraging more

---

[135] Cheney, 'Interdict', 309.   [136] Reg. Honorius III, no. 2622. Cheney, 'Interdict', 311.
[137] Reg. Alexander IV, no. 467; Reg. Innocent IV, nos. 8060, 8270.
[138] Reg. Urban IV, no. 635; Reg. Clement IV, no. 275.
[139] Hamilton, *Penance*, esp. 173–206, suggests, however, that penance was more widespread among the laity in the period 900–1050 than is often supposed, especially among royalty and nobility.

frequent confession. By 1215 Catholics were required to confess their sins to their parish priest at least once a year at Easter. Hence by the thirteenth century ecclesiastical authorities had to make provision for healthy as well as dying penitents during interdicts. The legate who promulgated the French interdict let parish priests hear confession and enjoin penance for individual penitents in church porches provided that others might not overhear. In 1209 Peter of Blois, Archdeacon of London, noted a similar arrangement made by his dean and chapter during the English interdict: penitents might confess their sins to a priest in a suitable place of his choice outside church.[140] A Canterbury source also stated that penance should be enjoined on both the healthy and sick during this interdict. Pilgrimage was a popular penance, and it was encouraged during the French and English interdicts as we have seen. Another important penitential activity for the laity was crusading, and thirteenth-century popes even sanctioned preaching of the cross in interdicted places.[141]

Official tolerance of confession and penitential works might console the living and stimulate popular piety, but most early thirteenth-century canonists suggested that only the dying might obtain absolution during interdicts. Admittedly Innocent III had ruled that crusaders and pilgrims might also receive it during the French interdict, but it was initially unclear whether the decretal in which this ruling appeared had general force, as we have already noted.[142] Indeed the only contemporary canonist who drew attention to Innocent's ruling was Johannes Teutonicus, who had included this decretal in *Compilatio quarta*, although Tancred later noted his remarks.[143] Any doubts about the decretal's place in canon law were settled by its inclusion in the *Liber extra*, after which canonists generally recognized that pilgrims and crusaders might be absolved together with the dying during interdicts. Moreover mid-thirteenth-century canonists, notably Bernard of Parma and Hostiensis, largely copied the commentary of Johannes Teutonicus on this ruling. He had explained that anyone setting out on a pilgrimage or crusade had reason to fear death and hence shared the same need for absolution as the dying.[144] But Bernard de Montmirat held that this

---

[140] Martène and Durand, iv.147 (France); *Peter of Blois*, 110 (Letter 24).

[141] England: Gervase, II, pp. xcii–xciii; Cheney, 'Interdict', 316. France: n. 140. See also papal grants in favour of crusaders and pilgrims at nn. 32, 44, 49, 87.

[142] See p. 141. A pupil of French canonist Petrus Brito noted on 1 Comp. 4.1.9 v. *penitentias*, Brussels, Bibliothèque royale MS 1407–9, fol. 59ra, that penance of the dying might not be extended to the infirm: 'Penitentia innotescenda est infirmis non imponenda, xxvi q.vii c.i [C.26 q.7 c.1].'

[143] See nn. 113 and 144.

[144] Johannes Teutonicus on 4 Comp. 5.14.3 v. *penitentiam*, BAV, Vat. lat. MS 1377, fol. 315va; Vat. lat. MS 2509, fol. 266ra; Borgh. lat. MS 264, fol. 308vb: 'Hoc est in eis speciale ut sine necessitate vel periculo mortis admittantur ad penitentiam, set certe ibi necessitas est quia non intelligo nisi cum proficiscuntur. Idem dico si aliqui proficiscuntur ad iustum bellum quia ibi est iusta causa timoris'. Cf. Goffredus de Trano, *Lectura* on X 5.38.11 v. *penitentia*, Vienna, Nationalbibliothek MS 2197, fol. 153rb; Bernard of Parma, ibid.; Hostiensis, *Lectura*, ibid. (vol. 2, fol. 101rb).

was only true of pilgrims travelling more than two leagues beyond their diocese, presumably because the dangers of their journey were otherwise insufficient to merit absolution.[145] Probably Innocent III had simply meant to reward the highest popular forms of penitential activity. He conceded absolution from sins, but not, as Johannes Teutonicus was careful to observe, from the interdict itself, for only those who occasioned the sentence might seek its removal, not its innocent sufferers.[146] In other words Innocent conceded absolution *in foro interno* but not *in foro externo*. Bernard of Parma and Hostiensis further concluded that since this concession was made specifically to crusaders and pilgrims (besides the dying), it was understood to be denied to other healthy penitents during interdicts. But this was a matter of canonistic controversy. Tancred had dared to argue that absolution might be granted to both the healthy and dying during interdicts, since it might be refused to nobody. This view was peculiar to him until its adoption by Vincentius Hispanus and Goffredus de Trano.[147] After Bernard and Hostiensis stated the contrary, the issue was still unresolved when John of Freiburg surveyed this canonistic debate (*c*.1280–98). Nevertheless he noted with approval the solution suggested by Hermann de Minden's treatise on interdicts: the healthy might confess all but venal sins, and their confessor might enjoin penance, including the taking of the cross, but not offer them absolution or prayers or otherwise act as a priest.[148] In other words priests might act as spiritual counsellors only for most healthy penitents, as they did during the English and French interdicts at the start of the century.

Indeed Hermann's cautious advice probably reflected approved practice more accurately than Tancred's radical opinion by the late thirteenth century. In addition to crusaders, pilgrims, and the dying the papacy offered few others express permission to receive absolution *in foro interno* during interdicts; they

---

[145] Bernard de Montmirat, *Lectura* on X 5.38.11 v. *peregrinis* (Ed. fol. 147ra), BAV, Vat. lat. MS 2542, fol. 81rb: 'Nunquid omnibus? Ita videtur cum indistincte loquatur hic. Sed quid, secundum hoc, si vadat ad ecclesiam non remotam ultra duas leucas causa peregrinationis? Nunquid habebit hoc privilegium? Dic quod non ... posset et satis probabiliter dici quod sufficiat si peregrinatio ultra duas dietas extra diocesim suam sit remota'. Johannes Andreae also doubted in his *Novella* on X 5.38.11 v. *morientibus* whether women close to childbirth were among the 'dying' who might obtain absolution during interdicts, and he conceded that this was true only if they were in imminent danger of death. An early-fourteenth-century German treatise also stated this view (Ludeco Cappel, *Summarius*, fol. 1r).

[146] Johannes Teutonicus (continued from n. 144): 'Sed quid si interdicta civitate aliqui vellent satisfacere, numquid in eis relaxandum esset interdictum? Non, quia aliquis sine culpa sua interdici potest, supra. de sponsal. Non est vobis [1 Comp. 4.1.13], <et> quia sic rigor ecclesie dissolveretur, ut supra. de privil. Ut privilegia lib. e. [4 Comp. 5.12.7].'

[147] Hostiensis, *Lectura* on X 5.38.11 v. *cum postulaverint* (vol. 2, fol. 101va). Bernard: as n. 144. Tancred on 1 Comp. 4.1.13 v. *morientium*, BAV, Vat. lat. MS 1377, fol. 64vb: 'Et etiam vivorum quoniam nulli deneganda est penitentia, infra. de penitentiis et re. Quod quidam, De pe. di. ult. c. ultimo. [4 Comp. 5.14.3; De pen. D.6 c.6] t.' Copied by Goffredus de Trano, *Lectura* on X 4.1.11 v. *morientium*, Vienna, Nationalbibliothek MS 2197, fol. 115vb; and Vincentius Hispanus, ibid., BAV, Vat. lat. MS 6769, fol. 104va.

[148] John of Freiburg, *Summa*, III, xxxiii, q.237–8, 245; Hermann de Minden, 'De interdictis', §79 (fol. 346va); cf. Monaldus, *Summa*, fol. 96v.

included the Dominicans by 1267 and Franciscans by 1288.[149] This implies, as Hostiensis and Bernard assumed, that it was normally prohibited by an interdict. However by 1298 Boniface VIII had enshrined Tancred's view as law in the *Liber sextus*, when he ruled that the sacrament of penance could be administered to the healthy and infirm as well as the dying during an interdict.[150] Nevertheless Boniface added that it was still to be refused to those who committed or supported the wrong that caused the interdict until they gave satisfaction for this wrong or adequate guarantee to do so. He thus adopted Johannes Teutonicus's distinction between absolution from sin and absolution from the sentence, in common with the more conservative commentators, synthesizing and settling canonistic debate.

4.2.7 Extreme Unction

The priest who administered final absolution and communion to the dying also usually conferred the last of the seven sacraments, extreme unction. This ritual anointing was meant to signify the spiritual healing and forgiveness of the dying and mirrored the use of chrism in baptism at the start of their lives.[151] However, the consecration of the oil used in these rituals was understood to be forbidden during interdicts by the beginning of the thirteenth century. Priests were, therefore, instructed to withhold extreme unction in interdicted France and England.[152] During the French interdict Innocent III had even affirmed in a decretal that it was prohibited for all by a general interdict, and although canonists were slow to recognize this decretal, its place in canon law was assured by 1234.[153] Papal concessions of extreme unction during an interdict to the Dominicans in 1267 and the Franciscans by 1288 were rare exceptions to this ban.[154] Even when Boniface VIII permitted consecration and use of chrism for baptism during interdicts, he did not lift the ban on extreme unction.

Priests might still perform other last rites during interdicts. They were allowed to commend departed souls to God in interdicted England, for example, provided that it was done privately in the house where the deceased was laid out and without a cross or holy water.[155] Innocent IV also taught that, after the final absolution, priests might pray for the dying and accept mortuary payments for attending on them in interdicted places.[156] Over a century later Johannes Calderinus agreed in his treatise on interdicts that all these practices, including commendation, were licit during interdicts. Another treatise attributed to him,

---

[149] Reg. Clement IV, no. 509; Reg. Nicholas IV, no. 205.
[150] VI 5.11.24. On this distinction see Guido de Baysio, *Lectura* on VI 5.11.24 v. *relaxatio* (fol. 125vb–6ra).
[151] Hamilton, *Religion*, 121; the scriptural basis for the sacrament is in James 5:14–15.
[152] Martène and Durand, i.813 (England), iv.147 (France).
[153] X 5.38.11 (= 4 Comp. 5.14.3). Addressed to the Bishop of Paris in Alan. 5.20.1 (see n. 65).
[154] See n. 149. On Boniface VIII's ruling see n. 95.
[155] Gervase, II, p. xciii; Martène and Durand, i.813.
[156] Innocent IV, *Apparatus* on X 5.31.18 v. *interdicti violationem*.

nevertheless, advised priests not to visit houses of the dead during interdicts for the sake of aspersing their bodies and saying prayers at their vigil unless they had caused the sentence and made amends before death.[157] Bartholomew of Pisa's *Summa* had indeed suggested (1338) that generally priests might hold vigils during interdicts only for deceased clerks.[158]

From birth till death an interdict thus inhibited participation in the sacraments to some degree. The extent of the ban was, however, gradually reduced by the papacy during the thirteenth century, and the course of this development is so complex that it needs to be briefly summarized. By the end of the twelfth century infant baptism and absolution of the dying were excepted from interdicts. Marriage was also understood to be unaffected, but not its solemnization. Innocent III then added further exceptions, notably confirmation of children in 1209. In 1200 he had also extended absolution to crusaders and pilgrims and permitted the Eucharist for the dying in interdicted France, but these rulings were not widely recognized as generally applicable until 1234, when Gregory IX also established the arrangements for consecrating the host for the dying. Finally in 1298 Boniface VIII mitigated the severity of the ban still further, allowing baptism and confirmation also for adults, the use of chrism in baptism, and absolution even of the living during interdicts. Ordination, extreme unction, and the Eucharist for the living remained under the ban on the sacraments, however, with few exceptions.

4.3 ECCLESIASTICAL BURIAL

In a decretal of 1200 Innocent III stated, as if a matter of accepted fact, that a general interdict forbade ecclesiastical burial, meaning burial with religious ceremony and in consecrated ground.[159] Though contemporary sentences rarely specified this third and final main effect of an interdict, the perfunctory nature of this papal statement implies that it was already widely understood. Those who died excommunicate had long been denied ecclesiastical burial under canon law. As early as the fifth century Pope Leo I had enunciated the principle that 'we may not communicate with those persons dead with whom we have not communicated when they lived'; and this had been included in Gratian's *Decretum*.[160] By 1031,

---

[157] Johannes Calderinus, 'De interdicto', Pt 1 §93, Pt 2 §7 (fols. 330va, 331va); id. (attrib.), *De censura*, BAV, Pal. lat. MS 797, fol. 14va (Ed. p. 281). Likewise according to an early fourteenth-century German treatise (Ludeco Cappel, *Summarius*, fol. 1r), priests or clergy might not attend the homes of the dead to read vigils or burn incense over them.

[158] Quoted by Nicholas Plowe, 'De interdicto', fol. 334ra.

[159] X 5.38.11 (= Alan. 5.20.1; 4 Comp. 5.14.3). Burial was thus prohibited by the interdicts recorded in Innocent III, Reg. 6, nos. 118, 148, 162; Innocent III, Reg. 11, no. 143; etc.

[160] C.24 q.2 c.1. See also n. 177 on Innocent III's invocation of this principle to regulate churchyards.

when an ecclesiastical council imposed a 'public excommunication' on Limoges diocese, this rule might apply to whole communities. The main effect of the conciliar sentence was that nobody might be buried in Limoges diocese or taken outside it for burial except clerks, visiting pilgrims, and infants under two years old.[161] Refusal of decent burial apparently became a fixed feature of such collective sentences once they were regularized and more often imposed as interdicts in the twelfth century. It was perhaps the most feared effect of an interdict, distressing not only to the dying but also to their family and friends. The same fate was allotted to suicides and executed criminals as well as excommunicates and other outcasts, hence denoting social shame and exclusion.[162] By Innocent III's time canonists were hardly unaware of the psychological effect of denying proper burial.[163] A pupil of the French canonist Petrus Brito noted that if a person died with significant debts, his heirs might be 'terrorized' into settling them through him being denied Christian burial 'in hatred of the heirs'. Alanus Anglicus similarly observed that when the sacrilegious refused to make amends at death and so were denied ecclesiastical burial, they brought shame on their heirs, and the sight of their bones being buried 'in the fields' might so affect the heirs that they would endeavour to give satisfaction to those robbed by the deceased. The refusal of ecclesiastical burial under an interdict was likewise intended to shame the guilty into repentance and provoke the innocent into compelling them to this end.

The ban on burial rarely meant no burial at all, as Alanus indicated in the case of the sacrilegious, but usually no burial in the normal place with the customary rites, i.e. ecclesiastical burial. The French interdict was unusually strict in this respect for it prohibited burial of any sort. The legate who promulgated the sentence forbade clergy to admit bodies to cemeteries to be buried or even left on the ground; they had to warn laity that it was a grave sin and usurpation of clerical office for them to bury the dead even in non-consecrated places.[164] This insistence on non-burial apparently met with compliance if the testimony of the *Gesta Innocentii III* is to be believed: corpses were not buried in cemeteries anywhere in interdicted France but left unburied everywhere, even lying on the ground. Ralph of Coggleshall claimed that corpses were simply left to rot, posing an offence to public health and popular sensibilities: 'the stench of these corpses infected the air, and the horrible sight of them struck terror into the hearts

---

[161] Mansi, xix.541.   [162] See Murray, *Suicide*, ii.16–17, 41–53, 467–71.

[163] Anon. on 1 Comp. 2.20.41 v. *tradendum sepulture*, Brussels, Bibliothèque royale MS 1407–09, fol. 29vb: 'Quando debitum evidens est ita quod heredes cognoscunt et tamen negant se solvere, locum habet quod hic dicit, et hoc in odium filiorum seu heredum, quando enim quis punitur propter delictum alterius, xvii. q.iiii. Miror [C.17 q.4 c.8]. Negatur sepultura ad terrorem ut de torneamentis'. Alanus on 1 Comp. 5.14.5 v. *penitentiam*, Munich, Bayerisches Staatsbibliothek Clm 3879, fol. 87vb: 'sed negatur sollempnis persone reconciliatio ad verecundiam heredum ... nam cum viderint ossa eius per campos sepeliri, lesi studebunt satisfacere rubore confecti.'

[164] Martène and Durand, iv.147. Cf. Murray, *Suicide*, ii.16–17, 464–71, on 'non-burial' of suicides.

of the living.'[165] Chroniclers often wrote with a moral purpose, however, and he perhaps intended this as a macabre warning to others to avoid an interdict. Roger of Howden's more sober account actually suggests that the ban on burial was not total; he recorded that the dead were buried outside French towns at the roadside.[166] The ecclesiastical authorities no doubt found it difficult to enforce the ban rigidly. They could withhold funeral services, but people might still make arrangements for the burial of their dead. In interdicted England ecclesiastical authorities even encouraged this and apparently limited the ban to ecclesiastical burial. According to the 'Forma interdicti' dead laity or clergy might be buried outside cemeteries wherever their friends wished, especially in places that passers-by would see and feel moved, but no priest might attend burials of laity. Roger of Wendover, albeit not the most trustworthy chronicler, recorded that this was indeed done, observing that the dead were carried out of towns and villages and buried 'like dogs' in ditches and highways without priests or prayers.[167] Suicides were also buried in such places, as Murray noted, especially spots that were visible to others, notably road junctions and boundaries such as ditches.[168] Likewise the 'Forma interdicti' recommended public places no doubt to provide a conspicuous reminder of the sentence's dangers, albeit a less disturbing one than decomposing bodies.

Special provision was made for burial of clergy during these interdicts, and as we have seen this had also been the case under the burial ban imposed by the council of Limoges in 1031. In a decretal of 1200 Innocent III had permitted clergy who died observing the French interdict to be buried at cemeteries in silence without ceremony. He had also mitigated the interdict on Lèon in this way in 1199, but it was not initially clear whether these mitigations applied to other interdicts.[169] The ruling on the French interdict was known to Peter of Blois, Archdeacon of London, but in 1209 he had to ask his bishop whether it might be observed in his diocese during the English interdict. In fact his bishop was one of the sentence's three executors, and if they indeed issued the 'Forma interdicti', they merely conceded there that the bodies of dead clerks might be deposited in marked hollow tree-trunks, or in lead coffins resting in the trees or on the walls of cemeteries, presumably to await burial on the interdict being lifted. Likewise the corpses of religious might be placed within their monastic precinct, but the ground of the cemetery was to remain unopened.[170]

---

[165] *Gesta* c.51 (*PL* 214. ccxiv); Coggleshall, *Chronicon*, 112–13. Older historians saw the *Gesta* as mere papal panegyric but more recently its value as a source, admittedly an insider's view from the curia, has been reassessed, notably by Bolton, 'Too Important to Neglect'.

[166] Howden, iv.138 (A. 1200). Cf. Murray, *Suicide*, ii.42–3.

[167] Martène and Durand, i.813 ('Forma'); Wendover, *Flores*, ii.46. The Dunstable annalist likewise recorded that the dead were buried outside cemeteries and without priests (*Annales*, iii.30).

[168] Murray, *Suicide*, ii.43–4, 46–50.

[169] France: X 5.38.11 (= Alan. 5.20.1; 4 Comp. 5.14.3). Lèon: Innocent III, Reg. 2, no. 72 (= 3 Comp. 4.15.1; X 4.20.5). On the Lèon interdict, see Krehbiel, 104–6.

[170] *Peter of Blois*, 120 (Letter 24); Martène and Durand, i.813 ('Forma').

In practice English monasteries largely seem to have closed their cemeteries in accordance with this ban, but rather than await the interdict's removal before burying their dead, they interred bodies in unconsecrated ground set aside specifically for this purpose, thus following the provision of the 'Forma interdicti' allowing burial outside cemeteries. At the Cistercian abbey of Meaux, for example, monks and *conversi* were not interred in the usual places, but beside its boundary wall in an orchard.[171] Similar arrangements were made by the monks of St Albans, Waverley, and Snellshall, where dedication of these *ad hoc* burial grounds was recorded after the interdict was relaxed. This was slightly more dignified provision than was made for most laity, if we accept Roger of Wendover's account, but the bodies of some laity were accepted by religious institutions for burial in such special plots. Papal privileges had long granted monastic houses the freedom to receive the bodies of laity who chose burial in their cemeteries rather than the local parish churchyard, provided that they did not die excommunicate or under interdict.[172] Such persons might no longer be buried in consecrated ground, but at Meaux a burial site marked with a wooden cross was provided for the abbey's servants, serfs, and neighbours on some waste ground near a chapel, and the monks of Snellshall buried local parishioners in a plot for their own dead during the interdict.[173]

It is not known what arrangements most secular clergy made for their own burial in interdicted England, but their superiors were apparently not spared from the common fate of burial in unhallowed ground. Before his death Robert, Bishop of Bangor, even provided for his burial in Shrewsbury marketplace. William de Montibus, chancellor of Lincoln Cathedral, was also buried in unconsecrated ground, but after the interdict his body was exhumed and re-interred in his church. The ban on ecclesiastical burial was thus applied to clergy and laity indiscriminately during the English interdict.[174]

The contemporary papal interdict on Narni also prohibited ecclesiastical burial specifically, forbidding its citizens to bury their dead in 'Christian' cemeteries on pain of excommunication, and this was seemingly the norm by the early

---

[171] Meaux: *Melsa*, ed. Bond, i.351. St Albans: Liebermann, 172 (Annales S. Albani, 1214). Waverley: *Annales*, ii.282 (A. 1214). Snellshall: *Cartulary*, ed. Jenkins, 7 (Tattenhoe charter 11, *c*.1218–24).

[172] E.g. Innocent III, Reg. 11, nos. 145, 193, 200, 282; 12, nos. 21, 166, 169; 13, nos. 51, 81; etc.

[173] See sources in n. 170. In 1209 the Bishop of London confirmed provision of an enclosed plot next to St Bartholomew's Hospital that the mayor and citizens of London had requested from its canons for the burial of dead citizens; brethren and inmates of the hospital and poor from elsewhere could be buried in a separate plot (*Records of St Bartholomew's*, 1. 109–10).

[174] Bishop of Bangor: *Annales*, 2. 273 (Waverley Annals A. 1213). William de Montibus: *Chronicle of Melrose*, 57 (A. 1213). The bones of Ralph prior of St Benet Holme were likewise translated (*Chronica Iohannis de Oxenedes*, 296). Geoffrey of Coldingham noted that Philip, Bishop of Durham, was buried by laymen outside his cathedral's precincts during the interdict (*Historiae Dunelmensis*, 26).

thirteenth century, as Innocent III's decretal of 1200 observed.[175] Canon law did
not regulate the private arrangements for unchristian burial during an interdict,
though they were presumably generally similar to those observed in interdicted
England.[176] Innocent III, however, regulated access to churchyards in his decretal
'Sacris' (1200), generally accepted by contemporary canonists. They understood
it to rule that if excommunicates and others denied Christian burial were buried
in cemeteries, their bones should be exhumed and cast out, provided that they
could be distinguished from the bones of the faithful. This reinforced Leo I's
teaching that when Communion was denied with persons when they were alive,
it was also denied after their death, thus maintaining their social exclusion beyond
the grave. Alanus even taught that mass might not be celebrated in any church
where such outcasts remained buried.[177] Such views were not confined to law
schools. In 1209, when Raymond of Toulouse asked the council of St Gilles to
lift the interdict on his lands, one of the preconditions set by the council was
that bodies buried during this interdict were to be disinterred by those who had
buried them and then re-interred solemnly after the sentence's removal, unless
they were excommunicated by name.[178]

Hence exclusion might be perpetual for those who died excommunicated,
but those dying under an interdict might be reconciled through reburial after
the sentence, no doubt a great comfort to their family and friends. The case
of William de Montibus has been noted. Likewise in 1237 Gregory IX ordered
that citizens of Reims who had died under an interdict might be buried in
churchyards after this sentence was relaxed, provided that they had received
final absolution from a priest, having shown signs of repentance at death.[179]
Innocent IV subsequently established this as standard doctrine; as a jurist he
held that if anyone showed signs of repentance on dying in an interdicted
place, they might be buried in a cemetery after the interdict was lifted. He
added that if such contrite persons were buried in a churchyard during an
interdict, their remains might not be disinterred subsequently. Once again an
interdict was to be mitigated in favour of the innocent, specifically those dying
at peace with the Church. And popes applied such moderation in practice. In
1290 when Nicholas IV ordered the lifting of the interdict on Strasbourg, he
conceded that if any of its citizens had shown signs of repentance at death

---

[175] Reg. Innocent III 11, no. 143. Cf. Honorius III, no. 4052. See n. 164 on Innocent
III's decretal.
[176] By the mid-fourteenth century Johannes Calderinus certainly accepted that the dead might
be buried without solemnity outside cemeteries in interdicted places; see his 'De interdicto' Pt 2
§22 (fol. 332va).
[177] 'Sacris': X 3.28.12 (= 3 Comp. 3.21.3). On Leo I's teaching quoted in 'Sacris', see
n. 159. Tancred on 2 Comp. 3.26.2 v. *excommunicatis*, BAV, Vat. lat. MS 1377, fol. 130rb:
'Immo nec missa celebratur ubi ossa excommunicatorum sunt, supra. de con. di. i. Ecclesiam [De
con. D.1 c.27], dummodo separari possunt ab ossibus fidelium, ut infra. de sepul. Sacris lib. iii.
A<lanus>.'
[178] *PL* 216.97–8; Krehbiel, 150–5, esp. 151.   [179] Reg. Gregory IX, no. 3540.

and been buried in ecclesiastical cemeteries during the sentence, their bodies might remain there.[180] But, according to Innocent IV, the penitent might not receive ecclesiastical burial even in non-interdicted places, if they were personally interdicted.

Canon law did not confirm these mitigations, but by 1234 it included Innocent III's decretal on the French interdict, hence giving general force to its ruling on clergy who died observing an interdict. They might be buried in consecrated ground but with no funeral service and almost secretly, as Hostiensis observed.[181] But this concession was apparently limited to general interdicts; Innocent IV and Hostiensis denied that it might be enjoyed where a church or the clergy were specifically interdicted. Besides this general concession, certain regular clergy held special burial privileges, notably the military orders. A canon of the Fourth Lateran Council indicates that papal grants of such privileges were not uncommon by the thirteenth century, and it summarized their terms: the privileged might hand over the corpses of brethren for ecclesiastical burial even if the deceased had belonged to an interdicted church, provided that they were not interdicted by name, excommunicates, or usurers; if prelates refused burial at their churches, these bodies might be taken to churches of their own order.[182] It was a matter of canonistic debate, however, whether Templars and Hospitallers might bury the dead at interdicted churches. A canon of the Third Lateran Council (1179) had ruled that their freedom to open a church in an interdicted place once a year did not allow them to conduct burials there. But most early thirteenth-century canonists, including Tancred, agreed that this applied not to burial of deceased brethren but only of dead outsiders; even Hostiensis considered this opinion valid.[183] According to Innocent IV, however, brethren of an interdicted church were not to be buried there but at another non-interdicted church, and their fellow lay parishioners might not enjoy this freedom unless their church was interdicted as a result of a violation or clerical wrongdoing.

In practice religious holding such privileges were burying persons other than members of their own community, notably laity who paid a small annual

---

[180] Innocent IV, *Apparatus* on X 5.31.18 v. *interdicti violationem*; Reg. Nicholas IV, no. 2679.

[181] X 5.38.11. Hostiensis, *Lectura* on X 5.38.11 v. *solemnitatibus* (vol. 2, fol. 101rb); on X 5.31.18 v. *post interdicti violationem* (vol. 2, fol. 72va). He also held that clergy who gave cause for an interdict forfeited their right to Christian burial during it; id. on X 5.38.11 v. *servaverint* (vol. 2, fol. 101rb).

[182] Lat. Conc. IV c.57 (= 4 Comp. 5.12.7; X 5.33.24). Examples of these burial privileges are found in Reg. Alexander IV, nos. 1553, 2037, 2373; Reg. Nicholas IV, no. 842; etc.

[183] Lat. Conc. III c.9 (= 1 Comp. 5.28.3; X 5.33.3). Tancred on 1 Comp. 5.28.3 v. *defunctorum*, BAV, Vat. lat. MS 1377, fol. 93rb: 'Nisi fratres eorum fuerunt, ut infra e. Simili modo [1 Comp. 5.28.5].' Cf. Alanus, ibid., Munich, Bayerisches Staatsbibliothek Clm 3879, fol. 92rb: 'Nisi cum fratres eorum fuerint, ut infra e. t. Simili ... et si ecclesia fuerit interdicta, ipsi mortui per hospitalarios tradantur semel in anno sepulture.' Hostiensis supported this view in his *Lectura* on X 5.33.24 v. *non negetur* (vol. 2, fol. 87rb) but ultimately agreed with Innocent IV, *Apparatus* on X 5.33.24 v. *non negetur* and v. *regularium*.

subscription to 'join' their order. Innocent III had denounced this practice in his Lateran ruling on burial privileges and restricted these to those who had entered the religious life fully, giving up all their property to their order and adopting its habit. However, subsequent thirteenth-century popes occasionally extended burial privileges to individuals outside monastic communities. In 1225 Honorius III required all Italian prelates to permit the burial of laity of the mendicant third orders at their churches during interdicts; and in 1246 Innocent IV made a similar concession to lay devotees of the Humiliati.[184] Some grants even rewarded lay charity to religious against the spirit of Innocent III's ruling. In 1221 Honorius III allowed the Holy Cross monastery, Coimbra, to grant its patrons ecclesiastical burial during an interdict, provided that these persons had not provoked the sentence. In 1257 Alexander IV extended traditional Hospitaller burial privileges to those admitted to the fraternity of Sens hospital for the price of an annual donation, the very abuse Innocent III's ruling had condemned.[185] Boniface VIII even recognized lay philanthropy in the community, when a confraternity formed to rebuild a road destroyed by floods was allowed to bury its members at a chapel near this road during general interdicts. A concern underlying such grants was that an interdict could harm the church's supporters, and in order to maintain their devotion it was expedient sometimes to spare them one of the sentence's harshest deprivations. When the Bishop of Constance told Innocent IV, for example, that some of his parishioners were aiding the Church against its political enemies in 1247, the pope granted ecclesiastical burial, at the bishop's request, for such parishioners belonging to interdicted churches.[186] But generally such grants to laity were rare and, except for the clergy, innocent and guilty alike suffered loss of ecclesiastical burial under interdicts. Admittedly the fourteenth-century canonist Johannes Calderinus speculated whether funeral services and burials were permitted on the four principal feast days when Boniface VIII allowed churches to be opened in interdicted places. But he observed that his teacher Johannes Andreae had rejected this conclusion and no other canonist had drawn it. Boniface VIII and his immediate successors had certainly not mitigated the interdict's ban on ecclesiastical burial; if anything they had sought to reinforce it, as we will see in the next chapter.[187]

The interdict constituted a severe disruption of the church's religious activities, but it was not meant to disturb the operation of church government. In interdicted England the 'Forma interdicti' encouraged continued administration of ecclesiastical justice to lay and clerical miscreants, though it required church

---

[184] Reg. Honorius III, no. 5740; Reg. Innocent IV, no. 2193.

[185] Ibid., no. 3129; Reg. Alexander IV, no. 2037.

[186] Reg. Boniface VIII, no. 104; Reg. Innocent IV, no. 2613.

[187] Calderinus, 'De interdicto', Pt 2 §15 (fol. 332ra). Cf. Andreae, *Novelle* on VI 5.11.24 v. *divinorum*.

courts to be held in cemeteries and priests' houses, not in churches closed by the interdict. In practice Cheney found that the judicial business of the English Church was not disrupted, though King John appears to have effectively impeded appeals to Rome from 1210.[188] According to the 'Forma interdicti' teaching was also to continue in the schools of interdicted England. The scholars of Oxford University admittedly dispersed, but, if Roger of Wendover is to be believed, this was a protest at the arbitrary lynching of some students by townsfolk rather than a direct result of the interdict, though town and gown were reconciled only after the interdict was lifted.[189] Nevertheless Innocent IV taught that masters who taught in the schools during an interdict violated it as much as one ministering in holy orders. But Hostiensis pointed out that a master did not discharge his duties by virtue of orders, and two fourteenth-century canonistic treatises indeed concluded that clerks might still carry out offices unrelated to orders during an interdict, including *magister scholarum* and notary public, since it only prohibited the functions of the ordained.[190] Cheney indeed found that much routine ecclesiastical business had continued as usual in interdicted England, notably appointments to benefices and sees (only occasionally affected by interdicts as we have seen) and church-building.[191] In addition the 'Forma interdicti' had urged parishioners to pay alms and other dues to the English Church as usual, even though it was refusing most of its ministrations. In fact King John seized much of its property, and, as the next chapter illustrates, when the Church's activities were disrupted during an interdict beyond the terms of the sentence, this usually arose from the reactions of secular princes and communities.

At the beginning of the thirteenth century the terms of the interdict were not specified in any detail by canon law. Innocent III began the gradual process of defining them in response to external demand, largely at the request of bishops instructed to enforce his interdicts. His rulings still left many points unclear and provided much scope for local variations in practice, but canonistic doctrine supplemented the law, providing general guidance on such issues, and at the end of the century the gaps in the law were largely filled by Boniface VIII. Boniface also revised some of Innocent's rulings and resolved points disputed among the canonists, to an extent redefining the terms of the interdict. In effect he completed the process of legal clarification of those terms; his successors did little to continue it. Indeed canon law and its commentators had defined the terms of the interdict in such detail by the early fourteenth century that an emerging genre of canonistic treatises on interdicts was largely devoted to

---

[188] Martène and Durand, i.813 ('Forma'); Cheney, 'Interdict', 308–13.

[189] Wendover, *Flores*, ii.51; Krehbiel, 145–8.

[190] Innocent IV, *Apparatus* on X 5.31.18 v. *violavit*; Hostiensis, *Lectura*, ibid. (vol. 2, fol. 76vb); Johannes Calderinus, 'De interdicto', Pt 1 §88 (fol. 330v); Ludeco Cappel, *Summarius*, fol. 3r.

[191] Cheney, 'Interdict', 309–12. See ibid. 301–7, and id., 'Reaction', on seizure of church property.

summarizing them; mnemonic poems were even written on the subject to guide clergy.[192]

In defining the terms of the interdict the papacy had largely sought to mitigate its severity for the innocent whilst maintaining its force against the guilty. As early as the twelfth century, even before popes began issuing general rules on the subject, they were granting mitigations of the interdict to certain regular clergy where they gave no cause for the sentence, notably the freedom to hold offices privately in their churches. By the thirteenth century even secular and ecclesiastical dignitaries and laity involved in pious activities were requesting these papal grants in ever-increasing numbers. It is understandable that popes gave clergy partial immunity from the effects of interdicts: interdicts were normally used to defend clergy against secular adversaries. Laity who opposed these enemies of the Church were also occasionally spared the sentence's full effects. But why did the papacy mitigate the interdict for the generality of laity, when canonists had articulated an elaborate justification of collective punishment, whereby the innocent rightly suffered for the sins of the guilty? This needs to be considered in the context of popular and princely responses to interdicts. The interdict's efficacy as a means of coercion largely depended on its effect on popular feeling, lay and clerical; thus its effect had to be well judged and such feeling taken into account by the Church authorities when laying an interdict. These issues will be explored in the next chapter.

---

[192] Two such poems are edited in my 'Interdict', 318–19. One inc. 'Tempore quando taces' was copied in a late-fifteenth-century hand on fol. 12r of a printed copy of Johannes Andreae, *De modo*; London, BL, IA. 10915. The other in German, written no later than 1494 and titled 'Wie man sych halden solle wan interdict yst' (inc. 'Halt messe'), was printed in Ludeco Cappel, *De interdicto*, fol. 4v.

5

The Interdict in Action

5.1 POPULAR AND PRINCELY RESPONSES TO INTERDICTS

An interdict was designed to compel those who provoked it to submit to ecclesiastical authority. As a collective sanction it was meant to achieve this by turning the innocent against the guilty. Indeed jurists and theologians held that the guilty could be coerced more effectively by making their innocent associates suffer than punishing them alone (see Chapter 1.1). In practice collective punishment occasionally had the desired effect. Abbot Geoffrey of Vendôme recounted that the county of Vendôme was interdicted in 1111 to punish its count's seizure of abbey property with the result 'that all the people who ... are much displeased by [the count's] iniquity ... proclaimed against him, and thus, since he did not wish to desist voluntarily from unjust action for the love of God, he desisted for both the clamour and fear of men or against his will'.[1] An interdict was meant not only to provoke such popular resistance to sinful rulers but also punish the lack of this resistance to the sin that caused the interdict in the first place. Peter the Chanter and subsequent canonists held that subjects had a collective duty to resist a sinful ruler and if they neglected this, they deserved punishment along with him.

But did general interdicts always have the desired effect? Popular reactions to the English interdict suggest otherwise. A contemporary monastic annalist noted that, when the dispute arose between Innocent III and King John that caused the interdict, all the laity, almost all the clergy, and many religious backed the king.[2] The pope was opposing John's interference in the appointment of the Archbishop of Canterbury, and the king's subjects doubtless sympathized more with royal claims of local custom than the pope's strict canonical position. Many English clergy owed their church offices to royal patronage, the system that the pope was fighting, and some even served in royal government. Contemporary verse condemned the Bishop of Winchester for taking the king's side and remaining at his desk in the royal exchequer while his colleagues who proclaimed the interdict

---

[1] *PL* 157.84.

[2] *Annales monastici*, i.28 (Margam annals). Incidentally Margam was one of three Cistercian abbeys accused of violating the interdict in the early days of the sentence; see p. 193.

fled into exile.[3] Evidently the conflict between pope and king tested loyalties, and the interdict merely exacerbated this.

Popular feelings were further confused by royal and papal propaganda. Before the sentence was declared, the pope had written letters to the episcopate of the English Church and magnates of England calling for their support.[4] He complained that some of the bishops were 'tepid and remiss' in the Archbishop of Canterbury's cause (which lends some credence to the annalist's claim above) and encouraged them all to defend ecclesiastical liberty. He likewise warned the nobles that in maintaining their fealty to an earthly king they should take care not to offend their heavenly king, and reminded them that they could not 'serve two masters' (Matthew 6:24). Hence he counselled them not to support John, for the king opposed God. This recalled Augustine's doctrine that Christians owed obedience to God before earthly rulers, well known to canonists from the *Decretum*; indeed Innocent's supposed teacher Huguccio had cited it to show that subjects had a duty to resist a king who defied God.[5] Similarly after the interdict was laid, the guidelines for its observance known as the 'Forma interdicti' required priests to preach to their parishioners that they had to obey God more than man (the apostles' teaching in Acts 5:29).[6] This weekly preaching was also to warn against fearing those with the power to kill them, i.e. John and his agents. Innocent had likewise warned the bishops and nobles to set aside such fear or rather to fear God more than man; God, as Augustine's doctrine pointed out, could inflict much harsher punishment, namely hell. Indeed priests were to admonish parishioners that those obedient to the Church might be saved but the disobedient should fear divine retribution. The 'Forma interdicti' also instructed priests to lead the faithful in prayers for the peace of the Church and for the king, that Christ might guide him towards the way of salvation and doing God's will. This was all designed to persuade the English to take the pope's side against the king.

This message was reinforced by a letter to the English people from Stephen Langton, for whose sake the interdict was imposed. Writing in exile shortly before it was declared, he entreated his compatriots not to consent to John's persecution of the English Church, reminding them of the canonistic teaching that a like penalty binds those doing wrong and those consenting to it. He defined this consent according to the classic scholastic distinction as both active support for sin and passive failure to resist it.[7] He especially reminded knights of their investiture by the Church and consequent duty to defend her, but rather than armed insurrection he called for use of persuasion to turn John away from wickedness and others from consent to it. Hence he expected people to react to

---

[3] *Political Songs*, 10.   [4] Innocent III, Reg. 10, no. 159; *SLI*, no. 32.
[5] C.11 q.3 c.97; on Huguccio see p. 43 n. 99.   [6] Martène and Durand, i.812–13.
[7] *Acta Stephani Langton*, 6. The letter was written at some point between 27 August 1207, when the Pope threatened the interdict, and the sentence's proclamation on 23 March 1208.

the interdict in accordance with theological and canonistic doctrine, namely to resist their king's wrongdoing, thereby compelling him to come to terms.

Innocent's letters and the 'Forma interdicti' shared this expectation, but it was countered by royal propaganda. In the week before the interdict's publication (on 23 March 1208) John sent agents to the shires with letters that told his side of the story.[8] One sent to the men of Kent instructed them to trust whatever its bearer, Reginald of Cornhill, told them on John's behalf about the wrong and injury done to him; a similar letter to the Durham diocese spoke of 'the injury inflicted on us by the lord pope'. The interdict thus generated a propaganda war between Church and Crown, but which side won? If we believe the Margam annalist, John's subjects were initially swayed by his claims but did the interdict eventually turn them against him? The *Gesta Innocentii III* alleged that soon after it came into force, John was forced to seek terms with the pope because of the 'general clamour'. This suggests that the interdict had its desired effect and provoked an immediate popular backlash against the king.[9] Innocent's biographer as a curial insider was perhaps expressing wishful thinking, however. His main source was the papal registers, and a letter copied there relates that John sought reconciliation with Innocent shortly after the interdict's publication, but not that he was prompted by public pressure; in any case subsequent negotiations failed.[10] Furthermore the English sources tell a different story. They imply that the interdict aroused public resentment, but against the Church authorities rather than John. In 1213 when Langton preached to a large crowd in London, hecklers interrupted him to complain that, although he was reconciled with John and the reason for the interdict had thereby ended, churches still remained closed and silent; the sentence was not actually relaxed till ten months later. Likewise in 1209 when the pope had permitted conventual clergy to hold mass once a week behind closed doors during the interdict, Peter of Blois observed that this caused scandal and grumbling among London laity, 'who saw unjust discrimination in it'.[11]

Stubbs rightly called an interdict 'that most … suicidal weapon of the medieval Church'. Not only could this backfire and turn people against the Church instead of its intended target, but it could also discourage religious devotion. Abbot John of Ford in 1210 lamented that piety was in danger of expiring in interdicted England unless God came to its aid, as the Eucharist had been withdrawn for so long. He admitted that this was still reserved to a few (i.e. conventual clergy) but added that the masses had been 'starved' of this for almost two years, and he feared that 'they will die on the road and completely cease to remember their fatherland if their hunger goes on increasing'.[12]

This withdrawal of religious ministrations was a test of orthodoxy that might have serious implications; this was recognized even before the English interdict.

---

[8] *RLP*, 80a; *Foedera*, I/i.100. [9] *Gesta* c.131 (*PL* 214. clxxvii).
[10] Letter: Innocent III, Reg. 11, no. 90; copied in *Gesta* c.132 (*PL* 214. clxxviii).
[11] Langton: Lacombe, 'Unpublished Document', 417. *Peter of Blois*, 120 (Letter 24).
[12] *Ioannis de Forda*, 300, 303. Stubbs quotation from Cheney, *England*, 303

Early in 1199 three Iberian prelates told Innocent III that a papal interdict was endangering the kingdom of León in three ways. Firstly various heresies were flourishing there, as the interdict stopped clergy from preaching against heretics and discouraged the king from persecuting them. Secondly it made León vulnerable to Saracen invasion, as the Church had stopped preaching holy war and giving remission of sins to those fighting the infidel; and without this ecclesiastical approval and because the people felt partly to blame for the interdict, they feared falling further into sin by going to war. Indeed there is some evidence that the interdict was inhibiting the realm's defence. Christian Spain was then threatened by the Almohads, a Muslim sect that had invaded southern Spain. Conflict between the kings of Castile and León stopped them from presenting a united front against the Almohads, but peace and an alliance was to be forged through the king of León marrying the king of Castile's daughter. However, the marriage was invalid and the interdict was meant to enforce its dissolution. The prelates' request for a marriage dispensation met with papal refusal, so they had to argue that the interdict exposed León to Muslim invasion in other ways.[13] They also alleged that, since clergy might not administer spiritual things to laity, laity refused temporal dues to the clergy, notably tithes, so that most clerks were reduced to begging and even working for Jews 'in ecclesie et totius Christianitatis opprobrium'.

The bishops perhaps exaggerated the negative effects of this interdict to secure its relaxation (the pope refused this), but during the thirteenth century clergy recorded several instances when interdicts resulted in the growth of anti-clericalism and heresy. After Bergamo fell under interdict because its citizens had taxed its clergy, its bishop petitioned the pope in early 1210 that the sentence had lasted so long that it had made some citizens less devout and more obdurate and let heretics spread their errors more easily; other sources indeed refer to Cathar sympathizers there at this time.[14] Hence an interdict inadvertently provided conditions for heresy to thrive, and Church authorities recognized this danger, especially in areas where heresy was already a major concern. Early thirteenth-century popes were notably concerned to eradicate the Cathar heresy in southern France, for example, but in 1234 the Bishop of Marseilles warned the pope that an interdict on his city had made it a safe haven for heretics, who were apparently flocking there from surrounding areas.[15] Presumably the sentence discouraged secular authorities and laity from cooperating with the inquisition, for the Bishop said that the heretics shrewdly considered that they could not be rooted out of Marseilles while the interdict was in force. He had therefore relaxed it to drive out the heretics more freely, and consequently he claimed to have handed over many of them to secular justice and several others for imprisonment.

[13] Innocent III, Reg. 2, no. 72; copied in *Gesta* c.58 (*PL* 214.cv–cvi). On the context see O'Callaghan, 'Innocent III', esp. 317–25.
[14] Innocent III, Reg. 13, no. 43. Lambert, 115.   [15] Reg. Gregory IX, no. 2020.

Admittedly popes exploited the interdict as a weapon against heresy, but even they recognized that this might be counter-productive. In 1213 Innocent III supported an interdict on Toulouse, since some of its citizens were Cathars and several others were *credentes*, supporters, or protectors of Catharism, so much so that Cathars were taking refuge there.[16] However, some thirty years later Innocent IV admitted to the Bishop of Toulouse that such sanctions had only made matters worse. He observed that general sentences of excommunication and interdict were laid so often in the bishop's diocese that ecclesiastical censure was scorned there, and some locals saw it as nothing, whilst the heretics, who naturally rejected ecclesiastical discipline, were rejoicing.[17] In order to strengthen orthodoxy and discourage heresy there he granted the city, diocese, and all communities of the lands of Toulouse immunity for five years from such sentences laid on papal authority without a specific mandate. In fact southern French Catharism was already in irretrievable decline, but Boniface VIII still associated it with popular defiance of an interdict on the southern French town of Béziers as late as 1297.[18]

French Cathars were not the only heretics accused of turning interdicts to their advantage. In Germany the papal–imperial conflict at its height under Innocent IV and Frederick II provoked anti-clericalism that in turn enabled Waldensianism to spread; the use of interdicts by pro-papal clergy in the struggle only exacerbated these effects. The Passau Anonymous wrote in his treatise on Waldensian heresy (*c.*1260) that its proponents rejoiced during these interdicts, since then they could 'corrupt' the faithful more easily. In particular Waldensians allegedly declared that it was wicked to refuse sacraments to the innocent under these sentences since it punished them for the sins of others (a fact that canonists had long tried to justify).[19] According to the Anonymous these heretics even claimed that interdicts deprived the souls of the dead in Purgatory of the Church's intercessions, and when they saw how interdicts also reduced religious devotion among the living, they discouraged the faithful from giving tithes. David of Augsburg, in a similar treatise (*c.*1260–72) based on his experiences as an inquisitor, also noted how Waldensians exploited and enflamed public hostility to German clergy as papal–imperial tensions climaxed in the 1240s, observing that the clergy themselves partly provoked this situation through excessive use of spiritual sanctions. Apparently these only added to the disruption of their pastoral and inquisitorial work that political circumstances had caused, enabling Waldensians to spread their views more easily.

It is hard to know whether interdicts often had such dramatic repercussions, as popular responses to them are not well documented, and the evidence discussed so far comes from clergy, who recorded events from their own peculiar viewpoint.

---

[16] Innocent III, Reg. 16, no. 48.   [17] Reg. Innocent IV, no. 541.
[18] See Lambert, 126–46.
[19] *Quellen*, 90–1 (Passau Anonymous); Preger, 'Tractat', 219 (David of Augsburg). Schneider, 97; Lambert, 148.

Boniface VIII nevertheless recognized by 1298 that the effect of interdicts on lay orthodoxy was a widespread problem. His constitution 'Alma mater' observed that, as a result of the withdrawal of sacraments and offices during general interdicts, 'the indevotion of the populace grows, heresies pullulate, and infinite spiritual dangers arise'.[20] Indeed the canonist Johannes Andreae commented on these words that he had heard of a place in the Marche which fell under an interdict for so long that when it was lifted, people in their thirties and forties had never heard mass there and derided priests who resumed celebration of it.[21] Similar observations on the dangers of interdicts for pastoral care were made in Boniface VIII's constitution 'Provide' (1302), which noted that overuse of interdicts was causing children and adolescents to grow up weak in the faith, since they participated so rarely in the sacraments.

How did popes address the pastoral problems raised by interdicts? Innocent III ordered that the interdict on Bergamo might be lifted once its podestà and citizens had made amends. Gregory IX likewise approved the decision of the Bishop of Marseilles to relax the interdict on his city in order better to suppress heresy there. In these cases the canonical preconditions for lifting interdicts were not disregarded, but these popes clearly saw no value in these sentences remaining in force. Nevertheless popes were reluctant to abandon the interdict completely as a means of coercion; they were more inclined to mitigate it in order to minimize its pastoral consequences. Innocent III had adopted this approach to the León interdict. He refused to relax it completely, but he agreed to its temporary and partial relaxation, permitting celebration of divine offices and burial of clergy in churchyards without solemnity. The king of León and his wife, who occasioned the interdict by refusing to break off their uncanonical marriage, were nevertheless excommunicated and subjected to an ambulatory interdict. Innocent thus reduced the interdict's severity for the innocent and intensified the punishment of the guilty; his aim was to make the interdict a more effective means of coercion. Boniface VIII also pursued this line in his constitution 'Alma mater' almost a century later. He attributed the dangers of the general interdict to its severity and therefore mitigated it in favour of the innocent, whilst denying his concessions to the guilty. Such pastoral concerns and pragmatism no doubt motivated other papal mitigations of the interdict.

The papacy also tried regulating usage of interdicts in order to avoid unwanted effects. As noted above, Innocent IV granted Toulouse immunity from interdicts since they had only encouraged the heresy that they were meant to combat. Boniface VIII's constitution 'Provide' likewise forbade general interdicts in debt cases, for he was not only alarmed at the pastoral effects of such sentences but also their misuse for such worldly ends. Clerical anxiety over these issues also underlay

---

[20] VI 5.11.24; Extrav. comm. 5.10.2 ('Provide').
[21] Johannes Andreae, *Glossa* on VI 5.11.24 v. *insurgunt*.

calls for further papal reform of the interdict in the fourteenth century.[22] These suggest that thirteenth-century attempts to reserve the interdict as a justified last resort had been insufficient; indeed the fourteenth-century canonist Johannes Andreae noted that there was a very great danger that all Italy and beyond might end up under interdicts.[23]

Even if popes perceived that overuse of the interdict and its negative effect on popular feeling might blunt its effectiveness as a political weapon, its success largely depended on the reaction of those it was meant to coerce. But if general interdicts did not always turn the innocent against the guilty, did the latter still fear the sentence? In the thirteenth century growing numbers of kings and nobles requested papal immunity from the interdict as well as freedom to hear private services during one; this suggests that increasingly they saw it as worth being free from. One secular ruler even claimed to find interdicts distressing. When the Archbishop of Esztergom interdicted Hungary, its king, András II, complained to Gregory IX in 1232 that the exclusion of him and his subjects from the bosom of the Church was a painful injustice and had undermined his reputation abroad.[24] The king's petition was calculated to secure the relaxation of this sentence, but it suggests that lay rulers did not regard interdicts with equanimity. They could and did appeal against a threatened interdict to have it quashed. But many rulers tried to stop interdicts by less canonical means.

First a ruler might prevent it from being published. As early as 1171 Henry II had tried to stop publication of an interdict on England which the Bishop of Senlis had already declared on his continental lands. The bishop was reacting to Henry's alleged complicity in Thomas Becket's recent murder; thus the king had good reason to fear that the pope would extend this papal interdict to England.[25] Henry admittedly approached Alexander III through proper channels, and his appeal to the curia stayed the pope's hand, but according to Gervase of Canterbury Henry remained sufficiently concerned to instruct his reeves at ports on both sides of the channel to arrest anyone bringing papal letters of interdict

---

[22] Auer, 'Verschollene Denkschrift'. In this 'Denkschrift' the German Dominican John of Dambach described the negative effects of John XXII's interdict on the lands of Lewis of Bavaria and his allies (see Kaufhold on this interdict). In 1348 Dambach proposed reform of the interdict to Clement VI, and his treatise probably comprises arguments he made before the pope; he addressed it to Emperor Charles IV in the hope that he would persuade the pope to carry out this reform (Nauclerus, *Chronica*, ii.894).

[23] Johannes Andreae, *Glossa* on Clem. 3.13.3 v. *interdicti*.

[24] D'Achery, *Spicilegium*, iii.610.

[25] Gervase, I, p. 234. See Barlow, 253–6, and Warren, 113–14. A source hostile to the king alleged that he sent agents with gifts to bribe the curia; a more credible account said that his representatives swore that he would submit to papal judgement on Becket's murder (*Materials*, iv.165–6; vii.473–4). Henry II had also famously sought to limit use of interdicts in clause 7 of the Constitutions of Clarendon (1164); this required that no tenant-in-chief or official of the king be excommunicated or their lands interdicted unless the king or his justiciar was first asked to grant justice in the matter (*Materials*, v. 75). This was one of the offensive clauses that Henry had to abjure in order to obtain papal absolution in 1172.

into England. His motive was perhaps legal since an unpublished sentence was technically invalid, although it is doubtful that Henry knew this at such an early date; more likely his reason was practical in that clergy could not enforce an interdict they were unaware of. Henry might resist an interdict in this way since his government was highly organized by late twelfth-century standards, with its network of loyal agents. We have seen how his son John later used this to spread anti-papal propaganda in 1208 when England was again threatened with a papal interdict.

If Roger of Wendover is to be trusted, John also used intimidation to dissuade the executors of this sentence from promulgating it, threatening physical violence and property seizures against clergy in England if they did so.[26] Admittedly he wrote with the benefit of hindsight; following the interdict's promulgation John indeed seized the goods of clergy who observed it. His account of John's blasphemous outburst against the tearful executors is also fanciful, with John swearing to send all Romans or papal clerks found in his lands back to Rome with their eyes torn out and noses cut off, but it is not wholly incredible. John was noted for cruelty, and the executors certainly fled into exile soon after declaring the interdict, doubtless fearful for their personal safety. According to the Evesham Abbey chronicle Romans had their goods sequestrated and were expelled on John's orders, including the abbey's own creditors, but not mutilated apparently. Nevertheless John of Ford warned in 1210 that clergy had to fear physical violence as well as loss of their property.[27] But, as Cheney noted, the evidence here is ambiguous. Shortly after the interdict's promulgation the king ordered that clerks and monks were not to be harmed, but a fourteenth-century chronicle claimed that he also forbade inquests into murders of clerks during the interdict, thus many died.[28] Cheney found few violations of clerical immunity, however, though there was the famous case that prompted Oxford University's dispersal in 1209. After a student accidentally slew a local woman and fled the scene, the mayor and townsfolk hanged two or three clerks who were room-mates of the fugitive, apparently with the king's support.[29]

As Cheney observed, 'John treated the interdict as tantamount to a declaration of war.'[30] And financial and physical coercion were his means of waging war against this weapon of the pope. It was a war in which each side fought to defend what it saw as its right. John defended the royal custom of controlling ecclesiastical appointments, while the pope sought to defend ecclesiastical liberty from such lay intrusions. But the king's surrender to the pope in 1213 after five years of conflict did not prevent further outbreaks of hostilities over such issues. In 1286 John's grandson Edward I exploited the archiepiscopal vacancy at York to present a royal clerk, Bonet de St Quentin, to a prebend at Southwell

---

[26] Wendover, *Flores*, iii.221–2.   [27] *Evesham*, 225; *Ioannis de Forda*, 300.
[28] *RLC*, i.111a; *Chronicles*, 8 (*Annales Londonienses*).
[29] Cheney, 'Interdict', 301; Wendover, *Flores*, iii.227–8, 274.   [30] Cheney, 'Interdict', 297.

Minster.[31] But Honorius IV had provided his chaplain, Rolando di Ferentino, to the same prebend, and when Bonet and the Southwell chapter blocked this provision, Rolando's executor suspended the chapter, interdicted the minster, and excommunicated Bonet. Edward reacted by having the executor jailed in the Tower of London; Nicholas IV called for his release in 1288 and was still seeking to enforce the provision in 1289. As in the Canterbury dispute under John, the interdict arose from the competing claims of pope and king to place their own man in the same benefice. It was not, however, the only time when Edward's interests conflicted with the Church's or his government resisted interdicts; Nicholas IV complained to Edward in 1292 that his officials sometimes did not tolerate ordinaries using ecclesiastical censures.[32]

Lay rulers elsewhere also defended their interests by retaliating against publication of interdicts. After Peter of Aragon displaced papally approved Angevin rule in Sicily in 1282, Martin IV issued an interdict and other sanctions against Peter and his allies, but Bishop Pontio of Majorca later complained that he had suffered persecution when he published these sentences. Peter's son Alfonso had invaded Majorca and seized the bishop's property and revenues, so the curia had to give Pontio and clerks who joined him in exile incomes from southern French benefices.[33] Peter doubtless saw Pontio's obedience to the pope as disloyalty to the Crown and hence deserving of retribution.

Not only royal but also city governments tried to stop interdicts being declared against them, notably at Verdun. Relations between its clergy and laity were turbulent for most of the thirteenth century as its citizens struggled repeatedly to win autonomy from their bishop's temporal jurisdiction. They finally exploited an episcopal vacancy in 1286–9 to proclaim self-government.[34] The cathedral chapter petitioned the pope to provide them with a bishop capable of restoring their church's rights, and Nicholas IV appointed noted jurist and curial auditor Jacques de Revigny in 1289. But the citizens resisted Revigny's attempt to recover episcopal authority, so in 1296 he sought papal intervention. He told Boniface VIII that citizens had seized clerks carrying his letters indicting them, torn up the letters, and threatened to kill or mutilate anyone who came to execute his mandates. Consequently when he sent priests to publish an interdict on Verdun, they were allegedly set upon by an armed mob that forced them to swear not to carry out his orders. He claimed that the city then responded with its own sanctions against the clergy, forbidding citizens to have contact with him even to give him food, a secular kind of excommunication, and revoking 'benefit of

---

[31] *CPR* 1281–92, 225. Bonet was a wardrobe clerk and trained lawyer whom Edward used in dealings with France over Gascony in 1285 (Prestwich, 143, 305). I am grateful to Dr Philip Saunders for these references. See his 'Royal Ecclesiastical Patronage' on similar clashes with the papacy.

[32] Reg. Nicholas IV, nos. 236, 657, 6859.

[33] Reg. Nicholas IV, no. 3793. On the context see Runciman, 237–80.

[34] Roussel, i.314–19; *Histoire*, ed. Girardot, 89, 91.

clergy', so that a layman might kill a clerk in a fight with impunity, and other laymen might be punished if they failed to aid him. Citizens were also accused of driving many clerks from Verdun and selling off their property.[35] No doubt some of these charges were not exaggerated; the interdicts on the towns of Dax, Bèziers, and San Gimignano treated below provoked similar reactions. However, Revigny's petition was designed to secure papal support, and Boniface responded by summoning the revolt's alleged ringleaders to the curia. No doubt like kings these men saw their resistance to the interdict as legitimate defence of their political claims.

Even more elaborate methods to counter publication of interdicts had featured in accusations made by Portuguese prelates against their king Afonso III. In 1266 the Archbishop of Braga and six bishops fled Portugal for the curia after interdicting their dioceses. They presented to the Pope forty charges of royal violations of ecclesiastical liberties, four of which regarded interdicts.[36] The first stated that if bishops or rectors interdicted places or excommunicated their parishioners for not paying tithes or other dues, the king had such clerks banished and their goods confiscated. The second held that prelates excommunicating the king's men or interdicting places were intimidated and their goods seized to force them to revoke these sentences, and if they refused, it was forbidden to communicate with them or receive them into anyone's home on pain of imprisonment and sequestration; prelates reckoned this secular 'excommunication' all the more humiliating in that the royal judges who imposed it were Jews. Thirdly if ecclesiastical judges, even judges delegate, interdicted a royal town or its inhabitants, the king or his officials allegedly retaliated with their own 'interdict' forbidding these clergy 'common commerce'; anyone disobeying this ban by offering them shelter, fire, or water could be punished. Like interdicts this ban was to be publicized widely. Such clergy were also to be distrusted and their property seized, inherited and ecclesiastical. Fourthly when a place was interdicted or any of its inhabitants were excommunicated, especially lay judges and other royal officials, the countermeasure generally adopted was to suspend tithes, bequests, or offerings for the churches concerned; other Iberian prelates had described a similar reaction to the León interdict over sixty years earlier.

Whatever truth lay behind these allegations, the main issue that had driven the Portuguese prelates to the curia was Afonso's resumption of the *inquirições* in 1258.[37] Originally instituted by his father in the 1220s, they inquired into the property titles of nobles and particularly of the clergy and sought to recover royal property, rights, and incomes, rather like Edward I's subsequent *Quo warranto* proceedings in England and equally resented. As a result of his *inquirições* Afonso

[35] Reg. Boniface VIII, no. 1253.
[36] Reg. Clement IV, no. 669. The charges appear with responses from Afonso's successor Diniz in Reg. Martin IV, no. 502, and Reg. Nicholas IV, no. 716.
[37] See Reuter, 61–82, and Linehan, 'Castile', 686–8.

had issued a law in 1265 which also foreshadowed Edward's *mortmain* legislation, ordering reversion to the Crown of royal lands obtained by those who paid the king no taxes, mainly property in the 'dead hand' of the Church. This threat to ecclesiastical wealth was mostly what prompted the bishops to approach the Pope, but that is not saying that their other allegations of royal persecution, including the countermeasures against interdicts, were concocted to win papal support. In 1250 when king and clergy were on good terms, the Bishop of Oporto complained that Afonso's men claimed not to give a straw for excommunication, and the king promised in the Cortes to curb such insolence and required all his subjects to observe such sentences.[38] Furthermore if the charges were largely false, it is doubtful that the bishops would have pursued them for over twenty years, most of them dying at the curia in the meantime. Admittedly they dropped some charges by the 1280s, but these had perhaps already been resolved, as Reuter argues, and none of these regarded interdicts. Afonso himself certainly opposed all charges almost till death, displaying 'a capacity for survival which amounted to genius'.[39] He showed no intention of making amends till January 1279 but he died a month later, leaving his son Diniz to negotiate a settlement with the bishops. In 1284 Diniz promised them that he had ordered none of the alleged countermeasures against interdicts, nor would he do so, and would punish subjects employing them and order restitution of property taken from clergy declaring interdicts and satisfaction for their ill-treatment. He gave similar assurances regarding the other charges, but further terms suggested by Martin IV were unacceptable to him, and the concordat between king and episcopate was only finally ratified in 1289.

Such countermeasures against interdicts were intended not only to discourage clergy from publishing these sentences but also from observing them. Some measures specifically had the latter aim in mind, though they largely comprised the same kinds of physical and financial coercion. After the French interdict was declared at a council of prelates of the kingdom in 1199, Philip Augustus of France persecuted bishops who had consented to the sentence and enforced it by having them expelled from their sees and their property confiscated.[40] The Bishops of Paris, Senlis, Amiens, Soissons, and Arras apparently enforced the sentence very strictly. Bishop Odo of Paris's disloyalty to the Crown especially enraged Philip and, according to Ralph of Coggleshall, Philip sent knights who seized Odo's horses, baggage, and other goods, forcing him to leave his diocese on foot; the Bishop of Senlis was said to have suffered the same indignity. Even lower clergy and canons were ejected from their benefices and had their goods sequestrated, presumably for refusing to celebrate. But several clergy did not observe the sentence initially, notably the Archbishop of Reims and Bishops of Laon, Noyons,

---

[38] *Portugaliae Monumenta Historica*, I/i.189.
[39] Quotation from Linehan, 'Castile', 687. See also Reuter, 83–114.
[40] *Recueil*, xvii.51 ('De gestis'), 387 ('Extraits'). See Krehbiel, 115–16.

Auxerre, Beauvais, Térouanne, Meaux, Chartres, and Orléans. Doubtless fear of royal persecution dissuaded them as well as deference to Philip, and they penned excuses to Innocent III, who had authorized the interdict, but promised to obey his sentence if he commanded them to do so, which he apparently did, though it is uncertain whether he secured the total compliance that his biographer claims.[41]

Dependent on spiritual sanctions to defend themselves, clergy were extremely vulnerable to lay coercion, and the strain that it put on their loyalties divided between king and pope must have been bewildering to many. King John readily exploited this situation in England.[42] Though it is suggested that he threatened clerks physically, he mainly used financial coercion to dissuade them from observing the papal interdict on England. His anti-papal propaganda included letters sent to Lincoln and Ely dioceses on 18 March 1208 which announced that on 24 March, the day after the interdict was to be published, his agents would seize all lands and goods of abbots, priors, religious, and clergy of these dioceses who refused to celebrate divine offices. Cheney assumed that such confiscations were ordered across the kingdom; chroniclers certainly suggest that they were widespread. Gerald of Wales observed that the interdict struck England with a double wound, involving both the withdrawal of divine offices and plundering of the clergy's goods.[43]   And several clerical commentators observed that four men in each parish were charged with guarding the barns of secular clerks in the king's name. Bishops were to retaliate by excommunicating any who seized ecclesiastical property, but many clergy negotiated to recover their possessions from the Crown.[44] Richardson and Sayles inferred that since property was taken from clerks for refusing to celebrate, it was restored to them in return for the resumption of church services. However, there is no evidence to support this assumption, and while Cheney found that John released most ecclesiastical property through grants and commissions often to its owners soon after it was seized, the sources suggest that this was done for a financial consideration. The biographer of St Hugh of Lincoln stated that most rectors redeemed their property from lay control with money.[45] John, nevertheless, retained goods of clergy who went into exile after the interdict's publication and of vacant sees and monasteries, in many cases until the interdict was lifted. He was admittedly exploiting the circumstances for financial gain but he was also trying to punish clergy for obeying the pope before him. One financial sanction was deliberately intended to embarrass the Church authorities. Several chroniclers report that John ordered royal custodians of the clergy's goods to arrest concubines of priests

---

[41] Coggleshall, *Chronicon*, 112. *Gesta* c.52 (*PL* 214.xcviii–xcix).

[42] Cheney, 'Interdict', 300–6; id., 'Reaction'.   [43] Gerald of Wales, *Opera*, viii.311.

[44] Cheney, 'Interdict', 302–4; id., 'Reaction', 130–1, 132–5. Martène and Durand, i.813 ('Forma interdicti'; the king, queen, and royal justiciar were to be excepted from this excommunication).

[45] *Magna Vita*, 303–4. See Richardson and Sayles, *Governance*, 346, and the critique of it by Cheney, 'A Recent View'.

and clerks and hold them to ransom. This mischievously drew attention to the widespread violation of clerical celibacy that reformers had long deplored. Abbot John of Ford, preaching in 1210, denounced as shameful priests who considered their mistresses' abduction the worst hardship of the interdict and hastened to secure their release with ransoms paid from ecclesiastical revenues.[46]

As Cheney has argued, John was fighting a war, in which the interdict was the opening shot, but it was a war against the pope, not the English Church itself. English clergy were victims of John's war since they obeyed the pope's interdict. The conflict was essentially about who controlled 'national' churches, popes or kings, and notably in John's England, church appointments. Rulers had gained extensive control over the churches in the contemporary Iberian kingdoms, especially in appointing bishops, and they were particularly determined to dissuade clergy from obeying interdicts imposed in defiance of that control. When Bishop Juan of Oviedo enforced a papal interdict on the kingdom of León in his diocese, he was driven into exile and fled to Rome in 1198 seeking papal support; Innocent III approved the interdict's removal on condition that Juan was reinstated.[47] Over ten years later, when Sancho I of Portugal tried to increase royal control over the churches of Oporto and Coimbra and their bishops resisted with interdicts, similar complaints of royal persecution ensued. Bishop Martinho of Oporto reached the curia 'almost naked' in 1210, alleging that after he had laid an interdict on his diocese, Sancho flouted it, ordering burial of the dead, and seized church property, presumably to compel clergy to disobey the interdict.[48] Innocent III had persuaded the king to make peace with Martinho in late 1210, but by then Sancho was involved in a similar clash with Bishop Pedro of Coimbra. Pedro accused him of many violations of ecclesiastical liberty, not least arresting clerks and trying them in the royal courts, and cast doubt on his orthodoxy, alleging that he consulted a witch daily. When he reacted to these charges with even more persecution, Pedro responded with an interdict on his diocese and an appeal to the pope, which only provoked the king further. He enlisted his friend the Archbishop of Braga to compel Pedro to relax the interdict, but Pedro's appeal was designed to block such a move. To prevent Pedro following in Martinho's footsteps to the curia, Sancho imprisoned him, but he still managed to smuggle out a letter to the pope. This alleged that Sancho (like the kings of France and England) had seized all goods of clerks observing the interdict, and he considered anyone receiving these clerks his enemy. When Pedro still refused to lift the interdict, Sancho like King John apparently threatened violence; clergy refusing to celebrate during the interdict were to be blinded in front of their friends and families. Pedro then lifted the sentence to avoid such

---

[46] *Ioannis de Forda*, 301; Cheney, 'Interdict', 306.
[47] Innocent III, Reg. 1, no. 125. See O'Callaghan, 'Innocent III', 320–1.
[48] Innocent III, Reg. 13, no. 57. See Reuter, 7–10.

atrocities.[49] Hence the charges of resisting interdicts which Portuguese bishops brought against Sancho's grandson Afonso III were not unprecedented.

Clergy made similar complaints to the curia that the communes of Verdun and San Gimignano violated their immunities during the interdicts on these towns later in the thirteenth century. Resistance by lay powers to interdicts was thus not uncommon at civic and national levels, and, as we have seen, it largely comprised seizing church property and attacking the persons and liberties of clergy. The ability of governments to resist interdicts depended partly on the sophistication of their organization.[50] From the late twelfth century the rulers of England, possibly the most centralized kingdom in the Latin West, could fight interdicts with increasing force as the apparatus of royal government developed. As town government also became more organized, communes are increasingly found defying interdicts by the end of the thirteenth century, notably in the progressive Italian city-states. But effective governmental machinery was not a necessary condition; the personalities of rulers and historical circumstance might also predispose them towards resisting interdicts. Iberian kings could exploit their status as defenders of a Christian frontier society against Muslim attack to increase their power over clergy behind the battle lines. Portuguese kings, especially Sancho I and Afonso III, resented the wealth and influence of the Portuguese Church and in their attempts to control it they fiercely resisted interdicts. Sancho was probably even anti-clerical, and was influenced in this direction by his 'aggressively secularist' chancellor Julião Pais and 'Romanist ideas he brought back from Bologna'.[51]

At the start of this chapter we noted that the aim of an interdict was to turn the innocent against the guilty, but in practice an interdict might turn the innocent against the Church and make the guilty even more defiant. Furthermore popes tried to address this problem by mitigating the interdict's severity for the innocent whilst maintaining its force against the guilty. But sometimes popes found this approach inadequate; hence from the late twelfth century they backed up ineffective interdicts with other sanctions. In such cases popes threatened to proceed both *spiritualiter* and *temporaliter* against those scorning interdicts. Further spiritual proceedings comprised excommunication of the main offenders if not already imposed, and this befell King John after he defied the English interdict for over a year.[52] A city might be threatened with loss of its see. As noted in Chapter 2, spiritual sanctions might increase in number and severity with the contumacy of the guilty, but a general interdict was usually the most extreme, laid when other spiritual measures, notably excommunication, failed. When it also failed, popes had to rely mainly on temporal sanctions for further coercion.

[49] Innocent III, Reg. 14, no. 8. See Krehbiel, 149, and Reuter, 10–11.

[50] See Trexler, 3 ff.   [51] As argued by Linehan, 'Castile', 688.

[52] The pope also considered extending the interdict on England and Wales to John's continental lands before the king's submission made it unnecessary; Innocent III, Reg. 16, no. 136.

Innocent III applied a whole range of these against the Lombard communes.[53] Principal among these were commercial sanctions, clearly designed to harm the chief source of these cities' growing power. Shortly after becoming pope Innocent imposed one on Parma and Piacenza. The cities had already been interdicted for harbouring the robbers of a legate, and Innocent also threatened to strip them of their diocesan status if they failed to return the stolen goods. Faced with continued defiance he wrote to the bishops and clergy of both cities in 1198 of the imminent effect of this threat and that he had called on the Empress Constance, the kings of France and England, the count and barons of Champagne, duke of Burgundy, and count of Maurienne to seize goods of Parman and Piacenzan merchants in their lands until the cities restored those stolen from the legate. Fighting fire with fire proved effective in Parma's case as it complied later that year, and Piacenza probably did so around the same time.[54]

No doubt this success encouraged Innocent to deploy similar measures against other Italian cities. He likewise threatened to instruct lay rulers to hold merchants with their goods from interdicted Treviso in 1199, any Lombard commune taxing its clergy in 1203, and Milan and Alessandria in 1212.[55] He was also prepared to ban trade with Treviso, Milan, Alessandria, and, in 1208, Narni; in the case of Milan and Alessandria this embargo was to be observed in both France and Italy, thus affecting long-distance as well as local trade. Such measures were not unprecedented. Innocent's predecessor Celestine III had also imposed a trade ban on interdicted Treviso, and Lucius III's 'Ad abolendam' ruled (1184) that a city not complying with this anti-heresy decree might be deprived of commerce with other cities and of its see.[56] Nevertheless the frequency with which Innocent applied such sanctions is remarkable. Trade bans admittedly relied on the cooperation of lay powers and merchants, but Innocent was ready to punish their non-compliance by excommunication and other sanctions, at least regarding Narni. Of course commercial and territorial rivalries between Italian cities provided an incentive to comply. Even the loss of a city's see enabled its neighbours to profit at its expense, not only in the spiritual sphere but also the temporal. When Piacenza was again under interdict in 1206 and had defied papal commands for three years, Innocent ordered its citizens to submit in a month; otherwise their see would be suppressed and its diocese divided among neighbouring ones. This implied the loss of the city's temporal county, and rather than endure this Piacenza quickly submitted. Like many Italian communes the city and its territory were nominally subject to their bishop's temporal jurisdiction; hence diocese and *contado* were one.[57]

[53] See Tillmann, 95 ff., and my 'Punishment of the Guiltless', 278–9.

[54] Innocent III, Reg. 1, nos. 121–2, 393. See Krehbiel, 101–2.

[55] Treviso: Innocent III, Reg. 2, no. 27. Lombard communes: Innocent III, Reg. 6, no. 182. Milan and Alessandria: Innocent III, Reg. 15, no. 189.

[56] Narni: Innocent III, Reg. 11, no. 143; Krehbiel, 104. 'Ad abolendam': 1 Comp. 5.6.11 (= X 5.7.9). Celestine's embargo is mentioned in Innocent's letter to Treviso (see n. 55).

Innocent III fought these communes, as Tillmann observed, with a rigour and unwillingness to compromise he rarely showed in his conflicts with kings. Doubtless he considered their rising power and ambitions a menace to the papal state; and some had allied with German emperors who invaded the papal state, notably Frederick I.[58] Following Innocent's example his successors would largely use temporal sanctions to defend papal territorial interests, and especially against disobedient Italian communes. This was particularly true of Martin IV. Shortly after he became pope in 1281, he was faced with a rebellion in Romagna within the papal state centred on the town of Forlì. A papal army was sent against the rebels and besieged Forlì but did not take the town or crush the revolt. By 1282 Martin had excommunicated the rebels and their leader, Guido da Montefeltro, and threatened to interdict papal communes that they occupied, notably Forlì, unless they surrendered after a month. In common with other interdicts this sentence was meant to make these communities hostile to the guilty and compel them to come to terms. The pope could also back it up with other collective sanctions. As these communes came under his temporal jurisdiction, he could enforce temporal sanctions against them without the aid of lay rulers. Indeed he threatened to proceed against them *spiritualiter et temporaliter*, even suppressing their sees, if they failed to coerce the rebels to withdraw. In March 1282 he extended the deadline for surrender and specified these further proceedings: towns harbouring rebels would lose rights, freedoms, privileges, and fiefs gained from the Roman or other churches; individual wrongdoers would incur similar penalties, including loss of public offices.[59]

The pope's enmity towards the rebels was deep-rooted. Their leader, Guido da Montefeltro, was an old enemy of the papacy, having supported the heirs of Frederick II. Earlier popes, notably Innocent IV, had regarded Frederick's personal union of the German empire and kingdom of Sicily as a threat to papal political power in Italy, and they had struggled against him and his heirs with unceasing vigour. This conflict split northern and central Italy into pro-papal and pro-imperial camps, the so-called Guelfs and Ghibellines. Even after Charles of Anjou had defeated the last of Frederick's heirs and supplanted them as king of Sicily with papal backing, these factions remained and the revolt in Romagna marked a Ghibelline resurgence. It was to become part of what Runciman termed a 'great international conspiracy' to oust Charles of Anjou from the papal fiefdom of Sicily. With Sicilian, Byzantine, Ghibelline, and Genoese support the king of Aragon conquered the island in 1282, claiming it by right of his wife, the last of Frederick II's descendants.[60]

---

[57] Innocent III, Reg. 9, nos. 156–9.   [58] Robinson, 491–4; Morris, 194–6.
[59] Reg. Martin IV, no. 266. See Runciman, 212.
[60] See Runciman, 222–50. Cf. papal measures against Conradin and his allies, notably Italian cities, in 1268: Reg. Clement IV, nos. 693, 694, 695, 699.

To Martin IV as a Frenchman (Charles was the French king's uncle) this was particularly intolerable. It provoked him to thunder a battery of spiritual and temporal sanctions against Ghibellines and other 'conspirators'. In November 1282 he warned Ghibellines that he would renew their excommunication and interdicts on towns where they held out in Romagna unless they submitted by Christmas. They and these towns would also be subjected to a trade ban and seizure of property outside papal temporal jurisdiction by the proper authorities. Hence the secular arm would be invoked against communities unmoved by interdicts as it often was against obdurate excommunicates. The deadline was not met and the trade ban came into force soon thereafter, as Martin issued warnings in February 1283 that commerce with the rebels, especially supplying them with arms and food, entailed excommunication for individuals and interdicts for towns and churches.[61] As with Innocent III, when the pope could not directly enforce temporal sanctions, he could threaten spiritual sanctions to persuade others to do so.

On the day when he threatened these sanctions against Ghibellines Martin IV declared similar measures against Sicilian rebels and the Aragonese invaders. He had already interdicted towns, notably Palermo and Messina, for their part in the 'Sicilian Vespers', the local uprising of Easter 1282 against Angevin rule. But their support of the subsequent Aragonese invasion convinced him that further sanctions were needed; hence he threatened to proceed against them *spiritualiter et temporaliter*. Towns that persisted in backing excommunicate 'occupier' Peter of Aragon against the pope and his Angevin vassal would be deprived of their sees and commerce with others.[62]

By January 1283 Martin IV had proclaimed Charles of Anjou's war to recover Sicily a 'crusade', and in March he declared Peter deposed from Aragon, a papal fief, and his vassals released from fealty to him, inviting Catholics chosen by the Holy See to occupy Aragon. Further measures against Peter's Sicilian supporters also followed; Martin renewed his interdict against the rebel towns and threatened them with loss of papal privileges and any fiefs or rights held from the Roman and other churches. As in Romagna he had the power to withdraw the latter as feudal overlord. Others, however, had to enforce the embargo on Sicily, and he specified its terms by November 1283.[63] Venice, Genoa, Pisa, Ancona, and other maritime towns might not buy from or sell to Sicilians, make contracts with them, admit them knowingly to their territory, approach Sicily, or export arms or other necessities there. Rulers of these towns were to compel their subjects to respect the embargo; violation of its terms entailed excommunication for individuals and interdict for communities. To reinforce the embargo further Martin ordered the Bishop of Castello in January 1284

---

[61] Reg. Martin IV, nos. 279–83, 309.

[62] Reg. Martin IV, nos. 270, 276. The sentences against Guido da Montefeltro and his supporters were renewed in ibid., nos. 268, 462.

[63] Reg. Martin IV, nos. 310, 460, 483, 490, 583, 587. See Runciman, 245, 246, 251, 265–6.

to announce its terms to the people and clergy of Venice in St Mark's Square; he issued similar instructions to the Archbishops of Genoa and Pisa. Genoa, Ancona, and Venice were specifically cautioned since they had supplied ships to Sicilian rebels in 1282, Genoa had perhaps sent them arms, and in 1283 the doge of Venice was even suspected of making overtures to the Aragonese. Admittedly Genoa, Pisa, and Venice had also provided ships for the Angevins, but this inconsistency doubtless only increased papal distrust of these cities.

Hence the interdict on Sicilian towns was accompanied by measures of social exclusion that normally followed excommunication. Even after Charles of Anjou and Martin died, leaving the island in Aragonese hands, Sicily's isolation was maintained by Nicholas IV, who crowned Charles's heir as its king in 1289. Admittedly Nicholas partly lifted the embargo later in 1289, letting Venetians sail to Sicily and have contact with Sicilians without fear of excommunication provided that they did not sell arms or otherwise support the rebels or Aragonese. But others remained bound by the original terms of the embargo. Sardinians could still be excommunicated for associating with Sicilians in 1291, when Nicholas authorized the Archbishop of Cagliari to absolve his subjects if they traded with Sicilian merchants provided that they did not support them otherwise. Despite such sanctions and the Angevin 'crusade', the Aragonese and their Sicilian allies were unmoved; a French invasion of Aragon had also failed in 1285. By 1302 Boniface VIII had to acknowledge Peter of Aragon's heirs as the real possessors of the kingdom of Aragon and island of Sicily.[64]

Though temporal sanctions mostly reinforced interdicts on Italian cities, partly for political motives and partly since papal claims of lordship over these towns eased their implementation, they occasionally accompanied interdicts north of the Alps for wider reasons of social control. When a band of knights attacked the Breton episcopal town of Tréguier, notably its churches, their property and clergy, in 1232 Gregory IX authorized an ambulatory interdict on the knights and ruled that if they failed to come to terms within a month, they might be deprived of any fiefs held from the Church. As in papal territory church authorities might inflict temporal sanctions by virtue of their temporal jurisdiction. But he added that the secular arm might be invoked if necessary 'so that the severity of human discipline coerces those whom the fear of God does not recall from evil'. Ecclesiastical judges proclaimed these sanctions, but over two years later the knights remained defiant and exercised lordship in those fiefs *de facto* which they had lost *de iure*. The secular arm was indeed invoked in the shape of the count of Brittany, but he ignored a papal request to compel those knights under his jurisdiction to submit. As Innocent III had found, spiritual sanctions had to be threatened to press temporal authority to place its power at the Church's disposal.[65]

---

[64] Reg. Nicholas IV, nos. 1390, 5578. On these later events see Runciman, 257–75.
[65] Reg. Gregory IX, nos. 757, 2158.

It is uncertain whether the count or knights complied, but this case shows how weak the Church authorities were in means of coercion. However much the thirteenth-century papacy asserted its power to intervene in the temporal sphere, even in places under its temporal jurisdiction, it ultimately relied on secular authorities to enforce its wishes. Its embargoes on Sicily and other places in Italy under papal suzerainty could not succeed without the cooperation of those outside its temporal rule, and it required Charles of Anjou's support to reinforce its political control over Italy, ill-fated as this partnership was. Its capacity to act independently in the temporal sphere, especially to impose temporal sanctions, was thus limited. Even in the spiritual sphere, where papal supremacy was largely undisputed, its sanctions did not go unchallenged by lay rulers. When it proceeded against them *spiritualiter*, it relied upon their piety and pressure of public opinion to compel them to submit, but its interdicts sometimes only succeeded in undermining lay orthodoxy and turning them even more against the Church. Royal and civic governments could use their resources to defy interdicts; their capacity and tendency to do so generally increased with their organization (ironically the latter was largely influenced by ecclesiastical institutions). Indeed by the later thirteenth century the papacy's claim to proceed against its opponents *spiritualiter* and *temporaliter* was seriously challenged by emerging nation-states. For example after the French city of Laon defied a papal interdict laid in 1296, Boniface VIII not only failed to act further *temporaliter*, as he threatened, but the French king Philip IV succeeded in intervening both *temporaliter*, abolishing Laon's commune, and *spiritualiter*, imposing penances on its citizens for their sins against the Church.[66] In the face of such challenges the papacy had demonstrated its reluctance to abandon the interdict as a political weapon; Boniface VIII significantly reduced the general interdict's severity for the innocent in order to reinvigorate the sanction. For him and previous popes the interdict ultimately tested their authority over the Church, so they were determined to enforce it and make it work. The next section examines how they tried to enforce observance of interdicts from the late twelfth century in the face of growing lay opposition.

5.2 THE ENFORCEMENT OF INTERDICTS

By Innocent III's time papal mandates imposing an interdict regularly instructed their executors to observe the sentence and have it observed inviolably. Indeed Innocent's decretal 'Petiistis' (1212) ruled that only if an interdict was not observed by clergy it was meant to defend, were others not obliged to observe it.[67] Even if an interdict was flouted by those who provoked it, others were not

---

[66] Denton, 'Laon', 89.   [67] X 5.33.20 (= 4 Comp. 5.12.3); Innocent III, Reg. 15, no. 162.

free to ignore it. This was basically a question of clerical obedience to ecclesiastical superiors. As Honorius III put it in a letter to exempt prelates in the Latin Empire of Constantinople, they were to enforce interdicts their patriarch pronounced on their subjects; otherwise they might give laity an excuse for rebellion and contempt when they should provide a model of obedience and devotion. The fact that clergy had to be told this indicates that they did not always respect interdicts. In fact three years before this letter, in 1222, Honorius had ejected monks from a Cistercian house in the patriarchate for scorning a legate's interdict.[68]

Only ordained clergy might celebrate offices and administer the sacraments and conversely withhold these religious comforts, but strict observance of interdicts did not depend on them alone. The passive compliance of the laity was also required, especially lay powers whom interdicts were meant to punish. As we have seen, royal and civic governments might compel clergy not to observe interdicts directed against them, and they were partially successful in doing so. Examples of this are found time and again across thirteenth-century Europe. A canon of Coimbra Cathedral petitioned Gregory IX in 1232 that fear drove him to celebrate offices for his king, Sancho II of Portugal, in interdicted places, since he was surrounded by spears, swords, and blades. Admittedly his petition was meant to obtain papal leniency for violating interdicts, but his excuse seems credible; Gregory received other reports of royal officials harrassing Portuguese clergy around this time.[69] As we have noted, such lay coercion comprised economic sanctions as well as physical violence. Indeed this canon alleged that when he ultimately refused to celebrate for those entering his church by force, they expelled him from his prebend and seized its revenues. Similar accusations were made against Conrad of Hohenstaufen two decades later after he claimed the kingdom of Sicily and German empire as Frederick II's heir in defiance of the papacy. According to English chronicler Matthew Paris, while the kingdom lay under a papal interdict, Conrad had forced clergy to celebrate offices in 1254. Conrad denied inflicting violence on these clerks and alleged that they violated the interdict of their own free will and were even doing so on his arrival in Sicily. His own letters apparently contradicted his version of events, but he maintained that these were issued without his consent and none of them compelled clergy to celebrate. Nevertheless it is hardly a coincidence that Conrad was also accused of intimidating clergy in the empire at this time. Early in 1254 monks of Scafusa Abbey in Constance diocese petitioned Innocent IV that Conrad had ordered them to celebrate for those under excommunication and interdict. When they refused, he had allegedly confiscated grain, livestock, and other goods of the abbey and gave its lands as fiefs to enemies of the papacy, presumably his own supporters.[70]

---

[68] Reg. Honorius III, nos. 3904, 5423.
[69] Reg. Gregory IX, no. 964. Cf. ibid. no. 810. See also Linehan, 'Castile', 683, and Reuter, 24–9.
[70] Matthew Paris, *Chronica*, vi.301. Reg. Innocent IV, no. 7635.

Clergy who observed interdicts directed against their lay rulers were evidently vulnerable to such attacks on their persons and property. Fear of royal persecution had even driven the bishops into exile who proclaimed Innocent III's interdict on England, and other English clergy followed them abroad once this fear was realized. Sometimes popes even advised clergy to leave places before interdicts came into force there; such precautions were meant not only to protect clergy from persecution but also reinforce observance of the sentences: clergy could hardly minister in interdicted places if they were not there to be forced into this. In 1203 when Innocent III threatened an interdict on Bergamo, he thus required its metropolitan the Archbishop of Milan and the Bishop of Vercelli to compel clergy to leave the city and its *contado* apparently at its bishop's request. Clergy were not to return until the commune made amends for its violations of ecclesiastical immunity; those who disobeyed were to incur excommunication and suspension. Innocent similarly instructed the Archbishop of Ravenna a year later when he authorized him to lay Modena under interdict for mistreating its clergy.[71] When an interdict was caused by persecution of clergy, it was clearly reasonable to assume that this might increase after the sentence was laid. But where could clergy find refuge and how could they sustain themselves away from their benefices? Papal mandates did not usually say. When Innocent III laid an interdict on Narni in 1208, he merely instructed its bishop and clergy to leave that city for 'nearby places'. Presumably churches there made *ad hoc* provision for them. Some eighty years later, when clergy left interdicted San Gimignano, they stayed at a church just a few miles away. Significantly they fled lay persecution apparently at their own initiative not an ecclesiastical superior's order. Nevertheless Innocent III's successors occasionally followed his example by ordering clergy to leave interdicted areas, normally in the papal state. Sometimes this must be inferred from the fact that clergy received papal permission to return to places where an interdict was to be relaxed.[72] But not all clergy were told to leave in the first place. After all interdicts did not forbid all religious ministrations. When Martin IV required the Bishop and clergy of Perugia to leave their interdicted city in 1282, he told them to leave behind sufficient priests to administer infant baptism and penance of the dying, sacraments normally permitted under general interdicts. Doubtless this provision was usual in these cases of clerical self-exile. Certainly it provoked popular outrage at San Gimignano when its 'exiled' clergy refused to release priests to perform ministrations allowed during the interdict there; its commune consequently resorted to hiring priests from elsewhere for this purpose.[73]

---

[71] Innocent III, Reg. 6, no. 182; 7, no. 41.

[72] Narni: as n. 56. San Gimignano: see p. 207. Papal permission: Reg. Gregory IX, no. 3839 (Todi); Reg. Boniface VIII, no. 1574 (Orvieto).

[73] Reg. Martin IV, no. 280. Cf. ibid. no. 281 (Spoleto). Perugian clergy received papal permission to return seventeen months later: ibid. no. 575. On San Gimignano see p. 208.

Another precaution designed to reinforce observance of interdicts was to take the host away from interdicted churches. After all priests were required to consecrate it weekly and keep it in their churches for the dying during interdicts by 1234. Even if they refused to administer it to the healthy, it might remain an object of veneration for those denied it. Indeed even outside of interdicts many laity attended masses simply to marvel at the elevation of the host and rarely received it. If they believed that it was as salutary to see the host as receive it, ecclesiastical authorities had to ensure that it was not exposed to public view lest the interdict appear to be flouted. Indeed it provoked a scandal in 1297 when consuls of interdicted Béziers had the host taken from its clergy to their town hall; it was not apparently distributed but presumably was on display to the faithful. It was not the first time that this danger arose or was anticipated at least. In 1234, shortly before weekly consecration of the host became a legal norm during interdicts, judges delegate had sought to reinforce an interdict on the land of a Breton nobleman by ordering removal of the *corpus Christi* from there. Likewise over sixty years later, when Laon Cathedral was violated in the rising of the city's commune and offices were suspended there, the dean and chapter had the Eucharist taken away from their closed church; it was apparently moved to Bruyères seven kilometres away.[74] In 1290, five years earlier, priests had allegedly even carried off other objects of popular adoration when they walked out of interdicted San Gimignano, namely altar paintings.

When clergy could not escape lay persecution during interdicts, the papacy, as we have seen, might impose additional sanctions including temporal ones. These were meant both to reinforce the interdict's purpose, in coercing the guilty to submit, and to compel them to respect the interdict itself, since their scorn for it provoked these extra measures. When Martin IV approved the interdict on Perugia in 1282, he ordered that if it was not observed and Perugians did not submit to him by a certain deadline, they would be deprived of all papal grants and all property held from the Roman or other churches.[75] Beyond such *ad hoc* measures the papacy made no provision in canon law against lay violators of interdicts until the council of Vienne (1311–12), and even then it was in response to external demand. At the council Clement V received complaints from prelates that some temporal lords coerced clergy to celebrate in their chapels and other churches in their interdicted lands and even had people called to hear mass there by church bells and public criers. Clement was also informed that some lords forbade excommunicates and those under interdict to leave church during mass when asked to do so by celebrants; thus services often had to be abandoned in order to avoid scandal. Pope and council responded with the canon 'Gravis', which placed

---

[74] Béziers: see p. 228. The judges acted against this nobleman since he continued persecuting the Bishop of Tréguier despite or perhaps because of this interdict: Reg. Gregory IX, no. 1765. Laon: Reg. Boniface VIII, nos. 355–6; Denton, 'Laon', 82. Cf. Trexler, 123–7 (host displayed in 1377 at interdicted Florence).

[75] Perugia: as n. 73.

excommunication on those committing such abuses and reserved absolution to the holy see. It is unclear whether such penalties were applied to laity other than lay powers. Ordinary citizens had, after all, defied interdicts at Béziers and Verdun in the 1290s, even if they did so partly at the direction of lay powers. Tancred had said (*c*.1220) that laity who scorned interdicts ought to be anathematized and cited a canon which required that those who still resisted ecclesiastical correction be condemned to exile by the judgement of their king. And over a century later a treatise attributed to Johannes Calderinus also argued that lay violators of interdicts who remained obdurate after excommunication should endure this sanction. Admittedly the aid of the 'secular arm' was often invoked by the church authorities against obdurate excommunicates by the fourteenth century, but no cases are known to concern laity resisting interdicts, at least in England.[76]

However, laity rarely violated an interdict *directly*, usurping clerical functions it banned, but usually *indirectly*, by encouraging clergy to flout the sentence. Clerical cooperation was not always extracted by force but sometimes given voluntarily. For instance, after the Bishop of Limoges interdicted his city in 1202, his clergy allegedly scorned his sentence, preaching in churches and even celebrating there after they were excommunicated.[77] The lay power collaborated with the clergy and unusually coerced not them but laity to disregard the sentence: burgesses of Limoges fined matrons and others who, fearing excommunication, refused to attend services held by these clergy or accept the Eucharist from their hands on Easter day. This does not necessarily mean that laity attending mass in interdicted places were automatically excommunicated; in this case they probably feared incurring this penalty as a result of communicating with excommunicates. Nevertheless this example illustrates how an interdict might test the authority of ecclesiastical superiors over clergy. In some cases local Church authorities instructed clergy to disregard an interdict imposed by higher ones. When Innocent III confirmed the Bishop of Modena's interdict on Cremona in 1203, he observed that the archpriest and archdeacon there had authorized priests to celebrate publicly.[78] Whilst such disobedience signalled tensions within the Church hierarchy, it might arise since local prelates supported the lay power at whom an interdict was directed. Innocent IV condemned the Bishop of Squillace in Sicily in 1253 for backing its king Frederick II after the latter's deposition as emperor in 1245 and for requiring priests and clergy of his diocese to celebrate despite the papal interdict on the kingdom. The bishop was in fact a nephew

---

[76] 'Gravis': Clem. 5.10.2. On Béziers see pp. 227–30. Tancred on 1 Comp. 4.1.13 v. *debitam*, BAV, Vat. lat. MS 1377, fol. 65ra; Vat. lat. MS 2509, fol. 61va: 'Pena debita hec est: clericus qui contempnit interdictum deponitur et laicus anathematizatur, ut infra. De clerico excommunicato ministrante c. ii et xi. q. iii. Si quis episcopus, Placuit universo [1 Comp. 5.23.2; C. 11 q. 3 c. 6, 9] t.' Johannes Calderinus (attrib.), *De censura*, BAV, Pal. lat. MS 797, fol. 15vb: 'Si laici fuerint et interdictum violaverint, excommunicari debent, et si moniti non destiterint ad requisitionem ecclesie, regis iudicio exilio deputentur.' England: Logan, 49–53.

[77] Innocent III, Reg. 6, no. 97; Krehbiel, 130–1.

[78] Innocent III, Reg. 6, no. 13.

of Frederick's chamberlain, who allegedly had engineered his election, and given that many prelates owed their posts to lay patronage, interdicts must often have tested whether their loyalty lay more with the temporal or spiritual power.[79]

In 1283, after Martin IV deposed Peter of Aragon, clergy along with other subjects of his even incurred interdict and excommunication for supporting him; unremarkably given their sympathies reports soon reached the pope that they were not observing the interdict.[80] Some prelates even used the same methods as lay powers to resist interdicts directed against them. In 1289 the Bishop of Perigeux complained to Nicholas IV that after he removed an abbot from office and interdicted the latter's abbey, the abbot celebrated there and compelled laity by seizure of their goods and even of their persons to attend services and receive the sacraments there. Indeed some thirty years later the canonist Johannes Andreae observed that bishops and other prelates might be excommunicated under Clement V's constitution 'Gravis' as well as temporal lords for coercing clergy to celebrate during interdicts.[81]

Even when secular clergy observed interdicts, religious were often accused of flouting them and this was a source of tension between seculars and regulars from the late twelfth century. Since then many religious had secured papal licences to celebrate offices in private during general local interdicts, and frequent episcopal complaints to Rome followed that they were admitting those under interdict to such private services, even though the licences required the exclusion of such persons.[82] The military orders were regularly accused of abusing the generous papal grants that they enjoyed during interdicts. Bishops were also frustrated since these and other religious holding similar freedoms often claimed immunity from episcopal correction; hence papal intervention was usually needed against such abuses. For example the Bishop of Hereford petitioned Alexander III that the papacy allowed Hospitallers to open interdicted churches once a year, but they were doing so more frequently in his diocese and even burying the dead there; the pope warned them not to violate their privileges in future or they might lose these freedoms. Though his ruling did not find a lasting place in canon law, this threat became enshrined as a canonistic principle. Similar episcopal complaints at the Third Lateran Council prompted Alexander to ban Templars and Hospitallers from burying the dead at interdicted churches. Subsequently canonists agreed that this ban did not apply to dead members of these orders, and Innocent III confirmed this in a canon of the Fourth Lateran Council. But such burial privileges were still not to be extended to laity, and Innocent III often had to correct religious on this point.[83]

---

[79] Reg. Innocent IV, no. 7259. See Pybus, 'Frederick II', 162–3.
[80] Reg. Martin IV, nos. 482, 489.
[81] Reg. Nicholas IV, no. 669. Johannes Andreae, *Glossa* on Clem. 5.10.2 v. *temporales*.
[82] E.g. Innocent III, Reg. 1, nos. 464, 476, 507; 5, no. 135; 6, no. 10; 9, no. 88; etc.
[83] 1 Comp. 5.28.7; see e.g. Ricardus Anglicus, ibid. v. *privilegium*, BAV, Pal. lat. MS 696, fol. 111vb: 'Solutio: Credo privilegium per abusionem amitti, idest per delictum quod committitur in

The papacy had to hedge such immunities with conditions in order to limit the scope for violation of interdicts. The terms of papal licences to celebrate in interdicted areas were especially strict. As we have seen, they required their recipients to shut the doors of their churches, excluding excommunicates and those under interdict, and not to ring the bells before celebrating in a low voice (so that nobody outside could hear). Consequently, when Innocent III heard in 1206 that some canons in Le Mans rang the bells of their church and celebrated with the doors open during an episcopal interdict, he intervened decisively. A legate had already condemned them at the local dean and chapter's request for violating the interdict, but their proctor claimed that their church was exempt and that, according to a custom recognized by the bishop, they might ring bells and celebrate offices in a loud voice even during general interdicts provided that excommunicates and those under interdict were not admitted. The pope responded by revoking this custom as going against strict observance of interdicts, replacing it with a licence for the canons to celebrate during general interdicts on their city but subject to the usual conditions.[84] This judgement quickly found a lasting place in canon law, but maintaining the balance it attempted to strike between protecting such immunities and enforcing interdicts remained a perennial problem for the papacy.

This difficulty was well illustrated by Innocent's interdict on England. Before his executors published it, he told them that it was to be observed in churches of both regular and secular clergy despite any freedoms or privileges.[85] But five months after they declared the interdict, they informed him that although all Cistercians in England had begun by observing it, after a few days some had resumed celebrating the offices; the monks concerned belonged to Margam, Meaux, and Beaulieu abbeys.[86] The Meaux Abbey chronicle indeed records that its members celebrated behind closed doors with excommunicates and those under interdict excluded as long as the interdict lasted. This represented them acting in accordance with their freedoms. In 1208 at the Cistercian General Chapter the abbot of Cîteaux hence acknowledged that the abbots of these houses had stood for the order's freedom and he imposed penances on other Cistercian abbots in England for observing the interdict 'contra immunitates ordinis'. Moreover he instructed all Cistercians in England and Wales to resume celebration of the offices in accordance with their freedoms, despite the interdict and the executors' orders, until they received a mandate from the pope telling them to stop.[87]

---

abutendum.' Lat. Conc. III c.9 (= 1 Comp. 5.28.3; X 5.33.3). Lat. Conc. IV c.57 (= 4 Comp. 5.12.7; X 5.33.24); see pp. 165–6 above. Innocent III, Reg. 1, nos. 464, 476, 507; 6, no. 10.

[84] Innocent III, Reg. 8, nos. 212 (= 3 Comp. 1.3.4; X 1.4.5), 213.

[85] *SLI*, no. 31. The English 'Forma interdicti' specifically forbade Hospitallers to open churches and bury in cemeteries (despite their freedoms), but priests might call people to hear them preach outside churches (Martène and Durand, i.813).

[86] Innocent III, Reg. 11, no. 141.

[87] *Melsa*, i.351. *Statuta*, i.351. Innocent III, Reg. 11, no. 235; Gervase, II, p. cix.

This situation embarrassed the pope. It appears that the executors had enforced his interdict more strictly than he intended, for he admitted to them by June 1208 that he would not have minded had monks been allowed to celebrate behind closed doors according to their privileges from the outset. This apparently contradicted his previous orders, and in another letter to the executors in August he had to refute allegations that he revealed his purpose first one way then another. However, his letter did not end the confusion but simply left the issue to his executors' discretion. Not until January 1209 did he allow celebration of the offices and weekly consecration of hosts for the dying in conventual churches provided that the interdict was observed there from the start.[88]

Although this seemed to confirm the Cistercians' freedoms, initially they were denied this concession. Innocent III regarded the abbot of Cîteaux's intervention as an affront to papal authority and chastised him in February 1209 for encouraging English Cistercians to violate the interdict. A copy of the executors' mandate concerning strict observance of the interdict was sent to him with orders to compel his English brethren to respect it, and he obediently did so. The pope's reaction seems excessive when they had apparently acted as their freedoms allowed, but a contemporary letter of his to the English episcopate suggests otherwise. He had received reports that some Cistercians had violated the interdict by flagrantly exceeding the terms of their privileges: ringing their churches' bells; bellowing chants with the doors open; and admitting outsiders to Communion celebrated with more than usual solemnity.[89] He instructed the bishops to investigate these rumours, compel offending houses to observe the interdict, and send their abbots or priors under suspension to Rome to account for themselves. Doubtless these allegations were exaggerated, and protests from the Cistercian General Chapter soon followed. In March 1209 he responded by acknowledging the order's freedom to celebrate during interdicts but expressed reservations about letting its English brethren enjoy this given their alleged conduct. But he issued a letter on the same day requiring his executors to mitigate the interdict for Cistercians in accordance with their freedom if they could do so without causing scandal and the interdict being broken. As Cheney judged, 'these confusing and contradictory orders … arose from the use of the interdict as an instrument of diplomacy'.[90] Although Innocent III was prepared to honour papal immunities, he was also concerned not to weaken the interdict against King John.

The situation also arose from a misunderstanding of Innocent's executors over his intentions and of Cistercians over the nature of their freedoms. Indeed after he had declared the interdict on France in 1199, Cistercians there also disputed

[88] *SLI*, no. 36, p. 109. Innocent III, Reg. 11, nos. 141, 214.

[89] Reg. Innocent III, 11, nos. 259, 260. His letter to the bishops was copied by Gervase, II, pp. xcvi–xcvii.

[90] Cheney, *England*, 306. Innocent III, Reg. 12, nos. 9, 10.

whether their immunities freed them from observing it, but here the General Chapter punished those disregarding it.[91] As the papacy established a common law of interdicts, such excuses wore thin and papal reprimands of religious violating interdicts became less common, which suggests that they increasingly understood the limits of their freedoms. In 1247, however, Innocent IV still had to tell Dominicans, Franciscans, Hospitallers, and other religious in Basel not to celebrate offices before its interdicted citizens. Alexander IV and Martin IV also had to correct exempt clergy for illicitly extending their freedoms to laity during interdicts.[92] Friars remained particular offenders in this respect, as we will see. And some religious still resisted interdicts aimed at them, especially by the local ordinary. In 1294 the Bishop of Mâcon complained to Celestine V that after he had interdicted a Cluniac church, four of its monks forced open the chancel door and places where chalices and ornaments were kept and celebrated with the church doors open and bells ringing.[93]

Since religious ministrations only continued during interdicts through clerical disobedience, voluntary or coerced, from the later twelfth century the papacy aimed a growing body of penalties for violation of interdicts mainly at clergy, and very little at laity as we have seen, though such measures were meant to counteract lay attempts to coerce clergy to disregard interdicts. Clergy increasingly found themselves under pressure from both ecclesiastical and lay directions. Indeed automatic penalties in canon law for clerical violation of interdicts were so numerous by the early fourteenth century that, according to the canonist Guillaume de Montlauzun, there were more of them than for violation of excommunication or suspension. In his view one reason for this was that the interdict was respected less and so disregarded more than these other sentences. Another reason, he added, was that its violation created more scandal than breaches of those sentences, for it was imposed on more people, more generally, and more publicly;[94] those sentences normally bound individuals only. Indeed an interdict was a very conspicuous test of the Church's authority over society, especially its own clergy, and one that faced growing princely and popular hostility in the thirteenth century, hence the papacy had to develop increasingly elaborate means to enforce it.

[91] Krehbiel, 116–17; *Statuta*, i.258.

[92] Reg. Innocent IV, no. 3109. Cf. Reg. Alexander IV, no. 1321; Reg. Martin IV, no. 530.

[93] Reg. Boniface VIII, no. 2142.

[94] Guillaume de Montlauzun, *Sacramentale* (c.1319), Oxford, Bodleian Library, Hamilton MS 24, fol. 81ra: 'Si queras que est ratio quod pluribus penis puniatur qui violat interdictum quam qui violat excommunicationem vel suspensionem cum alias omnia cetera sunt regulariter paria, dic quod hec est ratio quia aliqui credebant interdictum vilius et minus ceteris et ideo vilipendebant et negliebant ipsum, quare ut magis appareret, gravius punitur ad instar peccati in spiritum sanctum, ar. xxv di. Qualis et de pen. di. i. consimilibus [D.25 c.4; De pen. D.1 c.34]. Hoc est vel quia transgressio interdicti cum maiori scandali fit quam aliarum penarum pro eo quod in plures communius fertur et magis publice quam cetere pene, extra. de postul. prela. c.i et de of. or. Novit [X 1.5.1; 1.30.7].'

The earliest papal rulings on this issue, as on others, were issued in response to external demand, largely from prelates requesting advice on how to discipline clergy. Thus in an undated decretal, addressed in the *Liber extra* to the Bishop of London but in earlier collections to the Bishop of Tours or other prelates, Alexander III ruled that clergy who celebrated while under interdict or excommunication incurred permanent deposition. When many such offenders were reported to him from Toledo province, he introduced a distinction to this ruling in another undated decretal addressed to their archbishop. The pope instructed him to depose these priests from office in perpetuity if they were fewer than forty, but if they were more than forty, he might reserve this penalty for the more serious offenders and only temporarily suspend the rest. Hence clergy might be punished according to the severity of their violation. This applied a Roman law principle that punishment was to be mitigated in the case of a multitude of offenders, as canonists recognized.[95] Canonists also noted that those who returned to obedience might be dispensed from permanent deposition. Vincentius Hispanus held that a bishop might grant this dispensation, but Tancred agreed with Alanus and other canonists that this power was reserved to the pope. Tancred also shared Vincentius's doubts whether judges delegate might exercise this power on the pope's behalf. Later canonists generally accepted this reservation to the papacy; even Vincentius (*c.*1236) came around to it.[96] It was consistent with the nascent canonistic principle that only the authority imposing a penalty might lift it, which in the case of penalties attached to papal law was the pope himself. Indeed it appears that such violators of interdicts might be deposed only on papal authority. In 1221 when Honorius III heard that the Bishop of Hildesheim deposed a priest for celebrating before excommunicates during an interdict, he revoked this penalty since 'according to canonical sanctions' it might not be inflicted on mere episcopal authority.[97] Papal reservation of the correction of clergy violating interdicts also characterized rulings of Alexander III's successors.

---

[95] 1 Comp. 5.23.3, 4 (= X 5.27.3, 4). Cf. Anon. (*c.*1206) on 1 Comp. 5.23.4 v. *multitudinem*, Brussels, Bibliothèque royale MS 1407–9, fol. 85ra: 'Quia ubi multitudo est in causa detrahendum est ibi aliquid severitas pene, ut l. d. Ut constitueretur [D.50 c.25].'

[96] Vincentius on 1 Comp. 5.23.3 v. *admonitionem*, Leipzig Universitätsbibliothek MS 983, fol. 56ra: 'Ergo quod episcopus dispensare cum clerico ministrante, xi. q. iii. Si quis episcopus dampnatur [C.11 q.3 c.6].' Alanus on 1 Comp. 5.23.3 v. *redierint*, Munich, Bayerisches Staatsbibliothek Clm 3879, fol. 90va: 'Quod dictum est de dispensatione? ... Secundum quosdam quod alius a papa cum eis dispensare non potest, ar. xi. q. iii. Si quis damp., supra xi. q. iii. Placuit, Si quis episcopus [C.11 q.3 c.6, 9].' The latter gloss was copied by Tancred, ibid. v. *admonitionem* (manuscripts as follows). Id. on 1 Comp. 5.23.4 v. *presumpserint*, BAV, Vat. lat. MS 1377, fol. 91vb; Vat. lat. MS 2509, fol. 86vb: 'Sed nunquid potest delegatus dispensare cum talibus ut ministrent et videtur quoniam vicem pape gerit, supra. de sen. exco. Ad eminentiam lib. ii. [2 Comp. 5.18.9]. Non credo, ar. xi. q. iii. Si quis episcopus [C.11 q.3 c.6] ... Vinc.' Vincentius copied Alanus's gloss from Tancred on X 5.27.3 v. *nisi monita*, BAV, Vat. lat. MS 6769, fol. 131va. Cf. Innocent IV, *Apparatus* on X 5.27.4 v. *ad tempus*; Bernard of Parma on X 5.27.3 v. *moniti*, who held that a legate might grant such dispensations on the pope's behalf.

[97] Reg. Honorius III, no. 3321.

One such ruling was also prompted by another external request. The dean and prior of Cologne Cathedral asked Innocent III how to punish secular and regular clerks for celebrating in interdicted places, notably when they were already excommunicated for doing so. He replied in the decretal 'Postulastis' (1207) that secular clergy were to be deprived of their benefices; canonists also came to regard this as a consequence of the deposition incurred under Alexander III's rulings. Monks or nuns, Innocent added, were to be packed off to stricter monasteries to do penance. By 1210 'Postulastis' had found a lasting place in canon law alongside Alexander III's rulings.[98] Consequently its sanctions might be incurred likewise *ipso iure*. Certainly these penalties were also understood to be imposed on papal authority. In 1218 the Bishop of Prague solicited a faculty from Honorius III to strip prelates and clerks in his diocese of their benefices, as they had participated in offices, thereby violating an interdict laid by him. Honorius also authorized the removal of regular clergy who violated interdicts. And even before Innocent III had issued this ruling, bishops had sought his backing to discipline monks who violated interdicts, even religious subject to episcopal jurisdiction, presumably in order to prevent these monks appealing on the grounds of their immunities.[99]

Innocent III had also issued another less general ruling on clerical violation of interdicts in 1200. Although it was not solicited, it originated in response to a specific case referred to him.[100] The chapter of Sens had elected the Bishop of Auxerre as their archbishop and sent their precentor to ask the pope to endorse the bishop's translation. But Innocent refused since the bishop had not observed the papal interdict on France. His ruling in this case established the principle that the election to ecclesiastical office of anyone violating an interdict was invalid. It soon entered decretal collections where it attracted canonistic attention. Alanus included it in his own collection and observed that clergy nominating or electing such unworthy candidates were to lose their voting rights in accordance with other papal rulings. Most canonists accepted this view after Innocent's ruling passed into *Compilatio tertia* and the *Liber extra*.[101] Indeed Innocent had pointed out to the Sens chapter that he might remove its voting rights, but instead he let it choose a more suitable candidate; it had observed the interdict, he conceded, even

---

98 Innocent III, Reg. 10, no. 62; 3 Comp. 5.12.3; X 5.27.7.
99 Reg. Honorius III, no. 1722. Cf. Innocent III, Reg. 1, nos. 464, 476; 6, no. 10.
100 Alan. 1.5.5; 3 Comp. 1.4.1; X 1.5.1. See also *Gesta* c.56 (*PL* 214.ciii).
101 Alanus on Alan. 1.5.5 v. *privare*, Vercelli Cathedral Chapter MS 89, fol. 56rb: 'Nota quod postulantes indignum privari possunt iure postulandi, ut supra. e. c. i [Alan. 1.5.1], sicut et eligentes, ut supra. de elec. Cum in cunctis. lib. i., supra. de filiis presbiterorum. Innotuit. lib. ii, infra. de prebendis. Cum non ignores [1 Comp. 1.4.16; Gilb. 1.10.4; Alan. 3.4.3] contra ar.' This gloss was adopted by Johannes Galensis (*c*.1210) on 3 Comp. 1.4.1 v. *privare*, Munich, Bayerisches Staatsbibliothek Clm 3879, fol. 155rb. Tancred on 3 Comp. 1.4.1 v. *inmerito* noted that the canon 'Cum in cunctis' set the precedent for this and that it referred to those nominating or electing an unworthy candidate 'scienter' (BAV, Vat. lat. MS 1377, fol. 154vb; Vat. lat. MS 2509, fol. 146rb). Cf. Innocent IV, *Apparatus* on X 1.5.1 v. *privare*, and Bernard of Parma, ibid.

if its archbishop-elect had not. However, on subsequent occasions when electors violated interdicts, it seems that they lost their voting rights strictly in accordance with Alanus's teaching. When the chapter of Beauvais elected their dean as their bishop by a majority vote, canons who voted against him informed Gregory IX that he and most of his supporters had celebrated in Beauvais Cathedral although interdicted by the previous bishop.[102] For this and other reasons these canons proposed that those who had elected the dean should be deprived of their voting rights and his election blocked. In May 1238 Gregory suspended the interdict on the cathedral to allow a new election, although he did not expressly exclude from it electors accused of violating the sentence. Certainly ten years later monks of an abbey in Vienne could not elect a new abbot because they had celebrated during a papal interdict on that city, at least according to their mother house, which used this as a pretext to appoint an abbot for them.[103] Thus in practice it seems that violators of interdicts might neither elect nor be elected to church offices.

Over and above these rulings Gregory IX's decretal 'Tanta', after its inclusion in the *Liber extra*, was immediately recognized by canonists as the most significant on clerical violation of interdicts.[104] It was originally issued in 1232 with regard to clergy of Coimbra diocese who violated a papal interdict on Portugal. We noted above that a canon of Coimbra Cathedral petitioned Gregory that the Portuguese king and his men coerced him to celebrate for them during this interdict. He also alleged that his bishop ordered him to do so and when he refused, the bishop's agents seized his prebend. We have seen that some prelates did support their rulers in defying interdicts; 'Tanta' was largely occasioned by the bishop's admission of such complicity before the curia. His actions are comparable with those of lay rulers against clergy observing interdicts. He confessed to violating the interdict and forcing others to do so. He had exiled any who resisted, after confiscating both their own and their relatives' property and depriving them of their benefices, which he had conferred on his supporters; our canon claimed to be a victim of this.

'Tanta' was the pope's detailed response. Firstly clergy whom the bishop had deprived of benefices were to be reinstated and any who had received these benefices from him were to lose them and any others they held. Second the latter and any other clergy who violated the interdict were to be suspended from ecclesiastical offices and benefices. This was not unprecedented; in 1200 Innocent III ordered the suspension of clergy who did not observe his interdict on France from the start.[105] Thirdly Gregory required that any who laid violent hands on clergy observing the Portuguese interdict and their property were to be declared excommunicate; they would have incurred this sentence automatically under the canon 'Si quis suadente' in any case.[106] Finally all offenders had to represent

---

[102] Reg. Gregory IX, nos. 4078–9, 4358–60, 4365.   [103] Reg. Innocent IV, no. 4232.
[104] Reg. Gregory IX, no. 810; X 5.31.18.   [105] *Gesta* c.57 (*PL* 214.ciii); Krehbiel, 124.
[106] Lat. Conc. II c.15 (1139); C.17 q.4 c.29.

themselves before the Pope in four months, presumably to obtain absolution. Certainly 'Si quis suadente' required its violators to seek absolution from the Pope in person, and it was said that clergy suspended for violating the French interdict were similarly obliged to approach the holy see. When Raymond of Peñafort included 'Tanta' in the *Liber extra*, he amended this summons to the curia, limiting it to the excommunicate.[107] Nevertheless mid-thirteenth-century canonists would debate whether absolution from all its penalties was reserved to papacy, as we will see.

One of the most substantial and influential early commentaries on 'Tanta' was by Innocent IV. It was where he defined the interdict as forbidding religious rites that only the ordained might perform; hence clergy performing them violated the interdict and incurred suspension under 'Tanta'.[108] Accordingly Innocent argued that 'Tanta' applied to priests celebrating mass or other offices but not clergy chanting responses or reading lessons during offices. Hostiensis broadly agreed but added that the latter clergy only avoided suspension if they took part in offices out of devotion; the reverse was true if they did so out of contempt for ecclesiastical authority and had the offices celebrated in spite of an interdict.[109] There were clearly different kinds and degrees of violation. In 1266, for example, Clement IV heard how clergy in Volterra diocese had violated a papal interdict in various ways. He was concerned to vary their punishment according to the severity of their violation 'since a multitude is said to be at fault'. In other words he applied 'Tanta' in accordance with Alexander III's decretal for Toledo province. Clement thus ordered some violators to be suspended for longer than others: those who illicitly rang church bells for funerals might be suspended for twice as long as those who did so for the canonical hours.[110] This example also shows that Clement followed Hostiensis in applying 'Tanta' to those encouraging violation of an interdict, since church bells were rung to call laity to services.

Innocent IV and Hostiensis disagreed more strongly over whether the penalties stipulated in 'Tanta' were imposed by the law itself or ecclesiastical judges. The issue was important, for according to canonical procedure a penalty might only be lifted by the authority that imposed it. Innocent IV argued that clergy celebrating in interdicted places were suspended not by law but by the judge who imposed the interdict.[111] This implies that they had to obtain absolution from this judge, but Innocent did not say so explicitly. He did, however, question the canonistic assumption that they also incurred irregularity. This was a canonical impediment

[107] Raymond also cut the letter's final sentence which provided that the canons and others reduced to begging by the bishop's confiscations be compensated from his cathedral's property. On such editorial changes see Kuttner, 'Raymond of Peñafort'.

[108] Innocent IV, *Apparatus* on X 5.31.18 v. *violavit*.

[109] Hostiensis, *Lectura* on X 5.31.18 v. *violavit* (vol. 2, fol. 76vb).

[110] Reg. Clement IV, no. 348. A similar letter was copied into Benedict XII's formulary for the papal penitentiary (1334); see my 'Papal Penitentiary', 422–3.

[111] Innocent IV, *Apparatus* on X 5.31.18 v. *interdicti violationem*.

forbidding reception or exercise of holy orders; it might be overcome only by papal dispensation. Bernard of Parma made this assumption, as did Hostiensis, and Hostiensis also rejected Innocent's claim that those who imposed an interdict punished those who violated it. On the contrary he held that they were suspended by law.[112] The law in question and the penalty it contained were established by the papacy; hence this implies that those who violated interdicts had to ask the holy see for dispensation from irregularity and absolution from suspension.

Hostiensis apparently reflected reality where irregularity was concerned. Soon after 'Tanta' appeared in the *Liber extra*, it was understood in practice that clergy who celebrated during interdicts might incur irregularity and so require papal dispensation. Gregory IX himself dispensed some such clergy in Milan diocese seven months after the *Liber extra* was issued.[113] In 1247 even Innocent IV allowed the Bishop of Olmütz to dispense clerks in Bohemia who had celebrated during an interdict, allegedly out of fear of their king. Innocent's chancery was doubtless acceding to the bishop's request, but it is striking that the pope's views as a jurist did not shape his curial policy on this issue. Certainly his successors followed practice rather than his sceptical commentary. Increasingly they delegated their powers of dispensation in certain cases, as Innocent did in 1247, especially to legates and bishops.[114] But it was usually granted subject to certain conditions by the late thirteenth century. These normally included the proviso that clergy who violated an interdict 'in contempt of the keys' might not be dispensed; this echoed the remark in 'Tanta' that the Bishop of Coimbra had 'scorned the keys of St Peter' by violating a papal interdict.[115] According to papal mandates clergy might be dispensed if they celebrated during interdicts out of fear; this was the excuse of the Bohemian clergy in 1247. In this and most cases it normally meant fear of a lay power coercing them to celebrate.[116] Ignorance or naïvety (*simplicitas*) were also grounds for dispensation. They might arise from a genuine misunderstanding, as in a case referred to Honorius IV in 1285.[117] A canon of Tours had presumed to celebrate at an abbey in interdicted Blois for its monks enjoyed a papal grant to celebrate during interdicts, but he later realized that this did not apply to him as an outsider. He also pleaded old age as an

---

[112] Bernard of Parma on X 5.31.18 v. *inanes*; Hostiensis, *Lectura* on X 5.31.18 v. *post interdicti violationem* (vol. 2, fol. 77rb).

[113] Reg. Gregory IX, no. 2520.

[114] Reg. Innocent IV, no. 3063. Cf. Reg. Alexander IV, no. 1773 (cardinal); Reg. Martin IV, no. 382 (legate); Reg. Honorius IV, nos. 589, 608 (bishops); Reg. Nicholas IV, nos. 1007, 1387, 2133 (archbishops), 2201 (legate), 2736 (bishop), 2901, 2965 (mendicant provincials), 3185, 6590 (bishops and archbishops), 7211 (patriarch). Gregory IX had also delegated this power to the cardinal penitentiary by the late 1230s; see my 'Papal Penitentiary', 422.

[115] Reg. Honorius IV, no. 589; Reg. Nicholas IV, nos. 2133, 2736, 7211.

[116] Fear: Reg. Nicholas IV, nos. 2133, 2736. Lay coercion: Reg. Honorius IV, no. 589. Ignorance: Reg. Nicholas IV, no. 7211. Naïvety: ibid. nos. 2133, 2736. Cf. my 'Papal Penitentiary', 428–30.

[117] Reg. Honorius IV, no. 144. In 1227 Gregory IX had already accepted ignorance as an excuse provided that it was not crass or supine (X 5.27.9).

excuse for not approaching the pope in person for dispensation; hence Honorius instructed two ecclesiastical dignitaries in Tours to grant him it.

It is unclear whether Innocent IV's successors also reserved absolution from suspension in these cases, as it was not normally delegated along with dispensation. Admittedly in 1283 Martin IV instructed a legate to absolve a bishop suspended for violating a papal interdict, but another legate had laid the suspension and it is unclear whether his authority to do so was derived from the pope as judge enforcing his own interdict or as legislator.[118] Hence it is debatable whether Innocent IV or Hostiensis influenced practice on this point in the late thirteenth century. Certainly in this period popes threatened penalties for violation besides those prescribed by law and did as universal ordinary enforcing their own interdicts. In 1286, when James of Aragon was crowned king of Sicily in defiance of the papacy, Honorius IV told clergy to observe an ambulatory interdict against him or they would incur not only canonical penalties but also excommunication and loss of all offices and benefices.[119] This punishment was unusual in severity and scope. It applied not only to priests celebrating mass and those officiating in lesser orders but also those preaching at services, even if sermons were allowed during interdicts; this far exceeded Innocent IV's definition of violation. Excommunication was also an extraordinary penalty for those violating the interdicts Martin IV laid on Aragon and Castile, but apparently only those who celebrated might incur it.[120] It was presumably imposed on papal authority for Nicholas IV empowered various Spanish prelates to absolve such clergy from that sentence as well as dispense them from irregularity.

However, papal legislation did not react to the canonistic debate and practical developments following 'Tanta' until over sixty years after its publication in the *Liber extra*. In 1298 Boniface VIII issued several rulings in the *Liber sextus* which resolved various disputed points arising from 'Tanta' and confirmed many customary practices as law. For example his constitution 'Is qui' stated that clergy knowingly celebrating in interdicted places incurred irregularity, unless they might celebrate there by law or privilege. Hence Innocent IV's doubts on this point were set aside. And in accordance with practice and doctrine, Boniface confirmed that dispensation from this irregularity was reserved to the pope.[121] He added that such clergy were ineligible, not only in that they might not be elected to church office, as Innocent III had ruled, but also that they might not vote in such elections; they had long been excluded from them in practice.

Whilst 'Is qui' reinforced papal power to discipline violators, the constitution 'Episcoporum' responded to demands from bishops and other prelates. It was directed against secular and regular clergy regardless of their immunities, and addressed long-standing episcopal concerns about abuse of such freedoms during interdicts. Boniface also defined violation of interdicts in similar wide terms

---

[118] Reg. Martin IV, no. 382.   [119] Reg. Honorius IV, no. 807.
[120] Reg. Nicholas IV, nos. 1686, 2133, 2736, 2901, 2965, 3185.   [121] VI 5.11.18 §2.

to Hostiensis, including those who knowingly celebrated offices in interdicted places (except when allowed by law) and those who had them celebrated.[122] 'Episcoporum' also applied to clergy admitting those under interdict or known excommunicates to the offices, sacraments, or burial. All such violators incurred an interdict *ab ingressu ecclesie*. As Boniface explained in another constitution 'Is cui', clergy under such an interdict might not celebrate or act in their office, and if they did so, they also incurred irregularity. Moreover those who died under this interdict were denied ecclesiastical burial unless they had repented.[123] 'Episcoporum' added that this penalty remained in force until violators gave proper satisfaction to the judge whose interdict they had scorned. Therefore Boniface struck a compromise between the opposing views of Innocent IV and Hostiensis on whether violators were penalized by the judges laying interdicts or the law. 'Episcoporum' imposed the penalty, but it made violators accountable to both judges and the law.

Boniface's rulings were supplemented some two decades later by Clement V. Whereas Boniface had synthesized canonistic tradition and customary practice in his legislation, Clement largely reinforced the existing law and addressed specific abuses. For example his constitution 'Eos qui', allegedly sanctioned at the council of Vienne, supplemented the provisions of 'Episcoporum' on ecclesiastical burial.[124] It forbade on pain of excommunication the burial in cemeteries of anyone interdicted by name, known excommunicates and usurers, and anyone dying during interdicts. In the latter case, however, it conceded that the law made some exceptions; notably clergy dying during interdicts might be buried in hallowed ground if they had observed them.[125] It then concluded with two points based on 'Episcoporum'. Those excommunicated by 'Eos qui' had to give proper satisfaction to those injured by their actions, as the local bishop saw fit; otherwise they might not be absolved. The canonist Johannes Andreae suggested that injured parties included those on whose behalf the interdict was laid.[126] This was not necessarily the judge who laid the interdict, as in 'Episcoporum', though the local ordinary was assigned a role as arbitrator. Absolution was probably reserved to the pope, though this was not made explicit. Nevertheless 'Eos qui' made clear, as did 'Episcoporum', that no immunity might be claimed from it through exemption or other privileges. Clearly the abuse of burial privileges during interdicts condemned at the Third Lateran Council remained a concern over a century later. Indeed during an interdict on Laon (1295–7) some of the dead, including excommunicates, were said to be interred in local churches and cemeteries of the mendicant and military orders.[127]

---

[122] VI 5.7.8.   [123] VI 5.11.20.   [124] Clem. 3.7.1.

[125] X 5.38.11. See p. 162. Clergy who violated interdicts were presumably refused ecclesiastical burial during them; cf. VI 5.11.18, 20.

[126] Johannes Andreae, *Glossa* on Clem. 3.7.1 v. *sepelire*.

[127] X 5.33.3 §3. Laon: Reg. Boniface VIII, no. 1533; Denton, 'Laon', 85, 87–8. Boniface ordered the exhumation of these illicitly buried bodies.

By the early fourteenth century regular clergy were accused of other abuses of their freedoms during interdicts. In the preamble to Clement's bull 'Ex frequentibus', apparently issued in 1310 and included in the *Clementine*, he observed from his own experience and the 'frequent complaints of prelates' that religious abused the freedom to celebrate behind closed doors during interdicts.[128] They allegedly had holes bored or windows made in these doors, presumably so that excluded laity could witness the offices inside. Apparently such violations were widespread. Therefore Clement's bull ordered religious, even the exempt, to observe inviolably on pain of excommunication interdicts laid by papal or ordinary authority. It nevertheless affirmed Boniface VIII's concession in 'Alma mater' that clergy might celebrate behind closed doors.

The issue of lay access to the 'private' worship of regular clergy, only implied in 'Ex frequentibus', was directly confronted in another ruling of Clement V, 'Cum ex eo'.[129] Issued in 1306, it noted that Franciscans admitted members of their third order to hear offices in their churches during interdicts, and it claimed that this undermined respect for interdicts among those who remained excluded. The third order comprised lay men and women including married couples, and previous popes had allowed some of them to attend Franciscan services during interdicts. However, friars had long been criticized for receiving laity at their churches in interdicts. Müller noted an instance of special relevance to 'Cum ex eo'. After a legate had interdicted Strasbourg in 1283, he accused local Franciscans of admitting laity to their third order so that they might hear the offices in the friars' churches during his interdict. In 1287 the cardinal forbade the Franciscans on pain of excommunication from receiving tertiaries in their churches at that time.[130] 'Cum ex eo' extended this ban under the same penalty to the Franciscan order as a whole and in regard to any interdict; papal grants to the contrary were to be disregarded. Those incurring excommunication under 'Cum ex eo' might be absolved only by the pope, though he could delegate his power to absolve them to bishops. This curbing of mendicant privilege clearly met with the approval of prelates, for 'Cum ex eo' was renewed at the council of Vienne prior to its inclusion in the *Clementine*.

Decretal collections from their emergence in the late twelfth century down to the *Clementine* in 1317 thus record increasing pressure on clergy to enforce interdicts. The proliferation of laws against clerical violation of interdicts, especially from 1298, indicates how widespread the problem was becoming. Not only were clergy subject to growing lay coercion to violate interdicts, but also prelates often claimed that regular clergy abused their freedoms, admitting laity to their churches and cemeteries during interdicts. Automatic sanctions were especially needed against religious who claimed immunity from correction by local ordinaries. But the question remains whether popes and other Church

[128] Clem. 5.10.1. On the date of this constitution see Müller, *Vienne*, 546.
[129] Clem. 5.10.3.　　[130] Müller, *Vienne*, 545–7, esp. 546.

authorities could make interdicts work during the thirteenth century, despite growing lay opposition and clerical violations. In Chapters 2–4 we understood how the interdict was meant to work according to the canon law and canonists of the period. In the final parts of this chapter we will examine more closely how it actually worked in practice through detailed case studies of three thirteenth-century interdicts. As far as possible these have been based on the records of both the secular power and Church authorities in order to obtain a balance of views. All three interdicts provoked dramatic clashes between clergy and laity; and largely as a result the responses to them are well documented. Both these facts influenced my choice of these interdicts for close study.

5.3 THE INTERDICT ON SAN GIMIGNANO: A CLERICAL STRIKE AND ITS CONSEQUENCES

The strike has been defined as 'a temporary stoppage of work' designed 'to express a grievance or enforce a demand'. In many ways an interdict is comparable. The clergy likewise withdrew their labour during interdicts as an act of protest. The interdict that lay on the Tuscan commune of San Gimignano in *c*.1289–93 was notably comparable to modern industrial conflicts. The power against whom it was aimed tried to counter it in various ways, its deprivations provoked popular resentment, and an end to it was sought through a compromise negotiated by an independent arbitrator. Such elements of industrial disputes as the strikers' 'walk-out' and countermove of hiring 'blackleg' labour also featured at San Gimignano. The story of this 'strike' can be reconstructed in considerable detail, sometimes on a week-by-week basis, as the commune's records survive in some abundance at this time.[131] Like other thirteenth-century north Italian communes it had a very sophisticated form of popular government; regular meetings of its various committees were carefully minuted and its finances recorded in detailed ledgers. By contrast local ecclesiastical records of the dispute are sparse. Some were copied into a register of the commune and the clerical voice is echoed elsewhere in its records; a papal letter also reported clerical grievances during the interdict.

Before studying the sources, we need to examine the context. San Gimignano was a town with a small *contado* or county extending less than 10 km from it walls, in contrast to its powerful neighbours Florence and Siena. It had no bishop's see but lay within Volterra diocese, and its spiritual needs were served principally by the provost and secular canons of its collegiate church or *pieve*. A Bishop of

---

[131] The above definition of a strike is from Hyman, *Strikes*, 17. The medieval records of the commune are split between the Archivio Comunale di San Gimignano (ACSG) and Archivio di Stato di Firenze (ASF) and were selectively calendared by Davidsohn, *Forschungen*, II. The ACSG has recently been recatalogued; the new call numbers are cited here with the old ones cited by Davidsohn in brackets.

Volterra had founded the town *c.*929, and his successors steadily increased their temporal jurisdiction over the *castrum* and *terra* of San Gimignano till 1199 when its people formed a commune independent of episcopal control.[132] This phenomenon was indeed widespread among twelfth-century Italian towns ruled by bishops. Like such towns San Gimignano had, therefore, a difficult relationship with its local bishop long before he interdicted it in 1289. Strife between bishop and commune had broken out at least three times already in 1229, 1267, and 1277 and verged on armed warfare. The bishop had used spiritual sanctions against the commune on these occasions too, excommunicating its officials in 1267, and again in 1277, when he also interdicted the town.

The cause of these past conflicts was territorial: San Gimignano disputed the frontier with Volterra to its north-west, seeking especially to strengthen its weak hold over the castles of Ulignano and Gambassi. But the cause of our interdict is uncertain, nor do we know when it was laid, since no record of its proclamation has been found. Nevertheless Bishop Rainieri of Volterra had apparently declared it on the commune and excommunicated its officials by late December 1289. The commune's accounts at this time reveal that a judge Octavantus of Florence was paid for advice regarding the 'sentence of excommunication laid against us'.[133] A letter of the bishop addressed to the commune on 11 January 1290 also refers to the excommunication and interdict as already in force. It states that the sentences were incurred because the commune had made ordinances and statutes 'at the instigation of the devil', presumably contrary to ecclesiastical interests. But it does not specify what these were. It simply upbraids the commune for ignoring the bishop's warning to revoke this legislation (and thus secure his absolution) and for having proceeded to 'worse things'.[134] Such *peiora* were later specified in a petition of the town's clergy to Nicholas IV; its content was reported in the pope's reply of 5 November 1290 copied into his registers. This petition probably describes both the causes and effects of the interdict but does not distinguish between them. Hence we will return to it later.

Although the evidence hardly illuminates the interdict's cause, historians have proposed various causes. The authors of the two main histories of the town,

---

[132] The only political history of the town is Pecori, *San Gimignano*, recently supplemented by Waley, 'Guelfs and Ghibellines'. The town's medieval development is outlined by Luzzati, 'San Gimignano'.

[133] ASF, Comune di San Gimignano 171, fol. 7v; Davidsohn, *Forschungen*, II no. 1753. This jurist may be the 'dominus Actavianus' sent as the commune's envoy to seek 'concordia' with Bishop Rainieri on 23 January 1295 (ASF, Comune di San Gimignano 200, fol. 17r) and described as *plebanus* of Santa Maria Novella. This probably does not refer to the Dominican church in Florence as a *plebanus* headed a parish church and there is no evidence that it functioned as such or that any Octavantus or Actavianus was linked with it in this period. I am grateful to Michele Mulcahey for this information.

[134] ACSG, N.0069 (N.N.17), fol. 47r (edited in my 'San Gimignano', 298). Cf. Waley, *Siena*, 131: 'The [Sienese] bishop's occasional protest that certain statutes were "against ecclesiastical liberty" is so generic that it is sometimes difficult to know what was at stake.' Reg. Nicholas IV, no. 3581.

Coppi and Pecori (heavily reliant on Coppi), refer to a dispute between clergy and commune over *decime*. Indeed the commune sent three emissaries to speak to the provost of the *pieve* on 11 March 1290 'super facto clericorum pro decimis', but to no avail Coppi says.[135] Likewise, when the town council met on 18 April 1290 to consider an offer from two Florentine emissaries to mediate between commune and clergy, a councillor proposed that they be told everything 'quod clerici occasione decime faciebant'.[136] Three years later the commune was still negotiating with the clergy, when it instructed emissaries to promise whatever the provost and canons wanted regarding the *decima* and that the commune 'in dicta decima benigne se habebit'. But what *decima* means in the sources is ambiguous. It may mean tithes, and certainly the clergy claimed by November 1290 that the commune had forbidden payment of such *decime* to them, although this might have been a reaction to rather than cause of the interdict. Alternatively it may mean a 'tenth' levied by the commune, and clerical exemption from such secular taxation was increasingly contested by the late thirteenth century. Indeed the clergy also alleged by 1290 that the commune required them to pay a trade tax called *cabella* as if they were laity. No secular tenth is mentioned but the commune needed to tap clerical wealth at this time: it had to meet the costs of building a new *palazzo comunale*; supporting the Guelf league in wars against Arezzo and Pisa; and paying taxes to vicars of Charles II of Anjou. Certainly Waley indicates that both ecclesiastical and secular taxation were issues dividing laity and clergy in thirteenth-century Italian communes; but ultimately it is unclear which was at stake here.[137]

Volpe gives another, albeit finance-related, reason for the conflict.[138] Bishop Rainieri of Volterra was podestà of San Gimignano in 1289, governing it through a vicar. A podestà was usually well remunerated, and Volpe considered the commune's subsequent conflict with the clergy a reaction to the bishop's lucrative involvement in its affairs. Thus under Rainieri's successor as podestà it introduced the statutes against ecclesiastical liberty that provoked the bishop to lay the interdict. It seems a plausible explanation but, in the absence of clear evidence, highly speculative.

Ridolfi explains the background to the interdict differently again, claiming that commune and clergy were on bad terms from 1287 for another reason.[139] Apparently this arose from a dispute between the friars of San Galgano and

[135] Coppi, 152; Pecori, 115. ACSG, N.0068 (P.77), fol. 1v.

[136] ACSG, N.0069 (N.N.17), fol. 71v; Davidsohn, *Forschungen*, II, no. 1762 (18 April 1290). See also ASF, Comune di San Gimignano 195, fol. 24r (*c.*8 March–13 June 1293).

[137] Waley, *City-Republics*, 44. Bishop Rainieri's letter of 1290 (n. 134) may allude to the financial cause of the dispute: it laments that Sangimignanesi had strayed onto the paths of avarice ('averitatitis tramite deviare') and seeks to recall their souls from the fate of the greedy ('vestras animas apetatorum nexibus revocare').

[138] Volpe, 181, 183–4.

[139] Ridolfi, 'Ricordo', esp. 98–9. Pecori, 122, alluded to the dispute over this estate but dated it to 1276. Nevertheless on 28 October 1293 the commune paid for documents concerning its

provost and canons of San Gimignano over an estate bequeathed by a wealthy moneylender to the Church of Santa Maria Villacastello near the town. The friars alleged that he was murdered by a clerk of San Gimignano; the commune supported their accusations seeking the Bishop of Siena's intervention. According to Ridolfi the Bishop of Volterra had threatened an interdict if the commune continued to interfere, but the dispute only worsened so he carried out his threat. This story cannot be pure invention, but again it is impossible to substantiate. It may underlie the clergy's complaint to Nicholas IV that the commune disregarded their immunity from its secular jurisdiction.

If the interdict's origins are obscure and disputed, the immediate reactions to it are well documented. It is evident that by January 1290 clergy had staged a 'walk-out' leaving the town for the nearby Church of Santa Maria Villacastello. Indeed it was not uncommon for clergy of interdicted Italian towns to exile themselves, largely to avoid being forced by laity to ignore the interdict. Certainly our clergy claimed later in 1290 that the commune persecuted them so much that they had to abandon the town.[140]

It seems that before the clergy left, they had stripped the altars of the *pieve*. A meeting of the commune's general council was convened by the podestà, Benghus de Buondelmontibus of Florence, on 24 January 1290 to discuss the issue.[141] Two of the councillors called on Benghus to have the altars re-covered with whatever was taken. Another rejected this and proposed that the heads of the town's Franciscan and Austin friars be sent to ask the Bishop of Volterra what the commune had done that the clergy should despoil the *pieve*, its altars, and *tabule*. A majority vote backed this conciliatory proposal but most proposals at the meeting urged Benghus to identify and even punish those who had stripped the altars. Ultimately these hawkish voices prevailed, since the commune's accounts in October 1290 show that Gratia Andree was paid for recording proceedings against priests for 'stealing' *paramenta* and other pictures from altars of the *pieve*.[142] Indeed around then the clergy alleged that the commune had summoned clerks before its court, and the proceedings recorded by Gratia were apparently held in the first half of 1290 under Benghus. The clergy's action at the *pieve* and commune's reaction are illuminating in several respects. First, this is one of the earliest references to altar paintings in medieval Italy. Second, that clergy removed these images during an interdict suggests that they had a liturgical as well as devotional function.[143] After all interdicts forbade public liturgical ceremonies but not private devotional acts

dispute with the monastery of S. Galgano at the Bishop of Volterra's court (ASF, Comune di San Gimignano 193).

[140] Reg. Nicholas IV, no. 3581. The provost was at Santa Maria Villacastello by 11 March 1290 when the commune sent emissaries to him (n. 135), but he and other clergy had evidently left San Gimignano by January as the following indicates.

[141] ASCG, N.0069 (N.N.17), fols. 49v–50r.

[142] ASF, Comune di San Gimignano 178 (unfoliated; among entries for October 1290); ASCG, N.0070 (N.N.16), fol. 25v (among entries for 31 October 1290). Cf. Reg. Nicholas IV, no. 3581.

[143] I am grateful to Cordelia Warr and Donal Cooper for these observations.

like venerating images. Finally, that the commune charged priests with theft of the images shows not only disregard for privilege of clergy but also that it saw these objects not as exclusively church property but somehow its own. Doubtless they were donated by local townspeople, perhaps even the commune itself, and were symbols of communal pride like Duccio's *Maestà*, a massive altarpiece carried in civic processions at fourteenth-century Siena. The commune did not own the *pieve* (unlike at Bologna) but it acted as if it did, sometimes holding council meetings in the church's precincts. One of the clergy's grievances was that they had to ring bells to announce these. As Larner and Jones noted, secular and sacred blended in Italian towns to form a 'state religion'.[144]

Stripping the altars was not the only clerical act that scandalized the commune. Apparently from the outset clergy observed the interdict more strictly than canon law required. Infant baptism and absolution of the dying had long been allowed during an interdict, but seemingly none of the clergy returned from self-exile to administer these essential sacraments. In January and February 1290 four men acting for the commune asked canons of the *pieve* to baptize children there; they were doubtless refusing to do this. Demands of the town's laity for clergy of the *pieve* to baptize their children and absolve their dying were numerous; the commune owed a notary payment in October 1290 for writing ten *carte* full of them. The commune had even sent a messenger on 20 March 1290 to beg the provost to send back a priest from Santa Maria Villacastello to perform infant baptisms and 'alia necessaria' at the *pieve*; it is not recorded whether the mission was successful.[145]

In fact the commune devised its own solution to the problem by paying clergy to minister in their interdicted town, in effect hiring blackleg labour.[146] As early as 27 January 1290 two priests, Bonsignori and Jacobus, appear on the commune's payroll. They had been in its service since at least the start of January, soon after the interdict came into force, at a rate of four *soldi* per day. Their duties included burying the dead, absolving the dying, and baptizing babies born in the town and its county.[147] The latter two practices were of course licit, but an interdict banned burial in consecrated ground except for clergy who died observing the sentence. Ironically the town's exiled clergy later told Nicholas IV that the commune denied their burial rights during the interdict. Hence these priests were probably burying laity. This was licit in unhallowed ground but priests might not officiate at funerals even of clergy. Moreover on 5 March 1290 the commune sent an agent with two horses to fetch two priests to celebrate offices in the *pieve* and

---

[144] Larner, 250; Jones, 438. This grievance is described by Pecori, 122.

[145] ACSG, N.0068 (P.77), fols. 2r (20 March 1290), 11v (payment to four men; 29 April 1290). Notary paid: ACSG, N.0070 (N.N.16), fol. 38r (2 October 1290); same entry copied into ASF, Comune di San Gimignano 177 (unfoliated; among entries for 30 November 1290).

[146] It apparently did the same during an earlier interdict; Pecori, 104.

[147] They were paid for these and other services in February 1290 too; ASF, Comune di San Gimignano 176 (unfoliated; 27 January, 25 February 1290).

elsewhere at its pleasure, which the interdict also prohibited. Indeed the exiled clergy later informed Nicholas that the commune had had offices celebrated or 'rather profaned' by clerks who were not canonically instituted at the *pieve*.[148]

It certainly seems that the blacklegs did not belong to the town or its churches, notably the priest 'Lapus' who came on 21 March 1290 and stayed at the *pieve* for the commune. This admittedly happened the day after the commune sent for a priest from Santa Maria Villacastello, and Lapus's arrival was noted in a register of the commune after this request. Nevertheless it is unlikely that Lapus was an exiled priest who had returned on the provost's orders, for he was on the commune's payroll by 19 March at a similar rate to the other priests in the commune's service. He was clearly an outsider since the commune had to pay for him to be loaned a bed with two sheets, a cover, and pillow![149] Another priest, Iohannes, who was on the commune's payroll by July 1290, was also clothed at its expense; apparently this had also been done for Lapus.[150]

Local Church authorities learned by April 1290 that these priests were working in San Gimignano despite the interdict. Hence the commune had to defend its priestly employees against charges of violating the sentence. For example it sent a notary on 18 April 1290 to appeal to Bishop Rainieri, as he had initiated proceedings against the commune and a priest at its service, subsequently identified as Lapus. The bishop was clearly concerned to enforce his own interdict, and local prelates supported him. The day after the notary approached him, the commune sent two other agents to Florence to beg its bishop's vicar not to molest or trouble Lapus in his work for the commune. According to the commune this involved conferring sacraments and doing baptisms as these were necessary and might not be refused *de iure*.[151] Hence it claimed that its priests were doing no more than canon law permitted during interdicts.

Certainly its records do not substantiate the local clergy's allegation that these priests administered sacraments the interdict prohibited, even to excommunicated and interdicted persons. Early in 1290 the commune had engaged priests expressly to offer sacraments allowed during interdicts, as we have seen. Its records also substantiate its claim that Lapus was mainly doing baptisms. On 29 April 1290 it approved payments to two men for bringing water to fill fonts for baptisms and to another for a big candle lit on Sundays when Lapus was said to perform them.[152] Furthermore it was recorded that the commune twice sought chrism and holy oil. Hostiensis had taught that it was licit to anoint the baptized with

---

[148] Reg. Nicholas IV, no. 3581. ASCG, N.0068 (P.77), fol. 1v (4 March 1290).

[149] ACSG, N.0068 (P.77), fols. 2r (20 March 1290), 7r (19 March 1290), 10v (bedding; 29 April 1290).

[150] ASF, Comune di San Gimignano 178 (unfoliated; salaries to Iohannes and Lapus among monthly expenses for July–November 1290, and clothing allowance for them among September expenses).

[151] ACSG, N.0068 (P.77), fols. 3v (17, 19 April), 11v (payment to notary identifying Lapus; 29 April).

[152] Ibid., fol. 12r. Reg. Nicholas IV, no. 3581.

chrism during interdicts, but priests had to obtain fresh chrism every Maundy Thursday when it was blessed by their bishop, so the commune sent for chrism soon after this date in 1290 and 1291. On 23 March 1290 an agent of the commune went to ask the provost at Santa Maria Villacastello for 'unctionem cum qua fit baptismum'. The provost presumably refused this along with the recent request for a priest to do baptisms, for two days later the commune sent another envoy to seek chrism and holy oil for baptism from a priest even further away. On 28 March 1291 it reimbursed its priest Iohannes and another for fetching chrism and holy oil, probably for baptism. Certainly no evidence suggests that the dying were anointed with chrism in the interdicted town, the sacrament of extreme unction being banned during interdicts.[153]

Nevertheless the commune had solicited priests to perform some ministrations banned by the interdict, notably divine offices. The evidence for regular celebration of the offices is, however, indirect and ambiguous. Late in 1290 local clergy complained that the townsfolk had seized the *pieve* by armed force, throwing stones at its canons' houses, breaking down its doors, and snatching the keys to its bell-tower and sacristy from its clergy. They had then allegedly had the bells rung at all canonical hours and the offices celebrated there. The commune's records indicate that this story was not wholly exaggerated. Certainly the commune seems to have taken control of the *pieve* in January 1290; on 26 March 1290 it paid two men for guarding the *pieve* and its property day and night for over two months.[154] It is surely not coincidental that clergy of the *pieve* also left town by January 1290. The commune's accounts also include frequent wage payments to bell-ringers at the *pieve* from January 1290, but we can only assume that their role was to announce celebration of divine offices. Most of these payments were made for ringing the 'hours' night and day.[155] Apparently this was not simply to mark time but services, since two payments refer to 'customary hours' and another specifies the hours of terce, nones, and vespers. Apparently the *pieve*'s bells also announced the funerals conducted by the commune's priests, for it appointed a Muzzo Manonelli of Celluole on 2 November 1290 to ring them for the dead as well as the hours night and day.[156] He was also required to light lamps and perform other duties for the commune in the *pieve*; apparently he

---

[153] ACSG, N.0068 (P.77), fol. 2v (23, 25 March 1290; the second search for chrism was to Castiglione Fiorentino, 72 km away). ASF, Comune di San Gimignano 181 (unfoliated; 28 March 1291).

[154] Reg. Nicholas IV, no. 3581. ASCG, N.0068 (P.77), fol. 8r (26 March 1290).

[155] ASCG, N.0068 (P.77), fol. 9v (6 April 1290); N.0071 (N.N.20), fols. 26v, 38r (31 August and 28 September 1292); N.0072 (N.N.19), fol. 8r (1 December 1292). All the following are unfoliated: ASF, Comune di San Gimignano 176 (27 January 1290); 182 (29 July, 13 October 1291); 183 (August and October 1291); 187 (23 January, 'de die et nocte tempore rumoris'; 26 January; and January, February, March, and April 1292); 188 (1 September 1292).

[156] Customary hours: ASCG, N.0068, fols. 8r (26 March 1290; at the church of S. Giovanni), 10v (29 April 1290; Muzzo at the *pieve*). Both unfoliated: ASF, Comune di San Gimignano 177 (2 November 1290); 178 ('tercia ora et nona et vesperas'; September 1290).

was the *pieve*'s sacristan and continued in this office at the commune's request from January 1290. It had begun to pay him a monthly salary then for staying in the *pieve* 'ut hactenus consuevit', presumably in the sacristy whose keys the townsfolk had supposedly seized.[157]

It appears that the bells called laity to services at the *pieve* during the interdict, though no hard evidence has been found for these services; records of the commune's payments to its priests mainly describe their duties generically as *servitium communis*. Therefore it apparently disrupted observance of the interdict despite the opposition of local clergy. Its motives for sustaining religious life at San Gimignano were probably pious as well as political. Its podestà and judges, for example, had given three candles weighing 8 lb. to the *pieve* early in 1290 for the feast of the saint after whom the town was named (San Geminiano, 31 January).[158] The townsfolk's capture of the *pieve* and requests for infant baptism also suggest that the commune was responding to popular demand. Local clergy indeed provoked popular resentment by observing the interdict too strictly, and the commune was determined to restrain such anti-clerical feeling. It had set men to guard the *pieve* and its property, doubtless against further attacks of the kind already described. Indeed this suggests that it did not orchestrate the mob attack on the *pieve*. Moreover on 9 February 1290 its general council authorized the podestà to order throughout the *contado* that its inhabitants were not to make a *grida* or *rumor* against priests and clergy or harm their persons or property; otherwise they would face his judgement. Presumably the attack on the *pieve* also occasioned this ruling. It soon came into force: on 16 March 1290 the podestà was empowered to judge accusations of damage to the provost's property. Besides physical attacks the clergy had endured verbal ones, as the ruling of 9 February implied. Indeed it was further proposed on 27 May that the podestà declare throughout the *contado* that no male or female over the age of twelve might sing songs or start rumours about priests or clerks; otherwise they would be fined twenty *soldi* for singing and five for rumours.[159] Clearly the commune sought to pacify aggrieved local clergy; the February ruling was actually proposed on the grounds that clerks were defaming the commune and townsfolk. Such conciliatory measures were doubtless meant to help resolve the dispute with these clergy.

Indeed despite the commune's attempts to break their strike by hiring blackleg priests, it ultimately sought favourable terms with them and the interdict's relaxation. From an early stage both parties petitioned ecclesiastical judges to settle their dispute. As early as 11 January 1290 Bishop Rainieri, who had recently

[157] ASF, Comune di San Gimignano 176 (unfoliated; 27 January 1290).
[158] Ibid. (25 February 1290).
[159] ASCG, N.0069 (N.N.17), fols. 55r–v (9 February), 63v (16 March), 77r (27 May 1290); Davidsohn, *Forschungen*, II, no. 1766. Cf. ibid. no. 623 and Waley, 'Guelfs and Ghibellines', 199, on a similar ban on 'singing songs between Guelfs and Ghibellines' at San Gimignano in February 1252.

imposed the interdict, exhorted the commune to accept the Bishop of Pistoia as arbiter of its differences with the clergy. It presumably agreed to this proposal, since an envoy of the commune was paid twice in February 1290 for going to Pistoia. And on 17 April 1290 a member of the commune was sent there to learn of any progress in its dispute with the clergy. But progress was slow, for the commune continued to send envoys to the Bishop of Pistoia down to October 1291.[160] By this stage he was not the only third party involved. The Bishop of Florence's vicar was already taking action against the commune's priests by 19 April 1290 when the commune appealed to him. He was presumably responding to complaints from the Bishop of Volterra, for on 23 April the commune sent two judges to Florence to defend it against defamatory charges of the bishop's agents and bring accusations against the bishop and the clergy.[161] This war of words merely intensified and prolonged the dispute, and before the end of April it had already been referred to the papal curia.[162]

In fact the commune had been in frequent contact with the curia since December 1289, when the dispute first arose. The nature of its initial contacts is unclear, however, though members of the commune were apparently cited before the curia in January 1290. By 29 April 1290 the commune's records are explicit that its dealings at the curia concerned its dispute with local clergy. Proctors were then being used there to represent both the Eight for the defence, one of the commune's principal governing bodies, and Lapus, whom local church authorities had doubtless denounced to the curia as a 'strike-breaker'. Moreover on 27 May 1290 the Eight for the defence resolved that syndics and proctors be instructed at the curia to defend all members of the commune should any of them be cited there or any injury intended towards them. By September the commune was spending much and often on its dealings at the curia, including the gold florin paid to an advocate for defending the commune 'coram sede appostolicha vel suis auditoribus'. This extraordinary expenditure doubtless prompted the commune to assess its *contado* that month in order to raise 500 pounds in tax from its inhabitants. In late October it held several meetings to authorize payments totalling some 600 gold florins to the lawyers at the curia handling its dispute with local clergy. The commune raised such hefty sums not only by general taxation but by mortgaging all its property, and on 5 December it decided to obtain 500 gold florins by this means to meet its spiralling legal expenses at

[160] See n. 134 on Rainieri's letter. The commune's general council considered the bishop's proposal on 12 January: ASCG, N.0069 (N.N.17), fol. 48r. Envoys to Pistoia: ASCG, N.0068 (P.77), fol. 3v (17 April 1290); ASF, Comune di San Gimignano 176 (25 February 1290); 178 (August, October 1290); 182 (30 September, 13 October 1291); 183 (August 1291). All of these ASF registers are unfoliated.
[161] ASCG, N.0068 (P.77), fols. 3v (19 April), 4r (23 April 1290); Davidsohn, *Forschungen II*, no. 1763.
[162] ACSG, N.0068 (P.77), fols. 11r, 12r (29 April 1290). Expenses arising from contacts with the curia, December 1289–February 1290, are noted *passim* in ASF, Comune di San Gimignano, 176 (unfoliated).

the curia. Accordingly the commune's accounts record frequent payments in late 1290 to messengers and notaries for work concerning its case at the curia, but these only represent the tip of the iceberg. In October 1290 a notary was paid to keep a separate ledger of the commune's expenses arising from its dispute with the local clergy, but this does not appear to have survived; hence the total cost of the commune's case cannot be known.[163]

Nevertheless the commune was clearly expending much effort and money on settling its differences with the clergy, which shows that it took the interdict seriously. But the dispute was not to be resolved quickly or easily. The clergy of San Gimignano had brought serious allegations against the commune which are described in a letter of Nicholas IV addressed to the Bishop of Florence and dated 5 November 1290.[164] That the commune's legal expenses at the curia escalate around this time is no coincidence. The pope recounts that the clergy had recently clamoured and tearfully declared at the curia that the commune persecuted them so much that they had fled. They had done so in January, and probably their account largely portrays the commune's initial reaction to the interdict before it attempted a more conciliatory approach. Indeed the Bishop of Volterra had reprimanded the commune in a letter of 11 January 1290 for doing worse things then than before the interdict.[165] Some of these things have already been noted: the taxing of clergy on goods bought and sold; the ban on paying tithes; the attack on the *pieve*; the hiring of blackleg priests to celebrate the offices and administer banned sacraments there; and the refusal of ecclesiastical burial to local clergy. These clergy had also complained to Nicholas IV that if any of them brought a complaint against a member of the commune, justice was denied and a severe penalty inflicted on both the plaintiff and the notary who drew up his summons against the accused. It was further alleged that the commune forced clerks to appear before its court, and if they resisted, they were arrested and imprisoned in chains. Apart from infringing clerical immunity from lay justice the commune allegedly denied these clergy their legal rights, notably as plaintiffs, and was thus imposing the secular equivalent of excommunication. Like excommunicates the clergy apparently also suffered social exclusion: local labourers were forbidden to live or work on ecclesiastical lands or vineyards; nobody from the town might speak to its priests, visit their churches, or offer them any support or even human kindness (*humanitatis obsequium*). They were also subjected to the burial ban, despite their legal immunity from it during interdicts, as if they were excommunicate.

---

[163] ACSG, N.0069 (N.N.17), fol. 77r (27 May 1290). Expenses: ASF, Comune di San Gimignano, 177 (expenses for 29 November and 5–8, 13, 17, 26, 29–30 December 1290); 178 (September–November 1290); 179 (tax assessment; it tactfully excluded clergy but not labourers on church lands); ASCG, N.0070 (N.N.16), fols. 20r, 21r, 23r–v (meetings in late October), 27r, 28r, 28v (payment to notary), 34r, 35v, 38v, 39r (decision to mortgage property), 40v, 41v, 44r, 44v, 45v.

[164] Reg. Nicholas IV, no. 3581.   [165] See n. 134.

Though these seem apt countermeasures against the Church's sanctions, there is little evidence of them in the commune's records. The only documented instance when the commune tried clerks in its courts during the interdict was when it sought to prosecute those who stripped the *pieve*'s altars in early 1290. But another of the clergy's claims can be tested more fully, namely that the podestà and Eight for the defence forbade every *artifex* of the commune to work for them. In fact these officials instructed four men in January and February 1290 to compel all *artifices* and merchants of the town to swear an oath to serve its priests. This suggests that they were not doing so, but it does not necessarily mean that the commune forbade them to do so and then revoked this ban. The same four men were also told to ask canons of the *pieve* to baptize the townsfolk's children; hence it seems likely that local traders withdrew their services as a spontaneous reaction against clergy doing likewise, and that the commune sought to reconcile these two groups. It even paid a notary in October 1290 for 24 documents instructing local *quasi artisti* to serve the town's clergy.[166] Another clerical allegation finds some support in its records but also seems exaggerated, namely that some of the Eight were defamed as heretics. Some members of the commune, including the Eight, admittedly faced charges at the curia in 1290, but their nature is unclear. Nevertheless the commune was supplying provisions to an inquisitor and his entourage at the local Franciscan convent by October 1290.[167]

Whatever truth lay in the clergy's allegations, Nicholas IV took them seriously enough to instruct the Bishop of Florence to cite the podestà and some named past and present members of the Eight to appear in person at the curia within fifteen days of his summons accompanied by a syndic or proctor representing the commune. If they did not appear by this deadline, the pope would proceed to further spiritual and temporal penalties against them and their *contado*, if necessary invoking the aid of the secular arm in nearby towns. The commune complied; its council agreed on 3 December 1290 to send one or more syndics to Rome to defend the commune and its members, bring counter-accusations against its clergy, and accept papal judgement. A few days later the Eight left for the curia with the commune's syndic, the podestà's proctor, a notary, a porter, and an agent carrying 200 florins to meet their expenses.[168] The proceedings then dragged on for over fourteen months, as the commune's ever-rising expenditure at the curia shows, and the Eight had to answer another papal summons in June 1291. Meanwhile the case between commune and clergy was still being heard by the Bishop of Pistoia; the commune required three sheepskins to record its

[166] ACSG, N.0068 (P.77), fol. 11v (payment to the four men on 29 April 1290); N.0070 (N.N.16), fol. 25v (payment to the notary on 31 October 1290).

[167] ASF, Comune di San Gimignano 177 (unfoliated; 29 November, 16–17 December 1290); ACSG, N.0070 (N.N.16), fol. 34r (2 October 1290); Davidsohn, *Forschungen*, II, no. 1780.

[168] ACSG, N.0070 (N.N.16), fols. 38v, 39r, 40v, 41v, 44v, 45v (3, 5, 21, and 29 December 1290).

progress by December 1290.[169] Ultimately it was not settled by that bishop or the pope but another party.

In March 1292 both sides appointed Scolarius Ardinghelli, Archbishop of Tyre, as arbiter of their dispute and agreed to obey whatever settlement he decided, with the Bishop of Volterra's acquiescence.[170] Presumably they had wearied of their costly and fruitless litigation, and doubtless the clergy also found popular hostility towards them rising as the dispute continued despite the commune's efforts to protect them. Indeed it had ordered the restitution of corn to priests throughout the *contado* in August 1291, which implies that their share of the harvest was withheld, presumably as a protest.[171] Hence clergy and bishop must have particularly welcomed Ardinghelli's intervention. The commune perhaps proposed him as arbiter, as it had sent an ambassador with him to the curia on 21 February 1292, which also suggests that papal approval was sought for his arbitration.[172] In any case he was highly acceptable to both sides: he was born in San Gimignano and hence sensitive to local feelings, while as occupant of a distant see he was untainted by association with their dispute. After he heard and considered what both sides had to say, he gave his decision on 3 April 1292. It ordered the clergy to procure the removal of the interdict, which he identified as the dispute's cause, and absolution of anyone excommunicated in the *contado* because of it. They were also to drop all legal action against the commune or its members at the curia or elsewhere.[173] The commune considered his judgement in its favour so important that it was not only recorded in its *Libro bianco*, a kind of civic cartulary named after its white cover, but also summarized in an inscription painted on the back wall of the council chamber in its new *palazzo comunale*.

Ardinghelli required the clergy to carry out his instructions by the end of May; otherwise they would incur a penalty, and the inscription specifies this as a fine of one hundred silver marks. Despite this threat, they were reluctant to accept his judgement against them. On 12 July 1292, six weeks after the deadline, the commune's general council appointed a syndic to ask the clergy on the commune's behalf to comply with the arbitration. Indeed the clergy had not apparently ceased from legal action against the commune, as Ardinghelli required, for the syndic was also to represent and defend it in litigation regarding

---

[169] Pistoia: ibid. fol. 42r (21 December 1290). Papal summons: ASF, Comune di San Gimignano 184 (general council, c.8–16 June 1291). Expenses at curia: ASF, Comune di San Gimignano 182 (entries for 29 July, 27 August, 30 September, and 13 October 1291); 183 (expenses for July–October 1291).

[170] ACSG, *Libro bianco*, fols. 121v (commune's submission to his arbitration, 28 March 1292), 123r (provost's submission on behalf of clergy, 7 March 1292), 125v (bishop's consent, 23 March 1292).

[171] ASF, Comune di San Gimignano 182 (entries for 27 August 1291); 183 (expenses for September 1291).

[172] ASF, Comune di San Gimignano 187 (payment to ambassador on 23 February 1292).

[173] ASCG, *Libro bianco*, fol. 122r–v. On the inscription summarizing its terms in the *palazzo comunale* see my 'San Gimignano', 295 (photograph), 299–300 (text). It is also reproduced on the dust jacket of this book.

the dispute.[174] Nor, it seems, had they observed Ardinghelli's order to secure relaxation of the interdict. The priest Milliori, whom the commune had hired in March 1292, was still in its service at the usual rate of 4*d*. per day in June,[175] which implies that local clergy were still enforcing the interdict. Even in October and November 1292 it employed the priest Iacobus and a clerk at the Church of S. Matteo to visit the bodies of the dead, ring the hours, and carry out other duties. Presumably local clergy continued to accuse such priests of strike-breaking, for the commune had to send an envoy on behalf of Iacobus to Pistoia at this time, doubtless to defend him against such charges before the bishop there.[176] All of this can only have added to the clergy's unpopularity, and it seems that they feared reprisals: by December 1292 the commune was paying a night watchman to guard the priest Bartholus at Celluole (just outside San Gimignano) 'ne quis malefactor ledat eum'.[177]

Indeed the clergy did not hold out long. On 3 March 1293 at their request the Bishop of Volterra appointed a delegate to settle their differences with the commune; doubtless they thereby hoped to gain a more favourable decision. In response to this delegate's summons of 8 March, the general council decided the next day to appoint one or more syndics to represent the commune before him. On the podestà's advice it also agreed to set up a four-man committee to discuss the issues in dispute.[178] Perhaps this body drew up the proposals that two envoys of the commune had to present to the provost around this time.[179] These included a promise to observe whatever he and his canons wished regarding *decima* (one of the interdict's alleged causes). In return they were to cease all proceedings against the commune and its members before the curia, the Bishop of Volterra, or any delegate of his. Perhaps because of this approach, both sides were soon negotiating terms. On 10 April the general council voted the podestà full authority to make an agreement with the town's clergy and the Bishop of Volterra that respected Ardinghelli's arbitration, notably that the bishop was to lift the interdict and absolve those excommunicated. Accordingly the next day the podestà and council sent a syndic to the bishop to secure removal of these sentences and swear obedience to ecclesiastical mandates for the commune. Terms were not agreed immediately, but on 23 June seven canons of the *pieve* met

---

[174] ASF, Comune di San Gimignano 185; ACSG, N.0071 (N.N.20), fol. 6r; Davidsohn, *Forschungen*, II, no. 1804.

[175] ASF, Comune di San Gimignano 187 (expenses for March, April, and June 1292). May's expenses included payments to agents going to the Bishop of Volterra 'occasione concordie facte inter commune sancti Geminiani et clerum de sancto Geminiano et curte'.

[176] ACSG, N.0072 (N.N.19), fols. 8r, 13v, 22v, 37v; N.0073 (N.N.18), fols. 12v, 23v.

[177] ACSG, N.0072 (N.N.19), fols. 5v, 51r.

[178] ASF, Comune di San Gimignano 195, fol. 12v (letter of 8 March 1293); 191 (general council on 9 March 1293); 192 (payments on 10 February and 7 March 1293 to messengers for taking letters at the podestà's command to the bishop).

[179] ASF, Comune di San Gimignano 195, fol. 24 (*c*.8 March–13 June 1293). Around then the commune also asked the bishop to settle its dispute with the provost over 'novitates' at Gambasso (ibid. fol. 23r).

there with sixteen rectors of local parishes and resolved on behalf of their churches that their agents drop legal action against the commune and its members before the curia and judges acting on papal authority, and that their mandates to these agents be annulled. At the commune's request they gave written confirmation of this accord, which was then copied into the *Libro bianco*.[180]

Therefore, over a year after Ardinghelli's arbitration of their dispute with the commune, the clergy fulfilled one of its main requirements. But it is unclear whether they met another requirement, persuading their bishop to lift his sentences of interdict and excommunication. Certainly payments to blackleg priests no longer feature in the commune's accounts after 1292; thus we might assume that local clergy had returned and resumed their pastoral duties. Admittedly they agreed to abandon their case at the curia, but they still pursued their dispute before the Bishop of Volterra; the commune continued to make representations to him down to 1295. Two of the many references to these in its records suggest that the interdict continued after 1292. In August 1293 the commune paid a notary for drawing up a syndical instrument 'regarding the men interdicted by the lord bishop of Volterra', but this sounds like a sentence on specific individuals rather than the commune as a whole. The other reference is also allusive: in October 1294 the commune reimbursed a man for his expenses 'over the matter of the interdict', specifically for seeking advice from experts in canon law that might aid the commune 'regarding the grievance of the said interdict'.[181] Hence it is hard to say when the interdict and the dispute that caused it ended, although the commune sent an envoy to the Bishop of Volterra in January 1295 'pro facto concordie'. A document of the commune dated 21 March 1295 perhaps marked the final rapprochement of clergy and laity. It was a decree enacted 'for the honour, reverence and preservation of God's holy church and ecclesiastical liberty' binding the commune's podestà and officials to respect ecclesiastical liberty and clerical immunity in perpetuity, and forbidding them and other members of the commune from making or observing any ruling in prejudice of the same. But the commune's violations of the church's freedoms that occasioned the dispute with the clergy, the interdict, and ultimately the decree are not specified.[182] Over a year earlier, in February 1294 the commune had at the provost's request drawn up a ruling on financial dues to the *pieve* that were customary before the dispute. They were probably a key issue in the dispute, but doubtless there were other issues that the decree subsequently tried to resolve.

[180] ASCG, N.0074 (N.N.21), fols. 29v–30r, 31r–v, 42v (general council on 10 and 11 April and 26 June 1293; the last meeting authorized a syndic to receive clergy's undertaking to drop legal action); ASCG, *Libro bianco*, fol. 151r; ASF, Comune di San Gimignano 192 (expenses at Volterra regarding the dispute paid on 23 May and 23 June 1293); Davidsohn, *Forschungen*, II, nos. 1829, 1833.

[181] ASF, Comune di San Gimignano 194 (expenses for August 1293); 199, fol. 41r (October 1294).

[182] Archivio Vescovile di Volterra, Dec. X, no. 12, edited in my 'San Gimignano', 300–1; *Regesta*, ed. Schneider, no. 967. See n. 133 on the envoy of January 1295.

Clearly the commune took the interdict on San Gimignano seriously. The laity resented its withdrawal of spiritual comforts, particularly infant baptism and the final absolution. And even though the commune hired clergy to supply such wants, it still sought to make peace with clergy, observing the interdict and even restrained popular resentment against them. The commune's expenditure in its search for a settlement at the curia, Pistoia, and Volterra shows that it considered the interdict worth being free from. Even after an ecclesiastical arbitrator found in its favour, it was willing to make concessions to the clergy to secure their compliance, and the clergy apparently carried on enforcing the interdict until it did so. But whether lasting peace between commune and clergy was thereby achieved is debatable.

5.4 A TALE OF TWO CITIES: THE INTERDICTS ON DAX AND BÉZIERS

These interdicts are treated together for several reasons. Firstly, parallels and contrasts can be drawn between the towns they affected and reactions they elicited. Both towns lie in south-west France, Dax facing the Atlantic coast, Béziers the Mediterranean. By the time they fell under these interdicts, each had been subject to a distant royal power for under a century. Dax was taken by Henry II of England in 1177 and remained part of English Gascony until its recapture by the French in 1442. By contrast Béziers was part of the Languedoc incorporated in the French royal demesne after 1229 as a result of the Albigensian crusade. Though nominally controlled by agents of their respective rulers, both towns also developed their own self-governing bodies or communes. And the communes of Dax and Béziers reacted strongly to these interdicts.[183] In both cases clergy observing the interdict protested to the curia that the commune persecuted them for doing so and even usurped some of their spiritual functions in order to disrupt observance of the interdict. In doing so each commune opposed the bishop who had his see in its city. In both cases the dispute between commune and clergy was decided and the interdict relaxed through the intervention of a higher power: at Dax its secular overlord, the king of England; at Béziers the highest ecclesiastical authority, the pope. A less happy parallel is that local archives are not as rich for Dax and Béziers as for San Gimignano. But lay reactions to both interdicts are vividly described in contemporary papal letters, though these are based on petitions of aggrieved local clergy and hence describe events from a particular perspective. Nevertheless other views on events are provided by royal records and a civic cartulary for Dax and later accounts for Béziers.

---

[183] On the commune's origins at Dax: *Livre noir*, pp. xvii, xx, xxiii, xxvi–xxviii; De Sauviac, 177, 185–7; Marsh, 2. These historians also treated the interdict at Dax: *Livre noir*, pp. xxxii–xxxiii; De Sauviac, 188–91; Marsh, 106–10.

To begin with Dax, the interdict imposed there by late 1242 was not the first to fall on the town. The nineteenth-century historian of Dax, De Sauviac, recounts that a century earlier Guillaume de Falgars, the city's bishop since 1135, had interdicted his cathedral and other suburban churches. His interdict was provoked by a revolt against him. Its leaders were relatives and friends of a man whom he had excommunicated for seizing episcopal dues; the man had died unrepentant and the bishop's refusal to allow him ecclesiastical burial sparked the revolt. The bishop excommunicated its leaders as well as closing Dax's churches: De Sauviac observed that he punished Dax as if their accomplice (*témoin de cet acte inouï*). He then left Dax. Ultimately townsfolk sought him out begging him to return. On his rapturous reception at Dax he celebrated mass in the cathedral marking the end of his interdict and absolved the penitent rebels.[184]

There are notable parallels between this interdict and that imposed on the city by a later bishop, Navarre de Miossans, elected to the see of Dax in 1239. Firstly, the later interdict was also occasioned by lay opposition to episcopal authority, though its leaders were civic officials asserting communal rights rather than private individuals waging a personal feud. Secondly, Navarre likewise excommunicated the ringleaders, i.e. the officials, and interdicted the city, because its people, so he told the curia, had supported their opposition to him.[185] Indeed this reflected the canonistic teaching that those consenting to a wrong ought to be punished along with the wrongdoers. Thirdly, Navarre also fled from his enemies into exile and following a reconciliation agreed to return to a contrite public reception.

The dispute that provoked this interdict arose between him and the citizens of Dax before August 1242. King Henry III of England, then in Gascony, learned of it by 3 August, when he ordered that it be settled before the seneschal of Gascony, his chief agent in the region, or the viguier of Dax, another royal official, if the seneschal could not attend to it.[186] Although Henry wanted this to be decided 'sine ulteriori questione', his subjects at Dax were reluctant to come to terms. By November 1242 their bishop interdicted the city and excommunicated its officials, namely its *capdellus* or mayor, G. Arnauld de Gos, and justiciars (*iusticiarii*). The dispute that had occasioned these sentences concerned rival jurisdictional claims.[187] According to the bishop the mayor and justiciars had usurped jurisdiction over some men under his lordship and ignored his warnings to respect his rights; consequently he excommunicated these officials for their disobedience and interdicted Dax for backing them. Indeed, in May 1243, when the king intervened more decisively, the bishop identified the dispute's main object as the village of St-Vincent-de-Sentes, where citizens of Dax claimed certain seigneurial rights *de iure et de facto* that he contested. But by then other

---

[184] De Sauviac, 164–6. [185] Reg. Innocent IV, no. 201.

[186] *Rôles Gascons*, no. 590; London, National Archives, C66/52 (Patent roll, 26 Henry III); *CPR 1232–1247*, 337.

[187] As n. 185. On Henry's intervention of May 1243: *Livre noir*, 207–14, esp. 210, 213 on St-Vincent-de-Sentes. See also De Sauviac, 189–90.

issues had intensified the conflict between citizenry and bishop, not least their reaction to his interdict on Dax.

He alleged that the mayor and justiciars had some priests, including one called Durand de Vic, celebrate offices in his cathedral, administer sacraments, and grant the dead ecclesiastical burial under the interdict. These officials allegedly also fined those refusing to associate with these priests and forbade anyone to seek such ministrations from other priests. The bishop's allegations were substantiated when the king and his treasurer Pierre Chaceporc, canon of Poitiers, intervened in the dispute in May 1243. The king noted that the mayor and justiciars had fined those who refused to attend the offices in the interdicted cathedral and instead went to other churches; he ordered that such fines be refunded. Likewise Pierre Chaceporc found that corpses were buried in the cathedral cemetery during the interdict, and he decided that those of persons from other parishes nearby should be exhumed and reburied at their respective churches.

Clearly the dispute had divided the people of Dax but not simply along lay and clerical lines. On the one hand some renegade priests supported the commune against the bishop, violating his interdict. On the other hand some pious laity were unwilling to disobey it, attending churches outside the interdicted city in strict accordance with canonistic doctrine. Apparently such internal divisions only deepened after the Bishop of Bayonne intervened. On behalf of the local metropolitan, the Archbishop of Auch, he warned the mayor and justiciars to stop defying the Bishop of Dax and his interdict and forbade the renegade priests to support them and hold services on pain of eternal damnation and loss of their benefices and offices. When his threats and warnings went unheeded, he renewed the excommunication of the mayor and justiciars and extended it to their supporters, including these priests and other citizens, but to no avail.[188] The civic officials then apparently drove out of the cathedral some Dominicans who came to preach there on All Souls' Day (1 November 1242), and ordered that nobody might receive any sacrament from the cathedral chaplain; otherwise they would be punished. The Bishop of Dax and his archbishop had required this priest to baptize infants, hear confessions of the sick, and administer final communion to the dying. Ironically these canonical exceptions to the interdict's ban on sacraments were meant to curb popular resentment of the sentence. But the mayor and justiciars seemed resolved to supplant the ecclesiastical authorities in providing for the pastoral needs of their citizens during the interdict; these officials allowed only their clerical supporters to minister in Dax.

When these events were reported to the archbishop and his provincial council, they tried imposing their authority where his agent, the Bishop of Bayonne, had failed. They confirmed the bishop's excommunication of 'schismatic' priests and

---

[188] As n. 185. On the pious laity and Henry's instructions below: *Livre noir*, 208–9, 211–12. See p. 197 above on loss of benefices and excommunication as penalties for celebrating in interdicted places.

sent letters to the civic officials and their supporters, exhorting them to return to the unity of the Church within forty days of receiving these. But the Bishop of Dax claimed that their only response to this warning was to seize goods from him and some of his clergy. As we have seen, secular authorities often reacted to an interdict by imposing 'economic' sanctions on clergy observing it. Henry III certainly accepted that this had happened at Dax, for in May 1243 he instructed that the bishop, his chapter, and all his men be reinstated in their houses, revenues, and possessions. The king, nevertheless, implied that both sides in the dispute had suffered depredations, since he also ordered mutual restitution of all goods seized during the conflict. These losses probably occurred in the final most acrimonious stages of the dispute described by the Bishop of Dax.

Mayor G. Arnauld was succeeded by a new *capdellus* called Barthélemy, who intensified the dispute his predecessor instigated. He and his justiciars, so the bishop claimed, threatened to punish anyone giving, selling, or lending anything to clerks or other literate persons who refused to serve in churches under the 'schismatic' priests. Neither was anyone to buy from them, receive them in their homes, or show them any human kindness or familiarity. As at San Gimignano fifty years later, clergy obeying the interdict were to be ostracized in the same way as excommunicates. The commune thus countered the Church authorities' excommunication of its clerical supporters and conversely required citizens to associate with them despite that sentence. Apparently the social exclusion of clergy loyal to the bishop was enforced. The bishop reported that some country people sold them food, presumably in ignorance of the commune's ruling, and were overwhelmed by insults and injuries.

Seemingly it was not the only violence arising from the dispute. According to De Sauviac,[189] a citizen mob also besieged the cathedral canons in their houses facing the church, drove them out by force, and demolished some of their homes. The bishop certainly related that the attack on the country traders prompted him and other clergy to abandon their residences across the Dax and Bayonne dioceses, as they had reason to fear such violence against themselves. Seemingly hostilities also broke out between the commune's and the bishop's supporters, for Henry III observed in May 1243 that prisoners had been taken on both sides; he ordered their release and mutual restitution of goods seized during the conflict (*guerra*). A fatality had even occurred, for Henry's co-arbiter in the dispute, Pierre Chaceporc, heard that the bishop's servants (*valitores*) had killed a man; he clearly believed this since he ordered the bishop to have a priest pray for the man's soul for a year and send a servant on pilgrimage to the Holy Land for the same purpose. De Sauviac claimed on uncertain authority that the victim was renegade priest Durand de Vic and he was killed in the cathedral cemetery. Certainly Durand died under the interdict, and the bishop stated that his fellow excommunicates buried him beside the cathedral; Chaceporc later ordered his

---

[189] De Sauviac, 189.

exhumation and reburial at Divielle Abbey. But neither the bishop nor Chaceporc suggest that he met a violent end. Admittedly Chaceporc required the bishop to 'reconcile', i.e. ritually purify, the cathedral and its cemetery after the interdict, which would be required if violence had been committed there, but he did not give the reason for this and it could equally have been necessitated by burial of excommunicates there, notably Durand himself.[190]

During this ever-worsening dispute both sides looked to higher authorities to resolve it. Shortly after it broke out, Arnauld and his justiciars had tried referring it to the curia, but the bishop excommunicated them and interdicted Dax, considering their appeal groundless.[191] By any means there had been a papal vacancy effectively since Gregory IX's death in 1241. When the bishop himself later sought papal intervention, the new Pope Innocent IV did not respond till 20 October 1243, four months after his election.[192] But in the meantime Henry III had intervened.[193] After his failed attempt to end the dispute in August 1242, he had received a complaint from the men of Dax by December 1242 accusing the bishop of a hostile attack on them, when apparently three of them had been captured and another killed. This was presumably the fatality noted by Chaceporc in May 1243; it was also noted then that captives were held *but* on both sides. Either the men of Dax omitted this inconvenient detail or took prisoners after their complaint to the king. In any case on 15 December 1242 the king cited the men and Bishop of Dax to appear before him on 29 December to air these grievances. It is not recorded whether they appeared, but five days after this deadline Henry set a second hearing for 21 January 1243. The bishop was to appear before him again on 8 February 1243, but in late January he cancelled this hearing and delegated the case to an agent, whom he intended to send to Dax expressly in order to settle the dispute; he also warned the bishop not to harrass the men of Dax in the meantime. The agent was apparently unsuccessful, since fresh allegations had reached Henry by April 1243, this time from clergy of Dax. The mayor and justiciars apparently prevented cultivation of their vineyards and other lands; thus Henry ordered these officials on 19 April to stop doing this lest the clergy be deprived of produce.[194] Presumably, as at San Gimignano, this economic sanction was enforced by forbidding labourers to work on ecclesiastical estates and designed to discourage clergy from observing the interdict.

On 19 April 1243 Henry also promised the mayor and justiciars that he would resolve their differences with the clergy on reaching Dax. Four weeks later

---

[190] *Livre noir*, 209, 211 (prisoners); 210, 213–14 (Chaceporc's judgement).

[191] As n. 185.

[192] The vacancy after Gregory's death on 22 August 1241 was only interrupted by Celestine IV's brief pontificate (elected 25 October; died 10 November 1241) before Innocent's election on 25 June 1243.

[193] As n. 186. *Rôles Gascons*, no. 1591 (15 December 1242); London, National Archives, C54/55 (Close roll, 27 Henry III); *CCR 1242–1247*, 58.

[194] *Rôles Gascons*, nos. 952 (19 April), 1196 (3 January), 1201 (*c*.21–31 January 1243); London, National Archives, C66/53 (Patent roll, 27 Henry III); *CPR 1232–1247*, 374, 399.

he arrived and proposed that both sides submit to his arbitration in temporal matters and to Pierre Chaceporc's in spiritual matters.[195] Both sides agreed and offered guarantees to abide by this agreement before various ecclesiastical dignitaries on 15 May. Ten days later, on 25 May 1243, Henry and Chaceporc gave their judgement. Many of its terms have already been described: restititution of the bishop and chapter's property; surrender of goods and people seized by both sides; reimbursing of fines levied on those avoiding illicit services at the cathedral; exhumation of Durand de Vic and others buried there and their reburial elsewhere; and obligations on the bishop to reconcile the cathedral cemetery and atone for the murder attributed to his servants. The king further ordered that the commune compensate the bishop and chapter for damages, paying the former 120 *livres morlans* and the latter 100 *livres*, to be shared among the canons and other deserving persons at the discretion of the bishop and the minister of the Franciscans at Dax. These sums had to be paid by Michaelmas (29 September), while Henry's other conditions had to be fulfilled as early as Pentecost (31 May). Apparently the reburial of Durand de Vic and others was to be conducted promptly, as Chaceporc made this a precondition for the bishop's return to Dax. He also specified the arrangements for the latter and these strikingly recall the reconciliation of Navarre's predecessor Guillaume de Falgars to his flock following an interdict a century earlier. The community of Dax was to meet Bishop Navarre as he approached Dax in order to beg his forgiveness and lead him to his cathedral. Extraordinarily, though Chaceporc did not apparently act on higher ecclesiastical authority, he required the bishop to absolve G. Arnauld and other officials running the city during the dispute, as well as the rest of its citizens and their supporters. Mass was then to be celebrated, signifying the relaxation of the interdict. Guillaume de Falgars had performed such acts voluntarily, but Navarre was obliged to do so. Chaceporc also made demands on Dax's citizens: they and their neighbours had to pay tithes and ecclesiastical dues as they had done in the past. Evidently these were withheld during the interdict, presumably as one of the commune's sanctions against clergy observing it. Finally Henry and Chaceporc required both parties to obey their arbitration on pain of a thousand marks payable to the king.

But this arbitration did not settle the dispute that provoked the interdict. Henry left this to a commission of six citizens of Dax and six knights from outside Dax, who had to investigate the bishop's alleged jurisdictional rights over St-Vincent-de-Sentes that the commune disputed and decide the issue in the king's name by the Michaelmas deadline. Whether the arbitration led to peace between bishop and town is unclear. On 20 October, five months later, Innocent IV addressed the bishop's complaints against the commune.[196] Probably these were submitted to the curia before May, for he does not mention the arbitration. The

[195] *Livre noir*, 207–14 (25 May), 396–400 (15 May 1243).   [196] As n. 185.

papal vacancy to 25 June and Innocent's subsequent involvement in more urgent matters, notably his conflict with Frederick II, had clearly delayed this papal response. It was addressed to the Bishop, Archdeacon, and sacristan of Oloron, a see near Dax and subject to the same metropolitan. They were instructed to have Bishop Navarre's excommunication and interdict observed and renewed until clerical grievances were satisfied and Dax's mayor and justiciars sought absolution at the curia. Moreover clergy celebrating offices under the interdict were to be punished canonically and bodies of excommunicates exhumed from cemeteries; if necessary the aid of the secular arm was to be invoked. In fact the lay power had already intervened, giving the commune similar instructions to make amends to the clergy and disinter an excommunicate and others illicitly buried. Indeed the king's arbitration had required that differences between clergy and commune be settled by Michaelmas, three weeks before the pope's response; hence the latter was probably redundant. Nevertheless it ended by ordering its addressees to annul any settlement that was illicit or injurious to the bishop and clergy of Dax. It is doubtful that this was a cryptic allusion to the royal arbitration, but these instructions implicitly allowed for its revocation. His addressees might indeed have found such royal intervention in ecclesiastical affairs questionable, but since Dax's clergy had to turn to the king for justice in the absence of a pope and won favourable terms, the arbitration probably brought a lasting settlement. Certainly no further references to the dispute have been found, and the Bishop of Dax doubtless lifted his interdict once the necessary reparations were made.

A further royal intervention perhaps helped turn the May truce between clergy and commune into more lasting peace.[197] In September 1243 Henry ordered reform of Dax's administration. The *capdellus* and twenty justiciars that had apparently formed its government since the twelfth century were replaced by a mayor and twenty *jurati*. Citizens might elect the *jurati* and nominate three candidates for mayor annually, but the final choice of mayor lay with the seneschal of Gascony, the king's chief agent in the region. This measure was designed to increase royal control and improve stability by preventing concentration of power in the hands of any one faction. The *capdellus* G. Arnauld had indeed tried to expand the commune's jurisdiction and not only at the expense of the bishop but also of local nobility. In late 1242, after the dispute between bishop and commune had arisen, the knights of Dax had complained to Henry III that they were required to appear before the *capdellus* and justiciars in lawsuits.[198] On 26 December 1242 the king had ordered these civic officials to desist and confirmed the custom that the knights were subject only to his or his seneschal's

[197] *Rôles Gascons*, no. 1230 (9 September 1243); London, National Archives, C66/53 (Patent roll, 27 Henry III); *CPR 1232–1247*, 406. Marsh, 106–10; cf. ibid. 102–6 on a similar royal intervention around this time at Bayonne.

[198] *Rôles Gascons*, no. 1291 (26 December 1243); London, National Archives, C54/55 (Close Roll, 27 Henry III); *CCR 1242–1247*, 7. On the knights' role in the arbitration: *Livre noir*, 209–10, 212–13, 397, 398.

court. Hence these officials tried to exercise jurisdictional powers claimed by both king and bishop; this makes royal reorganization of the commune all the more understandable. The knights' dispute further indicates that divisions at Dax did not fall along lay and clerical lines. The Bishop and knights of Dax were united by their grievances against the commune, and the interdict arguably helped to consolidate if not forge this alliance. The bishop's lay allies during his interdict certainly included knights, for when he and his chapter swore to observe the royal arbitration on pain of 1000 marks, five knights, described as citizens of Dax, stood as guarantors of this sum. Furthermore Henry's decision to appoint six knights and six citizens to settle the dispute between bishop and commune was surely motivated by a concern to balance the commission in favour of both sides. Thus, even if the commune defied the interdict, the sentence influenced or reinforced a powerful section of public opinion against it; consequently the king intervened and reduced its autonomy. Indeed after his reform a mayor friendly to episcopal interests was elected. Arguably the interdict at Dax was, therefore, ultimately effective.

The interdict on Béziers some fifty years later was also caused by the city's commune extending its powers at local clergy's expense, in fact literally so for the issue at stake was lay taxation of church property. The Fourth Lateran Council (1215) had ruled that this was not licit without papal approval; lay rulers who compelled clergy to pay taxes faced anathema. But increasingly secular rulers taxed clergy in their lands with papal acquiescence; later thirteenth-century popes even assigned clerical taxes intended for crusades to kings who then used them for other purposes. Communes emerging across Europe since the twelfth century followed kings in disregarding clerical freedom from lay taxation. This possibly caused the interdict at San Gimignano, and lay resentment of this clerical privilege had certainly arisen at Béziers by 1283,[199] when the 'consuls' who governed Béziers complained about minor clergy abusing it. Apparently married clerks and others who had been tonsured but exercised an 'artem mechanicam' rather than church office refused to contribute to royal and civic taxes without papal consent. The consuls sought royal intervention, especially regarding property formerly subject to lay taxes but now in the dead hand of the Church. Béziers was subject to the French king, and in July 1283 he convened a *parlement*, the supreme tribunal of his realm, at Carcassone; petitions submitted to it included this request from nearby Béziers. Royal judges ruled that clerks living at Béziers 'non clericaliter' might be compelled to pay taxes, and if their bishop objected, the issue should be referred back to *parlement*. He probably objected, for a *parlement* at Carcassone in 1284 heard that local prelates and their officials (their deputies in judicial matters) tried to protect 'clericos mercatores', even married ones, from paying royal and civic taxes. It was apparently customary for their

---

[199] Langlois, 'Rouleaux', 198–9, 206; Given, 143. Lateran ruling: X 3.49.7.

fathers and predecessors to pay these; hence this *parlement* ruled that such clerks should not be excused from doing so. The seneschal of Carcassone, the principal royal agent in the region, apparently enforced this ruling in Béziers diocese too strictly, for the king ordered him on 15 June 1292 to stop making certain clerks there pay taxes at the will of the city's consuls. The king was doubtless responding to renewed protests from local Church authorities. Ironically in subsequent years the greatest lay attack on this clerical immunity was made by the king. As is well known, Philip IV introduced many taxes to fund a war against England, and French clergy came under increasing pressure to contribute. In 1294–5 he won clerical concessions to his tax demands at ecclesiastical assemblies across his kingdom.[200] Clergy of Narbonne province, which included Béziers diocese, even met at Béziers to approve additional royal subsidies in the spring of 1296. However, the issue of clerical taxation was soon brought to a head at a national and local level by Boniface VIII's famous bull 'Clericis laicos'.

It forbade lay taxation of ecclesiastical wealth without papal consent. It merely reaffirmed the earlier Lateran ruling admittedly, but it also reacted against subsequent political developments, notably recent clerical concessions to royal tax demands in both England and France. It partly responded to long-standing grievances of clergy who felt that such encroachments undermined their privileged status, as in Béziers diocese. It can also be seen as a naïve attempt to halt the Anglo-French war, for which clerical taxes were needed, and thereby reassert the papacy's traditional role in keeping peace between Christians. It was not only provocative at the level of high politics. Besides threatening excommunication on rulers who violated its terms (echoing the Lateran ruling's anathema), it also proclaimed an interdict on corporations that did so.[201] This challenged communes like Béziers. Its consuls claimed customary powers to tax local church property; an inquiry ordered by the French king on 1 January 1296 had found in their favour.[202] Ironically 'Clericis laicos' was drawn up around then, being dated 25 February 1296 in the papal register, but its impact was not immediate, for the pope delayed its promulgation until April 1296. News of it then spread quickly and copies of it gradually circulated in France. The Bishop of Béziers later informed the pope that it was publicized in his diocese and his official had even had it copied for the consuls so they could not claim ignorance of it.[203] Nevertheless they defied it, levying taxes on church property, even compelling

---

[200] Denton, 'Ecclesiastical Assemblies'; id. 'Taxation', esp. 241–4. Martin-Chabot, p. 111, no. 563 (15 January 1292).

[201] Reg. Boniface VIII, no. 1567; Po. 24291.

[202] 'Mémoire des consul de besiers', pp. 1–2; Montpellier, Archives départementales de l'Hérault G765. The handwritten 'Mémoire' is one of several dossiers in G765 compiled in the eighteenth century when another dispute arose at Béziers over civic taxation of church property. The dossiers refer to the dispute of 1296–8 and usefully cite documents now lost, notably the royal mandate of 1 January 1296. The 'Mémoire' relates that the latter was addressed to the seneschal of Carcassone, who with the royal judge of Béziers held this inquiry involving 49 witnesses.

[203] Reg. Boniface VIII, no. 2140 (7 October 1297).

some clergy to pay by seizing their goods. They were determined to exercise their customary right upheld by the recent royal inquiry, and their position paralleled Philip IV's, who was equally opposed to 'Clericis laicos'. Indeed, according to an eighteenth-century account, letters patent of the king dated 23 January 1297 required the seneschal of Carcassone and Béziers to compel local clergy to pay taxes on their property. If these clergy complained to the Church authorities, the seneschal was to have their temporalities confiscated; seemingly the consuls executed these letters by seizing goods of clergy who refused to pay them taxes.[204] Hence their defiance of 'Clericis laicos' began after 23 January but before October 1297 when the pope had learned of it.[205]

The city's cathedral chapter apparently reacted by seeking a fresh inquiry into the consuls' taxative powers, but this time under ecclesiastical auspices.[206] Mediators of the consuls and canons met in the latter's chapter house under the arbitration of the Archdeacon of Cabrières. Aided by two professors of canon and civil law they tried to determine whether civic taxes might be levied on ecclesiastical property, and whether the consuls might force clergy to pay them. This attempt at mediation failed, however. Although the consuls agreed to return goods seized from clergy for the sake of peace, they denied having done wrong or violating 'Clericis laicos'. A principle was at stake for both consuls and clergy, and neither side wished to compromise. Hence the Church authorities judged that the consuls were excommunicated and Béziers was interdicted under 'Clericis laicos'. Local clergy observed these sentences till May 1298 when the dispute was finally resolved.

The consuls and populace apparently defied these sentences to such an extent that the Bishop of Béziers, Bérenger Frédol, had to seek papal intervention. Boniface VIII's response is recorded in two lengthy papal letters dated 7 and 13 October 1297 respectively and preserved in his registers.[207] They contain the only extant account of lay reactions to the Béziers interdict; hence they must be treated with caution. Firstly, the poor survival of civic documents at Béziers for this period means that we have no secular sources against which to test these Church records as at San Gimignano. They might exaggerate lay hostility, especially when it was reported to the pope in order to secure his intervention. Secondly, the account in the first letter is based on the petition of the Bishop of Béziers, and while the second letter does not specify the source of its allegations, they probably came from him. But it is doubtful

---

[204] From the first page of a handwritten dossier titled 'Arret du Conseil de Renvoy en la Cour d'entre le maire et comune de la ville de Beziers et la Chapitre St. Nazaire de la dite ville. Extrait du Registre du Conseil d'Etat' (dated 9 August 1751) in Montpellier, Archives départementales de l'Hérault G765; St Nazaire was Béziers Cathedral. The contemporary 'Mémoire' (see n. 202), p. 2, alludes to several such letters sent by Philip to the seneschal of Carcasssone and Béziers in 1297 and 1298.

[205] See n. 203.   [206] Soucaille, 'Institutions Municipales', 236.

[207] Reg. Boniface VIII, nos. 2140–1. The second letter was edited by Raynaldus, *Annales*, xiv.513b–14a, and Du Plessis, *Collectio*, i.125; enregistered in ASV, Reg. Vat. 48, fol. 319r.

whether he witnessed the events he described, since he resided at the curia from November 1296 till early 1298. Apparently he was also absent from his see before November 1296, since he attended a synod of French clergy at Paris over the summer of 1296. He then went to Rome on the synod's behalf to obtain papal consent for royal taxation of the French Church as 'Clericis laicos' required.[208] Ironically it was during his absence on this business that the dispute broke out in his diocese over 'Clericis laicos'; tellingly his official brought the bull to the consuls' attention, not him. After his arrival in Rome, Boniface enlisted his collaboration on the *Liber sextus*, which prolonged his absence until shortly before its promulgation on 3 March 1298. The consuls clearly exploited this situation, and it doubtless contributed to their bald defiance of the interdict. As the saying goes, when the cat is away, the mice will play. Indeed the dispute at Béziers was not resolved nor the interdict lifted until after the bishop's return in early 1298.

According to the first papal letter the interdict's immediate effect was to make the consuls even more defiant of 'Clericis laicos', as they continued their campaign of confiscating church property to coerce clergy to pay taxes. During interdicts when the issue was not taxation secular rulers also seized the clergy's goods to discourage them from observing the sentence. The consuls perhaps shared this aim, as they apparently ensured that the interdict was not strictly enforced at Béziers. First, they allegedly had hosts seized from clergy and taken to the town hall. It is uncertain whether these were distributed in defiance of the interdict. Perhaps the consuls simply had them displayed for popular veneration, although Church authorities might still find this provocative, as Florentine councillors found eighty years later when they urged exposition of the host in their interdicted city.[209] Even if the consuls did not technically violate the interdict in this way, they allegedly did in another. They were said to have had the city's dead brought for burial in or close to the cemeteries of local churches and religious houses. Apparently crosses were carried before the funeral processions, and church bells were rung and citizens loudly chanted 'Kyrie eleison, Christe eleison' and 'Pater noster', as clergy did at funerals. Of course an interdict forbade Christian burial except for clerks who died observing it, and it even banned such solemnities at their funerals. Boniface VIII responded by ordering exhumation of bodies buried in contempt of this interdict; they were to be taken so far from churches that voices of clergy chanting offices could not be heard in places where they were dumped.

The pope reacted even more sternly to reports that unorthodox views underlay the consuls' defiance. The bishop claimed that when he threatened to interdict Béziers if they continued to tax clergy, one leading citizen allegedly responded that he and his fellow citizens did not care as the city was already interdicted and added that they had never been as happy and life had never been as good as during

---

[208] See Schmidt, 'Papst Bonifaz VIII', 227–8.   [209] Trexler, 123–7.

the interdict. This man was described as *consiliarius* of the consuls; doubtless his subversive views reflected theirs. When another *consiliarius* called Jacques Amelii was asked how he dared defy 'Clericis laicos', he apparently expressed even greater contempt for church authority, retorting with foul words that he would do nothing for the Roman pontiff. Boniface's first letter responded by ordering the local metropolitan, the Archbishop of Narbonne, to investigate these allegations. If he found that the consuls had taxed and seized clerical property; he was to enforce the interdict on Béziers. The consuls, their *consiliarii*, and other guilty citizens were to give satisfaction within a month of being warned, which presumably meant restitution of this property; otherwise the archbishop was to have it proclaimed throughout his province that they were to be shunned as excommunicates. He was also to identify the main ringleaders and summon them and Jacques Amelii to appear in person before the pope within two months. Boniface specifically suspected Amelii of unorthodoxy because of his anti-papal outburst. Indeed five years later he would state in his famous bull 'Unam sanctam' (1302) that obedience to the pope was essential to human salvation.[210] Apparently by 1297 he already equated opposition to papal authority with heresy: his second letter ordered the inquisitor for the Carcassone region to investigate Béziers for heresy.

This letter invites even less trust than the first because of its colourful rhetoric and extreme allegations. Firstly, it stated that several citizens of Béziers had aroused suspicions through their words and deeds that they wished to imitate their forefathers' wickedness. This referred to the Cathar heresy that flourished in the Languedoc until it was largely crushed by the early thirteenth-century Albigensian crusade. Indeed the letter added that these citizens ignored the fact that their ancestors had been punished by the sword for their wickedness and persecution of churches. This may specifically refer to the crusaders' massacre of the city's inhabitants in 1209; Simon de Montfort, military leader of the Albigensian crusade, had notoriously justified the indiscriminate attack with the claim that 'God would know his own'. The crusaders had slaughtered Catholics as suspected Cathars, and Boniface's belief that Catharism was resurgent at Béziers was equally misguided, as we will see.

Secondly, this letter stated that the citizens sought to overthrow ecclesiastical liberty by levying extraordinary taxes on churches and seizing the persons and goods of clergy by force. They apparently pressed clergy to accept statutes and agreements requiring them to pay these dues; this may refer to the royal letters of 23 January 1297 which stipulated this. They had consequently incurred excommunication and interdict under 'Clericis laicos' but apparently scorned these papal sentences in contempt of the keys. The letter described examples

---

[210] Extrav. comm. 1.8.1. Cf. Innocent III's decretal 'Vergentis' (1199), which famously equated heresy with treason (X 5.7.10); see my 'Punishment of the Guiltless', 272–8, and other literature on 'Vergentis' cited there.

of this which resemble those in the first letter, and they probably came from the same source, the Bishop of Béziers. Some of the citizens apparently claimed that things were better for them during the interdict than any other time; the first letter attributed similar remarks to a nameless *consiliarius*. They added that their food had lost none of its flavour and they had lost no sleep because of their excommunication. Such remarks suggested to Boniface that the citizens abhorred the sacraments forbidden by interdict and excommunication. Some of them allegedly had unorthodox attitudes towards church authority, since they said the vilest things about the papacy; this may refer to comments attributed to Jacques Amelii in the first letter. They had even appealed to the temporal power to remove the excommunication and interdict, although this was reserved to the spiritual power which laid these sentences. Hence, Boniface observed, the citizens acted as if the Church did not have the 'power to bind and to loose'; he meant this in the jurisdictional sense as the power to impose and remove canonical penalties.[211] Boniface added that some citizens had remained obdurate for two years or more under excommunication (presumably imposed before 'Clericis laicos'). He concluded that the behaviour of the citizenry smacked of heresy. Hence he instructed the inquisitor for the Carcassone region that if he found that these allegations were true, he was to prosecute suspected heretics at Béziers 'lest the weeds of heretical destruction are allowed to spread to the death of the catholic seed'.[212]

It is doubtful that the hostility to the interdict at Béziers was symptomatic of a Cathar revival, even if we accept the problematic evidence of these letters. Admittedly unorthodox views were reported, but the Bishop of Béziers attributed them to only two individuals albeit ones influential with the consuls, and Boniface perhaps distorted the evidence by crediting such opinions to groups of citizens in his second letter. It is thus questionable whether they were widely held at Béziers, and even if they were reported accurately, which is doubtful, they were not necessarily views of heretics. Apparently the religious rites that continued under the interdict had a popular following and hence might say more about the orthodoxy of the majority at Béziers. Chanting of the 'Pater noster' at funerals, for example, parallels its constant recitation by Cathar *perfecti*, but this practice 'was not unknown to thirteenth-century [orthodox] piety'.[213] In any case elaborate public funerals went against the Cathar dualist belief that the physical body was the creation of an evil God; hence Cathars were said to inter their dead at night in unconsecrated ground without ritual.[214] Appropriation of hosts also hardly

[211] Cf. Tierney, 30–6.
[212] ASV, Reg. Vat. 48, fol. 319r: 'officium inquisitionis heretice pravitatis in eadem civitate sic solerter studeas exercere ut perfidie filiis vipereis morsibus contra deum et eius sponsam ecclesiam insultantibus tamquam materni uteri corrosoribus, per quorum seductionem mundus inficitur et per eos velut per oves morbidas gregi fidelium gravior infligitur corruptela, exterminatis et penitus profugatis, heretice labis zizania non permittatur in necem catholici seminis pervagari'.
[213] Lambert, 106–11, 119 (quotation).   [214] Dossat, 'Cathares', 79, 80–1.

accorded with Cathar belief, which considered the Eucharist mere bread not the *corpus Christi*. Citizens probably revered the Eucharist, despite Boniface's claim that they scorned the sacraments. Indeed their participation in traditional religious rites during the interdict suggests that though they defied ecclesiastical authority, they were at least outwardly orthodox. Moreover Catharism had largely disappeared in the Languedoc by 1297.[215] After its last major stronghold had fallen there in 1243, the inquisition had gradually rooted out the heresy in southern France. By the 1270s most Cathar *perfecti* had fled persecution there to safer havens in northern Italy. Nevertheless the unceasing activity of inquisitors in the Languedoc provoked popular resentment which Church authorities might have interpreted as sympathy for heretics. At Carcassone a plot was supposedly hatched in 1284 to seize and destroy inquisition records and in 1295 citizens ran their inquisitor out of town and assaulted his fellow Dominicans.[216] Later events at nearby Béziers can only have confirmed official suspicions that Catharism still thrived in the area. Furthermore the Languedoc was home to radical Franciscan thinker Jean Pierre Olivi (d. 1296), whose strict views on Franciscan poverty had provoked conflict in his order and papal censure. Although officially rehabilitated by his death, he remained a focus for Spiritual Franciscans and attracted particular support at the Béziers convent. Indeed most nineteenth-century historians of Béziers and the Languedoc linked local sympathy for Olivi with Boniface VIII's decision to send the inquisition to Béziers.[217]

Boniface perhaps also had another motivation: he was determined to show that 'Clericis laicos' was not a dead letter despite considerable hostility to it in Béziers and elsewhere. Admittedly out of political expediency he had conceded in his bull 'Etsi de statu' (31 July 1297) that the French Crown might tax clergy without papal consent if it considered that a national emergency existed. But this only released the French king from observing 'Clericis laicos'. It still bound other lay powers, including the consuls of Béziers. This was shown by its reissue in the *Liber sextus* (March 1298), which the Bishop of Béziers helped to compile.[218] Arguably Boniface had already demonstrated its continuing force at Béziers in October 1297 by threatening the inquisition against those scorning 'Clericis laicos' and its penalties, notably the interdict. This threat was apparently effective, for the consuls came to terms in early 1298. Doubtless they were no longer confident of royal support. Admittedly the king had condemned inquisitors for persecuting innocent Catholics at Carcassone in May 1297, ordering its seneschal not to arrest such persons on mere suspicion of heresy. But after Boniface issued the constitution 'Ut inquisitionis' in the *Liber sextus*, requiring

---

[215] Lambert, 126–46, esp. 133–8; Dossat, 'Cathares', 75–7.

[216] Davis, 51–9; Given, 231.

[217] On Olivi: Burr; Lambert, 192–4. On alleged support for him at Béziers: Julia, 230–1; Sabatier, 274–5; De Vic and Vaisette, ix.199–200; *Histoire de Béziers*, 122–7.

[218] VI 3.23.3. Contemporary canonists certainly recognized its legal force, even in the French schools: Izbicki, 'Clericis laicos', esp. 181–3. On 'Etsi de statu' see Denton, 'Taxation', 249–53.

lay powers to cooperate with the inquisition, Philip called for observance of this ruling throughout his realm including Carcassone.[219] Boniface won his support by exempting him from 'Clericis laicos'. This allowed him to tax French clergy but did not necessarily predispose him towards local lay powers seeking to do the same. After royal taxes were levied on the lands of the Bishop of Béziers by virtue of Boniface's concession, Philip declared in a letter to all justiciars of his kingdom on 11 October 1297 that this did not derogate the traditional freedoms of the bishop and his lands.[220]

Nevertheless the terms that the consuls of Béziers initially offered the clergy did not imply submission to 'Clericis laicos'.[221] Eighteenth-century accounts claimed that the consuls agreed on 8 January 1298 to restitute goods seized from the clergy in order to secure absolution from excommunication and relaxation of the interdict. But they made it clear that they were not conceding an extension of clerical freedom at the expense of civic rights; in other words they were not prepared to abandon their claims to tax church property. Their terms were essentially those they had offered before the Archdeacon of Cabrières at the start of the dispute. The chapter of Béziers had rejected those terms then and enforced the interdict, and it had probably not come to find them acceptable in the meantime. Furthermore its bargaining position was strengthened by its bishop's return. He probably arrived in Béziers by early 1298, after completing his work on the *Liber sextus*. He certainly intervened in the dispute between consuls and clergy by May 1298, and this doubtless prompted the consuls to grant more generous terms, including acceptance of 'Clericis laicos'.

According to a nineteenth-century historian of Béziers,[222] the bishop Bérenger Frédol sought papal absolution for the consuls, offering assurances that they repented seizing clerical property. Doubtless his recent service at the curia partly accounted for Boniface's favourable response to his petition. Apparently the pope instructed Gerald Cardinal Bishop of Sabina to consider the consuls' plea for reconciliation. Gerald was told that they had promised to make restitution of goods seized from clergy in lieu of taxes and give them satisfaction for other losses incurred. Restitution and satisfaction were of course canonical preconditions for

---

[219] VI 5.2.18. On Philip's attitude to the inquisition at Carcassone: Paris, BN, Doat MS 32, fols. 264r–v (25 March 1296), 266r–7r (5 May 1297), 272v–4v ('Ut inquisitionis'), 275v–9v (*Vidimus* of the same; 6 February 1299), 280r–1v (order that the same be observed throughout the realm; 6 September 1298).

[220] Paris, BN, Doat MS 62, fol. 263v: 'nolumus quod dictis hominibus vel episcopo predicto possit in futurum preiudicium aliquod generari nec in dictis locis et terra sue ecclesie aliquam servitutem seu onera propter hoc imponere, non intendentes occasione dicte subventionis quocumque nomine censeatur libertatibus [vel] immunitatibus dicti episcopi terreque sue ... in aliquo derogare.' This was sent from Flanders where he needed such revenue to fund a campaign against an English invasion backed by the Flemish.

[221] Described in the 'Mémoire' (see n. 202), pp. 3–4, and 'Arret' (see n. 204).

[222] Soucaille, 'Institutions municipales', 236–9. Soucaille quotes at length the documents discussed here but unhelpfully gives their source as 'un unstrumen sur parchemin' that has proved impossible to trace. The 'Mémoire', p. 4, also refers to these documents.

absolution. On 13 May 1298 Gerald thus instructed a Raymond du Puy that once the consuls fulfilled these, as they promised, he might absolve them from excommunication and relax the interdict. Raymond was Bishop of Agde and like Bérenger a suffragan of the Archbishop of Narbonne. Hence Bérenger could again exploit his connections to help resolve the situation. Indeed he wrote to Raymond on 23 May that the consuls had made the required restitution and satisfaction; hence he requested that Raymond absolve them and lift the interdict in accordance with Gerald's mandate, provided that they or their proctor swore an oath before him to obey ecclesiastical mandates. Raymond replied a day later, on 24 May, that he intended to lift the interdict but first required proctors of the consuls to swear that the consuls would not violate 'Clericis laicos' but observe it in future. Indeed the consuls appointed proctors a week later, on 31 May, to ask him to remove sentences imposed on them and Béziers by 'Clericis laicos'. Presumably they gave the required oaths and the interdict was relaxed as a result. Raymond was certainly confident of a reconciliation on 24 May when he allowed Bérenger to admit the consuls, *consiliarii*, proctors, and citizens of Béziers to divine offices and the sacraments, notwithstanding the sentences of excommunication and interdict.

Evidently it concerned Bérenger that his diocese had fallen into such disorder, even alleged heresy, and he was anxious to prevent this reoccurring. Shortly after the *Liber sextus* appeared and he returned to Béziers, he compiled a treatise of instances in canon law where excommunication and interdict were incurred automatically; this naturally included 'Clericis laicos'. His treatise was designed, he wrote in its preface, 'for the common utility of all clergy and laity, especially our subjects, that they might avoid the ties' of these sentences.[223] He addressed it to the abbots, priors, rectors, and chaplains of his diocese, requiring that at least twice a year priests proclaim in every parish church in his diocese those instances where its laity might incur such sentences. Clearly he did not intend his subjects to forget the consequences of violating 'Clericis laicos' or other papal rulings, many of which he and his collaborators had included in the *Liber sextus* along with 'Clericis laicos'. Admittedly Clement V revoked 'Clericis laicos' and its penalties in 1306 as part of his conciliatory policy towards lay powers, but the clergy of Béziers remained defensive of their privileged status and were again resisting royal and civic taxes by the 1350s. Thus when the interdict at Béziers ceased in 1298, the tensions between its commune and clergy remained.[224]

Did any of our three interdicts actually work? According to canon law and canonists, how an interdict was meant to work was that clergy withdrew most of the sacraments, suspended divine offices, and refused ecclesiastical burial. In

---

[223] *Bérenger Frédol*, 24–5, 53 ('Clericis laicos'). On Bérenger and the interdict: Viollet, 'Bérenger Frédol', 71–2.

[224] Reg. Clement V, no. 906; incoporated in canon law as Clem. 3.17.un. Soucaille, 'Institutions municipales', 250 ff.; Pascal, 'Béziers', 110–13.

this sense the interdicts on our three towns largely worked, for most clergy observed them. However, the lay powers who occasioned these sentences tried to disrupt their enforcement. At Dax and San Gimignano civic authorities enlisted renegade priests to continue ministrations to the laity, including ecclesiastical burial. Laity even performed clerical functions by conducting funerals at Béziers. Nevertheless such defiance indicates that laity keenly felt the deprivations of these interdicts, notably at San Gimignano, even if at Béziers some allegedly expressed indifference. But this does not necessarily mean that these interdicts worked by turning popular resentment of their privations against the guilty. Conversely they appear to have turned laity against clergy observing these sentences, even provoking mob attacks on canons at Dax and San Gimignano as well as popular derision of clergy at Béziers and possibly San Gimignano. But commentators tend to note defiance rather than obedience to interdicts. Certainly the interdict at Dax elicited various responses; some laity obeyed it. No doubt this was also true at San Gimignano and Béziers though it went unrecorded. The interdict at Dax apparently united lay and clerical opponents of the guilty. Even when no lay support of the clergy is evident, the secular powers did not necessarily welcome the anti-clericalism an interdict provoked, notably at San Gimignano. Despite their initial defiance, lay authorities in these towns eventually found the interdict and associated conflict with clergy inconvenient; hence they came to terms to secure the sentence's relaxation. External pressures admittedly influenced civic officials at Dax and Béziers. At Dax these came from a temporal not spiritual superior; even at Béziers the papal threat of the inquisition carried the risk of being handed over to the secular arm for punishment. Political expediency was also a factor. Philip IV's reconciliation with the papacy deprived the consuls of Béziers of a key ally in their defiance of 'Clericis laicos' and its sanctions, for they claimed to tax clergy on royal authority. Moreover he had agreed to cooperate with the inquisition, which was then threatened against them. Cheney similarly found that the prospect of invasion from abroad and revolt at home had made it expedient for King John to seek an alliance with the pope and the lifting of the interdict on his kingdom. Cheney was unsure whether the interdict had contributed to these circumstances.[225] The interdict at Dax arguably brought to a head tensions between the city's rulers and their opponents, lay and clerical. In the thirteenth century secular powers could not long remain on bad terms with spiritual authorities but had to seek a *modus vivendi* of mutual benefit. And until they were prepared to do so, the church authorities carried on enforcing our three interdicts. The result was not necessarily lasting peace between laity and clergy but an interdict might not be lifted until the guilty sought at least a truce in their conflict with ecclesiastical authority, as we will see in the next chapter.

---

[225] Cheney, 'Interdict', 317.

6

The Lifting of Interdicts

An interdict's aim was not to punish but *persuade* the guilty to submit to ecclesiastical authority and make amends to injured parties for the offences that caused the interdict. Once this was achieved, it might be lifted or, canonically speaking, relaxed. Normally only the guilty could bring this about. According to Johannes Teutonicus the innocent victims of an interdict could not seek its removal by offering reparation for the guilty. By the mid-thirteenth century canonists generally agreed, including Innocent IV, who explained that the sin that occasioned the interdict was not theirs;[1] hence the innocent might not atone for it. They could only end interdicts indirectly by pressing the guilty to submit to ecclesiastical mandates; indeed general interdicts were meant to have this effect. However, when the guilty were unknown or dead, this norm was impracticable. For example the Lombard commune of Gravellona complained to Innocent III that an interdict laid on its territory for offences of its lords had never been relaxed, and it feared that spiritual dangers might arise from this. Innocent hence judged in 1213 that it might secure the interdict's relaxation by making amends to God, presumably since the injured parties were as intangible as the offenders.[2] But Johannes Teutonicus did not include this decision in *Compilatio quarta*; hence in his gloss on this collection of Innocent's later rulings Johannes still argued that only the guilty might make amends.

The canonical procedure for removing an interdict, like that for imposing one, broadly followed the rules concerning excommunication. Firstly Hostiensis and other thirteenth-century canonists held that as a rule only the judge who had laid a sentence might lift it, but they also admitted exceptions to this rule. They had recognized since at least the early thirteenth century that a judge's sentence might even be lifted by his superior in certain circumstances. Paulus Hungarus noted (*c*.1220), for example, that the pope might absolve someone

---

[1] Johannes: see p. 158 n. 146. Goffredus de Trano copied this gloss in his *Lectura* on X 5.38.11 v. *penitentia*, Vienna, Nationalbibliothek MS 2197, fol. 153rb–va. Cf. Innocent IV, *Apparatus* on X 5.38.11 v. *signum*; Bernard de Montmirat, *Lectura* on X 5.38.11 v. *crucis*, BAV, Borgh. lat. MS 231, fol. 132rb; MS 260, fol. 104vb (Ed. fol. 147ra); Monaldus, *Summa*, fol. 96vb; Anon. on X 5.38.11 v. *canonicas*, BAV, Borgh. lat. MS 228, fol. 167ra: 'Pone ista civitas est supposita ecclesiastico interdicto <et> unus vult satisfacere, numquid est satisfactio recipienda? Respondeo aut est persona qui dedit causam et tunc potest, de hereti. Ad abolendam [X 5.7.9], aut non est persona que dedit causam interdicti et tunc non potest ut hic.'
[2] Innocent III, Reg. 16, no. 20.

excommunicated by a judge delegate, and in practice popes had lifted interdicts laid by judges delegate since the late twelfth century.[3] But the judge here derived his power to lay and lift sentences from his superior, the pope. A local ordinary's interventions in the *ex officio* jurisdiction of his subordinates were technically subject to greater limitations. Alexander III had ruled that a bishop might not lift sentences of excommunication or interdict laid by an ordinary subject to him, specifically a *plebanus*, without the latter's knowledge. But Tancred commented that if a bishop ignored this ruling, his relaxation was still valid.[4] Nevertheless canonists agreed that a metropolitan might lift his suffragans' sentences in certain instances. For example Paulus noted that a decretal of Innocent III permitted a metropolitan to do so if his suffragan maliciously refused to grant absolution.[5] But normally a metropolitan could only intervene if the matter was referred to him on appeal, and we will return to appeals later.

A superior was not the only one who might intervene. The canonist Johannes Hispanus de Petesella argued (*c*.1236) that an excommunicate might be absolved by the delegate or successor of his excommunicator,[6] and apparently this principle also applied to interdicts. In practice the pope did not usually relax his interdicts in person but delegated the power to do so, just as he empowered subordinates to impose them. Indeed sometimes the pope ordered the same person to relax an interdict that he had authorized to lay it.[7] But this was not always the case. Johannes Teutonicus noted that if the pope ordered anyone to be excommunicated, the executor of this mandate might not absolve the excommunicate unless the pope granted him full cognizance over the latter's case, such as a judge delegate had.[8] Hence the pope might reserve absolution and order someone other than this executor to grant it. This certainly happened

---

[3] Hostiensis, *Summa* on X 5.39 §12 (fol. 294vb). Paulus Hungarus, *Notabilium* on 3 Comp. 1.20.5, BAV, Borgh. lat. MS 261, fol. 82rb: 'Item excommunicatus a delegato non potest absolvi nis<i> a papa vel ab illo qui ei succedit in honere hac honore.' Cf. Innocent III, Reg. 1, no. 221 (referring to Urban III (1185–7) lifting sentences laid by judges delegate).

[4] 1 Comp. 1.23.3 (= X 1.31.3). Tancred on 1 Comp. 1.23.3 v. *relaxetis*, BAV, Vat. lat. MS 1377, fol. 15ra: 'Sed pone quod episcopus relaxet talem sententiam eis inrequisitis, numquid tenet talis absolutio? utique eo quod est iudex ordinarius eorum, xi q. i. De persona, ar. in aut. de defensoribus civitatum in prin. [C.11 q.1 c.33; Nov. 15] ubi dicitur quod non prohibetur defensor civitatis, cui episcopus comparatur, cognoscere de causis inferiorum pretermissis municipalibus magistratibus. t.'

[5] Paulus Hungarus, *Notabilium* on 3 Comp. 1.20.2, BAV, Borgh. lat. MS 261, fol. 82rb: 'Item excommunicatus a suffraganeo potest metropolitanus absolvere si ille excommunicator malitiose noluerit absolvere.' Cf. id. on 3 Comp. 5.21.14, fol. 89rb: 'Item nota contra archiepiscopos quod excommunicatos a suis suffraganeis propter delictum manifestum non debent absolvere nisi illi malitiose illos non absolverint.'

[6] Johannes Hispanus de Petesella, *Summa*, §De sententia excommunicationis, BAV, Vat. lat. MS 2343, fol. 224r: 'Sed per quem est absolutio facienda? Respondeo per excommunicatorem vel eius superiorem vel delegatum ab eo, ut supra. de offic. del. Prudenciam §sextus. et infra. e. Sacro, supra. xi. q. iii. quasi per totum [X 1.29.21 §6; X 5.39.48; C.11 q.3], vel a successore excommunicatoris, ut supra. xi. q. iii. Si episcopus ante [C.11 q.3 c.40].'

[7] E.g. Reg. Innocent IV, no. 6038.

[8] Johannes Teutonicus on 3 Comp. 2.18.1 v. *absoluta* (Ed. pp. 309–10). Tancred copied this at 3 Comp. 2.18.1 v. *absolvi* (e.g. BAV, Vat. lat. MS 1377, fol. 210vb).

with some papal interdicts. For example, the one on France was proclaimed by the legate Peter of Capua but relaxed by another legate sent for this purpose, Cardinal Octavian. If an interdict was, as Cheney remarked, the Church's means of 'waging war', it made diplomatic sense to use a different agent to negotiate the peace. Indeed Philip II of France complained to Innocent III about the legate who published the interdict on his realm, and offered to submit before (other) legates or judges delegate.[9]

Clearly, as Johannes Teutonicus implied, nobody might relax a papal sentence unless authorized to do so. Thus Johannes also argued that a legate might not absolve anyone excommunicated by the pope or a judge delegate, unless, as Paulus Hungarus also noted, he had a specific mandate to do so. But Johannes added that a sentence laid by a legate might be lifted by the successor to his legation;[10] the French interdict is a case in point. Tancred adopted this view and likewise held that a judge delegate's sentence might be lifted by whoever replaced him in that capacity.[11] As we have seen, Johannes Hispanus de Petesella later extended this principle to sentences laid by any ecclesiastical judge. It was clearly expedient for a judge might die or otherwise vacate his office while his sentences were still in force. Indeed shortly before February 1238 the Bishop-elect of Beauvais relaxed an interdict laid on his cathedral by his deceased predecessor.[12] Moreover a bishop gained the judicial powers of his office on election to it, including the power to lift as well as lay interdicts. Hence such canonistic views were not only pragmatic but also based on the theoretical separation of the office and the person holding it; these powers inhered in the office not the person and thus might be delegated to another or pass to a successor.

While an office was vacant, however, alternative provision had to be made for lifting sentences imposed by its former occupant. Since the mid-twelfth century some canonists had argued that during episcopal vacancies a bishop's jurisdictional powers reverted to his chapter, though in practice it was one of several possible arrangements. Nevertheless, just as canonists had thereby inferred that a chapter might lay interdicts *sede vacante*, Jacobus de Albenga argued that it might also lift sentences then. Some later canonists adopted this view, and

[9] *Gesta* c.53 (*PL* 214.xcix). Similar considerations doubtless influenced Innocent's decision to instruct his legate Nicholas, Cardinal Bishop of Tusculum, to remove the interdict on England and Wales instead of the three English bishops who had proclaimed it and so alienated King John; *SLI*, pp. 164–5, 171–2.

[10] Johannes Teutonicus on 3 Comp. 1.6.19 v. *possit absolvere*; 1.19.2 v. *pontifici reservata*; 2.18.1 v. *absoluta* (Ed. pp. 85, 130, 310). Paulus Hungarus, *Notabilium* on 2 Comp. 5.18.9, BAV, Borgh. lat. MS 261, fol. 80ra: 'Ad eminentiam etc. Nota quod legati qui mittuntur a latere summi pontificis licet non habeant mandatum speciale absolvendi excommunicatos tamen possunt.'

[11] Tancred on 3 Comp. 1.18.5 v. *contestatione*, BAV, Vat. lat. MS 1377, fol. 177v; Vat. lat. MS 2509, fol. 168vb: 'Colligitur ex loco isto quod si iudex delegatus ante litem contestatam excommunicet aliquem pro contumacia, post annum non valet illum absolvere. Sed contra infra titulo secundo. Pastoralis [3 Comp. 1.20.5] ubi colligitur quod successor in dignitate qui successit in honore et honere illum absolvere possit.' Cf. n. 8.

[12] Reg. Gregory IX, no. 4078.

it became law when Boniface VIII ruled in his *Liber sextus* that if episcopal jurisdiction was transferred to a chapter *sede vacante*, it might lift sentences that its bishop would have lifted were he alive.[13]

Who might lift a sentence, however, if it was not laid by a judge but incurred under canon law? Some papal rulings that placed sentences on their violators reserved absolution to the pope, and the number of such reserved cases increased from the mid-twelfth century. For example, Boniface VIII's bull 'Clericis laicos' inflicted sentences of excommunication and interdict that might be removed only on papal authority.[14] In practice a pope authorized others to lift sentences in reserved cases, as with sentences he laid as a judge. For example, Boniface mandated a cardinal to lift the sentences laid on Béziers and its citizens under 'Clericis laicos'. Such mandates were not all specific to certain sentences but might be general. In 1291 Nicholas IV had given the abbot of St Denis a faculty to absolve anyone from excommunication, suspension, or interdict laid by canon law or a judge where absolution was reserved to the papacy.[15]

But not all papal rulings that imposed sentences expressly reserved absolution. Innocent III had commented in his decretal 'Nuper a nobis' (1199) that where this was the case, other Church authorities might lift these sentences. He specifically ruled that an excommunicate might be absolved by his bishop or priest in such cases. His ruling rapidly entered canon law,[16] but whether canonists understood it to apply to interdicts is unclear, nor is practice on this point evident from the thirteenth-century papal registers. Nevertheless it is doubtful that anyone less than the local ordinary could lift a general interdict *a iure*. Indeed Bérenger Frédol's treatise on such sentences states that he and his fellow compilers of Boniface VIII's *Liber sextus* suggested to Boniface that clergy below episcopal rank might not absolve from excommunication *a canone promulgata* unless the canon concerned authorized them. Apparently Boniface agreed to this but it did not result in a ruling in the *Liber sextus*.[17]

The competent authority normally relaxed an interdict after the guilty fulfilled certain conditions. These were defined in Innocent III's decretal 'Ex

---

[13] Jacobus de Albenga on 5 Comp. 1.18.1 v. *pro bono pacis*, London, BL, Royal MS 11.C.vii, fol. 251ra: 'Vacante sede capitulum potest absolvere excommunicatos, ut supra. de hereticis. Ad abolendam lib. i. [1 Comp. 5.6.11].' Id. on 5 Comp. 3.7.1 v. *in collationibus*, fol. 261va: 'Utrum mortuo episcopo qui excommunicavit transferatur potestas absolvendi ad capitulum dubitari consuevit et videtur quod non, ut xi. q. iii. Si episcopus [C.11 q.3 c.40]. Dicunt tamen doctores quod transferatur potestas absolvendi ad capitulum et hoc propter periculum animarum, et est ar. ad hoc supra. de maio et obe. c. i. in fi. lib. e. [5 Comp. 1.18.1].' Cf. Note added to Goffredus de Trano, *Summa*, §De sententia excommunicationis, BAV, Ottob. lat. MS 54, fol. 160rb: 'Nota quod pastore vacante capitulum potest excommunicare, iudicare et absolvere, ut supra. de hereticis. Ad abolendam. et supra. de maio. et obedientia c. Hiis que, prout ibi notatur et c. Cum olim. et ut notatur supra. de off. or. c. fin. [X 5.7.9; 1.33.11, 14; 1.31.20].' Boniface VIII: VI 1.17.un.

[14] VI 3.23.3. Cf. Hostiensis, *Summa* on X 5.39 §12 (fol. 294ra–va); *Bérenger Frédol*, 47.

[15] Reg. Nicholas IV, no. 6101.   [16] 3 Comp. 5.21.3 (= X 5.39.29).

[17] *Bérenger Frédol*, 50; Schmidt, 'Papst Bonifaz VIII', 230. But cf. VI 5.11.22.

parte' (1205).[18] It largely rationalized and clarified existing procedure and soon influenced practice, as it quickly entered canon law. First it distinguished that what the guilty should do to have an interdict or excommunication lifted depended on whether the sentence was laid for contumacy alone or also for an offence. Contumacy generally meant disobedience to ecclesiastical authority; 'Ex parte' defined it as the refusal to 'stand by the law' (*stare iuri*) when cited (summoned before a church court). 'Ex parte' thus concluded that in the case of contumacy a sufficient *cautio* to 'stand by the law' had to be given before a sentence might be lifted. Canonists generally understood this *cautio* to mean an oath or 'sworn caution' (*cautio iuratoria*).[19] Indeed letters of Innocent III before 'Ex parte' specified the latter as a prerequisite for lifting interdicts.[20] Sometimes the guilty had to swear this oath before the proper authorities *in person*. In 1213 Innocent III instructed judges to receive an oath sworn by Afonso II of Portugal *corporaliter* before relaxing the interdict on Portugal and absolving him from excommunication.[21] Such an express requirement suggests that usually this oath was sworn by representatives of the guilty. For example, when the officials and commune of Pistoia sought absolution from papal sentences of interdict and excommunication in 1266, they sent a proctor to the curia to swear on their souls that they would fully obey papal and ecclesiastical mandates.[22]

But what did it mean to swear an oath to 'stand by the law'? Innocent himself even recognized the phrase's ambiguity. When Philip II of France sought the lifting of the interdict on his realm and offered 'a sworn caution to stand by the law', apparently Innocent responded that Philip had to distinguish whether he meant the law as it stood (*iuri dictato*) or law to be stated (*iuri dictando*). If the former, he had to swear to leave his mistress and return to his wife, i.e. observe current canon law on marriage; his past refusal to do so had caused the interdict on France. If he meant the law to be stated, he had to accept judgement on his marriage's validity (which he disputed).[23]

Contemporary canonists drew similar distinctions. Tancred accepted Alanus's view that the oath might promise one of three things: to obey canon law, i.e. Innocent III's *ius dictatus*; to stand by ecclesiastical judgements or mandates, i.e. Innocent's *ius dictandus*; to obey the mandate of the prelate receiving the oath. The latter prelate was usually authorized to lift the sentence, and hence he might also have laid it. Hostiensis indeed later taught that if anyone was

[18] 3 Comp. 5.23.7 (= X 5.40.23).
[19] E.g. Tancred on 2 Comp. 1.3.7 v. *satisfactione*, BAV, Vat. lat. MS 1377, fol. 103ra: 'Ille qui excommunicatus est pro contumacia quia nolebat stare iuri vel in aliquo simili obedire in principio prestito iuramento debet absolvi ut in illa decretali "Quesitum" [1 Comp. 1.23.2].'
[20] Innocent III, Reg. 1, no. 92; 5, nos. 51, 136; 7, no. 136; 8, no. 125.
[21] Innocent III, Reg. 16, no. 52.
[22] Reg. Clement IV, no. 413. Cf. ibid. nos. 414, 694; Reg. Honorius III, nos. 827 (sworn caution to be received from one in the name of the whole populace of Pavia), 2637 (suitable proctors to stand by the law in Frederick II's name).
[23] See n. 9.

excommunicated by a judge whose mandates he had scorned, he had to swear to obey that judge's mandates to gain absolution.[24] This teaching reflected practice concerning papal interdicts. Thirteenth-century popes often required the guilty to swear obedience to papal mandates before papal interdicts might be lifted. Sometimes this requirement was stated only in generic terms, but frequently obedience was also required to mandates regarding the specific issues that caused the interdict. In 1213 Afonso II of Portugal had to swear such obedience. But sometimes it was only implied. After Innocent III had excommunicated the robber of a legate and interdicted his lands, the pope ordered in 1205 that he might be absolved on swearing an oath to obey papal mandates, but then he was to be instructed that this oath obliged him not to harass papal envoys in future.[25] And sometimes when an interdict was laid for disobedience to certain orders, it was lifted in return for obedience to those orders. After two legates had interdicted Pisa in 1198 for failing to join the Tuscan League as Innocent wished, the pope ordered them not to relax the interdict unless Pisa agreed to his wishes.[26]

However, Innocent observed that sentences might be laid for an offence as well as such disobedience. In his decretal 'Ex parte' he distinguished that if an offence was manifest rather than doubtful, the guilty had to make suitable satisfaction, i.e. amends, before the sentence might be lifted. This apparently confirmed normal practice; by the late twelfth century papal letters ordered that excommunicates might not be absolved until they gave satisfaction to injured parties.[27] Canonists had also recognized this as a legal principle even before 'Ex parte' and certainly did so thereafter.

Satisfaction took various forms. Often it meant restitution of property wrongly acquired. For example, after Parma was interdicted for harbouring a legate's robber, it promised the legate restitution. It agreed to pay him back half of the stolen money by 25 April 1199, making a first instalment of one hundred marks. In return he lifted the interdict and other sanctions, but he threatened to reimpose them if this deadline was not met. Sometimes restitution included compensation for income lost from property which was seized. In 1251 Innocent IV warned the duke of Swabia to make restitution of a castle seized from the Bishop of Turin and

---

[24] Tancred on 2 Comp. 5.18.4 v. *iuramentum*, BAV, Vat. lat. MS 1377, fol. 143va: 'Quidam dicunt illud esse quod parebunt iuri, ar. infra. e. t. Cum olim lib. iii. [3 Comp. 5.23.8]. Alii dicunt quod stabunt iudicio sive mandato ecclesie, ut hic et supra. de ap. Ad hec. lib. i. [1 Comp. 2.20.30]. Alii quod parebunt mandato prelati suscipientis sacramentum, ut supra. e. t. c. penult. lib. i. [1 Comp. 5.34.15] ... A<lanus>.' Hostiensis, *Summa* on X 5.39 §14 (fol. 295vb).

[25] Innocent III, Reg. 8, no. 125.

[26] Ibid. 1, no. 35; Krehbiel, 102–3. Cf. Reg. Honorius III, no. 5720: Bergamo fell under a papal interdict after electing a Cremonese as its podestà contrary to papal mandates and obtained its relaxation in 1225 with a sworn caution not to appoint anyone as their ruler contrary to papal prohibitions in future.

[27] As n. 18. Cf. e.g. Innocent III, Reg. 2, no. 27. See also n. 35.

of any profit derived from it on pain of interdict.[28] This issue arose not only when seizure of church property caused interdicts but also when it resulted from them. We have noted that lay rulers often reacted to an interdict on their lands by seizing the goods of clergy observing it. Philip II of France did so and had to give satisfaction to such clergy before the French interdict might be lifted in 1200. Likewise King John was required to make reparations for sequestrating property of clergy who observed the papal interdict on his realm. Cheney showed that most of these clergy had recovered this property by the time John came to terms with the pope; hence restitution concerned only a minority, mostly clergy who had been in exile during the interdict and whose estates John retained. But they included Stephen Langton; his exclusion from the see of Canterbury by John had provoked the interdict, and in 1213 the pope required that John restore ecclesiastical temporalities to Langton and others before the interdict might be lifted. Furthermore John had exploited church property financially while it remained in his hands, and most dispossessed clergy had probably paid him in order to recover it. Hence the legate Pandulf's mandate to lift the interdict told him to ensure such clergy received full compensation. By January 1214 it was arranged that John pay Pandulf 100,000 marks towards this compensation and the pope ordered that the interdict might be lifted once John swore an oath to pay this. John had already paid 27,000 marks in compensation by then, and a few months later the pope revised the arrangement, requiring John to bring this up to 40,000 before the interdict's removal and thereafter pay half-yearly instalments of 6,000 marks. But the only further compensation was 6,000 marks paid nearly six months after the interdict was lifted.[29] Nevertheless the total paid was still substantial and a major concession by John. He was desperate for a papal alliance against the combined threat of French invasion and baronial revolt, and made an even more striking concession to win papal support by surrendering his kingdom and Ireland to Innocent III as a fief.

But offenders were not always so obliging when major claims were made for compensation. When a secular lord attacked an abbey in Le Mans diocese, seized its property, held some of its monks to ransom, and drove the rest into exile, Gregory IX excommunicated him and interdicted his lands, and on papal orders the diocesan and his metropolitan assessed the abbey's damages at 4,000 marks. Even though Gregory approved this sum, the lord refused to pay it, offering a less generous settlement, and even continued harassing the abbey. Therefore in 1231 Gregory required its abbot, the diocesan, and his official to declare this lord a heretic and his vassals absolved of their fealty unless he relented. Though damages were usually determined by the competent Church authorities, as in this case, they were sometimes subject to negotiation between the guilty

---

[28] Parma: Innocent III, Reg. 1, no. 393; Krehbiel, 102. Swabia: Reg. Innocent IV, no. 5343.
[29] France: *Gesta* c.54 (*PL* 214.c); Krehbiel, 121–2. England: Cheney, 'Interdict', 301–6; id. 'Reaction'; *SLI*, pp. 171–2, 188–90.

and injured parties, notably when the former pleaded difficulties in meeting the claim. For example, when men of Noli allegedly destroyed a *castrum* of the Bishop of Savona, he had excommunicated them and the commune's officials and interdicted its other inhabitants and then a legate required it to pay 2,000 Genoese pounds toward rebuilding the *castrum*.[30] The commune appealed to the pope that it was too small and poor to pay this sum but still wished to obey ecclesiastical mandates; in other words it sought absolution. In May 1235 Gregory IX responded that if it reached an agreement with the bishop's successor over damages, the sentences might be lifted.

Thus satisfaction for manifest offences comprised not only restitution of goods seized but also compensation for goods damaged. Moreover when interdicts were laid in debt cases, it also meant repaying the debt, at least before Boniface VIII banned the use of interdicts to enforce debts in 1302. For instance when Sienese merchants sued the Bishop of Utrecht over money owed to them, they procured his excommunication and an interdict on his land. The bishop then agreed to settle with his creditors but he defaulted and later died. At their request Gregory IX intervened in 1235, requiring the bishop's successor to settle the debt and their expenses in pursuing it in church courts. This shows that satisfaction might also cover the injured party's costs in seeking legal redress, and that if an offender died before making satisfaction, his successor might be liable for it. Indeed Innocent III had often said that 'succedat in onere qui substituitur in honore'.[31]

Although Innocent ruled in 'Ex parte' that satisfaction had to be made before a sentence laid for a manifest offence might be lifted, this ruling was not always applied rigidly. Indeed Innocent himself was initially prepared to allow the English interdict's relaxation once King John merely promised the clergy satisfaction, albeit for offences that resulted from rather than caused the sentence. Likewise after the civic officials of Amiens were excommunicated and interdicted, Honorius III ordered in 1218 that they might be absolved on receipt of a caution that they would make satisfaction for losses inflicted on some monastery; such offences had doubtless provoked these sentences.[32] Hence assurances of future satisfaction might be enough to secure relaxation, at least from popes. But a *cautio* in this context might signify something more than an oath or promise. Generally a *cautio* meant money or goods pledged as a security. Sometimes canonists also understood it as such. Ricardus Anglicus argued that excommunicates might be absolved if a *cautio* was pledged 'de satisfaciendo', i.e. 'for the satisfaction to be made'.[33] Even after 'Ex parte' required that satisfaction precede relaxation, not all

---

[30] Reg. Gregory IX, nos. 734, 2579.

[31] Reg. Gregory IX, no. 2391. See e.g. Lat. Conc. IV c.46 (= X 3.49.7) for Innocent's punning maxim.

[32] Reg. Honorius III, no. 1160.

[33] Ricardus on 1 Comp. 2.20.15 v. *donec*, BAV, Pal. lat. MS 696, fol. 40va: 'Nota quod nullus est absolvendus ante cautionem prestitam de satisfaciendo, ut \extra. t. Vestra dixit [*recte* duxit]/, infra. xxiiii. q. ii. Legatur, infra. de pen. di. i. Neminem, infra. xxiiii. q. <ii.> Dampnationis, infra.

canonists interpreted this strictly; some still applied Ricardus's teaching in certain circumstances. Johannes Teutonicus commented on 'Ex parte' that if anyone was too poor to make satisfaction, it was enough to pledge a *cautio*. Anyone too poor even to offer a pledge might swear an oath instead, he added. Perhaps the officials of Amiens pleaded poverty as their excuse for offering a *cautio* instead of immediate satisfaction. Certainly this case suggests that the papacy and canonists agreed on the mitigation of 'Ex parte'. Furthermore many thirteenth-century canonists adopted Johannes's views, although some, notably Hostiensis, stuck more strictly to the letter of 'Ex parte'.[34]

Even if a *cautio* was not always an acceptable substitute for satisfaction, it was needed to secure relaxation in other instances. By the late twelfth century papal letters sometimes required a suitable or sufficient caution, and by the early thirteenth century canonists understood this to mean a pledge.[35] Sometimes it was needed when a *cautio* in the form of an oath was not considered a sufficient guarantee of obedience, notably when the papacy had reason to doubt the mere word of the guilty. For example, at the height of the crusade against the Cathars, Toulouse was interdicted in 1209 for refusal to hand over suspected Cathars, and when it sent messengers to seek papal relaxation of the interdict, Innocent III instructed a legate to grant this on receiving a 'sufficient caution'. A thousand pounds was agreed as the 'caution' in 1210, and this sum was to be raised by taxing the city.[36] Not only money might be pledged but also property. In 1218 Honorius III said that sentences of excommunication and interdict on citizens of Alessandria might be lifted, since they had sworn to stand by apostolic mandates and pledged a castle.[37] Moreover by the early thirteenth century canonists observed that *fideiussores* might act as guarantors of the guilty party's good faith and agree to give the pledge. When only half the sum required at Toulouse was paid, its citizens had to appease the legate by handing over hostages. Normally *fideiussores* pledged property rather than themselves. In 1266 Clement IV ordered that before sentences of interdict and excommunication on Pistoia might be relaxed, fifty or more merchants from there and Florence had to bind themselves and their goods as security that Pistoians would observe papal

xiiii. q. vi. Si res, infra. de usur. Cum tu sicut, infra. de raptoribus. Super eo [JL 9666; C.24 q.2 c.2; De pen. D.1 c.43; C. 24 q. c.2 c.5; C.14 q.6 c.1; 1 Comp. 5.15.5, 5.14.5].' Vincentius Hispanus copied this gloss at 1 Comp. 2.20.17 v. *iniuriam*, Leipzig Universitätsbibliothek MS 983, fol. 19vb.

34 Johannes Teutonicus on 3 Comp. 5.23.7 v. *contumacia*: http://faculty.cu.edu/Pennington/edit 517.htm. Cf. Tancred, ibid., BAV, Vat. lat. MS 1377, fol. 279rb; Goffredus de Trano, *Lectura* on X 5.40.23 v. *pro contumacia*, Vienna, Nationalbibliothek MS 2197, fol. 160ra; Bernard of Parma, ibid.; Hostiensis, *Summa* on X 5.39 §14 (fols. 295vb–6ra).

35 E.g. Tancred on 2 Comp. 2.7.3 v. *sufficienti cautione*, BAV, Vat. lat. MS 1377, fol. 111rb; Vat. lat. MS 2509, fol. 104va: 'Nota quod nomine cautionis simpliciter posito nuda solummodo intelligitur que sit solis verbis, ut C. de ver. si. Sancimus [Cod. 6.38.3], sed ex quo ydonea vel sufficiens ponitur pignorativa vel fideiussoria vel iuratoria intelligitur, ut ff. mandati. Si mandato Titii §ult. [Dig. 17.1.59].'

36 Innocent III, Reg. 12, no. 156; De Vic and Vaisette, viii.614–16; Krehbiel, 152–3.

37 Reg. Honorius III, no. 1686.

and ecclesiastical mandates. Pistoia had already sent a proctor to swear an oath to this effect and present *fideiussores* at the curia, but Clement clearly found them inadequate. The cardinal whom he ordered to absolve the Pistoians was to find the fifty merchants suitable in terms of the ease of summoning them and their ability to pay. Indeed he required them to pay fines on their pledged property if the Pistoians ever violated their oath.[38] In this instance not only might *fideiussores* forfeit pledges, but the relaxation that they had secured might also be forfeit. When Innocent III had ordered a legate to lift the interdict on Toulouse, he warned that if its citizens failed to give the caution required, they would fall back under the interdict again. Indeed when they had provided only half the sum required, the legate reimposed the sentence.[39]

By the mid-thirteenth century the canonist Bernard of Parma even understood that when 'Ex parte' required a sufficient caution before sentences laid for contumacy might be lifted, it meant a pledge or *fideiussores*. Though his gloss on 'Ex parte' was *ordinaria*, Hostiensis and other canonists still interpreted a caution in this context as an oath.[40] But a sufficient caution in the sense of a pledge was usually prerequisite for lifting of sentences laid for an 'offensa dubia'. This term came from 'Ex parte', where Innocent III ruled that if a sentence was laid for a 'doubtful offence', it might be lifted once a 'security' was given that the offender would obey ecclesiastical mandates.[41] In practice Innocent's successors interpreted this 'security' as a pledge. But when was an offence manifest rather than doubtful, and thus satisfaction more fitting? The countess of Blois asked Innocent exactly this question, for 'Ex parte' specifically concerned an interdict on her lands. In another decretal 'Cum olim pro canonicis' (1207) he replied that a manifest offence was proven by a confession or other evidence beyond denial;[42] this gloss on 'Ex parte' accompanied it in canonical collections from 1210. Innocent's clarification implied that a doubtful offence was not proven but contested between the alleged offender and their accuser. Consequently it appears that the pledge bound the accused to submit to ecclesiastical judgement on the disputed offence and, if this was proven, to make satisfaction. For example, the Bishop of Chalon-sur-Saône interdicted the duchess of Burgundy's lands since, according to him, she had destroyed

---

[38] Reg. Clement IV, no. 413; issued with a similar mandate requiring thirty *fideiussores* from Pistoia's neighbour Prato. Cf. Reg. Martin IV, no. 130: the Bishop of Parma was ordered to lift a papal interdict on his city when suitable *fideiussores* swore obedience to papal mandates on behalf of its commune.

[39] See n. 36. Cf. Reg. Nicholas IV, no. 616: renewal of a papal interdict on Bologna was authorized if restitution and satisfaction were not made within eight days of its relaxation.

[40] Bernard of Parma on X 2.24.7 v. *sufficienti cautione*; X 3.21.8 v. *cautionem idoneam*; X 5.40.23 v. *sufficiens*. Hostiensis: see n. 34. Cf. Johannes Hispanus de Petesella, *Summa* §De sententia excommunicationis, BAV, Vat. lat. MS 2343, fol. 224ra; Borgh. lat. MS 163, fol. 80ra: 'est absolvendus prestita cautione quod stabit iuri, si pro contumacia fuit ligatus, <et etiam> iuramento quod stabit mandatis ecclesie'.

[41] As n. 18.   [42] Innocent III, Reg. 8, no. 31; 10, no. 66. 3 Comp. 5.23.8 (= X 5.40.24).

some iron chains in Chalon that belonged to him.[43] In 1219 Honorius III intervened, presumably at the duchess's request, and instructed the Bishop, dean, and precentor of Auxerrre to relax the interdict once she gave them a 'sufficient caution' to stand by the law on the disputed matter. Presumably such mediation was often necessary where the judge who laid an interdict also made the accusations that occasioned it.

The distinction between manifest and doubtful offences could be hard to draw in practice, and sometimes both kinds might be in question. Indeed by Honorius III's time papal mandates to lift interdicts sometimes contain a catch-all formula, requiring both satisfaction for manifest offences and a sufficient caution for doubtful ones. In the case of Noli above Gregory IX required it to fulfil this dual obligation before the sentences there might be lifted.[44] But papal mandates rarely specified what the pledge or satisfaction should comprise. In some cases it was left to papal executors to determine, but their decisions are rarely known. Nevertheless details sometimes emerge. Gregory IX in 1236 defined the prerequisites for lifting an interdict on Arezzo and absolving from excommunication its podestà and councillors. First, the latter had to offer a caution, comprising an oath and pledge of a thousand pounds, such that they would obey papal mandates and annul civic statutes contrary to ecclesiastical liberty. Second, the Bishop and churches of Arezzo diocese had to receive three hundred pounds in satisfaction of their losses; the chapter of Arezzo Cathedral determined that the losses did not exceed this amount. Third, two *castra* seized by the city had to be restored to the chapter and their former inhabitants ordered to return, they having been forced to live in Arezzo.[45] In this case there was admittedly no coupling of manifest and doubtful offences, but a more common combination of contumacy and manifest offence, which required both a caution and satisfaction.

Once the requisite caution or satisfaction was given, the competent authority might relax the interdict. Unlike absolution from excommunication, this involved no solemn ritual, according to Hostiensis. He taught that an interdict might be relaxed by words alone just as it was laid by them. Later canonists widely adopted his teaching as it apparently reflected current practice, where these words were usually expressed in a public proclamation.[46] Indeed in 1234 when judges delegate had revoked the count of Brittany's excommunication and an interdict on his lands, this was declared in places where the sentences were published, namely in neighbouring parts and throughout the French kingdom. But it is unclear whether this was standard procedure; Clement IV in 1266

---

[43] Reg. Honorius III, no. 2295.
[44] Ibid. nos. 1054, 1991. Cf. Reg. Gregory IX, nos. 2376, 4080, 4736. Cf. also n. 30 (Noli).
[45] Reg. Gregory IX, no. 3083.
[46] Hostiensis, *Summa* on X 5.39 §14 (fol. 296va). Cf. John of Freiburg, *Summa*, III, xxxiii, q.269; Petrus Bonetus on X 2.28.37, BAV, Borgh. lat. MS 228, fol. 112vb: 'in absolutione interdicti nulla forma sollempnis est statuta, ymo sicut nudo verbo profertur, sic nudo verbo relaxari potest'.

simply required a cardinal to make similar proclamations in places where he saw fit.[47] The removal of sentences might also be announced in writing. Canon law did not require this, even if Innocent IV ruled in 1245 that sentences had to be promulgated *in scriptis*. Nevertheless some thirty years earlier Johannes Teutonicus had advised that former excommunicates ought to preserve their letters of absolution carefully as proof of their absolution. Doubtless those released from interdicts sought similar safeguards against allegations that they remained interdicted. In 1296, for example, the rulers and commune of Orvieto obtained letters from Boniface VIII stating that all sentences and penalties on them, including an interdict, were revoked.[48]

Although canon law did not prescribe a ritual to lift interdicts, it did to end the cessation of worship in violated or polluted churches. The canons 'Ecclesiis' and 'Si motum' in Gratian's *Decretum* required reconsecration of such churches.[49] But by the late twelfth century the papacy provided a simpler ceremony. Alexander III's decretal 'Significasti' (1172–3) ordered the 'reconciliation' of such churches by aspersion with holy water. This responded to a case where a woman committed adultery with a priest in church; the church's 'reconciliation' was meant to parallel the penance enjoined on the woman. Penitents were aspersed with holy water on reconciliation to the church to signify the cleansing of their sins, just as aspersing violated churches literally washed away the stains of sin. 'Ecclesiis' similarly compared consecration to baptism, stating that, just as a person should not be rebaptized, a church should not be reconsecrated unless it were violated. This exception to a logical theological argument had perhaps made Alexander III, a theologian himself, uncomfortable. There was still unease over the issue when Innocent III was asked for an alternative to reconsecration in the case of a church violated by murder and bloodshed. He had studied theology, and perhaps this also led him to confirm in the decretal 'Proposuisti' (1207) that the church might be 'reconciled' with holy water mixed with ash and wine; penitents similarly had their faces ritually smeared with ash to signify their humble contrition. These papal rulings were incorporated in canon law and generally accepted among canonists by the early thirteenth century.[50] This legal change was already reflected in a papal letter of 1198, which stated that the Archbishop of Lund had prohibited celebration of divine offices in a violated church until its 'reconciliation'. But it is unclear whether this illustrates reception of 'Significasti' at Lund or awareness of that decretal in the papal chancery where this letter was drawn up.[51]

---

[47] Reg. Gregory IX, no. 2190; Reg. Clement IV, no. 413.
[48] Innocent IV: see p. 107. Johannes Teutonicus on 3 Comp. 1.18.10 (Ed. p. 127). Reg. Boniface VIII, no. 1651.
[49] D.68 c.3 (repeated at De con. D.1 c.20); De con. D.1 c.19.
[50] 1 Comp. 5.13.6 (= X 5.16.5); 3 Comp. 3.31.3 (= X 3.40.4).
[51] Innocent III, Reg. 1, no. 450 (= 3 Comp. 5.16.1; X 5.33.11, where misaddressed to the Archbishop of Lyons, i.e. 'Lugdunensi' instead of 'Lundensi').

Gregory IX further clarified the law on 'reconciliation' in 1233 at the request of the Bishop of Astorga in Portugal. The bishop had apparently asked whether priests might 'reconcile' violated churches, as was customary in the province of Braga where his diocese lay. The pope replied that the power to 'reconcile' was reserved to bishops but they might delegate it to priests. A year later this ruling was published in the *Liber extra*.[52] Although it thereby became common law, some sixty years later bishops and other prelates, including abbots, still considered it necessary to seek papal permission to delegate to priests their power to 'reconsecrate' violated churches.

Absolved excommunicates likewise had to undergo a ritual 'reconciliation' to the church before they might be readmitted to the sacraments and divine offices. The authority who absolved them might also enjoin a penance on them for the offence that provoked their excommunication.[53] This was also true of those whose offence caused interdicts as they were normally excommunicated on this account. But it was unusual to impose penances on an interdicted community, though when this occurred, heavier penances fell on those whose offence caused the interdict. In 1213 the legate Nicholas, Bishop of Tusculum, enjoined penance on burgesses of Oxford responsible for hanging some clerks of Oxford University; this violation of clerical immunity from lay justice had caused an interdict on Oxford and the university's dispersal in 1209. According to Roger of Wendover the penitents had to visit every church in Oxford unshod, naked, and carrying scourges and ask its priest for absolution by reciting Psalm 50.[54] In order to prolong their penance and better deter them and others from repeating this sin, they were to visit only one church a day. On 25 June 1214 Nicholas also placed obligations on all citizens of Oxford which were partly penitential.[55] First, for ten years students were to be charged for lodgings half the rent they paid before the university dispersed; rents on lodgings built since then were to be fixed by a committee of four masters and four burgesses. Secondly, annually the city had to provide 52 shillings to support poor scholars and a feast on St Nicholas day for a hundred poor scholars; such alms-giving was a common penance enjoined on excommunicates.[56] Besides other conditions that citizens had to swear to observe, including selling food and other goods to scholars at just and reasonable prices, Nicholas enjoined a further penitential act to be performed after the interdict was relaxed. Citizens found guilty of hanging the clerks had to go to their victims' graves without shoes, belts, hats, and cloaks, followed by the rest of the citizens, and move the clerks' bodies to a cemetery designated by the clergy. Nicholas declared that if the burgesses did not comply, they would incur excommunication and, along with Oxford, fall back

---

[52] Reg. Gregory IX, no. 1324 (= X 3.40.9). Cf. Reg. Nicholas IV, nos. 1595, 2014, 2132, 2845, 3028, 3382, 4091, 5161, 5196, 5531, 5845.

[53] Logan, 143–4.   [54] Wendover, *Flores*, ii.94; Krehbiel, 145–8.

[55] *Munimenta*, i.1–4.   [56] E.g. William Sampson in Logan, 143.

under the interdict; they presumably complied, as there is no further record of this interdict.

A comparable case has been noted at Laon.[57] Like Oxford this French city was interdicted owing to violation of clerical and ecclesiastical immunity. In 1295 leading citizens stormed its cathedral, dragged out two laymen and a clerk taking refuge there, and wounded them violating the church; civic officials later jailed the clerk despite his immunity from lay justice. The Bishop of Laon held the whole community responsible for these events; hence he interdicted it and excommunicated the ringleaders. Although the pope enforced these sentences, the citizens came to terms owing to royal not papal intervention. In 1298 the French king required them to do certain penances before the sentences might be lifted, a striking intrusion of temporal power into spiritual affairs. These included a barefoot procession bearing gifts of wax figures to the cathedral and the endowment of a chapel in that church. But otherwise in the thirteenth century such collective penances were not associated with lifting of interdicts or specified by canon law and its commentators as prerequisite to this.

Occasionally the papacy lifted an interdict even when the guilty did not repent, or rather because it failed to move them to repentance. For example, Gregory IX lifted an interdict on Pisa and the excommunication of its officials when the sentences failed to compel restitution of certain *castra* to the Bishop of Lucca. This was no climbdown. His idea was to mollify the Pisans into submission, but when they remained obdurate, he threatened to reimpose the sentences in 1237 unless they capitulated.[58] Innocent IV responded with similar pragmatism when interdicts laid in Germany during his clash with Frederick II proved counter-productive. In 1247 Innocent allowed the Bishop of Constance to relax the interdict on his diocese for up to two months so that he 'might better attract everyone to devotion to the church'.[59] As seen in Chapter 5, interdicts might not only increase the defiance of the guilty but also reduce the devotion of the innocent. In the latter case the papacy might also deem it pragmatic to relax interdicts. For example, Urban IV lifted the 'ambulatory' interdict on Afonso III of Portugal and his consort Beatriz in 1263 on hearing from two Portuguese bishops that it had caused serious spiritual dangers, loss to clergy, and popular scandal.[60] Moreover it no longer had any purpose. Alexander IV had authorized it when Afonso refused to abandon his bigamous consanguineous marriage to Beatriz and return to his first wife, but she had died by 1259 and Beatriz had since borne him three children, including a male heir.[61] Hence Urban's decision was prompted by both political and pastoral expediency.

---

[57] Denton, 'Laon', 88–92 (including edition of royal document specifying the penances at pp. 90–2).

[58] Reg. Gregory IX, no. 3630.

[59] Reg. Innocent IV, no. 2616: 'ut ad devotionem ecclesie possis melius attrahere universos'.

[60] Reg. Urban IV, no. C376.   [61] Linehan, 'Castile', 686.

Boniface VIII revoked similarly 'obsolete' interdicts in 1296, largely because they brought ecclesiastical discipline into disrepute. Franciscans in Cologne province told him that these sentences were laid on the lands of some nobles there so long ago that hardly anyone remembered this and nobody cared about observing them. Indeed when these friars tried observing them, apparently the province's inhabitants did not act likewise but rather 'to the disturbance and scandal' of these sentences. Boniface thus declared that the friars might disregard these *antiquate* sentences.[62] Presumably, like the Gravellona interdict noted earlier, they became irrelevant since the grievances that prompted them no longer mattered or were even known. Occasionally popes even overlooked such grievances and relaxed interdicts as a political favour. In 1297 when Boniface's famed clash with the Colonna turned into open war, his allies included the commune of Fermo but it lay under an interdict and various other sentences and fines. In 1298 he revoked these penalties, ordering the Bishop of Fermo to lift the interdict in view of Fermo's military services to the papacy 'contra Columpnenses scismaticos et rebelles'.[63] Indeed the interdict's purpose had already been served, namely to compel obedience to ecclesiastical authority, since Fermo had returned to papal obedience.

Thirteenth-century popes thus understood that an interdict had to serve its proper ends; otherwise, it might be counter-productive spiritually and politically. We saw in Chapter 3 how they legislated and intervened to curb usage of interdicts for improper ends. For example, interdicts might not be laid without 'manifest and reasonable cause', but such a principle would be ineffectual without a mechanism to enforce it. The appeals' system that evolved in the Church from the mid-twelfth century provided this. Indeed the Fourth Lateran Council (1215) which established this principle ruled that if judges violated it, an appeal might be made to their superior to remove their unjust sentences. In fact by the 1170s Alexander III had already provided for appeals from sentences to a superior. He even specified in his decretal 'Qua fronte' (c.1174–81) that those under 'unreasonable' sentences of excommunication or interdict might appeal for absolution even if judges who imposed such sentences objected.[64] This decretal was addressed to the Archbishop of Canterbury, and Alexander was expressly providing for appeal from a bishop's sentence to his metropolitan. But appeals did not necessarily have to go to a judge's immediate superior. Decretal law also allowed appeals directly to the pope as 'universal ordinary', and interdict cases involving appeals to Rome abound in the thirteenth-century papal registers. The earliest examples show 'Qua fronte' in action. In 1198 when monks of Saint-Vaast Abbey, Arras, had petitioned Innocent III about interdicts laid on their churches by local prelates, he ordered the relaxation of such 'unreasonable' sentences. In this case he applied Alexander III's term 'unreasonable' to sentences

---

[62] Reg. Boniface VIII, no. 1307.   [63] Ibid. nos. 2552, 2555.
[64] 1 Comp. 2.20.41 (= X 2.28.25). Cf. his ruling at 1 Comp. 1.23.2 (c.1171–80).

laid 'without manifest and reasonable cause', anticipating his later ruling at the Fourth Lateran Council that such sentences might be removed on appeal. Indeed before 1215 he gave Saint-Vaast and other beneficiaries immunity from interdicts laid without manifest and reasonable cause. Such grants allowed them to appeal to Rome if they were aggrieved in this way and declared that sentences laid after such appeals were not binding.[65] But he did not restrict such appeals to those so privileged prior to his Lateran ruling. He responded favourably to appeals from Le Puy and Laon in 1207 and 1211, respectively, against interdicts laid without reasonable cause.[66] Indeed such appeals often prompted his grants of immunity from such sentences, as in the case of Laon and Saint-Vaast. Hence Innocent recognized a general right of appeal from such sentences on the basis of Alexander III's decretal 'Qua fronte' and simply confirmed this in his Lateran ruling.

Another influential ruling of Alexander III on appeal from interdicts was his decretal 'Ad hec'. The Bishop of Norwich had asked him how to deal with those who appealed from an interdict and then refused to observe it. He responded in 'Ad hec' that they might not avoid an interdict's effects by appealing after it was laid.[67] This signalled a departure from Romano-canonical procedure, the rules then being devised for the church courts. Normally appeals suspended proceedings against appellants in the church courts from which they appealed. But canonists quickly learned from 'Ad hec' that interdicts were not suspended by subsequent appeals.[68] Alanus explained that generally no sentence that came into immediate effect might be relieved by an appeal. Innocent III gave this explanation in his decretal 'Pastoralis' (1204) when he extended the ruling in 'Ad hec' to excommunication, and it was generally accepted by later thirteenth-century canonists.[69] This principle aside, the aim of such legislation was to curb frustratory appeals. As 'Ad hec' indicated, appeals might be used as an excuse to ignore interdicts. Even after 'Ad hec' circulated in *Compilatio prima*, the Archbishop of Arles still lamented in 1206 that those he laid under excommunication or interdict appealed to Rome 'in elusionem ecclesiastice discipline'. Nevertheless

---

[65] Innocent III, Reg. 1, nos. 160 (Saint-Vaast), 511; 2, no. 43; 7, no. 62; 10, nos. 120; 168; 14, no. 45.

[66] Ibid. 10, no. 85; 14, no. 63. Cf. ibid. 7, no. 151; 15, no. 124; 16, no. 57.

[67] 1 Comp. 2.20.46 (= X 2.28.37).

[68] E.g. Johannes Teutonicus on 3 Comp. 2.19.13 v. *suspendendum* (Ed. pp. 358–9); this gloss was copied by Tancred, ibid. (BAV, Vat. lat. MS 1377, fol. 218rb) and Bernard of Parma on X 2.28.55 v. *suspendendum*. Alanus on 1 Comp. 2.20.46 v. *declinare*, Munich, Bayerisches Staatsbibliothek Clm 3879, fol. 36va: 'Generaliter omnis sententia que secum trahit executionem per appellationem non <res>cinditur'.

[69] 3 Comp. 2.19.11 (= X 2.28.53). See e.g. Anon. on 1 Comp. 2.20.46 v. *declinare*, Brussels, Bibliothèque royale MS 1407–9, fol. 30rb: 'Patet quod executio annexa est interdicto sicut excommunicationi, tamen tam interdictus quam excommunicatus appellare potest, <ut> iii. q.ix. Revera, supra. de officio ord. Quesitum [C.3 q.9 c.12; 1 Comp. 1.23.2], sed tamen appellatio non relevat sententiam sed facit quod causa transferatur ad superiorem.' Cf. Tancred on 3 Comp. 1.20.2 v. *suspendatur*, BAV, Vat. lat. MS 1377, fol. 181ra: 'Hoc ideo quia illa sententia secum trahit suam executionem ut infra. de appell. Pastoralis'. Cf. also Vincentius Hispanus on 1 Comp. 1.23.2 v. *sententia*, Leipzig Universitätsbibliothek MS 983, fol. 9ra.

in accordance with 'Ad hec' popes often insisted that interdicts remain in force despite a subsequent appeal. In 1238 Gregory IX ordered that the interdict on Corbie and excommunication of its mayor and *jurati* be obeyed though the latter had appealed to him. The abbot of Corbie laid these sentences since these officials had led townsfolk in attacking his abbey and seizing some of its property. He told the pope that their appeal was frivolous and a mere pretext to continue defying his authority. Allegedly townsfolk had buried those under excommunication and interdict in the abbey cemetery, even building an *atrium* for such burials, presumably a walled enclosure. The pope ordered its demolition and publication of these sentences throughout the local province until Corbie's inhabitants came to terms. Evidently an appeal was no excuse for disregarding existing interdicts; clergy who did so could incur the canonical penalties for violating interdicts. In 1235 clergy in Milan diocese informed the pope that they were so confident of an appeal to him, they had not observed an interdict but hence now feared that they were irregular. Accordingly when Gregory IX relaxed this interdict, he granted those who celebrated during it provisional dispensation from irregularity.[70]

While early thirteenth-century canonists agreed that an appeal did not suspend an interdict already in force, they conceded that it might refer the appellant's case to a higher court.[71] Laurentius even held that a superior might absolve such an appellant if his appeal seemed justified, a view later adopted by Tancred.[72] But the issue was more problematic in practice. When an interdict was threatened on a city or region, its ruler was normally the appellant. Indeed Vincentius Hispanus admitted that a prince might appeal against his land being interdicted for another's fault.[73] The problem was that if the fault was his, church authorities might excommunicate him as well as interdict his land, and Innocent III had ruled in his decretal 'Per tuas' (1203) that excommunicates might not appeal until after their absolution.[74] Excommunication deprived a person of the right to act in court even if interdicts did not. Furthermore Hostiensis argued that one

---

[70] Arles: Innocent III, Reg. 9, no. 27. Corbie and Milan: Reg. Gregory IX, nos. 2520, 4498.

[71] See n. 69 (Brussels gloss). Cf. *Apparatus* 'Servus appellatur' on 3 Comp. 5.21.14 v. *videtur*, Bamberg Staatsbibliothek MS Can. 19, fol. 219vb: 'Appellatio non relevat, transfert tamen ad superiorem, extra. de ap. Qua fronte et iii. q.viiii. Revera [1 Comp. 2.20.41; C.3 q.9 c.12].' Tancred on 3 Comp. 1.20.2 v. *obiectum*, BAV, Vat. lat. MS 1377, fol. 181ra: 'Appellare potest non ut excommunicationem relevet sed ut causam transferat ad superiorem, supra. de appell. Qua fronte lib. i. infra. de sen. ex. Per tuas [1 Comp. 2.20.41; 3 Comp. 5.21.14] ... Vinc.'

[72] Tancred on 3 Comp. 5.23.7 v. *terram*, BAV, Vat. lat. MS 1377, fol. 279ra; Vat. lat. MS 2509, fol. 229ra: 'per appellationem hec absolutio ad superiorem refertur si appellatio iusta appareret, ut supra. de appell. Cum in ecclesia. lib. ii [2 Comp. 2.19.11] la.' Cf. McManus, 'Laurentius', 619.

[73] Vincentius Hispanus on Lat. Conc. IV c.42 v. *ne clerici* (*Constitutiones*, 348). By 1207 the Bishop of Auxerre had appealed against an interdict on his city, which was subject to his temporal jurisdiction, as Pierre Sampsona noted on X 2.28.55 v. *civitatis*, Vienna, Nationalbibliothek MS 2083, fol. 29vb; MS 2113, fol. 51rb: 'Nota hic quod episcopus appellat nomine sue civitatis vel nomine suorum subiectorum'. Cf. his pupil Bernard de Montmirat, *Lectura* on X 2.28.55 v. *se et suum*, BAV, Vat. lat. MS 2542, fol. 52ra; Borgh. lat. MS 231, fol. 77rb; MS 260, fol. 61vb (Ed. fol. 90ra).

[74] 3 Comp. 5.21.14 (= X 5.39.40).

might not even appeal from an interdict in force unless it was suspended. Clearly the appeal could not suspend it, but Hostiensis taught that it could be suspended for a time by the one who laid it and appeals lodged. Early thirteenth-century canonists had disagreed whether appeals from suspended interdicts were valid, as Hostiensis noted. Nevertheless his teaching was widely accepted by later canonists, especially Johannes Andreae and Johannes Calderinus, albeit Johannes de Legnano still judged the matter open to debate after an interdict on Bologna was suspended in 1357.[75]

Nevertheless appeals to Rome were sometimes made against interdicts already in force, as thirteenth-century papal registers reveal. Even Innocent III had entertained such appeals; hence contemporary canonists rightly described practice in arguing that they might be referred to higher courts. Indeed when the Archbishop of Arles decried his subjects' frustratory appeal against his sentences in 1206, Innocent still conceded that it might be prosecuted; and he appointed judges delegate to hear a similar appeal in 1212.[76] But it is hard to say whether Hostiensis's view described or even caused a change in papal practice later in the thirteenth century. No appeals against suspended interdicts are known from the papal registers, which might illustrate Hostiensis's point, though examples of popes suspending interdicts occur there. Nevertheless by the end of the century popes appear less sympathetic to appeals from those under interdict. In 1291 Nicholas IV rejected such an appeal from clergy in Lyon, Vienne, and Besançon provinces and Cambrai, Liège, Metz, Toul, and Verdun dioceses. They refused to pay a tenth granted by him in aid of the French Crown and he had authorized its collectors to compel them to do so; thus they were interdicted and their archbishops and bishops excommunicated. Their defiance was understandable in regions not considered part of the French kingdom; hence they appealed to the pope despite these sentences that they were not obliged to pay this tax to the French Crown.[77] Nicholas reacted by ordering his collectors to continue coercing them regardless of any appeal.

Even before the right to appeal against interdicts in force became problematic, papal registers referred more to appeals made before rather than after sentences were laid, notably under Innocent III.[78] Canon law had long favoured such advance appeals and the warning required before a sentence allowed sufficient opportunity for them. In the 1170s Alexander III had already ruled that excommunication was not binding if it was laid on anyone after they appealed.

---

[75] Hostiensis, *Lectura* on X 2.28.37 v. *illud* (vol. 1, fol. 180rb); Johannes Andreae, *Novella* on X 2.28.37; Johannes Calderinus (Andreae's pupil), 'De interdicto', Pt 2 §31 (fol. 333ra); id. (attrib.), *De censura*, BAV, Pal. lat. MS 797, fol. 15r (Clarke, 'Theory', 284–5). Legnano, 'De interdicto'; the latter text abridges that in BAV, Vat. lat. MS 2639, fols. 292vb–300rb (McCall, 'Legnano', 417, 420), where the explicit records that Legnano debated this question in Bologna on 13 January 1358.

[76] Innocent III, Reg. 15, no. 12. Arles: n. 70.

[77] Reg. Nicholas IV, no. 6316; Denton, 'Assemblies', 4–6.

[78] E.g. Innocent III, Reg. 1, nos. 58, 131, 240; 5, no. 136; 6, no. 42; 8, no. 31; 9, no. 27; 10, nos. 120, 189, 190, 194; 14, no. 133; 15, nos. 119, 192; etc.

By 1198 Innocent III was applying this rule to interdicts, declaring them null if an appeal had preceded them.[79] In 1203 he amplified on Alexander III's ruling in his decretal 'Per tuas': if a sentence of excommunication was laid after an appeal or contained an 'intolerable error', those subject to it did not need absolution to prosecute their appeal. But he conceded that it was papal custom to absolve them 'provisionally' (*ad cautelam*). Apparently he was extending this custom to interdicts by 1209, when he provisionally relaxed sentences of excommunication, suspension, and interdict imposed after an appeal to Rome.[80] The distinction between declaring such sentences not binding and relaxing them provisionally was not purely semantic; provisional relaxation implied that they might be reimposed if the appeals preceding them were not upheld. In this instance absolution might be secured only by fulfilling the usual preconditions: swearing obedience to ecclesiastical mandates and offering satisfaction. A decretal of Honorius III suggests as much. It responded to an appeal of the Bishop of Le Mans against his suspension by his metropolitan. Honorius agreed to relax this sentence provisionally once he had sworn that he would obey his metropolitan's mandates if he were found guilty of whatever provoked the sentence.[81] Jacobus de Albenga commented on this decretal that if he was suspended *ex culpa vel offensa*, he should have given satisfaction before he could be absolved.

Such an oath of obedience might be required of appellants seeking provisional relaxation of interdicts, especially after Honorius's decretal was included in the *Liber extra* (1234).[82] For example, in 1235 Gregory IX required the Bishop of Ascoli Puglia to relax provisionally an interdict placed on an abbey after an appeal, but its abbot and monks first had to give a 'sufficient caution' to obey ecclesiastical mandates on issues that occasioned the interdict. Such mandates doubtless comprised those of the cardinal appointed to hear their appeal and of the Archbishop of Bari who had laid the interdict. An oath was not the only precondition for such appellants from ecclesiastical censure. A Third Lateran Council canon (1179) required them to prosecute their appeal within the deadline set by the appeal judge; otherwise they had to pay the other party's costs. Incidentally it also required that a warning precede a sentence, hence enabling appeals before it was imposed. By the mid-thirteenth century this right of appeal was subject to further limitations. At the First Council of Lyon Innocent IV ruled that provisional absolution was denied if the judge who laid the sentence (or another opponent) could prove in eight days that a manifest offence had caused it. Faced with such opposition absolution might be granted only on fulfilment of

---

[79] Ibid. 1, nos. 131, 240; 5, no. 136; 6, no. 42; 10, nos. 20, 189, 194; 14, no. 133. Alexander III: n. 64.

[80] Innocent III, Reg. 11, no. 205; 3 Comp. 1.3.7 (= X 1.4.8). 'Per tuas': n. 74.

[81] 5 Comp. 5.18.4 (= X 5.39.52). Jacobus de Albenga on 5 Comp. 5.18.4 v. *parebit*, London, BL, Royal MS 11.C.VII, fol. 270vb: 'In hoc fecit bene quia si erat suspensus ex culpa vel offensa prius deberet satisfacere quam absolveretur, ut supra. de v. sig. Ex parte. lib. iii. [3 Comp. 5.23.7].'

[82] Reg. Gregory IX, no. 2712.

the usual preconditions, including a suitable caution to obey the law regarding an *offensa dubia*. Moreover Innocent ruled in his decretal 'Venerabilibus' (1254) that a sentence might be relaxed provisionally if it followed an appeal made on legitimate and provable (*probabili*) grounds; doubtless the reverse was true where these were lacking.[83]

This legislation was meant to discourage frustratory appeals, i.e. those made to frustrate the legal process generally and threatened sentences specifically. The papacy was certainly concerned about this abuse by the mid-thirteenth century. Indeed after a legate excommunicated the king of Hungary and interdicted his court, the Archbishop of Esztergom apparently not only refused to publish these sentences but also appealed to prevent others doing so; Gregory IX upbraided him for this in 1234. Nevertheless, if judges thought an appeal frustratory, they sometimes enforced sentences regardless, and occasionally popes even authorized them to do so against notorious offenders. In 1243 Innocent IV empowered the Archbishop of Cologne to use ecclesiastical censure, barring any appeal, against those persecuting clergy and churches in his diocese, even interdicting their land if necessary, and in particular he could ignore frivolous appeals 'habitually launched in destruction of ecclesiastical discipline'.[84] Indeed the canonist Alanus had distinguished that frustratory appeals were invalid in the case of notorious crimes or when they were a means to persist in a crime or the grounds for appeal were clearly unjust. Canonists even taught that such appeals might be ignored altogether after a ruling of Innocent III in 1203.[85] The concern was that not only might subjects escape ecclesiastical discipline but archbishops might also exercise appellate jurisdiction at their suffragans' expense. In 1245 Innocent IV learned from bishops of Reims province that sentences of excommunication or interdict laid by them or their officials were illicitly lifted by their metropolitan and his officials owing to frivolous appeals. Appellants seeking to avoid their judgement allegedly secured archiepiscopal rescripts in favour of their appeals before these sentences were published, even when no grievance was stated as grounds for appeal. Innocent's decretal 'Romana Ecclesia' replied to such allegations by limiting the archbishop's right to hear appeals from and absolve suffragans' subjects; and such restrictions were meant to apply generally.[86]

Nevertheless during the thirteenth century canonists identified an increasing number of legal reasons why a superior might relax a sentence provisionally. A

---

[83] Lat. Conc. III c.6 (= X 2.28.26); VI 5.11.2, 7 §2.

[84] Reg. Gregory IX, no. 203; Reg. Innocent IV, no. 354.

[85] Alanus on 1 Comp. 2.20.42 v. *ingressum*, Munich, Bayerisches Staatsbibliothek Clm 3879, fol 36vb: 'Frustratoria enim tenet appellatio, ut s. e. t. Consuluit, extra. t. Prudentiam [1 Comp. 2.20.16; 2 Comp. 2.19.16], nisi in casibus ut in notorio crimine, ut supra. Ex querimoniis [1 Comp. 2.20.33], et ubi pretextu appellationis in crimine vult perseverare, ut supra. e. Relatum [1 Comp. 2.20.21], et ubi manifeste iniustam causam appellandi assignat ut supra. e. t. Relatum'. Cf. 3 Comp. 2.19.11 (= X 2.28.53) and Johannes Teutonicus on 3 Comp. 2.19.11 v. *indulgetur expresse* (Ed. pp. 350–1).

[86] Reg. Innocent IV, no. 1625; VI 5.11.5.

prior appeal, whether frustratory or not, was one. Another was specified along with this in Innocent III's decretal 'Per tuas' (1203), namely an 'intolerable error' in the sentence. An early commentary on 'Per tuas' understood this to mean that the sentence was laid because of something that could not give rise to contumacy, such as belief in God. In other words the sentence's cause was uncanonical; Innocent defined contumacy as the main canonical cause of a sentence.[87] Likewise Vincentius argued that an 'intolerable error' was an error of law, notably excommunicating someone for being obedient, i.e. the opposite of contumacy. Johannes Teutonicus agreed, but added that an intolerable error might be an error of fact, notably excommunicating someone for a deed they had not done.[88] He also taught that this error might involve a mortal sin, a view Vincentius noted but later rejected. Johannes nevertheless accepted his argument that appeal was unnecessary in the case of intolerable error, since the sentence was automatically null. Johannes's commentary on 'Per tuas' was largely copied by Tancred into his gloss on *Compilatio tertia* and later canonists treated this gloss as *ordinaria*; thus they adopted Johannes's definition of 'intolerable error', though not apparently his view on appeal as unnecessary.[89] Nevertheless the basic idea of intolerable error as something against canon law was influential, and the grounds for provisional relaxation which canonists identified beyond those in 'Per tuas' were largely instances of this.

First, since the late twelfth century canonists had stated the maxim that a sentence laid on anyone by someone who was not their judge was null.[90] By the early thirteenth century this argument was recognized in practice as grounds for appeal. For example, in 1213 Countess Matilda of Flanders sought papal

---

[87] *Apparatus* 'Servus appellatur' on 3 Comp. 5.21.14 v. *errorem*, Bamberg Staatsbibliothek MS Can. 19, fol. 219vb: 'Quod intelligo quandocumque excommunicat eum pro tali facto ex quo non potest surgere contumacia puta "Excommunico te quia facis quod debes", vel "Excommunico te quia credis in deum" vel "quia credis articulos fidei", alias non'.

[88] Vincentius on 3 Comp. 5.21.14 v. *errorem*, Bamberg Staatsbibliothek MS Can. 20, fol. 178vb: 'Cum enim errorem continet nec etiam appellare necesse est, ar. ff. que sen. sine ap. res. l.i. §1 [Dig. 49.8.1] ... Sed quis erit error? Dicunt quidam quodlibet peccatum mortale peccatum, xxviii. q. i. Uxor, xiii. di. Nervi [C.28 q.1 c.4; D.13 c.2]. Ego intelligo errorem iuris de quo agitur unde si excommunicat <eum> quia non adulteratur, tenet excommunicatio, vel quia non interficit hominem. Si autem excommunicat eum quia est obediens, non tenet quia pro sola contumacia quis est excommunicatus, xi q.iii. Certum [C.11 q.3 c.43].' Johannes on 3 Comp. 5.21.14 v. *intollerabilem*: http://faculty.cu.edu/Pennington/ edit517.htm

[89] Tancred on 3 Comp. 5.21.14, copied Johannes's gloss at v. *errorem* and the first part of Vincentius's gloss before 'Sed quis erit error?' at v. *intollerabilem*; BAV, Vat. lat. MS 1377, fol. 277va. Vincentius (c.1236) on X 5.39.40 v. *errorem*, Paris, BN, MS lat. 3967, fol. 206v, copied Johannes's gloss too but added: 'dico ego quod error mortalis peccati non est contra naturam excommunicationis expresse ut "Excommunico te quia <non> interficis hominem, adulteraris vel non furaris" non offendit excommunicationem, licet quidam dicant contra ius'. Johannes's gloss was also copied by Goffredus de Trano on X 5.39.40 v. *intollerabilem*, Vienna, Nationalbibliothek MS 2197, fol. 157rb. Cf. Bernard of Parma on X 5.39.40 v. *intollerabilem errorem*.

[90] Ricardus Anglicus on 1 Comp. 1.23.2 v. *appellationem*, BAV, Pal. lat. MS 696, fol. 17rb: 'Nota quod sententia a non suo iudice de causa nulla est, ut ii. q. i. Inprimis [C.2 q.1 c.7].' Copied with additional allegations by Tancred, ibid.; BAV, Vat. lat. MS 1377, fol. 14vb.

justice as the Archbishop of Reims had excommunicated her and interdicted her lands though she claimed to hold nothing in his diocese. The pope hence understood that she was not subject to the archbishop's jurisdiction, and ordered that his sentences against her be declared null unless her case had been referred to him on appeal or delegated to him. It is unclear whether canonists recognized such exceptions, but Johannes Andreae later stated that even sentences laid by delegated authority might be null if they went against the delegator's intentions.[91]

Another instance of nullity canonists identified by the early thirteenth century was a variation on the maxim above.[92] Those directly subject to the pope and immune from ordinary jurisdiction, notably the exempt, could not be laid under valid sentences except by papal authority. As the local ordinary was not their judge, they might appeal against his sentences. Two undated decretals of Alexander III acknowledged this right and declared such sentences not binding *de iure*. Hence almost a century later a priory claiming exemption from episcopal jurisdiction appealed to Rome when the Bishop of Orvieto excommunicated its monks and others associated with it and interdicted it and a church subject to it. A cardinal appointed by Innocent IV to hear their appeal judged in 1257 that the bishop had acted wrongly and his sentences were invalid as the priory and church were exempt; Alexander IV confirmed this.[93]

Further instances of nullity largely concerned violations of judicial procedure. And these instances grew as the rules of procedure governing the interdict multiplied. For instance, following the ruling at the Third Lateran Council (1179) that a warning should precede a sentence, sentences might be declared null if laid without a warning. Certainly this was true under Innocent III, and as we have seen, he was also prepared to declare sentences null if laid without manifest and reasonable cause even before he made the latter a legal requirement in his Fourth Lateran Council ruling.[94] Innocent IV reinforced these rulings at the First Council of Lyon, adding that a sentence should be proclaimed in writing. Hence the canonist Pierre Sampsona could remark by the mid-thirteenth century that a sentence might be annulled as unjust if laid without warning, reasonable cause, or written form (*sine scriptis*).[95] By *c*.1302 Johannes

[91] Innocent III, Reg. 15, no. 199; cf. Reg. Honorius III, no. 2166. Johannes Andreae, *Glossa* on VI 5.11.10 v. *ad cautelam.*

[92] Vincentius Hispanus on 1 Comp. 2.20.7 v. *excommunicationis*, Leipzig Universitätsbibliothek MS 983, fol. 19rb: 'Sed contra nonne exemptus est ab eius iudicio? Si ergo iuste sententiavit in eum, non tenuit, x. q.ii. c.i. [C.10 q.2 c.1].' Tancred on 2 Comp. 5.13.3 v. *tenere*, BAV, Vat. lat. MS 1377, fol. 141vb: 'Eos eximit dominus papa a iurisdictione sui prelati unde sententia talis iure communi tamquam a non suo iudice lata non tenet, ut xi. q.i c. penult. et C. si a non compe. iudice l. ult. supra. de iudic. At si clerici. lib. i. [C.11 q.1 c.46; Cod. 7.48.4; 1 Comp. 2.1.6] ... A<lanus>.'

[93] 1 Comp. 2.1.6; 3.25.4. Reg. Alexander IV, no. 2448; cf. Reg. Gregory IX, no. 1299.

[94] Lat. Conc. III c.6 (= X 2.28.26). Innocent III, Reg. 1, no. 240; 10, no. 120 (immunity from sentences laid without warning and freedom to appeal against them).

[95] Coll. III 36; (= VI 5.11.1). Pierre Sampsona on X 1.29.36 v. *postulanti*, Vienna, National-bibliothek MS 2083, fol. 13va: 'Aut dicitur sententia esse nulla aut annullanda tamquam iniusta, aut quia lata est monitione non premissa aut absque causa rationabili, ut infra. de sententia

Andreae could list twelve instances where excommunication might be declared null and provisionally absolved. Bérenger Frédol even claimed that provisional absolution was to be granted to anyone seeking it around this time.[96]

Nevertheless provisional absolution was only possible in certain instances, and Gregory X even outlawed it altogether regarding general local interdicts at the Second Council of Lyon. According to the first commentators on this ruling, Johannes Garsias Hispanus and William Durand, it responded to the fact that canonists doubted whether these interdicts might be lifted provisionally.[97] Certainly canonists justified the ruling readily. Durand noted that though the innocent punished by general interdicts seemed to deserve provisional relaxation more than excommunicates (who might still seek it), excommunication had graver spiritual consequences. It separated from communion of men while interdicts only forbade the sacraments and even then not all of them. It also bound the soul and might consign the latter to eternal damnation, whereas nobody was delivered to Satan by general interdicts; hence there was less urgency to relax them.

Johannes Andreae largely adopted these views in his gloss on the *Liber sextus* (considered *ordinaria* at Bologna) after this ruling was included there. He also agreed with Durand and Garsias Hispanus that, since its ban on provisional relaxation related to general interdicts, this did not apply to specific interdicts, at least on persons.[98] But Guido de Baysio distinguished that it applied to specific interdicts on places, notably individual churches, but not admittedly on persons. Nevertheless Johannes Monachus, whose gloss on the *Liber sextus* was *ordinaria* at Paris, argued that specific interdicts might be lifted provisionally even on churches. As with excommunication the reason given was the greater severity of such sentences; he and Garsias Hispanus argued that the mitigations of the interdict, notably infant baptism, applied to general not specific sentences.[99] Monachus apparently reflected current practice.

---

excommuni. Sacro [X 5.39.47], aut sine scriptis et ita contra constitutionem novam, infra. de sententia excommuni. Cum medicinalis [Coll. III 36] … dicatur annullanda tamquam iniusta ex tribus causis predictis'.

[96] Johannes Andreae, *Glossa* on VI 5.11.10 v. *ad cautelam*; he simply added four cases to the eight already listed by Hostiensis, *Summa* on X 5.27 §4 (fol. 258rb). *Bérenger Frédol*, 4. See also Logan, 118–19.

[97] Lugd. Conc. II c.30 (= VI 5.11.10). Johannes Garsias Hispanus on Lugd. Conc. II c.30, v. *Presenti*, BAV, Pal. lat. MS 629, fol. 285ra: 'sed dubitatur utrum sicut observabatur in sententia excommunicationis ita observaretur in sententia interdicti promulgata in civitatem vel castrum'. Cf. William Durand on Lugd. Conc. II c.30 (fol. 103r).

[98] Johannes Andreae, *Glossa* on VI 5.11.10 v. *declaramus*; v. *generaliter*. William Durand on Lugd. Conc. II c.30 (fols. 103v–104r).

[99] Guido de Baysio on VI 5.11.10 v. *sive*; v. *non habere* (Ed. fol. 123ra). Johannes Monachus on VI 5.11.10 (Ed. fol. 407vb). Johannes Garsias Hispanus on Conc. Lugd. II c.30 v. *ad cautelam*, BAV, Pal. lat. MS 629, fol. 285ra: 'Sed quid de suspensione vel de interdicto specialiter promulgato? Nunquid relaxabitur ad cautelam? Dic quod sic ar. hoc a contrario sensu et ar. supra. e. Solet [Coll. III 37], maius enim periculum est in interdicto speciali quam in generali, cum in generali baptismus

For example the chapter of a collegiate church in Tèrouanne diocese told Boniface VIII that, despite their prior appeal to him, their bishop interdicted them and their church and excommunicated its clergy. The sentences were technically null; hence the chapter sought their revocation, at least provisionally. Boniface acceded in 1298, four months after reissuing Gregory X's ruling in the *Liber sextus*.[100] This case also illustrates that personal interdicts were still lifted provisionally in practice, and indeed canonists agreed that specific personal interdicts might be, for, as Johannes Andreae argued, they forbade all sacraments like excommunication.

Certainly provisional absolution was crucial for excommunicates to prosecute appeals. Without it they might not act in court, whereas those under interdicts were not deprived of such rights; thus Gregory's ruling did not necessarily inhibit appeals from general interdicts. Durand even argued that a lord might obtain provisional absolution of sentences on him and his family by reason of a prior appeal, even if an interdict on his land might not be lifted while the appeal was pending. Durand's earlier arguments excused the continuing punishment of the lord's innocent subjects which this implied. Nevertheless Johannes Andreae pointed out that interdicts might be suspended; hence provisional relaxation was unnecessary.[101] Although we have noted no evidence that interdicts were suspended for the sake of an appeal, they were certainly suspended for other reasons: to facilitate resolution of disputes, notably between clergy and laity;[102] reward a city's devotion to the papacy;[103] permit an episcopal election;[104] allow those preaching the crusade to celebrate in interdicted places, and presumably recruit better there.[105] Normally an interdict might be suspended only by the one who laid it and for a specific period; after this it came back into force unless the guilty had come to terms in the meantime.[106] But this period might be extended to allow the guilty extra time to do so. In 1300 Boniface VIII ordered a legate to suspend an interdict on Spoleto until All Saints' Day since it opposed his enemies at nearby Gubbio.[107] It had provoked the sentence by seizing a *castrum* under papal overlordship; on the suspension expiring he ordered the legate to extend it and secure restitution of that *castrum* in the meantime.

---

parvulorum et penitentie morientium excipiantur et predicatio verbi dei et confirmatio episcopalis, supra. e. c. Responso et c. Permittimus, de spon. Non est [X 5.39.43, 57; 4.1.11]. Sed specialiter interdicto omnia ista denegantur ante absolutionem'.

[100] Reg. Boniface VIII, no. 3051.

[101] William Durand on Lugd. Conc. II c.30 (fol. 104v). Johannes Andreae, *Glossa* on VI 5.11.10 v. *generaliter*.

[102] Reg. Clement IV, no. 671; Reg. Nicholas IV, no. 7211; Reg. Boniface VIII, nos. 2034, 2374.

[103] Reg. Boniface VIII, nos. 932, 4211.

[104] Reg. Gregory IX, nos. 3894, 4358. See pp. 154–6 above.

[105] Reg. Urban IV, nos. 385, C321.

[106] See e.g. Hostiensis, *Lectura* on X 2.28.37 v. *illud* (vol. 1, fol. 180r). Cf. Reg. Boniface VIII, no. 932.

[107] Reg. Boniface VIII, nos. 3727, 3731, 3897.

What this chapter has sought to illustrate is that an interdict's aim was not retribution but reconciliation, both between wrongdoers and wronged and between ecclesiastical authority and those disobeying it. It thus differed strikingly from the vindictive forms of contemporary secular punishment. Medieval churchmen believed in the possibility of redemption for sinners; thus their sanctions were meant to induce repentance. Once the one who had provoked an interdict complied with their demands and gave the required pledge or satisfaction, the sentence might be relaxed. Hence it was a means to an end rather than an end in itself. Sometimes it was lifted without such preconditions being fulfilled, notably when it was failing to serve this end or even impeding it. Moreover interdicts might be relaxed provisionally when they were null, and grounds for nullity expanded during the thirteenth century. Nevertheless in his decretal 'Per tuas' (1203) Innocent III distinguished that sentences appealed as unjust rather than null remained binding. His decretal concerned excommunication but Hostiensis understood that this distinction also extended to interdicts. Early thirteenth-century canonists had held that obedience to unjust sentences was meritorious and meant that ecclesiastical discipline was feared.[108] When later canonists accepted that an unjust interdict was valid and the ban on provisionally relaxing general local interdicts justified, they likewise held that the suffering of innocents under such sentences was excusable. Although an interdict was not meant to be vindictive, its effect was undeniably harsh on the innocent. Their suffering was underscored by their impotence since they might bring about the lifting, and indeed the laying, of general interdicts only indirectly. The initiative in provoking such sentences and securing their removal ultimately lay with the guilty.

---

[108] Hostiensis: as n. 75; cf. Johannes Andreae, *Novella* on X 2.28.37. Laurentius Hispanus cited the argument for obeying unjust sentences on 3 Comp. 2.19.11 v. *cum executionem excommunicatio secum trahat* (McManus, 'Laurentius', 442), attributing it to Petrus Hispanus; cf. *Apparatus* 'Servus appellatur' (probably by a pupil of Laurentius) on 3 Comp. 2.19.11 v. *excommunicatis*, Bamberg, Staatsbibliothek MS Can. 19, fol. 170r. Laurentius's gloss was copied by Johannes Teutonicus on 3 Comp. 2.19.11 v. *secum trahat* (Ed. p. 352) and Tancred, ibid. v. *executionem* (BAV, Vat. lat. MS 1377, fol. 217va).

Conclusion

This book has largely treated the interdict as a collective sanction, though it might be placed on individuals and sometimes was. Its application to entire communities posed a major moral and legal problem, for it involved punishing the innocent together with the guilty. The writings of twelfth- and thirteenth-century canonists and theologians do much to illuminate why contemporary popes and prelates thought such indiscriminate punishment was justified. Firstly the schoolmen recognized that a penalty that struck at those close to an offender might be more effective than one that affected him alone. Secondly they recognized the Pauline doctrine that those consenting to evil deserved punishment along with the evildoer. And they distinguished between two main forms of consent. It might be 'express', involving active collaboration and support, or 'tacit', meaning the failure to resist others' sins. Admittedly some reserved this correction of others' sins to those in authority, but several, notably Peter the Chanter and Huguccio, argued that it was a universal duty and might even be exercised against the powerful by their subjects. The Chanter, Huguccio, and some early-thirteenth-century canonists even suggested that this responsibility weighed even more on subjects as a group than as individuals, for their power to resist sins lay in their numbers. Hence the group that failed in this duty deserved punishment more. These writers specifically had in mind Jewish failure to stop Christ's Crucifixion, but their argument clearly had wider, more contemporary, political resonances. Innocent III, trained at Paris in the Chanter's day and at Bologna when Huguccio was the leading canonist there, hinted more than once that interdicts fell on realms where subjects failed to resist their prince's disobedience to the Church. Likewise Stephen Langton, a pupil of the Chanter, warned King John's subjects not to consent to royal defiance of the Church shortly before his kingdom was interdicted. Churchmen and the schoolmen who taught them considered that subjects owed greater loyalty to ecclesiastical than secular authority, especially when lay and clerical powers clashed. Clergy had to preach to John's subjects under the interdict on his realm that they had to fear and obey divine power more than human. Such views partly derived from the doctrine of the reform papacy that popes had a right to depose unfit rulers and release their subjects from obedience. Kern even credited the reform papacy with enshrining an 'ecclesiastical right of resistance', such that subjects had a duty to resist princes condemned by ecclesiastical authority.[1] Schoolmen backing this right in the twelfth and thirteenth centuries were also reacting to organized forms of lay government emerging at that time, whose claims over their subjects increasingly rivalled the Church's own. Churchmen largely used interdicts to defend ecclesiastical claims against the secular power and to reinforce their authority over clergy and laity. However, although they imposed interdicts to incite subjects to resist errant rulers and punish past failure to do so, they and their teachers thereby advocated peaceful protest not armed uprising. They recognized that royal power was ordained by God and hence to be obeyed even when misused against his Church.

The interdict and scholastic doctrine that justified it thus sought to reinforce a sense of collective responsibility, if not collective guilt, among subjects for the faults of their rulers. Canonistic thought in this regard and many others drew on late twelfth-century theology, as shown by the remarkable unanimity of Huguccio and the Chanter on this matter. But Roman law and its commentators began to replace theology as the main external influence on canonistic thought by the early thirteenth century, notably on ideas of collective responsibility.[2] This change indeed carried such ideas in a new direction as canonists began to explore them within the context of corporation theory. Roman law supplied canonists with the notion *universitas*, an organized community or corporation. Although they largely applied it to ecclesiastical bodies like a bishop and his chapter, they recognized that it also described the city communes emerging across Europe, particularly in northern Italy where the most famous canonists taught. By the mid-thirteenth century canonists reached a consensus that a *universitas* might be held responsible for crimes of its rulers or agents done with its prior consent or subsequent approval and that it might be penalized accordingly; Innocent IV who crystallized this view specified the interdict as an appropriate penalty. This affirmed that a community was capable of 'express' consent to its leaders' faults, not only tacit consent as earlier theologians and canonists had argued. Organized ecclesiastical and civic communities were indeed run on the basis of express and collective consent, notably in the election of their leaders. Jurists increasingly observed that those invested with power by such a community were its representatives and thus it might be held responsible for whatever they did in this capacity. Hence consent included a general mandate to act in another's name, not just approval of specific acts. This was based on another area of interaction between Roman and canon law: Romano-canonical procedure. This defined the rules governing the growing system of church courts, notably the appointing of proctors or legal representatives. Such rules provided that litigants might issue a general mandate to a proctor and canonists agreed by the early thirteenth century that this bound them to whatever the proctor

---

[1] Kern, *Divine Right*, 81–133, esp. 97–117.
[2] Cf. Meyer, 243–6, 252–7, 265, 271–3.

did on their behalf provided that it came within the mandate's terms. It is not hard to see how this principle came to be applied more generally when thirteenth-century canonists increasingly saw the head of an ecclesiastical body as its proctor. Even in the secular sphere governments might issue general mandates to their agents, notably ambassadors; Edward I of England required that the representatives of local communities attend Parliament with *plena potestas* to bind those communities to whatever was decided there, largely tax grants.[3] However, in most thirteenth-century communities, especially kingdoms, tacit consent to authority remained the norm, and even when kings were crowned with their subjects' acclamation and they summoned popular assemblies to approve their taxes, such consent was rarely free if express. But feudal ties could also justify interdicts on kingdoms and other domains. Those holding lands from the lord of such a domain owed him financial and military aid and counsel. Consequently this might involve them in supporting him against the Church and hence their punishment along with him under a general local interdict might seem deserved.

Although such thinking on consent and representation might justify interdicts on communities, the thirteenth-century papacy had misgivings about such collective sanctions. It recognized that they did not always have the desired effect of turning the innocent against the guilty. Frequently the innocent turned against Church authorities for depriving them of religious ministrations and the guilty became even more defiant and resisted observance of interdicts. Sometimes the innocent supported the guilty in their defiance. In addition, the papacy observed that interdicts could have undesirable side effects. The lack of pastoral care could weaken the faith of many and encourage the growth of heresy, especially when interdicts disinclined rulers from persecuting it. But the interdict was too valuable as a means of coercion for the papacy to abandon it completely, though sometimes popes were prepared to lift an interdict simply because it was proving counter-productive. Generally they insisted upon strict enforcement of interdicts in the teeth of popular and princely opposition. Popes from Alexander III to Clement V issued laws that inflicted automatic penalties on clergy ignoring interdicts. And when lay rulers defied interdicts, popes sometimes threatened to proceed against them further both *spiritualiter* and *temporaliter*. Temporal proceedings usually meant an embargo, though when popes applied these outside their temporal jurisdiction, they clearly depended on the cooperation of foreign rulers.

Popes also strove to make the interdict work more effectively by mitigating its severity for the innocent whilst maintaining its force against the guilty. By the twelfth century infant baptism and penance of the dying were traditionally excluded from the interdict's ban on the sacraments. From the late twelfth century the papacy introduced further exceptions. Firstly they granted certain regular clergy and others freedoms in interdicted lands, notably the right to celebrate behind closed doors, usually provided that these beneficiaries had not provoked

---

[3] Post, 91–162.

the interdict. Such grants were even made to secular dignitaries and other laity, especially to reward service to the Church and pious activities like almsgiving and crusading. But most went to clergy mostly to spare them from sanctions normally imposed on their behalf; interdicts were largely weapons of self-defence against lay infringements of clerical immunities. In 1298 Boniface VIII's constitution 'Alma mater' made it the common right of all clergy to celebrate offices behind closed doors during general local interdicts, and further conceded that the laity might be admitted to these services on certain feast days. Hence the thirteenth-century papacy reduced the severity of such sentences not only by grants to specific groups or individuals but also by rulings that acquired general force. At the start of the century these were normally issued in relation to individual sentences, notably Innocent III's interdict on France, and they were applied to other interdicts mainly as a result of their inclusion in decretal collections compiled by canonists. As popes seized the initiative from canonists in creating such collections, notably Gregory IX with the *Liber extra*, they became more self-conscious as legislators. For example Gregory wrote a ruling for his own collection, that the host was to be consecrated for the dying weekly in all interdicted lands. This movement towards direct general legislation culminated in the *Liber sextus*, where 'Alma mater' appeared. Indeed this constitution represented the most self-conscious papal attempt to reform interdicts; Boniface VIII recognized the need to do so in its preamble, observing that during general interdicts 'the indevotion of the populace grows, heresies pullulate, and infinite spiritual dangers arise'.

In addition to softening the terms of the interdict, the papacy also attempted to curb misuse of the sanction which might otherwise limit its effectiveness. Innocent III heard appeals from interdicts on the grounds that they had no manifest and reasonable cause, even granting some appellants immunity from such sentences, and he made it a general rule that such sentences were null. His successors introduced more procedural rules concerning interdicts that increased the grounds for appeal from the sanction and encouraged judges to use it only as a last resort, where other means of coercion failed. Popes especially discouraged general interdicts in cases involving the faults of private individuals such as debts; popes and canonists agreed that a community might be held accountable and punished only for faults of its public figures. But interdicts doubtless became more frequent as ecclesiastical jurisdiction expanded, and such regulation was probably a reaction to this. Indeed by the thirteenth century the power to interdict was technically limited to ecclesiastical judges, but the growing business of church courts, especially the curia, meant that this power was increasingly delegated and passed into ever more hands, particularly at the lower end of the clerical hierarchy. Not only were there ever more men able to lay interdicts (and only men since this power was denied to women) but ever more papal laws imposed an automatic interdict on their violators. Such laws were so numerous by the early fourteenth century that treatises listing them proliferated.

Indeed since the late twelfth century a substantial body of papal law and legal doctrine on interdicts had developed. Early papal rulings on the interdict arose largely in response to external demand, since local ecclesiastical authorities asked the pope to clarify how it was meant to work. Subsequently, as argued above, papal lawmaking became more self-conscious and less related to individual cases, but it maintained the pragmatic concern of earlier rulings to make the interdict more effective as a means of coercion. Its operation was thus regulated at the end of the thirteenth century far more closely than at the start; and papal letters and other sources show that increasingly the interdict worked in accordance with canon law and canonistic thought. But did all this regulation yield the effect popes desired? Our studies of interdicts at Béziers, Dax, and San Gimignano suggest that, despite municipal and popular defiance, clergy of these towns could enforce these sentences until the canonistic preconditions for lifting them were fulfilled, i.e. satisfaction, oaths, or pledges; albeit at San Gimignano it is difficult to say exactly what this involved. How far papal reform and regulation of the interdict made these sentences effective is debatable. Certainly new laws imposing penalties on clergy who violated interdicts may have reinforced observance, but some clergy were willing to flout the interdicts at San Gimignano and Dax while laity circumvented the law by usurping clerical functions at interdicted Béziers. Even clergy observing these interdicts did so in their own interest, since the sentences were laid in defence of their liberties and property. Moreover papal mitigations of the interdict did not necessarily make these sentences effective either. City officials even impeded clerical observance of such mitigations at Dax, expelling Dominicans who came to preach in the cathedral and banning reception of the permitted sacraments from its chaplain. Admittedly such preaching might persuade people to take the Church's side, but Dax's officials did not stop clergy observing such mitigations so that popular resentment of the Church might increase and the interdict's efficacy decrease for the want of them. These clergy were boycotted since they observed the interdict according to canon law and were obedient to ecclesiastical authority. Indeed Dax's officials encouraged renegade priests to offer ministrations banned by the interdict in defiance of canon law and episcopal authority. Nevertheless some laity observed the interdict canonically, shunning these priests and attending churches outside Dax. The latter option and other exceptions to the interdict doubtless encouraged their loyalty to the Church but grievances shared with the clergy against the city's officials seem a stronger factor. However, it indicates some popular awareness of what was officially permitted during interdicts. This was also evident at San Gimignano when many laity solicited clergy to baptize their children and absolve the dying; the refusal of such customary mitigations doubtless contributed to popular resentment of these clergy and the interdict as well as the commune's decision to hire its own priests to perform these rites. Nevertheless even when canonical mitigations were respected, they did not bring universal compliance with the interdict, since laity in all three towns participated in rites banned by it, and civic authorities enabled them to do so at Dax and San Gimignano.

Despite such civic and popular defiance, those who occasioned these interdicts eventually sought to be free from them, which meant coming to terms with the Church authorities, or at least lengthy litigation and negotiation in the case of San Gimignano. And growing requests from laity and clergy for papal immunities from the interdict in the thirteenth century indeed suggest that it was increasingly seen as something worth being free from. It was thus a potent weapon in the hands of churchmen, even if papal reform of the sanction had not entirely reduced its unwanted side effects, as our case studies show. Interdicts were especially valuable to the papacy as it faced deepening opposition to its claims to intervene in secular affairs by the later thirteenth century. The interdict was a tool of this interventionism, and resistance to this sanction sprang increasingly from resentment of the ecclesiastical claims it was used to defend. Such resentment culminated under Boniface VIII, and it is no coincidence that he made the biggest contributions to papal law on the interdict. He thereby sought to reinvigorate it as a means to counter the growing challenges to traditional papal claims. Indeed some of his laws inflicted an automatic interdict on violators of the clerical immunities they upheld, notably his bull 'Clercis laicos'. Its arenga described the laity as traditionally hostile to the clergy, which can be seen as a rationale for interdicts and his attempts to reinvigorate them. Indeed the whole history of the evolution of canonical thought and procedure on interdicts in the thirteenth century is one of growing papal determination to bolster the spiritual power in its relations with temporal rulers and reinforce a sense of corporate identity in Christian society over and beyond, if not always in derogation of, individual liberties.

Bibliography

MANUSCRIPTS CITED

Admont Stiftsbibliothek

MS 7 (Huguccio, *Summa* on the *Decretum*)

Avranches, Bibliothèque municipale

MS 149 (*Forma interdicti* on England)

Bamberg Staatsbibliothek

MS Can. 19 (*Apparatus* 'Servus appellatur' on 3 Comp.)
MS Can. 20 (Vincentius Hispanus on 3 Comp.)
MS Can. 42 (*Summa* 'Animal est substantia' on the *Decretum*)

Brussels, Bibliothèque royale

MS 1407–9 (Anonymous French pupil of Petrus Brito on 1 Comp.)

Cambridge, Gonville and Caius College

MS 283/676 (Anonymous Anglo-Norman glosses on the *Decretum*)

Cambridge, Peterhouse

MS 112 (Stephen Langton on 1–4 Kings)

Cambridge, Trinity College

MS O.10.2 (Laurentius Hispanus, *Glossa Palatina* on the *Decretum*)

Cambridge University Library

MS Dd. 7. 20 (*Decretum* with *glossa ordinaria*)
MS Ii. 4. 23 (Stephen Langton on Peter Lombard's gloss on Romans)

Durham Cathedral

MS A.I.7 (Stephen Langton on Exodus, Leviticus, Deuteronomy)
MS A.III.12 (Stephen Langton on Exodus)

Eton College

MS 14 (Peter the Chanter on Genesis, Exodus)
MS 16 (Peter the Chanter on Deuteronomy, 1–4 Kings)

Laon, Bibliothèque communale

MS 371bis, fols. 83r–170v (*Summa* 'De iure canonico tractaturus' on the *Decretum*)

Bibliography

267

Leipzig Universitätsbibliothek

MS 983 (Vincentius Hispanus on 1 Comp.)

London, British Library

Arundel MS 492 (Pilius, *Summa super Tres Libros*)
Royal MS 2.C.viii (Peter the Chanter on Leviticus)
Royal MS 10.C.v (Peter the Chanter on Psalms)
Royal MS 11.C.vii (Jacobus de Albenga on 5 Comp.)

Munich, Bayerisches Staatsbibliothek

Clm 3879 (Alanus Anglicus on 1 Comp.; Johannes Galensis on 3 Comp.)

Oxford, Bodleian Library

Bodley MS 371 (Peter the Chanter on 1–4 Kings)
Hamilton MS 24 (Guillaume de Montlauzun, *Sacramentale*)
Rawlinson MS C.427 (Stephen Langton on 1–4 Kings)

Oxford, Merton College

MS 212 (Peter the Chanter on Matthew)

Oxford, Trinity College

MS 65 (Stephen Langton on Genesis, Exodus, Deuteronomy)

Paris, Bibliothèque de l'Arsenal

MS 44 (Peter the Chanter on Genesis, Exodus, Leviticus, Deuteronomy, 1–4 Kings)

Paris, Bibliothèque Nationale

MS lat. 3967 (Vincentius Hispanus on the *Liber extra*)
MS lat. 14443 (Stephen Langton on Peter Lombard's gloss on Romans)
MS lat. 15393 (Alanus Anglicus, *Apparatus* 'Ius naturale' on the *Decretum*)
MS lat. 15585 (Peter the Chanter on Matthew)
MS lat. 16793 (Peter the Chanter on Ezechiel)
MS lat. nouv. acq. 1576 (*Apparatus* 'Ecce vicit leo' on the *Decretum*)

Tours, Bibliothèque municipale

MS 565 (Zoen Tencarius on 5 Comp.)

Vatican City, Biblioteca Apostolica Vaticana

Arch. S. Pietro C.114 (Huguccio, *Summa* on the *Decretum*)
Barb. lat. MS 1626 (Vincentius Hispanus on the *Liber extra*)
Borgh. lat. MS 71 (Johannes Faventinus, *Summa* on the *Decretum*)
Borgh. lat. MS 163 (Johannes Hispanus de Petesella, *Summa* on the *Liber extra*)
Borgh. lat. MS 228 (Petrus Bonetus and anonymous glossator on the *Liber extra*)
Borgh. lat. MS 231 ('Abbas Antiquus' on the *Liber extra*)

Borgh. lat. MS 260 ('Abbas Antiquus' on the *Liber extra*)
Borgh. lat. MS 261 (Damasus, *Questiones*; Paulus Hungarus, *Notabilia* on 2 Comp. and 3 Comp.)
Borgh. lat. MS 264 (Tancred on 1–3 Comp.; Johannes Teutonicus on 4 Comp.)
Ottob. lat. MS 54 (Goffredus de Trano, *Summa* on the *Liber extra*)
Pal. lat. MS 629 (Johannes Garsias Hispanus on the canons of Lyons II)
Pal. lat. MS 653 (Sicard of Cremona, *Summa* on the *Decretum*)
Pal. lat. MS 656 (Pierre Sampsona, *Distinctiones*)
Pal. lat. MS 658 (Laurentius Hispanus, *Glossa Palatina* on the *Decretum*)
Pal. lat. MS 696 (Ricardus Anglicus on 1 Comp.)
Pal. lat. MS 797 (Johannes Andreae (attrib.), *De modo*; Johannes Calderinus (attrib.), *De censura ecclesiastica*)
Reg. lat. MS 106 (Peter the Chanter, *Verbum abbreviatum*)
Reg. lat. MS 1061 (*Summa Reginensis* on the *Decretum*)
Ross. lat. MS 595 (Alanus Anglicus, *Apparatus* 'Ius naturale' on the *Decretum*)
Vat. lat. MS 1365 (Bernardus Compostellanus junior, *glossa ordinaria* on Innocent IV's *Novelle*)
Vat. lat. MS 1367 (*Decretum* with *glossa ordinaria*)
Vat. lat. MS 1377 (Tancred on 1–3 Comp.; Johannes Teutonicus on 4 Comp.)
Vat. lat. MS 1378 (Vincentius Hispanus on 3 Comp.)
Vat. lat. MS 2280 (Huguccio, *Summa* on the *Decretum*)
Vat. lat. MS 2343 (Johannes Hispanus de Petesella, *Summa* on the *Liber extra*)
Vat. lat. MS 2509 (Tancred on 1–3 Comp.; Johannes Teutonicus on 4 Comp.)
Vat. lat. MS 2542 ('Abbas Antiquus' on the *Liber extra*)
Vat. lat. MS 2546 (Vincentius Hispanus on the *Liber extra*)
Vat. lat. MS 2639 (Johannes de Legnano, *De interdicto* and other treatises)
Vat. lat. MS 6769 (Vincentius Hispanus on the *Liber extra*)

Vercelli Cathedral

MS 89 (Alanus Anglicus's decretal collection with his own glosses)

Vienna, Nationalbibliothek

MS 2083 (Pierre Sampsona on the *Liber extra*)
MS 2113 (Pierre Sampsona on the *Liber extra*)
MS 2197 (Goffredus de Trano on the *Liber extra*)

ARCHIVAL SOURCES

Carlisle, Cumbria County Record Office
DRC/1/2

Florence (Firenze), Archivio di Stato

Comune di San Gimignano, 171; 176; 177; 178; 179; 181; 182; 183; 184; 185; 187; 188; 191; 192; 193; 194; 195; 198; 199; 200

London, National Archives
C54/55; C66/52; C66/53

Montpellier, Archives départementales de l'Hérault

G765

Paris, Bibliothèque Nationale

Doat MSS 32 and 62

San Gimignano, Archivio Comunale

Libro bianco; N.0068; N.0069; N.0070, N.0071; N.0072; N.0073; N.0074

Vatican City, Archivio Segreto Vaticano

A. A. Arm. C.139; Reg. Vat. 48

Volterra, Archivio Vescovile

Pergamene, Dec. X, no. 12

PRINTED SOURCES

'Abbas Antiquus' (Bernard de Montmirat), *Lectura super quinque libros decretalium*, in *Perillustrium doctorum tam veterum quam recentiorum in libros decretalium aurei commentarii*, vol. 1 (Venice 1588), fols. 2–152.

Accursius: see *Corpus iuris civilis.*

Acta Stephani Langton Cantuariensis Archiepiscopi, ed. K. Major, Canterbury and York Society, Series L (Oxford, 1950).

The Acts of Welsh Rulers 1120–1283, ed. H. Pryce (Cardiff, 2005).

Alan.: see von Heckel under SECONDARY LITERATURE.

Annales monastici, ed. H. R. Luard, 5 vols., Rolls Series 36 (London, 1864–9).

Auer, A., 'Eine verschollene Denkschrift über das grosse Interdikt des 14. Jahrhunderts', *Historisches Jahrbuch*, 46 (1926), 532–49.

Augustine, *Enarrationes in Psalmos I-L*, ed. E. Dekkers and J. Fraipont, *CCSL* 38 (Turnhout, 1956).

Azo, *Summa super Codicem* (Pavia, 1506; repr. Turin, 1966).

Baldus de Ubaldis, *Lectura in prima parte Digesti ueteri* (Lyon, 1585).

Bérenger Frédol: Le 'Liber de Excommunicacione' du Cardinal Bérenger Frédol, ed. E. Vernay (Paris, 1912); it comprises Frédol's treatises 'De absolucione ad cautelam' (pp. 1–18) and 'De excommunicacione et interdicto' (pp. 24–58).

Bernard de Montmirat: see 'Abbas Antiquus'.

Bernardus Papiensis (Bernard of Pavia), *Summa Decretalium*, ed. T. Laspeyres (Ratisbon, 1860).

Bernardus Parmensis (Bernard of Parma), *Glossa ordinaria*: see *Decretales.*

Biblia latina cum glossa ordinaria, 4 vols. (Strassburg, 1480–1; repr. Turnhout, 1992).

The Cartulary of Snellshall Priory, ed. J. G. Jenkins, Buckinghamshire Record Society 10 ([Aylesbury], 1952).

Chronica Iohannis de Oxenedes, ed. H. Ellis, Rolls Series 13 (London, 1859).

The Chronicle of Melrose, ed. A. O. Anderson and M. O. Anderson (London, 1936).

Chronicles of the Reigns of Edward I and Edward II, ed. W. Stubbs, 2 vols., Rolls Series 76 (London, 1882–3).

Chronicon monasterii de Melsa, ed. E. A. Bond, 2 vols., Rolls Series 43 (London, 1866).

Clementinas: Constitutiones Clementis quinti quas Clementinas vocant (with *glossa ordinaria* of Johannes Andreae) (Venice, 1567).

Codex Chronologico-Diplomaticus Episcopatus Ratisbonensis, ed. T. Ried (Ratisbon, 1816).

Coggleshall, *Chronicon*: Ralph of Coggleshall, *Chronicon Anglicanum*, ed. J. Stephenson, Rolls Series 66 (London, 1875).

Constitutiones Concilii quarti Lateranensis una cum Commentariis glossatorum, ed. A. Garcia y Garcia, Monumenta Iuris Canonici, Series A, 2 (Città del Vaticano, 1981).

Corpus iuris canonici, ed. E. Friedberg, 2 vols. (Leipzig, 1879–81; repr. Graz, 1995).

Corpus iuris civilis with the *glossa ordinaria* of Accursius (Venice, 1488; repr. Turin, 1969).

Corpus iuris civilis, ed. T. Mommsen, P. Krueger, and A. Schoell, 3 vols. (Berlin, 1872–95; repr. Frankfurt-am-Main, 1968–70).

Coventry, *Memoriale*: Walter of Coventry, *Memoriale*, ed. W. Stubbs, 2 vols., Rolls Series 58 (London, 1873).

CCR 1242–1247: Calendar of Close Rolls: Henry III, A.D. 1242–1247 (London, 1916).

CPR 1232–1247: Calendar of Patent Rolls: Henry III, A.D. 1232–1247 (London, 1906).

CPR 1281–1292: Calendar of Patent Rolls: Edward I, A.D. 1281–1292 (London, 1893).

D'Achery, L., *Spicilegium sive collectio veterum aliquot scriptorum* … , 3 vols. (Paris, 1723).

Damasus, *Apparatus in constitutiones concilii quarti Lateranensis*: see *Constitutiones*.

——, 'Brocarda', in *Tractatus ex variis iuris interpretibus collecta* (Lyon, 1549), vol. 17.

Decretales Gregorii IX (with *glossa ordinaria* of Bernard of Parma) (Paris, 1529).

'De Gestis Philippi Augusti Francorum Regis', printed in *Recueil des Historiens des Gaules et de la France*, vol. 17 (Paris, 1878; repr. Farnborough, 1968), 1–62.

Du Plessis, C., *Collectio iudiciorum de novis erroribus* (Paris, 1728).

'Editio Romana': *Corpus iuris canonici* (Rome, 1582).

Evesham, ed. Macray: *Chronicon abbatiae de Evesham ad annum 1418*, ed. W. D. Macray, Rolls Series 29 (London, 1863).

'Extraits des Chroniques de S. Denis', printed in *Recueil des Historiens des Gaules et de la France*, vol. 17 (Paris, 1878; repr. Farnborough, 1968), 346–422.

Foedera, conventiones, litterae … , ed. T. Rymer, 4 vols., Record Commission (London, 1816–30).

Geoffrey of Vendôme (Goffridus Abbas Vindocinensis), *Epistolae* in *PL* 157.33–212.

Gerald of Wales (Giraldus Cambrensis), *Opera*, ed. J. S. Brewer (vols. 1–4), J. F. Dimock (vols. 5–7), and G. F. Warner (vol. 8), Rolls Series 21 (London, 1861–91).

Gervase of Canterbury, *Historical Works*, ed. W. Stubbs, 2 vols., Rolls Series 73 (London, 1880).

Gesta (Innocentii III) in *PL* 214.xviii–ccxxxviii.

Glossa ordinaria on Genesis-Apocalypse: see *Biblia sacra*.

Goffredus de Trano, *Summa in titulis decretalium* (Venice, 1564).

Gregory the Great, *Moralia in Iob*, ed. M. Adriaen, CCSL 143, 143A, 143B (Turnhout, 1979–85).

Guido de Baysio, *Lectura super Sexto decretalium* (Lyon, 1547).

——, *Rosarium Decretorum* (Venice, 1481).

Hermann of Minden (attrib.), 'De interdictis civitatis, castri vel alterius loci', in *Tractatus universi iuris*, vol. 14, fols. 345rb–346va.

Historiae Dunelmensis scriptores tres, ed. J. Raine, Surtees Society 9 (London, 1839).

Horace, *Epistulae*, ed. J. Préaux (Paris, 1968).

Hostiensis, *Lectura*: Henricus de Segusio, *In primum-sextum librum decretalium commentaria*, 2 vols. (Venice, 1581).

_____, *Summa aurea* (Lyons, 1537; repr. Darmstadt, 1962).

Howden: *Chronica Rogeri de Hovedon*, ed. W. Stubbs, 4 vols., Rolls Series 51 (London, 1868–71).

Innocent III, *Lotharii cardinalis (Innocentii III) De miseria conditionis humanae*, ed. M. Maccarone (Lucca, 1955).

_____, Reg. 1, 2, 5, 6, 7, 8: *Die Register Papst Innocenz' III*, ed. O. Hageneder et al., vols. 1, 2, 5, 6, 7, 8 (Rome–Vienna, 1964–2001).

_____, Reg. 9–16: *PL* 215.801–1102 (Reg. 9), 1103–1340 (Reg. 10), 1339–1612 (Reg. 11); 216.9–194 (Reg. 12), 193–378 (Reg. 13), 377–540 (Reg. 14), 539–782 (Reg. 15), 781–994 (Reg. 16).

_____, *RNI: Regestum super negotio Romani imperii*, ed. F. Kempf, Miscellanea Historiae Pontificiae 12 (Rome, 1947).

_____, *Sermones* in *PL* 217.309–690.

_____, Suppl. in *PL* 217.9–308.

Innocent IV, *Apparatus super quinque libros decretalium* (Strassburg 1478).

_____, *Apparatus super quinque libros decretalium* (Venice 1578).

Ps. Jerome, *Quaestiones Hebraice in libros Regum et Paralipomenon* in *PL* 23. 1329–1402.

Johannes Andreae, *Glossa (ordinaria)*: see *Liber sextus* and *Clementinas*.

_____, *Novella commentaria super quinque libros decretalium* (Venice, 1489).

_____, *Novelle in Sextum librum decretalium* (Rome, 1476).

_____ (attrib.), *Tractatus utillissimus de modo observandi interdictum* (Magdeburg 1483); this tract is also edited from BAV, Pal. lat. MS 797, fols. 5va–10va, by Clarke, 'Theory', 289–311 (see SECONDARY LITERATURE).

Johannes Calderinus, 'De interdicto ecclesiastico' in *Tractatus universi iuris*, vol. 14, fols. 325rb–333rb.

_____ (attrib.), *De censura ecclesiastica*, part edited from BAV, Pal. lat. MS 797, fols. 11ra–16ra, by Clarke, 'Theory', 264–88 (see SECONDARY LITERATURE).

Ioannis de Forda sermones, ed. E. Mikkers and H. Costello, Corpus Christianorum Continuatio Medievalis 17 (Turnhout, 1970).

Johannes Friburgensis (John of Freiburg), *Summa confessorum* (Lyons, 1518).

Johannes Legnano, 'De ecclesiastico interdicto', in *Tractatus universi iuris*, vol. 14, fols. 335ra–336ra.

Johannes Monachus, *Glosa aurea super Sexto decretalium libro* (Paris, 1535).

_____, *Glossa* on *Extravagantes communes*, printed with the text in *Extravagantes tum viginti Ioannis vigesimisecundus tum communes* (Venice, 1567).

Johannes Nauclerus, *Chronica ... ab initio mundi ad annum Christi nati MCCCCC*, 2 vols. (Cologne, 1544).

Johannes Teutonicus, *Apparatus glossarum in Compilationem tertiam*, ed. K. Pennington, vol. 1, Monumenta Iuris Canonici, Series A, 3 (Vatican City, 1981).

Lacombe, G., 'An Unpublished Document of the Great Interdict (1207–13)', *Catholic Historical Review*, 15 (1929–30), 408–20.

Liber Papiensis, ed. A. Boretius in *Monumenta Germaniae Historica, Legum* IV (Hanover, 1869), 290–585.

Liber sextus decretalium (with *glossa* of Johannes Andreae) (Venice, 1567).

Liebermann, F., *Ungedruckte anglo-normannische Geschichtsquellen* (Strassburg, 1879).

Le livre noir et les établissements de Dax, ed. F. Abbadie, Archives historiques du département de la Gironde 37 (Bordeaux, 1902).

Lombarda Casinensis: rubrics and incipits listed by F. Bluhm in *Monumenta Germaniae Historica, Legum* IV (Hanover, 1869), 607–23.

Ludeco Cappel, *Summarius de interdicto excommunicationis* [sic] (Erfurt, 1494).

Magna Vita sancti Hugonis Lincolniensis, ed. J. F. Dimock, Rolls Series 37 (London, 1864).

Mansi: *Sacrorum conciliorum nova et amplissima collectio*, ed. J. D. Mansi, 31 vols. (Florence–Venice, 1759–98).

Martène, E., and U. Durand (eds.), *Thesaurus novus anecdotorum*, 5 vols. (Paris, 1717).

Materials for the History of Thomas Becket, Archbishop of Canterbury, eds. J. C. Robertson (vols. 1–6) and J. G. Sheppard (vol. 7), Rolls Series 67 (London, 1875–85).

Matthew Paris, *Chronica majora*, ed. H. R. Luard, 7 vols., Rolls Series 57 (London, 1872–83).

McManus, B. J., 'The Ecclesiology of Laurentius Hispanus (c. 1180–1248) and his Contribution to the Romanization of Canon Law Jurisprudence with an Edition of the *Apparatus glossarum Laurentii Hispani in Compilationem tertiam*' (edition at pp. 213–907), PhD dissertation, University of Syracuse, 1991.

Melsa, ed. Bond: *Chronica monasterii de Melsa*, ed. E. A. Bond, 2 vols., Rolls Series 43 (London, 1866).

Monaldus, *Summa*: Johannes Monaldus, *Summa perutilis atque aurea de iure canonici* (Lyon, 1516)

Munimenta academica Oxoniensis, ed. H. Anstey, 2 vols., Rolls Series 50 (London, 1868).

Nicholas Plowe, 'De ecclesiastico interdicto', in *Tractatus universi iuris*, vol. 14, fols. 333rb–334vb.

Paucapalea, *Summa* on the *Decretum*, ed. J. F. Schulte (Giessen, 1890).

Peter of Blois, *Speculum iuris canonici*, ed. T. A. Reimarus (Berlin, 1937).

The Later Letters of Peter of Blois, ed. E. Revell, Auctores Britannici medii aevi 13 (Oxford, 1993).

Peter the Chanter, *Summa de sacramentis et animae consilio*, ed. J.-A. Dugauquier, AMN 4, 7, 11, 16, 21 (Louvain-Lille, 1954–67).

———, *Verbum abbreviatum* in *PL* 205.21–554.

Peter Lombard, *Collectanea in omnes D. Pauli apostoli epistolas* in *PL* 191.1297–1696.

———, *Commentaria in Psalmos* in *PL* 191.61–1296.

The Political Songs of England from the Reign of John to That of Edward II, ed T. Wright, Camden Society, old series, 6 (London, 1839).

Portugaliae monumenta historica, vol. I/i: *Leges et consuetudines* (Lisbon, 1857).

W. Preger, 'Der Tractat des Davids von Augsburg über die Waldesier', *Abhandlungen der (königlichen) bayerischen Akademie der Wissenschaften*, III (Historische) Klasse, 14/2 (1878), 181–235.

Quellen zur Geschichte der Waldenser, eds. A. Patschovsky and K.-V. Selge, Texte zur Kirchen- und Theologie-geschichte 18 (Gütersloh, 1973).

Quinque compilationes antiquae, ed. E. Friedberg (Leipzig 1882; repr. Graz, 1956).

Raymond of Peñafort, *Summa de casibus penitentiae* (Verona, 1744).

Raynaldus, O., *Annales ecclesiastici* (Cologne, 1692).

The Records of St Bartholomew's, Smithfield, ed. E. A. Webb, 2 vols. (Oxford, 1921).

Reg. Alexander IV: *Les Registres d'Alexandre IV*, ed. C. Bourel de la Roncière et al., 3 vols., Ecole Française de Rome (Paris, 1895–1960).

Reg. Boniface VIII: *Les Registres de Boniface VIII*, ed. G. Digard et al., 4 vols., Ecole Française de Rome (Paris, 1884–1939).

Reg. Clement IV: *Les Registres de Clément IV*, ed. E. Jordan, Ecole Française de Rome (Paris, 1893–1945).

Reg. Clement V: *Regestum Clementis papae V*, ed. monks of the Benedictine order, 8 vols. (Rome, 1885–92); indices in 2 vols., Ecole Française de Rome (Paris, 1948–57).

Reg. Gregory IX: *Les Registres de Grégoire IX*, ed. L. Auvray et al., Ecole Française de Rome (Paris, 1890–1955).

Reg. Gregory X: *Les Registres de Grégoire X*, ed. J. Guiraud, Ecole Française de Rome (Paris, 1892–1906).

Reg. Honorius III: *Regesta Honorii III*, ed. P. Pressutti, 2 vols. (Rome, 1888–91).

Reg. Honorius IV: *Les Registres d'Honorius IV*, ed. M. Prou, Ecole Française de Rome (Paris, 1886–8).

Reg. Innocent IV: *Les Registres d'Innocent IV*, ed. E. Berger, 4 vols., Ecole Française de Rome (Paris, 1884–1921).

Reg. Martin IV: *Les Registres de Martin IV*, ed. F. Olivier-Martin et al., Ecole Française de Rome (Paris, 1901–35).

Reg. Nicholas III: *Les Registres de Nicolas III*, ed. J. Gay, Ecole Française de Rome (Paris, 1898–1938).

Reg. Nicholas IV: *Les Registres de Nicolas IV*, ed. E. Langlois, 2 vols., Ecole Française de Rome (Paris, 1887–93).

Reg. Urban IV: *Les Registres d'Urbain IV*, ed. J. Guiraud, 4 vols., Ecole Française de Rome (Paris, 1899–1958).

RLC: Rotuli litterarum clausarum, ed. T. D. Hardy, 2 vols., Record Commission (London, 1833–44).

RLP: Rotuli litterarum patentium, ed. T. D. Hardy, 2 vols., Record Commission (London, 1833–44).

Rolandus, *Die Sentenzen*, ed. A. M. Gietl (Freiburg, 1891).

———, *Summa: Die Summa Magistri Rolandi*, ed. F. Thaner (Innsbruck, 1874).

Rôles Gascons, ed. F. Michel and C. Bemont, 4 vols. (Paris, 1885–1906).

Rufinus, *Summa Decretorum*, ed. H. Singer (Paderborn, 1902).

Select Cases from the Ecclesiastical Courts of the Province of Canterbury c. 1200–1301, ed. N. Adams and C. Donahue, Selden Society 95 (London, 1981).

SLI: Selected Letters of Pope Innocent III Concerning England (1198–1216), ed. C. R. Cheney and W. Semple, Nelson Medieval Texts (London, 1953).

Statuta capitulorum generalium ordinis Cisterciensis, ed. J. M. Canivez, 8 vols. (Louvain, 1933–41).

Stephen Langton: see *Acta*.

Stephen of Tournai, *Summa*: Stephan von Doornick, *Die Summa über das Decretum Gratiani*, ed. J. F. Schulte (Giessen, 1891).

Summa Parisiensis (on the *Decretum*), ed. T. P. McLaughlin (Toronto, 1952).

Thomas Aquinas, *Scriptum super libros Sententiarum*, ed. P. Madonnet and M. F. Moos, 4 vols. (Paris, 1929–47).

——, *Summa theologiae*, ed. T. Gilby et al., 61 vols. (London, 1964–80).

Varin, P., *Archives administratives de la ville de Reims* (Paris, 1839).

Vincentius Hispanus, *Apparatus in constitutiones concilii quarti Lateranensis*: see *Constitutiones*.

Wendover, *Flores*: Roger of Wendover, *Flores Historiarum*, ed. H. O. Coxe, 5 vols. (London, 1841–4).

William Durand the Elder (Willelmus Durandus senior), *In sacrosanctum Lugdunensem concilium ... commentarius* (Fano, 1569).

——, *Speculum iudiciale* (Strassburg, 1473).

Wilmart, A., 'Les mélanges de Mathieu, préchantre de Rievaulx', *Revue Bénédictine*, 52 (1940), 15–84.

SECONDARY LITERATURE

Abulafia, D., *Frederick II* (London, 1988).

Anciaux, P., *La théologie du sacrement de pénitence au XIIe siècle* (Gembloux-Louvain, 1949).

Baldwin, J. W., *Masters, Princes and Merchants: The Social Views of Peter the Chanter and his Circle*, 2 vols. (Princeton, 1970).

Barlow, F., *Thomas Becket* (London, 1986).

Benson, R. L., *The Bishop-Elect: A Study in Medieval Ecclesiastical Office* (Princeton, 1968).

Bertram, M., 'Angeblicke Originale des Dekretalenapparats Innocenz' IV', in S. Kuttner and K. Pennington, eds., *Proceedings of the Sixth International Congress of Medieval Canon Law*, Monumenta Iuris Canonici, Series C, 8 (Vatican City, 1985), 41–7.

——, 'Le commentaire de Guillaume Durand sur les constitutions du deuxième concile de Lyons', in P.-M. Gy, ed., *Guillaume Durand, evêque de Mende, canoniste, liturgiste et homme politique* (Paris, 1992), 95–105.

——, 'Pierre de Sampson and Bernard de Montmirat. Two French canonists of the XIIIth century', *Cahiers de Fanjeaux*, 29 (1994), 37–74.

——, 'Zur Wissenschaftlichen Bearbeitung der Konstitutionen Gregors X', *Quellen und Forschungen aus italienischen Archiven und Bibliotheken*, 53 (1973), 459–67.

Histoire de Béziers, ed. J. Sagnes ([Toulouse], 1986).

Boase, T. S. R., *Boniface VIII* (London, 1933).

Bolton, B. M., 'Too Important to Neglect: The *Gesta Innocentii PP. III*', in G. A. Loud and I. N. Wood, eds., *Church and Chronicle in the Middle Ages: Essays presented to John Taylor* (London 1991), 87–99; repr. in her *Innocent III: Studies on Papal Authority and Pastoral Care* (Aldershot, 1995), Ch. 4.

Brucker, G. A., 'Ecclesiastical Courts in Fifteenth Century Fiesole and Florence', *Mediaeval Studies*, 53 (1991), 228–57.

Brundage, J. A., 'The Cambridge Faculty of Canon Law and the Ecclesiastical Courts of Ely', in P. N. R. Zutshi, ed., *Medieval Cambridge: Essays on the Pre-Reformation*

University, History of the University of Cambridge: Texts and Studies 2 (Woodbridge, 1993).

———, *Medieval Canon Law* (Harlow, 1995).

Buc, P., *L'Ambiguïté du livre. Prince, pouvoir et peuple dans les commentaires de la Bible au moyen âge* (Paris, 1994).

Burr, D., *Olivi and Franciscan Poverty: The Origins of the* usus pauper *Controversy* (Philadelphia, 1989).

A Catalogue of Canon and Roman Law Manuscripts in the Vatican Library, I: *Codices Vaticani latini 541–2299*; II: *Codices Vaticani latini 2300–2746*, Studi e testi 322 and 328 (Città del Vaticano, 1986–7).

Cheney, C. R., 'A Recent View of the General Interdict on England, 1208–1214', *Studies in Church History*, 3 (1966), ed. G. J. Cuming, 159–68; repr. in his *The Papacy*, Ch. 11.

———, *Episcopal Visitation of Monasteries in the Thirteenth Century* (repr. Manchester, 1983).

———, *From Becket to Langton: English Church Government 1170–1213* (Manchester, 1956).

———, 'King John and the Papal Interdict', *BJRL* 31 (1948), 295–317; repr. in his *The Papacy*, Ch. 9.

———, 'King John's Reaction to the Interdict on England', *Transactions of the Royal Historical Society*, 4th series, 31 (1949), 129–50; repr. in his *The Papacy*, Ch. 10.

———, *Pope Innocent III and England*, Päpste und Papsttum 9 (Stuttgart, 1976).

———, *The papacy and England 12th–14th centuries* (London, 1982).

Clarke, P. D., 'The Collection of Gilbertus and the French Glosses in Brussels, Bibliothèque Royale, MS 1407–09, and an Early Recension of *Compilatio secunda*', *ZRGKA* 86 (2000), 132–84.

———, 'A Fragment of a Collection of Boniface VIII's *extravagantes* and a Gloss to *Unam sanctam* from Carlisle', *BMCL*, new series, 24 (2001–2), 130–3.

———, 'Innocent III, Canon Law and the Punishment of the Guiltless', in J. C. Moore, ed., *Pope Innocent III and His World* (Aldershot, 1999), 271–85.

———, 'Innocent III, the Interdict, and Medieval Theories of Popular Resistance', in F. Andrews and C. Eggar, eds., *Pope, Church and City: Essays in honour of Brenda M. Bolton* (Leiden, 2004), 77–97.

———, 'The Interdict on San Gimignano, *c.* 1289–93: A Clerical Strike and Its Consequences', *Papers of the British School at Rome*, 67 (1999), 281–302.

———, 'Peter the Chanter, Innocent III and Theological Views on Collective Guilt and Punishment', *Journal of Ecclesiastical History*, 52 (2001), 1–20.

———, 'A Question of Collective Guilt: Popes, Canonists and the Interdict *c.* 1140–*c.* 1250', *ZRGKA* 85 (1999), 104–46.

———, 'The records of the Papal Penitentiary as a Source for the Ecclesiastical Interdict', in A. Meyer, C. Rendtel, and M. Wittmer-Batsch, eds., *Päpste, Pilger, Pöniteniarie. Festschrift für Ludwig Schmugge zum 65. Geburtstag* (Tübingen, 2004), 411–33.

———, 'The Theory and Practice of the Ecclesiastical Interdict in the Age of the Decretalists', PhD dissertation, University of Manchester, 1995.

———, 'Two Constitutions of Boniface VIII: An Insight into the Sources of the *Liber Sextus*', *BJRL* 83 (2001), 115–28.

Coppi, G. V., *Annali, memorie ed huomini illustri di San Gimignano* (Florence, 1695).

Davidsohn, R., *Forschungen zur Geschichte von Florenz* II: *Aus den Stadtbüchern und Urkunden von San Gimignano (13. und 14. Jahrhundert)* (Berlin, 1900).

Davis, G. W., *The Inquisition at Albi, 1299–1300* (New York, 1948).

Denifle, H. S., and F. Ehrle, *Archiv für Literatur- und Kirchen-geschichte des Mittelalters* (Berlin, 1886; repr. Graz, 1956).

Denton, J. H., 'Philip the Fair and the Ecclesiastical Assemblies of 1294–5', *Transactions of the American Philosophical Society*, 81 (1991).

——, 'The Second Uprising at Laon and its Aftermath, 1295–98', *BJRL* 72 (1990), 79–92.

——, *English Royal Free Chapels, 1100–1300: A Constitutional Study* (Manchester, 1970).

——, 'Taxation and the Conflict between Philip the Fair and Boniface VIII', *French History*, 11 (1997), 241–64.

De Vic, C., and J. Vaisette, *Histoire générale de Languedoc*, 16 vols. (Toulouse, 1872–1905).

Dictionnaire de droit canonique, ed. R. Naz, 7 vols. (Paris, 1935–65).

Dompnier de Sauviac, A., *Chroniques de la cité et du diocèse d'Acqs* (Dax, 1869–73).

Dossat, Y., 'Les Cathares d'après les documents de l'inquisition', *Cahiers de Fanjeaux*, 3 (1968), 71–104.

Duggan, C., *Twelfth-Century Decretal Collections and Their Importance in English History* (London, 1963).

Eschmann, T., 'Studies on the Notion of Society in St Thomas Aquinas: I. St Thomas Aquinas and the Decretal of Innocent IV "Romana Ecclesia: Ceterum"', *Mediaeval Studies*, 7 (1946), 1–42.

Gagnér, S., *Studien zur Ideengeschichte der Gesetzgebung*, Acta Universitatis Upsaliensis, Studia iuridica Upsaliensia 1 (Upsala, 1960).

Gierke, O., *Das deutsche Genossenschaftsrecht*, 4 vols. (Berlin, 1868–1913).

Given, J. B., *State and Society in medieval Europe: Gwynedd and Languedoc* (Ithaca, NY/London, 1990).

Hamilton, B., *Religion in the Medieval West* (London, 1986).

Hamilton, S., *The Practice of Penance 900–1050* (Woodbridge, 2001).

Helmholz, R. H., 'Excommunication as a Legal Sanction: The Attitudes of the Medieval Canonists', *ZRGKA* 68 (1982).

——, ' "Si quis suadente" (C.17 q.4 c.29): Theory and Practice', in P. Linehan, ed., *Proceedings of the Seventh International Congress of Medieval Canon Law*, Monumenta Iuris Canonici, Series C, 8 (Vatican City, 1988), 425–38.

——, *The Spirit of Classical Canon Law* (London, 1996).

Hinschius, P., *System des katholischen Kirchenrechts*, 6 vols. (Berlin, 1869–97).

Histoire de Verdun, ed. A. Girardot (Toulouse, 1982).

Howland, A. C., 'The Origin of the Local Interdict', *Reports of the American Historical Association*, 1 (1899), 429–48.

Huizing, P., 'The Earliest Development of Excommunication *latae sententiae* by Gratian and the Earliest Decretists', *Studia Gratiana*, 3 (1955), 277–320.

Hyman, R., *Strikes* (Glasgow, 1977).

Izbicki, T. M., '*Clericis laicos* and the Canonists', in S. Chodorow and J. R. Sweeney, eds., *Popes, teachers and canon law in the middle ages* (New York, 1989), 179–90.

Johanek, P., 'Studien zur Überlieferung der Konstitutionen des II. Konzils von Lyon (1274)', *ZRGKA* 65 (1979), 149–216.

Jones, P. J., *The Italian City-State: From Commune to Signoria* (Oxford, 1997).

Julia, H., *Histoire de Béziers ou recherches sur la province de Languedoc* (Paris, 1845).

Kaeppeli, T., *Scriptores ordinis praedicatorum medii aevi*, 4 vols. (Rome, 1970–93).

Kantorowicz, E., *The King's Two Bodies* (Princeton, 1957).

Kaufhold, M., *Gladius spiritualis: das päpstliche Interdikt über Deutschland in der Regierungszeit Ludwigs des Bayern (1324–1347)* (Heidelberg, 1994).

Kern, F., *The Divine Right of Kings and the Right of Resistance in the Early Middle Ages*, trans. S. B. Chrimes (Oxford, 1939).

Kessler, P. J., 'Untersuchungen über die Novellen-Gesetzgebung Papst Innozenz' IV', in three parts (I-III Teile): *ZRGKA* 31 (1942), 142–320; 32 (1943), 300–83; 33 (1944), 56–128.

Knowles, D., *The Evolution of Medieval Thought* (London 1962).

——, 'The Growth of Monastic Exemption', *Downside Review*, 1 (1950), 201–31, 396–436.

Kober, F., 'Das Interdict', *Archiv für katholisches Kirchenrecht*, 21 (1869), 3–45, 291–341; 22 (1869), 3–53.

Krehbiel, E. B., *The Interdict: Its History and Operation with Especial Attention to the Time of Pope Innocent III 1198–1216*, Prize essay of the American Historical Association for 1907 (Washington, 1909).

Kuttner, S., 'Conciliar Law in the Making: The Lyonese Constitutions of Gregory X in a Manuscript at Washington', *Miscellanea Pio Paschini*, II (Rome 1949), 39–81, repr. with *retractiones* in his *Medieval councils*, Ch. 12.

——, 'Decretalistica', *ZRGKA* 26 (1937), 436–70.

——, 'Die Konstitutionen des ersten allgemeinen Konzils von Lyon', *Studia et documenta historiae et iuris*, 6 (1940), 70–131; repr. with *retractiones* in his *Medieval councils*, Ch. 11.

——, 'Joannes Andreae and his Novella on the Decretals of Gregory IX: An Introduction', *The Jurist*, 24 (1964), 393–408.

——, *Kanonistische Schuldlehre von Gratian bis auf die Dekretalen Gregors IX systematisch auf Grund der handschriftlichen Quellen dargestellt*, Studi e testi 64 (Vatican City, 1935).

——, *Medieval Councils, Decretals and Collections of Canon Law* (London, 1980; 2nd edn, 1992).

——, 'Raymond of Peñafort as Editor: The *decretales* and *constitutiones* of Gregory IX', *BMCL* 12 (1982), 65–80.

——, *Repertorium der Kanonistik (1140–1234): Prodomus corporis glossarum*, Studi e testi 71 (Vatican City, 1937).

——, 'The Collection of Alanus: A Concordance of its Two Recensions', *Rivista di storia del diritto italiano*, 26 (1953), 37–53.

——, 'Wer war der Dekretalist "Abbas antiquus"?', *ZRGKA* 26 (1937), 471–87.

Kuttner, S., (with E. Rathbone), 'Anglo-Norman Canonists of the Twelfth Century', *Traditio*, 7 (1949–51), 279–358; repr. with *retractiones* in his *Gratian and the Schools of Law 1140–1234* (London, 1983), Ch. 8.

Kuttner, S., (with B. Smalley), 'The *Glossa ordinaria* to the Gregorian Decretals', *English Historical Review*, 60 (1945), 97–105; repr. with *retractiones* in his *Studies in the History of Medieval Canon Law* (London, 1990), Ch. 13.

Lambert, M. D., *Medieval Heresy: Popular Movements from the Gregorian Reform to the Reformation*, 2nd edn (Oxford, 1992).

Landau, P., 'Die Bedeutung des kanonischen Rechts für die Entwicklung einheitlicher Rechtsprinzipien', *Arbeiten zur Rechtsvergleichung*, 177, ed. H. Scholler (Baden-Baden, 1996), 23–47.

Landgraf, A., 'Die Vererbung der Sünden der Eltern auf die Kinder nach der Lehre des 12. Jahrhunderts', *Gregorianum*, 21 (1940), 203–47.

Langlois, C. V., 'Rouleaux d'arrêts de la cour du roi au XIIIe siècle', *Bibliothèque de l'Ecole des Chartes*, 48 (1887), 177–206.

Larner, J., *Italy in the Age of Dante and Petrarch 1216–1380* (London, 1980).

Lawrence, C. H. (ed.), *English Church and the Papacy in the Middle Ages* (London, 1965).

Le Bras, G., 'Boniface VIII, symphoniste et modérateur', *Mélanges d'histoire du moyen âge dédiés à la mémoire de Louis Halphen* (Paris, 1951), 383–94.

——, *Institutions ecclésiastiques de la Chrétienté médiévale* (Paris, 1964).

Linehan, P., 'Castile, Portugal, and Navarre', in D. Abulafia, ed., *New Cambridge Medieval History*, v: *c. 1198–c. 1300* (Cambridge, 1999), 668–99.

Little, L. K., *Benedictine Maledictions: Liturgical Cursing in Romanesque France* (Ithaca, NY/London, 1993).

Logan, F. D., *Excommunication and the Secular Arm in Medieval England* (Toronto, 1968).

Luzzati, M., 'Un comune di poche miglia quadrate: San Gimignano', in G. Galasso, ed., *Storia d'Italia*, VII/i, (Turin, 1987), 601–3.

Maisonneuve, H., 'L'interdit dans le droit classique de l'Eglise', *Mélanges d'histoire du moyen âge dédiés à la mémoire de Louis Halphen* (Paris, 1951), 465–81.

Marsh, F. B., *English Rule in Gascony 1199–1259*, University of Michigan Historical Studies 2 (Ann Arbor, 1912).

Martin-Chabot, E., *Les archives de la cour des comptes. Aides et finances de Montpellier* (Paris, 1907).

McCall, J. P., 'The Writings of John of Legnano with a List of Manuscripts', *Traditio*, 23 (1967), 415–38.

Melloni, A., *Innocenzo IV : La concezione e l'esperienza della cristianità come regimen unius personae* (Genoa, 1990).

Menache, S., *Clement V* (Cambridge, 1998).

Meyer, C. H. F., *Die Distinktionstechnik in der Kanonistik des 12. Jahrhunderts : Ein Beitrag zur Wissenschaftsgeschichte des Hochmittelalters*, Mediaevalia Lovaniensia Series 1, Studia 29 (Leuven, 2000).

Michaud-Quantin, P., 'Remarques sur l'oeuvre législative de Grégoire IX', *Etudes d'histoire du droit canonique dédiées à Gabriel Le Bras*, 1 (Paris, 1965), 273–81.

——, *Universitas: expressions du mouvement communitaire dans le moyen âge* (Paris, 1970).

Mollat, G., *Introduction à l'étude du droit canonique et du droit civil* (Paris, 1930).

Moorman, J. R. H., *Church Life in England in the Thirteenth Century* (Cambridge, 1946).

Morris, C., *The Papal Monarchy: The Western Church from 1050 to 1250* (Oxford, 1989).

Müller, P. E., *Das Konzil von Vienne, 1311–1312*, Vorreformationgeschichtliche Forschungen 12 (Münster-in-Westfalen, 1934).

Müller, W. P., *Huguccio: The Life, Works, and Thought of a Twelfth-Century Jurist* (Washington, DC, 1994).

Muratori, L. A., *Antiquitates Italicae medii aevi*, 6 vols. (Milan, 1738–42).

Murray, A., *Excommunication and Conscience in the Middle Ages* (London, 1991).

———, *Suicide in the Middle Ages*, ii: *The Curse on Self-Murder* (Oxford, 2000).

Noonan, J. R., 'Who was Rolandus?', in K. Pennington and R. Somerville, eds., *Law, Church and Society: Essays in honor of Stephan Kuttner* (Philadelphia, 1977), 21–48.

O'Callaghan, J. F., 'Innocent III and the Kingdoms of Castile and Leon', in J. C. Moore, ed., *Pope Innocent III and his world* (Aldershot, 1999), 317–35.

Ochoa Sanz, J., *Vincentius Hispanus, canonista Boloñes del siglo XIII* (Rome–Madrid, 1960).

Parker, T. M., 'The Terms of the Interdict of Innocent III', *Speculum*, 11 (1936), 258–60.

Pascal, J., 'Béziers au XIVe siècle d'aprés la chronique de Jacme Mascaro', thése, University of Montpellier, 1967.

Pecori, L., *Storia della terra di San Gimignano* (Florence, 1853).

Pennington, K., 'An Earlier Recension of Hostiensis's *Lectura* on the Decretals', *BMCL* 17 (1987), 77–90; repr. in his *Popes*, Ch. 17.

———, 'The Formation of the Jurisprudence of the Feudal Oath of Fealty', *Rivista internazionale di diritto comune*, 15 (2004), 57–76.

———, 'Further Thoughts on Pope Innocent III's Knowledge of Law', *ZRGKA* 72 (1986), 417–28; repr. in his *Popes*, Ch. 2.

———, 'Henricus de Segusio (Hostiensis)', in his *Popes*, Ch. 16.

———, 'The Legal Education of Pope Innocent III', *BMCL* 4 (1974), 70–7; repr. in his *Popes*, Ch. 1.

———, 'The Making of a Decretal Collection: The Genesis of *Compilatio tertia*', in S. Kuttner and K. Pennington, eds., *Proceedings of the Fifth International Congress of Medieval Canon Law*, Monumenta Iuris Canonici, Series C, 6 (Vatican City, 1980), 67–92; repr. in his *Popes*, Ch. 8.

———, *Pope and Bishops: The Papal Monarchy in the Twelfth and Thirteenth Centuries* (Pennsylvania, 1984).

———, *Popes, Canonists and Texts 1150–1550* (Aldershot, 1993).

———, '*Pro peccatis patrum puniri*: A Moral and Legal Problem of the Inquisition', *Church History*, 47 (1978), 137–54; repr. in his *Popes*, Ch. 11.

Piergiovanni, V., *La punibilità degli innocenti nel diritto canonico dell'età classica*, 2 vols. (Milan, 1971–4).

Pontal, O., 'Quelques remarques sur l'oeuvre canonique de Pierre de Sampson', *Annuarium historiae conciliorum*, 8 (1976), 126–42.

Post, G., *Studies in Medieval Legal Thought* (Princeton, 1964).

Prestwich, M., *Edward I* (London, 1988).

Pybus, H. J., 'The Emperor Frederick II and the Sicilian Church', *Cambridge Historical Journal*, 3 (1929–30), 134–63.

Regesta chartarum Italiae I: *Regestum Volterranum*, ed. F. Schneider (Rome, 1907).

Reuter, A. E., *Königtum und Episkopat in Portugal im 13. Jahrhundert* (Berlin, 1928).

Richardson, H. G., and G. O. Sayles, *The Governance of Medieval England from the Conquest to Magna Carta* (Edinburgh, 1963).

Richter, W., *De origine et evolutione interdicti usque ad aetatem Ivonis Carnotensis et Paschalis II*, Textus et documenta, Series theologica 12–13 (Rome, 1934).

Ridolfi, A., 'Ricordo di Scolaio Ardinghelli nel palazzo comunale di S. Gimignano', *Miscellanea storica della Valdelsa*, 36 (1928), 98–102.

Robinson, I. S., *The Papacy 1073–1198: Continuity and Innovation* (Cambridge, 1990).

Rodriguez, M. J., 'Innocent IV and the Element of Fiction in Juristic Personalities', *The Jurist*, 22 (1962), 287–318.

Roussel, N., *Histoire ecclésiastique et civile de Verdun*, 2 vols. (Bar-le-Duc, 1863–4).

Runcimann, S., *Sicilian Vespers* (Cambridge, 1958).

Russo, F., 'Pénitence et excommunication. Etude historique sur les rapports entre la théologie et le droit canonique dans le domaine pénitentiel du XIe au XIIIe siècle', *Recherches de science religieuse*, 33 (1946), 257–79, 431–61.

Sabatier, E., *Histoire de la ville et des évèques de Béziers* (Paris, 1854).

Saunders, P. J., 'Royal Ecclesiastical Patronage from Winchelsey to Stratford', *BJRL* 83 (2001), 95–114.

Sayers, J. E., *Papal Government and England during the Pontificate of Honorius III* (Cambridge, 1984).

Schedario Baumgarten, ed. G. Battelli and S. Pagano, 4 vols. (Vatican City, 1965–86).

Schmidt, T., 'Frühe Anwendungen des Liber Sextus Papst Bonifaz' VIII', in P. Landau and J. Müller, eds., *Proceedings of the Ninth International Congress of Medieval Canon Law*, Monumenta Iuris Canonici, Series C, 10 (Vatican City, 1997), 117–34.

———, 'Papst Bonifaz VIII als Gesetzgeber', in S. Chodorow, ed., *Proceedings of the Eighth International Congress of Medieval Canon Law*, Monumenta Iuris Canonici, Series C, 9 (Vatican City, 1992), 227–45.

Schneider, M., *Europäisches Waldensertum im 13. und 14. Jahrhundert* (Berlin/New York, 1981).

Schreiber, G., 'Studien zur Exemptionsgeschichte der Zisterzienser. Zugleich ein Beitrag zur Veroneser Synode von Jahre 1184', *ZRGKA* 4 (1914), 74–112.

Schulte, J. F., *Die Geschichte der Quellen und Literatur des Canonischen Rechts*, 3 vols. (Stuttgart, 1875–80).

Somerville, R., *Pope Alexander III and the Council of Tours (1163)* (Berkeley, 1977).

Soucaille, A., 'Institutions municipales: le consulat de Béziers (1131–1789)', *Bulletin de la société archéologique de Béziers*, 3e série, 1 (1895–6); also printed separately as a monograph (Béziers, 1896).

Tierney, B., *The Foundations of the Conciliar Theory* (Cambridge, 1956).

Tillmann, H., *Pope Innocent III*, trans. W. Sax (Amsterdam, 1980).

Trexler, R. C., *The Spiritual Power: Republican Florence under Interdict*, Studies in Medieval and Reformation Thought 9 (Leiden, 1974).

Ullmann, W., 'The Delictal Responsibility of Medieval Corporations', *Law Quarterly Review*, 64 (1948), 77–96; repr. in his *Scholarship and Politics in the Middle Ages* (London, 1978), Ch. 12.

Viollet, P., 'Bérenger Frédol, canoniste', in *Histoire littéraire de la France*, 34 (1914), 62–178.

Vodola, E., *Excommunication in the Middle Ages* (London, 1986).

_____, 'Interdict', in J. R. Strayer, ed., *Dictionary of the Middle Ages*, vol. vi (New York, 1985), 493–7.

Volpe, G., *Volterra: storia dei vescovi signori, di istituti comunali, di rapporti tra stato e chiesa nella città nei secoli XI–XV* (Florence, 1923).

von Heckel, R., 'Die Dekretalensammlungen des Gilbertus und Alanus nach den Weingartner Hanschriften', *ZRGKA* 29 (1940), 116–357.

Waley, D. P., *The Italian City-Republics*, 2nd edn (London, 1978).

_____, 'Guelfs and Ghibellines at San Gimignano, *c.* 1260–*c.* 1320: A Political Experiment', *BJRL* 72 (1990), 199–212.

_____, *Siena and the Sienese in the Thirteenth Century* (Cambridge, 1991).

Warren, W. L., *Henry II* (London, 1973).

Watt, J. A., 'Parisian Theologians and the Jews: Peter Lombard and Peter Cantor', in P. Biller and B. Dobson, eds. *The Medieval Church: Universities, Heresy and the Religious Life*, Studies in Church History, Subsidia 11 (1999), 55–76.

_____, *The Theory of Papal Monarchy in the Thirteenth Century: The Contribution of the Canonists* (London, 1965).

Winkler, A., 'The Excommunicated Castle: Clerical Power and the Natural World', in A. J. Duggan, J. Greatrex, and B. M. Bolton, eds., *'Omnia disce': Medieval Studies in Memory of Leonard Boyle, O.P.*, (Aldershot, 2005), 245–57.

Winroth, A., *The Making of Gratian's* Decretum (Cambridge, 2000).

Zurowski, M., 'Die Erstreckung der Strafsanktion auf nicht schuldige Personen die zum Straffalligen in Beziehung stehen nach der Lehre der Dekretisten und Dekretalisten', *ZRGKA* 59 (1973), 175–90.

_____, 'Penal Responsibility of Organised Communities in the Writings of the Decretalists: A Study in Evolution', in S. Kuttner and K. Pennington, eds., *Proceedings of the Sixth International Congress of Medieval Canon Law*, Monumenta Iuris Canonici, Series C, 7 (Vatican City, 1980), 518–31.

Index

Johannes Andreae, *Glossa ordinaria* on the
  Clementine (*cont.*)
  5.10.1: 74 n. 63
  5.10.2: 192 n. 81
Johannes Andreae, *Novella* on the *Liber extra*
  (X) 11
  1.5.1: 67 n. 31
  2.28.37: 252 n. 75; 259 n. 108
  5.38.11: 158 n. 145
Johannes Andreae, *Novelle* on the *Liber sextus*
  (VI) 11
  5.11.5: 61 n. 8
  5.11.16: 78 n. 75; 79 n. 78
  5.11.24: 139 n. 55; 151 n. 115; 166 n.
  187
Johannes Andreae (attrib.), *De modo* 65 n. 23,
  68 n. 35, 70 n. 42, 83 n. 90, 151 n. 113,
  152 n. 118, 168 n. 192
Johannes Calderinus, 'De interdicto' 12; 67 n.
  31; 72 n. 53; 72–3 n. 54; 79 n. 78, n. 81;
  80 n. 82; 93 n. 37; 133 n. 19; 142 n. 70;
  143; 144 n. 85; 145; 152; 153; 154; 160
  n. 157; 164 n. 176; 166 n. 187; 167 n.
  190; 252 n. 75
Johannes Calderinus (attrib.), *De censura* 61 n.
  8, 76 n. 69, 83 n. 90, 87–8, 112, 144 n.
  84, 152 n. 118, 155 n. 134, 160 n. 157,
  191 n. 76, 252 n. 75
John of Dambach, OP 175 n. 22
Johannes de Deo 72
Johannes Faventinus, *Summa* 5
  D.83 d.a.c.1: 29 n. 53; 33 n. 69; 45 n.
  110
  D.86 c.1: 29 n. 56; 33 n. 69
  D.86 c.21: 32 n. 66
  C.16 q.6 c.3: 52 n. 136
John of Freiburg, OP, *Summa* 61 n. 8; 62 n.
  11; 66 n. 27; 77; 143 n. 76; 144 n. 82, n.
  84; 147 n. 95; 158 n. 148; 245 n. 46
Johannes Galensis 7, see also *Compilatio
  secunda*
Johannes Galensis, *Apparatus* on 3 Comp. 7
  1.4.1: 51 n. 128; 197 n. 101
  1.6.1: 155 n. 131
  3.26.5: 50 n. 126
  3.29.un.: 51 n. 128
  5.2.5: 55 n. 148
  5.2.6: 31 n. 63
  5.14.3: 55 n. 148
  5.21.3: 46 n. 113
  5.21.16: 147 n. 96
Johannes Garsias Hispanus, *Apparatus* on
  Lugd. Conc. II 11
  c.17: 73 n. 58; 74 n. 61
  c.30: 257 n. 97; 257–8 n. 99
Johannes Hispanus de Petesella, *Summa* 10,
  97 n. 49, 122 n. 178, 236, 244 n. 40

Johannes de Legnano, *De interdicto* 12 n. 41,
  252
Johannes Monachus, *Glossa* on the *Liber
  sextus* 11
  5.11.5: 27 n. 49
  5.11.10: 257 n. 99
  5.11.24: 140 n. 57
Johannes Monachus, *Glossa* on the
  Extravagantes communes
  5.10.2: 121
Johannes Teutonicus 7, 9, 58, 97 n. 49, 99,
  235, 237, see also *Compilatio quarta*;
  Glossa ordinaria on the *Decretum*
Johannes Teutonicus, *Apparatus* on 3 Comp. 7
  1.3.7: 155 n. 132
  1.4.1: 51 n. 129; 61 n. 9; 106 n. 93; 107
  1.6.19: 237 n. 10
  1.18.10: 246 n. 48
  1.19.2: 237 n. 10
  1.19.5: 91 n. 25
  1.20.1: 100 n. 62
  2.3.1: 51 n. 129
  2.4.un.: 47 n. 117
  2.18.1: 236 n. 8; 237 n. 10
  2.19.11: 254 n. 85; 259 n. 108
  2.19.13: 94 n. 42; 250 n. 68
  3.5.1: 47–8
  3.31.3: 72 n. 53
  5.2.2: 23 n. 37
  5.4.1: 19 n. 24
  5.21.14: 255 n. 88, n. 89
  5.21.16: 147 n. 96; 151 n. 113
  5.23.7: 243 n. 34
Johannes Teutonicus, *Apparatus* on 4
  Comp. 8, 9
  1.12.1: 51 n. 129
  1.13.1: 74 n. 60
  1.14.2: 100 n. 62
  2.10.2: 100 n. 63
  5.12.8: 136
  5.14.3: 157 n. 144; 158 n. 146; 235
  5.15.3: 36 n. 77
  5.15.5: 105 n. 88
John of Tynemouth 5
Jones, Phillip 208
Juan, bishop of Oviedo 181
judges delegate, papal 62, 86, 90–91, 109,
  111, 178, 190, 196, 236, 237, 252
  subdelegate 90–91
Julião Pais, royal chancellor of Portugal 182

Kent 171
Kern, Fritz 260
keys, power of 86–8, 200
Kilmacduagh, archdeacon and bishop of 91
2 Kings 24: 20; 41; 52